DS-DX

D1613755

History of Asia, Africa, Australia, New Zealand, etc.

Library of Congress Classification
2012

Prepared by the Policy and Standards Division
Library Services

LIBRARY OF CONGRESS
LIBRARY OF CONGRESS   Cataloging Distribution Service
Washington, D.C.

This edition cumulates all additions and changes to subclasses DS-DX through List 2012/06, dated June 6, 2012. Additions and changes made subsequent to that date are published in lists posted on the World Wide Web at

<http://www.loc.gov/aba/cataloging/classification/weeklylists/>

and are also available in *Classification Web*, the online Web-based edition of the Library of Congress Classification.

Library of Congress Cataloging-in-Publication Data

Library of Congress.
    Library of Congress classification. DS-DX. History of Asia, Africa, Australia, New Zealand, etc. / prepared by the Policy and Standards Division, Library Services. — 2012 ed.
        p. cm.
    "This edition cumulates all additions and changes to subclasses DS-DX through List 2012/06, dated June 16, 2012. Additions and changes made subsequent to that date are published in lists posted on the World Wide Web ... and are also available in *Classification Web*, the online Web-based edition of the Library of Congress classification."— T.p. verso.
    Includes index.
    ISBN 978-0-8444-9556-9 (alk. paper)
    1. Classification, Library of Congress. 2. Classification—Books—History. 3. Classification—Books—Asia. 4. Classification—Books—Africa. 5. Classification—Books—Oceania. 6. Classification—Books—Australia. 7. Classification—Books—Romanies. I. Library of Congress. Cataloging Policy and Support Office. II. Title. III. Title: History of Asia, Africa, Australia, New Zealand, etc.

    Z696.U5D53 2012
    025.4'69—dc23

                        20122028469

For sale by the Library of Congress Cataloging Distribution Service,
101 Independence Avenue, S.E., Washington, DC 20541-4912.
Product catalog available on the Web at **www.loc.gov/cds**.

PREFACE

Class D, *History*, was first drafted in 1901 and after undergoing revision was published in 1916. Two supplements were published: *European War* (first edition, 1921; second edition, 1933; reprinted in 1954 with additions and changes), and *Second World War* (1947). The second edition of class D was published in 1959, containing additions and changes through June 1957. A reprint edition was published in 1966, containing a supplementary section of additions and changes through July 1965. The third edition was published in five parts between 1987 and 1990: D-DJ, DJK-DK, DL-DR, DS, and DT-DX. Subclasses DS-DX, History of Asia, Africa, Australia, New Zealand, etc., were published in a single edition in 1998, complemented by a 2001 edition of D-DR. A subsequent edition was published in 2008. This 2012 edition of DS-DX cumulates all additions and changes that have been made since the publication of the 2008 edition.

Classification numbers or spans of numbers that appear in parentheses are formerly valid numbers that are now obsolete. Numbers or spans that appear in angle brackets are optional numbers that have never been used at the Library of Congress but are provided for other libraries that wish to use them. In most cases, a parenthesized or angle-bracketed number is accompanied by a "see" reference directing the user to the actual number that the Library of Congress currently uses, or a note explaining Library of Congress practice.

Access to the online version of the full Library of Congress Classification is available on the World Wide Web by subscription to Classification Web. Details about ordering and pricing may be obtained from the Cataloging Distribution Service at

<http://www.loc.gov/cds/>

New or revised numbers and captions are added to the L.C. Classification schedules as a result of development proposals made by the cataloging staff of the Library of Congress and cooperating institutions. Upon approval of these proposals by the editorial meeting of the Policy and Standards Division, new classification records are created or existing records are revised in the master classification database. Lists of newly approved or revised classification numbers and captions are posted on the World Wide Web at

<http://www.loc.gov/aba/cataloging/classification/weeklylists/>

Janis L. Young, senior subject cataloging policy specialist in the Policy and Standards Division, is responsible for coordinating the overall intellectual and editorial content of class D and its various subclasses. Kent Griffiths and Ethel Tillman, assistant editors, create new classification records and their associated index terms, and maintain the master database.

Barbara B. Tillett, Chief
Policy and Standards Division

July 2012

OUTLINE

History of Asia **DS**

History of Africa **DT**

History of Oceania (South Seas) **DU**

History of Romanies **DX**

TABLES

INDEX

DS1-937	History of Asia
DS5.95-10	Description and travel
DS11	Antiquities
DS13-28	Ethnography
DS31-35.2	History
DS35.3-35.77	The Islamic World
DS36-39.2	Arab countries
DS36.9	Ethnography
DS37-39.2	History
DS41-66	Middle East. Southwestern Asia. Ancient Orient. Arab East. Near East
DS51-54.95	Local history and description
DS54-54.95	Cyprus
DS58-59	Ethnography
DS61-66	History
DS67-79.9	Iraq (Assyria, Babylonia, Mesopotamia)
DS69-70.5	Antiquities
DS70.8	Ethnography
DS70.82-79.9	History
DS80-90	Lebanon (Phenicia)
DS80.5-80.55	Ethnography
DS80.7-87.6	History
DS92-99	Syria
DS94.7-94.8	Ethnography
DS94.9-98.3	History
DS99	Provinces, regions, cities, etc.
DS101-151	Israel (Palestine). The Jews
DS109-109.94	Jerusalem
DS111-111.9	Antiquities
DS113.2-113.8	Ethnography. Tribes of Israel
DS114-128.2	History
DS133-151	Jews outside of Palestine
DS153-154.9	Jordan. Transjordan
DS153.5-153.55	Ethnography
DS153.7-154.55	History
DS155-156	Asia Minor
DS161-195.5	Armenia
DS173-195.5	History
DS201-248	Arabian Peninsula. Saudi Arabia
DS218-219	Ethnography
DS221-244.63	History
DS247-248	Local history and description

OUTLINE

History of Asia - Continued

DS251-326	Iran (Persia)
DS260.7-262	Antiquities
DS268-269	Ethnography
DS270-318.85	History
DS324-326	Local history and description
DS327-329.4	Central Asia
DS331-349.9	Southern Asia. Indian Ocean Region
DS349.8-349.9	Islands of the Indian Ocean
DS350-375	Afghanistan
DS354.5-354.6	Ethnography
DS355-371.3	History
DS374-375	Local history and description
DS376-392.2	Pakistan
DS380	Ethnography
DS381-389.22	History
DS392-392.2	Local history and description
DS393-396.9	Bangladesh. East Pakistan
DS393.82-393.83	Ethnography
DS394.5-395.7	History
DS396.8-396.9	Local history and description
DS401-(486.8)	India (Bharat)
DS430-432	Ethnography. Sects
DS433-481	History
DS483-(486.8)	Local history and description
DS488-490	Sri Lanka
DS489.2-489.25	Ethnography
DS489.5-489.86	History
DS491-492.9	Bhutan
DS493-495.8	Nepal
DS498-498.8	Goa. Portuguese in India
DS501-518.9	East Asia. The Far East
DS518.15-518.9	Relation of individual countries to East Asia
DS520-560.72	Southeast Asia
DS524-526.7	History
DS527-530.9	Burma
DS531-560.72	French Indochina
DS541-553.7	History
DS554-554.98	Cambodia
DS555-555.98	Laos
DS556-559.93	Vietnam. Annam
DS557-559.9	Vietnamese Conflict
DS560-560.72	Democratic Republic (North Vietnam), 1945-

History of Asia
Southeast Asia - Continued
DS561-589   Thailand (Siam)
DS569-570   Ethnography
DS570.95-586   History
DS588-589   Local history and description
DS591-599   Malaysia. Malay Peninsula. Straits Settlements
DS595-595.2   Ethnography
DS595.8-597.215   History
DS597.22-599   Local history and description
DS597.33-597.34   Sabah. British North Borneo
DS597.36-597.39   Sarawak
DS600-605   Malay Archipelago
DS608-610.9   Singapore
DS611-649   Indonesia (Dutch East Indies)
DS631-632   Ethnography
DS633-644.46   History
DS646.1-646.15   Sumatra
DS646.17-646.29   Java
DS646.3-646.34   Borneo. Kalimantan, Indonesia
DS646.4-646.49   Celebes. Sulawesi
DS646.5-646.59   Timor
DS646.6-646.69   Moluccas. Maluku
DS650-650.99   Brunei
DS651-689   Philippines
DS665-666   Ethnography
DS667-686.62   History
DS688-689   Local history and description
DS701-799.9   China
DS730-731   Ethnography
DS733-779.32   History
DS781-796   Local history and description
DS781-784.2   Manchuria
DS785-786   Tibet
DS796.H7   Hong Kong
DS798   Outer Mongolia. Mongolian People's Republic
DS798.92-799.9   Taiwan
DS801-897   Japan
DS833-891.5   History
DS894.215-897   Local history and description
DS901-937   Korea
DS904.8-922.4642   History
DS918-921.8   War and intervention, 1950-1953

OUTLINE

History of Asia

Korea - Continued

DS924-925   Local history and description

DS930-937   Democratic People's Republic, 1948-

DT1-3415   History of Africa

DT7-12.25   Description and travel

DT15-16   Ethnography

DT17-39   History

DT43-154   Egypt

DT56.8-69.5   Antiquities

DT63-63.5   Pyramids

DT68-68.8   Religious antiquities

DT71-72   Ethnography

DT73   Local antiquities

DT74-107.87   History

DT115-154   Local history and description

DT139-153.5   Cairo

DT154.1-159.9   Sudan. Anglo-Egyptian Sudan

DT154.8   Antiquities

DT155-155.2   Ethnography

DT155.3-157.67   History

DT159.6-159.9   Local history and description

DT160-177   North Africa

DT167-176   History

DT168-169.5   Carthaginian period

DT179.2-179.9   Northwest Africa

DT181-346   Maghrib. Barbary States

DT211-239   Libya

DT223-223.2   Ethnography

DT223.3-236   History

DT238-239   Local history and description

DT241-269   Tunisia (Tunis)

DT253-253.2   Ethnography

DT253.4-264.49   History

DT268-269   Local history and description

DT271-299   Algeria

DT283-283.6   Ethnography

DT283.7-295.55   History

DT298-299   Local history and description

DT301-330   Morocco

DT313-313.6   Ethnography

DT313.7-325.92   History

History of Africa
　　Maghrib. Barbary States
　　　Morocco - Continued
DT328-329　　　　Local history and description
DT330　　　　　　Spanish Morocco
DT331-346　　　　Sahara
DT348-363.3　　Central Sub-Saharan Africa
DT365-469　　　Eastern Africa
DT365.5-365.78　　History
DT367-367.8　　　Northeast Africa
DT371-390　　　　Ethiopia (Abyssinia)
DT380-380.4　　　　Ethnography
DT380.5-390　　　　History
DT391-398　　　　Eritrea
DT401-409　　　　Somalia. Somaliland and adjacent territory
DT402.3-402.45　　　Ethnography
DT402.5-407.3　　　History
DT409　　　　　　Local history and description
DT411-411.9　　　Djibouti. French Territory of the Afars and Issas.
　　　　　　　　　　French Somaliland
DT411.42-411.45　　Ethnography
DT411.5-411.83　　　History
DT411.9　　　　　Local history and description
DT421-432.5　　　East Africa. British East Africa
DT433.2-433.29　　Uganda
DT433.242-433.245　　Ethnography
DT433.252-433.287　　History
DT433.29　　　　　Local history and description
DT433.5-434　　　Kenya
DT433.542-433.545　　Ethnography
DT433.552-433.584　　History
DT436-449　　　　Tanzania. Tanganyika. German East Africa
DT443-443.3　　　　Ethnography
DT443.5-448.25　　　History
DT449.Z2　　　　　Zanzibar
DT450-450.49　　　Rwanda. Ruanda-Urundi
DT450.24-450.25　　Ethnography
DT450.26-450.437　　History
DT450.49　　　　　Local history and description
DT450.5-450.95　　Burundi
DT450.64-450.65　　Ethnography
DT450.66-450.855　　History
DT450.95　　　　　Local history and description

History of Africa
Eastern Africa - Continued
DT468-469   Islands (East African coast)
DT469.M21-.M38   Madagascar
DT469.M39   Mascarene Islands
DT469.M4-.M495   Mautitius (Ile de France)
DT469.M4975   Mayotte
DT469.R3-.R5   Reunion
DT469.S4-.S49   Seychelles
DT470-671   West Africa. West Coast
DT477   Upper Guinea
DT479   Lower Guinea
DT491-516.9   British West Africa
DT507   Ashanti Empire
DT509-509.9   Gambia
DT509.42-509.45   Ethnography
DT509.5-509.83   History
DT509.9   Local history and description
DT509.97-512.9   Ghana (Gold Coast)
DT510.42-510.43   Ethnography
DT510.5-512.34   History
DT512.9   Local history and description
DT515-515.9   Nigeria
DT515.42-515.45   Ethnography
DT515.53-515.842   History
DT515.9   Local history and description
DT516-516.9   Sierra Leone
DT516.42-516.45   Ethnography
DT516.5-516.82   History
DT516.9   Local history and description
DT521-555.9   French West Africa. French Sahara. West Sahara.
     Sahel
DT541-541.9   Benin. Dahomey
DT541.42-541.45   Ethnography
DT541.5-541.845   History
DT541.9   Local history and description
DT543-543.9   Guinea
DT543.42-543.45   Ethnography
DT543.5-543.827   History
DT543.9   Local history and description
DT545-545.9   Côte d'Ivoire. Ivory Coast
DT545.42-545.45   Ethnography
DT545.52-545.83   History

History of Africa
  West Africa. West Coast
    French West Africa. French Sahara. West Sahara.
    Sahel
     Côte d'Ivoire. Ivory Coast - Continued

D545.9	Local history and description
DT546.1-546.49	French-speaking Equatorial Africa
DT546.1-546.19	Gabon (Gaboon, Gabun)
DT546.142-546.145	Ethnography
DT546.15-546.183	History
DT546.19	Local history and description
DT546.2-546.29	Congo (Brazzaville). Middle Congo
DT546.242-546.245	Ethnography
DT546.25-546.283	History
DT546.29	Local history and description
DT546.3-546.39	Central African Republic. Central African Empire.
	Ubangi-Shari
DT546.342-546.345	Ethnography
DT546.348-546.3852	History
DT546.39	Local history and description
DT546.4-546.49	Chad (Tchad)
DT546.442-546.445	Ethnography
DT546.449-546.483	History
DT546.49	Local history and description
DT547-547.9	Niger
DT547.42-547.45	Ethnography
DT547.5-547.83	History
DT547.9	Local history and description
DT548	West Sahara
DT549-549.9	Senegal
DT549.42-549.45	Ethnography
DT549.47-549.83	History
DT549.9	Local history and description
DT551-551.9	Mali. Mali Federation. Sudanese Republic.
	French Sudan
DT551.42-551.45	Ethnography
DT551.5-551.82	History
DT551.9	Local history and description
DT554-554.9	Mauritania
DT554.42-554.45	Ethnography
DT554.52-554.83	History
DT554.9	Local history and description

OUTLINE

History of Africa
French West Africa. French Sahara. West Sahara.
Sahel - Continued

DT555-555.9   Burkina Faso. Upper Volta
DT555.42-555.45   Ethnography
DT555.517-555.837   History
DT555.9   Local history and description
DT561-581   Cameroon (Cameroun, Kamerun)
DT570-571   Ethnography
DT572-578.4   History
DT581   Local history and description
DT582-582.9   Togo. Togoland
DT582.42-582.45   Ethnography
DT582.5-582.82   History
DT582.9   Local history and description
DT591-615.9   Portuguese-speaking West Africa
DT613-613.9   Guinea-Bissau. Portuguese Guinea
DT613.42-613.45   Ethnography
DT613.5-613.83   History
DT613.9   Local history and description
DT615-615.9   Sao Tome and Principe
DT615.42-615.45   Ethnography
DT615.5-615.8   History
DT615.9   Local history and description
DT619-620.9   Spanish West Africa
DT620-620.9   Equatorial Guinea (Spanish Guinea)
DT620.42-620.45   Ethnography
DT620.46-620.83   History
DT620.9   Local history and description
DT621-637   Liberia
DT630-630.5   Ethnography
DT630.8-636.53   History
DT639   Congo (Kongo) River region
DT641-665   Zaire. Congo (Democratic Republic). Belgian Congo
DT649.5-650   Ethnography
DT650.2-663   History
DT665   Local history and description
DT669-671   Islands
DT671.C2   Cape Verde
DT1001-1190   Southern Africa
DT1054-1058   Ethnography
DT1062-1182   History
DT1190   Local history and description

History of Africa - Continued

DT1251-1465   Angola
DT1304-1308   Ethnography
DT1314-1436   History
DT1450-1465   Local history and description
DT1501-1685   Namibia. South-West Africa
DT1554-1558   Ethnography
DT1564-1651   History
DT1670-1685   Local history and description
DT1701-2405   South Africa
DT1754-1770   Ethnography
DT1757   Apartheid
DT1758-1760   Blacks
DT1772-1974   History
DT1991-2054   Cape Province. Cape of Good Hope
DT2075-2145   Orange Free State. Oranje Vrystaat
DT2181-2278   KwaZulu-Natal. Natal
DT2291-2378   Transvaal. South African Republic
DT2421-2525   Botswana. Bechuanaland
DT2454-2458   Ethnography
DT2464-2502   History
DT2541-2686   Lesotho. Basutoland
DT2592-2596   Ethnography
DT2604-2660   History
DT2680-2686   Local history and description
DT2701-2825   Swaziland
DT2744-2746   Ethnography
DT2754-2806   History
DT2820-2825   Local history and description
DT2831-2864   British Central Africa. Federation of Rhodesia and Nyasaland
DT2871-3025   Zimbabwe. Southern Rhodesia
DT2910-2913   Ethnography
DT2914-3000   History
DT3020-3025   Local history and description
DT3031-3145   Zambia. Northern Rhodesia
DT3054-3058   Ethnography
DT3064-3119   History
DT3140-3145   Local history and description
DT3161-3257   Malawi. Nyasaland
DT3189-3192   Ethnography
DT3194-3237   History
DT3252-3257   Local history and description

OUTLINE

History of Africa - Continued

DT3291-3415	Mozambique
DT3324-3328	Ethnography
DT3330-3398	History
DT3410-3415	Local history and description

DU1-950	History of Oceania (South Seas)
DU28.11-68	History
DU80-398	Australia
DU108-117.2	History
DU120-125	Ethnography
DU125	Australian aborigines
DU145	Australian Capital Territory. Canberra
DU150-180	New South Wales
DU170-172	History
DU178-180	Local history and description
DU182-198	Tasmania. Van Diemen's Land
DU190-195.3	History
DU200-230	Victoria
DU220-222	History
DU228-230	Local history and description
DU250-280	Queensland
DU270-272	History
DU278-280	Local history and description
DU300-330	South Australia
DU320-322	History
DU328-330	Local history and description
DU350-380	Western Australia
DU370-372	History
DU378-380	Local history and description
DU390	Central Australia
DU391	Northern Australia
DU392-398	Northern Territory of Australia
DU400-430	New Zealand
DU419-422	History
DU422.5-424.5	Ethnography
DU422.8-424	Maoris
DU428-430	Local history and description
DU490	Melanesia (General)
DU500	Micronesia (General)
DU510	Polynesia (General)
DU520-950	Smaller island groups
DU620-629	Hawaiian Islands. Hawaii

History of Oceania (South Seas)
 Smaller island groups - Continued
DU739-747   New Guinea
DU810-819   Samoan Islands

DX101-301   History of Romanies

	History of Asia
1	Periodicals. Societies. Serials
1.5	Congresses
2	Sources and documents
	Collected works (nonserial)
3.A2	Several authors
3.A3-Z	Individual authors, A-Z
4	Gazetteers. Dictionaries, etc.
4.8	Guidebooks
5	General works
5.5	Pictorial works
5.9	Historical geography
5.92	Geography
	Description and travel
	Cf. DK750 Soviet Central Asia
	Cf. DK751+ Siberia
	Cf. DK845+ Russian Central Asia
	Cf. DS41+ Levant
	Cf. DS327+ Central Asia
	Cf. DS411+ East Indies (General)
	Cf. DS501+ Far East
	Cf. DS611+ Dutch East Indies
5.95	History of voyages and discoveries. History of travel
6	Through 1491
7	1492-1800
8	1801-1900
9	1901-1950
10	1951-
11	Antiquities
12	Social life and customs. Civilization. Intellectual life
	Cf. CB253+ Oriental civilization
	Ethnography
13	General works
	Indo-Europeans
	Cf. GN539 Indo-Europeans (General)
15	General works
15.3	Indo-Iranians
16	Semites
	Cf. GN547 Semitic race (General)
17	Ural-Altaic peoples
18	Altaic peoples
	Mongols
	Cf. GN548 Mongolian race (General)
19	General works
21	Early to 12th century
22	Genghis Khan, 1162-1227
22.1	Jochi, d. 1227

	Ethnography
	Mongols -- Continued
22.3	Ogotai dynasty (China, etc.)
22.4	Güyüg, Khan of Mongolia, 1206-1248
22.5	Jagatai dynasty (Central Asia)
22.7	Khanate of Kiptchak (Golden Horde)
23	Timur, 1336-1405
23.1	Timurides
24	Kazakhs
	Cf. DK855.5.K33 Kazakhs in West Turkestan
	Cf. DS793.E2 Lazakhs in Sinkiang (East Turkestan)
25	Tatars
25.5	Tibeto-Burman peoples
	Turkic peoples
26	General works
	Kazakhs see DS24
	Tatars see DS25
	Seljuks
	Including Battle of Malazgirt, 1071; etc.
27	General works
	Biography
27.2	Collective
27.22.A-Z	Individual, A-Z
27.5	Kara Koyunlu
27.52	Ak Koyunlu
27.53	Mengüceks
27.54	Karapapaks
27.55	Yuruks
27.56	Uighur
	Ottomans see DR434+
28.A-Z	Other individual elements in the population, A-Z
28.A35	Africans
28.J3	Japanese
	For Japanese in Southeast Asia see DS509.5.J3
28.P67	Portuguese
28.W46	Whites
	History
31	Dictionaries. Chronological tables, outlines, etc.
32	Biography (Collective)
	Historiography
32.5	General works
	Biography of historians, area studies specialists,
	archaeologists, etc.
32.6	Collective
32.7.A-Z	Individual, A-Z
	Study and teaching
32.8	General works

	History	
	Study and teaching -- Continued	
32.9.A-Z	By region or country, A-Z	
	Under each country:	
	.x	*General works*
	.x2A-.x2Z	*Special schools. By place, A-Z*
33	General works	
33.1	General special	
33.2	Addresses, essays, lectures	
	Political and diplomatic history	
33.3	General works	
33.4.A-Z	Asian relations of individual countries, A-Z	
	By period	
33.5	Ancient and medieval	
33.7	Early modern	
34	19th century	
	For Central Asian question see D378+	
	20th century	
	For Central Asian question (1801-1914) see D378+	
	For Central Asian question (1914-) see D471	
	For Near East see DS61+	
	For Far Eastern question see DS515	
35	General works	
35.2	1945-	
	The Islamic world	
	Cf. BP1+ Islam	
	Cf. BV2625+ Missions among Muslims	
	Cf. DR1+ Turkey, Bulgaria, etc.	
	Cf. DS36+ Arab countries, including North Africa, Islamic Empire, Islamic civilization	
	Cf. DS41+ Near East	
	Cf. DS350+ Afghanistan, Pakistan, etc.	
	Cf. DS591+ Malaysia, Indonesia	
	Cf. DT43+ Egypt, North Africa	
	Cf. DT348+ Sub-Saharan Africa	
35.3	Periodicals. Societies. Sources	
35.32	Congresses	
	Collected works (nonserial)	
35.4.A2	Several authors	
35.4.A3-Z	Individual authors, A-Z	
35.53	Gazetteers. Guidebooks. Dictionaries. Directories, etc.	
35.56	Geography	
35.57	Description and travel	
35.6	General works	

	The Islamic world -- Continued
35.62	Social life and customs. Civilization. Intellectual life
	For the civilization of the individual countries, see the country
	For the modern Arab countries in general, including North Africa see DS36.8+
	For medieval Islamic civilization in general, as well as medieval Islamic civilization of the Near East see DS36.85+
	For the Near East in general, including Islamic civilization in the modern period see DS57
	Ethnography
35.625.A1	General works
35.625.A2-Z	Individual elements in the population, A-Z
35.625.S55	Slavs
	History
	Periodicals. Societies. Serials see DS35.3
35.627	Dictionaries. Chronological tables, outlines, etc.
35.63	General works
35.64	Biography (Collective)
	For individual biography, see the specific country or region
	Historiography
35.65	General works
	Biography of historians, area studies specialists, archaeologists, etc.
35.67.A1	Collective
35.67.A2-Z	Individual, A-Z
35.68	Study and teaching
35.684	Addresses, essays, lectures. Anecdotes, etc.
35.687	Military history
35.69	Political history
35.7	Panislamism
	Foreign and general relations
	For general works on the diplomatic history of a period, see the period
35.73	General works
	For works on relations with a specific country regardless of period see DS35.74.A+
35.74.A-Z	By region or country, A-Z
35.74.U6	United States
	By period
	Early to 1900, see DS35.63
35.77	20th century
	Arab countries
	Including North Africa
	For general works on the eastern Arab countries, including Egypt see DS41+
	For general works on North Africa see DT160

	Arab countries -- Continued
	Periodicals. Societies. Serials
36	General
36.2	League of Arab States
36.23	Majlis al-Taʻāun al-ʻArabī. Arab Cooperation Council
36.28	Congresses
36.3	Sources and documents
	Collected works (nonserial)
36.4	Several authors
36.5	Individual authors
36.55	Gazetteers. Dictionaries. Guidebooks. Directories, etc.
36.57	Historical geography
	Including the Islamic Empire as a whole
	For the Middle East see DS44.9
36.58	Geography
	Description and travel
36.59	History of travel
36.6	Early to 1800
	Cf. G93 Arabic geographers
36.65	1800-
36.7	General works
36.75	Antiquities
	Social life and customs. Civilization. Intellectual life
	For the Islamic countries in general, including India, Indonesia, Sub-Saharan Africa, etc. see DS35.62
	For the Eastern Arab countries only, and Near East in general see DS57
36.77	General works
36.78	Addresses, essays, lectures
36.79.A-Z	Special topics, A-Z
36.79.B42	Bears
36.79.C35	Camels
36.79.S47	Serpents
	Civilization and culture. Intellectual life
36.8	General works
	Foreign influences
36.82.A2	General works
36.82.A3-Z	By country, civilization, etc., A-Z
	e.g.
36.82.C45	Christian
	Europe see DS36.82.O3
36.82.G7	Greece
36.82.I7	Iran
36.82.O3	Occident. Europe
36.82.S7	Spain
	By period
36.84	Early to 622

Arab countries
  Social life and customs. Civilization. Intellectual life
    Civilization and culture. Intellectual life
      By period -- Continued
        622-1517. Medieval Islamic civilization (General)
          Including Islamic civilization in the Mediterranean region,
            western and central Asia during this period

36.85	General works
36.855	General special
36.86	Addresses, essays, lectures
	By country
	see the individual country
36.87	1517-1798
36.88	1798-

Ethnography
  For ethnographic works on Arabs in general see
    GN549.A7

36.9.A1	General works
36.9.A3	Psychology
36.9.A5-Z	Individual elements in the population, A-Z
36.9.B4	Bedouins
	Christians see BR1067.A7
36.9.D47	Dhimmis
	Jews see DS134.2+
36.9.K87	Kurds
36.9.Q38	Qays
	Romanies see DX300

Arabs in foreign countries (General)
  For Arabs in a particular country, see the country

36.95	General works
36.96	Arabs (Muslims) in Europe and the Mediterranean islands during the Middle Ages

History

37	Dictionaries. Chronological tables, outlines, etc.
37.2	Biography (Collective)
	For medieval biography alone see DS38.4.A2+

Historiography

37.4	General works
	Biography of historians, area studies specialists, archaeologists, etc.
37.5.A2	Collective
37.5.A3-Z	Individual, A-Z

Study and teaching
  Including area studies

37.6.A2	General works
37.6.A3-Z	Individual schools, A-Z
37.65.A-Z	Local, A-Z

	Arab countries
	History -- Continued
37.7	General works
37.8	Military and naval history
	Political and diplomatic history and foreign and general relations see DS62.8+
	Arab nationalism, Panarabism see DS63.6
	Arab-Israeli wars see DS126.9
	Jewish-Arab relations see DS119.7+
37.9	Addresses, essays, lectures
	By period
38	Early to 622
	For Pre-Islamic Arabia see DS231
38.1	622-661, Hegira to the Omayyad period
	Including the Arab conquest (Futūh)
	Caliphs, 632-1517
38.14	Sources and documents
	Historiography
38.16	General works
	Biography of historians
38.17	Collective
38.18.A-Z	Individual, A-Z
	General works
38.2	Early to 1800
38.3	1801-
	Biography and memoirs of caliphs, etc.
38.4.A2	Collective
38.4.A23-Z	Individual, A-Z
	e.g.
38.4.H3	Hārūn al-Rashīd, caliph
38.4.K5	Khālid ibn al-Walīd
38.4.S2	Saladin, Sultan of Egypt and Syria
	By period
38.5	Omayyad period, 661-750
	Cf. DP97.3+ Omayyads in Spain
	Cf. DS97.2 Omayyads
38.6	Abbasid period, 750-1258
	Cf. DS76.4 Abbasids
38.7	1258-1517
	For Mameluke see DT96+
38.8	Ottoman period, 1517-1918
38.9	1798-
	1914-
39	General works
	Biography and memoirs
39.2.A2	Collective
39.2.A3-Z	Individual, A-Z

Middle East. Southwestern Asia. Ancient Orient. Arab East.
 Near East
41   Periodicals. Societies. Serials
41.5   Congresses
42   Sources and documents
                Collected works (nonserial)
42.4   Several authors
42.5   Individual authors
43   Gazetteers. Guidebooks. Dictionaries. Directories, etc.
44   General works
44.5   Pictorial works
44.9   Historical geography
44.96   Geography
                Description and travel
                  Including Levant, Bible lands, and countries bordering on the
                    eastern Mediterranean; also overland journeys from Asia
                    Minor by various routes to the Persian Gulf and India
                Palestine (and Egypt) see DS103+
                Palestine and Syria see DS103+
44.98   History of travel
45   Through 700
46   701-1453
                1453-1800
47   General Levant: (Greece), Turkey, Asia Minor, Palestine,
                    Egypt
47.2   Aleppo, Mesopotamia, Tigris, Euphrates to Persian Gulf
47.3   Anatolia, with Armenia and Kurdistan
47.5   (Asia Minor), Armenia, Kurdistan, Assyria, Babylonia,
                    Persia, India
                1801-1900
48   General Levant: (Greece), Turkey, Asia Minor, Palestine,
                    Egypt
48.2   Aleppo, Mesopotamia, Tigris, Euphrates to Persian Gulf
48.3   Anatolia, with Armenia and Kurdistan
48.5   (Asia Minor), Armenia, Kurdistan, Assyria, Babylonia,
                    Persia, India
                1901-1950
49   General Levant: (Greece), Turkey, Asia Minor, Palestine,
                    Egypt
                    As of 1950: (Greece), Turkey, Syria, Lebanon, Palestine
                      (Jordan, Israel), Egypt
49.2   Aleppo, Mesopotamia, Tigris, Euphrates to Persian Gulf
                    As of 1950: Syria, Iraq
49.3   Anatolia, with Armenia and Kurdistan
                    As of 1950: Turkey in Asia, Armenia, Kurdistan

	Middle East. Southwestern Asia. Ancient Orient. Arab East. Near East
	Description and travel
	1901-1950 -- Continued
49.5	(Asia Minor), Armenia, Kurdistan, Assyria, Babylonia, Persia, India
	As of 1950: Turkey in Asia, Iraq, Iran, Afghanistan, Pakistan, India
49.7	1951-
	Local history and description
	Red Sea region see DT39
51.A-Z	Turkish provinces, regions, cities, islands, etc., A-Z
	e.g.
	For provinces, regions, etc., in European Turkey see DR701.A+
	For ancient states, cities, etc., including archaeological sites see DS156.A+
51.A15	Collective
51.A2	Adana
51.A33	Alibey Adasi
	Anatolia see DS47+
51.A6	Ankara. Angora
51.A64	Antalya İli
51.A66	Ararat, Mount
51.A73	Artvin (Province)
(51.B35)	Baluchistan
	see DS392.B2+
51.B57	Black Sea Coast
51.B63	Bolu
51.D37	Demirci (Manisa İli)
51.D4	Denizli
51.D57	Diyarbakır
51.E27	Eastern Turkey
51.E76	Ereğli (Zonguldak)
	Cf. DS156.H47 Heraclea Pontica
51.E8	Erzurum
51.G3	Gazipaşa. Pazarli
(51.H3)	Hacin. Hadjin
	see DS51.S16
51.H347	Harran
51.H35	Hatay. Alexandretta (Sanjak)
51.I47	İmroz Island
51.I7	Ismid. İzmit
51.I9	Izmir (City)
51.K144	Karaman İli
51.K2	Kastamonu. Kastamuni
51.K5	Konya. Konia

Middle East. Southwestern Asia. Ancient Orient. Arab East.
  Near East
  Local history and description
    Turkish provinces, regions, cities, islands, etc., A-Z --
      Continued

51.K67	Kütahya
51.M322	Marmara Island
51.M324	Marmara Sea Region
(51.P75)	Princes Islands
	see DR738.5.P74
51.S16	Saimbeyli. Hacin
51.S36	Şemdinli
51.S5	Sivas
	Smyrna see DS51.I9
51.T2	Tarsus
51.T7	Trabazon. Trebizond
51.V3	Van

    Archipelago (Islands of the Aegean)
      see DF220.5, DF261.A177, DF895
    Greek islands of the Aegean see DF901.A+
    Turkish islands of Aegean see DS51.A+
    Cyprus

54.A2	Periodicals. Societies. Sources and documents. Collections
	Museums, exhibitions, etc.
54.A25	General works
54.A26A-.A26Z	Individual. By place, A-Z
54.A28	Gazetteers. Dictionaries, etc.
54.A285	Place names (General)
54.A288	Guidebooks
54.A3	General works
54.A33	Historical geography
54.A35	Geography
54.A4-Z	Description and travel
54.3	Antiquities
54.35	Social life and customs. Civilization. Intellectual life
	For specific periods, see the period or reign
	Ethnography
54.4	General works
54.42.A-Z	Individual elements in the population, A-Z
54.42.A75	Armenians
54.42.G74	Greeks
54.42.M82	Muslims
54.42.S94	Swedes
54.42.T87	Turks
54.44	Cypriots in foreign countries (General)
	For Cypriots in a particular country, see the country

Middle East. Southwestern Asia. Ancient Orient. Arab East.
Near East
Local history and description
Cyprus -- Continued
History

54.5	General works
	Political and diplomatic history. Foreign and general relations
54.55	General works
54.56.A-Z	Relations with individual countries, A-Z
	By period
	Early to 1571
54.6	General works
	Biography and memoirs
54.62	Collective
54.63.A-Z	Individual, A-Z
54.66	Turkish Conquest, 1570-1571
54.7	1571-1878. Turkish era
	1878-1960. British period
54.8	General works
	Biography and memoirs
54.82	Collective
54.83.A-Z	Individual, A-Z
54.85	October Uprising, 1931
54.86	War for Union with Greece, 1955-1959
	Republic, 1960-
54.9	General works
	Biography and memoirs
54.92	Collective
54.93.A-Z	Individual, A-Z
54.95.A-Z	Local, A-Z
	e.g.
54.95.A52	Amathus
	Bamboula Site (Kition) see DS54.95.K58
	Bamboula Site (Kourion) see DS54.95.K68
54.95.B34	Bamboulari tis Koukouninas Site
	Citium see DS54.95.L37
54.95.E54	Enkomi Site
54.95.H34	Hala Sultan Teke
54.95.I3	Idhalion
54.95.K58	Kition. Bamboula Site
	Kouklia see DS54.95.O43
54.95.K68	Kourion. Bamboula Site
54.95.L37	Larnaca
54.95.M35	Malloura Valley
54.95.M4	Maroni Petrera Site
54.95.N47	New Paphos

	Middle East. Southwestern Asia. Ancient Orient. Arab East. Near East
	Local history and description
	Cyprus
	Local, A-Z -- Continued
54.95.N53	Nicosia
54.95.N58	Nitovikla
54.95.N67	Northern Cyprus
54.95.O43	Old Paphos. Kouklia
54.95.P52	Phaneromeni Site
54.95.P94	Pyla-Kokkinokremos Site
54.95.S2	Salamis
54.95.S64	Soli
54.95.S68	Sotira Kaminoudhia Sita
54.95.T46	Themokrēnē Site
	Turkish Republic of Northern Cyprus see DS54.95.N67
54.95.V68	Vounous Site
56	Antiquities. Social antiquities
	For local antiquities see DS51.A+
57	Social life and customs. Civilization.
	For works on Arab civilization in general see DS36.77+
	For medieval Islamic civilization see DS36.85+
	Ethnography
58	General works
59.A-Z	Individual elements in the population, A-Z
59.A7	Arameans
59.A73	Armenians
59.A75	Assyrians
59.B34	Baluchi
	Bedouins see DS36.9.B4
59.B55	Blacks
59.B75	British
	Including English
	Chaldean Catholics see DS59.A75
59.C48	Christians
	Cimmerians see DK34.C56
59.C57	Circassians
59.D47	Dhimmis
59.D78	Druzes
59.E27	East Indians
	English see DS59.B75
59.G47	Germans
59.G8	Greeks
59.H8	Hurrians
59.J25	Jacobites (Syrian Christians)
59.J3	Japanese
59.K3	Kaskans

	Middle East. Southwestern Asia. Ancient Orient. Arab East. Near East
	Ethnography
	Individual elements in the population, A-Z -- Continued
59.K86	Kurds
59.L86	Luwians
59.M34	Malays
	Negroes see DS59.B55
	Nestorians see DS59.A75
59.S86	Sunnites
59.S94	Syriac Christians
59.T8	Turks
	History
	For history of Arab countries in general (including North Africa) see DS37.7
	For history of Islamic Empire see DS38.1
61	Dictionaries. Chronological tables, outlines, etc.
	Biography
61.5	Collective
	Class here general biography
	For rulers, caliphs, and successors of Muhammed see DS38.4.A2+
	For Arab (Islamic Empire) see DS201+
61.52.A-Z	Individual, A-Z
	Class here biographies not elsewhere provided for under special countries and periods
	Historiography
61.6	General works
	Biography of historians, area studies specialists, archaeologists, etc.
61.7.A1	Collective
61.7.A2-Z	Individual, A-Z
	Study and teaching
	Including area studies
61.8	General works
61.85	Orientalism. Western views or concepts of the Middle East
61.9.A-Z	By region or country, A-Z
	Under each country:
	.x *General works*
	.x2A-.x2Z *Special schools. By place, A-Z*
62	General works
	By period
	Early to 622 A.D.
	For Macedonian Empire see DF234+
	For Assyro-Babylonian Empire see DS71+
	For Persian Empire see DS281+

Middle East. Southwestern Asia. Ancient Orient. Arab East.
Near East
History
By period
Early to 622 A.D. -- Continued

62.2	General works
	By period
62.23	Through 1 A.D.
62.25	1 A.D.-622
	Medieval see DS38.1
	Modern, 1517-
62.4	General works
62.6	1517-1914
62.7	19th century
	20th century
62.8	General works
62.9	Through 1914
	1914-1945
63	General works
63.04	1914-1923
	1945-
63.1	General works
63.12	Biography and memoirs

For individual biography, see the specific country

63.15	Military and naval history

For individual campaigns and engagements, see the period

Political and diplomatic history. Foreign and general
relations
For general works on the diplomatic history of a period, see
the period
For works on relations with a specific country
regardless of period see DS63.2.A+

63.17	Sources and documents
63.18	General works
63.2.A-Z	Relations with individual countries, A-Z
	e.g.
63.2.U5	United States
63.3	Arab propaganda in foreign countries
	Nationalism
63.5	General works
63.6	Arab nationalism. Arabism. Panarabism

Cf. DS36.2 League of Arab States

Islam and nationalism see BP173.55
Panislamism see DS35.7
Palestine problem. Jewish-Arab relations see DS119.7+

64	Addresses, essays, lectures
65	Elam

	Middle East. Southwestern Asia. Ancient Orient. Arab East.
	Near East
	History -- Continued
66	Hittites
66.4	Mitanni. Mitannians
	Iraq (Assyria, Babylonia, Mesopotamia)
67	Periodicals. Societies. Serials
	Collected works (Modern)
67.4	Several authors
67.5	Individual authors
67.8	Dictionaries. Gazetteers. Guidebooks
68	Sources and documents
	Antiquities
	Including ancient social life and customs, civilization, etc.
	Museums, exhibitions, etc.
69.A2	General works
69.A3-Z	By city and museum, A-Z
	e.g.
69.L6B7	London. British Museum
69.1	Dictionaries
	General works
69.3	Through 1899
69.5	1900-
69.6	General special
	History of excavations
69.9	Through 1825
70	1826-
70.5.A-Z	Local antiquities, A-Z
70.5.A43	Adab
70.5.A46	Aḥmad al-Ḥa Hū, Tall
70.5.A5	al Anbār
70.5.A7	Assur
70.5.B3	Babylon
70.5.B35	Balāwāt
70.5.B6	Borsippa
	Burj 'Aqarqūf see DS70.5.D87
70.5.C3	Calah
70.5.D57	Diyala River Region
70.5.D73	Drehem
70.5.D87	Dur-Kurigalzu
70.5.D89	Dur-Sharrukin
70.5.E65	Erech
70.5.E67	Eridu
70.5.E7	Eshnunna
70.5.G38	Gawra, Tepe
70.5.G57	Girsu (Extinct city)
70.5.H24	Haradum

Iraq (Assyria, Babylonia, Mesopotamia)
  Antiquities
    Local antiquities, A-Z -- Continued

70.5.H27	Ḥarmal, Tall
70.5.H3	Hatra
70.5.I44	Imlīḥīyah, Tall
70.5.I75	Isin
70.5.K37	Karana
70.5.K435	Khans
70.5.K44	Khatuniyeh Site
70.5.K5	Kish
70.5.K52	Kissūrah
70.5.L35	Larsa
70.5.M37	Mashkan-shapir
70.5.N35	Nemrik 9 Site
70.5.N47	Nineveh
70.5.N5	Nippur
70.5.N9	Nuzi
70.5.O93	Oueili, Tall al-
70.5.Q47	Qermez Dere
70.5.R54	Rijim, Tall
70.5.S45	Seleucia on the Tigris. Seleucia Babylonia
70.5.S55	Sippar
70.5.U4	Ukheidar
70.5.U44	Umma
70.5.U7	Ur
70.5.Z35	Zamār (Nīnawá)
70.6	General works
70.61	Pictorial works
70.62	Juvenile works
70.63	Historical geography
70.64	Geography
70.65	Description and travel
70.7	Social life and customs. Civilization

      Cf. DS69+ Antiquities, ancient social life and customs, etc.

  Ethnography
    Cf. DS71+ Ancient peoples

70.8.A1	General works
70.8.A2-Z	Individual elements in the population, A-Z
70.8.A74	Armenians
70.8.A89	Assyrians
70.8.B4	Bedouins
70.8.C45	Christians
70.8.K5	Khazā'il
70.8.K8	Kurds
70.8.M37	Marsh Arabs

	Iraq (Assyria, Babylonia, Mesopotamia)

Iraq (Assyria, Babylonia, Mesopotamia)
    Ethnography
        Individual elements in the population, A-Z -- Continued

70.8.M86	Muntafiq
70.8.S55	Shiites
70.8.T85	Turkomans
70.8.T86	Turks
70.8.Y49	Yezidis

    History

70.82	Dictionaries. Chronological tables, outlines, etc.
70.85	Biography (Collective)

      Historiography

70.87	General works

        Biography of historians, area studies specialists, archaeologists, etc.

70.88.A2	Collective
70.88.A3-Z	Individual, A-Z
70.9	General works
70.92	Military and naval history

          For individual campaigns and engagements, see the period or reign

      Political and diplomatic history. Foreign and general relations

70.95	General works
70.96.A-Z	Relations with individual countries A-Z

      By period
        Ancient
          Including Media and Chaldea

71	General works
72	Sumerians
72.3	Akkadians
72.5	Amorites
72.52	Sutaeans

        By period

73.1	4500-2200 B.C. Earliest rulers

          2400-607 B.C. First dynasty to fall of Assyrian monarchy

73.2	General works
73.25	2400-2100. First dynasty

            2100-1700. Second dynasty

73.3	General works
73.35	Hammurabi, ca. 1800

            1731-1154. Third dynasty

73.4	General works
73.45	Shalmaneser I, 1330-1310

            1160-1081. Fourth dynasty

73.5	General works

Iraq (Assyria, Babylonia, Mesopotamia)
History
By period
Ancient
By period
2400-607 B.C. First dynasty to fall of Assyrian
monarchy
1160-1081. Fourth dynasty -- Continued
73.53   Tiglath-Pileser I, 1115-1100
73.58   Assurbelkala, 1100-1080
73.6   1000-900. Fifth to seventh dynasties
910-607. Eighth dynasty. Fall of Assyrian monarchy
73.7   General works
73.72   Ashurnasirpal II, 885-860
73.73   Shalmaneser II, 860-824
73.74   Semiramis, ca. 800
73.75   Shalmaneser III, 782-772
73.76   Tiglath-Pileser III, 745-727
73.78   Shalmaneser IV, 727-722
73.8   Sargon II, 722-705
73.83   Sennacherib, 705-681
73.85   Esarhaddon, 681-668
73.87   Assurbanipal (Sardanapalus), 668-626
625-539 B.C. New Babylonian or Chaldean Empire
73.9   General works
73.91   Nabopolassar, 625-604
Including Fall of Nineveh, 612
73.92   Nebuchadnezzar II, 604-561
73.93   Nabonidus, 555-538
73.94   Invasion of Babylon by Cyrus, 539
73.95   539-333 B.C.
74   Addresses, essays, lectures
333 B.C.-638 A.D.
Including Hellenistic period
75   General works
75.2   Characene (Kingdom)
Medieval period, 638-1517
76   General works
76.4   Abbasids, 750-1258
77   Turkish period, 1517-1918
1919-1958
79   General works
79.5   Faisal I, 1921-1933
79.52   Ghazi I, 1933-1939
79.53   Faisal II, 1939-1958
Including Regency, 1939-1953
Biography and memoirs

	Iraq (Assyria, Babylonia, Mesopotamia)
	History
	By period
	1919-1958
	Biography and memoirs -- Continued
79.6.A2	Collective
79.6.A3-Z	Individual, A-Z
	Republic, 1958-
79.65	General works
	Biography and memoirs
79.66.A2	Collective
79.66.A3-Z	Individual, A-Z
79.7	Hussein, Saddam, 1979-2003
	For biography of Hussein see DS79.66.A2+
	Iran-Iraq War, 1980-1988 see DS318.85
79.718	Anfal Campaign, 1986-1989
	Persian Gulf War, 1990-1991. Iraq-Kuwait Crisis, 1990-1991
79.719	Causes. Origins. Aims
79.72	General works. Military operations
79.722	Pictorial works
79.723	Juvenile literature
79.724.A-Z	By region or country, A-Z
	Including foreign relations, participation in the conflict
	For other topics in a specific country, see the topic at DS79.736+
	Military operations
	General see DS79.72
79.735	Local events, battles, etc. By place, A-Z
79.736	Atrocities. War crimes. Destruction and pillage
79.738	Economic aspects. Commerce, finance, etc. (General)
79.739	Press. Censorship. Publicity. Propaganda
79.74	Personal narratives
79.744.A-Z	Other topics, A-Z
79.744.A47	Aerial operations
	Including history of individual units
79.744.A75	Armored operations
	Including history of individual units
	Biological warfare see DS79.744.C46
79.744.C46	Chemical warfare. Biological warfare
	Civil affairs see DS79.744.C58
79.744.C58	Civilian relief. Civil affairs
79.744.D55	Diplomatic history. Peace negotiations, etc.
79.744.E58	Environmental aspects
	Health aspects see DS79.744.M44
79.744.L64	Logistics

	Iraq (Assyria, Babylonia, Mesopotamia)
	History
	By period
	Republic, 1958-
	Hussein, Saddam, 1979-2003
	Persian Gulf War, 1990-1991. Iraq-Kuwait Crisis, 1990-1991
	Other topics, A-Z -- Continued
79.744.M42	Medals
79.744.M44	Medical and health aspects
79.744.N38	Naval operations
	Including history of individual units
	Peace negotiations see DS79.744.D55
79.744.P74	Protest movements
79.744.P78	Psychological aspects
79.744.R44	Religious aspects
79.744.S25	Sanctions
79.744.S34	Science and technology. Weapons
79.744.V47	Veterans
	Weapons see DS79.744.S34
79.744.W65	Women
	Post-Persian Gulf War, 1991-2003
79.75	General works
79.755	Military history
	Including works on the containment of Iraqi military operations, and/or compliance with inspections of UNSCOM (UN Special Commission on Iraq)
	Iraq War, 2003-
79.757	Causes. Origins. Aims
79.76	General works
79.761	Diplomatic history
79.762	Pictorial works
79.763	Juvenile literature
79.7635	Pamphlets, addresses, sermons, etc.
	Military operations
	Including aerial operations and insurgency
	General works see DS79.76
79.764.A-Z	Individual campaigns, battles, etc., A-Z
79.764.A93	A'zamīyah
79.764.B35	Baghdad
	Including Battle of Sadr City, 2008
79.764.F35	Fallujah
79.764.M33	Maḥmūdīyah
79.764.M34	Majarr al-Kabīr
79.764.N35	Najaf
79.764.N37	Nasiriyah
79.764.R36	Ramādī

DS

	Iraq (Assyria, Babylonia, Mesopotamia)
	History
	By period
	Republic, 1958-
	Iraq War, 2003-
	Military operations
	Individual campaigns, battles, etc., A-Z -- Continued
79.764.T55	Tikrit
	Including Operation Iron Triangle
79.765.A-Z	By country, A-Z
	Including regimental histories
	e.g.
79.765.F8	France
79.765.G7	Great Britain
79.765.I72	Iraq
	United States
	General works see DS79.76
79.765.U6	Regimental histories. Subarrange by main entry
	Biography. Personal narratives
	For personal narratives limited to a campaign, battle, etc., special troops, or topic see the campaign, battle, etc., troops or topic, e. g. DS79.764.F35, Fallujah, Battle of; DS79.767.D38, Detainees; DS79.765.U6, U.S. Army 101st Airborne Division
79.766.A1	Collective
79.766.A2-Z	Individual, A-Z
79.767.A-Z	Special topics, A-Z
79.767.A87	Atrocities
	For individual atrocities see DS79.764.A+
79.767.C37	Casualties
	Censorship see DS79.767.P74
	Charities see DS79.767.R43
79.767.C55	Children
79.767.C58	Civilian relief
79.767.C66	Conscientious objectors
79.767.C85	Cultural property
79.767.D38	Detainees. Prisoners of war
	Displaced persons see DS79.767.R43
79.767.E26	Economic aspects
	For specific topics or for individual countries, see HC, HF, HJ
79.767.E58	Environmental aspects
	Hospitals see DS79.767.M43
79.767.I53	Indians
	Insurgency see DS79.76352+
	Journalism see DS79.767.P74
79.767.M37	Mass media

	Iraq (Assyria, Babylonia, Mesopotamia)
	History
	By period
	Republic, 1958-
	Iraq War, 2003-
	Special topics, A-Z -- Continued
79.767.M43	Medical care. Hospitals
	Military intelligence see DS79.767.S75
79.767.M67	Moral and ethical aspects
79.767.M68	Motion pictures and the war
79.767.P74	Press. Journalism. Censorship
	Prisoners of war see DS79.767.D38
79.767.P76	Protest movements
79.767.P79	Psychological aspects
79.767.P83	Public opinion
	Refugees see DS79.767.R43
79.767.R43	Relief work. Charities. Protection. Refugees. Displaced persons
79.767.R45	Religious aspects
	Secret service see DS79.767.S75
79.767.S63	Social aspects
79.767.S75	Spies. Secret service. Military intelligence
79.767.W66	Women
79.769	Reconstruction
79.89.A-Z	Provinces, regions, etc., A-Z
79.9.A-Z	Cities, towns, etc., A-Z
	e.g.
79.9.B25	Baghdad
79.9.I85	Isin
79.9.M6	Mosul
79.9.S3	Samarra
79.9.T54	Tikrit
	Lebanon (Phenicia)
80.A2	Periodicals. Societies. Serials
80.A3	Sources and documents
80.A5	Dictionaries. Gazetteers. Guidebooks
80.A7-Z	General works
80.15	Geography
80.2	Description and travel
80.3	Antiquities
80.4	Social life and customs. Civilization. Intellectual life
	Ethnography
80.5	General works
80.55.A-Z	Individual elements in the population, A-Z
80.55.A45	Americans
80.55.A75	Armenians
80.55.B43	Bedouins

	Lebanon (Phenicia)
	Ethnography
	Individual elements in the population, A-Z -- Continued
80.55.D78	Druzes
80.55.K87	Kurds
80.55.M37	Maronites
80.55.P34	Palestinians
80.55.S54	Shī'ah
80.6	Lebanese in foreign countries
	For Lebanese in a particular country, see the country
	History
80.7	Chronological tables
80.73	Collected works
80.75	Biography (Collective)
	Historiography
80.8	General works
	Biography of historians, area studies specialists, archaeologists, etc.
80.82	Collective
80.825.A-Z	Individual, A-Z
80.9	General works
80.92	Military and naval history
	For individual campaigns and engagements, see the period or reign
	Political and diplomatic history. Foreign and general relations
80.95	General works
80.96.A-Z	Relations with individual countries, A-Z
	By period
81	Ancient. Phenicians
82	333 B.C.-638 A.D.
83	Medieval, 638-1517
	Turkish period, 1517-1918
84	General works
85	Autonomy, 1861-1918
86	French Mandate and occupation, 1919-1945
	Republic, 1941-
87	General works
	Biography and memoirs
87.2.A2	Collective
87.2.A3-Z	Individual, A-Z
	Civil War, 1975-1990
87.5	General works
87.52	Hostage taking. Hostages

	Lebanon (Phenicia)
	History
	By period
	Republic, 1941-
	Civil War, 1975-1990 -- Continued
87.53	Israeli intervention, 1982-1984
	Including the massacre of Palestinian Arabs in Sabrā and Shātīlā, and the bombing of the U.S. Marine headquarters
	1990-
87.54	General works
87.6	Israeli intervention, 1996
87.65	Lebanon War, 2006
	Regions, cities, etc.
89.A1	Phenician colonies (Collectively)
89.A2-Z	Individual, A-Z
89.B3	Baalbek
89.B35	Barāghīth Valley
89.B39	Batrūn
89.B4	Beirut
89.B9	Byblos
89.G45	Ghasīl, Tall al-
89.G47	Ghazīr
89.K27	Kāmid al-Lawz Site
(89.S37)	Sarepta
	see DS89.Z36
89.S5	Sidon
89.T36	Tannūrīn
89.T8	Tyre
	Cf. DF234.4 Siege, 332 B.C.
89.Z36	Zarephath. Sarepta
90	Philistines
	Syria
92	Periodicals. Societies. Serials
	Museums, exhibitions, etc.
92.2	General works
92.25.A-Z	Individual. By place, A-Z
92.3	Congresses
92.4	Sources and documents
	Collected works (nonserial)
92.5	Several authors
92.55	Individual authors
92.6	Gazetteers. Dictionaries, etc.
92.7	Place names (General)
92.8	Directories
92.9	Guidebooks
93	General works

	Syria -- Continued
93.2	Pictorial works
93.5	Geography
94	Description and travel
	For works on Palestine and Syria see DS103+
94.5	Antiquities
94.6	Social life and customs. Civilization. Intellectual life
	Ethnography
94.7	General works
94.8.A-Z	Individual elements in the population, A-Z
	Alawites see DS94.8.N67
94.8.A43	Algerians
	Arameans see DS94.8.S94
94.8.A83	Armenians
94.8.B4	Bedouins
94.8.C57	Circassians
94.8.D8	Druses
94.8.K8	Kurds
94.8.N67	Nosairians. Alawites
	For religious aspects see BP195.N7+
94.8.P64	Poles
94.8.S94	Syriac Christians. Arameans
	History
94.9	Dictionaries. Chronological tables, outlines, etc.
94.93	Biography (Collective)
	Historiography
94.95	General works
	Biography
94.97.A2	Collective
94.97.A3-Z	Individual, A-Z
95	General works
	Political and diplomatic history. Foreign and general relations
95.5	General works
95.6.A-Z	Relations with individual countries, A-Z
	By period
96	Early to 333 B.C.
96.2	333 B.C.-634 A.D.
	634-1516
	Cf. DS195.3.A2+ Latin Kingdom of Jerusalem, 1099-1291
97	General works
97.15	634-660
97.2	Omayyads, 660-750
97.3	750-1260
97.4	Mamelukes, 1250-1516
	Turkish period, 1517-1918

	Syria
	History
	By period
	Turkish period, 1517-1918 -- Continued
97.5	General works
	Biography and memoirs
97.6.A2	Collective
97.6.A3-Z	Individual, A-Z
	e.g.
97.6.A8	Asmar, Maria Theresa, princess
	French mandate, 1918-1945
98	General works
	Biography and memoirs
98.12	Collective
98.13.A-Z	Individual, A-Z
	1946-1971
98.2	General works
	Biography and memoirs
98.3.A2	Collective
98.3.A3-Z	Individual, A-Z
	1971-2000
98.4	General works
	Biography and memoirs
98.5.A2	Collective
98.5.A3-Z	Individual, A-Z
	2000-
98.6	General works
	Biography and memoirs
98.7	Collective
98.72.A-Z	Individual, A-Z
99.A-Z	Provinces, regions, cities, etc., A-Z
	e.g.
99.A13	'Abd, Tall al-
99.A14	Abila
99.A24	Abu Danné, Tall
99.A44	Afis, Tall
99.A56	Aleppo
99.A58	Armana, Tall
99.A6	Antioch
99.A7	Apamea
99.A93	'Ayn Dārah, Tall
99.B28	Barri, Tell
99.B29	Bāsiṭ Site
99.B48	Beydar, Tell
99.B57	Birak, Tall
99.B67	Bostra
99.D3	Damascus

DS

Syria
 Provinces, regions, cities, etc., A-Z -- Continued
99.D34   Dayr al-Zawr
99.D78   Dūr-Katlimmu
99.D8   Dura-Europos
99.E25   Ebla
99.E34   Ekatte
99.E52   Emar
99.G55   Gindaros
99.G65   Golan Heights. Jawlān
99.H25   Habūba Kabira Site
99.H26   el Hajj, Tall
99.H293   Hamman al-Turkman, Tall
99.H296   Hana Kingdom
99.H3   Hauran
99.H34   Hayr ash sharqī, Qaṣr
99.H37   Hazna, Tall
99.H82   Hūarte Site
99.H85   'al Hushsh, Tall
                 Jawlān see DS99.G65
99.K48   Khirbat al Bayḍā
99.L3   Latakia
99.M3   Mari
99.M33   Mastuma, Tall
(99.M64)   Mozan, Tall
                     see DS99.U74
99.P17   Palmyra. Tadmur
                 Qalaat al Mudik, Tall see DS99.A7
99.Q225   Qal'at al-Ḥiṣn
                 Qal'at Shayzar Site see DS99.S395
99.Q228   Qarqur, Tall
                 Ras Shamra see DS99.U35
99.R87   Rusafa
99.S27   Ṣaydnāyā
99.S39   Shaykh Ḥasan Site
99.S395   Shayzar
99.S44   Shubat-Enlil
99.S5   Shuwayrah, Tall
99.S55   Sin, Tall
99.S75   Sūkās, Tall
99.S86   Sweyhat, Tell
99.S95   Syrian Desert
                 Tadmur see DS99.P17
99.T47   Terqa
99.T54   Til Barsip
99.T86   Tuqan, Tell
99.T88   Tuttul (Extinct city)

	Syria
	Provinces, regions, cities, etc., A-Z -- Continued
99.U35	Ugarit
99.U46	Umm al Marā, Tall
99.U74	Urkesh
99.Z45	Zenobia
	Israel (Palestine). The Jews
	Cf. BM1+ Judaism
101	Periodicals. Societies. Serials
101.5	Congresses
102	Sources and documents
	Collected works (nonserial)
102.4	Several authors
102.5	Individual authors
102.8	Encyclopedias. Dictionaries
102.9	Directories
102.95	General works
	Description and travel
	Cf. DS47+ Southwestern Asia
103	Guidebooks
103.5	Place names
	To 70 A.D.
104	Contemporary and early works through 1800
104.3	Modern works, 1801-
104.5	70-500
105	500-1453
106	1453-1800
107	1800-1900
107.3	1900-1948
107.4	1948-1980
107.5	1980-
108.5	Monumental and picturesque. Pictorial works
108.9	Historical geography. History of Palestine exploration, etc.
108.92	Geography
	Jerusalem
	Description. Antiquities and exploration
109	To 1981
109.15	1981-
109.2	Pictorial works
109.25	Cemeteries
	Temple Mount
109.28	General works
109.3	Temple
	Cf. NA243 Architecture
109.32.A-Z	Other structures on the Temple Mount, A-Z
	e.g.
	Aqsá Mosque see DS109.32.M38

Israel (Palestine). The Jews
  Jerusalem
    Description. Antiquities and exploration
      Temple Mount
        Other structures on the Temple Mount, A-Z

109.32.M38	Masjid al-Aqsá. Aqsá Mosque
109.32.R6	Dome of the Rock
109.32.W47	Western Wall
109.4	Holy Sepulcher
	Including Church of the Holy Sepulchre
109.8.A-Z	Other special places and objects, A-Z
	e.g.
109.8.A75	Armenian Quarter
109.8.B35	Bet ha-Kerem
109.8.B38	Bet ha-nasi
109.8.B39	Bet Yiśra'el
109.8.C5	Citadel
109.8.C54	City of David
	David, City of see DS109.8.C54
	Dome of the Rock see DS109.32.R6
109.8.G4	Garden of Gethsemane
109.8.G58	Giv'at Sha'ul
	Ḥabashim, Shekhunat ha- see DS109.8.S45
	'Ir David see DS109.8.C54
109.8.J38	Jerusalem Forest
109.8.J4	Jerusalem National Park
109.8.J45	Jewish Quarter
109.8.K37	Ḳaṭamon
109.8.M34	Maḥaneh Yiśra'el
109.8.M4	Mea Shearim. Me'ah She'arim
109.8.M47	Mishkenot sha'ananim
109.8.M5	Mitḥam Roṭshild
109.8.M54	Mitḥam Ṭerah Sanṭah
109.8.M57	Morashah
109.8.M58	Moshavah ha-Germanit
109.8.M6	Mount Herzl
109.8.N34	Naḥla'ot
109.8.O33	Ohel Moshe
109.8.O4	Olives, Mount of
109.8.O62	Ophel Archaeological Garden
109.8.Q65	Qomemiyyut
109.8.R35	Ramot Alon
109.8.R45	Reḥavyah
109.8.S36	Scopus, Mount
109.8.S44	Sheikh Jarrah
109.8.S45	Shekhunat ha-Ḥabashim
109.8.S5	Pool of Siloam

	Israel (Palestine). The Jews
	Jerusalem
	Description. Antiquities and exploration
	Other special places and objects, A-Z -- Continued
109.8.Y45	Yemin Moshe
	History
	Biography and memoirs
109.85	Collective
109.86.A-Z	Individual, A-Z
109.9	General works
	By period
109.912	Through 70 A.D.
	Fall of Jerusalem, 70 A.D see DS122.8
109.913	70 A.D. to 637
109.916	637 to 1099, Muslim period
	1099-1291. Latin Kingdom see D175+
	1244-1917, Muslim-Turkish period
109.92	General works
109.925	1800-1917
	1917-
109.93	General works
	Fall of Jerusalem, 1918 see D568.7
109.94	1967-1993
109.95	1993-
110.A-Z	Regions, towns, etc., A-Z
	Class here regions, towns, etc., west of the Jordan River, regardless of political jurisdiction
	e.g.
110.A22	Abu Ghaush
110.A25	Abu-Shushah, Tel
110.A27	Ābūd
110.A3	Acre
110.A34	Afeq Site. Aphek (Extinct city). Antipatris (Extinct city)
110.A38	Ahwat Site
	Akhziv, Tel see DS110.T23
110.A65	Anafa Site
	Antipatris (Extinct city) see DS110.A34
	Aphek (Extinct city) see DS110.A34
110.A67	Aqabah
110.A683	Arabah Valley
110.A685	'Arad
110.A689	Arbela Site
(110.A7)	Armageddon
	see DS110.M4
110.A73	Arsuf (Extinct city)
110.A754	Ashdod
110.A76	Ashḳelon

Israel (Palestine). The Jews
Regions, towns, etc., A-Z -- Continued

110.A764	Aṣīrah al-Shamālīyah
110.A78	ʻAtlit
110.A8	Avedat
110.A96	ʻAyn Ghazāl (Palestine)
110.B228	Balʻamah Site
110.B23	Balfuryah
110.B25	Banī Naʻīm
110.B26	Baqāh al-Gharbīyah
110.B27	Barṭaʻa
110.B28	Bashīt
110.B297	Bat-Shelomoh
110.B3	Bat Yam
110.B3125	Bayt Jirjā
110.B3127	Bayt Ṣafāfā
110.B313	Bayt Saḥūr
110.B315	Bayt Ummar
110.B316	Baytīn
110.B3213	Beʻeri Region
110.B3213	Beʼer Ṭoviyah
110.B35	Beersheba
110.B364	Beit Jann
110.B367	Belmont Castle Site
110.B372	Bene Berak
110.B3724	Bene Tsiyon
110.B3725	Benjamin, Territory of (Israel and West Bank)
110.B3728	Beśor Region
110.B373	Besor River
110.B3925	Bet Gan
110.B393	Bet She'an
110.B3933	Bet Sheʻarim
110.B394	Bet Shemesh
110.B395	Bet Yeraḥ, Tel
110.B398	Bethany
110.B4	Bethlehem
110.B476	Bethsaida (Extinct city)
110.B56	Binyaminah
110.B57	Biʻr Zayt
110.B83	Budrus
110.B97	Buqeiʻa
110.C13	Caesarea
110.C15	Capernaum
110.C2	Carmel, Mount
110.C27	Castra Site
	Cave of the Letters see DS110.L37
110.D3	Dalit Site

Israel (Palestine). The Jews
Regions, towns, etc., A-Z -- Continued

110.D322	Dāliyat al-Karmil
110.D33	Dan (Extinct city)
110.D335	Dayr Ayyūb
110.D374	Dayr Site
110.D38	Dead Sea
110.D4	Deganyah Alef
110.D67	Dor (Extinct city)
110.D69	Dothan Site
110.E23	Ebal, Mount
110.E455	Efrat
110.E458	Ekron (Extinct city)
110.E46	Elat
110.E47	Elot Region
110.E5	Emmaus
110.E58	'En Besor Site
110.E63	'En Gedi
110.E643	'En Hatsevah Site
110.E645	En Hod
110.E65	En Shadud
110.E76	Even-Yehudah
110.E95	Ezyon Bloc
110.G2	Galilee
110.G22	Gan-Yavneh
110.G3	Gaza Strip
110.G4	Gederah
110.G46	Gerizim, Mount
110.G47	Gesher Site
110.G48	Gevat
110.G5	Gezer
110.G52	Gezer (Region)
110.G557	Gilat Site
110.G572	Gilgal Site
110.G574	Gimzo
110.G577	Ginegar
110.H25	Haderah
110.H257	Hafets-Hayim
110.H28	Haifa
110.H285	Halif Site
110.H286	Hamadyah
110.H288	Hamāmah
110.H292	Hammat Gader Site
110.H295	Hamran, Mount
110.H32	Hanitah-Shelomi Forest
110.H346	Haror, Tel
110.H348	Haruvit

Israel (Palestine). The Jews
Regions, towns, etc., A-Z -- Continued

	Hasi Site see DS110.T4
110.H37	Har-Ṭov
	Ḥazeva Site see DS110.E643
110.H4	Hebron
110.H47	Hertseliyah
110.H475	Ḥiṭṭīn
110.H53	Ḥizma Site
110.H55	Hod ha-Sharon
110.H6	Ḥolon
110.H77	Hula Valley
110.H78	Ḥurfaysh
110.I68	ʻIra Site
110.I93	ʻIzbet Sarṭah
110.J3	Jaffa
110.J3	Jabaʻ
110.J37	Jenin
110.J4	Jericho
110.J44	Jifnā
110.J58	Jīyah
110.J6	Jordan River
110.J78	Judaea (Region)
110.J8	Judaea, Wilderness of
110.J83	Judean Hills
110.J85	Jūlis
110.K2	Ḳabri Site
110.K23	Ḳadimah Forest
110.K27	Karkom Mountain
110.K313	Ḳarmi'el
110.K316	Katif Bloc
110.K34	Kefar ʻAzah
110.K36	Kefar Bar'am
110.K375	Kefar ʻEtsyon
110.K394	Kefar ha-Roʻeh
110.K395	Kefar Ḥabad
110.K396	Kefar 'Otnai Site
110.K397	Kefar Pines
110.K4345	Kefar Sirḳin
110.K4346	Kefar Tavor
110.K44	Kefar Yeḥezḳel
110.K45	Kefar Yehoshu'a
110.K46	Kefar Yonah
110.K53	Khān Yūnus
110.K54	Khirbat Fattir
110.K55	Kineret
110.K553	Ḳiryat Arbaʻ

Israel (Palestine). The Jews
Regions, towns, etc., A-Z -- Continued

110.K554	Ḳiryat Byaliḳ
110.L3	Lachish (Tell ed Duweir)
110.L37	Letters, Cave of the
110.L45	Little Triangle. Meshulash ha-ḳaṭan. Muthallath
110.L63	Lod
110.L83	Lūbiyā (Palestine)
110.M218	Ma'aleh Adumim
110.M26	Maḥanayim
110.M27	Majd al-Kurūm
110.M274	Majdal Yābā
110.M276	Malḥatah, Tel
110.M277	Mallāḥah
110.M33	Masada
110.M36	Mazkeret-Batyah
110.M4	Megiddo (Extinct city)
	Meshulash ha- ka tan. see DS110.L45
110.M44	Menaḥemiyah
	Mezada see DS110.M33
110.M54	Migdal
110.M557	Misgav
110.M57	Mishmar ha-'Emeḳ
110.M6	Modi'in
110.M66	Motsa
110.M85	Munhata Site
	Muthallath see DS110.L45
110.N2	Nablus
110.N23	Nahalal
110.N25	Nahali'el
110.N26	Nahariyah
110.N28	Natsrat 'Ilit
110.N3	Nazareth
110.N4	Negev
110.N434	Nes Harim
110.N46	Netanyah
110.N47	Netsarim
110.N475	Netser Sireni
110.N48	Neveh Etan
110.N57	Nir 'Am
110.N58	Nitsanim
110.O7	Or Yehudah
110.P34	Parḳ ha-Sharon
110.P4	Petaḥ Tiḳvah
110.P67	Poriyyah
110.Q23	Qabāṭīyah
110.Q25	Qālūniyā

Israel (Palestine). The Jews
Regions, towns, etc., A-Z -- Continued

110.Q317	Qashish Site
110.Q58	Qitmit Site
110.Q75	Qubaybah
110.Q8	Qumran Site
110.Q84	Qūqān
110.R22	Ra'ananah
110.R24	Rahaṭ
110.R324	Rām Allāh
110.R325	Ramat-Gan
110.R326	Ramat ha-Kovesh
110.R327	Ramat ha-Sharon
110.R3273	Ramat Hanadiv (Region)
110.R328	Ramat Menasheh
110.R34	Ramat Raḥel
110.R348	Ramat Yishai
110.R36	Ramlah
110.R365	Ramon, Mount
110.R4	Reḥovot
110.R48	Revivim
110.R49	Rinatyah
110.R5	Rishōn le-Tsiyon
110.R57	Rosh ha-'Ayin
110.R6	Rosh Pinah
110.R65	Rosh Zayit Site
110.S2	Sa'adim Site
110.S3	Samaria Region
110.S43	Sepphoris (Extinct city)
110.S5	Sha'ar ha-Golan Site
110.S53	Sharon, Plain of
110.S534	Sharonah
110.S543	Shechem (Extinct city)
110.S546	Shefar'am
110.S555	Shephelah
110.S557	Shikmonah (Extinct city)
110.S558	Shiloh (Extinct city)
110.S57	Shiltā
110.S58	Shivta (Extinct city)
110.S585	Shomerah. Tarbīkhā
110.S59	Shuyūkh
110.S83	Ṣūbā
110.S85	Sumaq Site
110.S86	Ṣummeil (Palestine)
110.S87	Susita (Extinct city)
110.T13	Taanach (Extinct city)
110.T15	Ta'anakh Region

	Israel (Palestine). The Jews
	Regions, towns, etc., A-Z -- Continued
110.T2	Tabor, Mount
110.T22	Tanninim Site
110.T225	Ṭanṭūrah
	Tarbīkhā see DS110.S585
110.T227	Tarshīḥā
110.T23	Tel Akhziv
110.T3-.T395	Tel Aviv (Table DS-DX4)
	Tel Hasi
	see DS110.T4
110.T397	Tel-Yosef
	Tell Duweir (Tell ed Duweir, Lachish)
	see DS110.L3
110.T4	Tell el Hasī
110.T5	Tell en-Nasbeh
110.T6	Tiberias
110.T62	Tiberias Lake
110.T63	Timna Site
110.T66	Tirat Karmel
110.T77	Tsefat
110.T82	Tsovah
110.U65	Upper Zohar
110.U99	ʻUza Site
110.W47	West Bank
	Cf. DS109.8.S36 Mount Scopus
110.Y26	Yagur
110.Y27	Yāmūn
110.Y29	Yanoaḥ
110.Y387	Yavneʻel
110.Y42	Yesud ha-Maʻalah
110.Y53	Yirka
110.Y64	Yoḳneʻam
110.Z38	Zebulon Valley
110.Z5	Zikhron Yaʻaḳov
110.Z53	Ziḳim Site
110.Z64	Zirʻīn
110.Z75	Zubaydāt
	Trans-Jordan see DS153+
110.45	Gulf of Aqaba. Straits of Tiran
(110.5)	Sinai Peninsula
	see DT137.S55
(110.7)	Petra
	see DS154.9.P48
	Antiquities
111.A1	Periodicals. Societies. Museums
111.A2	Sources and documents

Israel (Palestine). The Jews
  Antiquities -- Continued
111.A3-Z	General works
111.1	General special
111.2	Public and political
111.3	Roman
	Social (Family, woman, slavery, etc.), see DS112

111.5	Economic conditions (Industry, commerce)
111.6	Military
111.7	Religious (Festivals, sacrifices, priesthood, temples)
111.8	Art. Music
111.9	Other (Costumes, etc.)

Social life and customs. Civilization. Intellectual life
112	General works
113	Intellectual life. Culture

Ethnography. Tribes of Israel
    For ancient period see DS116+
113.2	General works
113.3	Israeli national characteristics, identity, etc.
113.4	Post-Zionism

    Cf. DS149+ Zionism
Ten lost tribes see DS131
113.5.A-Z	Individual tribes, A-Z

Arabs. Palestinian Arabs
113.6	General works

    Including works on Palestinian Arabs in foreign countries collectively
    For works on Palestinians in individual countries, see the country

Arabs in Israel
113.7	General works
113.72	Druzes
113.74	Lebanese
113.75	Bedouins
113.8.A-Z	Other elements in the population, A-Z
113.8.A35	Algerian Jews
113.8.A4	Americans
113.8.A72	Argentine Jews
113.8.A74	Armenians
113.8.A8	Ashkenazim
113.8.A84	Asian Jews
113.8.A88	Austrian Jews
113.8.B44	Belarusian Jews
113.8.B7	British
113.8.B84	Bulgarians
113.8.C35	Canadian Jews
113.8.C37	Caucasian Jews

	Israel (Palestine). The Jews
	Ethnography. Tribes of Israel
	Other elements in the population, A-Z -- Continued
113.8.C5	Circassians
113.8.C94	Czech Jews
113.8.D8	Dutch Jews
	Ethiopian Jews see DS113.8.F34
113.8.E48	Egyptian Jews
113.8.F34	Falashas
113.8.F73	French Jews
113.8.G37	Georgian (South Caucasian) Jews
113.8.G4	German Jews
113.8.G95	Gypsies. Romanies
113.8.H85	Hungarian Jews
113.8.I7	Iranians
113.8.I72	Iraqi Jews
113.8.I8	Italian Jews
113.8.K9	Kurdish Jews
113.8.L37	Latin American Jews
113.8.L38	Latvian Jews
113.8.L52	Libyan Jews
113.8.L58	Lithuanian Jews
113.8.M66	Moroccan Jews
113.8.N6	North Africans
	Oriental Jews see DS113.8.S4
113.8.P64	Polish Jews
113.8.R65	Romanian Jews
	Romanies see DS113.8.G95
113.8.R87	Russian Jews
113.8.S4	Sephardim
113.8.S65	South African Jews
	Soviet Jews see DS113.8.R87
113.8.S72	Spaniards
113.8.T3	Tajiks
113.8.T83	Tunisian Jews
113.8.T85	Turkish Jews
113.8.T86	Turkmen
113.8.U4	Ukrainian Jews
113.8.U92	Uzbeks
113.8.Y4	Yemenites
113.8.Y83	Yugoslavian Jews
	History
	For history of Jerusalem see DS109.9
114	Dictionaries. Chronological tables, outlines, etc.

Israel (Palestine). The Jews
  History -- Continued
    Biography
      Class here collective biography not limited to one country
      For biography of Jews in a particular country, class in the
        number appropriate for Jews in that country

115	General works
115.2	Women
115.3	Public men
	Historiography
115.5	General works
	Biography of historians, area studies specialists, archaeologists, etc.
115.7	Collective
115.9.A-Z	Individual, A-Z
	e.g.
115.9.J6	Josephus, Flavius
	Cf. DS116 Works by Josephus
	Study and teaching
115.95.A-.Z8	General works
115.95.Z9	Catalogs of audiovisual materials
	General works
116	To 1800
	Including the collected works of Flavius Josephus
117	1801-
118	Compends. Popular and juvenile works
118.5	Questions and answers on Palestine and the Jews
119.2	Military and naval history
	Political and diplomatic history. Foreign and general relations
119.6	General works
119.65	Boundaries
	Jewish-Arab relations. Palestine problem. Arab-Israeli conflict
	For economic aspects see HC415.15
119.7	To 1993
	Cf. DS127.6.O3 Territories occupied by Israel in 1967 Israel-Arab War
	Cf. DS128.183 Peace efforts following 1973 Israel-Arab War
119.75	Intifada, 1987-
	1993-
119.76	General works
119.765	Al-Aqsa Intifada, 2000-
119.767	Gaza War, 2008-2009
119.8.A-Z	Relations with individual countries, A-Z
120	Addresses, essays, lectures

Israel (Palestine). The Jews
History -- Continued
By period
Earliest to 70 A.D.
121   General works
                              For the collected works of Flavius Josephus see
                                  DS116
121.A2   Sources and documents
121.3   Addresses, essays, lectures
121.4   Canaanites
121.5   Jews in Egypt
121.55   Exodus to Death of Solomon
121.6   Divided Kingdom
121.65   Babylonian Exile to Maccabean period (586-168 B.C.)
                              Including Hellenistic period (332-168 B.C.)
                              For works on both Hellenistic and Roman periods
                                  see DS122
                           Maccabees. Hasmonean period (168-63 B.C.)
121.7   General works
121.8.A-Z   Biography, A-Z
121.8.J8   Judas Maccabaeus
                           63 B.C.-70 A.D. Roman period
                              Cf. DS111.3 Roman antiquities
122   General works
122.1   Addresses, essays, lectures
122.3   Herod I the Great, 37-4 B.C.
122.4   Archelaus, 4 B.C.-6 A.D. Judea, Samaria, Idumea
122.5   Herod Antipas, 4 B.C.-39 A.D. Galilee, Perea
122.6   Herod Philip, 4 B.C.-33 A.D. Batanea, Trachonitis,
                                  Auranitis
122.7   Herod Agrippa I, 37-44. Perea, Galilee, Judea,
                                  Samaria, Idumea
122.8   Herod Agrippa II, 53-70. Batanea, Trachonitis,
                                  Auranitis
122.9   Roman domination after the destruction of Jerusalem,
                                  70-324
                                  Including Bar Kokhba Rebellion, 132-135
                           70 A.D.-
123   General works
                                  For works on Roman domination after the
                                      destruction of Jerusalem, 70-324, including Bar
                                      Kokhba Rebellion, 132-135 see DS122.9
123.3   Addresses, essays, lectures
123.5   70-638. Mishnaic and Talmudic period
124   General medieval and early modern to 1800
                           19th-20th centuries
125   General works

Israel (Palestine). The Jews
   History
     By period
      70 A.D.-
        19th-20th centuries -- Continued
         Biography and memoirs
          For Zionists see DS151.A+

125.3.A2	Collective
125.3.A3-Z	Individual, A-Z
	e.g.
125.3.B37	Ben-Gurion, David
125.3.T7	Trumpeldor, Joseph
125.3.W45	Weizmann, Chaim
125.5	Period of World War I, 1914-1918
	Cf. D568.7 World War I
	Cf. DS109.9 Jerusalem
	1919-1948. Period of British control
126	General works
126.3	Period of World War II, 1939-1945
	Cf. D810.J4 World War II
126.4	1945-1948
	Republic, 1948-
	Cf. DS154.5 Jordan
126.5	General works
	Biography
126.6.A2	Collective
126.6.A3-Z	Individual, A-Z
126.7	Addresses, essays, lectures
126.75	Israeli-Zionist propaganda in foreign countries
126.8	Independence Day celebrations
126.82	Yom ha-zikaron (Memorial Day)
126.9	Arab War, 1948-1949. War of Liberation
	Including military operations
126.9.A1	Periodicals. Collections
126.9.A2-.A4	Sources and documents
126.9.A5-Z	General works
126.91	Pictorial works. Satire, caricatures, etc.
126.915	Juvenile works
	Diplomatic history
126.92	General works
126.93.A-Z	Individual countries, A-Z
126.94.A-Z	Regimental and unit histories, A-Z
126.95	Registers, lists of dead and wounded, etc.
126.952	Prisoners and prisons
126.954	Medical and sanitary services. Relief. Refugees
126.96.A-Z	Other topics, A-Z
126.96.A3	Aerial operations

Israel (Palestine). The Jews
  History
    By period
      70 A.D.-
        19th-20th centuries
          Republic, 1948-
            Arab War, 1948-1949. War of Liberation
              Other topics, A-Z -- Continued

126.96.F67	Fortification
126.96.M4	Memorials. Monuments
126.96.M65	Motion pictures about the war
126.96.N3	Naval operations
126.96.O3	Occupied territories
126.96.P8	Public opinion
	Refugees see DS126.954
126.96.R4	Religious aspects
126.96.S94	Supplies
126.96.T4	Territorial questions
126.97	Personal narratives
126.98	Armistices
126.983	Peace
126.985	Influence and results
126.99.A-Z	Local, A-Z

          1967-1993
           For Israeli intervention in Lebanon, 1982-1984 see DS87.53

126.995	General works
	Arab War, 1967
	Including military operations
127.A1	Periodicals. Collections
127.A2-.A4	Sources and documents
127.A5-Z	General works
127.1	Pictorial works. Satire, caricatures, etc.
127.15	Juvenile works
	Diplomatic history
127.2	General works
127.3.A-Z	Individual countries, A-Z
127.4.A-Z	Regimental and unit histories, A-Z
127.5	Registers, lists of dead and wounded, etc.
127.52	Prisoners and prisons
127.54	Medical and sanitary services. Relief. Refugees
127.6.A-Z	Other topics, A-Z
	For list of topics see DS126.96.A+
127.6.O3	Occupied territories
	Cf. DS119.7 Jewish-Arab relations to 1993
127.7	Personal narratives
127.8	Armistices

	Israel (Palestine). The Jews
	History
	By period
	70 A.D.-
	19th-20th centuries
	1967-1993
	Arab War, 1967 -- Continued
127.83	Peace
127.85	Influence and results
127.9.A-Z	Local, A-Z
127.95	War of Attrition, 1969-1970
	Arab War, 1973
	Including military operations
128.1.A1	Periodicals. Collections
128.1.A2-.A4	Sources and documents
128.1.A5-Z	General works
128.11	Pictorial works. Satire, caricatures, etc.
128.115	Juvenile works
	Diplomatic history
128.12	General works
128.13.A-Z	Individual countries, A-Z
128.14.A-Z	Regimental and unit histories, A-Z
128.15	Registers, lists of dead and wounded, etc.
128.152	Prisoners and prisons
128.154	Medical and sanitary services. Relief. Refugees
128.16.A-Z	Other topics, A-Z
	For list of topics see DS126.96.A+
128.17	Personal narratives
128.18	Armistices
128.183	Peace
	Cf. DS119.7 Jewish-Arab relations to 1993
128.185	Influence and results
128.19.A-Z	Local, A-Z
128.2	1993-
	Special topics
129	Samaritans
	Cf. BM900+ Religious sect
131	Ten lost tribes of Israel. Anglo-Israelism
	Cf. BX8643.L66 Lost tribes of Israel (Mormonism)
132	The Jewish state and Jews outside of Palestine. Israel and the diaspora
	Jewish diaspora
	Including Sephardim
	Cf. BM182 Ashkenazim and Sephardim in the history of Judaism
133	Periodicals
	Cf. AP91 General periodicals for Jewish readers

Israel (Palestine). The Jews
    Special topics
      Jewish diaspora -- Continued

134	General works
	Biography and memoirs see DS115+
	By region or country
	Germany
134.2	Serials. Collections
134.22	General works
	History
134.23	General works
134.24	To 1800
134.25	1800-1933
134.255	1933-1945
134.26	1945-1990
134.27	1990-
	Local
134.3	Berlin
134.32	Frankfurt
134.34	Hamburg
134.36.A-Z	Other, A-Z
	Biography
134.4	Collective
134.42.A-Z	Individual, A-Z
	Poland
134.5	Serials. Collections
134.52	General works
	History
134.53	General works
134.54	To 1800
134.55	19th-20th centuries
134.56	2000-
	Local
	For Former Polish Eastern Territories see
	DS135.F67
134.6	Krakow
134.62	Lodz
134.64	Warsaw
134.66.A-Z	Other, A-Z
	Biography and memoirs
134.7	Collective
134.72.A-Z	Individual, A-Z
	Russia (Federation)
	Including Russian Empire, Soviet Union as a whole
	For individual republics of the Soviet Union see the
	modern country in DS135.A-Z
134.8	Serials. Collections

DS

Israel (Palestine). The Jews
Special topics
Jewish diaspora
By region or country
Russia (Federation) -- Continued

134.82	General works
	History
134.83	General works
134.84	To 1917
134.85	1917-1991
134.86	1991-
134.9.A-Z	Local, A-Z
	Biography and memoirs
134.92	Collective
134.93.A-Z	Individual, A-Z
135.A-Z	Other regions or countries, A-Z
	For North and South American countries, see E-F
135.A23	Afghanistan
135.A25	Africa
135.A28	Albania
135.A3	Algeria
135.A68	Arab countries
	Arabia
135.A7	General works
135.A75A-.A75Z	Local, A-Z
	Biography and memoirs
135.A8A1-.A8A19	Collective
135.A8A2-.A8Z	Individual, A-Z
135.A83	Armenia
135.A85	Asia
135.A86	Asia, Central
135.A88-.A883	Australia (Table DS-DX7)
	Austria (Austria-Hungary)
135.A9	General works
135.A92A-.A92Z	Local, A-Z
	Czechoslovakia see DS135.C95+
	Hungary see DS135.H9+
	Biography and memoirs
135.A93A1-.A93A19	Collective
135.A93A2-.A93Z	Individual, A-Z
135.A96	Azerbaijan
135.B2	Babylonia
135.B26-.B263	Bahrain (Table DS-DX7)
135.B3	Balkan Peninsula
135.B337	Baltic Sea Region
135.B34	Baltic States
135.B38-.B383	Belarus (Table DS-DX7)

Israel (Palestine). The Jews
  Special topics
    Jewish diaspora
      By region or country
        Other regions or countries, A-Z -- Continued

135.B4-.B43	Belgium (Table DS-DX7)
135.B54-.B543	Bosnia and Hercegovina (Table DS-DX7)
	Bulgaria
135.B8	General works
135.B83	Local, A-Z
	Biography and memoirs
135.B85A1-.B85A19	Collective
135.B85A2-.B85Z	Individual, A-Z
135.B87	Burma. Myanmar
	Canada see F1035.J5
135.C33	Canary Islands
135.C35	Cape Verde
	Central America see F1440.J48
135.C5	China
135.C66	Congo (Democratic Republic)
	Costa Rica see F1557.J4
135.C75	Croatia
135.C88	Cyprus
	Czechoslovakia. Czech Republic
135.C95	General works
135.C96A-.C96Z	Local, A-Z
	Biography and memoirs
135.C97A1-.C97A19	Collective
135.C97A2-.C97Z	Individual, A-Z
135.D4-.D43	Denmark (Table DS-DX7)
135.E2-.E23	East (Far East) (Table DS-DX7)
135.E4-.E43	Egypt (Table DS-DX7)
	England. Great Britain
135.E5A2-.E5A4	Serials. Collections
135.E5A5-.E5Z	History
135.E55	Local, A-Z
	Biography and memoirs
135.E6A1-.E6A19	Collective
135.E6A2-.E6Z	Individual, A-Z
135.E64	English-speaking countries
135.E68	Eritrea
135.E73	Estonia
135.E75	Ethiopia
	Including Falashas
135.E77	Eurasia
	Europe
	Including Eastern Europe in general

DS

Israel (Palestine). The Jews
Special topics
Jewish diaspora
By region or country
Other regions or countries, A-Z
Europe -- Continued

135.E8A2-.E8A4	Serials. Collections
	History
135.E8A5-.E8Z	General
135.E81	Early and medieval
	Cf. BM182 Ashkenazim and Sephardim in the history of Judaism
135.E82	1601-1815
135.E83	19th-20th centuries
135.E84	21st century
	Biography
135.E89	Collective
135.E9A-.E9Z	Individual, A-Z
135.F54	Finland
135.F67	Former Polish Eastern Territories
	France
135.F8A2-.F8A4	Serials. Collections
	History
135.F8A5-.F8Z	General
135.F81	Early and medieval
135.F82	1601-1815
135.F83	19th-20th centuries
135.F84	21st century
135.F85	Local, A-Z
	Biography
135.F89	Collective
135.F9A-.F9Z	Individual, A-Z
135.G28	Georgia (Republic)
(135.G3-.G5)	Germany
	see DS134.2+
	Great Britain see DS135.E5+
135.G7-.G73	Greece (Table DS-DX7)
135.H9-.H93	Hungary (Table DS-DX7)
135.I6-.I63	India (Table DS-DX7)
135.I64-.I643	Indonesia (Table DS-DX7)
135.I65-.I653	Iran (Table DS-DX7)
	Iraq
135.I7	General works
135.I712A-.I712Z	Local, A-Z
	Biography and memoirs
135.I713A1-.I713A19	Collective
135.I713A2-.I713Z	Individual, A-Z

Israel (Palestine). The Jews
  Special topics
    Jewish diaspora
      By region or country
        Other regions or countries, A-Z -- Continued

135.I72	Ireland
	Islamic countries see DS135.L4
	Italy
135.I8	General works
135.I85A-.I85Z	Local, A-Z
	e.g.
135.I85E53	Emilia-Romagna
135.I85M3	Mantua
135.I85N3	Naples
135.I85R6	Rome
	Biography and memoirs
135.I9A1-.I9A19	Collective
135.I9A2-.I9Z	Individual, A-Z
135.J3-.J33	Japan (Table DS-DX7)
135.K39-.K393	Kazakhstan (Table DS-DX7)
135.K45	Kenya
135.K8	Kurdistan
135.K97	Kyrgyzstan
135.L3-.L33	Latvia (Table DS-DX7)
135.L34	Lebanon
135.L4	Levant. Near East. Islamic countries
	Libya
135.L44	General works
135.L45A-.L45Z	Local, A-Z
	Biography and memoirs
135.L46A1-.L46A19	Collective
135.L46A2-.L46Z	Individual, A-Z
135.L5-.L53	Lithuania (Table DS-DX7)
135.L8-.L83	Luxemburg (Table DS-DX7)
135.M23	Macedonia
135.M234	Mali
135.M26	Malta
135.M3	Mauritania
135.M33	Mauritius
135.M43	Mediterranean Region
135.M64	Moldova
	Morocco
135.M8	General works
135.M85A-.M85Z	Local, A-Z
	Biography and memoirs
135.M9A1-.M9A19	Collective
135.M9A2-.M9Z	Individual, A-Z

Israel (Palestine). The Jews
  Special topics
    Jewish diaspora
      Other regions or countries, A-Z

135.M95	Mozambique
	Myanmar see DS135.B87
	Netherlands
135.N4	General works
135.N5A-.N5Z	Local, A-Z
	Biography and memoirs
135.N6A1-.N6A19	Collective
135.N6A2-.N6Z	Individual, A-Z
135.N65-.N653	New Zealand (Table DS-DX7)
135.N72	Nigeria
135.N8-.N83	Norway (Table DS-DX7)
	Panama see F1557.J4
135.P45	Philippines
(135.P6-.P63)	Poland
	see DS134.5+
	Portugal
135.P7	General works
135.P75A-.P75Z	Local, A-Z
	Biography and memoirs
135.P8A1-.P8A19	Collective
135.P8A2-.P8Z	Individual, A-Z
135.R7-.R73	Romania (Table DS-DX7)
(135.R9-.R95)	Russia. Soviet Union
	see DS134.8+
135.S24	San Marino
135.S26	Sao Tome and Principe
135.S32	Scandinavia
135.S34	Senegal
135.S35-.S353	Serbia (Table DS-DX7)
135.S44	Singapore
135.S55-.S553	Slovakia (Table DS-DX7)
135.S57-.S573	Slovenia (Table DS-DX7)
135.S57	Slovenia
135.S6-.S63	South Africa (Table DS-DX7)
	Soviet Union see DS134.8+
	Spain
	Cf. BM182 Ashkenazim and Sephardim in the history of Judaism
135.S7	General works
135.S75	Local, A-Z
	Biography and memoirs
135.S8A1-.S8A19	Collective
135.S8A2-.S8Z	Individual, A-Z

	Israel (Palestine). The Jews
	Special topics
	Jewish diaspora
	By region or country
	Other regions or countries, A-Z -- Continued
	Spanish America
	see F
135.S85	Sudan
	Sweden
135.S87	General works
135.S88A-.S88Z	Local, A-Z
	Biography and memoirs
135.S89A1-.S89A19	Collective
135.S89A2-.S89Z	Individual, A-Z
135.S9-.S93	Switzerland (Table DS-DX7)
135.S95	Syria
135.T34	Tajikistan
135.T54	Thailand
135.T7-.T73	Tunisia (Table DS-DX7)
135.T8-.T83	Turkey. Ottoman Empire (Table DS-DX7)
135.T85	Turkmenistan
135.U32	Uganda
135.U4-.U43	Ukraine (Table DS-DX7)
	United States see E184.3+
135.U92	Uzbekistan
135.Y4	Yemen
135.Y8-.Y83	Yugoslavia (Table DS-DX7)
135.Z35	Zambia
135.Z56	Zimbabwe
	Political and social conditions
140	General works
140.5	Economic conditions
141	Jewish question
143	The modern Jew. Jewish identity
145	Antisemitism
	"Protocols of the Wise Men of Zion"
145.P49	Russian. By date
145.P5	English. By date
145.P6A-.P6Z	Other languages, A-Z
145.P7	Criticism
146.A-Z	By region or country, A-Z
	e.g.
146.A67	Arab countries
146.E85	Europe. Europe, Western
146.E8515	Europe, Central
146.E852	Europe, Eastern
	Europe, Western see DS146.E85

	Israel (Palestine). The Jews
	Special topics
	Jewish diaspora
	Antisemitism
	By region or country, A-Z -- Continued
146.U6	United States
147	Civil emancipation
148	Assimilation
	Zionism
	Cf. BS649.J5 Prophecies about Jews in Palestine
	Cf. DS113.4 Post-Zionism
149.A1	Periodicals. Societies
149.A4	Congresses
149.A5-Z	General works
149.5.A-Z	By region or country, A-Z
150.A-Z	Special movements, A-Z
	Choveve Zion (Hoveve Zion). Hibbat Zion
150.C44	Periodicals. Congresses
150.C45	General works
150.C451-.C459	Organizations within Choveve Zion
	Subarrange alphabetically
	For local organizations see DS150.C46A+
150.C46A-.C46Z	By region or country, A-Z
	"General" Zionism
150.G4	Periodicals. Congresses
150.G5	General works
150.G51-.G59	Organizations within General Zionism
	Subarrange alphabetically
	For local organizations see DS150.G6A+
150.G6A-.G6Z	By region or country, A-Z
	Hadassah
150.H3	Periodicals. Societies
150.H4	General works
150.H41-.H49	Organizations within Hadassah
	Subarrange alphabetically
	For local organizations see DS150.H5A+
150.H5A-.H5Z	By region or country, A-Z
	Labor Zionism
150.L3	Periodicals. Societies
150.L4	General works
150.L41-.L49	Organizations within Labor Zionism
	Subarrange alphabetically
	e.g.
150.L43	Hashomer Hatzair
	For local see DS150.L5A+
150.L5A-.L5Z	By region or country, A-Z
	Religious Zionism

                                        Israel (Palestine). The Jews
                                            Special topics
                                            Jewish diaspora
                                                Zionism
                                                    Special movements, A-Z
                                                        Religious Zionism -- Continued
150.R3   Periodicals. Congresses
150.R32   General works
150.R33-.R38   Organizations within Religious Zionism
                                                                Subarrange alphabetically
                                                                e.g.
150.R35   Mizrachi
                                                                    For local see DS150.R39A+
150.R39A-.R39Z   By region or country, A-Z
                                                        Revisionist Zionism
150.R4   Periodicals. Congresses
150.R5   General works
150.R51-.R59   Organizations within Revisionist Zionism
                                                                Subarrange alphabetically
                                                                For local organizations see DS150.R6A+
150.R6A-.R6Z   By region or country, A-Z
150.5   Christian Zionism
                                                    Biography and memoirs of Zionists
151.A2   Collective
151.A3-Z   Individual, A-Z
                                                            e.g.
                                                            Aḥad Ha'am see DS151.G5
151.G5   Ginzberg, Asher
151.H4   Herzl, Theodor
                                                            Jabotinsky, Vladimir see DS151.Z5
151.R6   Rothschild, Edmond, baron de
151.W7   Wolfsson, David
151.Z5   Zhabotinskii, Vladimir Evgen'evich
                                        Jordan. Transjordan
                                            Official name: Hashemite Kingdom of Jordan
153.A2   Periodicals. Societies
153.A3   Sources and documents
153.A4   Guidebooks
153.A5-Z   General works
153.122   Gazetteers. Dictionaries, etc.
153.123   Place names (General)
153.198   Geography
153.2   Description and travel
153.3   Antiquities
153.4   Social life and customs. Civilization. Intellectual life
                                            Ethnography
153.5   General works

Jordan. Transjordan
   Ethnography -- Continued

153.55.A-Z	Individual elements in the population, A-Z
153.55.A45	Āl Zaydān
153.55.B43	Bedouins
153.55.C44	Chechens
153.55.C57	Circassians
153.55.K86	Kurds
153.55.P34	Palestinian Arabs
153.55.S34	Ṣakhr
153.55.Y46	Yemenis
	History
153.7	Chronological tables
153.8	Biography (Collective)
153.9	Historiography
154	General works
154.13	Military history
	Foreign and general relations
154.15	General works
154.16.A-Z	Relations with individual countries, A-Z
	By period
	Ancient
154.2	General works
154.215	Ammonites
154.22	Nabataeans
154.3	Medieval
154.4	Turkish period, 1517-1918
	1919-
154.5	General works
	Biography and memoirs
154.52.A2	Collective
154.52.A3-Z	Individual, A-Z
154.53	Abdullah I, 1946-1951
154.54	Talal I, 1951-1952
154.55	Hussein I, 1952-1999
	Including Regency, 1952-1953
154.6	Abdullah II, 1999-
154.9.A-Z	Regions, towns, etc., A-Z
	e.g.
	For regions, towns, etc., west of Jordan River see DS110.A+
154.9.A24	Abila
154.9.A28	Abu al-Kharaz, Tell
154.9.A5	Amman
154.9.A55	Amman Airport Site
154.9.A7	Araq el-Emir Site
154.9.B32	Bāb edh-Dhrā Site

	Jordan. Transjordan
	Regions, towns, etc., A-Z -- Continued
154.9.B34	Bādīyah al-Shamāliyah
154.9.C34	Callirrhoe Site
154.9.D34	Dayr ‘Allā, Tall
154.9.D48	Dhrā‘ el Khān Site
154.9.E83	Ezion-geber
154.9.G47	Gerasa
154.9.H39	Hayyat, Tell el-
154.9.H57	Hisbān, Tall
154.9.H86	Humaymat Site
154.9.J38	Jāwā
154.9.J39	Jawa, Tall (Amman)
154.9.J54	Johfiyeh, Tell
154.9.M33	Ma'dabā
154.9.M35	Mafraq
154.9.M36	Mafraq Province
154.9.M39	Mazar, Tall al-
154.9.M6	Moab
154.9.P43	Pella of the Decapolis
154.9.P48	Petra
154.9.Q36	Qaṣr Kharāna
154.9.S22	Sa‘īdīyah, Tall
154.9.S27	Samrā' Site
154.9.T38	Tawilan Site
154.9.T57	Ṭiwāl al-Sharqī Site
154.9.U4	‘Umayri, Tall al-
154.9.U45	Umm al-Jimāl Site
154.9.U47	Umm Hammad, Tall
154.9.Z35	Zahrat adh-Dhra' 1
154.9.Z37	Zarqā'
	Asia Minor
155	General works on Asia Minor before 1453
	Including Greek city-states and colonies
156.A-Z	Ancient states, regions, cities, etc., A-Z
	Including archaeological sites
	e.g.
	For modern provinces, regions, cities, etc. see DS51.A+
156.A45	Alaca Höyük
156.A556	Antioch
156.A557	Antioch in Pisidia
	Apamea on the Euphrates see DS156.Z48
	Ararat see DS156.U7
156.A63	Aphrodisias
156.A64	Arykanda
156.A7	Assos
	Bergama see DS156.P4

	Asia Minor
	Ancient states, regions, cities, etc., A-Z -- Continued
156.B6	Bithynia
156.C3	Cappadocia
	Caunus see DS156.K33
156.C5	Cilicia
	Clazomenae see DF261.C6
156.C87	Cyme
156.C9	Cyzicus
156.D45	Dereağzı Site
156.D5	Didyma
156.E2	Edessa (Urfa)
	Ephesus see DF261.E5
	Gordion see DS156.G6
156.G6	Gordium. Gordion
156.G73	Gritille Site
156.H3	Halicarnassus (Bodrum)
156.H47	Heraclea Pontica
	Cf. DS51.E76 Ereğli (Zonguldak)
156.H48	Herakleia
156.I6	Ionia
156.I82	Isauria
156.K27	Kapikaya site
156.K33	Kaunos. Caunus
156.K46	Keramos
156.K59	Kızılbel Tomb
156.K67	Korucutepe
156.K92	Kyaneai
	Kyme see DS156.C87
156.L34	Lagina
156.L8	Lycia
156.L9	Lydia. Croesus
156.M33	Magnesia ad Maeander
	Miletus see DF261.M5
156.M56	Mina Site
156.M95	Myra. Kale
156.N42	Neandria
156.N45	Nemrut Dağı Mound
156.N5	Nicaea
156.O49	Olympos
156.O8	Osrhoene
	Cf. DS156.E2 Edessa
156.P27	Pamphylia
156.P3	Paphlagonia
156.P37	Pepuza
156.P38	Perga
156.P4	Pergamum (Bergama)

	Asia Minor
	Ancient states, regions, cities, etc., A-Z -- Continued
156.P5	Phrygia
156.P58	Pisidia
156.P8	Pontus
156.S25	Sagalassos
156.S3	Sardis
	Seleucia on the Euphrates see DS156.Z48
156.S6	Sinope
156.T45	Teichiussa (Extinct city)
156.T54	Tille Mound
156.T55	Tilmen (Extinct city)
	Troy see DF221.T8
156.T79	Trysa (Extinct city)
156.U7	Urartu (Kingdom)
156.Z48	Zeugma. Apamea on the Euphrates. Seleucia on the Euphrates
	Armenia
	Class here works on the historic kingdom and region of Armenia as a whole
	For works on the territories incorporated into other countries after 1920, see the country e.g. DK511.A68+, Armenian S.S.R., DS51+, Turkey
161	Periodicals. Societies. Serials
162	Sources and documents
162.23	Gazetteers. Dictionaries, etc.
162.24	Place names (General)
163	Guidebooks
165	General works. Description and travel
166	Pictorial works
166.5	Historical geography
166.7	Geography
167	Antiquities
171	Social life and customs. Civilization. Intellectual life
172	Ethnography
172.2	Armenians in foreign countries (General)
	For Armenians in a particular country, see the country
	History
173	Dictionaries
174	Biography (Collective)
	Historiography
174.7	General works
	Biography of historians, area studies specialists, archaeologists, etc.
174.8	Collective
174.9.A-Z	Individual, A-Z
	Study and teaching

	Armenia
	History
	Study and teaching -- Continued
174.92	General works
174.93.A-Z	By region or country, A-Z

Under each country:

.x	General works
.x2A-.x2Z	Special schools. By place, A-Z

175	General works
	Political and diplomatic history. Foreign and general relations
175.3	General works
175.4.A-Z	Relations with individual countries, A-Z
176	Addresses, essays, lectures
	By period
	Earliest to 428. Armenian dynasties
181	General works
183	Addresses, essays, lectures
	Biography and memoirs
184.A2	Collective
184.A3-Z	Individual, A-Z
	428-1522. Sassanids, etc.
186	General works
	Biography and memoirs
188.A2	Collective
188.A3-Z	Individual, A-Z
	1522-1800. Turkish rule
191	General works
	Biography and memoirs
193.A2	Collective
193.A3-Z	Individual, A-Z
	e.g.
193.S6	Spandarîan, Suren Spandarovich
	1801-1900
194	General works
	Biography and memoirs
194.5.A2	Collective
194.5.A3-Z	Individual, A-Z
	1901-
195	General works
	Biography and memoirs
195.3.A2	Collective
195.3.A3-195.Z	Individual, A-Z
195.5	1914-1923
	Including independence and massacre by the Turks until the Treaty of Lausanne in 1923

	Armenia -- Continued
(199)	Local

see the appropriate local numbers in Iran, Turkey or Armenia (Republic)

Arabian Peninsula. Saudi Arabia
    Cf. DS36+ Modern Moslem world
    Cf. DS36.85+ Medieval Arab Empire

201	Periodicals. Societies. Serials
201.2	Gulf Cooperation Council
202	Sources and documents
202.2	Gazetteers. Dictionaries, etc.
202.3	Place names (General)
202.4	Directories
203	Guidebooks, etc.
204	General works
204.2	Pictorial works
204.25	Juvenile works
204.45	Geography
	Description and travel
204.5	History of travel
205	Through 1100
206	1100-1800
207	1801-1950
208	1951-
211	Antiquities
	For local antiquities see DS247+
215	Social life and customs. Civilization. Intellectual life
	Ethnography
218	General works
219.A-Z	Individual elements in the population, A-Z
219.A3	'Ād
219.A4	Āl Murrah
219.A53	'Anazah (Arab tribe)
219.A8	al-'Awāzim
219.A85	'Awlaqī (Arab tribe)
219.A93	Azd
219.B34	Bakr ibn Wā'il
219.B345	Balī (Arab tribe)
219.B35	Banī Shahr (Arab tribe)
219.B36	Banū Khālid (Arab tribe)
219.B4	Bedouins
219.B56	Blacks
219.D32	Dabba
219.D38	Dawāsir
219.D48	Dhubyān
219.F83	Fuḍūl
219.G43	Ghāmid

	Arabian Peninsula. Saudi Arabia
	Ethnography
	Individual elements in the population, A-Z -- Continued
219.H34	Hadrami
219.H38	Hawāzin
219.H59	Hizzān
219.H78	Hudhayl
219.H785	Huwala
219.H8	al-Ḥuwayṭāt
219.K43	Khazraj
219.K48	Khuzā'ah
219.K5	Kilāb
219.M33	Ma'āḍīd
219.M34	Makhzūm
	Otaybay see DS219.U73
219.Q7	Quraysh
219.S38	Shammar
219.S43	Sharārāt
219.S45	Shaybān
219.S47	Shiites
219.S58	Shuḥūḥ
219.S84	Sulaym
219.T32	Taghlib
219.T34	Tamim
219.T38	Tay'
219.T45	Thamud
219.T47	Thaqif
219.U72	'Uqayl (Arab tribe)
219.U73	'Utaybah. Otaybah
219.Y34	Yāfi'
219.Z34	Zahrān
219.Z39	Zayd ibn Layth
	History
221	Dictionaries
222	Biography (Collective)
	Historiography
222.7	General works
	Biography of historians, area studies specialists, archaeologists, etc.
222.8	Collective
222.9.A-Z	Individual, A-Z
	e.g.
222.9.N5	Niebuhr, Carsten
	Study and teaching
222.92	General works
222.93.A-Z	By region or country, A-Z
	Subarrange by author

	Arabian Peninsula. Saudi Arabia
	History -- Continued
223	General works
225	Addresses, essays, lectures
	Political and diplomatic history. Foreign and general relations
227	General works
228.A-Z	Relations with individual countries, A-Z
	By period
231	Earliest to 622
232	622-661

For works on the first four caliphs and the Arab conquests see DS38.1

	661-1517
	General works
234	Oriental authors to 1800
	European, modern Oriental, and other
235	To 1800
236	1800-
237	Addresses, essays, lectures
	Biography and memoirs
238.A1	Collective
238.A2-Z	Individual, A-Z
	By period
238.3	661-750
238.5	750-1258
238.7	1258-1517
239	1517-1635
241	1635-1740
242	1740-1873. Wahhabi movement

For works by and about Muḥammad ibn 'Abd al-Wahhāb and the religious aspects of the Wahhabi movement see BP195.W2+

243	1873-1914
	1914-1932
244	General works
	Biography and memoirs
244.49	Collective
244.5.A-Z	Individual, A-Z
	1932-
244.512	General works
	Kingdom of Saudi Arabia, 1932-
	Including history of the Sa'ud family
244.52	General works
	Biography and memoirs
244.525	Collective
244.526.A-Z	Individual, A-Z

	Arabian Peninsula. Saudi Arabia
	History
	By period
	1932-
	Kingdom of Saudi Arabia, 1932- -- Continued
	By period
244.53	Ibn Saʻūd, 1932-1953
244.56	Saʻūd, 1953-1964
244.6	Fayṣal, 1964-1975
244.63	1975-
	Local history and description
247.A-Z	Regions, sultanates, emirates, etc., A-Z
	For regions, provinces, etc., of Saudia Arabia see DS247.9.A+
247.A1-.15	Regions
247.A13-.A138	Persian Gulf States (Table DS-DX5)
247.A14-.A148	Southern Arabia (Table DS-DX5)
247.A18-.A188	Abū Ẓaby (Table DS-DX5)
247.A2-.A28	Aden. Yemen (People's Democratic Republic). Federation of South Arabia (Table DS-DX5)
247.A54-.A548	Ajmām (Table DS-DX5)
(247.A8-.A88)	Asir Region
	see DS247.9.A83
(247.B17-.B178)	Bāḥah
	see DS247.9.B34
247.B2-.B28	Bahrain (Table DS-DX5)
247.B8-.B88	Buraimi (Oasis) (Table DS-DX5)
247.D7-.D78	Dubai (Table DS-DX5)
247.F34-.F348	Failaka Island (Table DS-DX5)
247.F84-.F848	Fujayrah (Table DS-DX5)
247.H3-.H38	Hadramaut (Table DS-DX5)
(247.H394-.H3948)	Hasa Oasis
	see DS247.9.H37
(247.H4-.H48)	Hejaz
	see DS247.9.H45
(247.J3-.J38)	Al Jaww
	see DS247.9.J38
(247.J57-.J578)	Jāzān
	see DS247.9.Q58
247.K8-.K88	Kuwait (Kuweit) (Table DS-DX5)
247.M8-.M88	Muscat (Table DS-DX5)
	Najd see DS247.9.N35
(247.N47-.N48)	Nejd
	see DS247.9.N35
247.O6-.O68	Oman (Table DS-DX5)
247.Q3-.Q38	Qatar (Table DS-DX5)
247.R37-.R378	Ras al Khaimah (Table DS-DX5)

	Arabian Peninsula. Saudi Arabia
	Local history and description
	Regions, sultanates, emirates, etc., A-Z -- Continued
247.R8-.R88	Rub'al Khālī (Table DS-DX5)
247.S4-.S48	Sealand (Table DS-DX5)
247.S5-.S58	ash Shāriqah (Table DS-DX5)
(247.S62-.S628)	Sharqīyah (Saudi Arabia)
	see DS247.9.S52
247.T8-.T88	Trucial Oman. Trucial States. United Arab Emirates
	(Table DS-DX5)
247.U45-.U458	Umm al-Nār Island (Table DS-DX5)
(247.U5-.U58)	'Unayzah
	see DS247.9.U52
(247.Y35-.Y358)	Yamāmah
	see DS247.9.Y24
247.Y4-.Y48	Yemen (Table DS-DX5)
	Yemen (People's Democratic Republic) see DS247.A2+
	Cities, towns, etc.
247.2.A-Z	Places in Bahrain, A-Z
247.3.A-Z	Places in Kuwait, A-Z
247.4.A-Z	Places in Oman, A-Z
247.5.A-Z	Places in Qatar, A-Z
	Places in Saudi Arabia see DS248.A+
247.6.A-Z	Places in United Arab Emirates, A-Z
247.7.A-Z	Places in Yemen, A-Z
	e.g.
247.7.S52	Shabwa
247.9.A-Z	Regions, provinces, etc., of Saudi Arabia, A-Z
	e.g.
247.9.A83	Asir Region
247.9.B34	Bāḥah
247.9.H35	Hāil
247.9.H37	Hasa Oasis
247.9.H45	Hejaz
247.9.J38	al Jaww
247.9.N35	Najd
247.9.Q28	Qaṭīf
247.9.Q58	Qīzān
247.9.S52	Shariqīyah
247.9.U52	'Unayzah
247.9.Y24	Yamāmah
248.A-Z	Cities, towns, etc. of Saudi Arabia, A-Z
	e.g.
248.J5	Jiddah
248.M4	Mecca
248.M5	Medina
248.Q37	Qaryat al-Fāu

	Arabian Peninsula. Saudi Arabia
	Local history and description
	Cities, towns, etc. of Saudi Arabia, A-Z -- Continued
248.R5	Riyadh
(248.S55)	Shabwa
	see DS247.7.S52
	Iran (Persia)
251	Periodicals. Societies. Serials
251.5	Congresses
252	Sources and documents
	Collected works
252.4	Several authors
252.5	Individual authors
253	Gazetteers. Dictionaries, etc.
254	Guidebooks
254.5	General works
254.7	Pictorial works
254.75	Juvenile works
254.8	Historical geography
254.9	Geography
	Description and travel
255	Oriental authors
	European and other authors
255.5	History of travel
256	Earliest to 226 A.D.
257	226-1800
258	1801-1950
259	1951-1979
259.2	1980-
	Antiquities
	Museums, exhibitions, etc.
260.7	General works
260.8.A-Z	By region or country, A-Z
	Subarrange by author
261	General works
262.A-Z	Local antiquities, A-Z
262.A57	Anshan
262.B36	Bani Surmah Site
262.B37	Bastam
262.B56	Bīshāpūr
262.B57	Bisutun Site
262.C45	Chogha Bonut Site
262.C46	Chogha Mish
262.D57	Djubi Gauhar Site
262.D87	Dur-Untash
262.F37	Farrokhabad, Tepe
262.G6	Godin Tepe

Iran (Persia)
  Antiquities
    Local antiquities, A-Z -- Continued

262.H34	Haft Tepe
262.H37	Hasanlu
262.H57	Hissar Tepe
262.K32	Kabūd Gonbad, Khorasan
262.M37	Marlik Site
262.P35	Pasargadae
262.P4	Persepolis
262.P84	Pūskān Site
262.Q26	Qaṣr-i Abū Naṣr Site
262.S27	Sarab Site
262.S48	Shāh'dizh
262.S515	Shahr-i Sokhta
262.S52	Shāpūr
262.S57	Sīrāf
262.S59	Siyalk, Tepe
262.S9	Susa
262.T35	Takht-i-Sulayman
262.T4	Tāq-e Bostān Site
262.W37	War Kabud Site
262.Y3	Yahya, Tapah-ye
262.Z58	Ziwiyē

Social life and customs. Civilization. Intellectual life

266	General works
267	Earliest (Zoroastrian)

Ethnography

268	General works
269.A-Z	Individual elements in the population, A-Z
269.A23	'Abd al-Malikis
269.A34	Afghans
269.A36	Afshar (Turkish tribe)
269.A73	Arabs
269.A75	Armenians
269.A88	Assyrians
269.A94	Azerbaijanis. Azeris
269.B3	Bakhtiari
269.B33	Baluchi
269.B36	Baseri tribe
269.B39	Bayat (Turkic people)
269.B57	Bīrānvand
269.C34	Cadusii
269.G46	Georgians (South Caucasians)
269.K25	Ka'b (Arab people)
269.K27	Karapapaks
269.K3	Kashgai (Turkic people). Qashqāʾī (Turkic people)

	Iran (Persia)
	Ethnography
	Individual elements in the population, A-Z -- Continued
269.K65	Komachi
269.K87	Kurds
269.L87	Lurs
269.M36	Mandaeans. Sabians. St. John's Christians
269.P3	Papis
	Qashqāī (Turkic people) see DS269.K3
	Sabians see DS269.M36
	St. John's Christians see DS269.M36
269.S53	Shahsevan
269.T38	Tats
269.T8	Turkomans
269.T82	Turks
269.Z65	Zoroastrians
	History
270	Dictionaries. Chronological tables, outlines, etc.
271	Biography (Collective)
	For individual biography, see the specific period, reign or place
	Historiography
271.5	General works
	Biography of historians, area studies specialists, archaeologists, etc.
271.6	Collective
271.7.A-Z	Individual, A-Z
	Study and teaching
271.8	General works
271.9.A-Z	By region or country, A-Z

Under each country:

.x	General works
.x2A-.x2Z	Individual schools. By name, A-Z

272	General works
273	Addresses, essays, lectures
273.3	Military history
	For individual campaigns and engagements see the special period or reign
	Political and diplomatic history. Foreign and general relations
274	General works
274.2.A-Z	Relations with individual countries, A-Z
	By period
	Ancient to 226 A.D.
275	General works
276	Earliest through 640 B.C.
	Median Empire, 640-558 B.C.

Iran (Persia)
History
By period
Ancient to 226 A.D.
Median Empire, 640-558 B.C. -- Continued

278	General works
279	Deioces, 708-655
279.3	Phraortes, 655-633
279.5	Cyaxares, 633-593
279.7	Astyages, 593-558
	Persian Empire, 558-330 B.C. Achaemenidae
281	General works
282	Cyrus, 558-529
282.5	Cambyses, 529-522
282.6	Smerdis, 521
282.7	Darius I, 521-485
283	Xerxes I, 485-465
284	Artaxerxes I, 465-424
284.2	Xerxes II, 424
284.3	Darius II, 424-405
284.4	Artaxerxes II, 405-359
	Cf. DF231.32 Expedition of Cyrus
284.5	Artaxerxes III, 358-338
284.6	Arses, 338-336
284.7	Darius III, 336-330
284.9	330/323-246 B.C. Seleucids
285	Parthian Empire, 246 B.C.-226 A.D. Arsacidae
	Cf. DS324.P37 Parthia
	Modern, 226-
	General works see DS272
	Sassanian empire, 226-651
286	General works
286.2	Ardashir (Artaxerxes) I, 226-241
286.3	Shapur I, 241-272
286.31	Hormizd I, 272-273
286.33	Bahram I, 273-276
286.35	Bahram II, 276-293
286.37	Bahram III, 293
286.4	Narseh, 293-302
286.45	Hormizd II, 302-310
286.5	Shapur II, 310-379
286.51	Ardashir II, 379-383
286.53	Shapur III, 383-388
286.55	Bahram IV, 388-399
286.57	Yazdegerd I, 399-420
286.6	Bahram V, 420-438
286.7	Yazdegerd II, 438-457

	Iran (Persia)
	History
	By period
	Modern, 226-
	Sassanian empire, 226-651 -- Continued
286.75	Hormizd III, 457-459
286.8	Peroz, 457-484
287	Balash, 484-488
287.1	Kavadh I, 488-531
287.2	Djamasp, 496-498
287.3	Chosroes I, Anushirvan, 531-579
287.4	Hormizd IV, 579-590
287.45	Bahrām VI, 590 (Bahrām Chubin)
287.5	Chosroes II, 590-628
287.6	Kavadh II, 628
287.7	Ardashir III, 628-630
287.8	Yazdegerd III, 632-651
	Arab and Mongol rule, 640-1500
288	General works
	Arab and pre-Mongol rule, 640-1256
288.3	General works
288.4	821-873. Tahirids
288.5	874-999. Samanids
288.56	931-1090. Ziyarids
288.6	932-1094. Buwayhids
288.7	977-1187. Ghaznevids
288.8	1037-1192. Seljuks
288.9	1148-1287. Salghurids
	Mongol and Timurids rule, 1256-1500
288.95	General works
289	1256-1353. Ilkhanids
289.2	1248-1383. Beni Kurt
289.3	1335-1392. Muzaffarids
289.4	1335-1381. Sarbadarids
289.5	1336-1432. Jalāyirids
289.6	1337-1355. Jubanians
289.7	1369-1505. Timurids
289.8	1400-1508. Ak-Kuyunli
290	Other dynasties
	Safawids and Afghans, 1500-1736
292	General works
292.3	Ismail I, 1500-1524
292.4	Tahmasp I, 1524-1576
292.5	Ismail II, 1576-1577
292.51	Mohammed Mirza, 1577-1586
292.53	Hamza, 1586
292.55	Ismail III, 1586-1587

Iran (Persia)
History
By period
Modern, 226-
Safawids and Afghans, 1500-1736 -- Continued

292.6	Abbas I the Great, 1587-1629
292.7	Safi I, 1629-1642
292.8	Abbas II, 1641-1668
292.9	Safi II (Suleiman), 1668-1694
293	Afghan wars, etc.
293.2	Hosain, 1694-1722
293.3	Mir Waiz, 1708-1715
293.4	Mir Abdallah, 1715-1716
293.5	Mahmud, 1716-1725
293.6	Ashraf, 1725-1729
293.7	Tahmasp II, 1729-1732
293.8	Abbas III, 1732-1736
	1736-1794
293.9	General works
294	Nadir Shah, 1736-1747
	1747-1794
295	General works
297	Loṭf- 'Alī Khān, 1789-1794
	Qajar dynasty, 1794-1925
298	General works
299	General special
300	Social life and customs. Civilization. Intellectual life
301	Agha Mohammed, 1794-1797
302	Fath Ali, 1797-1834
305	Mohammed, 1834-1848
	Nasr-ed-Din, 1848-1896
307	General works
307.5	War with Great Britain, 1856-1857
311	Muzaffar-ed-Din, 1896-1907
313	1905-1911
	Including Mohammed Ali, 1907-1909
	Ahmed, 1909-1925
315	General works
315.4	Coup d'état, 1921
	Biography and memoirs
315.9	Collective
316.A-Z	Individual, A-Z
	e.g.
316.H4	Hedāyat, Mehdī-Qolī
	Pahlavi dynasty, 1925-1979
316.2	Periodicals. Societies. Serials
316.22	Congresses

Iran (Persia)
History
By period
Modern, 226-
Pahlavi dynasty, 1925-1979 -- Continued
316.23 Sources and documents
316.24 Collected works (nonserial)
316.25 Historiography
316.3 General works
316.32 General special
316.33 Addresses, essays, lectures
316.4 Social life and customs. Civilization. Intellectual life
316.5 Military history
316.55 Naval history
316.6 Political history
316.8 Foreign and general relations
Biography and memoirs
316.85 Collective
316.9.A-Z Individual, A-Z
317 Reza Shah Pahlavi, 1925-1941
Mohammad Reza Pahlavi, 1941-1979
318 General works
318.5 Writings of Mohammad Reza Pahlavi
318.6 Mohammad Mosaddeq, Prime Minister, 1951-1953
Including Coup of 1953 and Anglo-Iranian Oil
Dispute, 1951-1954
318.7 2500th anniversary celebration of the founding of
Iran, 1971
Islamic Republic, 1979-
318.72 Periodicals. Societies. Serials
318.73 Congresses
318.74 Sources and documents
318.75 Collected works (nonserial)
318.77 Historiography
318.8 General works
318.81 General special
318.815 Addresses, essays, lectures
318.82 Social life and customs. Civilization. Intellectual life
318.822 Military history
318.825 Political history
318.83 Foreign and general relations
Biography and memoirs
318.839 Collective
318.84.A-Z Individual, A-Z
e.g.
318.84.K48 Khomeini, Ruhollah
Iran Hostage Crisis, 1979-1981 see E183.8.A+

	Iran (Persia)
	History
	By period
	Modern, 226-
	Islamic Republic, 1979- -- Continued
318.85	Iran-Iraq War, 1980-1988
318.9	1997-
	Local history and description
324.A-Z	Provinces, regions, etc., A-Z
	e.g.
324.A9	Azerbaijan
324.B23	Baluchistan
324.E4	Elburz Mountains
324.F3	Fars
324.K49	Khūzestān. Arabístan
324.K5	Kirman (Kerman)
324.M28	Masīleh Basin
324.P37	Parthia
	Cf. DS285 Parthian Empire
	Cities, towns, etc.
325.A2	Collective
325.A3-Z	Individual, A-Z
	e.g.
325.M4	Meshed
325.O7	Ormus
	Persepolis see DS262.P4
	Susa see DS262.S9
325.T3	Teheran
326	Persian Gulf (General)
	Central Asia
	For Soviet Central Asia see DK845+
327	Periodicals. Societies. Serials
327.25	Congresses
327.3	Sources and documents
327.4	Guidebooks
327.5	General works
327.6	Historical geography
327.65	Geography
	Description and travel
327.7	Through 1980
327.8	1981-
328	Antiquities
328.2	Social life and customs. Civilization. Intellectual life
	Ethnography
328.3	General works
328.4.A-Z	Individual elements in the population, A-Z
328.4.A43	Alani

Central Asia
  Ethnography
    Individual elements in the population, A-Z -- Continued
328.4.E64   Ephthalites
328.4.H85   Huns
328.4.I53   Indo-Europeans
328.4.K6   Koreans
328.4.M87   Muslims
328.4.O57   Oirats
328.4.S35   Saka
  History
      For the history of the Mongols see DS19+
      For the history of the Tatars see DS25
      For the history of the Turks see DS26+
329.4   General works
  Historiography
329.6   General works
      Biography of historians, area studies specialists,
        archaeologists, etc.
329.7   Collective
329.8.A-Z   Individual, A-Z
Southern Asia. Indian Ocean Region
331   Periodicals. Societies. Sources and documents. Collections
331.5   Congresses
334   Gazetteers. Dictionaries
334.5   Guidebooks
335   General works
336   General special
336.9   Geography
337   Description and travel
                Cf. DS411+ Southern and Southeast Asia combined,
                  1498-1761
338   Antiquities
339   Social life and customs. Civilization. Intellectual life
  Ethnography
339.2   General works
339.3.A-Z   Individual elements in the population, A-Z
339.3.A34   Africans
339.3.C45   Chakma
339.3.E28   East Indians
339.3.E97   Eurasians
339.3.K56   Khokhar Rajput
339.3.K84   Kuki Chin
339.3.M87   Muslims
339.3.S53   Siddiquis
339.4   South Asians in foreign countries (General)
                For South Asians in a particular country, see the country

	Southern Asia. Indian Ocean Region -- Continued
	History
	Study and teaching
339.8	General works
339.9.A-Z	By region or country, A-Z
	Subarrange by author
340	General works
	Political and diplomatic history. Foreign and general relations
341	General works
341.3.A-Z	Relations with individual countries, A-Z
	Islands of the Indian Ocean
	For works on the islands of the East African coast see DT468+
349.8	General works
349.9.A-Z	Individual islands, A-Z
	Amirante Islands see DT469.A6
	Andaman Islands see DS486.5.L3
349.9.A57	Amsterdam Island (Terre australes et antarctiques françaises)
349.9.C42	Chagos Archipelago (British Indian Ocean Territory)
349.9.C45	Christmas Island. Kiritimati
	Cocos Islands see DS349.9.K43
	Comoros see DT469.C7
349.9.C75	Crozet Islands
349.9.D53	Diego Garcia
349.9.H42	Heard Island
349.9.K43	Keeling Islands. Cocos Islands
349.9.K47	Kerguelen Islands
	Laccadive Islands see DS486.5.L3
	Madagascar see DT469.M21+
349.9.M34-.M3495	Maldives. Maldive Islands (Table DS-DX2)
	Mascarene Islands see DT469.M39
	Mauritius see DT469.M4+
	Nicobar Islands see DS486.5.A52
	Nossi-Bé see DT469.M37N67
	Réunion see DT469.R3+
	Rodrigues see DT469.M492
	Seychelles see DT469.S4+
	Zanzibar see DT449.Z2+
	Afghanistan
350	Periodicals. Societies. Sources and documents. Collections
351	Gazetteers. Guidebooks
351.5	General works
351.9	Geography
352	Description and travel

	Afghanistan -- Continued
353	Antiquities
	For local antiquities see DS374.A+
354	Social life and customs. Civilization
	Ethnography
354.5	General works
354.58	Pushtuns
354.6.A-Z	Other elements in the population, A-Z
354.6.A7	Arabs
354.6.B35	Baluchi
354.6.G67	Gorbat
354.6.H3	Hazāras
354.6.H55	Hindus
354.6.K3	Kafirs. Nuristani
354.6.K57	Kirghiz
	Nuristani see DS354.6.K3
354.6.P37	Pashai
354.6.S9	Sum
354.6.T35	Tajiks
354.6.T87	Turkmen
354.6.U82	Uzbeks
354.6.W34	Wakhi
	History
354.9	Dictionaries. Chronological tables, outlines, etc.
355	Biography (Collective)
	Historiography
355.2	General works
	Biography of historians, area studies specialists, archaeologists, etc.
355.3	Collective
355.4.A-Z	Individual, A-Z
356	General works
357	Addresses, essays, lectures
	Political and diplomatic history. Foreign and general relations
357.5	General works
357.6.A-Z	Relations with individual countries, A-Z
	By period
358	Earliest to 1747
	1747-1826. Durani dynasty
359	General works
359.2	Ahmed Shah, 1747-1773
359.3	Timur, 1773-1793
359.4	Humayun, 1793
359.5	Zaman Shah, 1797-1800
359.6	Mahmud Shah, 1800-1819
359.7	Shuja Shah, 1803-1843

	Afghanistan
	History
	By period
	1747-1826. Durani dynasty -- Continued
359.8	Azim I, 1819-1833
	19th-20th centuries
	1826-1973
361	General works
363	Dost Mohammed, 1826-1863
	Including British Intervention, 1839-1842
363.5	Herat emirat, 1819-1863
	Shere Ali, 1863-1879
364	General works
364.2	Ufzul, 1866-1867
364.4	Azim II, 1867-1868
364.6	Yakub, 1879-1880
	Abdur Rahman, 1880-1901
365	General works on reign
366	Biography
367.A-Z	Biography and memoirs, 1826-1900, A-Z
368	Habibullah, 1901-1919
369	Amanullah Khan, 1919-1929
369.2	Habibullah Ghazi, 1929 (January 17-October 16)
369.3	Muhammad Nadir Shah, 1929-1933
369.4	Muhammad Zahir Shah, 1933-
	Biography and memoirs, 1901-
371.A2	Collective
371.A3-Z	Individual, A-Z
371.2	1973-1989
	Including Soviet occupation, 1979-1989
	1989-2001
	Including Taliban regime, 1996-2001
371.3	General works
	Biography and memoirs
371.32	Collective
371.33.A-Z	Individual, A-Z
	2001-
371.4	General works
	Afghan War, 2001-
371.412	General works. Military operations (General)
371.4123.A-Z	Individual campaigns, battles, etc., A-Z
	e. g.
371.4123.O64	Operation Anaconda, 2002
371.4123.S56	Shok Valley, Battle of, 2008
371.413	Personal narratives
371.4135	Press. Censorship. Publicity
371.414	Prisoners and prisons

DS

	Afghanistan
	History
	By period
	19th-20th centuries
	2001-
	General works
	Afghan War, 2001- -- Continued
371.415	Relief work. Charities. Refugees. Displaced persons
	Biography and memoirs
371.42	Collective
371.43.A-Z	Individual, A-Z
	e.g.
371.43.K37	Karzai, Hamid, 1957-
	Local history and description
374.A-Z	Provinces, regions, etc., A-Z
	e.g.
	Bactria see DS374.B28
374.B28	Balkh. Bactria
374.H39	Hazarajat
374.H5	Hindu Kush Mountains
374.K2	Kafiristan. Nuristan
374.K5	Khyber Pass
	Nuristan see DS374.K2
375.A-Z	Cities, towns, etc., A-Z
	e.g.
375.A84	Ātishkadah-i Surkh Kutah Site
375.A95	Aykhānom
375.B3	Bamian
375.B4	Beghram (Bagram)
375.H5	Herat
375.K2	Kabul
375.S47	Shortughai Site
375.S59	Skandar, Tapa
	Pakistan
376	Periodicals. Societies. Sources and documents. Collections
	Museums, exhibitions, etc.
376.2	General works
376.3.A-Z	By place, A-Z
	Subarrange by author
376.8	Gazetteers. Guidebooks
376.9	General works
376.98	Geography
377	Description and travel
378	Antiquities
	For local antiquities see DS392+
379	Social life and customs. Civilization. Intellectual life

	Pakistan -- Continued
	Ethnography
380.A1	General works
380.A2-Z	Individual elements in the population, A-Z
380.A35	Afghans
380.A37	Afridis
380.A68	Arains
380.A94	Awans
380.B3	Baluchi
380.B36	Bangash
380.B5	Bhatias
380.B7	Brahui
380.B74	British
380.B83	Bugti
380.C47	Christians
380.D48	Dhund
380.G46	Georgians (South Caucasians)
380.G52	Gichki
380.G85	Gujars
380.H38	Hazāras
380.K34	Kalash
380.K37	Kamboh
380.K87	Kurds
380.M46	Memons
380.M63	Mohmands
380.M83	Muhajir
380.P36	Panjabis
380.P38	Parsees
380.P8	Pushtuns
380.Q35	Qalandar
380.R32	Rajput
	Cf. DS432.R3 Rajput in India
380.S45	Shahwani
380.S53	Sindhi
380.S55	Siraiki
380.T3	Tanawalis
380.T35	Tanoli
380.Y85	Yusufzais
380.5	Pakistanis in foreign countries (General)
	For Pakistanis in a particular country, see the country
	History
381	Biography (Collective)
381.4	Historiography
381.7	Study and teaching
382	General works. Dictionaries
383	Addresses, essays, lectures
383.2	Military and naval history

	Pakistan
	History -- Continued
	Political and diplomatic history. Foreign and general relations
383.5.A2	General works
383.5.A3-Z	Relations with individual countries, A-Z
	By period
	Early through 1946 see DS451+
	1947-1988
384	General works
	Biography and memoirs
385.A2	Collective
385.A3-Z	Individual, A-Z
	e.g.
385.J5	Jinnah, Mahomed Ali
385.K5	Khan, Liaquat Ali
	Conflict with India, 1947-1949
385.9.A2	Sources and documents
385.9.A3-Z	General works
	Conflict with India, September, 1965
386.A2	Sources and documents
386.A3-Z	General works
387	Tashkend Conference
	Conflict with India, 1971-
388.A2	Sources and documents
388.A3-Z	General works
388.2	Simla Summit
389	1988-
	Biography and memoirs
389.2	Collective
389.22.A-Z	Individual, A-Z
	e. g.
389.22.M87	Musharraf, Pervez
	Local history and description
392.A-Z	Minor kingdoms, states, regions, etc., A-Z
	e.g.
	Baluchistan
392.B2	Periodicals, etc.
392.B23	General works
392.B24	Description and travel
392.B25	Antiquities
392.B26	Social life and customs
392.B28	History
392.B35	Bannú
392.H86	Hunza
392.K35	Karakoram Range
	For Karakoram Range in India see DS485.K193

	Pakistan
	Local history and description
	Minor kingdoms, states, regions, etc., A-Z -- Continued
	Khyber Pakhtunkhwa see DS392.N67
	Majha see DS485.M3493
392.N67	North-West Frontier Province. Khyber Pakhtunkhwa
392.P8	Punjab, West
	Sind
392.S5	Periodicals, etc.
392.S53	General works
392.S54	Description and travel
392.S55	Antiquities
392.S56	Social life and customs
392.S58	History
392.T5	Tirah
392.T54	Tirich Mīr Mountain
392.W3	Waziristan
392.2.A-Z	Cities, towns, etc., A-Z
	e.g.
392.2.A44	Allāhdino site
392.2.A95	Aziz Dheri Site
392.2.B57	Bīr-koṭ-ghwaṇḍai Site
392.2.C53	Chanhu-daro
392.2.H3	Harappa
392.2.K3	Karachi
392.2.L3	Lahore
392.2.M6	Mohenjo-daro
392.2.N36	Nanga Parbat
392.2.O73	Oshibat Site
392.2.P57	Pirak
392.2.R64	Rohtas Fort
392.2.S24	Saidu Sharif I Site
392.2.T3	Taxila
392.2.Z37	Zar Dheri Site
	Bangladesh. East Pakistan
393	Periodicals. Societies. Serials
393.2	Sources and documents
393.3	Directories. Gazetteers. Guidebooks
393.4	General works
393.5	Description and travel
393.6	Antiquities
	Social life and customs. Civilization. Intellectual life
393.8	General works
393.812.A-Z	Special topics, A-Z
393.812.C65	Communalism
	Ethnography
393.82	General works

DS

Bangladesh. East Pakistan
Ethnography -- Continued

393.83.A-Z	Individual elements in the population, A-Z
393.83.A35	Adivasis
393.83.B38	Baum Chin
393.83.B5	Bihari
393.83.C48	Chakma
393.83.G37	Garos
393.83.H35	Hajong
393.83.H54	Hindus
393.83.J86	Jumma
393.83.K37	Kārāra
393.83.K45	Khasi
393.83.M3	Maghs
393.83.M34	Mahali (Indic people)
393.83.M44	Meitheis
393.83.M78	Mru
393.83.M87	Muslims
393.83.O73	Oraon
393.83.P33	Paharia
393.83.P36	Panika
393.83.R34	Rākshāina
393.83.R64	Rohingya
393.83.S36	Santal
393.83.S43	Shandar
393.83.T57	Tipura
	History
	Historiography
394.2	General works
	Biography of historians, area studies specialists, archaeologists, etc.
394.22	Collective
394.24.A-Z	Individual, A-Z
394.3	Study and teaching
394.5	General works
394.6	Addresses, essays, lectures
	Political and diplomatic history. Foreign and general relations
394.7	General works
394.73.A-Z	Relations with individual countries, A-Z
	By period
	Early to 1946 see DS485.B46+
395	1947-1971
	1971-
395.5	General works
	Biography and memoirs
395.7.A2	Collective

	Bangladesh. East Pakistan
	History
	By period
	1971-
	Biography and memoirs -- Continued
395.7.A3-Z	Individual, A-Z
	e.g.
395.7.M9	Mujibur Rahman, Sheikh
	Local history and description
396.8.A-Z	Minor kingdoms, states, regions, etc., A-Z
	e.g.
396.8.C45	Chittagong Hill Tracts
396.8.G46	Ganges River. Ganges River Region
	Class here works on the Ganges River restricted to Bangladesh
	Class general works on the Ganges River and works on the Ganges River restricted to India in DS485.G25
	Cf. DS485.G25 Ganges River in India
396.8.S9	Sundarbans
396.9.A-Z	Cities and towns, etc., A-Z
	e.g.
396.9.D3	Dacca
396.9.M33	Mahasthan Site
396.9.P35	Paharpur Site
	India (Bharat)
401	Periodicals. Societies. Serials
	Museums, exhibitions, etc.
402.A1	General works
402.A2-Z	Individual. By place, A-Z
402.5	Congresses
403	Sources and documents
	Collected works
404	Several authors
404.5	Individual authors
405	Gazetteers. Dictionaries. Directories, etc.
406	Guidebooks
407	General works
408	Monumental and picturesque
408.5	Historical geography
408.6	Geography
	Description and travel
409	Through 1000
410	1001-1497

	Southeast Asia
	India (Bharat)
	Description and travel
	1498-1761. General East Indies. Voyages and accounts
	Class here works dealing with the East Indies in its broad historical concept as the area of South and Southeast Asia.
	Class works on individual regions, e.g. Indonesia, Malay Archipelago, etc., with the region
411	English
411.1	Dutch
	Cf. DS618 Dutch East Indies, 1595-1800
411.5	French
411.7	Portuguese
411.9	Other
412	1762-1858
413	1859-1946
414	1947-1980
414.2	1981-
	Antiquities
	Cf. DS483+ Local history and description
416	Periodicals. Societies. Serials
417	Collections
418	General works
419	General special
	Social life and customs. Civilization. Intellectual life
421	General works
421.5	Addresses, essays, lectures
422.A-Z	Special topics, A-Z
422.C3	Caste. Dalits (Untouchables)
	For individual castes see DS432.A+
	Cf. HT720 Social aspects
422.C64	Communalism
	Dalits see DS422.C3
	Human sacrifice see DS422.S2
422.I5	Infanticide
422.S2	Sacrifice, Human
	Scheduled castes see DS422.C3
	Scheduled tribes see GN635.I4
422.S43	Secularism
	Suttee see GT3370
422.T5	Thugs
	Untouchables see DS422.C3
	Civilization and culture. Intellectual life
423	General works
425	Earliest civilization
426	Buddhist civilization

	India (Bharat)
	Social life and customs. Civilization. Intellectual life
	Civilization and culture. Intellectual life -- Continued
427	Muslim civilization
	Cf. DS432.M84 Muslims as an element in the population
427.5	Portuguese civilization
428	Anglo-Indian society
428.2	1947-
	Ethnography. Sects
430	General works
432.A-Z	Individual elements in the population, A-Z
432.A19	Abor. Adi
	Adi see DS432.A19
432.A2	Adivasis
432.A25	Africans
432.A3	Agaria
432.A34	Agarwals
432.A38	Ahirs
432.A39	Ahom
432.A44	Akas
432.A46	Ambastha Kayasthas
432.A48	Anal
432.A488	Anavil Brahmans
432.A54	Andamanese
432.A546	Angami
432.A55	Anglo-Indians
432.A56	Anwal
432.A57	Ao
432.A6	Apatani. Apa Tanis
432.A65	Arabs
432.A67	Arains
432.A7	Armenians
432.A74	Arunthathiyars
432.A8	Asur
432.A9	Audumbara
432.B25	Badaga
432.B26	Baḍaganāḍu Brāhmaṇas
432.B27	Bagdis
432.B275	Bagta
432.B3	Baiga
432.B312	Bailpattars
432.B314	Bairwas
432.B316	Bais Kshatriyas
432.B32	Bakrawallah
432.B324	Balija
432.B326	Baluchi

India (Bharat)
Ethnography. Sects
Individual elements in the population, A-Z -- Continued

432.B33	Bāncharā
432.B34	Bangladeshis
(432.B35)	Banjaras
	see DS432.L34
432.B353	Bants
432.B355	Barela
432.B357	Bāroṭas
432.B36	Basadevā
432.B367	Bauddhatantis
432.B37	Bauris
432.B373	Bavanīlu
432.B376	Bawaria
432.B38	Bazigar
432.B383	Beary
432.B39	Beldar
432.B4	Bengali
432.B412	Berads
432.B413	Berias
432.B414	Bhairas
432.B416	Bhamta
432.B417	Bhangis
432.B4177	Bhansalis
432.B4185	Bhāradvājas
432.B419	Bharia
432.B42	Bharvads
432.B43	Bhāṭarā
432.B45	Bhil
432.B453	Bhimmā
432.B454	Bhojpuri
432.B455	Bhoksa
432.B456	Bhotias
432.B458	Bhovis
432.B46	Bhṛgus
432.B47	Bhumij
432.B475	Bhunjia
432.B48	Bihari
432.B49	Binjhwar
432.B5	Birhor
432.B52	Bisnoīs
432.B63	Bodo
432.B64	Bokar
432.B65	Bondo
432.B66	Bongcher
432.B67	Bori

India (Bharat)
Ethnography. Sects
Individual elements in the population, A-Z -- Continued

432.B73	Brahmans
432.B8	Budga Jangams
432.B87	Buxas
432.C38	Caupāla
432.C43	Chakkiliyans
432.C46	Chakma
432.C48	Chamārs
432.C483	Chandreseniya Kayastha Prabhus
432.C4845	Changpa
432.C485	Charans
432.C486	Chaudri. Chodhri
432.C488	Chenchu
432.C49	Cheros
432.C495	Chik Baraik
432.C5	Chinese
432.C52	Chiru
432.C524	Chitpawan Brahmans
(432.C53)	Chodhri
	see DS432.C486
432.C54	Cholanaickan
432.C55	Christians
432.C57	Chuar
(432.C6)	Coorg
	see DS432.K56
432.D3	Dafla
432.D32	Daivadnya Brahmans
432.D35	Dakkalas
432.D38	Delki Khadia
432.D4	Deori
432.D43	Desasthas
432.D437	Devangas
432.D44	Dewar
432.D45	Dharalas
432.D47	Dheds
432.D476	Dhimal
432.D48	Dhimars
432.D49	Dhodias
432.D494	Dhors
432.D5	Dhurwas
432.D53	Didayi
432.D58	Dogras
432.D587	Dom
432.D59	Dombaru
432.D593	Dombidasas

India (Bharat)
    Ethnography. Sects
        Individual elements in the population, A-Z -- Continued

432.D595	Dongria Kondh
432.D6	Dorla
432.D7	Dravidians
432.D87	Dusadhs
432.E6	Ephthalites
432.E88	Europeans
432.E95	Ezhavas
432.F73	French

            Cf. DS462+ French in India, 1664-1765
            Cf. DS485.P66 Pondicherry, French India (General)

432.G27	Gabada
432.G275	Gaddis
432.G3	Gallong
432.G32	Gamit
432.G325	Gamokkalu
432.G33	Gandas
432.G335	Garewālas
432.G34	Garo
432.G37	Gauḍa Sārasvata Brāhmaṇas
432.G38	Gaudas
432.G43	Ghānchīs
432.G5	Ghasis
432.G56	Goans
432.G58	Golla
432.G59	Gomativala Brahmans
432.G6	Gond
432.G63	Gondhalis
432.G65	Gorava
432.G67	Goravālas
432.G68	Gosangis
432.G7	Grasia
432.G74	Great Andamanese
432.G85	Gujaratis
432.G86	Gujars
432.G87	Gurkhas
432.H28	Hajong
432.H3	Hakas
432.H32	Hakki Pikki
432.H327	Hālakki Okkaligas
432.H33	Halams
432.H38	Havyaka Brahmins
432.H44	Hill Kharia
432.H5	Hmar
432.H6	Ho

India (Bharat)
Ethnography. Sects
Individual elements in the population, A-Z -- Continued

432.H68	Hoysaḷa Karnāṭaka Brahmans
432.I32	Idangai
432.I37	Idu
432.I75	Iranians
432.I77	Irukkuvēḷirs
432.I78	Irulas
432.I94	Iyers
432.J223	Jains
432.J225	Jaintia
432.J227	Jalaris
432.J229	Jarawa
432.J23	Jatapu
432.J25	Jatavs
432.J27	Jatigaras
432.J3	Jats
432.J35	Jaunsari
432.J37	Jayantira Panos
432.J64	Jogi-Nath
432.J84	Juang. Patua
432.J94	Jyeshṭhimalla
432.K15	Kachari
432.K155	Kachhwaha
432.K158	Kadamba
432.K16	Kadar
432.K167	Kaibartas
432.K17	Kaikōlar
432.K174	Kaithala Vaisyas
432.K176	Kalbelia
432.K177	Kalitās
432.K18	Kallans
432.K187	Kamar
432.K188	Kamboh
432.K19	Kammas
432.K1905	Kānaḍa Gavaḷīs
432.K1907	Kanarese
432.K191	Kanaura
	Kanbis see DS432.P43
432.K192	Kandh
432.K1922	Kanikkaran
432.K1923	Kañjārabhāṭa
432.K1924	Kansari
432.K194	Kānyakubja Brahmans
432.K196	Kapoḷas
432.K198	Karana Kayasthas

India (Bharat)
    Ethnography. Sects
        Individual elements in the population, A-Z -- Continued

432.K1985	Karbis
432.K199	Kammälans
432.K1996	Karbong
432.K2	Karens
432.K25	Karhade Vainyas
432.K27	Kashmiri Pandits
432.K28	Kathodi
432.K285	Kattunaicken
432.K287	Kawar
432.K289	Kayamkhanis
432.K29	Kayasthas
	Kayasthas, Karana see DS432.K198
432.K37	Kelas
432.K42	Khairwar
432.K44	Khamti
432.K46	Khandelwals
432.K47	Khangārota
432.K48	Kharia
432.K5	Khasi
432.K52	Khatris
432.K53	Khattaks
432.K533	Khiamnungan
432.K54	Killekyatha
432.K545	Kinnaura
432.K55	Kiranti
432.K559	Koda
432.K56	Kodagu. Coorg
432.K565	Kohalī
432.K57	Kokna
432.K58	Kolami. Kolam
432.K583	Kolgha
432.K585	Koli
432.K586	Koloi
432.K588	Koltas
432.K5885	Kom
432.K5886	Konda Reddis
(432.K5888)	Konkani
	see DS432.K57
(432.K589)	Konkans
	see DS432.K57
432.K59	Koragas
(432.K6)	Korava
432.K62	Korku
432.K626	Korrirāju

India (Bharat)
  Ethnography. Sects
    Individual elements in the population, A-Z -- Continued

432.K63	Korwa
432.K66	Kota
432.K7	Kshatriyas
432.K72	Kucabandiyā
432.K73	Kudumbis
432.K75	Kuki
432.K754	Kūḷabī
432.K758	Kulalars
432.K76	Kulins
432.K77	Kulu
432.K778	Kumauni
432.K779	Kumawat Kshatriyas
432.K78	Kumbavats
432.K785	Kumhars
432.K7853	Kunbi
432.K7854	Kunchitigas
432.K786	Kurichiya
432.K787	Kurmis
432.K8	Kurumba
432.K84	Kutia Kondh
432.L23	Ladakhi
432.L24	Lakher
432.L26	Lalungs
432.L34	Lambadi
432.L4	Lepcha
432.L5	Licchavis
432.L55	Limbus
432.L56	Lingayats
432.L57	Lisu (Southeast Asian people)
432.L6	Lodha
432.L62	Lōhaṇās
432.L63	Lohars
432.L65	Lois
432.L8	Lushai
432.M13	Madigas
432.M146	Mahadeo Koli
432.M15	Mahali
432.M154	Mahars
432.M16	Mahesri
432.M17	Mahisyas
432.M18	Mahiyā
432.M2	Mahrattas. Marathas. Marathi
	Cf. DS485.M349 Maharashtra
432.M23	Maithil Brahmans

India (Bharat)
  Ethnography. Sects
    Individual elements in the population, A-Z -- Continued

432.M235	Māladhārī
432.M24	Malaiyalis
432.M243	Malapandaram
432.M245	Malas
432.M246	Malayalis
432.M247	Malekudiya
432.M248	Maler
432.M249	Mālī-Sainīs
432.M2493	Malia Kondh
432.M2495	Mallahs
	Malpaharia see DS432.M25
432.M25	Malto. Malpaharia
432.M2515	Mandaheccus
432.M253	Mang
432.M2533	Mangalas
432.M254	Mankidia
432.M257	Maram
	Marathas see DS432.M2
432.M26	Maravars
432.M267	Maria
432.M27	Maring
432.M28	Marwaris
432.M3	Mate
432.M315	Mēdas
432.M32	Meghavaṃsīs
432.M325	Mehtas
432.M33	Meitheis
432.M34	Memons
432.M35	Meo
432.M37	Mer
432.M38	Mhamais
432.M42	Mikir
432.M424	Millang
432.M43	Mina
432.M434	Minyong
432.M44	Miri
432.M45	Mishmi
432.M48	Mogaveeras
432.M6	Mohmands
432.M63	Monpa
432.M64	Moothans
432.M65	Moplahs
432.M66	Moria
432.M67	Mowāmārīya

India (Bharat)
  Ethnography. Sects
    Individual elements in the population, A-Z -- Continued

432.M74	Muduvar
432.M77	Mukkuvars
432.M78	Mulakānaḍu Brāhamaṇas
432.M8	Munda
432.M83	Muria
432.M836	Musahar
432.M84	Muslims
	Cf. DS427 Muslim civilization
432.N25	Nadars
432.N26	Nadavas
432.N28	Nagar Brahmans
432.N3	Naga
432.N313	Nagesia
432.N32	Naika
432.N324	Nairs
432.N35	Namasudras
432.N354	Nambudiris
432.N36	Nangudi Vellalas
432.N38	Nattukottai Chettiars
432.N42	Navayats
432.N46	Nepalese. Nepali speaking people
432.N53	Nicobarese
432.N59	Niyogi Brahmans
432.N62	Noatia
432.N63	Nocte
432.N87	Nūrbāsh
432.O4	Okkaligas
432.O53	Onge
432.O7	Oraon
432.O8	Oriya
432.O85	Oswāls
432.P2	Padagas
432.P2115	Padam
432.P212	Padma Sālēs
432.P213	Pailibo
432.P214	Paite (Asian people)
432.P215	Pal Kshatriyas
432.P218	Paliyan (Indic people)
432.P22	Pallars
432.P23	Pallis
432.P2315	Pang
432.P232	Panjabis
432.P2325	Pañjiriyarava
432.P233	Panos

India (Bharat)
    Ethnography. Sects
        Individual elements in the population, A-Z -- Continued

432.P235	Paravas
432.P236	Pardhan
432.P2365	Pardhis
432.P237	Pareek Brahmans
432.P24	Parhaiyas
432.P25	Pariahs
432.P255	Parits
432.P26	Parji
432.P3	Parsees
432.P36	Pasis
432.P4	Pathans. Pushtuns
432.P43	Patidars
432.P45	Pattanavars
	Patua see DS432.J84
432.P46	Paudi Bhuyan
432.P47	Paundra Kshatriyas
432.P55	Pengo
432.P56	Perikas
432.P6	Pindarees
432.P65	Pnar
432.P67	Poles
432.P68	Poravālas
432.P73	Pramalai Kallans
432.P76	Pulayan (Indic people)
432.P78	Pulayas
432.P8	Purum
432.P84	Pushkarna Brahmans
	Pushtuns see DS432.P4
432.R13	Rabaris
432.R2	Rabha
432.R232	Rabi Das
432.R236	Raghuvaṃsīs
432.R238	Raigaras
432.R24	Rajapurohitas
432.R25	Rajbangsi
432.R27	Rājī
432.R3	Rajput
	Cf. DS380.R32 Rajput in Pakistan
432.R314	Rajuar
432.R317	Rāmakṣatriya
432.R32	Ramgarhia
432.R33	Ramo
432.R39	Reddys
432.R44	Rengma

India (Bharat)
   Ethnography. Sects
      Individual elements in the population, A-Z -- Continued

432.R5	Riang
432.R65	Rohilla
	Romanies see DX283
432.R86	Rūpīni
432.S13	Sadāna
432.S15	Saharia
432.S16	Sangar
432.S17	Saṅkēti
432.S18	Sansi
432.S2	Santal
432.S22	Santia
432.S25	Sapua Kelas
432.S3	Saraks
432.S35	Saraswats
432.S357	Sarayūpārin Brahmans
432.S359	Satnāmīs
432.S36	Saurashtra. Saurashtrians
432.S37	Savara
432.S42	Sentinelese
432.S45	Sherdukpen
432.S455	Shivalli Brahmans
432.S46	Shompen
432.S47	Shudras
432.S49	Siddi. Siddhi
432.S5	Sikhs
	Cf. DS485.P88 Punjab
432.S6	Sikligars
432.S64	Sindhi
	Cf. DS380.S53 Sindhi in Pakistan
432.S66	Sindhoḷḷus
432.S69	Soligas
432.S7	Somanis
432.S73	Somavasī Kshatriyas
432.S735	Sonowal Kachari
432.S74	Soods
432.S76	Sri Lankans
432.S77	Srimali Brahmans
432.S78	Srngavāla Brahmans
432.S83	Stodpa
432.S86	Subarnabaniks
432.S87	Sudugadusiddha
432.S88	Sulung
432.S9	Sumarā
432.S94	Sunuwar

India (Bharat)
   Ethnography. Sects
      Individual elements in the population, A-Z -- Continued

432.S965	Syriac Christians
432.T17	Tagin
432.T26	Tai (Southeast Asian people)
432.T27	Tai Phakes
432.T28	Tai Turung
432.T29	Tamburi
432.T3	Tamil
432.T32	Tangkhul
432.T33	Tangsa
432.T4	Telugu
432.T46	Thado
432.T48	Thakuri
432.T49	Tharu
432.T495	Thoti
432.T5	Tibetans
432.T52	Tigalas
432.T53	Tikhak
432.T54	Tipura
432.T56	Tiyars
432.T6	Toda
432.T66	Toto
432.T8	Tulu
432.U25	Ucai
432.U4	Ulladans
432.U65	Uppina Kolaga Okkaligas
432.V29	Vāḍabalija
432.V33	Vāgheras
432.V34	Vaidu
432.V35	Vaiphei
432.V36	Vaiṣṇava Okkaligas
432.V37	Vaisyas
432.V376	Valangai
432.V38	Valayars
432.V39	Vanavarayar
432.V4	Vellalas
432.V48	Vettuvar
432.W27	Waghri
432.W3	Warli
432.Y3	Yanadi
432.Y35	Yaudheya
432.Y44	Yerava
432.Y47	Yerukala. Korava
432.Z44	Zeliangrong
432.Z46	Zeme

	India (Bharat)
	Ethnography. Sects
	Individual elements in the population, A-Z -- Continued
432.Z68	Zou
432.5	East Indians in foreign countries (General)
	For East Indians in a particular country, see the country
	History
433	Dictionaries. Chronological tables, outlines, etc.
434	Biography (Collective)
	For individual biography, see the specific period, reign or place
	Historiography
435	General works
	Biography of historians
435.5	Collective
435.7.A-Z	Individual, A-Z
435.8	Study and teaching
	General works
436.A1	Works by Oriental authors to 1850
436.A2	Works by European authors to 1850
436.A3-Z	Works by modern authors
437	Addresses, essays, lectures
	General special
441	Several parts of the country treated together
	Military history
442.A2	Sources and documents
442.A3-Z	General works
442.2	Early and medieval
442.3	1526-1761
442.5	1761-1900
442.6	1901-
443	Naval history
	Political and diplomatic history. Foreign and general relations
444	Sources and documents
445	General works
446	Early to 1761
	1761-
446.3	General works
446.5	1761-1858
447	19th century
448	20th century
449	21st century
450.A-Z	Relations with individual countries, A-Z
	By period
	Earliest to 997
451	General works

	India (Bharat)
	History
	By period
	Earliest to 997 -- Continued
451.5	Asoka
	Including historical studies of the edicts and inscriptions of his reign
451.8	Gurjara-Pratihāras, ca. 740-1036
	Biography of early rulers and others
451.9.A2	Collective
451.9.A3-Z	Individual, A-Z
	e.g.
451.9.C5	Chandragupta Maurya, Emperor of Northern India
451.9.H3	Harshadeva, King of Thānesar, 606-647
	997-1761. Moslem rule
452	General works
	997-1526
457	General works
	Ghazni dynasty, 997-1196
458	General works
458.3	Mahmud, 997-1030
	Ghor dynasty, 1186-1206
458.5	General works
458.7	Mohammed, 1193-1203
	Slave kings of Delhi, 1206-1290
459	General works
459.1	Kutb-ud-din, 1206-1210
459.15	Iltutmis, 1211-1236
	Khilji dynasty, 1290-1320
459.2	General works
459.3	Ala-ud-din, 1296-1316
	Tughlak dynasty, 1320-1414
459.4	General works
459.5	Mohammed, 1325-1351
459.52	Firūz Shāh III, 1351-1388
459.6	Sayyid dynasty, 1414-1451
	Lodi Dynasty, 1451-1526
459.7	General works
459.8	Bahlol, 1451-1489
459.9	Sikandar, 1489-1517
459.95	Ibrahim, 1517-1526
	Biography and memoirs
460.A2	Collective
460.A3-Z	Individual, A-Z
	e.g.
460.M3	Maḥmūd Gāwā
	1526-1761. Mogul Empire

India (Bharat)
  History
    By period
      997-1761. Moslem rule
        1526-1761. Mogul Empire -- Continued

461	General works
461.1	Babar, 1526-1530
461.2	Humayun, 1530-1556
	Akbar, 1556-1605
461.3	General works
461.4	Other
461.5	Jahangir, 1605-1627
461.6	Shāhjahān, 1627-1658
461.7	Aurangzib, 1658-1707
461.8	1707-1761
	Biography and memoirs
461.9.A1	Collective
461.9.A2-Z	Individual, A-Z
	e.g.
461.9.B3	Baji Rao I, peshwa
461.9.C45	Chānd Bībī, Sultana, d. 1600
461.9.D3	Dārā Shikūh, prince, son of Shāhjahān
461.9.S4	Shēr Shah, sultan of Delhi
461.9.S5	Shivājī, Raja

French in India, 1664-1765. 17th-18th centuries
  Including French East India Company
  Cf. DS432.F73 French as an element in the
    population
  Cf. DS485.P66 Pondicherry, French India (General)

462	General works
462.5	Addresses, essays, lectures
462.8.A-Z	Biography and memoirs, A-Z
	e.g.
462.8.B8	Bussy-Castelnau, Charles Joseph P., marquis de
462.8.D8	Dupleix, Joseph François, marquis
462.8.L3	La Bourdonnais, Bertrand Francois M., comte de
462.8.M3	Madec, René Marie
462.8.M4	Martin, François

Portuguese in India see DS498+
English rule, 1761-1947

463	General works
464	Biography (Collective)
465	East India Company, 1600-1858
	Cf. HF486.A+ English commerce
	1761-1798
468	General works
469	General special

	India (Bharat)
	History
	By period
	English rule, 1761-1947
	1761-1798 -- Continued
470.A-Z	Biography and memoirs of contemporaries not identified with any particular administration, A-Z
	Including Hindu rulers of this period
	e.g.
470.C6	Chamberlain, Sir Neville Bowles
470.H2	Ḥaidar Shāh, called Ḥaidar Alī, khan bahadur, nawab of Mysore
470.I5	Impey, Sir Elijah
470.M2	Madhu Rao I, peshwa
470.N5	Nizām Alī Khān, nizam of Hyderabad
470.T6	Tīpū Sultān, Fatḥ Alī nawab of Mysore
	Lord Clive, 1751-1767
471	Life and administration
472	Administration
472.8.A-Z	Biography and memoirs of contemporaries, A-Z
	e.g.
472.8.F6	Forde, Francis
472.9	Verelst, Harry, 1767-1769
	Warren Hastings, 1772-1785
	Including Maratha War, 1775-1782
473	General works
473.3	General special
473.5	Addresses, essays, lectures
474	Sir John Macpherson, 1785-1786
474.1	Marquis Cornwallis, 1786-1793
	Cf. DS475.35 His administration, 1805
474.2	Sir John Shore (Lord Teignmouth), 1793-1798
	1798-1862. 19th century
475	General works
475.1	General special
	Biography and memoirs
	Cf. DS479.1.A2+ Biography and memoirs, 1862-1914
475.2.A2	Collective
475.2.A3-Z	Individual, A-Z
	e.g.
475.2.A5	Ahmad Khan, Sir Syed, 1817-1898
475.2.B25	Baji Rao II, peshwa of the Mahrattas
475.2.C7	Colvin, John Russell
475.2.E4	Elphinstone, Mountstuart
475.2.G7	Grant, Charles
475.2.G8	Gulāb Singh, maharajah of Kashmir

India (Bharat)
  History
    By period
      English rule, 1761-1947
        1798-1862. 19th century
          Biography and memoirs
            Individual, A-Z -- Continued

475.2.H2	Havelock, Sir Henry, Bart.
475.2.H4	Hodgson, Brian Houghton
475.2.L4	Lawrence, Sir Henry Montgomery
475.2.L84	Low, Sir John
475.2.M9	Munro, Sir Thomas
475.2.N5	Nicholson, John
475.2.O8	Outram, Sir James, Bart.
475.2.R18	Rāmamohana Rāya, raja
475.2.R2	Ranjit Singh, Maharaja of the Punjab
475.3	Marquis Wellesley, 1798-1805
	Including Maratha War, 1805
475.35	Marquis Cornwallis, 1805
	Cf. DS474.1 His administration of 1786-1793
475.4	Sir George Barlow, 1805-1807
475.5	Earl of Minto, 1807-1813
	Including Mutiny of 1809
475.6	Earl of Moira (Marquis of Hastings), 1813-1823
	Including Maratha War, 1816-1818; etc.
475.7	Earl of Amherst, 1823-1828
	Including First Anglo-Burmese War, 1824-1826
475.8	Lord Bentinck, 1828-1835
475.9	Lord Metcalf, 1835-1836
476	Earl of Aukland, 1836-1842
477	Earl of Ellenborough, 1842-1844
477.1	Viscount Hardinge, 1844-1844
	Including Sikh War, 1845-1846; etc
	Marquis of Dalhousie, 1848-1856
477.5	Life and administration
477.6	Administration
477.63	Sikh War, 1848-1849
477.65	Second Anglo-Burmese War, 1852
477.67	General special
	Earl Canning, 1856-1862
477.8	Life and administration
	Sepoy Rebellion, 1857-1858
478.A1	Sources and documents
478.A2-Z	General works
478.3	Addresses, essays, lectures
	1862-1914
479	General works

                          India (Bharat)
                            History
                              By period
                                English rule, 1761-1947
                                  1862-1914 -- Continued
                                    Biography and memoirs
479.1.A2   Collective
479.1.A3-Z   Individual, A-Z
                                          e.g.
479.1.D4   Dhuleep Singh, maharajah
479.1.G6   Gokhale, Gopal Krishna
479.1.P4   Pennell, Theodore Leighton
479.1.R3   Ramabai Sarasvati, pandita
479.1.R32   Ranade, Mahadev Govind, rao bahadur
479.1.T54   Tilak, Bal Gangadhar
479.1.W3   Wedderburn, Sir William, Bart.
479.15   Earl of Elgin, 1862-1863
479.2   Lord Lawrence, 1864-1868
479.3   Earl of Mayo, 1869-1872
479.4   Earl of Northbrook, 1872-1876
479.5   Earl of Lytton, 1876-1880
479.6   Marquis of Ripon, 1880-1884
479.7   Marquis of Dufferin, 1884-1888
                                          Including Sikhim Expedition, 1888; Third Anglo-
                                             Burmese War, 1885
479.8   Marquis of Lansdowne, 1888-1894
479.9   Earl of Elgin, 1894-1899
480   Marquis Curzon of Kedleston, 1899-1905
480.2   Earl of Minto, 1905-1910
480.3   Lord Hardinge, 1910-1916
480.4   1914-1919
                                   1919-1947
480.45   General works
480.5   Viscount Chelmsford, 1916-1921
                                          Including Amritsar Massacre, 1919; etc.
480.6   Marquis of Reading, 1921-1926
480.7   Earl of Halifax, 1926-1931
480.8   Marquis of Willingdon, 1931-1936
480.82   Marquis of Linlithgow, 1936-1943
                                          Including Quit India Movement, 1942; etc.
480.83   Earl of Wavell, 1943-1947
                                   1947-1977
                                      For India-Pakistan Conflict (September 1965) see
                                         DS386+
480.832   Periodicals. Societies. Serials
480.84   General works
480.842   Partition, 1947

	India (Bharat)
	History
	By period
	1947-1977 -- Continued
480.85	Chinese border dispute, 1957
480.852	National Emergency, 1975-1977
480.853	1977-
	Biography and memoirs
481.A1	Collective
481.A2-Z	Individual, A-Z
	e.g.
481.B6	Bose, Subhas Chandra
481.G23	Gandhi, Indira Nehru
481.G25	Gandhi, Kasturbai
481.G3	Gandhi, Mahatma, 1869-1948
481.N35	Nehru, Jawaharlal
481.P3	Pandit, Vijaya Lakshmi (Nehru)
481.P35	Patel, Vallabhbhai Jhaverbhai, sardar
481.S36	Savarkar, Vinayak Damodar
481.S8	Sultan Muhammad Shah, Sir, agha khan
	Local history and description
	Larger geographical divisions
483-483.95	Northeast (Table DS-DX1)
484-484.95	South (Table DS-DX1)
485.A-Z	Minor kingdoms, states, regions, etc., A-Z
	e.g.
	Agra see DS485.U6+
485.A2	Ajmer-Merwara
485.A3	Alwar
	Andaman and Nicobar see DS486.5.A5+
485.A55-.A5595	Andhra. Andhra Pradesh (Table DS-DX2)
	Arunāchal Pradesh see DS485.N68
	Assam
485.A82	Periodicals, etc.
485.A83	Biography (Collective)
485.A835	General works
485.A84	Description and travel
485.A85	Antiquities
485.A852	Social life and customs. Civilization
485.A86	Ethnography
	History
485.A87	General works
485.A88	Modern
485.B15	Baltisan (Little Tibet)
485.B34	Baroda. Vadodara
485.B38	Bastar

	India (Bharat)
	Local history and description
	Minor kingdoms, states, regions, etc., A-Z -- Continued
	Bengal
	For East Bengal see DS393+
485.B39	Periodicals, etc.
485.B395	Biography (Collective)
485.B4	Gazetteers, etc.
485.B41	General works
485.B42	Description and travel
485.B43	Antiquities
485.B44	Social life and customs
	Ethnography
485.B45	General works
485.B4512A-.B4512Z	Individual elements in the population, A-Z
485.B4512M8	Muslims
	History
485.B46	General works
485.B47	Early and medieval
485.B48	1701-1850
485.B49	1851-1947
485.B493	Bengal, West
485.B498	Bhagalpur
485.B5	Bhopal
(485.B503)	Bhutan
	see DS491+
485.B51-.B5195	Bihar. Bihar and Orissa (Table DS-DX2)
	Cf. DS485.O6+ Orissa
485.B52	Bikaner
	Bombay
485.B59	Periodicals, etc.
485.B6	Gazetteers, etc.
485.B61	General works
485.B62	Description and travel
485.B63	Antiquities
485.B64	Social life and customs
485.B65	Ethnography
	History
485.B66	General works
485.B67	Early and medieval
485.B68	1701-1850
485.B69	1851-1947
485.B692	1948-
485.B7	Bundelkhand
485.B74	Burdwan
	Burma see DS527+
485.C2	Cambay

	India (Bharat)
	Local history and description
	Minor kingdoms, states, regions, etc., A-Z -- Continued
485.C24	Carnatic
485.C3-.C395	Central Provinces. Madhya Pradesh (Table DS-DX2)
485.C53	Champaran
	Chin Hills see DS530.8.C45
485.C6	Chota Nagpur
485.C64	Cochin
485.C69	Coorg. Kodagu
485.C8	Cutch. Kachchh
485.D14	Daman
485.D17	Dardistan
485.D2	Darjeeling
	Deccan
485.D23	Description and travel
485.D24	Antiquities
485.D242	Social life and customs
485.D25	History
485.D3	Delhi
485.D5	Diu
	East Punjab see DS485.P8+
485.E3	Eastern Bengal and Assam
	Cf. DS485.A84 Assam
	Cf. DS485.B39+ Bengal
485.G25	Ganges River. Ganges River Region
	Class here general works and works restricted to discussions of the Ganges River in India
	Class works on the Ganges River in Bangladesh in DS396.8.G46
	Cf. DS396.8.G46 Ganges River in Bangladesh
	Goa. Goa, Daman, and Diu
	Class here general or chronologically comprehensive works on Goa or on Goa, Daman, and Diu, and works covering predominantly the period after 1961.
	For Portuguese colonial Goa see DS498+
	Cf. DS485.D14 Daman
	Cf. DS485.D5 Diu
485.G56	General works
	History
485.G563	General works
	By period
	Early to 1961 see DS498+
485.G564	1962-
485.G6	Gondal
485.G8-.G895	Gujarat (Table DS-DX2)
485.G9	Gwalior

	India (Bharat)
	Local history and description
	Minor kingdoms, states, regions, etc., A-Z -- Continued
485.H34-.H3495	Haryana (Table DS-DX2)
485.H5	Himachal Pradesh
485.H6	Himalaya Mountains. Himalaya region
(485.H62)	Himalayan States (Collective)
	see DS485.H6
485.H9	Hyderabad
485.I5	Indore
485.J25	Jaipur
	Jammu see DS485.K2+
485.J48-.J4895	Jharkhand (Table DS-DX2)
485.J6	Jodhpur
	Kachchh see DS485.C8
485.K193	Karakoram Range
	For Karakoram Range in Pakistan see DS392.K35
	Karnataka see DS485.M83+
	Kashmir. Jammu and Kashmir
485.K2	Periodicals. Societies. Serials
485.K22	Gazetteers. Dictionaries
485.K225	Directories
485.K226	Guidebooks
485.K23	General works
485.K233	Historical geography
485.K24	Description and travel
485.K245	Antiquities
485.K246	Social life and customs. Civilization. Intellectual life
485.K247	Ethnography
	History
485.K2485	Biography (Collective)
	For individual biography see the period
485.K25	General works
485.K255	Through 1500
485.K256	1500-1850
485.K26	1850-1947
485.K27	1947-
485.K3	Káthiáwár
485.K4-.K495	Kerala (Table DS-DX2)
	Cf. DS485.C64 Cochin
	Cf. DS485.T7 Travancore
485.K5	Kishtwar
	Kodagu see DS485.C69
485.K8	Kunáwár
	Laccadives see DS486.5.L3
485.L2	Ladakh
485.L3	Lalitpur

	India (Bharat)
	Local history and description
	Minor kingdoms, states, regions, etc., A-Z -- Continued
485.L8	Lushai Hills
	Madhya Pradesh see DS485.C3+
	Madras. Tamil Nadu
485.M25	Periodicals, etc.
485.M26	Gazetteers. Dictionaries
485.M27	Description and travel
485.M275	Antiquities
485.M276	Social life and customs. Civilization
485.M277	Ethnography
485.M28	History
485.M29	Madura
485.M32	Magadha
	Maharashtra
485.M34	Periodicals. Sources and documents
485.M342	General works
485.M343	Description and travel
485.M3435	Gazetteers
485.M344	Biography (Collective)
485.M345	Antiquities
485.M346	Social life and customs. Civilization
485.M347	Ethnography
	History
485.M348	General works
485.M349	Marathas
	Cf. DS432.M2 Ethnography
485.M3493	Majha
485.M35	Malabar
485.M38	Malwa
	Manipur
485.M42	Periodicals. Sources and documents
485.M425	General works
485.M43	Biography
485.M44	Description and travel
485.M45	Ethnography
485.M46	Antiquities
485.M47	Social life and customs
	History
485.M48	General works
485.M49	Modern
485.M494	Mathura. Muttra
485.M5	Mayurbhanj
485.M58	Meghalaya
485.M6	Merwara
	Mewar see DS485.U3

India (Bharat)
  Local history and description
    Minor kingdoms, states, regions, etc., A-Z -- Continued

485.M7	Monghyr
(485.M8)	Muttra
	see DS485.M494
	Mysore. Karnataka
485.M83	Periodicals. Sources and documents
485.M835	Biography (Collective)
485.M84	Gazetteers
485.M843	Guidebooks
485.M845	General works
485.M85	Description and travel
485.M86	Antiquities
485.M87	Social life and customs. Civilization
485.M9	History
485.N27	Nāgāland
485.N3	Nawangar
485.N5	Nilgiri Hills
485.N68	North East Frontier Agency. Arunāchal Pradesh
	Orissa
	Cf. DS485.B51+ Bihar and Orissa
485.O6	Periodicals. Societies. Serials
485.O62	Gazetteers. Dictionaries
485.O625	Directories
485.O626	Guidebooks
485.O63	General works
485.O633	Historical geography
485.O64	Description and travel
485.O645	Antiquities
485.O646	Social life and customs. Civilization. Intellectual life
485.O647	Ethnography
	History
485.O6485	Biography (Collective)
	For individual biography see the period
485.O65	General works
485.O655	Through 1500
485.O656	1500-1850
485.O66	1850-1947
485.O67	1947-
	Oudh
485.O9	Description and travel
485.O92	Gazetteers
485.O94	History
485.P66	Pondicherry
	Including French India (General)
485.P72	Prakasam

	India (Bharat)
	Local history and description
	Minor kingdoms, states, regions, etc., A-Z -- Continued
485.P79	Pudukkottai
	Punjab
485.P8	Biography (Collective)
485.P82	Gazetteers
485.P83	General works
485.P84	Description and travel
485.P85	Antiquities
485.P86	Social life and customs
	History
485.P87	General works
485.P88	Sikhs
	Cf. DS432.S5 Ethnography
485.P89	Punjab, East
	Punjab, West see DS392.P8
485.P9	Puri
485.P92	Purnea
	Rajasthan. Rajputana
485.R18	Periodicals, etc.
485.R19	General works
485.R2	Description and travel
485.R21	Gazetteers
485.R22	Biography (Collective)
485.R23	Antiquities
485.R24	Social life and customs. Civilization
485.R25	Ethnography
485.R26	History
485.S37	Saraswati River Valley
485.S48	Shahabad
485.S5-.S595	Sikkim (Table DS-DX2)
485.S794	Surapura (Princely State)
	Tamil Nadu see DS485.M25+
485.T7	Travancore
485.T8	Tripura
485.U3	Udaipur. Mewar
	United Provinces of Agra and Oudh. Uttar Pradesh
	Cf. DS485.O9+ Oudh
485.U6	General works
485.U61	Gazetteers
	Biography
485.U62A1-.U62A19	Collective
485.U62A2-.U62Z	Individual, A-Z
485.U63	Antiquities
485.U64	History
	Uttar Pradesh see DS485.U6+

	India (Bharat)
	Local history and description
	Minor kingdoms, states, regions, etc., A-Z -- Continued
	Uttarakhand see DS485.U693
485.U693	Uttaranchal. Uttarakhand
	Vadodara see DS485.B34
485.V432	Veerapuram Site
485.V6	Vijayayanagar
	West Bengal see DS485.B493
486.A-Z	Cities, towns, etc., A-Z
	e.g.
486.A29	Agiabir Site
486.A3	Agra
	Including Taj Mahal, etc.
486.A483	Alagankulam Site
486.A6	Amaraoti (Amaravati, Amravati)
	Arikamedu Site see DS486.P53
486.A86	Atranjīkherā Site
486.B345	Balathal Site
486.B3698	Bekal
	Including Bekal Fort
486.B4	Benares. Vārānasi
486.B7	Bombay
486.B9	Buddha Gayá
486.C2	Calcutta
486.C28	Carāideu Site
486.C37	Chandraketugarh Site
486.C459	Charda Jamogh
486.C48	Chitor Fort
486.D18	Dangawada Site
486.D3	Delhi. New Delhi
486.D46	Dholavira Site
486.F36	Farmana Site
486.F37	Fatehpur-Sikri
486.G3	Gaur
486.G6	Golconda
486.G8	Gwalior
486.H3	Hampi
486.J48	Jhusi Site
486.J65	Jokṣer Danga Site
486.K236	Kakrehta Site
486.K266	Kalli Khera Mound
486.K3	Kānchenjunga
486.K325	Kaothe Site
486.K3565	Katanera Site
486.K366	Kaundinyapura Site
486.K37	Kausambi

India (Bharat)
  Local history and description
    Cities, towns, etc., A-Z -- Continued

486.K514	Khangabok Site
486.L63	Lothal
486.L9	Lucknow
486.M2	Madras
486.M8	Mysore
486.N259	Nageswar Site
486.N28	Nanda Devi
(486.N3)	Nanga Parbat
	see DS392.2.N36
486.N314	Nantipuram (Ancient city)
	New Delhi see DS486.D3
486.O6	Ootacamund
486.O75	Oriyo Timbo
486.P26	Patna
	Including Bankipore (Bankipur), Pataliputra
486.P44	Phanigiri Site
486.P53	Podouké. Arikamedu Site
486.P58	Pondicherry
486.P74	Puhār
486.R33	Ramgarh Hill Cave Theatre
486.R63	Rojdi Site
486.S13	Sahasraliṅga Site
486.S2	Sanchi
486.S5	Simla
486.S576	Sisupalgarh
486.S94	Surkotada Site
486.T37	Tarkhanewala-Dera Mound
486.T484	Thapli Site
486.T7	Tranquebar
486.T75	Trilokpur Mound
486.T84	Tumain Site
486.U295	Udayagiri Site
486.V3	Vaiśālī
	Vārānasi see DS486.B4
486.W37	Warangal
486.5.A-Z	Islands, A-Z
	Andaman (and Nicobar)
486.5.A5	General works
486.5.A52	Nicobar
486.5.L3	Laccadives. Lakshadweep
	Maldives see DS349.9.M34+
	Nicobar see DS486.5.A52

	India (Bharat)
	Local history and description -- Continued
(486.8)	French in India
	For works limited to the 17th-18th centuries, see DS642+
	For works on Pondicherry, French India (General), see DS485.P66
	Portuguese in India see DS498+
	Sri Lanka
488	Periodicals. Societies. Serials
	Museums, exhibitions, etc.
488.12	General works
488.13.A-Z	Individual. By place, A-Z
488.2	Sources and documents
488.3	Addresses, essays, lectures
488.9	Directories. Gazetteers. Guidebooks
489	General works. Description and travel
489.1	Antiquities
489.15	Social life and customs
	Ethnography
489.2	General works
489.25.A-Z	Individual elements in the population, A-Z
489.25.A43	Ambattans
489.25.B85	Burghers
489.25.C45	Chetties
489.25.D87	Durawa
489.25.E3	East Indians
489.25.E95	Europeans
489.25.J38	Javanese
489.25.K3	Karavas
489.25.M32	Malaiyaha Tamil
489.25.M37	Malays
489.25.M46	Memons
489.25.M8	Muslims
489.25.P35	Pallis
489.25.R63	Rodiya
489.25.S25	Salagama
489.25.S5	Sinhalese
489.25.T3	Tamil
489.25.V4	Veddahs
489.25.X56	Xhosa
489.3	Biography (Collective)
	For individual biography, see the special period or locality
	History
489.5	General works
489.55	Addresses, essays, lectures

	Sri Lanka
	History -- Continued
489.56	Military history
	For individual campaigns and engagements, see the special period or reign
	Political and diplomatic history. Foreign and general relations
489.57	General works
489.59.A-Z	Relations with individual countries, A-Z
	By period
	Early to 1505
489.6	General works
	Biography and memoirs
489.62	Collective
489.63.A-Z	Individual, A-Z
	1505-1948
489.7	General works
	Biography and memoirs
489.72	Collective
489.73.A-Z	Individual, A-Z
	1948-1978
489.8	General works
	Biography and memoirs
489.82	Collective
489.83.A-Z	Individual, A-Z
	e.g.
489.83.B28	Bandaranaike, Sirimavo R.D., 1916-
489.83.B3	Bandaranaike, Solomon West Ridgeway Dias
489.83.K6	Kotelawala, Sir John Lionel
	1978-
489.84	General works
	Biography and memoirs
489.85	Collective
489.86.A-Z	Individual, A-Z
490.A-Z	Sections, districts, cities, etc., A-Z
	e.g.
490.A2	Adam's Peak
490.A6	Anuradhpura
490.C8	Colombo
490.J3	Jaffna
490.K3	Kandy
	Bhutan
491	Periodicals. Societies. Serials
491.3	Guidebooks
491.4	General works
491.42	Pictorial works
491.5	Description and travel

Bhutan -- Continued

491.6	Antiquities
	For local antiquities see DS492.9.A+
491.7	Social life and customs. Civilization. Intellectual life
	Ethnography
491.75	General works
491.76.A-Z	Individual elements in the population, A-Z
491.76.D69	Doya
491.76.M66	Monpa
	History
492	General works
492.4	Foreign and general relations
	For general works on the diplomatic history of a period, see the period
	For works on relations with a specific country regardless of period, see DS492.5.A+
492.5.A-Z	Relations with individual countries, A-Z
	By period
	Through 1907
492.6	General works
	Biography
492.62	Collective
492.63.A-Z	Individual, A-Z
	1907-
492.7	General works
	Biography
492.72	Collective
492.73.A-Z	Individual, A-Z
492.9.A-Z	Local history and description, A-Z
	Nepal
493	Periodicals. Societies
493.15	Congresses
493.2	Sources and documents
493.3	Gazetteers. Dictionaries, etc. Guidebooks
493.32	Place names (General)
493.4	General works
493.42	Pictorial works
493.49	Historical geography
493.495	Geography
	Description and travel
493.5	Earliest through 1768
493.52	1769-1950
493.53	1951-
493.6	Antiquities
	Social life and customs. Civilization. Intellectual life
493.7	General works

	Nepal
	Social life and customs. Civilization. Intellectual life --
	Continued
493.73	Caste
	For individual castes, see DS493.9+, e. g. DS493.9.D24,
	Dalits
	Ethnography
493.8	General works
493.9.A-Z	Individual elements in the population, A-Z
493.9.A87	Atris
493.9.B36	Baniyas
493.9.B37	Baram
493.9.B4	Bhaṭṭharāīs
493.9.B45	Bhotias
493.9.B47	Bhujela
493.9.B68	Bote
493.9.B72	Brahmans
493.9.C46	Chantel
493.9.C47	Chantyāla
493.9.C48	Chepang
493.9.C49	Chhetris
493.9.C53	Chyamlung
493.9.D24	Dalits
493.9.D38	Darai
493.9.D44	Dhimal
493.9.D87	Durā
493.9.E28	East Indians
493.9.E47	Ekthariya Chhetris
493.9.G38	Gautamas
493.9.G8	Gurkhas
493.9.G84	Gurungs
493.9.K37	Kārkīs
493.9.K43	Khaling
493.9.K45	Khamma
493.9.K48	Khas
493.9.K57	Kiranti
493.9.K64	Koirālā
493.9.K83	Kucabandiyā
493.9.L44	Lepcha
493.9.L5	Limbus
493.9.M3	Magars
493.9.M35	Mahatas
493.9.M43	Mech
493.9.M87	Muslims
493.9.N3	Nakarmīs
493.9.N35	Nauthars
493.9.N4	Newars

	Nepal
	Ethnography
	Individual elements in the population, A-Z -- Continued
493.9.N92	Nyinba
493.9.N94	Nyishangba
493.9.P35	Pāndes
493.9.R34	Rai
493.9.R35	Rajbangsi
493.9.R36	Rājī
493.9.R38	Raute
493.9.R55	Rimālas
493.9.S25	Śākyas
493.9.S26	Santal
493.9.S5	Sherpas
493.9.S74	Śreshthas
493.9.S94	Sunuwar
493.9.S965	Suvedīs
493.9.S97	Suyala Th+ap+as
493.9.T35	Tamang
493.9.T45	Thakali
493.9.T47	Tharus
493.9.T53	Tibetans
493.9.W35	Walung
493.9.W36	Wambule Rai
493.9.Y35	Yakha
493.9.Y36	Yamphu
494	Biography (Collective)
	For individual biography, see the special period or locality
	History
494.4	Historiography
494.5	General works
494.6	Addresses, essays, lectures
494.65	Military history
	For individual campaigns and engagements, see the special period or reign
	Political and diplomatic history. Foreign and general relations
	For specific periods, see the special period or reign
494.7	General works
494.8.A-Z	Relations with individual countries, A-Z
	By period
	Earliest to 1768
495	General works
	Biography and memoirs
495.2	Collective
495.22.A-Z	Individual, A-Z
	1768-1951

	Nepal
	History
	By period
	1768-1951 -- Continued
495.3	General works
	Biography and memoirs
495.32	Collective
495.33.A-Z	Individual, A-Z
	1951-1990
495.5	General works
495.58	Foreign and general relations
	Biography and memoirs
495.59	Collective
495.592.A-Z	Individual, A-Z
	1990-
495.6	General works
495.64	Foreign and general relations
	Biography and memoirs
495.65	Collective
495.652.A-Z	Individual, A-Z
495.8.A-Z	Local history and description, A-Z
	e.g.
495.8.A5	Annapurna
495.8.D45	Dhaulāgiri Himāl
495.8.E9	Everest, Mount
495.8.K3	Kathmandu
495.8.M3	Manaslu Peak
	Portuguese colonial Goa. Portuguese in India
	For general or chronologically comprehensive works on Goa or on Goa, Daman, and Diu, and works covering predominantly the period after 1961, see DS485.G56+
	Cf. DS485.D14 Daman
	Cf. DS485.D5 Diu
498	General works
	Early to 1600
498.3	General works
498.5.A-Z	Biography and memoirs, A-Z
	e.g.
498.5.A3	Albuquerque, Affonso de
498.5.C3	Castro, Joao de
498.5.C7	Castro, Diogo do
498.7	1600-1961
(498.8)	1962-
	see DS485.G564
	East Asia. The Far East
501	Periodicals. Societies. Serials
501.5	Congresses. Conferences, etc.

East Asia. The Far East -- Continued

502	Directories
503	Sources and documents
	Collected works
503.4	Several authors
503.5	Individual authors
504	Gazetteers. Dictionaries, etc. Guidebooks
504.5	General works
504.7	Historical geography
504.8	Geography
	Description and travel
505	Through 1500
506	1501-1800
507	1801-1900
508	1901-1950
508.2	1951-
509	Antiquities
509.3	Social life and customs. Civilization. Intellectual life
	Ethnography
509.5.A1	General works
509.5.A2-Z	Individual elements in the population, A-Z
509.5.C5	Chinese
509.5.E3	East Indian
509.5.E9	Eurasian
509.5.H66	Hmong
509.5.J3	Japanese
509.5.R87	Russians
509.5.T3	Tai
509.5.U35	Ukrainians
	Biography and memoirs
510	Collective
510.5.A-Z	Individual, A-Z
	History
	Including Far Eastern question
	Study and teaching
510.7	General works
510.8.A-Z	Individual schools, A-Z
511	General works
513	Addresses, essays, lectures
	By period
514	Early through 1500
514.3	1501-1800
515	1801-1904
	Cf. DS740.6+ China and the Far Eastern question
	Russo-Japanese War, 1904-1905
516	Sources and documents
516.A2-.A3	Japanese

East Asia. The Far East
 History
  By period
   Russo-Japanese War, 1904-1905
    Sources and documents -- Continued

516.A5-.A6	Russian
516.A8-Z	Other countries, A-Z
516.5	Pictorial works
517	General works
517.1	Naval history
517.13	Political and diplomatic history

Special events, battles, etc.

517.15	Battle of Yalu, 1904
517.3	Siege of Port Arthur (Lüshun), 1904-1905
517.4	Battle of Mukden (Shenyang), 1905
517.5	Battle of Tsushima, 1905
517.7	Treaty of Portsmouth, 1905
517.8	Addresses, essays, lectures
517.9	Other

Including reminiscences, etc.

518	1904-1945

For works on control of the Pacific, the Panama
Canal, and the Far Eastern question see DU29

518.1	1945-

Relation of individual countries to East Asia

518.15	China, 1945-

For works on China and the Far Eastern question to
1945 see DS740.6+

518.2	France
518.3	Germany
518.4	Great Britain
518.42	India
518.45	Japan
518.47	Korea
518.5	Netherlands
518.6	Portugal
518.7	Soviet Union. Far Eastern Republic
518.8	United States
518.9.A-Z	Other countries, A-Z

Southeast Asia

520	Periodicals. Societies. Serials
520.3	Congresses
520.4	Sources and documents

Collected works (nonserial)

520.5	Several authors
520.6	Individual authors
520.7	Gazetteers. Dictionaries, etc.

	Southeast Asia -- Continued
520.9	Guidebooks
521	General works
521.2	General special
521.3	Pictorial works
521.6	Historical geography
521.62	Geography
	Description and travel
522	Through 1500
522.2	1501-1800
522.3	1801-1900
522.4	1901-1950
522.5	1951-1975
522.6	1975-
523	Antiquities
523.2	Social life and customs. Civilization. Intellectual life
	For specific periods, see the period
	Ethnography
523.3	General works
523.4.A-Z	Individual elements in the population, A-Z
523.4.A73	Arabs
523.4.C45	Chinese
523.4.E28	East Indians
523.4.E87	Eurasians
523.4.E89	Europeans
523.4.J36	Japanese
523.4.J38	Jarai
523.4.L33	Lahu
523.4.M35	Malay
523.4.M65	Mon
523.4.M87	Muslims
523.4.T35	Tai
523.4.Y36	Yao
	History
	Periodicals. Societies. Serials see DS520
524	Dictionaries. Chronological tables, outlines, etc.
524.2	Biography (Collective)
	For individual biography, see the specific period, reign or place
	Historiography
524.4	General works
	Biography of historians, area studies specialists, archaeologists, etc.
524.5	Collective
524.6.A-Z	Individual, A-Z
	Study and teaching
524.7	General works

	Southeast Asia
	History
	Study and teaching -- Continued
524.8.A-Z	By region or country, A-Z
	Subarrange by author
525	General works
525.3	Juvenile works
525.32	Addresses, essays, lectures
525.7	Political history
	For specific periods, see the period
	Foreign and general relations
525.8	General works
525.9.A-Z	Relations with individual countries, A-Z
	By period
526.3	Through 1500
526.4	1500-1900
526.6	1900-1945
526.7	1945-
526.9	Golden Triangle (Southeast Asia)
	Burma. Myanmar
527	Periodicals. Societies. Serials
527.2	Sources and documents
527.3	Gazetteers. Guidebooks. Directories, etc.
527.4	General works
	Description and travel
527.5	Through 1823
527.6	1824-1945
527.7	1945-
527.8	Antiquities
527.9	Social life and customs. Civilization. Intellectual life
	Ethnography
528	General works
528.2.A-Z	Individual elements in the population, A-Z
	Akha see DS528.2.K37
528.2.A73	Arakanese
528.2.B7	Brahmans
528.2.C42	Chakma
528.2.C44	Chinese
528.2.C45	Chins
528.2.E9	Eurasians
528.2.G63	Goanese
528.2.G9	Gurkhas
528.2.H3	Hakas
528.2.K22	Ka nan'''
528.2.K3	Kachin
528.2.K35	Karen
528.2.K37	Kaw. Akha

	Southeast Asia
	Burma. Myanmar
	Ethnography
	Individual elements in the population, A-Z -- Continued
528.2.K38	Kayah
528.2.K84	Kuki Chin
528.2.L35	Laotu
528.2.L57	Lisu
528.2.L87	Lushai
528.2.M33	Maru
528.2.M58	Moken. Selung
528.2.M6	Mon
528.2.M78	Mrui
528.2.M9	Muslims
528.2.N33	Naga
528.2.P3	Palaungs
528.2.P95	Pyu
528.2.R64	Rohingya
(528.2.S34)	Selung
528.2.S5	Shans
528.2.T38	Taungtha
528.2.T43	Telugu
528.2.T45	Thado
528.2.T65	Toṅ'sā"
528.2.W32	Wa
528.3	Biography (Collective)
	History
528.34	Dictionaries. Chronological tables, outlines, etc.
	Historiography
528.4	General works
	Biography of historians, area studies specialists, archaeologists, etc.
528.42	Collective
528.43.A-Z	Individual, A-Z
528.5	General works
528.6	Military history
	For individual campaigns and engagements, see the special period or reign
	Political and diplomatic history. Foreign and general relations
528.7	General works
528.8.A-Z	Relations with individual countries, A-Z
	By period
529.2	Earliest to 1287. Pagan kingdom
529.3	1287-1824

	Southeast Asia
	Burma. Myanmar
	History
	By period -- Continued
529.7	1824-1885
	For First Anglo-Burmese War, 1824-1826 see DS475.7
	For Second Anglo-Burmese War, 1852 see DS477.65
	For Third Anglo-Burmese War, 1885 see DS479.7
	1885-1945
530	General works
	Biography and memoirs
530.3	Collective
530.32.A-Z	Individual, A-Z
	e.g.
530.32.A9	Aung San, U
	'On' Chan", Buil'khyup', 1915-1947 see DS530.32.A9
	1945-
530.4	General works
	Biography and memoirs
530.52	Collective
530.53.A-Z	Individual, A-Z
	e.g.
530.53.N9	Nu, U
	1948-1962
530.54	General works
	Biography and memoirs
530.55	Collective
530.56.A-Z	Individual, A-Z
	1962-1988
	Including struggle for democracy, 1988
530.6	General works
	Biography and memoirs
530.62	Collective
530.63.A-Z	Individual, A-Z
	1988-
530.65	General works
	Biography and memoirs
530.67	Collective
530.68.A-Z	Individual, A-Z
	Local history and description
530.8.A-Z	Minor kingdoms, states, regions, etc., A-Z
	e.g.
530.8.C45	Chin Hills. Chin State
530.8.M47	Mergui Archipelago

	Southeast Asia
	Burma. Myanmar
	Local history and description
	Minor kingdoms, states, regions, etc., A-Z -- Continued
530.8.S45	Shan State. Shan States. Federated Shan States
530.9.A-Z	Cities, towns, etc., A-Z
	e.g.
530.9.K34	Kalasāpūra (Extinct city)
530.9.M3	Mandalay
530.9.R3	Rangoon
	French Indochina
531	Periodicals. Societies. Serials
531.5	Congresses. Conferences, etc.
532	Sources and documents
532.5	Directories. Gazetteers. Guidebooks
532.8	General works
	Description and travel
533	Through 1787
534	1788-1950
535	1951-
536	Antiquities
	See also Local history and description
537	Social life and customs. Civilization. Intellectual life
	Ethnography
538	General works
539.A-Z	Individual elements in the population, A-Z
539.C5	Chinese
539.F74	French
539.K5	Kha Tahoi
539.M58	Mnong
539.M6	Moi
539.R3	Rade
539.T36	Tamil
	Biography and memoirs
540.A2	Collective
540.A3-Z	Individual, A-Z
540.P3	Pavie, Auguste
	History
541	General works
542	Addresses, essays, lectures
544	Military history
545	Naval history
545.5	Political history
	For specific periods, see the period

DS

Southeast Asia
>French Indochina
>>History -- Continued
>>>Foreign and general relations
>>>>For general works on the diplomatic history of a period, see the period
>>>>For works on relations with a specific country regardless of period see DS546.5.A+

546	General works
546.5.A-Z	Relations with individual countries, A-Z
	By period
547	Earliest to 1787
548	1787-1884
549	1884-1945. Sino-French War, 1884-1885
	Cf. DS559.92.T6 Tongking
	1945-
550	General works
	Indochinese War, 1946-1954
553.A1	Periodicals. Collections
553.A2-Z	Sources and documents
553.1	General works. Military operations (General)
553.2	Pictorial works. Satire, caricature, etc.
553.3.A-Z	Individual campaigns, battles, etc., A-Z
553.3.D5	Diên Biên Phû
553.4.A-Z	Regimental and unit histories (not A-Z)
553.5	Personal narratives
553.6	Armistices. Peace negotiations
553.7	Other topics (not A-Z)
	Cambodia
554	Periodicals. Societies. Serials
554.2	Sources and documents
554.25	Gazetteers. Dictionaries, etc. Guidebooks
554.3	General works
	Description and travel
554.34	Earliest through 1800
554.36	1801-1950
554.38	1951-1974
554.382	1975-
554.4	Antiquities
554.42	Social life and customs. Civilization. Intellectual life
	Ethnography
554.44	General works
554.45	Khmers
554.46.A-Z	Other elements in the population, A-Z
554.46.B78	Bru
554.46.C45	Cham
554.46.C5	Chinese

	Southeast Asia
	French Indochina
	Cambodia -- Continued
554.47	Biography (Collective)
	For individual biography, see the specific period, reign or place
	Study and teaching
554.49	General works
554.492.A-Z	Local, A-Z
	History
554.5	General works
	Diplomatic history. Foreign and general relations
554.57	General works
554.58.A-Z	Relations with individual countries, A-Z
	By period
	Earliest to 1863
554.6	General works
554.62	Khmer Empire
	Biography and memoirs
554.63	Collective
554.64.A-Z	Individual, A-Z
	1863-1954
554.7	General works
	Biography and memoirs
554.72	Collective
554.73.A-Z	Individual, A-Z
	1954-
554.8	General works
	Biography and memoirs
554.82	Collective
554.83.A-Z	Individual, A-Z
	e.g.
554.83.N6	Norodom Sihanouk Varmam
	Sihanouk see DS554.83.N6
	Cambodian-Vietnamese Conflict, 1977-
554.84	Sources and documents
554.842	General works
554.98.A-Z	Local history and description, A-Z
	e.g.
554.98.A5	Angkor
554.98.F85	Funan (Kingdom)
	Laos
555	Periodicals. Societies. Serials
555.2	Sources and documents
555.25	Gazetteers. Dictionaries, etc. Guidebooks
555.3	General works
	Description and travel

	Southeast Asia
	French Indochina
	Laos
	Description and travel -- Continued
555.34	Earliest through 1800
555.36	1801-1950
555.38	1951-1974
555.382	1975-
555.4	Antiquities
555.42	Social life and customs. Civilization. Intellectual life
	Ethnography
555.44	General works
555.45.A-Z	Individual elements in the population, A-Z
555.45.C5	Chinese
	Hmong see DS555.45.M5
555.45.K37	Katu
555.45.K45	Khmu
555.45.L36	Lamet
555.45.L37	Lao
555.45.M5	Miao. Hmong
555.45.N67	Norweigans
555.45.T35	Tai
555.45.T36	Talieng
555.45.T48	Thai Deng
555.45.V54	Vietnamese
555.47	Biography (Collective)
	For individual biography, see the special period or locality
	History
555.5	General works
	Diplomatic history. Foreign and general relations
555.57	General works
555.58.A-Z	Relations with individual countries, A-Z
	By period
	Earliest to 1893
555.6	General works
	Biography and memoirs
555.62	Collective
555.63.A-Z	Individual, A-Z
	1893-1954
555.7	General works
	Biography and memoirs
555.72	Collective
555.73.A-Z	Individual, A-Z
	1954-1975
555.8	General works
	Biography and memoirs
555.82	Collective

	Southeast Asia
	French Indochina
	Laos
	History
	By period
	1954-1975
	Biography and memoirs -- Continued
555.83.A-Z	Individual, A-Z
	1975-
555.84	General works
	Biography and memoirs
555.85	Collective
555.86.A-Z	Individual, A-Z
555.98.A-Z	Local history and description, A-Z
	Vietnam. Annam
	Including the Republic of Vietnam (South Vietnam)
	For works on the Democratic Republic of Vietnam see DS560+
556	Periodicals. Societies. Serials
	Museums, exhibitions, etc.
556.12	General works
556.13.A-Z	Individual. By place, A-Z
556.14	Congresses
556.2	Sources and documents
556.25	Gazetteers. Dictionaries, etc. Guidebooks
556.3	General works
556.328	Historical geography
556.33	Geography
	Description and travel
556.34	Earliest through 1800
556.36	1801-1954
556.38	1955-1975
556.39	1976-
556.4	Antiquities
556.42	Social life and customs. Civilization. Intellectual life
	Ethnography
556.44	General works
556.45.A-Z	Individual elements in the population, A-Z
556.45.A43	Amerasians
556.45.A73	Arem
556.45.B3	Bahnar
556.45.C5	Chams
556.45.C55	Chinese
556.45.C57	Ching
556.45.C58	Chrau
556.45.C586	Chru
556.45.C59	Chut

Southeast Asia
French Indochina
Vietnam. Annam
Ethnography
Individual elements in the population, A-Z -- Continued

556.45.C83	Cua
556.45.G53	Giay
556.45.H35	Hani
556.45.H56	Hmong
556.45.J3	Jarai
556.45.K5	Khmers
556.45.K54	Khmu'
556.45.K63	Koho
556.45.L37	Lati
556.45.L65	Lolo
556.45.M22	Mã Liêng
556.45.M36	Mang
556.45.M6	Montagnards (General)
556.45.M84	Muong
556.45.N85	Nung
556.45.R48	Rhade
556.45.R63	Roglai
556.45.R82	Ruc
556.45.S24	San Chay
556.45.S25	San Diu
556.45.S44	Sedang
556.45.S5	Si La
556.45.S75	Stieng
556.45.T35	Tai
556.45.T39	Tay Nung
556.45.T53	Thai Deng
556.45.T58	Thos
556.45.U66	Upper Ta'oih
556.45.V34	Van Kieu
556.45.X56	Xinh Mun
556.45.Y36	Yao
556.455	Vietnamese in foreign countries (General)

For Vietnamese in a particular country, see the country

556.47   Biography (Collective)

For individual biography, see the special period or locality

History
Historiography

556.487   General works

Biography of historians, area studies specialists,
archaeologists, etc.

556.488   Collective
556.489.A-Z   Individual, A-Z

	Southeast Asia
	French Indochina
	Vietnam. Annam
	History -- Continued
556.49	Study and teaching
556.5	General works
556.54	Military history
	For individual campaigns and engagements, see the special period or reign
556.55	Naval history
	For individual campaigns and engagements, see the special period or reign
	Diplomatic history. Foreign and general relations
556.57	General works
556.58.A-Z	Relations with individual countries, A-Z
	By period
	Earliest to 1225
556.6	General works
	Biography and memoirs
556.62	Collective
556.63.A-Z	Individual, A-Z
	1225-1802
556.7	General works
	Biography and memoirs
556.72	Collective
556.73.A-Z	Individual, A-Z
	e.g.
556.73.N5	Nguyen Hue, King of Vietnam (Quang Trung)
	1802-1954
	For works on the Democratic Republic of Vietnam see DS560+
556.8	General works
556.815	August Revolution, 1945
	Biography and memoirs
556.82	Collective
556.83.A-Z	Individual, A-Z
	1954-1975
	For works on the Democratic Republic of Vietnam see DS560+
556.9	General works
	Biography and memoirs
556.92	Collective
556.93.A-Z	Individual, A-Z
	e.g.
	Diêm, Ngô Dinh see DS556.93.N5
556.93.N5	Ngô Dinh Diêm, President
	Vietnam War

Southeast Asia
French Indochina
Vietnam. Annam
History
By period
1954-1975
Vietnam War -- Continued
557	Periodicals. Societies. Serials
557.3	Congresses. Conferences, etc.
557.4	Sources and documents
557.5	Biography (Collective)

For individual biography, see the individual
countries in DA-F

557.6	Causes. Origins. Aims
557.7	General works. Military operations (General)
557.72	Pictorial works. Satire, caricature, etc.
557.73	Motion pictures about the war
557.74	Study and teaching
557.8.A-Z	Individual campaigns, battles, etc., A-Z

e.g.

557.8.C3	Cambodia
557.8.E23	Easter Offensive, 1972
557.8.K5	Khe Sanh
557.8.K56	Kontum, 1972
557.8.L3	Laos
557.8.L66	Long Tân
557.8.S6	Sontay Raid, 1970
557.8.T4	Tet Offensive, 1968

By country
Including foreign relations, participation in the
conflict, etc.
United States

558	General works
558.2	General special
558.4	Armies, divisions, regiments, etc.
558.5	Democratic Republic (North Vietnam)

Cf. DS560.4 Effect of war in North Vietnam

558.6.A-Z	Other, A-Z

Military operations see DS557.7
Armies, divisions, regiments, etc. see DS558.4

558.7	Naval operations

Including history of individual units

558.8	Aerial operations

Including history of individual units

558.85	Engineering operations
558.9.A-Z	Other services, A-Z
558.9.A75	Armor

Southeast Asia
French Indochina
Vietnam. Annam
History
By period
1954-1975
Vietnam War
Other services, A-Z -- Continued

558.9.A77	Artillery
558.92	Guerrilla operations
	Medals, badges, decorations of honor
	Including lists of recipients and individual recipients of medals
558.98	General works
558.99.A-Z	By region or country, A-Z
559	Registers, lists of dead and wounded, etc.
559.2	Atrocities. War crimes
559.3	Destruction and pillage
559.4	Prisoners and prisons
559.42	Economic aspects. Commerce, finance, etc. (General)
	For individual countries, see HC, HF, HJ
559.44	Medical and sanitary services
559.46	Press. Censorship. Publicity
559.5	Personal narratives
	Protest movements, anti-war demonstrations, public opinion
559.6	General works
559.62.A-Z	By region or country, A-Z
	For individual demonstrations, see the city where held
559.63	Relief work. Charities. Refugees. Displaced persons
559.64	Moral and religious aspects
559.7	Peace negotiations, treaties, etc.
	Veterans
559.72	General works
	For specific services for veterans see UB356+
559.73.A-Z	By region or country, A-Z
559.8.A-Z	Other topics, A-Z
559.8.A4	Amnesty
559.8.A78	Art and the war
	Biological warfare see DS559.8.C5
559.8.B55	Blacks
	Burials see DS559.8.D38
	Cemeteries see DS559.8.D38

Southeast Asia
French Indochina
Vietnam. Annam
History
By period
1954-1975
Vietnam War
Other topics, A-Z -- Continued

559.8.C5	Chemical warfare. Biological warfare. Defoliation
559.8.C53	Children. Orphans
559.8.C54	Churches
559.8.C6	Communications
559.8.C63	Conscientious objectors
559.8.D38	Dead, Care of. Repatriation of the dead. Burials. Cemeteries
	Defoliation see DS559.8.C5
559.8.D4	Desertions
559.8.D7	Draft resisters
559.8.F83	Fuel supplies
559.8.J35	Japanese Americans
559.8.L64	Logistics
559.8.M39	Mexican Americans
559.8.M44	Military intelligence
559.8.M5	Missing in action
	Negroes see DS559.8.B55
	Orphans see DS559.8.C53
559.8.P65	Propaganda
559.8.P7	Psychological aspects
559.8.R43	Reconnaissance operations
	Repatriation of the dead see DS559.8.D38
559.8.S3	Science and technology
559.8.S4	Search and rescue operations
559.8.S6	Social aspects
559.8.S9	Supplies
	Technology see DS559.8.S3
559.8.T7	Transportation
559.8.T85	Tunnels
559.8.W6	Women
	Celebrations. Memorials. Monuments
	For memorials to special divisions, etc., see the history of the division
559.82	General works
	By region or country
	United States
559.825	General works
559.83.A-Z	Local, A-Z

	Southeast Asia
	French Indochina
	Vietnam. Annam
	History
	By period
	1954-1975
	Vietnam War
	Celebrations. Memorials. Monuments
	By region or country -- Continued
559.832.A-Z	Other regions or countries, A-Z
559.9.A-Z	Local history, A-Z
	1975- . Reunification. Socialist Republic of Vietnam
	For Cambodian-Vietnamese Conflict see DS554.84+
559.912	General works
	Biography and memoirs
559.913	Collective
559.914.A-Z	Individual, A-Z
	Sino-Vietnamese Conflict, 1979
559.915	Sources and documents
559.916	General works
	Local history and description
559.92.A-Z	Protectorates, regions, minor kingdoms, etc., A-Z
	e.g.
559.92.A5	Annam
	Class here works on the French protectorate only
559.92.C5	Champa
559.92.C6	Cochin China
559.92.T6	Tongking (Tonkin)
559.93.A-Z	Cities, towns, etc., A-Z
	e.g.
559.93.C65	Cô-Loa
559.93.D66	Dông-Dâu Site
559.93.H36	Hanoi
	Ho Chi Minh City see DS559.93.S2
559.93.H63	Hoa Lu'
559.93.S2	Saigon. Ho Chi Minh City
	Democratic Republic (North Vietnam), 1945-1975
560	Periodicals. Societies. Serials
560.2	Sources and documents
560.25	Gazetteers. Dictionaries, etc. Guidebooks
560.3	General works
560.4	Description and travel
560.42	Antiquities
560.5	Social life and customs. Civilization. Intellectual life
	Ethnography
560.54	General works

	Southeast Asia
	French Indochina
	Democratic Republic (North Vietnam), 1945- 1975
	Ethnography
560.56.A-Z	Individual elements in the population, A-Z
	History
560.6	General works
	Diplomatic history. Foreign and general relations
560.68	General works
560.69.A-Z	Relations with individual countries, A-Z
	Biography and memoirs
560.7	Collective
560.72.A-Z	Individual, A-Z
560.72.H6	Hô Chi Minh
	Local history and description see DS559.92+
	Thailand (Siam)
561	Periodicals. Societies. Serials
561.5	Congresses
562	Sources and documents
563	Directories. Gazetteers. Guidebooks
563.5	General works
563.7	Historical geography
563.9	Geography
	Description and travel
564	Through 1800
565	1801-1950
566	1951-1975
566.2	1976-
567	Antiquities
	Cf. DS588+ Local history and description
568	Social life and customs. Civilization. Intellectual life
	Ethnography
569	General works
570.A-Z	Individual elements in the population, A-Z
570.A35	Akha
570.A44	Americans
570.B55	Black Tai
570.B87	Burmese
570.C5	Chinese
570.E37	East Indians
	Hmong see DS570.M5
570.J38	Japanese
	Kah So see DS570.S65
570.K37	Karen
570.K48	Khmers
570.K84	Kui
570.L26	Lahu

Southeast Asia
  Thailand (Siam)
    Ethnography
      Individual elements in the population, A-Z -- Continued

570.L28	Lao
570.L3	Lawa
570.L56	Lisu
570.M3	Malays
570.M5	Miao. Hmong
570.M57	Moken
570.M6	Mon
570.M85	Muslims
570.N67	Northern Thai
570.N92	Nyahkur
570.P48	Phi Tong Luang
570.P49	Phu Thai
570.P52	Phuan
570.S42	Semang
570.S44	Senoi
570.S46	Sgaw Karen
570.S52	Shans
570.S65	So. Kah So
570.T34	Tai Yong
570.U73	Urak Lawoi'
570.V5	Vietnamese
570.Y35	Yao
570.5	Biography (Collective)
	For individual biography, see the specific period, reign or place

History
  Historiography

570.95	General works
	Biography of historians, area studies specialists, archaeologists, etc.
570.96	Collective
570.97.A-Z	Individual, A-Z
	Study and teaching
570.98	General works
570.99.A-Z	By region or country, A-Z
	Subarrange by author
571	General works
572	Addresses, essays, lectures
573	Military history
574	Naval history
	Political and diplomatic history
575	General works
575.5.A-Z	Foreign relations with individual countries, A-Z

	Southeast Asia
	Thailand (Siam)
	History -- Continued
	By period
576	Earliest to 638
	638-1809
577	General works
	Biography and memoirs
577.2	Collective
577.22.A-Z	Individual, A-Z
577.9	Čhao Phrayā Čhakkrī (Phutthayōtfā Čhulālōk) (Rama I), 1782-1809
	19th-20th centuries
578	General works
	Biography and memoirs
578.3	Collective
578.32.A-Z	Individual, A-Z
	For biography of an individual ruler, see the period or reign
579	Phra Budalot La (Rama II), 1809-1824
580	Phra Nang Klao (Rama III), 1824-1851
581	Mongkut (Rama IV), 1851-1868
582	Chulalongkorn (Rama V), 1868-1910
583	Vajiravudh (Rama VI), 1910-1925
584	Prajadhipok (Rama VII), 1925-1935
585	Ananda Mahidol (Rama VIII), 1935-1946
586	Bhumibol Adulyadej (Rama IX), 1946-
	Including Regency, 1946-1950
	Local history and description
588.A-Z	Provinces, regions, etc., A-Z
589.A-Z	Cities, towns, etc., A-Z
	e.g.
589.B2	Bangkok
589.N3	Nakon Patom (Nakhon Pathom)
589.P4	Petchaburi (Phetburi)
	Malaysia. Malay Peninsula. Straits Settlements
591	Periodicals. Sources and documents. Collections
591.5	Directories. Gazetteers. Guidebooks
592	General works
592.2	Pictorial works
592.3	Historical geography
592.35	Geography
	Description and travel
592.4	Through 1900
592.5	1901-1945
592.6	1946-

Southeast Asia

Malaysia. Malay Peninsula. Straits Settlements -- Continued

593	Antiquities
	Cf. DS597.22+ Local history and description
594	Social life and customs. Civilization. Intellectual life
	Ethnography
595	General works
595.2	Individual elements in the population
595.2.B38	Batek
595.2.B74	British
595.2.B84	Bugis
595.2.C47	Chewong
595.2.C5	Chinese
595.2.D88	Dutch
595.2.E2	East Indians
595.2.J27	Jah Hut
595.2.J3	Jakun
595.2.K35	Kanaq
595.2.M34	Mah-Meri
595.2.M35	Malays
595.2.O73	Orang Asli
595.2.P44	Penan
595.2.P67	Portuguese
595.2.S3	Sakai. Senoi
595.2.S37	Seletar
595.2.S4	Semang
595.2.S43	Semelai
	Senoi see DS595.2.S3
595.2.S55	Sikhs
595.2.S64	Sri Lankans
595.2.T36	Tamil
595.2.T45	Temuan
595.2.T53	Thais
595.5	Biography (Collective)
	For individual biography, see the specific period, reign or place
	History
595.8	Historiography
595.9	Study and teaching
596	General works
	Political and diplomatic history. Foreign and general relations
596.3	General works
596.4.A-Z	Relations with individual countries, A-Z
	By period
	Early to 1511. Malacca Kingdom
596.5	General works

	Southeast Asia
	Malaysia. Malay Peninsula. Straits Settlements
	History
	By period
	Early to 1511. Malacca Kingdom -- Continued
	Biography and memoirs
596.52	Collective
596.53.A-Z	Individual, A-Z
	1511-1946
596.6	General works
	Biography and memoirs
596.62	Collective
596.63.A-Z	Individual, A-Z
	1946-1963 (Federation)
597	General works
	Biography and memoirs
597.14	Collective
597.15.A-Z	Individual, A-Z
	1963-
597.2	General works
	Biography and memoirs
597.214	Collective
597.215.A-Z	Individual, A-Z
	Local history and description
	East Malaysia (General)
597.22	General works
	Sabah. British North Borneo
597.33	General works
597.332	Description and travel
597.333	Social life and customs. Civilization. Intellectual life
	Ethnography
597.334	General works
597.335.A-Z	Individual elements in the population, A-Z
597.335.B35	Bajau
597.335.B84	Bugis
597.335.D88	Dusun
597.335.H34	Hakka
597.335.I43	Ilanun
(597.335.I73)	Iranun
	see DS597.335.I43
597.335.R85	Rungus
597.336	History
	Biography and memoirs
597.337.A2	Collective
597.337.A3-597.Z	Individual, A-Z
597.34.A-Z	Local, A-Z
	e.g.

DS

	Southeast Asia
	Malaysia. Malay Peninsula. Straits Settlements
	Local history and description
	East Malaysia (General)
	Sabah. British North Borneo
	Local, A-Z -- Continued
597.34.K5	Kinabula, Mount
	Sarawak
597.36	General works
597.364	Description and travel
597.3645	Antiquities
597.365	Social life and customs. Civilization. Intellectual life
	Ethnography
597.366	General works
597.367.A-Z	Individual elements in the population, A-Z
597.367.B47	Berawan
597.367.B56	Bisaya
597.367.C55	Chinese
597.367.D93	Dyaks
597.367.I23	Ibans
597.367.K44	Kelabit
597.367.K47	Kenya
597.367.M34	Malays
597.367.M44	Melanau
597.367.M87	Murut
597.37	History
	Biography and memoirs
597.38.A2	Collective
597.38.A3-Z	Individual, A-Z
	e.g.
597.38.B7	Brooke, Sir James
597.39.A-Z	Local, A-Z
	e.g.
597.39.K8	Kuching
598.A-Z	Other states, regions, etc., A-Z
	e.g.
598.J7	Johor
598.K3	Kelantan
	Penang see DS598.P5
598.P4	Perak
598.P5	Pinang. Pulau Pinang
	Singapore see DS608+
599.A-Z	Cities, towns, etc., A-Z
	e.g.
599.K8	Kuala Lumpur
599.M3	Malacca. Melaka
	Malay Archipelago

	Southeast Asia
	Malay Archipelago -- Continued
600	Dictionaries
601	General works. Description and travel
603	History
605	Other
	Singapore
608	Periodicals. Societies. Serials
608.2	Museums, exhibitions, etc.
608.3	Congresses
608.4	Sources and documents
608.5	Gazetteers. Dictionaries, etc.
608.7	Directories
608.8	Guidebooks
609	General works
609.2	Pictorial works
609.3	Historic monuments, landmarks, scenery, etc.
	For local see DS610.9.A+
609.4	Geography
	Description and travel
609.5	Early through 1900
609.6	1901-1980
609.7	1981-
609.8	Antiquities
	For local antiquities see DS610.9.A+
609.9	Social life and customs. Civilization. Intellectual life
	By period
	see the specific period
	Ethnography
610	General works
610.25.A-Z	Individual elements in the population, A-Z
610.25.A7	Arabs
610.25.A74	Armenians
610.25.E37	East Indians
610.25.E87	Eurasians
610.25.G47	Germans
610.25.H34	Hakka
610.25.I75	Irish
610.25.J34	Japanese
610.25.M34	Malays
610.25.M87	Muslims
610.25.P47	Peranakan
610.25.S54	Sikhs
610.25.T34	Tamil
	History
610.3	Biography (Collective)
	For individual biography, see the specific period

	Southeast Asia
	Singapore
	History -- Continued
610.34	Historiography
610.37	Study and teaching
610.4	General works
	Foreign and general relations
	For general works on the diplomatic history of a period, see the period
610.45	General works
	For works on relations with a specific country regardless of period see DS610.47.A+
610.47.A-Z	Relations with individual countries, A-Z
	By period
	Early to 1945
610.5	General works
	Biography and memoirs
610.52	Collective
610.53.A-Z	Individual, A-Z
610.55	1942-1945. Japanese occupation
	1945-1965
610.6	General works
	Biography and memoirs
610.62	Collective
610.63.A-Z	Individual, A-Z
	1965-
610.7	General works
	Biography and memoirs
610.72	Collective
610.73.A-Z	Individual, A-Z
610.9.A-Z	Local, A-Z
	Indonesia (Dutch East Indies)
611	Periodicals. Societies. Serials
	Museums, exhibitions, etc.
611.2	General works
611.3.A-Z	Individual. By place, A-Z
612	Congresses
613	Sources and documents
	Collected documents
613.5	Several authors
613.7	Individual authors
614	Gazetteers. Guidebooks. Directories, etc.
615	General works
	Historic monuments, landmarks, scenery, etc. (General)
	For local see DS646.1+
615.4	General works
615.5	Preservation

	Southeast Asia
	Indonesia (Dutch East Indies) -- Continued
	Description and travel
617	Through 1594
618	1595-1800
	For Dutch accounts see DS411+
619	1801-1945
620	1946-1980
620.2	1981-
621	Antiquities
	Cf. DS646.1+ Individual islands
625	Social life and customs. Civilization. Intellectual life
	Ethnography
631	General works
632.A-Z	Individual elements in the population, A-Z
	Cf. DS646.32.A1+ Borneo and Kalimantan
	Cf. DU744.35.A+ Irian Jaya
632.A25	Achinese
632.A45	Alas
632.A52	Anakalang
632.A54	Angkola
632.A73	Arabs
	Atoni see DS632.T35
632.B23	Badui
632.B24	Bajau
632.B25	Balinese
632.B27	Bantian
632.B3	Batak
632.B35	Bawo
632.B42	Benuaq
632.B44	Betawi
632.B46	Betew
632.B85	Bugis
632.B87	Bunak
632.B88	Buton
632.C57	Christians
632.D68	Dou Donggo
632.E9	Eurasians
632.G25	Galela
632.G26	Gane
632.G3	Gayo
632.H64	Hoga Sara
632.I53	Indos
632.J38	Javanese
632.K27	Kaili
632.K28	Kalang
632.K3	Karo-Batak

Southeast Asia
  Indonesia (Dutch East Indies)
    Ethnography
      Individual elements in the population, A-Z -- Continued

632.K45	Kemak
632.K46	Kenya
632.K47	Keo
632.K6	Kodi
632.K75	Krui
632.K78	Kubu
632.K785	Kulawi
632.K8	Kurai
632.L33	Lamaholot
632.L34	Lamboya
632.L35	Lampung
632.L37	Lauje
632.L55	Lio
632.M25	Makasar
632.M27	Malays
632.M275	Maloh
632.M28	Mambai
632.M285	Mandailing
632.M287	Manggarai
632.M289	Manusela
632.M29	Manyuke
632.M3	Maporese
632.M35	Mentawai
632.M38	Minahasa
632.M4	Minangkabau
632.M65	Moluccans, South
632.N33	Naga
632.N35	Nage
632.N52	Niasese
632.N83	Nuaulu
632.O85	Osing
632.P3	Pakpak
632.R44	Rejang
632.R46	Rembong
632.S32	Sahu
632.S33	Sakudei
632.S34	Saluan
632.S35	Sangir
632.S37	Sarmi
632.S38	Sasak
632.S39	Sawu
632.S45	Senoi
632.S5	Simelungun

	Southeast Asia
	Indonesia (Dutch East Indies)
	Ethnography
	Individual elements in the population, A-Z -- Continued
632.S89	Sumbanese
632.S9	Sundanese
632.T35	Talang Mama
632.T36	Tanimbar
632.T38	Tenggerese
632.T4	Tetum
632.T5	Timor
632.T62	Toba-Batak
632.T63	Tobelo
632.T65	Tolaki
632.T7	Toradjas
632.T95	Tundjung
632.W34	Wana
632.W48	Wewewa
	Natives of foreign countries in Indonesia
632.3.A1	General works
632.3.A2-632.Z	Individual elements, A-Z
632.3.A7	Arabs
632.3.C5	Chinese
632.3.D88	Dutch
632.3.G4	Germans
632.3.J3	Japanese
632.3.Y45	Yemenis
632.4	Indonesians in foreign countries
	For Indonesians in a particular country, see the country
632.5	Biography (Collective)
	History
633	Dictionaries. Chronological tables, outlines, etc.
	Historiography
633.5	General works
	Biography of historians, area studies specialists, archaeologists, etc.
633.6	Collective
633.7.A-Z	Individual, A-Z
633.8	Study and teaching
634	General works
635	Addresses, essays, lectures
636	Military history
637	Naval history
	Political and diplomatic history. Foreign and general relations
638	General works
640.A-Z	Relations with individual countries, A-Z

	Southeast Asia
	Indonesia (Dutch East Indies)
	History -- Continued
	By period
641	Earliest to 1478. Hindu-Buddhist era
641.5	1478-1602. Moslem rule
	1602-1798. Dutch East India Company
642	General works
	Biography and memoirs
642.2	Collective
642.22.A-Z	Individual, A-Z
	1798-1942. Colonial period
643	General works
	Biography and memoirs
643.2	Collective
643.22.A-Z	Individual, A-Z
643.5	1942-1945
	Class here works on the period of World War II, and works on the Japanese occupation
	1945-1966
	Class here works on the Proclamation of Indonesian Republic, August 1945; the struggle with the Netherlands, 1945-1949; the United States of Indonesia, December 1949; and the Republic of Indonesia, 1950-
644	General works
	Biography and memoirs
644.1.A2	Collective
644.1.A3-Z	Individual, A-Z
	e.g.
644.1.S8	Sukarno, president
644.2	Addresses, essays, lectures. By original date of publication
	Subarrange by author
644.3	National holiday celebrations
644.32	Coup d'etat, 1965
	1966-1998
644.4	General works
	Biography and memoirs
644.45	Collective
644.46.A-Z	Individual, A-Z
	1998-
644.5	General works
	Biography and memoirs
644.6	Collective
644.62.A-Z	Individual, A-Z
	Islands

	Southeast Asia
	Indonesia (Dutch East Indies)
	Islands -- Continued
	Sumatra
646.1	General works
646.129	History
	Biography and memoirs
646.13.A1	Collective
646.13.A2-Z	Individual, A-Z
646.15.A-Z	Local, A-Z
	e.g.
646.15.A8	Aceh. Nanggroe Aceh Darussalam
	For Achin Wars see DS643
	Minangkabau see DS646.15.S76
	Nanggroe Aceh Darussalam see DS646.15.A8
646.15.P3	Palembang
646.15.S76	Sumatera Barat. Minangkabau
646.15.S8	Sumatera utara
	Java
646.17	Periodicals. Societies. Serials
646.18	General works
	Description and travel
646.19	Through 1800
646.2	1801-1945
646.21	1946-
646.22	Antiquities
646.23	Social life and customs. Civilization. Intellectual life
	Biography and memoirs
646.25	Collective
646.26.A-Z	Individual, A-Z
	e.g.
646.26.K3	Karatini, raden adjeng
646.26.R3	Raffles, Sir Thomas Stamford
646.27	History
646.29.A-Z	Local history and description, A-Z
	e.g.
646.29.B23	Bandung
646.29.B25	Bantam
646.29.B6	Boro-Budur
646.29.D5	Djakarta. Batavia
646.29.E15	East Java
	Jawa Timur see DS646.29.E15
	Jogjakarta see DS646.29.Y63
646.29.K5	Kedu
646.29.P7	Priangan (Preanger)
646.29.R37	Ratu Baka site
646.29.S8	Surabaya

	Southeast Asia
	Indonesia (Dutch East Indies)
	Islands
	Java
	Local history and description, A-Z -- Continued
646.29.Y63	Yogyakarta. Jogjakarta
	Borneo. Kalimantan, Indonesia
	For Sabah see DS597.33+
	For Sarawak see DS597.36+
	For Brunei see DS650+
646.3	General works
646.312	Description and travel
	Ethnography
646.32.A1	General works
646.32.A2-646.Z	Individual elements in the population, A-Z
	Bajau see DS666.B3
646.32.B34	Banjar
646.32.B46	Bentian Dayak
646.32.C5	Chinese
	Dayak see DS646.32.D9
646.32.D86	Dusuns
646.32.D9	Dyak. Dayak
646.32.I2	Iban
646.32.K36	Kantu
646.32.K38	Kayan
646.32.M2	Maanyans
	Maloh see DS632.M275
646.32.M64	Modang
646.32.N45	Ngaju
646.32.P58	Pitap
646.32.P85	Punan
646.32.T35	Taman
646.34.A-Z	Local history and description, A-Z
	e.g.
646.34.B3	Bandjarmasin. Banjermasin (Sultanate)
646.34.P6	Pontianak
(646.35)	Brunei
	see DS650+
(646.36-.38)	Sarawak
	see DS597.36+
	Celebes. Sulawesi
646.4	General works
646.42	Description and travel
646.47	History
646.49.A-Z	Local, A-Z
	e.g.
646.49.M35	Makasar (Macassar). Udjung Pandang

	Southeast Asia
	Indonesia (Dutch East Indies)
	Islands
	Celebes. Sulawesi
	Local, A-Z -- Continued
	Udjung Pandang see DS646.49.M35
	Papua (Indonesia). Irian Jaya. Irian Barat. Netherlands New Guinea see DU744.5
	Timor
646.5	General works
646.57	History
646.59.A-Z	Local, A-Z
	East Timor see DS649.2+
	Timor-Leste see DS649.2+
	Timor Timur see DS649.2+
	Moluccas. Malaku
646.6	General works
	Ethnography
646.65	General works
646.66.A-Z	Individual elements in the population, A-Z
646.66.H82	Huaulu
646.67	History
646.69.A-Z	Local, A-Z
	e.g.
646.69.S69	South Moluccas
647.A-Z	Other islands, regions, and political jurisdictions larger than islands, A-Z

Under each island:

| .x | General works |
| .x2A-.x2Z | Local, A-Z |

e.g.

647.B2-.B22	Bali
647.B25-.B252	Banda Islands
647.B6-.B62	Billiton
647.E6-.E62	Engano
647.K2-.K22	Kei Islands
647.K5-.K52	Kisar
647.K6-.K62	Komodo
647.L8-.L82	Lombok
647.M6-.M62	Mentawi Islands
647.N5-.N52	Nias
647.S3-.S32	Sangihe Islands
647.S8-.S82	Sunda Islands, Lesser
648	British possessions
	Borneo see DS646.3+
649	German possessions (Former)
	Timor-Leste. East Timor. Timor Timur. Portuguese Timor

Southeast Asia
  Timor-Leste. East Timor. Timor Timur. Portuguese Timor --
    Continued

649.2	Periodicals. Societies. Serials
649.23	Congresses
649.25	Sources and documents
649.29	Guidebooks
649.3	General works
649.4	Description and travel
649.42	Antiquities
649.43	Social life and customs. Civilization. Intellectual life
	History
649.5	General works
	By period
	Earliest to 1975
649.53	General works
	Biography and memoirs
649.54	Collective
649.55.A-Z	Individual, A-Z
	1975-2002
649.6	General works
	Biography and memoirs
649.62	Collective
649.63.A-Z	Individual, A-Z
	2002-
649.7	General works
	Biography and memoirs
649.72	Collective
649.73.A-Z	Individual, A-Z
649.9.A-Z	Local history and description, A-Z
	Brunei
650	Periodicals. Societies. Serials
650.15	Sources and documents
650.2	Directories. Dictionaries. Gazetteers
650.23	Guidebooks
650.3	General works
650.34	Historical geography
650.35	Description and travel
650.39	Antiquities
	For local antiquities see DS650.98+
650.4	Social life and customs. Civilization. Intellectual life
	For specific periods, see the period
	Ethnography
650.42	General works
650.43.A-Z	Individual elements in the population, A-Z
650.43.C45	Chinese
650.43.D87	Dusuns

	Southeast Asia
	Brunei
	Ethnography
	Individual elements in the population, A-Z -- Continued
650.43.I23	Ibans
650.43.M87	Muruts
	History
650.44	Biography (Collective)
	For individual biography, see the specific period, reign or place
650.46	Historiography
650.48	Study and teaching
650.5	General works
	Political history. Foreign and general relations
	For specific periods, see the period
	For works on relations with a specific country
	regardless of period see DS650.55.A+
650.54	General works
650.55.A-Z	Relations with individual countries, A-Z
	By period
650.56	Early to 1400
650.6	1400-1906
	1906-1959
650.64	General works
	Biography and memoirs
650.65	Collective
650.66.A-Z	Individual, A-Z
	1959-1984
650.7	General works
	Biography and memoirs
650.72	Collective
650.73.A-Z	Individual, A-Z
	1984-
650.8	General works
	Biography and memoirs
650.82	Collective
650.83.A-Z	Individual, A-Z
	Local history and description
650.98.A-Z	Districts and regions, A-Z
650.99.A-Z	Cities and towns, etc., A-Z
	e.g.
650.99.B35	Bandar Seri Begawan
	Philippines
651	Periodicals. Societies. Serials
	Museums, exhibitions, etc.
652	General works
652.2.A-Z	Individual. By place, A-Z

	Southeast Asia
	Philippines -- Continued
653	Sources and documents
	Collected works
653.4	Several authors
653.5	Individual authors
653.7	Biography (Collective)
	For individual biography, see the specific period, reign or place
654	Gazetteers. Dictionaries, etc. Guidebooks
655	General works
656	Addresses, essays, lectures
656.2	Pictorial works
657	Historic monuments, landmarks, etc. (General)
	For local see DS688+
	Description and travel
	Through 1762 see DS674+
658	1763-1897
659	1898-1945
660	1946-
661	Antiquities
	Cf. DS688.A+ Local history and description
	Social life and customs
663	General works
664	Civilization. Intellectual life
	Ethnography
665	General works
666.A-Z	Individual elements in the population, A-Z
666.A3	Aetas
666.A33	Alangan
666.A38	Amerasians
666.A4	Americans
666.B27	Bagobo
666.B3	Bajau
666.B33	Basques
666.B34	Batak
666.B36	Batan
666.B54	Bikol
666.B57	Bisayas
666.B58	Blaan
666.B6	Bontoks
666.B74	British
666.B78	Buhid
666.B8	Bukidnon
666.B85	Bulakeños
666.C36	Catalans
666.C5	Chinese

	Southeast Asia
	Philippines
	Ethnography
	Individual elements in the population, A-Z -- Continued
666.G3	Gaddang
666.H54	Hiligaynon
666.I12	Ibaloi
666.I13	Ibanag
666.I15	Ifugaos
666.I2	Igorot
666.I37	Ilokanos
666.I4	Ilongot
666.I7	Isneg
666.I77	Itawis
666.I85	Iwaak
666.J3	Japanese
666.K3	Kalinga
666.K4	Kenney
666.M23	Magindanao
666.M25	Mamanuas
666.M3	Mangyans
666.M34	Manobos
666.M37	Maranao
666.M8	Muslims
666.N4	Negritos
666.P34	Palawan
666.P35	Pampangan
666.P36	Panjabis
666.R85	Russians
666.S3	Samals
666.S34	Sangir
666.S8	Subanuns
666.S85	Sulod
666.T2	Tagalos (Tagals)
666.T3	Tagbanuas
666.T32	Tasaday
666.T33	Tausug
666.T36	Tboli
666.T5	Tinguianes
666.T6	Tiruray
666.Y33	Yakans
	History
667	Dictionaries. Chronological tables, outlines, etc.
	Historiography
667.2	General works
	Biography of historians, area studies specialists, archaeologists, etc.

	Southeast Asia
	Philippines
	History
	Historiography
	Biography of historians, area studies specialists, archaeologists, etc. -- Continued
667.25	Collective
667.26.A-Z	Individual, A-Z
667.28	Study and teaching
	General works
668.A2	Through 1800
668.A3-Z	1801-
669	Addresses, essays, lectures
670	Outlines, syllabi, etc.
671	Military history
	Naval history
672	General works
672.5	Pirate wars
	Political and diplomatic history. Foreign and general relations
	For works on a specific period, see the period
672.8	General works
673.A-Z	Special, A-Z
	Friars
673.F6	Sources and documents
673.F7	General works
673.J3	Japan
	By period
673.8	Earliest to 1521
	Spanish rule, 1521-1898
674	General works
674.5	Battle of Playa Honda, 1617
674.8	English in Manila, 1762
674.9.A-Z	Biography and memoirs, A-Z
	e.g.
674.9.A6	Anda y Salazar, Simón de
674.9.L4	Legazpi, Miguel Lopéz de
	19th century
675	General works
675.5	Cavite Mutiny, 1872
	Biography and memoirs, 1801-1894
675.78	Collective
675.8.A-Z	Individual, A-Z
	e.g.
675.8.P5	Pilar Gat-Maytan, Marcelo Hilario del
675.8.R5	Rizal y Alonso, José
	1894-1901

	Southeast Asia
	Philippines
	History
	By period
	1894-1901 -- Continued
676	General works
676.5	General special
	Biography and memoirs
676.8.A1	Collective
676.8.A2-Z	Individual, A-Z
	e.g.
676.8.A3	Aguinaldo y Famy, Emilio
676.8.R4	Retana y Gamboa, Wenceslao Emilio
678	1894-1897
679	1898-1901
	Cf. E714+ War of 1898 (Spanish-American War)
	1901- see DS685+
	Political and diplomatic history
	For works on a specific period, see the period
681	General works
681.3	Addresses, essays, lectures
681.5	Congressional documents (United States)
	Reports of commisions and committee hearings.
	By date
681.5.U3	Senate
681.5.U33	House
681.5.U39	Senate and House
681.5.U4-.U43	Speeches
681.5.U4	Senate
681.5.U43	House
681.5.U5	Other documents. By date
681.7	Diplomatic history
	Military history
	e.g. Insurrections of 1896-1898 and 1899-1901; etc.
682.A1-.A3	General works
682.A5-Z	Special events, battles, etc.
	e.g.
682.B2	Bacalod, Battle of, 1903
683.A-Z	Regimental histories. By state, A-Z
	e.g.
	Kansas
683.K34	General works
683.K342	Regiments, etc.
	Oregon
683.O6	General works
683.O7	Regiments, etc.

                                Southeast Asia
                                   Philippines
                                     History
                                       By period
                                           1894-1901 -- Continued
                                           Naval history
                                               Cf. E717.7 Philippine campaign and Battle of
                                                     Manila Bay, 1898

683.3	General works
683.5	Addresses, essays, lectures
683.7	Personal narratives, etc.
684	Prisons, hospitals, etc.
684.2	Songs, etc.
684.3	Pictorial works

                                     1901-
                                         Class here works on the Philippines under United States
                                           rule, 1901-1935
                                       Including political history

685	General works
	Biography and memoirs
685.8.A2	Collective
685.8.A3-Z	Individual, A-Z
	Commonwealth, 1935-1946
686	General works
	Biography and memoirs
686.2.A2	Collective
686.2.A3-686.Z	Individual, A-Z
	e.g.
686.2.L3	Laurel, José Paciano
686.2.R6	Romulo, Carlos Pena
686.3	Quezon, 1935-1944
686.4	Period of World War II, 1942-1945. Japanese occupation. Osmeña, 1944-1946
	1946-1986
686.5	General works
	Biography and memoirs
686.6.A2	Collective
686.6.A3-Z	Individual, A-Z
	e.g.
686.6.M3	Magsaysay, Ramón
686.6.M35	Marcos, Ferdinand
686.6.Q5	Quirino, Elpidio
686.6.R6	Roxas y Acuña, Manuel
	1986-
686.614	General works
	Biography and memoirs
686.615	Collective

	Southeast Asia
	Philippines
	History
	By period
	1901-
	1986-
	Biography and memoirs -- Continued
686.616.A-Z	Individual, A-Z
686.62	Revolution, 1986
	Local history and description
688.A-Z	Provinces, islands, etc., A-Z
	e.g.
688.A7	Albay
688.B2	Bataan
688.B3	Batangas
688.B5	Benguet
688.B6	Bisayas. Visayan Islands
688.B8	Bulacan
688.C3	Cagayan Sulu
688.C36	Camarines Sur
688.C4	Cebu
688.D3	Davao
688.I3	Ilocos Norte
688.L9	Luzon
688.M2	Mindanao
688.M5	Mountain (Province)
688.N5	Negros Islands
688.N9	Nueva Vizcaya
688.P15	Palawan
688.P19	Pampanga
688.P2	Panay
688.S9	Sulu Archipelago
	Visayan Islands see DS688.B6
689.A-Z	Cities, towns, etc., A-Z
	e.g.
689.B2	Baguio
689.C5	Cebu
689.M2	Manila
689.M24	Marzo Site
689.P3	Paete
	China
701	Periodicals. Societies. Serials
702	Congresses, conferences, etc.
703	Sources and documents
	Collected works
703.4	Several authors
703.5	Individual authors

	China -- Continued
705	Gazetteers. Dictionaries, etc. Guidebooks
706	General works
706.3	Monumental and picturesque. Castles, temples, monuments, etc.
706.5	Historical geography
706.7	Geography
	Description and travel
707	Earliest through 1500
708	1501-1800
709	1801-1900
710	1901-1948
711	1949-1975
712	1976-
	Antiquities
	Cf. DS781+ Local history and description
714	Museums. Collections of national antiquities
715	General works
719	General special
	Social life and customs. Civilization. Intellectual life
721	General works
	Early to 221 B.C. see DS741.65
	221 B.C.-960 A.D see DS747.42
	960-1644 see DS750.72
	1644-1912 see DS754.14
	1912-1949 see DS775.2
	1949-1976 see DS777.6
	1976- see DS779.23
	Women, children, etc. see HQ792.A+
727	Other special
	Ethnography
730	General works
731.A-Z	Individual elements in the population, A-Z
731.A25	Achang
731.A53	Amdo
	Bai see DS731.P34
731.B55	Blacks
	Bonan see DS731.P36
	Bouyei see DS731.P84
731.B76	'Broṅ-pa (Tibetan people)
731.C35	Canadians
731.C48	Ch'iang. Qiang
731.C488	Ching (Vietnamese people)
731.C49	Ching-p'o. Jingpo
731.C495	Chino
731.C5	Chuang. Zhuang
731.D33	Dagur

	China
	Ethnography
	Individual elements in the population, A-Z -- Continued
	Dai see DS731.T27
	Dong see DS731.T77
	Dongxiang see DS731.T78
731.E36	East Indians
731.E82	Europeans
731.E85	Evenki
731.F74	French
731.G36	Gelo
731.G4	Germans
731.H3	Hakkas
731.H34	Hani
	Hezhen see DS731.H6
	Hmong see DS731.M5
731.H6	Ho-che. Hezhen
731.H85	Hui
731.J3	Japanese
	Jingpo see DS731.C49
731.K37	Karluk (Turkic people)
731.K38	Kazakhs
731.K46	Khmu' (Southeast Asian people)
731.K57	Kirghiz
731.K6	Koreans
731.L33	Lahu
731.L5	Li (Hainan people)
731.L57	Lisu (Southeast Asian people)
	Lolos see DS731.Y5
731.L64	Lopa
731.M35	Manchus
731.M36	Maonan
731.M45	Menba. Moinba
731.M5	Miao. Hmong
	Min-chia see DS731.P34
	Moinba see DS731.M45
731.M64	Mongols
731.M65	Monguors
(731.M7)	Moso
	see DS731.N39
731.M84	Mulao
731.M87	Muslims
731.N39	Naxi
731.N48	New Zealanders
731.N82	Nu (Chinese people)
(731.O16)	O-wen-k'o
	see DS731.E85

DS

	China
	Ethnography
	Individual elements in the population, A-Z -- Continued
731.O43	Olcha
731.O73	Ordos (Mongolian people)
731.O76	Oroqen
731.P34	Pai. Bai
731.P35	Palaungs
731.P36	Pao-an. Bonan
731.P64	Poles
731.P84	Pu-i. Bouyei
731.P844	P'u-mi. Pumi
731.P85	Pulang (Southeast Asian people)
	Pumi see DS731.P844
	Qiang see DS731.C48
731.R9	Russians
731.S24	Salar (Chinese people)
731.S54	She (Chinese people)
731.S57	Sibo
731.S63	Sogdians
731.S88	Sui (Chinese people)
731.S95	Sushen (Manchurian people)
731.T27	Tai (Southeast Asian people)
731.T29	Tajiks
731.T3	Tanka
731.T34	Tatar
731.T53	Thais
731.T56	Tibetans
731.T6	Tokhari
731.T74	Tujia
731.T76	Tulung (Tibeto-Burman people)
731.T77	Tung. Dong
731.T78	Tung-hsiang. Dongxiang
731.T8	Tungusic peoples
731.U4	Uighur (Turkic people)
731.U8	Uzbeks
731.V53	Vietnamese
731.W32	Wa (Burmese people)
731.W35	Wang-ku (Turkic people)
731.Y3	Yao
731.Y5	Yi
731.Y83	Yugur
	Zhuang see DS731.C5
732	Chinese in foreign countries (General)
	History
733	Dictionaries. Chronological tables, outlines, etc.

	China
	History -- Continued
734	Biography (Collective)
	For individual biography, see the specific period, reign or place
	Historiography
734.7	General works
	Biography of historians
734.8	Collective
734.9.A-Z	Individual, A-Z
	e.g.
734.9.K8	Ku, Chieh-kang
	Study and teaching
734.95	General works
734.96	Audiovisual materials
734.97.A-Z	By region or country, A-Z
	Subarrange by author
	General works
735.A2	Through 1800
735.A3-Z	1801-
736	Addresses, essays, lectures
736.5	Philosophy of Chinese history
737	Several parts of the empire treated together
738	Military history
739	Naval history
	Political and diplomatic history
	For special periods or reigns, see the period or reign
740	General works
740.2	General special
	Diplomatic history. Foreign and general relations
740.4	General works
	Early to 1644 see DS750.82
	1644-1912 see DS754.18
	1912-1949 see DS775.8
	1949-1976 see DS777.8
	1976- see DS779.27
740.5.A-Z	Relations with individual countries, A-Z
	e.g.
	Germany
740.5.G2	International relations
740.5.G3	German territory in China. Kiao-chou
	Great Britain
740.5.G5	International relations
740.5.G6	Local, A-Z
	e.g.
740.5.G6C5	Chinkiang
740.5.G6H6	Hong Kong

China

   History

      Political and diplomatic history

         Diplomatic history. Foreign and general relations

            Relations with individual countries, A-Z -- Continued

               United States see E183.8.A+

         China and the Far Eastern question

740.6	General works
740.61	Early through 1800
740.62	1801-1860
740.63	1861-1945
	1945- see DS518.15

        By period

           Early to 221 B.C.

741	Periodicals. Societies. Serials
741.12	Congresses
741.15	Sources and documents
741.22	Collected works (nonserial)
741.25	Historiography
	General works
741.3	Through 1800
741.5	1801-
741.55	General special
741.62	Addresses, essays, lectures
741.65	Social life and customs. Civilization. Intellectual life
741.72	Military history
741.75	Political history
	Biography and memoirs
741.82	Collective
741.85.A-Z	Individual, A-Z
	Legendary period
742	General works
742.2	General special
743	Xia (Hsia) dynasty, ca. 2205-1766 B.C.
	Biography and memoirs see DS741.82+
	Shang (Yin) Dynasty, 1766-1122 B.C.
744	General works
744.2	General special
	Biography and memoirs see DS741.82+
	Zhou (Chou) dynasty, 1122-221 B.C.
	Western Zhou, 1122-771 B.C.; Eastern Zhou, 771-256 B.C.
747	General works
747.13	General special
747.15	Spring and Autumn period, 722-481 B.C.
747.2	Warring States, 403-221 B.C.
	Biography and memoirs

China
  History
    By period
      Early to 221 B.C.
        Zhou (Chou) dynasty, 1122-221 B.C.
          Biography and memoirs -- Continued
747.22   Collective
747.23.A-Z   Individual, A-Z
        221 B.C.-960 A.D.
747.28   Periodicals. Societies. Serials
747.32   Congresses
747.33   Sources and documents
747.34   Collected works (nonserial)
747.35   Historiography
747.37   General works
747.38   General special
747.39   Addresses, essays, lectures
747.42   Social life and customs. Civilization. Intellectual life
747.43   Military history
747.45   Political history
747.46   Foreign and general relations
747.48   Biography and memoirs (Collective)
                            For individual biography, see the specific period, reign or
                            place
          Qin (Ch'in) dynasty, 221-207 B.C.
747.5   General works
747.6   General special
                          Biography and memoirs
747.8   Collective
747.9.A-Z   Individual, A-Zd
          Han Dynasty, 202 B.C.-220 A.D.
                            Western Han, 202 B.C.-9 A.D.; Eastern Han, 25-220
748   General works
748.13   General special
                          Biography and memoirs
748.15   Collective
748.16.A-Z   Individual, A-Z
          Xin (Hsin) dynasty, 9-23
748.162   General works
748.164   General special
                          Biography and memoirs see DS748.15+
          220-589
                            Wei, Jin (Chin), Southern, and Northern dynasties; or Six
                            dynasties
748.17   General works
748.18   General special

	China
	History
	By period
	221 B.C.-960 A.D.
	220-589 -- Continued
748.19	Biography and memoirs (Collective)
	For individual biography, see the specific period, reign or place
	Three Kingdoms, 220-265
	Including Shu, 221-264; Wei, 220-265; Wu, 220-280
748.2	General works
748.25	General special
	Biography and memoirs
748.28	Collective
748.29.A-Z	Individual, A-Z
	Jin (Chin) dynasty, 265-419
	Western Jin, 265-317; Eastern Jin, 317-419
748.4	General works
748.42	General special
	Biography and memoirs
748.43	Collective
748.44.A-Z	Individual, A-Z
	Five Hu and Sixteen Kingdoms, 304-439
748.45	General works
748.46	General special
	Biography and memoirs
748.47	Collective
748.48.A-Z	Individual, A-Z
	Northern and Southern Dynasties, 386-589
	For Southern Dynasties, Northern Dynasties, or individual countries see DS748.6+
748.5	General works
748.55	General special
	Biography and memoirs
748.58	Collective
	Individual see DS748.66.A+; DS748.76.A+
	Southern Dynasties
	Including Liu Song (Sung) dynasty (Former Song dynasty), 420-479; Qi (Ch'i) dynasty, 479-502; Liang dynasty, 502-557; Chen(Ch'en) dynasty, 557-589
748.6	General works
748.62	General special
	Biography and memoirs
748.64	Collective
748.66.A-Z	Individual, A-Z

China
History
By period
221 B.C.-960 A.D.
220-589
Northern and Southern Dynasties, 386-589 --
Continued
Northern Dynasties
Including Northern Wei dynasty, 386-534; Eastern
Wei dynasty, 534-550; Western Wei dynasty,
553-556; Northern Qi (Ch'i) dynasty, 550-557;
Northern Zhou (Chou) dynasty, 557-581

748.7	General works
748.72	General special
	Biography and memoirs
748.74	Collective
748.76.A-Z	Individual, A-Z
	Sui Dynasty, 581-618
749.2	General works
749.25	General special
	Biography and memoirs
749.28	Collective
749.29.A-Z	Individual, A-Z
	Tang (T'ang) dynasty, 618-907
749.3	General works
749.35	General special
	Biography and memoirs
749.4	Collective
749.42.A-Z	Individual, A-Z
749.46	An Lushan Rebellion, 755-763
749.47	Huang Chao Rebellion, 874-884

Five Dynasties, and the Ten Kingdoms, 907-979
For Five dynasties, the Ten Kingdoms or individual
countries see DS749.6+

749.5	General works
749.55	General special
	Biography and memoirs
749.58	Collective
	Individual see DS749.66.A+
749.6-.66	Five dynasties, 907-960

Including Later Liang dynasty, 907-923; Later Tang
dynasty, 923-936; Later Jin (Ch'in) dynasty, 936-
947; Later Han dynasty, 947-950; Later Zhou
(Chou) dynasty, 951-960

749.62	General special
	Biography and memoirs
749.64	Collective

	China
	History
	By period
	221 B.C.-960 A.D.
	Five Dynasties, and the Ten Kingdoms, 907-979
	Five dynasties, 907-960
	Biography and memoirs -- Continued
749.66.A-Z	Individual, A-Z
	Ten Kingdoms, 902-979
	Including Wu, 902-937; Southern Tang 937-975; Southern Ping (Jing Nan), 924-963; Earlier Shu, 907-925; Chu, 927-951; Later Shu, 934-965; Wuyue, 907-978; Min, 909-944; Southern Han, 917-971; Northern Han, 951-979
749.7	General works
749.72	General special
	Biography and memoirs
749.74	Collective
749.76.A-Z	Individual, A-Z
	960-1644
750.52	Periodicals. Societies. Serials
750.54	Congresses
750.56	Sources and documents
750.58	Collected works (nonserial)
750.62	Historiography
750.64	General works
750.66	General special
750.68	Addresses, essays, lectures
750.72	Social life and customs. Civilization. Intellectual life
750.74	Military history
750.76	Naval history
750.78	Political history
750.82	Foreign and general relations
750.86	Biography and memoirs (Collective)
	For individual biography, see the specific period or dynasty
	Song (Sung) dynasty, 960-1279
	Northern Song, 960-1126; Southern Song, 1127-1279
751	General works
751.3	General special
	Biography and memoirs
751.5	Collective
751.6.A-Z	Individual, A-Z
	Liao Dynasty, 947-1125. Khitan Mongols
751.72	General works
751.74	General special
	Biography and memoirs

	China
	History
	By period
	960-1644
	Liao Dynasty, 947-1125. Khitan Mongols
	Biography and memoirs -- Continued
751.76	Collective
751.78.A-Z	Individual, A-Z
	Xi Xia (Hsi Hsia) dynasty, 1038-1227. Tangut
751.82	General works
751.84	General special
	Biography and memoirs
751.86	Collective
751.88.A-Z	Individual, A-Z
	Jin (Chin) dynasty, 1115-1234. (Juchen or Ruzhen dynasty)
751.92	General works
751.94	General special
	Biography and memoirs
751.96	Collective
751.98.A-Z	Individual, A-Z
	Yuan dynasty, 1260-1368
752	General works
752.3	General special
	Biography and memoirs
752.5	Collective
752.6.A-Z	Individual, A-Z
	Ming Dynasty, 1368-1644
753	General works
753.2	General special
	Biography and memoirs
753.5	Collective
753.6.A-Z	Individual, A-Z
	e.g.
	Cheng, Ch'eng-kung see DS753.6.K6
	Chongzhen, Emperor of China, 1611-1644 see DS753.6.M45
	Ch'ung-chen, Emperor of China see DS753.6.M45
	Huaizong, Emperor of China, 1611-1644 see DS753.6.M45
753.6.K6	Koxinga, 1624-1662
753.6.M45	Ming Huaizong. Chongzhen, Emperor of China, 1611-1644
753.65	Li Zicheng Rebellion, 1628-1645
753.7	Tatar Conquest, 1643-1644
753.75	Southern Ming dynasty, 1644-1662

	China
	History
	By period -- Continued
	Qing (Ch'ing) dynasty, 1644-1912
753.82	Periodicals. Societies. Serials
753.84	Congresses
753.86	Sources and documents
753.88	Collected works (nonserial)
753.92	Historiography
754	General works
754.12	General special
754.13	Addresses, essays, lectures
754.14	Social life and customs. Civilization. Intellectual life
754.15	Military history
754.16	Naval history
754.17	Political history
754.18	Foreign and general relations
754.19	Biography and memoirs (Collective)
	For individual biography, see the specific period or reign
	1644-1795. 18th century
754.2	General works
754.25	General special
754.3	Biography and memoirs (Collective)
	For individual biography, see the specific period or reign
	Shunzhi, 1644-1661
754.5	General works on life and reign
754.52	General special
	Biography and memoirs of contemporaries
754.53	Collective
754.54.A-Z	Individual, A-Z
	Kangxi, 1662-1722
754.6	General works on life and reign
754.62	General special
	Biography and memoirs of contemporaries
754.63	Collective
754.64.A-Z	Individual, A-Z
754.66	Rebellion of Three Feudatories, 1673-1681
	Yongzheng, 1723-1735
754.7	General works on life and reign
754.72	General special
	Biography and memoirs of contemporaries
754.73	Collective
754.74.A-Z	Individual, A-Z
	Qianlong, 1736-1795
754.8	General works on life and reign
754.82	General special

China
History
By period
Qing (Ch'ing) dynasty, 1644-1912
1644-1795. 18th century
Qianlong, 1736-1795 -- Continued
Biography and memoirs of contemporaries
754.83   Collective
754.84.A-Z   Individual, A-Z
1796-1861. 19th century
755   General works
Some titles may be subarranged by editor, e.g.
755.C5   Chung-kuo chin tai shih
Subarrange by editor
755.C52   Chung-kuo ko ming shih
Subarrange by editor
755.2   General special
755.3   Biography and memoirs (Collective)
For individual biography, see the specific period or
reign
Jiaqing, 1796-1820
756   General works on life and reign
756.2   General special
Biography and memoirs of contemporaries
756.22   Collective
756.23.A-Z   Individual, A-Z
White Lotus Rebellion, 1796-1804
756.3   Sources and documents
756.32   Historiography
756.33   General works
Personal narratives
756.35   Collective
756.36   Individual
756.37.A-Z   Other topics, A-Z
Daoguang, 1820-1850
757   General works on life and reign
757.2   General special
Biography and memoirs of contemporaries
757.22   Collective
757.23.A-Z   Individual, A-Z
Opium War, 1840-1842
757.4   Sources and documents
757.45   Historiography
757.5   General works
757.55   General special
757.6   Addresses, essays, lectures
Personal narratives

DS

China
 History
  By period
   Qing (Ch'ing) dynasty, 1644-1912
    1796-1861. 19th century
     Daoguang, 1820-1850
      Opium War, 1840-1842
       Personal narratives -- Continued

757.63	Collective
757.66	Individual
757.7.A-Z	Other topics, A-Z
	Xianfeng, 1850-1861
758	General works on life and reign
758.2	General special
	Biography and memoirs of contemporaries
758.22	Collective
758.23.A-Z	Individual, A-Z
	Taiping Rebellion, 1850-1864. Tai Ping Tian Guo
758.7	Sources and documents
758.8	Historiography
759	General works
759.15	General special
759.2	Addresses, essays, lectures
	Personal narratives
759.3	Collective
759.35	Individual
759.4.A-Z	Other topics, A-Z
759.5	Nian Rebellion, 1853-1868
760	Foreign intervention, 1857-1861
	1861-1912
761	General works
761.2	General special
763.A2	Biography and memoirs (Collective)
	For individual biography, see the specific period or reign
	Tongzhi, 1861-1875
763.5	General works on life and reign
763.6	General special
	Biography and memoirs of contemporaries
763.62	Collective
763.63.A-Z	Individual, A-Z
763.65	Self-strengthening Movement, 1861-1895
763.7	Tianjin Massacre, 1870
	Guangxu, 1875-1908
764	General works on life and reign
764.2	General special
	Biography and memoirs of contemporaries

China
  History
    By period
      Qing (Ch'ing) dynasty, 1644-1912
        1861-1912
          Guangxu, 1875-1908
            Biography and memoirs of contemporaries --
              Continued

764.22	Collective
764.23.A-Z	Individual, A-Z
	Sino-French War, 1894-1895 see DS549
	Sino-Japanese War, 1894-1895
764.4	Sources and documents
764.6	Historiography
765	General works
765.5	General special
767	Addresses, essays, lectures
	Personal narratives
767.3	Collective
767.4	Individual
767.6.A-Z	Other topics, A-Z
768	Reform Movement, 1898
	Boxer Rebellion, 1899-1901
770	Sources and documents
770.5	Historiography
771	General works
771.5	General special
771.7	Addresses, essays, lectures
	Personal narratives
772	Collective
772.2.A-Z	Individual, A-Z
772.3.A-Z	Other topics, A-Z
	Xuantong, 1908-1912
773	General works on life and reign
773.2	General special
	Biography and memoirs of contemporaries
773.22	Collective
773.23.A-Z	Individual, A-Z
	Revolution of 1911-1912
773.32	Sources and documents
773.35	Historiography
773.4	General works
773.42	General special
773.45	Addresses, essays, lectures
	Personal narratives
773.5	Collective
773.52	Individual

DS

China
History
By period
Qing (Ch'ing) dynasty, 1644-1912
1861-1912
Xuantong, 1908-1912
Revolution of 1911-1912 -- Continued
773.55.A-Z   Local revolutionary history. By place, A-Z
773.6.A-Z   Other topics, A-Z
Republic, 1912-1949. 20th century
773.83   Periodicals. Societies. Serials
773.86   Congresses
773.89   Sources and documents
773.92   Collected works (nonserial)
773.94   Historiography
774   General works
774.5   General special
774.7   Addresses, essays, lectures
775.2   Social life and customs. Civilization. Intellectual life
775.4   Military history
775.5   Naval history
775.7   Political history
775.8   Foreign and general relations
776   Biography and memoirs (Collective)
        For individual biography, see the specific period
1912-1928
776.4   General works
776.6   General special
    Biography and memoirs
776.8   Collective
    Individual
    Sun, Yat-sen
    Writings
777.A2   Collected works. By date
777.A25   Selected works. By date
777.A3   Autobiography
777.A4   Letters. By date
777.A5   Speeches. By date
    Separate works
777.A515   Chien kuo fang lueh
777.A519   Chien kuo ta kang
777.A52   Min ch'üan ch'u pu
777.A53   San min chu i. Criticism of San min chu i
    Wu ch'uan hsien fa
      see class K
    Biography and criticism
777.A595   Periodicals. Societies. Serials

China
  History
    By period
      Republic, 1912-1949. 20th century
        1912-1928
          Biography and memoirs
            Individual
              Sun, Yat-sen
                Biography and criticism -- Continued

777.A597-Z	General works
777.15.A-Z	Others, A-Z
777.2	Revolution, 1913 (Second Revolution)
777.25	Revolution, 1915-1916 (Third Revolution)
777.36	Warlord period, 1916-1928
777.38	Restoration Attempt, 1917
777.4	Movement to Protect the Constitution, 1917-1923
777.43	May 4th Movement, 1919
777.45	May 30 Movement, 1925
	Northern Expedition, 1926-1928
777.46	General works
777.462	Tsinan (Jinan) Incident, 1928
	1928-1937
777.47	General works
777.48	General special
	Biography and memoirs
777.487	Collective
777.488.A-Z	Individual, A-Z
	e.g.
777.488.C5	Chiang, Kai-shek, 1887-1975
	Sino-Japanese Conflict, 1931-1933
	For Manchu Kuo see DS783
	For Conflict in Manchuria see DS783.7
	For Mukden Incident see DS783.8
777.5	General works
777.51	Shanghai Invasion, 1932
	Long March, 1934-1935
777.5132	Sources and documents
777.5133	Historiography
777.5134	General works
777.5135	General special
777.5136	Addresses, essays, lectures
	Personal narratives
777.5137	Collective
777.5138	Individual
777.5139.A-Z	Other topics, A-Z
777.51392	Huabei Incident, 1935
777.51393	December Ninth movement, 1935

DS

	China
	History
	By period
	Republic, 1912-1949. 20th century
	1928-1937 -- Continued
777.514	Sian (Xi'an) Incident, 1936
	1937-1945
777.518	General works
777.519	General special
	Biography and memoirs
777.5194	Collective
777.5195.A-Z	Individual, A-Z
	Sino-Japanese War, 1937-1945
777.52	Sources and documents
777.525	Historiography
777.53	General works
777.5313	Addresses, essays, lectures
	Personal narratives
777.5314	Collective
777.5315	Individual
777.5316.A-Z	Individual campaigns, battles, etc., A-Z
777.532	Foreign participation
777.533.A-Z	Other topics, A-Z
777.533.A35	Aerial operations
777.533.A78	Art and the war
777.533.A86	Atrocities
777.533.B55	Biological warfare. Chemical warfare
	Charities see DS777.533.R45
	Chemical warfare see DS777.533.B55
777.533.C47	Children. Orphans
777.533.C64	Collaborationists
	Displaced persons see DS777.533.R45
777.533.E38	Education
777.533.E56	Entertainment and recreation for soldiers
	Espionage see DS777.533.S65
	Health aspects see DS777.533.M42
	Hospitals see DS777.533.M42
777.533.I53	Indemnity and reparation
777.533.M3	Marco Polo Bridge Incident, 1937
777.533.M42	Medical care. Hospitals. Health aspects
	Military intelligence see DS777.533.S65
	Orphans see DS777.533.C47
777.533.P75	Prisoners and prisons
777.533.P76	Propaganda
	Protection see DS777.533.R45
777.533.P78	Protest movements
	Public opinion

China
  History
    By period
      Republic, 1912-1949. 20th century
        1937-1945
          Sino-Japanese War, 1937-1945
            Other topics, A-Z
              Public opinion -- Continued

777.533.P82	General works
777.533.P825A- .P825Z	By region or country, A-Z
	Refugees see DS777.533.R45
777.533.R45	Relief work. Charities. Protection. Refugees. Displaced persons
	Reparation see DS777.533.I53
	Secret service see DS777.533.S65
777.533.S62	Social aspects
777.533.S65	Spies. Secret service. Military intelligence
777.533.T73	Transportation
777.533.U53	Underground movements
777.533.W37	War work
777.533.W65	Women
777.534	Southern Anhui Incident, 1941

        1945-1949

777.535	General works
777.536	General special
	Biography and memoirs
777.5365	Collective
777.5366.A-Z	Individual, A-Z
	Civil War, 1945-1949
777.537	Sources and documents
777.538	Historiography
777.54	General works
777.542	General special
777.5424	Addresses, essays, lectures
777.5425.A-Z	Individual campaigns, battles, etc., A-Z
	Personal narratives
777.543	Collective
777.5435	Individual
777.544.A-Z	Other topics, A-Z

      Republic, 1949- see DS799
      People's Republic, 1949-
        1949-1976
          Including comprehensive works on the People's Republic

777.545	Periodicals. Societies. Serials
777.546	Congresses
777.547	Sources and documents

DS

	China
	History
	By period
	People's Republic, 1949-
	1949-1976 -- Continued
777.548	Collected works
777.549	Historiography
777.55	General works
777.56	General special
777.58	Addresses, essays, lectures
777.6	Social life and customs. Civilization. Intellectual life
777.65	Military history
777.7	Naval history
777.75	Political history
777.8	Foreign and general relations
	Biography and memoirs
778.A1	Collective
778.A2-Z	Individual, A-Z
	e.g.
778.C593	Chou, En-lai, 1898-1976. Zhou, Enlai
778.D46	Deng, Xiaoping, 1904-
778.M3	Mao, Zedong, 1893-1976
	Teng, Hsiao-p'ing, 1904- see DS778.D46
	Zhou, Enlai see DS778.C593
778.4	Hundred Flowers Campaign, 1956
778.5	Anti-rightist Campaign, 1957-1958
778.7	Cultural Revolution, 1966-1976
	1976-2002
779.15	Periodicals. Societies. Serials
779.16	Congresses
779.17	Sources and documents
779.18	Collected works (nonserial)
779.19	Historiography
779.2	General works
779.215	General special
779.22	Addresses, essays, lectures
779.23	Social life and customs. Civilization. Intellectual life
779.24	Military history
779.25	Naval history
779.26	Political history
779.27	Foreign and general relations
	Biography and memoirs
779.28	Collective
779.29.A-Z	Individual, A-Z
	e.g.
779.29.H8	Hua, Guofeng
	Sino-Vietnamese Conflict, 1979 see DS559.915+

	China
	History
	By period
	People's Republic, 1949-
	1976-2002 -- Continued
779.32	Tiananmen Square Incident, 1989
	2002-
779.35	Periodicals. Societies. Serials
779.36	Congresses
779.37	Sources and documents
779.39	Historiography
779.4	General works
779.43	Social life and customs. Civilization. Intellectual life
779.44	Military history
779.45	Naval history
779.46	Political history
779.47	Foreign and general relations
	Biography and memoirs
779.48	Collective
779.49.A-Z	Individual, A-Z
	Local history and description
	Manchuria
781	Periodicals. Sources and documents. Collections
781.5	Gazetteers. Dictionaries. Directories, etc.
782	General works
782.3	Description and travel
782.5	Antiquities
782.8	Social life and customs. Civilization. Intellectual life
782.9	Ethnography
	For individual elements see DS731.A+
	History
782.95	Biography (Collective)
	For individual biography, see the specific period, reign or place
783	General works
	By period
783.4	Early to 1800
783.7	19th-20th centuries
	League of Nations Commision of Enquiry (The Lytton Commission)
783.7.L4C6	Memoranda presented by China. By date
783.7.L4J3	Memoranda presented by Japan. By date
783.7.L42	Summary. Report. By date
783.7.L42C6	China's discussion. By date
783.7.L42J3	Japan's discussion. By date
783.7.L43	Verdict of the League. Report. By date

DS

	China
	Local history and description
	Manchuria
	History
	By period
	19th-20th centuries
	League of Nations Commision of Enquiry (The Lytton Commission) -- Continued
783.7.L45	Summary and discussions by individual authors, A-Z
783.8	Mukden Incident, 1931
784	Manchoukuo. P'u-i, 1932-1945
784.2	1945-
	Tibet
785.A1	Periodicals. Societies. Congresses
785.A2-.A4	Documents
	General works. History and description
785.A5-Z	Through 1950
786	1951-
793.A-Z	Provinces, dependencies, regions, etc., A-Z
	e.g.
	For national municipalities and special administrative regions see DS795+
	For counties see DS797.22.A+
	Anhui see DS793.A6
793.A6	Anhwei. Anhui
793.C3	Chekiang. Zhejiang
	Chihli see DS793.H6
	Dzungaria see DS793.S7
793.E2	East (Chinese) Turkestan
	Area of the Tarim basin south of the Tien Shan
	Including Thian Shan Mountains (China)
	Fujian see DS793.F8
793.F8	Fukien. Fujian
	Gansu see DS793.K2
793.G6	Gobi
793.G67	Great Wall
	Guangdong see DS793.K7
	Guangxi Zhuang Autonomous Region see DS793.K6
	Guizhou see DS793.K8
793.H3	Hainan (Island)
	Hebei see DS793.H6
	Heilongjiang see DS793.H44
793.H44	Heilungkiang. Heilongjiang
	Henan see DS793.H5
793.H47	Ho-hsi
793.H5	Honan. Henan

	China
	Local history and description
	Provinces, dependencies, regions, etc., A-Z -- Continued
793.H6	Hopei (Hopeh). Hebai
	Hubei see DS793.H75
793.H7	Hunan
793.H75	Hupeh. Hubei
	Inner Mongolia see DS793.M7
793.J4	Jehol
	Jiangsu see DS793.K45
	Jiangxi see DS793.K4
	Jilin see DS793.K54
	Jungaria see DS793.S7
793.K2	Kansu. Gansu
793.K4	Kiangsi. Jiangxi
793.K45	Kiangsu. Jiangsu
793.K54	Kirin. Jilin
793.K593	Kunlun Mountains
793.K6	Kwangsi. Guangxi Zhuang Autonomous Region
793.K7	Kwangtung. Guangdong
793.K8	Kweichow. Guizhou
793.L5	Liaoning
793.L6	Lop Nur
793.M7	Mongolia. Inner Mongolia
	Cf. DS19+ Mongols
	For the Mongolian People's Republic see DS798.A1+
793.N5	Ningsia. Ningxia Hui Autonomous Region
	Ningxia Hui Autonomous Region see DS793.N5
793.N6	Northwest
793.N7	Nosuland
793.O5	Omei (Mountain)
793.P59	Po-hai (Kingdom)
	Qinghai see DS793.T7
	Shaanxi see DS793.S5
	Shandong see DS793.S4
793.S3	Shansi. Shanxi
793.S4	Shantung. Shandong
	Shanxi see DS793.S3
793.S5	Shensi. Shaanxi
	Sichuan see DS793.S8
793.S6	Sinkiang (River and Valley)
793.S62	Sinkiang. Xinjiang Uighur Autonomous Region
	For Turkestan see DS793.E2
	For Dzungaria see DS793.S7
793.S644	Southeast
793.S6445	Southwest
793.S7	Sungaria

China
  Local history and description
    Provinces, dependencies, regions, etc., A-Z -- Continued
793.S8   Szechwan. Sichuan
                          Thian Shan Mountains see DS793.E2
793.T337   Takla Makan Desert
793.T7   Tsinghai. Qinghai
                          Xinjiang Uighur Autonomous Region see DS793.S62
793.Y3   Yangtze River Valley
793.Y8   Yunnan
                          Zhejiang see DS793.C3
    Cities, towns, counties, prefectures, etc.
      National municipalities and special administrative regions
795-795.95   Beijing (Peking. Peiping) (Table DS-DX3)
796.A-Z   Other national municipalities and special administrative
                              regions, A-Z
(796.C2)   Canton
                                see DS797.32.G836
796.C592-.C59295   Chongqing. (Ch'ung-ch-ing shih. Chungking) (Table
                                DS-DX4)
(796.H3)   Hankow
                                see DS797.48.H365
(796.H4)   Harbin
                                see DS797.42.H373
796.H7-.H795   Hong Kong (Hongkong) (Table DS-DX4)
(796.J4)   Jehol
                                see DS797.39.C546
(796.K4)   Khotan
                                see DS797.84.H673
796.M2-.M295   Macau (Macao) (Table DS-DX4)
(796.M8)   Mukden
                                see DS797.62.S546
(796.N2)   Nanking
                                see DS797.56.N365
796.S2-.S295   Shanghai (Table DS-DX4)
796.T5-.T595   Tianjin (Tientsin) (Table DS-DX4)
(796.T7)   Tsingtao
                                see DS797.72.Q354
(796.T84)   T'u-mo't'e-yu ch'i
                                see DS797.54.T866
(796.Y5)   Ying-k'ou
                                see DS797.62.Y564
      Other cities, towns, counties, prefectures, arranged by
        province
797.22.A-Z   Anhui Sheng, A-Z
797.26.A-Z   Fujian Sheng, A-Z
797.28.A-Z   Gansu Sheng, A-Z

China
  Local history and description
    Cities, towns, counties, prefectures, etc.
      Other cities, towns, counties, prefectures, arranged by
        province -- Continued

797.32.A-Z	Guangdong Sheng, A-Z
	e. g.
797.32.G836	Guangzhou (Canton)
797.33.A-Z	Guangxi Zhuangzu Zizhiqu, A-Z
797.35.A-Z	Guizhou Sheng, A-Z
797.37.A-Z	Hainan Sheng, A-Z
797.39.A-Z	Hebei Sheng, A-Z
	e. g.
797.39.C546	Chengde (Ch'eng-te. Jehol)
797.42.A-Z	Heilongjiang, A-Z
	e. g.
797.42.H373	Harbin
797.44.A-Z	Henan Sheng, A-Z
	e.g.
797.44.L84	Luoyang
797.48.A-Z	Hubei Sheng, A-Z
	e. g.
797.48.H365	Hankou (Hankow)
797.52.A-Z	Hunan Sheng, A-Z
797.54.A-Z	Inner Mongolia, A-Z
	e. g.
797.54.T866	Tumd Youqi (Qi) (T'u-mo-t'e-yu ch'i)
797.56.A-Z	Jiangsu Sheng, A-Z
	e. g.
797.56.N365	Nanjing (Nanking)
797.57.A-Z	Jiangxi Sheng, A-Z
797.59.A-Z	Jilin Sheng, A-Z
797.62.A-Z	Liaoning Sheng, A-Z
	e. g.
	Andong see DS797.62.D363
797.62.A574	Anshan
797.62.C536	Chaoyang
797.62.D355	Dalian (Dairen)
797.62.D363	Dandong (Andong)
797.62.F874	Fushun
797.62.J567	Jinxi (Chin-hsi)
797.62.J569	Jinzhou (Chin-chou)
797.62.L874	Lüshun (Port Arthur)
797.62.S546	Shenyang (Mukden)
797.62.Y564	Yingkou
797.64.A-Z	Ningxia Huizu Zizhiqu, A-Z
797.66.A-Z	Qinghai Sheng, A-Z

China
  Local history and description
    Cities, towns, counties, prefectures, etc.
      Other cities, towns, counties, prefectures, arranged by
        province -- Continued

797.68.A-Z	Shaanxi Sheng, A-Z
797.72.A-Z	Shandong Sheng, A-Z
	e. g.
797.72.Q354	Qingdao (Tsingtao. Tsingtau. Ch'ingtao)
797.75.A-Z	Shanxi Sheng, A-Z
797.77.A-Z	Sichuan Sheng, A-Z
797.82.A-Z	Tibet, A-Z
797.84.A-Z	Xinjiang Uygur Zizhiqu, A-Z
	e. g.
797.84.H673	Hotan (Khotan)
797.86.A-Z	Yunnan Sheng, A-Z
797.88.A-Z	Zhejiang Sheng, A-Z

Mongolia. Mongolian People's Republic

798.A1	Periodicals. Societies
798.A3	Sources and documents. Serials
798.A5-Z	General works
798.2	Description and travel. Guidebooks. Gazetteers
798.3	Antiquities
798.4	Social life and customs. Civilization. Intellectual life

  Ethnography

798.42	General works
798.422.A-Z	Individual elements in the population, A-Z
798.422.B67	Borjigid
798.422.B87	Buriats
798.422.D37	Darkhat
798.422.K39	Kazakhs
798.422.K48	Khalka
798.422.K49	Khatagin
798.422.O57	Oirats
798.422.T34	Taïlakh (Kazakh people)
798.422.T67	Torghuts
798.422.T85	Tuvinians

  History
    Historiography

798.43	General works
	Biography of historians, area studies specialists, archeologists, etc.
798.44	Collective
798.45.A-Z	Individual, A-Z
798.5	General works
798.6	Biography (Collective)

  Political history. Foreign and general relations

	Mongolia. Mongolian People's Republic
	History
	Political history. Foreign and general relations -- Continued
798.62	General works
	By period
	see the specific period
798.63.A-Z	Relations with individual countries, A-Z
	By period
	Early
798.65	General works
	Biography and memoirs
798.66.A2	Collective
798.66.A3-Z	Individual, A-Z
	Colonial
798.7	General works
	Biography and memoirs
798.72.A2	Collective
798.72.A3-Z	Individual, A-Z
	20th century
	Including Independence movement, 1911
798.75	General works
	Biography and memoirs
798.76.A2	Collective
798.76.A3-Z	Individual, A-Z
	Independent
	Including Revolution, 1921; etc.
798.8	General works
	Biography and memoirs
798.82.A2	Collective
798.82.A3-Z	Individual, A-Z
	1990
798.84	General works
	Biography and memoirs
798.86.A2	Collective
798.86.A3-Z	Individual, A-Z
798.9.A-Z	Local, A-Z
798.9.K37	Karakorum (Extinct city)
	Taiwan
798.92	Periodicals. Societies. Serials
	Museums, exhibitions, etc.
798.93	General works
798.935.A-Z	Individual. By place, A-Z
798.94	Congresses
798.945	Sources and documents
	Collected works (nonserial)
798.95	Several authors
798.955	Individual authors

	Taiwan -- Continued
798.96	Gazetteers. Dictionaries, etc.
798.965	Guidebooks
799	General works
799.13	Historic monuments, landmarks, scenery, etc. (General)
	For local see DS799.9.A+
799.14	Historical geography
	Description and travel
799.15	Early through 1944
799.2	1945-1974
799.24	1975-
799.3	Antiquities
799.4	Social life and customs. Civilization. Intellectual life
	For specific periods, see the period
	Ethnology
799.42	General works
799.43.A-Z	Individual elements in the population, A-Z
799.43.A44	Amis
799.43.A85	Atayal
799.43.B85	Bunun
799.43.H35	Hakka
799.43.J3	Japanese
	Kavalan see DS799.43.K88
799.43.K48	Ketagalan
799.43.K88	Kuvalan. Kavalan
799.43.P34	Paiwan
799.43.P39	Pazeh
799.43.P89	Puyuma
799.43.R85	Rukai
799.43.S24	Saisiyat
799.43.S57	Siraya
799.43.S73	Spaniards
799.43.T42	Taokas
799.43.T45	Thao
799.43.T66	Truku
799.43.T74	Tsou
799.43.Y35	Yami
	History
799.44	Dictionaries. Chronological tables, outlines, etc.
	Historiography
799.45	General works
	Biography of historians
799.46	Collective
799.47.A-Z	Individual, A-Z
	Study and teaching
799.48	General works

	Taiwan
	History
	Study and teaching -- Continued
799.49.A-Z	By region or country, A-Z
	Subarrange by author
799.5	General works
799.6	Biography (Collective)
	For individual biography, see the specific period
799.615	Military history
799.62	Political history
	For the specific periods, see the period
	Foreign and general relations
	For general works on the diplomatic history of a period, see the period
	For works on relations with a specific country regardless of period see DS799.63.A+
799.625	General works
799.63.A-Z	Relations with individual countries, A-Z
	By period
	Early to 1895
799.64	Periodicals. Societies. Serials
799.642	Congresses
799.643	Sources and documents
799.644	Historiography
799.65	General works
799.652	Social life and customs. Civilization. Intellectual life
799.654	Military history
799.656	Political history
799.658	Foreign and general relations
	Biography and memoirs
799.66.A2	Collective
799.66.A3-Z	Individual, A-Z
799.67	Dutch rule, 1624-1661
	1895-1945
799.69	Periodicals. Societies. Serials
799.692	Congresses
799.693	Sources and documents
799.694	Historiography
799.7	General works
799.712	Social life and customs. Civilization. Intellectual life
799.714	Military history
799.716	Political history
799.718	Foreign and general relations
	Biography and memoirs
799.72.A2	Collective
799.72.A3-Z	Individual, A-Z

	Taiwan
	History
	By period -- Continued
	1945-1975
	Including works on Taiwan since 1945
799.77	Periodicals. Societies. Serials
799.78	Congresses
799.783	Sources and documents
799.785	Historiography
799.8	General works
799.812	Social life and customs. Civilization. Intellectual life
799.814	Military history
799.816	Political history
799.818	Foreign and general relations
	Biography and memoirs
799.82.A2	Collective
799.82.A3-Z	Individual, A-Z
799.823	February Twenty Eighth Incident, 1947
	1975-1988
799.83	General works
	Biography and memoirs
799.832	Collective
799.833.A-Z	Individual, A-Z
799.834	Kaohsiung Incident, 1979
	1988-
799.84	Periodicals. Societies. Serials
799.8415	Congresses
799.842	Sources and documents
799.843	Historiography
799.844	General works
799.845	Social life and customs. Civilization. Intellectual life
799.846	Military history
799.847	Political history
799.848	Foreign and general relations
	Biography and memoirs
799.8485	Collective
799.849.A-Z	Individual, A-Z
799.9.A-Z	Local history and description, A-Z
	Japan
801	Periodicals. Societies. Serials
802	Congresses
803	Sources and documents
	Collected works
804	Several authors
804.5	Individual authors
805	Gazetteers. Dictionaries, etc. Place names
805.15	Directories

	Japan -- Continued
805.2	Guidebooks
806	General works
806.3	Monumental and picturesque. Castles, temples, monuments, etc.
806.4	Historical geography
806.5	Historical accounts of disasters (General)
	For individual disasters see DS895.A+
	Description and travel
807	Earliest through 1500
808	1501-1800
809	1801-1900
810	1901-1945
811	1946-1989
812	1990-
815	Antiquities
	For local antiquities see DS894.2+
	Social life and customs. Civilization. Intellectual life
820.8	Periodicals, societies, etc.
821	General works
	Foreign influences
821.5.A1	General
821.5.A2-Z	By region or country, A-Z
	By period
822	Early
822.2	Medieval to 1868
822.25	1868-
822.3	1868-1912
822.4	1912-1945
822.5	1945-
824	Court life
824.5	Coronations
	Women, children, etc. see HQ792.A+
827.A-Z	Other special, A-Z
	Costume see GT1560
827.D34	Daimyo
827.D4	Death
827.F34	Fads
	Hairdressing see GT2290+
827.H37	Hatamoto
827.I35	Iemoto
827.N63	Nobility
827.Q5	Quietude
827.S3	Samurai
827.S46	Seppuku
	Ethnography
830	General works

Japan
     Ethnography -- Continued
831.A-Z   Individual elements in the population, A-Z
832   Ainu
832.5   Japanese in foreign countries (General)
           For Japanese in a particular country, see the country
        Natives of foreign countries in Japan
832.7.A1   General works
832.7.A2-Z   By element, A-Z
            For individual elements in the population of a particular place,
              see the place
832.7.A6   Americans (U.S.)
832.7.A8   Asians
832.7.B34   Bangladeshis
832.7.B73   Brazilians
832.7.B74   British
832.7.C5   Chinese
832.7.D8   Dutch
832.7.E8   Europeans (General)
832.7.F54   Filipinos
832.7.F74   French
832.7.G4   Germans
832.7.I77   Israelis
832.7.I83   Italians
832.7.K6   Koreans
832.7.P47   Peruvians
832.7.P67   Portuguese
832.7.R8   Russians
       History
833   Dictionaries. Chronological tables, outlines, etc.
834   Biography (Collective)
            For individual biography, see the specific period, reign or
              place
834.1   Rulers. Imperial family
        Houses, noble families, etc.
834.5.A1   Collective
834.5.A2-Z   Individual, A-Z
            e.g.
834.5.M5   Mitsui family
       Historiography
834.7   General works
        Biography of historians, area studies specialists,
          archaeologists, etc.
834.8   Collective
834.9.A-Z   Individual, A-Z
       Study and teaching
834.95   General works

Japan
  History
   Study and teaching -- Continued
834.96   Criticism of textbooks
834.98   Philosophy of Japanese history
835   General works
836   Special aspects
837   Juvenile works
   Military history
    For individual campaigns and engagements, see the period
838   General works
    By period
838.5   Early to 1868
838.7   1868-
   Naval history
    For individual campaigns and engagements, see the special period or reign
839   General works
    By period
839.5   Early to 1868
839.7   1868-
   Political and diplomatic history
    Cf. DS850 Individual periods, reigns, etc.
840   Sources and documents
841   General works
842   Early
843   General special
844   Addresses, essays, lectures
   Diplomatic history. Foreign and general relations
    For general works on the diplomatic history of a period, see the period
    For works on relations with a specific country regardless of period see DS849.A+
845   General works
847   Addresses, essays, lectures
849.A-Z   Individual countries, A-Z
    For relations with regions, see the region
    Cf. DS518.15+ Far Eastern question
   By period
    Earliest to 1600
849.7   Sources and documents
850   General works
    Earliest to 1185
851   General works
     Biography and memoirs
852.A1   Collective

DS

Japan
  History
    By period
      Earliest to 1600
        Earliest to 1185
          Biography and memoirs -- Continued

852.A2-Z   Individual, A-Z
                      e.g.
852.S4   Shōtoku Taishi
854   General special
                 To 794
                   Including the original texts, translations, and general
                     and historical studies of Kojiki and Nihon shoki.
                   For the religious and mythological aspects of
                     these works see BL2217.2+
                   For literary and linguistic studies of Kojiki see
                     PL784.K6
                   For literary and linguistic studies of Nihon shoki
                     see PL784.N5
855   General works
855.3   General special
855.5   Asuka period, 592-645
855.6   Taika reform, 646-710
                 Nara period, 710-794
855.68   Sources and documents
855.7   General works
855.73   General special
                   Biography see DS852.A1+
                 Heian period, 794-1185
855.87   Sources and documents
856   General works
856.3   General special
                   Biography and memoirs
856.7   Collective
856.72.A-Z   Individual, A-Z
               1185-1603. Medieval to early modern
856.75   Sources and documents
857   General works
857.5   Foreign and general relations
                   Kamakura period, 1185-1333
858   Sources and documents
859   General works
                     Biography
860.A1   Collective
860.A2-Z   Individual, A-Z

	Japan
	History
	By period
	Earliest to 1600
	1185-1603. Medieval to early modern
	Kamakura period, 1185-1333 -- Continued
861	Period of Hojo rule as regents, 1219-1338
	Including attempted Mongol invasions, 1274 and 1281; etc.
863	Kenmu Restorations, 1333-1336
	Muromachi period, 1336-1573. Ashikaga Shogunate
863.75	Sources and documents
864	General works
	Biography
865.A1	Collective
865.A2-Z	Individual, A-Z
	Period of northern and southern courts, 1336-1392
865.4	Sources and documents
865.5	General works
	Period of civil wars, 1480-1603. Sengoku period
868	General works
868.2	General special
868.6	Foreign and general relations
	Biography
869.A1	Collective
869.A2-Z	Individual, A-Z
	e.g.
869.O3	Oda, Nobunaga
869.T6	Toyotomi, Hideyoshi
	Azuchi-Momoyama period, 1568-1603
869.4	Sources and documents
869.5	General works
869.6	General special
	Japanese invasions of Korea, 1592-1598 see DS913.4
	Tokugawa period, 1600-1868. Edo period
870	Sources and documents
870.3	Collected works (nonserial)
871	General works
871.5	General special
871.7	Foreign and general relations
871.75	Biography and memoirs (Collective)
	For individual biography, see the specific period or reign
	1600-1709
871.77	General works
871.78	General special
	Biography and memoirs

               Japan
                 History
                   By period
                     Tokugawa period, 1600-1868. Edo period
                       1600-1709
                         Biography and memoirs -- Continued

872.A1	Collective
872.A2-Z	Individual, A-Z
873	Akō Vendetta. Forty-seven Rōnin
	1709-1853
874	General works
875	General special
	Biography and memoirs
876	Collective
877.A-Z	Individual, A-Z
881	1790-1853. Early to mid-nineteenth century
	1853-1868. Bakumatsu period
	Including the Meiji Restoration
881.2	Sources and documents
881.3	General works
881.4	General special
881.45	Foreign and general relations
	Biography and memoirs
881.5.A1	Collective
881.5.A2-Z	Individual, A-Z
	e.g.
881.5.T62	Tokugawa, Yoshinobu
881.5.Y6	Yoshida, Shōin
881.8	United States Naval Expedition to Japan, 1852-1854 (Perry Expedition)
	Civil War, 1868-1869. Boshin War
881.83	General works
881.84	Individual campaigns, battles, etc.
	Modern, 1868-
881.85	Collected works (nonserial)
881.9	General works
881.95	General special
881.96	Foreign and general relations
881.97	Biography (Collective)
	For individual biography, see the specific period, reign or place
	Meiji (Mutsuhito), 1868-1912
881.98	Periodicals. Societies. Serials
881.987	Sources and documents
882	General works on reign
882.5	General special
	Sino-Japanese War, 1894-1895 see DS764.4+

Japan
History
By period
Modern, a868-
Meiji (Mutsuhito), 1868-1912
Russo-Japanese War, 1904-1905 see DS516+

882.6	Foreign and general relations
	Biography and memoirs
882.7	Meiji (Mutsuhito)
	Other
883	Collective
884.A-Z	Individual, A-Z
	e.g.
884.I8	Ito, Hirobumi, Prince
884.N7	Nogi, Maresuke, Count
884.O4	Ōkuma, Shigénobu, Count
884.S3	Saionji, Kimmochi, Prince
884.T6	Tōgō, Heihachirō, Count
	20th century
884.5	Periodicals. Societies. Serials
885	General works
885.2	General special
885.48	Foreign and general relations
	Biography and memoirs
885.5.A1	Collective
885.5.A2-Z	Individual, A-Z
	e.g.
885.5.K6	Konoye, Fumimaro, Prince
885.5.N5	Nitobe, Inazō
885.5.T6	Tōyama, Mitsuru
	Taishō (Yoshihito), 1912-1926
885.8	Periodicals. Societies. Serials
886	General works on life and reign
886.13	Foreign and general relations
	Biography and memoirs
	Royal family
886.15	General works
886.2	Yoshihito, 1912-1926
886.22.A-Z	Other members, A-Z
887	Period of World War I, 1914-1918
888	Special
	e.g. Earthquake of 1923
	Shōwa (Hirohito), 1926-1989
888.15	Collected works (nonserial)
888.2	General works on reign
888.25	General special

DS

	Japan
	History
	By period
	Modern, 1868-
	20th century
	Showa (Hirohito), 1926-1989 -- Continued
	1926-1945
	Including works on February 26, 1936 Incident, etc.
	Cf. D731+ World War II
	Cf. D777.5.A+ Sino-Japanese Conflict, 1931-1933
	Cf. DS777.52+ Sino-Japanese War, 1937-1945
888.4	Sources and documents
888.5	General works
	1945-1989. Postwar period
888.84	Collected works (nonserial)
889	General works
889.15	General special
889.16	Allied occupation, 1945-1952
	Propaganda in other countries (General)
889.2	General works
889.3.A-Z	Individual countries, A-Z
	e.g.
889.3.U6	United States
889.5	Foreign and general relations
	Biography and memoirs
	Royal family
889.7	General works
889.8	Hirohito, 1901-
889.9.A-Z	Other members, A-Z
	Akihito, 1933- see DS891.4
	Contemporaries
890.A1	Collective
890.A2-Z	Individual, A-Z
	1980-1989
890.3	Foreign and general relations
	Heisei (Akihito), 1989-
891	General works on reign
891.2	Foreign and general relations
	Biography and memoirs
	Royal family
891.3	General works
891.4	Akihito, 1933-
891.42.A-Z	Other members, A-Z
	Contemporaries
891.48	Collective
891.5.A-Z	Individual, A-Z

	Japan -- Continued
	Local history and description
	By major region subarranged by other local subdivisions except cities. Under all major regions, except Hokkaidō, the administrative subdivisions will be prefectures. Subarrange these subdivisions by Table DS-DX6 except when otherwise provided for
	For cities see DS896+
894.2-.285	Hokkaidō (Table DS-DX8)
	Formerly Ezo
894.29.A-Z	Administrative subdivisions, subregions, etc., A-Z
894.29.A22-.A2295	Abashiri-shichō (Table DS-DX6)
894.29.H53-.H5395	Hidaka-shichō (Table DS-DX6)
894.29.H59-.H5995	Hiyama-shichō (Table DS-DX6)
894.29.I28-.I2895	Iburi-shichō (Table DS-DX6)
894.29.I84-.I8495	Ishikari-shichō (Table DS-DX6)
894.29.K34-.K3495	Kamikawa-shichō (Table DS-DX6)
894.29.K87-.K8795	Kushiro-shichō (Table DS-DX6)
894.29.N44-.N4495	Nemuro-shichō (Table DS-DX6)
894.29.O83-.O8395	Oshima-shichō (Table DS-DX6)
894.29.R84-.R8495	Rumori-shichō (Table DS-DX6)
894.29.S44-.S4495	Shiretoko Peninsula (Table DS-DX6)
894.29.S45-.S4595	Shiribe-shichō (Table DS-DX6)
894.29.S65-.S6595	Sorachi-shichō (Table DS-DX6)
894.29.S69-.S6995	Sōya-shichō (Table DS-DX6)
894.29.T63-.T6395	Tokachi-shichō (Table DS-DX6)
894.295.A-Z	Natural features such as mountains, rivers, lakes, etc., A-Z
894.3-.385	Tōhoku region (Table DS-DX8)
	Also known as Ōu
894.39.A-Z	Prefectures, subregions, etc., A-Z
894.39.A39-.A3995	Akita (Table DS-DX6)
	Formerly Ugo and Rikuchu provinces
894.39.A55-.A5595	Aomori (Table DS-DX6)
	Formerly Mutsu province
894.39.D4-.D495	Dewa region (Table DS-DX6)
894.39.F83-.F8395	Fukishima (Table DS-DX6)
	Formerly Iwashiro and Iwaki provinces
894.39.I92-.I9295	Iwate (Table DS-DX6)
	Formerly Rikuchu province
894.39.M59-.M5995	Miyagi (Table DS-DX6)
	Formerly Rikuzen province
894.39.M87-.M8795	Mutsu region (Table DS-DX6)
894.39.N35-.N3595	Nambu region (Table DS-DX6)
894.39.S26-.S2695	Sanriku region (Table DS-DX6)
894.39.Y34-.Y3495	Yamagata (Table DS-DX6)
	Formerly Uzen province

Japan

Local history and description

Tohoku region -- Continued

894.395.A-Z	Natural features such as mountains, rivers, lakes, etc., A-Z
894.4-.485	Kantō region (Table DS-DX8)
894.49.A-Z	Prefectures, subregions, etc., A-Z
894.49.C45-.C4595	Chiba (Table DS-DX6)
	Formerly Awa, Kazusa, and Shimōsa provinces
894.49.G85-.G8595	Gunma (Table DS-DX6)
	Formerly Kozuke province
894.49.I22-.I2295	Ibaraki (Table DS-DX6)
	Formerly Hitachi province
894.49.K34-.K3495	Kanagawa (Table DS-DX6)
	Formerly Sagami province
894.49.M87-.M8795	Musashino region (Table DS-DX6)
	Covers part of Tokyo and Saitama
894.49.S24-.S2495	Saitama (Table DS-DX6)
	Formerly Musashi province
894.49.T62-.T6295	Tochigi (Table DS-DX6)
	Formerly Shimotsuki province
	Tokyo see DS896+
894.495.A-Z	Natural features such as mountains, rivers, lakes, etc., A-Z
894.5-.585	Chubu region (Table DS-DX8)
894.59.A-Z	Prefectures, subregions, etc., A-Z
894.59.A35-.A3595	Aichi (Table DS-DX6)
	Covers the former Owari and Mikawa provinces
894.59.A83-.A8395	Asama Mountain region (Table DS-DX6)
894.59.F83-.F8395	Fukui (Table DS-DX6)
	Covers the former Echizen and Wakasa provinces
894.59.G53-.G5395	Gifu (Table DS-DX6)
	Covers the former Hida and Mino provinces
894.59.H63-.H6395	Hokuriku region (Table DS-DX6)
894.59.I53-.I5395	Ina region (Table DS-DX6)
894.59.I83-.I8395	Ishikawa (Table DS-DX6)
	Covers the former Kaga and Noto provinces
894.59.K6-.K695	Kōshū Kaido (Table DS-DX6)
894.59.N33-.N3395	Nagano (Table DS-DX6)
	Covers the former Shinano province
894.59.N36-.N3695	Nakasendō (Table DS-DX6)
894.59.N54-.N5495	Niigata (Table DS-DX6)
	Covers the former Echigo province and Sado Island
894.59.S45-.S4595	Shizuoka (Table DS-DX6)
	Covers the former Izu, Suruga, and Tōtomi provinces
894.59.T63-.T6395	Tōkai region (Table DS-DX6)
	Including the Tokaido

Japan
  Local history and description
    Chubu region
      Prefectures, subregions, etc., A-Z -- Continued

894.59.T67-.T6795	Tōsan region (Table DS-DX6)
894.59.T69-.T6995	Toyama (Table DS-DX6)
	Covers the former Etchū province
894.59.Y34-.Y3495	Yamanashi (Table DS-DX6)
	Covers the former Kai province
894.595.A-Z	Natural features such as mountains, rivers, lakes, etc., A-Z
894.6-.685	Kinki region (Table DS-DX8)
894.69.A-Z	Prefectures, subregions, etc., A-Z
894.69.H95-.H9595	Hyōgo (Table DS-DX6)
	Covers the former Awaji, Harima, western Settsu, Tajima, and western Tamba provinces
894.69.K35-.K3595	Kansai region (Table DS-DX6)
894.69.K5-.K595	Kinai region (Table DS-DX6)
894.69.K85-.K8595	Kumano region (Table DS-DX6)
894.69.K95-.K9595	Kyōto (Table DS-DX6)
	Covers the former Tamba, Tango, and Yamashiro provinces
894.69.M5-.M595	Mie (Table DS-DX6)
	Covers the former Iga, Ise, and Shima provinces
894.69.N36-.N3695	Nara (Table DS-DX6)
	Covers the former Yamato province
894.69.O82-.O8295	Ōsaka (Table DS-DX6)
	Covers Izumi, Kawachi, and Settsu provinces
894.69.S45-.S4595	Shiga (Table DS-DX6)
	Covers the former Ōmi province
894.69.W33-.W3395	Wakayama (Table DS-DX6)
	Covers the former Kii province
894.695.A-Z	Natural features such as mountains, rivers, lakes, etc., A-Z
894.7-.785	Chūgoku region (Table DS-DX8)
894.79.A-Z	Prefectures, subregions, etc., A-Z
894.79.H56-.H5695	Hiroshima (Table DS-DX6)
	Covers the former Bingo and Aki provinces
894.79.I54-.I5495	Inland Sea (Setonaikai) (Table DS-DX6)
	Including Inland Sea region
894.79.O37-.O3795	Okayama (Table DS-DX6)
	Covers the former Bizen, Bitchu and Mimasaka provinces
894.79.S25-.S2595	San'in region (Table DS-DX6)
	Including the San'indō
894.79.S29-.S2995	San'yō region (Table DS-DX6)
	Including the San'yōdō

	Japan
	Local history and description
	Chugoku region
	Prefectures, subregions, etc., A-Z -- Continued
894.79.S45-.S4595	Shimane (Table DS-DX6)
	Including the former Iwami, Izumo, and Oki provinces
894.79.T67-.T6795	Tottori (Table DS-DX6)
	Covers the former Hōki and Inaba provinces
894.79.Y34-.Y3495	Yamaguchi (Table DS-DX6)
	Including Chōshū-han
	Covers the former Nagato and Suwō provinces
894.795.A-Z	Natural features such as mountains, rivers, lakes, etc., A-Z
894.8-.885	Shikoku region (Table DS-DX8)
894.89.A-Z	Prefectures, subregions, etc., A-Z
894.89.E35-.E3595	Ehime (Table DS-DX6)
	Covers the former Iyo province
894.89.K33-.K3395	Kagawa (Table DS-DX6)
	Covers the former Sanuki province
894.89.K62-.K6295	Kōchi (Table DS-DX6)
	Covers the former Tosa province
894.89.T63-.T6395	Tokushima (Table DS-DX6)
	Covers the former Awa province
894.895.A-Z	Natural features such as mountains, rivers,lakes, etc., A-Z
894.9-.985	Kyushu region (Table DS-DX8)
894.99.A-Z	Prefectures, subregions, etc., A-Z
894.99.F83-.F8395	Fukuoka (Table DS-DX6)
	Covers the former Buzen, Chikugo, and Chikuzen provinces
894.99.H59-.H5995	Hizen (Table DS-DX6)
	Covers the Nagasaki and Saga prefectures
894.99.K33-.K3395	Kagoshima (Table DS-DX6)
	Covers the former Satsuma and Ōsumi provinces
894.99.K84-.K8495	Kumamoto (Table DS-DX6)
	Covers the former Higo province
894.99.M59-.M5995	Miyazaki (Table DS-DX6)
	Covers the former Hyūga province
894.99.N33-.N3395	Nagasaki (Table DS-DX6)
	Covers the former Iki, Tsushima, and part of Hizen provinces
894.99.O36-.O3695	Ōita (Table DS-DX6)
	Covers the former Bungo and part of Buzen provinces
894.99.O37-.O3795	Okinawa (Table DS-DX6)
	Covers only Okinawa, Miyako, and Yaeyama groups of islands.
	For the entire Ryuku archipelago, see Ryukyu Islands

	Japan
	Local history and description
	Kyushu region
	Prefectures, subregions, etc., A-Z -- Continued
	Ryukyu Islands see DS895.R9+
894.99.S36-.S3695	Saga (Table DS-DX6)
	Covers part of the former Hizen province
894.995.A-Z	Natural features such as mountains, rivers, lakes, etc., A-Z
895.A-Z	Other regions, etc., A-Z
(895.F68-.F77)	Formosa. Taiwan
	see DS798.92+
	Ryukyu Islands
895.R9A2-.R9A29	Periodicals. Serials
895.R9A3-.R9A39	Sources and documents
895.R9A5-.R9Z	General works
895.R92	Description and travel. Guidebooks. Gazetteers
895.R93	Cultural property. Castles, temples, monuments, etc.
895.R935	Antiquities
895.R94	Social life and customs. Civilization
	History
895.R95	General works
895.R96	Biography and memoirs (Collective)
	For individual biography, see the specific period or place
	By period
895.R97	Early to 1879
895.R975	1879-1945
895.R98	1945-1972
895.R985	1972-
	For works on Okinawa Prefecture see DS894.99.O37+
895.3.A-Z	Former dependencies, A-Z
	e.g.
	Formosa see DS798.92+
895.3.K86	Kuril Islands
895.4.A-Z	Mountains, rivers, valleys and other natural features not contained within the boundaries of any one of the major regions, A-Z
	Tokyo
	For counties, regions, islands in Tōkyō-to see DS896.7.A+
	For cities and towns in Tōkyō-to see DS897.A+
896	Periodicals. Societies. Sources and documents
896.1	Directories. Dictionaries. Gazetteers
	Biography
896.2.A1	Collective

196

	Japan
	Tokyo
	Biography -- Continued
896.2.A2-Z	Individual, A-Z
	General works. Description and travel. Pictorial works
896.3	Early to 1868
896.35	1868-
896.38	Guidebooks
896.39	Cultural property
896.4	Antiquities
896.5	Social life and customs. Civilization. Intellectual life
	History (General)
896.6	General works
896.62	Through 1868
896.64	1868-1945
896.66	1945-
896.7.A-Z	Subregions, districts, sections, etc., A-Z
	e.g.
896.7.C5	Chiyoda-ku
896.7.G5	Ginza
896.7.S5	Shinjuku-ku
	Parks, squares, circles
896.75	Collective
896.76.A-Z	Individual, A-Z
	Streets. Bridges
896.77	Collective
896.8.A-Z	Individual, A-Z
	Buildings
896.9.A1	Collective
896.9.A2-Z	Individual, A-Z
	e.g.
896.9.E3	Edojō
896.95.A-Z	Natural features such as mountains, rivers, etc., A-Z
897.A-Z	Other cities, towns, etc., A-Z
	e.g.
897.H5	Hiroshima
897.K3	Kamakura
897.K612-.K61295	Kobe (Table DS-DX4)
897.K8-.K895	Kyoto (Table DS-DX4)
897.N27	Nagano
897.N29-.N2995	Nagasaki (Table DS-DX4)
897.N31-.N3195	Nagoya (Table DS-DX4)
897.N35	Nara
897.O81-.O8195	Osaka (Table DS-DX4)
897.Y3	Yamaguchi
897.Y6-.Y695	Yokohama (Table DS-DX4)

	Korea
	Class here general works on Korea and South Korea
	For North Korea see DS930+
901	Periodicals. Societies. Serials
	Museums, exhibitions, etc.
901.2	General works
901.3.A-Z	Individual. By place, A-Z
901.6	Congresses
901.62	Sources and documents
	Collected works (nonserial)
901.7	Several authors
901.72	Individual authors
901.8	Gazetteers. Dictionaries, etc.
901.82	Place names (General)
	For etymological studies, see class P
901.9	Directories
901.95	Guidebooks
902	General works
902.12	General special
902.14	Pictorial works
	Historic monuments, landmarks, scenery, etc. (General)
	For local see DS924+
902.15	General works
902.16	Preservation
902.17	Historical geography
902.18	Geography
	Description and travel
902.2	Through 1900
902.3	1901-1953
902.4	1954-
903	Antiquities
	For local antiquities see DS924+
904	Social life and customs. Civilization. Intellectual life
	For specific periods, see the period or reign
	Ethnography
904.5	General works
904.52	National characteristics
904.6.A-Z	Individual elements in the population, A-Z
904.6.A6	Americans (U.S.)
904.6.C5	Chinese
904.6.J3	Japanese
904.7	Koreans in foreign countries (General)
	For Koreans in a particular country, see the country
	History
	Periodicals. Societies. Serials see DS901
904.8	Dictionaries. Chronological tables, outlines, etc.
	Biography (Collective)

	Korea
	History
	Biography (Collective) -- Continued
905	General works
905.2	Rulers, kings, etc.
	Houses, noble families, etc.
905.5	Collective
905.52.A-Z	Individual houses, families, etc., A-Z
905.55	Statesmen
905.57	Women
	Historiography
905.7	General works
	Biography of historians
905.8	Collective
905.82.A-Z	Individual, A-Z
	Study and teaching
905.9	General works
905.92.A-Z	By region or country, A-Z
	Subarrange by author
	General works
907.14	Through 1800
907.16	1801-1976
907.18	1977-
907.2	Pictorial works
907.4	Juvenile works
907.6	Addresses, essays, lectures. Anecdotes, etc.
908.2	Philosophy of Korean history
(908.4)	History of several parts of Korea treated together
	see DS907.14+
	Military history
	For individual campaigns and engagements, see the specific period or reign
909	Sources and documents
909.2	General works
	Naval history
	For individual campaigns and engagements, see the specific period or reign
909.5	Sources and documents
909.7	General works
	Political history
	For specific periods, see the period or reign
909.95	Sources and documents
910	General works

	Korea
	History -- Continued
	Foreign and general relations
	For general works on the diplomatic history of a period, see the period
	For works on relations with a specific country regardless of period see DS910.2.A+
910.16	Sources and documents
910.18	General works
910.2.A-Z	Relations with individual countries, A-Z
	By period
	Early to 935
911	Periodicals. Societies. Serials
911.13	Congresses
911.15	Sources and documents
911.17	Collected works (nonserial)
911.19	Historiography
911.2	General works
911.25	General special
911.26	Addresses, essays, lectures
911.27	Social life and customs. Civilization. Intellectual life
911.31	Military history
911.35	Political history
911.37	Foreign and general relations
	Biography and memoirs
911.5	Collective
911.52.A-Z	Individual, A-Z
911.62	Kojosŏn Kingdom, 2333 B.C.-108 B.C.
	Silla Kingdom, 57 B.C.-935 A.D.
911.715	Periodicals. Societies. Serials
911.716	Congresses
911.72	General works
911.723	Social life and customs. Civilization. Intellectual life
911.725	Political history. Foreign and general relations
911.726	Military history
	Biography and memoirs
911.727	Collective
911.728.A-Z	Individual, A-Z
	Koguryŏ Kingdom, 37 B.C.-668 A.D.
911.735	Periodicals. Societies. Serials
911.736	Congresses
911.74	General works
911.743	Social life and customs. Civilization. Intellectual life
911.745	Political history. Foreign and general relations
911.746	Military history
	Biography and memoirs
911.747	Collective

Korea

History

By period

Early to 935

Koguryŏ Kingdom, 37 B.C.-668 A.D.

Biography and memoirs -- Continued

911.748.A-Z   Individual, A-Z

Paekche Kingdom, 18 B.C.-660 A.D.

911.755	Periodicals. Societies. Serials
911.756	Congresses
911.76	General works
911.763	Social life and customs. Civilization. Intellectual life
911.765	Political history. Foreign and general relations
911.766	Military history
	Biography and memoirs
911.767	Collective
911.768.A-Z	Individual, A-Z
	Kaya Confederacy, 42-562 A.D.
911.775	Periodicals. Societies. Serials
911.776	Congresses
911.78	General works
911.783	Social life and customs. Civilization. Intellectual life
911.785	Political history. Foreign and general relations
911.786	Military history
	Biography and memoirs
911.787	Collective
911.788.A-Z	Individual, A-Z
911.86	T'aebong Kingdom, 901-918
	Koryŏ period, 935-1392
912	Periodicals. Societies. Serials
912.13	Congresses
912.15	Sources and documents
912.17	Collected works (nonserial)
912.19	Historiography
912.2	General works
912.25	General special
912.26	Addresses, essays, lectures
912.27	Social life and customs. Civilization. Intellectual life
912.31	Military history
912.35	Political history
912.37	Foreign and general relations
	Biography and memoirs
912.38	Collective
912.382.A-Z	Individual, A-Z
	Mongolian invasions, 1231-1270
912.4	Sources and documents
912.42	General works

	Korea
	History
	By period
	Koryo period, 935-1392
	Mongolian invasions, 1231-1270 -- Continued
912.43	General special
	Chosŏn (Yi) dynasty, 1392-1910
913	Periodicals. Societies. Serials
913.13	Congresses
913.15	Sources and documents
913.17	Collected works (nonserial)
913.19	Historiography
913.2	General works
913.25	General special
913.26	Addresses, essays, lectures
913.27	Social life and customs. Civilization. Intellectual life
913.31	Military history
913.33	Naval history
913.35	Political history
913.37	Foreign and general relations
	Biography and memoirs
913.39	Collective
913.392.A-Z	Individual, A-Z
	1392-1637
913.39312	Sources and documents
913.39313	General works
913.39314	Social life and customs. Civilization. Intellectual life
913.39316	Political history. Foreign and general relations
	Biography and memoirs
913.39318	Collective
913.39319.A-Z	Individual, A-Z
	Japanese invasions, 1592-1598
913.395	Sources and documents
913.4	General works
913.43	General special
	Biography and memoirs
913.44	Collective
913.45.A-Z	Individual, A-Z
	Manchu invasions, 1627-1637
913.615	Sources and documents
913.62	General works
913.65	General special
	Biography and memoirs
913.67	Collective
913.675.A-Z	Individual, A-Z
	1637-1864
914	Periodicals. Societies. Serials

Korea
  History
    By period
      Chosŏn (Yi) dynasty, 1392-1910
        1637-1864 -- Continued

914.13	Congresses
914.15	Sources and documents
914.19	Historiography
914.2	General works
914.27	Social life and customs. Civilization. Intellectual life
914.31	Military history
914.35	Political history
914.37	Foreign and general relations
	Biography and memoirs
914.49	Collective
914.5.A-Z	Individual, A-Z
	19th century. 1864-1910
915	Periodicals. Societies. Serials
915.13	Congresses
915.15	Sources and documents
915.17	Collected works (nonserial)
915.19	Historiography
915.2	General works
915.25	General special
915.26	Addresses, essays, lectures
915.27	Social life and customs. Civilization. Intellectual life
915.31	Military history
915.35	Political history
915.37	Foreign and general relations
	Biography and memoirs
915.49	Collective
915.5.A-Z	Individual, A-Z
915.52	Imo Incident, 1882
915.522	Kapsin Incident, 1884
915.53	Tonghak Incident, 1894
	20th century
915.56	Periodicals. Societies. Serials
915.57	Congresses
915.572	Sources and documents
915.58	Collected works (nonserial)
915.59	Historiography
916	General works
916.25	General special
916.26	Addresses, essays, lectures
916.27	Social life and customs. Civilization. Intellectual life
916.35	Political history
916.37	Foreign and general relations

Korea

  History

    By period

      20th century -- Continued

        Biography and memoirs

916.5.A1	Collective
916.5.A3-916.Z	Individual, A-Z
	e.g.
916.5.R5	Rhee, Syngman

        Japanese rule, 1910-1945

916.525	Periodicals. Societies. Serials
916.53	Sources and documents
916.535	Collected works (nonserial)
916.54	General works
916.55	General special
916.56	Political history

          Biography and memoirs

916.57	Collective
916.58.A-Z	Individual, A-Z

          Resistance movements, 1905-1945

916.59	Periodicals. Societies. Serials
916.592	Sources and documents
916.593	General works
916.594.A-Z	Local, A-Z
	Including overseas activities

           Biography

916.595	Collective
916.596.A-Z	Individual, A-Z
916.597	Independence movement, 1919

        1945-

916.6	Periodicals. Societies. Serials
916.65	Congresses
916.7	Sources and documents
916.8	Collected works (nonserial)
916.85	Historiography
917	General works
917.25	General special
917.26	Addresses, essays, lectures
917.27	Social life and customs. Civilization. Intellectual life
917.3	Military history
917.35	Political history
917.37	Foreign and general relations

         Biography and memoirs

917.4	Collective
917.42.A-Z	Individual, A-Z
917.43	Partition, 1945

         Reunification question, 1945-

	Korea
	History
	By period
	20th century
	1945-
	Reunification question, 1945- -- Continued
917.44	Periodicals. Societies. Serials
917.442	Congresses
917.443	Sources and documents
917.444	General works
	Allied occupation, 1945-1948
917.5	Sources and documents
917.52	General works
917.55	General special
	1948-1960
917.6	Periodicals. Societies. Serials
917.65	Sources and documents
917.655	Collected works (nonserial)
917.7	General works
917.75	General special
917.76	Addresses, essays, lectures
917.77	Social life and customs. Civilization. Intellectual life
917.8	Political history
917.82	Foreign and general relations
	Biography and memoirs
917.9	Collective
917.92.A-Z	Individual, A-Z
	War and intervention, 1950-1953
	Including military operations
918.A1	Periodicals. Collections
918.A15	Museums, exhibitions, etc.
	Sources and documents
918.A2-.A4	Serials
918.A5-.A55	Nonserials
	Biography
918.A553	Collective
918.A554	Individual
	see the country of the individual, D+ or other appropriate class for biography; for personal narratives, see DS921.6
918.A555	Causes. Origins. Aims
918.A56-Z	General works
918.15	Pictorial works. Satire, caricature, etc.
918.16	Motion pictures about the war
918.2.A-Z	Individual campaigns, battles, etc., A-Z
	Regimental histories
918.4	South Korea

Korea
History
By period
20th century
1945-
1946-1960
War and intervention, 1950-1953
Regimental histories -- Continued
918.6 North Korea
Foreign participation
Including armies, divisions, regiments, etc.
918.8 General works
By country
919 United States
919.2 Canada
919.3 Great Britain
919.4 Turkey
919.5 China
919.7.A-Z Other, A-Z
Military operations see DS918.A56+
Naval operations
920.A2 General works
920.A3-Z Individual engagements, ships, etc.
Aerial operations
920.2.A2 General works
920.2.A3-Z By region or country, A-Z
920.4 Engineering operations
Medals, badges, decorations of honor
Including lists of recipients and individual recipients
of medals
920.44 General works
920.45 By region or country, A-Z
920.5.A-Z Other services, A-Z
Medical and sanitary services see DS921.25
920.6 Registers, lists of dead and wounded, etc.
920.6.A2 General
920.6.A3-Z By region or country, A-Z
Atrocities
920.8 General works
920.9 Germ warfare charges
Prisoners and prisons
921 General works
921.2 Repatriation
921.25 Medical and sanitary services. Hospital services
921.3 Relief work. Charities. Protection. Refugees.
Displaced persons
921.4 Religious aspects

Korea

  History

    By period

      20th century

        1945-

          1946-1960

            War and intervention, 1950-1953 -- Continued

921.5.A-Z	Other topics, A-Z
921.5.B6	Boy Scouts
921.5.D4	Destruction and pillage
921.5.G8	Guerrillas
	Military intelligence see DS921.5.S7+
921.5.M5	Missing persons
921.5.P46	Photography
921.5.P74	Press coverage. Television coverage
921.5.P78	Psychological aspects. Psychological warfare
	Psychological warfare see DS921.5.P78
921.5.S4	Search and rescue operations
921.5.S63	Social aspects
	Spies. Secret service. Military intelligence
921.5.S7	General works
921.5.S8	Individual spies, A-Z
921.5.T35	Tank warfare
	Television coverage see DS921.5.P74
921.5.W64	Women
921.6	Personal narratives
921.7	Armistice
921.75	Peace
921.8	Reconstruction
	Celebrations. Memorials. Monuments
	For memorials to special divisions, etc., see the history of the division
921.9	General works
921.92.A-Z	By region or country, A-Z
	1960-1988
922	Periodicals. Societies. Serials
922.13	Congresses
922.15	Sources and documents
922.17	Collected works (nonserial)
922.2	General works
922.25	General special
922.26	Addresses, essays, lectures
922.27	Social life and customs. Civilization. Intellectual life
922.35	Political history
922.37	Foreign and general relations
	Biography and memoirs
922.4	Collective

	Korea
	History
	By period
	20th century
	1945-
	1960-1988
	Biography and memoirs -- Continued
922.42.A-Z	Individual, A-Z
922.43	April Revolution, 1960
922.44	May Revolution, 1961
922.445	Kwangju Uprising, 1980
	1988-2002
922.46	Periodicals. Societies. Serials
922.4613	Congresses
922.4615	Sources and documents
922.462	General works
922.463	Social life and customs. Civilization. Intellectual life
922.4635	Political history
922.4637	Foreign and general relations
	Biography and memoirs
922.464	Collective
922.4642.A-Z	Individual, A-Z
	21st century
922.5	Periodicals. Sources and documents. Collections
922.6	General works
922.7	Social life and customs. Civilization. Intellectual life
922.8	Political history
	2002-
923	Periodicals. Societies. Serials
923.13	Congresses
923.15	Sources and documents
923.2	General works
923.23	Social life and customs. Civilization. Intellectual life
923.25	Political history
923.27	Foreign and general relations
	Biography and memoirs
923.283	Collective
923.284	Individual, A-Z
	Local history and description
924.A-Z	Provinces, regions, etc., A-Z
	e.g.
924.C39	Cheju-do
925.A-Z	Cities, towns, etc., A-Z
	Subarrange each by main entry only unless otherwise indicated
	e.g.
925.P8	Pusan

Korea
  Local history and description
    Cities, towns, etc., A-Z -- Continued

925.S4-.S495	Seoul (Table DS-DX4)

Democratic People's Republic, 1948-

930	Periodicals. Societies. Serials
	Museums, exhibitions, etc.
930.2	General works
930.3.A-Z	Individual. By place, A-Z
930.5	Congresses
930.6	Sources and documents
	Collected works (nonserial)
930.7	Several authors
930.72	Individual authors
930.8	Gazetteers. Dictionaries, etc.
930.82	Place names (General)
	For etymological studies, see class P
930.9	Directories
930.95	Guidebooks
932	General works
932.2	General special
932.23	Pictorial works
	Historic monuments, landmarks, surveys, etc. (General)
	For local see DS936+
932.3	General works
932.35	Preservation
932.4	Description and travel
932.5	Antiquities
	For local antiquities see DS936+
932.7	Social life and customs. Civilization. Intellectual life
	Ethnography
933	General works
933.3.A-Z	Individual elements in the population, A-Z
933.3.J3	Japanese
933.5	North Koreans in foreign countries (General)
	History
	Periodicals. Societies. Serials see DS930
933.7	Dictionaries. Chronological tables, outlines, etc.
	Biography
	Collective
934	General works
934.5	Rulers, kings, etc.
934.55	Statesmen
934.57	Women
934.6.A-Z	Individual, A-Z
934.7	Historiography
934.8	Study and teaching

	Korea
	Democratic People's Republic, 1948-
	History -- Continued
935	General works
935.2	Pictorial works
935.25	Juvenile works
935.27	Addresses, essays, lectures
935.3	General special
935.31	Military history
	Political history
935.4	Sources and documents
935.5	General works
935.55	General special
	Foreign and general relations
935.6	Sources and documents
935.65	General works
935.7.A-Z	Relations with individual countries, A-Z
	By period
	1948-1994
935.75	General works
935.754	Political history
	Biography and memoirs
935.7552	Collective
935.7553	Individual, A-Z
	1994-
935.773	General works
935.774	Political history
935.775	Foreign and general relations
	Biography and memoirs
935.7772	Collective
935.7773	Individual, A-Z
	Local history and description
936.A-Z	Provinces, regions, etc., A-Z
	e.g.
936.P9	P'yŏngan-pukto
937.A-Z	Cities, towns, etc., A-Z
	e.g.
937.P9	P'yŏngyang

	History of Africa
1	Periodicals. Societies. Sources and documents. Serials
1.5	Congresses. Conferences, etc.
2	Gazetteers. Dictionaries, etc. Guidebooks
2.5	Directories
3	General works. History of explorations
	Cf. G220+ History of discoveries, explorations, and travel
4	General special
4.5	Pictorial works
5	Compends
6	Pamphlets
6.5	Addresses, essays, lectures
6.7	Geography
	Description and travel
	For North Africa see DT160+
	For Central Sub-Saharan Africa see DT348+
	For East Africa see DT365+
	For West Africa see DT470+
	For Southern Africa see DT1001+
7	Through 1700
	Cf. DT24 Africa as known to the ancients
8	1701-1800
11	1801-1900
12	1901-1950
12.2	1951-1977
12.25	1978-
13	Antiquities
14	Social life and customs. Civilization. Intellectual life
	Ethnography
	Cf. GN643+ Anthropology
15	General works
16.A-Z	Individual elements in the population not limited to specific territorial divisions, A-Z
16.A72	Arabs
16.B2	Bantus
16.B58	Blacks
	Class here works on blacks who have emigrated to Africa from other continents
16.C48	Chinese
16.E17	East Indians
16.E95	Europeans
16.J34	Japanese
16.P8	Pygmies
16.R87	Russians
16.S35	Scots
16.S94	Swabians
16.W45	Whites

	Ethnography -- Continued
16.5	Africans in foreign countries. African diaspora
	History
17	Dictionaries. Chronological tables, outlines, etc.
18	Biography (Collective)
	Historiography
19	General works
	Biography of historians, area studies specialists, archaeologists, etc.
19.5	Collective
19.7	Individual
	Study and teaching
19.8.A-.Z8	General works
19.8.Z9	Catalogs of audiovisual materials
19.9.A-Z	By region or country, A-Z
19.95.A-Z	Individual schools, A-Z
20	General works
21	General special
21.5	Military history
22	Juvenile works
	By period
24	Africa as known to the ancients. History and description
	Cf. DT50 Egypt
	Cf. DT168+ Carthage, etc.
25	Early through 1500
26	1501-1700
27	1701-1800
28	1801-1884
29	1884-1945
	1945-1960
30	General works
30.2	Addresses, essays, lectures
30.5	1960-
	Political and diplomatic history. Partition. Colonies and possessions
31	General works
	By period
	see the specific period
	Relations with individual countries
	England. Great Britain
32	Comprehensive description and history
32.1	General special
32.3	Early history through 1800
32.5	1800-1960
32.7	1960-
	France
33	Comprehensive description and history

History
    Political and diplomatic history. Partition. Colonies and
        possessions
    Relations with individual countries
        France -- Continued
33.1   General special
33.3   Early history through 1800
33.5   1800-1960
33.7   1960-
        Germany
34   Comprehensive description and history
34.1   General special
34.3   Early history through 1800
34.5   1800-1960
34.7   1960-
        Italy
35   Comprehensive description and history
35.1   General special
35.3   Early history through 1800
35.5   1800-1960
35.7   1960-
        Portugal
36   Comprehensive description and history
36.1   General special
36.3   Early history through 1800
36.5   1800-1960
36.7   1960-
        Spain
                    Cf. DT653.5.A+ Congo question
37   Comprehensive description and history
37.1   General special
37.3   Early history through 1800
37.5   1800-1960
37.7   1960-
        United States
38   Comprehensive description and history
38.1   General special
38.3   Early history through 1800
38.5   1800-1960
38.7   1960-
38.9.A-Z   Other regions or countries, A-Z
                    e.g.
38.9.S65   Soviet Union
39   Red Sea coast. Red Sea region
            Including Asian portion of the Red Sea region
            Cf. DT367+ Northeast Africa
    Egypt

Egypt -- Continued
43	Periodicals. Societies. Sources and documents. Serials
44	Directories
45	Guidebooks. Gazetteers. Dictionaries. Directories, etc.
	Including Upper and Lower Egypt
46	General works
47	Monumental and picturesque
48	General special
49	Juvenile works
49.9	Historical geography
	Description and travel
49.98	History of travel
50	Ancient through 637
51	638-1797
53	1798-1848
54	1849-1900
55	1901-1950
56	1951-1980
56.2	1981-
	Antiquities
56.8	Periodicals. Societies. Serials
56.9	General works
	By period
	Ancient Egypt. Egyptology
	Cf. PJ1051+ History of Egyptology
57	Periodicals. Societies. Serials
	e.g. Egypt exploration fund
57.5	Private collections
58	Dictionaries
	Museums, exhibitions, etc.
58.9	General works
59.A-Z	Individual. By place, A-Z
	e.g.
59.P2	Paris. Musée National du Louvre
60	General works
60.5	Forgeries
61	General special. Civilization, culture, etc.
62.A-Z	Special topics, A-Z
62.A5	Amulets
62.A55	Animals
	Arrows see DT62.B6
62.A9	Axes
62.B27	Baskets. Basketry
62.B3	Baths
62.B46	Block statues
62.B5	Board games
	Boats see DT62.S55

Egypt
  Antiquities
    By period
      Ancient Egypt. Egyptology
        Special topics, A-Z -- Continued

62.B6	Bows and arrows
	Canes see DT62.W34
62.C3	Canopic jars
62.C48	Chariots
62.C64	Coffins
62.C76	Crowns
	Funeral customs see DT62.T6
	Grave goods see DT62.T6
62.H44	Headrests
62.I92	Ivories
62.L34	Lamps
62.L42	Leatherwork
62.M5	Metals
62.M58	Mirrors
62.M7	Mummies
62.O2	Obelisks
62.O88	Ostraka
	Cf. PJ1675 Hieratic literature
	Cf. PJ1829 Demotic literature
62.P34	Palettes
62.P54	Plant remains
62.P72	Pottery
	Pyramids see DT63+
62.Q8	Quarries
62.S3	Scarabs
62.S55	Ships. Boats
62.S57	Shoes
62.S67	Sparterie
62.S7	Sphinxes
62.S73	Spoons
62.S8	Steles
62.T24	Talismans
	Temples see DT68.8
62.T45	Tiles
62.T5	Toilet articles
62.T6	Tombs. Grave goods
	For tomb of Tutankhamen see DT87.5
	Cf. BL2450.F8 Funeral rites and ceremonies
62.T65	Tools
62.U84	Ushabti
62.V47	Vessels
62.W34	Walking sticks. Canes

	Egypt
	Antiquities
	By period
	Ancient Egypt. Egyptology -- Continued
	Pyramids
63	General works
63.5	Pamphlets, etc.
64	Pamphlets, etc.
65	Public and political antiquities
66	Private antiquities
	Religious antiquities
	Cf. BL2428+ Egyptian mythology
68	General works
	Cultus
68.2	General works
68.3	Cult of the pharaohs
68.4	Festivals
68.8	Temples, altars, etc.
	Cf. NA215+ Egyptian architecture
69	Christian period
	Cf. BR130+ Christian religious antiquities
69.5	Islamic period. Islamic antiquities
70	Social life and customs. Civilization. Intellectual life
	Cf. DT61 Ancient Egyptian civilization
	Ethnography
71	General works
72.A-Z	Individual elements in the population, A-Z
72.A73	Arameans
72.A75	Armenians
72.B4	Bedouins
72.B45	Beja
72.C53	Circassians
72.C7	Copts
72.F7	French
72.G4	Germans
72.G7	Greeks
72.I8	Italians
72.K8	Kukus
72.L43	Lebanese
72.M55	Minoans
72.N67	North Africans
72.N83	Nubians
72.P35	Palestinian Arabs
	Romanies see DX293
72.R87	Russians
72.S25	Ṣaʻīdīs (Ṣaʻāyidah). صعيدي . صعيدية
72.S9	Syrians

	Egypt
	Ethnography
	Individual elements in the population, A-Z -- Continued
72.Y44	Yemenites
73.A-Z	Local antiquities, A-Z
73.A13	Abū Jirāb. أبو جراب
73.A134	Abū Mīna. أبو مينة
73.A137	Abū Rawwāsh. أبو رواش
73.A14	Abu Sir Site. (Jīzah). جيزة
73.A15	Abū Sunbul. أبو صنبل
73.A16	Abydos
73.A17	Adaima
73.A28	Akhmīm. اخميم
73.A29	Akoris
73.A3	Al-Mîna
73.A4	Alexandria
73.A7	Antinoopolis
73.A75	Aphroditopolis
73.A8	Armant
73.A812	Arminnā West (Site)
73.A8127	Arsinoe
73.A813	Arsinoites
73.A82	al 'Asāsīf. العساسيف
73.A85	el Ashmūnein. Hermopolis Magna
73.A88	Aswân. أسوان
73.A9	Asyūt
73.A92	Asyut Province
73.A93	Athribis
73.A937	'Aydhāb
73.A94	'Ayn al Labakhah Site. عين اللبخة
73.A95	'Ayn Wāqifah Site. عين واقفة
73.B3	Bacchis
73.B33	Bahariya Oasis
73.B34	Balāmūn, Tall al-. تل البلامون
73.B35	Balat Site
	Banī Ḥasan Site see DT73.B4
73.B375	Barānīs. برانيس
73.B38	Bawit
73.B4	Beni Hasan (Bani or Beni Hassan)
73.B44	Bibân el Molûk. Valley of the Kings
73.B56	Bir Umm Fawakhir Site
73.B8	Bubastis Site
73.C55	Clysma
73.D25	ad Dab'ah
73.D27	Dābūd (Temple). دابود
73.D3	Dahshûr. دهشور
73.D33	Dakhla Oasis

	Egypt
	Local antiquities, A-Z -- Continued
73.D4	Dandara
	Dayr al-Bahrī Site see DT73.D45
(73.D43)	Dayr al-Ballas Site
	see DT73.D46
73.D44	Dayr al-Barshā. دير البرشا
	Dayr al-Madīnah Site see DT73.D47
73.D45	Deir el-Bahri Site
73.D46	Deir el-Ballas Site
73.D465	Deir el-Gebrawi Site
73.D47	Deir el-Medina Site
73.D48	Deir el-Shelwit Site
	Delta Region see DT73.N54
73.D49	Dendūr
73.D492	el-Derr. Rock Temple of el-Derr
73.D54	Dīmay
73.D56	Dionysias. Qaṣr Qārūn
73.E27	Eastern Desert
73.E43	El-Kab
73.E45	Elephantine
73.F36	Farkha, Tell el-
73.F38	Fayyūm. فيوم
	Gebel el-Silsila see DT73.S56
73.G42	Gebelein Site
73.G47	Gerf Hussein (Temple)
73.G5	Gizeh
73.G85	Gurob
73.H25	Haram Zāwiyat al 'Urbān
73.H3	Hawara
73.H34	Hawawish Site
73.H42	Heliopolis
73.H44	Heracleopolis Magna
73.H45	Hermopolite Nome
73.H57	Ḥisn, Kawm al- (Egypt)
73.I25	Ibis Nome
73.I27	Ibrim. Qasr Ibrim
73.I3	Idfū. ادفو
(73.I46)	Imlīḥīyah, Tall
	see DS70.5.I44
73.I8	Isnā (Site)
73.K28	Kahun
73.K33	Karanis
73.K4	Karnak. Temple of Ammon
73.K45	Kawa
73.K453	al Kawm al Ahmar. Hierakonpolis
73.K47	Kellia Site

	Egypt
	Local antiquities, A-Z -- Continued
73.K5	Kharga (Oasis)
73.K54	Khelua Site
	Kom el-Nana Site see DT73.T25
73.K66	Kom Firin Site
	Koptos see DT73.Q54
73.K75	Kuntillat Jurayyah
73.K8	Kush
73.K95	Kysis
73.L33	El Lāhūn
	Lake Nasser (Egypt and Sudan) see DT73.N27
73.L47	el-Lessiya
73.L6	Lisht
73.M23	Madīnat Wāṭifah, Kawn
73.M233	Magdolum
73.M24	Malkata Site
73.M245	Marea
73.M254	Marsá Maṭrūḥ. مرسى مطروح
73.M257	Maryūt (Lake)
73.M3	Medinet Habu
73.M35	Medinet Madi. Narmouthis
73.M4	Meidum Site
	Including Meidum Pyramid
73.M5	Memphis
73.M54	Mendes
73.M72	Minshāt abū 'Umar Site
73.M75	Minyā (Province). منيا
73.M8	Moeris (Lake)
73.M85	Mons Claudianus Site
73.N18	Nag' el-Scheima Site
73.N2	Naga-ed-Dêr
73.N26	Naqādah. نقادة
	Narmouthis see DT73.M35
73.N27	Nasser, Lake (Egypt and Sudan)
73.N28	Naṭrūn Valley
73.N3	Naucratis
73.N54	Nile River Delta
73.O8	Oxyrhynchus
73.P4	Pelusium
73.P47	Per-Sopdu
73.P5	Philae
73.P58	Pi-Ramesse
73.P8	Ptolemais
73.Q33	Qarara Site
73.Q35	Qasr al-Sagha Region. Temple of Qasr al-Sagha
	Qasr Ibrim see DT73.I27

DT

	Egypt
	Local antiquities, A-Z -- Continued
73.Q38	Qaṣr wa-al-Ṣayyād Site
73.Q54	Qifṭ. Koptos
73.Q72	Qubbat al-Hawā' Site
73.Q75	el-Qurna
73.Q76	Qurnat Murā'i. قرنة مراعي
73.Q77	Qusayr al-Qadīm. قصير القديم
73.R5	Rizeiqāt
	Rock Chapel of Horemheb see DT73.S56
	Rock Temple of el-Derr see DT73.D492
73.S3	Sakkara
73.S35	Sarābīṭ al-Khādim Site. سرابيط الخادم
73.S38	Sayyālah. سيالة
73.S5	Shanhūr. شنهور
73.S53	Sharīqiyah (Governorate). شرقية
73.S54	Shārūnah Site
73.S56	Silsila, Gebel el-. Rock Chapel of Horemheb
73.S85	Sūhāj (Province). سوهاج
73.T2	Tanis
73.T23	Taphis
73.T24	el-Tarif Site
73.T244	Tarkhan Site
73.T247	Tebtunis Site
73.T25	Tell el-Amarna
	Including Kom el-Nana Site
	Tell el-Farkha see DT73.F36
	Temple of Qasr al-Sagha see DT73.Q35
	Thebes. Temple of Luxor
73.T3	General works
73.T32	Memnon statue. Mortuary Temple of Amenhotep III
73.T33	Ramesseum
73.T74	Tree Shelter Site
73.T85	Tūnat al-Jabal Site
73.T87	Ṭūr. طور
	Valley of the Kings see DT73.B44
73.V34	Valley of the Queens
73.Z35	Zāwiyat al-Amwāt Site
73.Z39	Zayt Mountain
	History
74	Dictionaries. Chronological tables, outlines, etc.
76	Biography (Collective)
	Historiography
76.7	General works
	Biography
76.8	Collective
76.9.A-Z	Individual, A-Z

	Egypt
	History -- Continued
	Study and teaching
76.93.A-.Z8	General works
76.93.Z9	Catalogs of audiovisual materials
76.95.A-Z	By region or country, A-Z
	Subarrange by author
77	General works
79	Pamphlets, etc.
80	General special
81	Military history
	Political and diplomatic history. Foreign and general relations
82	General works
82.5.A-Z	Relations with individual countries, A-Z
	By period
	Ancient and early to 638 A.D.
83	General works
83.A2	Through 1800
83.A3-Z	1801-
	Old and middle kingdoms, 1st-17th dynasties 3400-1580 B.C.
85	General works
86	Hyksos
	18th-20th dynasties, 1580-1150 B.C.
87	General works
87.15	Hatshepsut, 1503-1482
87.2	Thutmose III, 1479-1447. Megiddo
87.3	Amenhotep II, 1427-1400
87.38	Amenhotep III, 1417-1379
	Amenhetep IV, 1375-1358 (Ikhnaton)
87.4	General works
87.45	Nefertiti (Nofretete), Consort of Amenhetep IV
87.5	Tutenkhamûn, 1358-1350
87.8	Horemheb, 1319-1292
88	Ramses II, 1292-1225
88.5	Period of Jewish captivity
	For history of the Jews see DS121+
88.8	Ramses III, 1198-1167
88.82	Ramses IV, 1166-1160
89	1150-663 B.C., 21st-24th dynasties
90	663-525 B.C., 25th-26th dynasties
91	Persian rule, 525-332 B.C.
	Alexander and Ptolemies, 332-30 B.C.
	General works
92.A2	Through 1800
92.A3-Z	1801-

	Egypt
	History
	By period
	Ancient and early to 638 A.D.
	Alexander and Ptolemies, 332-30 B.C. -- Continued
92.7	Cleopatra
	Roman rule, 30 B.C.-638 A.D.
	General works
93.A2	Through 1800
93.A3-Z	1801-
	Modern
94	General works
	Moslems, 638-1798
95	General works
	638-1250
95.5	General works
95.55	Conquest. Omayyads. Abbasids. 638-868
	Tulūnids, 868-905. طلونيون
95.6	General works
	Biography and memoirs
95.64.A2	Collective
95.64.A3-Z	Individual, A-Z
	Ikhshīdids, 935-969. Interregnum, 905-935.
	اخشيديون
95.65	General works
	Biography and memoirs
95.69.A2	Collective
95.69.A3-Z	Individual, A-Z
	Fatimids, 909-1171. فاطميون
95.7	General works
	Biography and memoirs
95.78.A2	Collective
95.78.A3-Z	Individual, A-Z
	Ayyūbids, 1169-1250. ايوبيون
95.8	General works
	Biography and memoirs
95.88.A2	Collective
95.88.A3-Z	Individual, A-Z
	1250-1517. Mamelukes. ماليك
96	General works
	Biography and memoirs
96.3.A2	Collective
96.3.A3-Z	Individual, A-Z
	By period
96.4	Bahri line, 1250-1390
96.7	Burji line, 1382-1517
	1517-1798. Turkish rule

Egypt
History
By period
Modern
Moslems, 638-1798
1517-1798. Turkish rule -- Continued

97	General works
98.5	Ali Bey, 1766-1773

1798-1879. 19th century

100	General works
	Biography and memoirs
102.A2	Collective
102.A3-Z	Individual, A-Z
	e.g.
102.S2	Salt, Henry
103	1798-1805
	Cf. DC225+ French expedition to Egypt
104	Mohammed Ali, 1805-1848
104.5	Ibrahim, 1848
104.7	Abbas I, 1848-1854
105	Mohammed Said, 1854-1863
106	Ismail, 1863-1879
	1879-1952
	For Sudan see DT154.1+
107	General works
	Biography and memoirs
107.2.A2	Collective
107.2.A3-Z	Individual, A-Z
	e.g.
107.2.A5	Ahmad Seif-ed-Din, Prince
107.2.B16	Baker, Sir Samuel White
107.2.C7	Cromer, Evelyn Baring, 1st Earl of
107.2.T3	Tāhā Husayn. طه حسين
	Tawfīq, 1879-1892
107.3	General works
107.4	Ahmad ʿUrābī (Arabi Pasha). Anglo-Egyptian War, 1882
107.6	Abbas II (Abbas Hilmi), 1892-1914
107.7	Hussein Kamil, 1914-1917
107.8	Fuad I, 1917-1936
107.82	Fārūq I, 1936-1952
	Republic, 1952-
107.821	Periodicals. Societies. Serials
107.822	Congresses
107.823	Sources and documents
107.824	Historiography
107.825	General works

	Egypt
	History
	By period
	Modern
	Republic, 1952- -- Continued
107.8255	Addresses, essays, lectures
107.826	Social life and customs. Civilization. Intellectual life
107.8265	Military history
107.827	Political history
107.8275	Foreign and general relations
	Biography and memoirs
107.828.A2	Collective
107.828.A3-Z	Individual, A-Z
	By period
107.83	Nasser, Gamal Abdel, 1952-1970
	For War of Attrition, 1969-1970 see DS127.95
107.85	Sadat, Anwar, 1970-1981
107.87	Mubārak, Muḥammad Ḥusnī, 1981-. مبارك، محمد حسني
	Local history and description
	Nile River (General)
	For the Nile River in individual countries, see the country, e.g.
	DT159.6.N54, Sudan
115	General works
116	Nile in Egypt
117	Sources of the Nile
	Cf. DT361+ Ruwenzori Mountains
137.A-Z	Governorships, provinces, regions, etc., A-Z
	e.g.
137.B8	al-Buḥayrah. البحيرة
137.D26	Damietta region
137.G5	al-Gharbīyah. الغربية
	Nubia see DT159.6.N83
137.S55	Sinai Peninsula
137.T3	Taḥrīr (Province). تحرير
137.T54	Tīh Plateau. تيه
137.W4	Western Desert
	Cities, towns, etc.
	Cairo
139	Periodicals. Societies. Serials
141	Directories. Dictionaries. Gazetteers
142	Guidebooks
143	General works
	Description and travel
144	General works
144.2	Early and medieval
144.3	Pictorial works

	Egypt
	Local history and description
	Cities, towns, etc.
	Cairo -- Continued
145	Antiquities
146	Social life and customs. Civilization. Intellectual life
	Ethnography
146.5	General works
146.6.A-Z	Individual elements in the population, A-Z
146.6.S83	Sudanese
	History
147	Biography (Collective)
	For individual biography, see the specific period, reign, or place
148	General works
	By period
149	Early and medieval
	Sections, districts, suburbs, etc.
150	Collective
150.5.A-Z	Individual, A-Z
	Monuments, statues, etc.
151	Collective
151.5.A-Z	Individual, A-Z
	Parks, squares, circles
152	Collective
152.5.A-Z	Individual, A-Z
	Buildings
153	Collective
153.5.A-Z	Individual, A-Z
154.A-Z	Other cities, towns, etc., A-Z
	e.g.
	For extinct cities, towns, and archaeological sites see DT73.A+
154.A4	Alexandria
154.H5	Helwan
154.K6	Kharga (Oasis)
154.P7	Port Said
154.S5	Siwa (Oasis)
154.S9	Suez (Isthmus and Canal)
	Sudan. Anglo-Egyptian Sudan
	For South Sudan see DT159.915+
154.1	Periodicals. Societies. Serials
	Museums, exhibitions, etc.
154.2	General works
154.25.A-Z	Individual. By place, A-Z
154.3	Congresses
154.32	Sources and documents

Sudan. Anglo-Egyptian Sudan -- Continued
Collected works (nonserial)

154.33	Several authors
154.34	Individual authors
154.4	Gazetteers. Dictionaries, etc.
154.45	Directories
154.5	Guidebooks
154.6	General works
154.65	General special
154.67	Pictorial works
154.68	Historic monuments, landmarks, scenery, etc. (General)
	For local see DT159.6+
154.69	Historical geography
	Description and travel
154.7	History of travel
154.72	Early through 1800
154.73	19th century
154.74	20th century through 1955
154.75	1956-
154.8	Antiquities
	For local antiquities see DT159.6+
154.9	Social life and customs. Civilization. Intellectual life
	For specific periods, see the period or reign
	Ethnography
155	General works
155.2.A-Z	Individual elements in the population, A-Z
(155.2.A35)	Acoli
	see DT159.927.A35
155.2.A53	Amaa
(155.2.A68)	Anuaks
	see DT159.927.A58
155.2.A78	Arabs (General)
155.2.A79	Atuot
(155.2.A93)	Azande. Zande
	see DT159.927.Z36
155.2.B34	Baggara
(155.2.B37)	Bari
	see DT159.927.B37
155.2.B44	Beja
155.2.B47	Berti
(155.2.B65)	Bongo
	see DT159.927.B66
155.2.C65	Copts
155.2.D36	Danagla
(155.2.D53)	Didinga
	see DT159.927.D56
155.2.D56	Dinka

	Sudan. Anglo-Egyptian Sudan
	Ethnography
	Individual elements in the population, A-Z -- Continued
	For see DT155.2.F87
	Forawa see DT155.2.F87
155.2.F84	Fula
155.2.F87	Fur. For. Forawa
155.2.G74	Greeks
155.2.H32	Hadendowa
155.2.H34	Halab
155.2.H36	Hassaniyeh
155.2.H38	Hausas
155.2.J33	Ja'aliyyīn
155.2.J86	Jumū'īyah
155.2.K32	Kababish
155.2.K38	Kawāhla
155.2.K46	Kenuz
155.2.K65	Koma
(155.2.K74)	Kreish
	see DT159.927.G32
155.2.K75	Krongo
(155.2.L37)	Latuka. Latuko
	see DT159.927.L68
(155.2.L86)	Luo. Lwoo
	see DT159.927.L86
(155.2.M36)	Mandari
	see DT159.927.M36
(155.2.M87)	Murle
	see DT159.927.M87
155.2.N55	Nilotic peoples (General)
155.2.N82	Nuba
	Nubians see DT159.6.N83
(155.2.N85)	Nuer
	see DT159.927.N84
(155.2.P37)	Päri
	see DT159.927.P37
155.2.R37	Rashāyidah
155.2.R83	Rufa'a al-Hoi
155.2.S45	Shaikia
155.2.S46	Shilluks
155.2.T36	Taaisha
155.2.T45	Thracians
155.2.U38	Uduk
155.2.Z34	Zaghawa
	History
	Periodicals. Societies. Serials see DT154.1
155.3	Dictionaries. Chronological tables, outlines, etc.

	Sudan. Anglo-Egyptian Sudan
	History -- Continued
	Biography (Collective)
	For individual biography, see the specific period, reign, or place
155.4	General works
155.42	Rulers, kings, etc.
	Houses, noble families, etc.
155.44	General works
155.45.A-Z	Individual houses, families, etc., A-Z
155.46	Statesmen
	Historiography
155.5	General works
	Biography of historians, area studies specialists, archaeologists, etc.
155.52	Collective
155.53.A-Z	Individual, A-Z
	Study and teaching
155.55	General works
155.56.A-Z	By region or country, A-Z
	Subarrange by author
	General works
155.58	Through 1800
155.6	1801-
155.62	Addresses, essays, lectures. Anecdotes, etc.
155.64	Military history
	For individual campaigns and engagements, see the special period or reign
155.7	Political history
	For specific periods, see the period or reign
	Foreign and general relations
	For general works on the diplomatic history of a period, see the period
	For works on relations with a specific country regardless of period see DT155.9.A+
155.78	Sources and documents
155.8	General works
155.9.A-Z	Relations with individual countries, A-Z
	By period
156	Early to 641
	641-1821
156.3	General works
156.35	1504-1821. Funj dynasty
	1821-
156.4	General works
	19th century
156.5	General works

Sudan. Anglo-Egyptian Sudan
History
By period
1821-
19th Century -- Continued
1881-1899. Mahdiyah. Gordon. Kitchener. المهدية
Cf. DT363 Emin Pasha

156.6	General works
156.65	Battle of Omdurman, 1898
156.7	1900-1955
	Republic, 1956-
157	Periodicals. Societies. Serials
157.1	Congresses
157.2	Sources and documents
157.23	Collected works (nonserial)
157.25	Historiography
157.3	General works
157.33	General special
157.36	Addresses, essays, lectures
157.4	Social life and customs. Civilization. Intellectual life
157.43	Military history
157.5	Political history
157.6	Foreign and general relations
	Biography and memoirs
157.63	Collective
157.65.A-Z	Individual, A-Z
	1956-1985
157.66	General works
157.67	Civil War, 1956-1972. Southern Sudan question
157.672	Civil War, 1983-2005
157.673	1985-2011
	Including Coup d'état, 1985
157.675	2011-
	Including partition, 2011
	Local history and description
159.6.A-Z	Provinces, regions, etc., A-Z
	e.g.
159.6.B34	Bahr al Ghazāl Province
	For Bahr al Ghazāl region see DT159.977.B37
159.6.D27	Darfur
159.6.K67	Kordofan
159.6.N54	an Nil al Azraq
159.6.N83	Nubia
	Including Egyptian Nubia
159.6.S46	Sennar
(159.6.S73)	Southern Region
	see DT159.915+

	Sudan. Anglo-Egyptian Sudan
	Local history and description -- Continued
	Cities, towns, etc.
159.7	Khartum. Greater Khartum
159.9.A-Z	Other cities, towns, etc., A-Z
	e.g.
159.9.A35	Akāshah Site
159.9.A37	Aksha
159.9.B34	Begrawia Site
159.9.B85	Buhen
159.9.G33	Gabati Site
159.9.H36	Hambukol Site
159.9.J32	Jabal Mayyah Site
159.9.K37	Karmah
159.9.L55	Lion Temple of Naq'a
159.9.M44	Meinarti
159.9.M47	Meroe
159.9.M57	Mirgissa
159.9.S47	Serra East Site
159.9.T33	Tabo Site
	South Sudan
159.915	Periodicals. Societies. Serials
159.916	Congresses
159.917	Sources and documents
159.9175	Gazetteers. Dictionaries, etc.
159.9177	Place names (General)
159.9179	Directories
159.918	Guidebooks
159.92	General works
159.923	Pictorial works
	Historic monuments, landmarks, etc.
	For local see DT159.977+
159.9234	General works
159.9235	Preservation
159.924	Historical geography
159.9244	Geography
159.9245	Description and travel
159.925	Antiquities
	For local antiquities see DT159.977+
159.9255	Social life and customs. Civilization. Intellectual life
	By period, see the specific period or reign
	Ethnography
159.926	General works
159.9265	South Sudanese in foreign countries (General)
	For South Sudanese in a particular country, see the country
159.9266	National characteristics
159.927.A-Z	Individual elements in the population, A-Z

South Sudan
Ethnography
Individual elements in the population, A-Z -- Continued

159.927.A35	Acholi
159.927.A58	Anuak
159.927.B36	Banda
159.927.B37	Bari
159.927.B66	Bongo
159.927.D56	Didinga
159.927.D57	Dinka
159.927.G32	Gbaya. Kreich
159.927.I5	Ik
159.927.K66	Koma
	Kreich see DT159.927.G32
159.927.K85	Kuku
159.927.L68	Lotuko
159.927.L86	Lwoo
159.927.M36	Mandari
159.927.M87	Murle
159.927.N84	Nuer
159.927.P37	Päri
159.927.S55	Shilluk
159.927.U38	Uduk
159.927.Z36	Zande

History
Periodicals. Societies. Serials see DT159.915

159.928	Dictionaries. Chronological tables, outlines, etc.
	Biography (Collective)
	For individual biography, see the specific period, reign, or place
159.9285	Rulers, kings, etc.
	Houses, noble families, etc.
159.9286	General works
159.92862.A-Z	Individual, A-Z
	Historiography
159.92865	General works
	Biography of historians, area studies specialists, archaeologists, etc.
159.928666	Collective
159.928667.A-Z	Individual, A-Z
159.9287	Study and teaching
159.929	General works
159.9292	Pictorial works
159.9293	Military history
	For individual campaigns and engagements, see the period or reign
159.9295	Political history

           South Sudan
             History -- Continued
               Foreign and general relations
                 Class general works on the diplomatic history of a period with
                    the period
                 For works on relations with a specific country
                    regardless of period see DT159.9298.A+

159.9296	Sources and documents
159.9297	General works
159.9298.A-Z	Relations with individual countries, A-Z
	By period
	2011-
159.9399	Periodicals. Societies. Serials
159.93995	Congresses
159.93996	Sources and documents
159.93997	Historiography
159.94	General works
159.942	Social life and customs. Civilization. Intellectual life
159.943	Military history
159.944	Political history
159.945	Foreign and general relations
	Biography and memoirs
159.946	Collective
159.947.A-Z	Individual, A-Z
	Local history and description
159.977.A-Z	States, regions, etc., A-Z
	e.g.
159.977.B37	Bahr al Ghazāl region
	Including the states of Northern Bahr el Ghazal, Western Bahr el Ghazal, Lakes, and Warrap treated collectively
159.977.C46	Central Equatoria
159.977.E27	Eastern Equatoria
159.977.J66	Jonglei
159.977.U65	Unity
159.977.U67	Upper Nile
159.977.W37	Warrap
159.977.W47	Western Bahr el Ghazal
159.977.W48	Western Equatoria
159.978.A-Z	Cities, towns, etc., A-Z
	e.g.
159.978.J82	Juba
	North Africa
	Including Egypt and Maghrib (Collectively)
160	Periodicals. Societies. Serials
161.9	Guidebooks
162	General works
	Description and travel

	North Africa
	Description and travel -- Continued
163	Early through 1800
	Cf. DG59.A4 Roman province of Africa
164	1801-1900
165	1901-1950
165.2	1951-
165.9	Pamphlets, etc.
	Ethnography see DT193+
	History
167	General works
	By period
	Carthaginian period
	For works on Carthage and its Empire see DT269.C3+
	Cf. DG241+ Roman conquest, 264-133 B.C.
168	General works
169	General special
169.5	Pamphlets, etc.
170	Roman period, 146 B.C.-439 A.D.
171	Vandals, 439-534
	Cf. D139 Migrations
172	Byzantine period
173	Arab conquest (to ca. 1516 or 1524)
174	16th-18th centuries
176	19th-20th centuries
176.2	21st century
177	Other
	Northwest Africa
	Including Maghrib, Mali, Mauretania, and other Sahara countries west of Libya (Collectively)
179.2	Periodicals. Societies. Serials
179.3	Guidebooks. Gazetteers
179.4	General works
179.5	Description and travel
179.6	Antiquities
179.7	Social life and customs. Civilization. Intellectual life
179.8	Ethnology
179.9	History
	Maghrib. Barbary States
	Including Libya, Tunisia, Algeria and Morocco (Collectively)
181	Periodicals. Societies
181.5	Congresses
182	Collections
183	Biography (Collective)
184	Guidebooks. Gazetteers. Directories, etc.
185	General works

	Maghrib. Barbary States -- Continued
	Description and travel
188	Early through 1800
189	1801-1900
190	1901-1950
190.2	1951-
191	Antiquities
192	Social life and customs. Civilization. Intellectual life
	Ethnography
193	General works
193.5.A-Z	Individual elements in the population, A-Z
193.5.A83	Atarantes
193.5.B45	Berbers
193.5.P64	Poles
	History
193.95	Historiography
194	General works
	Political and diplomatic history. Foreign and general relations
197	General works
197.5.A-Z	Relations with individual countries, A-Z
	By period
198	Early to 647
199	647-1516
	1516-1830. Period of piracy
	For relations with the United States see E335
201	General works
202	16th century
204	19th-20th centuries
205	21st century
	Libya
211	Periodicals. Societies
212	Collections
213	Biography (Collective)
214	Guidebooks. Gazetteers
215	General works
216	Historical geography
	Description and travel
218	Early through 1800
219	1801-1900
220	1901-1950
220.2	1951-1980
220.22	1981-
221	Antiquities
222	Social life and customs. Civilization. Intellectual life
	Ethnography
223	General works

Maghrib. Barbary States
Libya
Ethnography -- Continued
223.2.A-Z   Individual elements in the population, A-Z
223.2.B43   Bedouins
223.2.I73   Italians
223.2.T83   Tuaregs
223.2.T85   Turks
223.2.Z87   Zuwaya
History
223.3   Dictionaries. Chronological tables, etc.
Historiography
223.6   General works
Biography
223.8.A2   Collective
223.8.A3-Z   Individual, A-Z
224   General works
Political and diplomatic history. Foreign and general
relations
227   General works
227.5.A-Z   Relations with individual countries, A-Z
By period
228   Early to 642
229   642-1551
1551-1912
231   General works
1801-1912
233   General works
War with the United States see E335
234   Turco-Italian War, 1911-1912
235   1912-1951
235.5   1951-1969
236   1969-
Local history and description
238.A-Z   Provinces, regions, etc., A-Z
e.g.
238.C8   Cyrenaica. Barqah
238.F5   Fezzan
238.S3   Sahara
238.T5   Tibesti Mountains
Cf. DT546.4+ Chad
238.T8   Tripolitania
239.A-Z   Cities, towns, etc., A-Z
e.g.
239.C9   Cyrene
239.D4   Derna
239.J35   Jarmah

	Maghrib. Barbary States
	Libya
	Local history and description
	Cities, towns, etc., A-Z -- Continued
239.J4	Jebel Nefusa
239.L4	Leptis Magna
239.S115	Sabratha
239.S87	Surt Site
239.T6	Tolemaide
239.T7	Tripoli
	Tunisia (Tunis)
241	Periodicals. Societies
242	Collections
243	Biography (Collective)
244	Guidebooks. Gazetteers. Directories, etc.
245	General works
247.9	Historical geography
247.95	Geography
	Description and travel
248	Early through 1800
249	1801-1900
250	1901-1950
250.2	1951-
251	Antiquities
252	Social life and customs. Civilization. Intellectual life
	Ethnography
253	General works
253.2.A-Z	Individual elements in the population, A-Z
253.2.A43	Algerians
253.2.E8	Europeans
253.2.G74	Greeks
253.2.H35	Hammām (Arab tribe)
253.2.I8	Italians
253.2.M6	Moriscos
253.2.N65	Nomads
253.2.R8	Russians
	History
	Historiography
253.4	General works
	Biography of historians
253.5.A2	Collective
253.5.A3-Z	Individual, A-Z
254	General works
	Political and diplomatic history. Foreign and general relations
257	General works
257.5.A-Z	Relations with individual countries, A-Z

	Maghrib. Barbary States
	Tunisia
	History -- Continued
	By period
258	Early to 647
259	647-1516
	1516-1830. Period of piracy
261	General works
262	16th century
	Including Siege of Goletta, 1573
	1830-1881. 19th century
263	General works
	Biography and memoirs
263.75	Collective
263.76.A-Z	Individual, A-Z
	French protectorate, 1881-1956
263.9	Periodicals. Societies. Serials
263.95	Sources and documents
264	General works
264.25	Social life and customs. Civilization. Intellectual life
264.26	Military and naval history
264.27	Political history
264.28	Foreign and general relations
	Biography and memoirs
264.29	Collective
264.3.A-Z	Individual, A-Z
	e.g.
264.3.B6	Bourguiba, Habib, 1903-2000
264.3.L3	Lakdar, Mohamed
	1956-1987. Independence. Bourguiba administration
264.35	Periodicals. Societies. Serials
264.36	Congresses
264.37	Sources and documents
264.38	Collected works (nonserial)
264.39	Historiography
264.4	General works
264.42	General special
264.43	Addresses, essays, lectures
264.44	Social life and customs. Civilization. Intellectual life
264.45	Military and naval history
264.46	Political history
264.47	Foreign and general relations
	Biography and memoirs
264.48	Collective
264.49.A-Z	Individual, A-Z
	Bourguiba, Habib, 1903-2000 see DT264.3.B6
265	Battle of Bizerte, 1961

Maghrib. Barbary States
  Tunisia
    History
      By period -- Continued
        1987- . Bin 'Alī administration
          Including demonstrations, 2010-

266	Periodicals. Societies. Serials
266.2	Congresses
266.3	Sources and documents
266.4	General works
266.5	Social life and customs. Civilization. Intellectual life
266.6	Military and naval history
266.7	Political history
266.8	Foreign and general relations
	Biography and memoirs
266.9	Collective
266.92.A-Z	Individual, A-Z

Local history and description

268.A-Z	Districts, regions, etc., A-Z
	e.g.
	Jarbah see DT268.J4
268.J4	Jerba. Jarbah
268.N4	Nefzaoua
269.A-Z	Cities, towns, etc., A-Z
	e.g.
269.A23	Acholla (Extinct city)
269.A48	Althiburos (Tunisia)
269.B37	Belalis Maior
269.B6	Bizerta
269.B85	Bulla Regia
269.B98	Byzacena
	Carthage. Carthaginian Empire
	Cf. DG225.C37 Carthaginians in Italy
269.C3	Periodicals. Societies. Serials
269.C32	General works
269.C33	Antiquities
269.C34	Social life and customs. Civilization. Intellectual life
269.C35	History
	For Punic wars see DG242
269.C38	Carthaginian (Punic) colonies (Collectively)
269.C54	Cillium
269.H3	Hammamet
269.K3	Kairwan
269.K37	Kerkouane
269.K4	Khumir
269.L46	Leptis Minor
269.M28	Mactaris

	Maghrib. Barbary States
	Tunisia
	Local history and description
	Cities, towns, etc., A-Z -- Continued
269.M34	Mahrine Site
269.M6	Monastir
269.M87	Musti
269.P85	Pupput Site
269.Q24	Qafṣah
269.R35	Raqqada
269.S4	Ṣafāquis. Sfax
269.S57	Simithu
269.T48	Thugga
269.T52	Thysdrus
269.T8	Tunis
269.U73	Ureu
269.U78	Uthina
269.U8	Utica
	Algeria
271	Periodicals. Societies
	Museums, exhibitions, etc.
271.2	General works
271.3.A-Z	Individual. By place, A-Z
271.4	Congresses
272	Collections
273	Biography (Collective)
274	Guidebooks. Gazetteers. Directories, etc.
275	General works
276	Pictorial works
	Description and travel
277.8	History of travel
278	Early through 1800
279	1801-1900
280	1901-1950
280.2	1951-1980
280.3	1981-
281	Antiquities
282	Social life and customs. Civilization. Intellectual life
	For specific periods, see the period or reign
	Ethnography
283	General works
	Individual elements in the population
	Berbers
283.2	General works
283.3.A-Z	Individual groups, A-Z
	Kabyles see DT298.K2
	Arabs

Maghrib. Barbary States
  Algeria
    Ethnography
      Individual elements in the population
        Arabs -- Continued

283.4	General works
283.5.A-Z	Individual groups, A-Z
283.5.B44	Bedouins
283.6.A-Z	Other, A-Z
283.6.A44	Ajjer
283.6.C48	Christians
283.6.E95	Europeans
283.6.F7	French. Pieds noir
283.6.G47	Germans
283.6.I73	Italians
283.6.M35	Maltese
283.6.M55	Minorcans
283.6.N6	Nomads
283.6.P64	Poles
283.6.S62	Spaniards
283.6.T83	Tuaregs
	History
283.7	Dictionaries. Chronological tables, etc.
	Historiography
283.8	General works
	Biography
283.9	Collective
283.92.A-Z	Individual, A-Z
	Study and teaching
283.93	General works
283.94.A-Z	Local, A-Z
284	General works
285	General special
	Political and diplomatic history. Foreign and general relations
287	General works
287.5.A-Z	Relations with individual countries, A-Z
	By period
288	Early to 647
289	647-1516
	1516-1830. Period of piracy
291	General works
292	16th century
	War with the United States see E335
294	1830-1901
	1901-1945
294.5	General works

<table>
<tbody>
<tr><td></td><td>Maghrib. Barbary States</td></tr>
<tr><td></td><td>Algeria</td></tr>
<tr><td></td><td>History</td></tr>
<tr><td></td><td>By period</td></tr>
<tr><td></td><td>1901-1945 -- Continued</td></tr>
<tr><td></td><td>Biography and memoirs</td></tr>
<tr><td>294.7.A1</td><td>Collective</td></tr>
<tr><td>294.7.A2-Z</td><td>Individual, A-Z</td></tr>
<tr><td></td><td>e.g.</td></tr>
<tr><td>294.7.A3</td><td>'Abd al-Qādir ibn Muḥyī al-Dīn, Amir of Mascara.</td></tr>
<tr><td></td><td>عبد القادر محي الدين</td></tr>
<tr><td>294.7.E2</td><td>Eberhardt, Isabelle</td></tr>
<tr><td>294.7.E8</td><td>Étienne, Eugène</td></tr>
<tr><td>294.7.I52</td><td>Imache, Amar, 1895-1960</td></tr>
<tr><td>294.7.T5</td><td>Tidjani, Aurélie (Picard)</td></tr>
<tr><td></td><td>1945-1962</td></tr>
<tr><td></td><td>Including the Algerian Revolution, 1954-1962</td></tr>
<tr><td>295</td><td>General works</td></tr>
<tr><td></td><td>Biography and memoirs</td></tr>
<tr><td>295.3.A1</td><td>Collective</td></tr>
<tr><td>295.3.A2-Z</td><td>Individual, A-Z</td></tr>
<tr><td></td><td>e.g.</td></tr>
<tr><td>295.3.B6</td><td>Boupacha, Djamila</td></tr>
<tr><td></td><td>1962-1990</td></tr>
<tr><td>295.5</td><td>General works</td></tr>
<tr><td></td><td>Biography and memoirs</td></tr>
<tr><td>295.55.A1</td><td>Collective</td></tr>
<tr><td>295.55.A2-Z</td><td>Individual, A-Z</td></tr>
<tr><td></td><td>1990-</td></tr>
<tr><td>295.6</td><td>General works</td></tr>
<tr><td></td><td>Biography and memoirs</td></tr>
<tr><td>295.65</td><td>Collective</td></tr>
<tr><td>295.652.A-Z</td><td>Individual, A-Z</td></tr>
<tr><td>296</td><td>Other</td></tr>
<tr><td></td><td>Local history and description</td></tr>
<tr><td>298.A-Z</td><td>Departments, regions, etc., A-Z</td></tr>
<tr><td></td><td>e.g.</td></tr>
<tr><td>298.C7</td><td>Constantine</td></tr>
<tr><td>298.E7</td><td>Erg, El</td></tr>
<tr><td>298.K2</td><td>Kabylia (Great and Little)</td></tr>
<tr><td>298.O8</td><td>Oran</td></tr>
<tr><td>298.S6</td><td>Southern Territories</td></tr>
<tr><td>299.A-Z</td><td>Cities, towns, etc., A-Z</td></tr>
<tr><td></td><td>e.g.</td></tr>
<tr><td>299.A5</td><td>Algiers</td></tr>
<tr><td>299.B5</td><td>Biskra</td></tr>
<tr><td>299.B7</td><td>Bougie</td></tr>
</tbody>
</table>

	Maghrib. Barbary States
	Algeria
	Local history and description
	Cities, towns, etc., A-Z -- Continued
299.C5	Cherchel
299.C6	Constantine
299.N34	Nādōr Site
299.O7	Oran
	Thamugadi City see DT299.T5
299.T5	Timgad
299.T55	Tlemcen
299.T7	Touggourt. Tuggurt
	Tuggurt see DT299.T7
	Morocco
301	Periodicals. Societies
302	Collections
303	Biography (Collective)
304	Guidebooks. Gazetteers. Directories, etc.
305	General works
305.2	Pictorial works
306.5	Geography
	Description and travel
307	History of travel
308	Early through 1800
309	1801-1900
310	1901-1950
310.2	1951-1980
310.3	1981-
311	Antiquities
312	Social life and customs. Civilization. Intellectual life
	Ethnography
313	General works
	Individual elements in the population
	Berbers
313.2	General works
313.3.A-Z	Individual groups, A-Z
313.3.A35	Ahansala
313.3.A37	Ait Atta
313.3.A53	Amānūz. امانوز
313.3.A93	Ayash
	Beni Urriaghel see DT313.3.W35
313.3.B46	Beni Zerual
313.3.I33	Idaw Martini
313.3.I57	Īnūlatān. Oultanu. Ultānu. اينولتان
313.3.I65	Iqar'iyen
313.3.N4	Ndhir
	Oultanu see DT313.3.I57

Maghrib. Barbary States
Morocco
Ethnography
Individual elements in the population
Berbers
Individual groups, A-Z -- Continued
313.3.R53   Rif
313.3.S44   Seksawa
Ultānu see DT313.3.I57
313.3.W35   Waryaghel. Beni Urriaghel
Arabs
313.4   General works
313.5.A-Z   Individual groups, A-Z
313.5.U4   Ulad Stut
313.6.A-Z   Others, A-Z
313.6.F73   French
313.6.M67   Moriscos
History
313.7   Dictionaries. Chronological tables, outlines, etc.
313.75   Biography (Collective)
Historiography
313.8   General works
Biography of historians
313.82   Collective
313.83.A-Z   Individual, A-Z
314   General works
315   General special
316   Military and naval history
For individual campaigns and engagements, see the
special period or reign
317   Political and diplomatic history. Foreign and general
relations
For special periods, reigns, etc. see DT318+
317.5.A-Z   Relations with individual countries, A-Z
By period
318   Early to 647. Mauretania
319   647-1516
1516-1830. Period of piracy
321   General works
322   16th century
323.5   Ismail, 1672-1727
1830-1955
324   General works
Biography and memoirs
324.9   Collective
324.92.A-Z   Individual, A-Z
e.g.

	Maghrib. Barbary States
	Morocco
	History
	By period
	1830-1955
	Biography and memoirs
	Individual, A-Z -- Continued
324.92.A3	Abd el Krim, 1883-1963
324.92.M6	Muḥammad V, King of Morocco, 1909-1963
	1955-
325	Periodicals. Societies. Serials
325.15	Congresses
325.2	Sources and documents
325.23	Collected works (nonserial)
325.3	Historiography
325.4	General works
325.42	General special
325.45	Addresses, essays, lectures
325.5	Social life and customs. Civilization. Intellectual life
325.6	Military history
325.7	Political history
325.8	Foreign and general relations
	Biography and memoirs
325.9	Collective
325.92.A-Z	Individual, A-Z
	e.g.
325.92.B55	Bin Barakah, al-Mahdi, 1920-. المهدي ، بن بركة
325.92.H37	Hassan II, King of Morocco, 1929-
326	Moroccan-Spanish War, 1957-1958
326.3	Mohammed VI, 1999-
	Local history and description
328.A-Z	Regions, islands, etc., A-Z
	e.g.
328.A8	Atlas Mountains
328.P3	Peregil Island
328.R5	Rif Mountains
329.A-Z	Cities, towns, etc., A-Z
	e.g.
329.A7	Arzila
329.B35	Basra (Extinct city)
329.C3	Casablanca
329.C5	Ceuta (Spain)
329.E84	Essaouirá
329.L59	Lixus
329.M3	Marrakesh
329.M4	Melilla (Spain)
329.S12	Safi

Maghrib. Barbary States
  Morocco
    Local history and description
      Cities, towns, etc., A-Z -- Continued

329.T16	Tangier Zone. International Zone
329.T4	Tétouan
329.V6	Volubilis
330	Spanish Morocco

        Including Ifni; Northern and Southern Zones
    Sahara
      Cf. DT346.S7 Spanish Sahara
      Cf. DT548 West Sahara

331	Periodicals. Societies. Serials
332	Guidebooks. Gazetteers
333	General works. History. Description and travel
334	Juvenile works
335	Antiquities
337	Social life and customs. Civilization. Intellectual life
339	Other
346.A-Z	Regions, tribes, etc., A-Z
346.C5	Chaamba
346.D38	Daza
346.M5	Mekhadma
346.O8	Ouled Naïl
	Rio de Oro see DT346.S7
	Sekia el Hamra see DT346.S7
346.S7	Spanish Sahara. Western Sahara. Rio de Oro. Sekia el Hamra
346.T4	Teda. Tibbu
346.T7	Tuaregs
346.T8	Twat
	Western Sahara see DT346.S7

  Central Sub-Saharan Africa
    Including Sahara to Congo basin, travel across the continent by Congo and Lake Region, etc., to 1950, and biographies of explorers of the region
    For works by and about Sir Henry Morton Stanley see DT351.S6+
    For works by Theodore Roosevelt see SK252

348	Periodicals. Societies. Serials
	Museums, exhibitions, etc.
348.4	General works
348.5.A-Z	Individual. By place, A-Z
349	Congresses
349.2	Sources and documents
	Collected works (nonserial)
349.3	Several authors
349.4	Individual authors

	Central Sub-Saharan Africa -- Continued
349.5	Gazetteers. Dictionaries, etc.
349.6	Place names (General)
349.7	Directories
	Communication of information
349.72	General works
349.74	Electronic information resources
	Including computer network resources
349.8	Guidebooks
351	General works
351.5	Pictorial works
	Historic monuments, landmarks, etc. (General)
	For local, see specific countries
351.6	General works
351.7	Preservation
351.9	Geography
	Description and travel
	Early works through 1950 see DT351
352	1951-1980
352.2	1981-
352.3	Antiquities
352.4	Social life and customs. Civilization. Intellectual life
	Ethnography
352.42	General works
352.43.A-Z	Individual elements in the population, A-Z
352.43.E16	East Indians
352.43.G74	Greeks
352.43.M87	Muslims
352.43.P65	Poles
352.43.Z35	Zande
	History
	Study and teaching see DT19.8+
352.5	General works
352.6	Biography and memoirs
	By period
352.65	Early
352.7	Colonial
352.8	Independent
	Political and diplomatic history
353	General works
353.5.A-Z	Relations with individual countries, A-Z
	British Central Africa see DT2831+
	Wadai see DT546.49.W33
356	West Central Africa. West Sudan
	Including works by Paul Du Chaillu, Mungo Park, etc.
	Cf. DT470+ West coast and Guinea

Central Sub-Saharan Africa -- Continued
360   Niger River
      Cf. DT470+ West Coast
      Cf. DT521+ French West Africa
      Cf. DT547+ French Niger
    Lake Chad see DT546.49.L34
    East Central (Lake region)
      Including Ruwenzori Mountains (Mountains of the Moon)
      Cf. DT117 Sources of the Nile
      Cf. DT365+ East coast
361   Description and travel
    History
      Biography and memoirs
362   Collective
363   Emin Pasha. Exploration and relief expedition
363.2.A-Z   Other individual, A-Z
363.3   General works
    Eastern Africa
365   Periodicals. Societies. Serials
365.13   Sources and documents
365.15   Gazetteers. Dictionaries, etc.
365.17   Guidebooks
365.18   General works
365.19   Pictorial works
365.196   Geography
365.2   Description and travel
365.3   Antiquities
      For local antiquities see DT367+
365.4   Social life and customs. Civilization. Intellectual life
      For specific periods, see the period
    Ethnography
365.42   General works
365.45.A-Z   Individual elements in the population, A-Z
365.45.B87   Burji
365.45.S93   Swahili-speaking peoples
    History
365.47   Biography (Collective)
      For individual biography, see the specific period, reign, or place
365.5   General works
365.58   Military history
365.59   Political history
      For specific periods, see the period

	Eastern Africa
	History -- Continued
	Foreign and general relations
	For general works on the diplomatic history of a period, see the period
	For works on relations with a specific country regardless of period see DT365.63.A+
365.62	General works
365.63.A-Z	Relations with the individual countries, A-Z
	By period
365.65	Early to 1886
	Biography and memoirs
	Class biography under individual country except for those persons who are associated with more than one country or who inhabited a region that does not correspond to a modern jurisdiction
365.654	Collective
365.655.A-Z	Individual, A-Z
	1886-1960
365.7	General works
	Biography and memoirs
	Class biography under individual country except for those persons who are associated with more than one country or who inhabited a region that does not correspond to a modern jurisdiction
365.74	Collective
365.75.A-Z	Individual, A-Z
365.76	1886-1918
365.77	1918-1960
365.78	1960-
	Northeast Africa
	Including Sudan, Ethiopia, Somalia and Djibouti (Collectively)
367	Periodicals. Societies. Serials
367.13	Sources and documents
367.17	Guidebooks
367.18	General works
367.19	Pictorial works
367.2	Description and travel
367.4	Social life and customs. Civilization. Intellectual life
	For specific periods, see the period
	Ethnography
367.42	General works
367.45.A-Z	Individual elements in the population, A-Z
367.45.C86	Cushites
	History
367.5	General works

	Eastern Africa
	Northeast Africa
	History -- Continued
367.59	Political history
	For specific periods, see the period
	Foreign and general relations
	For general works on the diplomatic history of a period, see the period
	For works on relations with a specific country regardless of period see DT367.63.A+
367.62	General works
367.63.A-Z	Relations with individual countries, A-Z
	By period
367.65	Early to 1900
	1900-1974
367.75	General works
	Biography and memoirs
	Class biography under individual country except for those persons who are associated with more than one country or who inhabited a region that does not correspond to a modern jurisdiction
367.76	Collective
367.77.A-Z	Individual, A-Z
367.8	1974-
	Local history and description
	see the individual country
	Ethiopia (Abyssinia)
371	Periodicals. Societies. Serials
371.2	Congresses
371.5	Gazetteers. Dictionaries, etc.
372	Guidebooks
373	General works
374	General special
374.3	Pictorial works
	Description and travel
375	Early through 1400
376	1401-1700
377	1701-1900
378	1901-1950
378.2	1951-1980
378.3	1981-
379	Antiquities
379.5	Social life and customs. Civilization. Intellectual life
	Ethnography
380	General works
380.4.A-Z	Individual elements in the population, A-Z
380.4.A33	Afar

	Eastern Africa
	Ethiopia (Abyssinia)
	Ethnography
	Individual elements in the population, A-Z -- Continued
380.4.A43	Amhara
380.4.A68	Arbore
380.4.A69	Argobba
380.4.A7	Armenians
380.4.B37	Bashada
380.4.B45	Beja
380.4.B6	Bogos
380.4.B64	Boran
380.4.D3	Dasanetch
380.4.D37	Dawro
380.4.D57	Dizi
380.4.D67	Dorze
	Falashas see DS135.E75
	Gallas see DT390.G2
380.4.G19	Gamo
380.4.G35	Gimiras
380.4.G66	Gonga
380.4.G72	Greeks
380.4.G85	Gurage
380.4.H33	Hadiya
380.4.H36	Hamar
380.4.H38	Harari
380.4.K34	Kambata
380.4.K36	Karrayu
380.4.K45	Kemants
380.4.K65	Konsos
380.4.M3	Majangirs
380.4.M32	Male
380.4.M45	Mekan
380.4.M85	Murzu
380.4.M87	Muslims
380.4.N54	Nilotic peoples
380.4.N84	Nuer
380.4.N92	Nyangatom
380.4.O23	Ochollo
	Oromo see DT390.G2
380.4.S5	Sidamas
380.4.S65	Somalis
380.4.S87	Suri
380.4.S94	Swedes
380.4.T54	Tigrinya
380.4.Z39	Zay
	History

	Eastern Africa
	Ethiopia (Abyssinia)
	History -- Continued
	Historiography
380.5	General works
	Biography of historians, area studies specialists, archaeologists, etc.
380.6	Collective
380.62.A-Z	Individual, A-Z
	Study and teaching
380.8.A-.Z8	General works
380.8.Z9	Catalogs of audiovisual materials
380.85.A-Z	By region or country, A-Z
380.9.A-Z	Individual schools, A-Z
381	General works
382	Pamphlets, etc.
	Political and diplomatic history. Foreign and general relations
382.3	General works
382.5.A-Z	Relations with individual countries, A-Z
	By period
383	Early through 1500
384	16th-18th centuries
	19th-20th centuries
386	General works
386.3	Theodore II, 1855-1868
	John IV, 1872-1889
386.7	General works on life and reign
	Biography and memoirs
386.72	Collective
386.73.A-Z	Individual, A-Z
	Menelik II, 1889-1913
387	General works
387.3	War with Italy, 1895-1896
	Biography and memoirs
387.33	Collective
387.34.A-Z	Individual, A-Z
387.5	Lij Yasu, 1913-1916
387.6	Waizeru Zauditu and Ras Taffari (Tafari) Makonnen, 1916-1928
	Haile Selassie I, 1928-1974
387.7	General works
387.8	Italo-Ethiopian War, 1935-1936
387.8.A1	Collections
	Documents
387.8.A2	League of Nations (as author)
387.8.A3-.A5	Italy

                              Eastern Africa
                                Ethiopia (Abyssinia)
                                  History
                                    By period
                                      19th-20th centuries
                                        Haile Selassie I, 1928-1974
                                          Italo-Ethiopian War, 1935-1936
                                            Documents -- Continued
387.8.A6   Ethiopia
387.8.A7A-.A7Z   Other countries, A-Z
387.8.A8-Z   General works. By author
387.9   1936-1974
                                            Biography and memoirs of contemporaries
387.92.A2   Collective
387.92.A3-Z   Individual, A-Z
                                          1974-1991
387.95   General works
387.952   Somali-Ethiopian Conflict, 1977-
                                            Biography and memoirs
387.953   Collective
387.954.A-Z   Individual, A-Z
                                          1991-
388   General works
                                            Biography and memoirs
388.33   Collective
388.34.A-Z   Individual, A-Z
388.35   Eritrean-Ethiopian War, 1998-
390.A-Z   Kingdoms, regions, cities, etc., A-Z
                                         e.g.
390.A3   Addis Ababa
                                         Afar see DT390.D28
                                         Aksum Kingdom see DT390.A88
390.A88   Axum. Aksum Kingdom
390.B5   Blue Nile
390.D28   Danakil. Afar
390.G2   Gallas (Galla, Oromo)
                                           Including territory
390.H3   Harar
390.K3   Kaffa (Kafa)
390.O33   Ogaden
390.T5   Tigré
390.T8   Tsana (Tana) Lake
                                  Eritrea
391   Periodicals. Societies. Serials
392.8   Guidebooks
393   General works
393.34   Description and travel

	Eastern Africa
	Eritrea -- Continued
393.35	Antiquities
	For local antiquities see DT398.A+
393.4	Social life and customs. Civilization. Intellectual life
	For specific periods, see the period or reign
	Ethnography
393.5	General works
393.55.A-Z	Individual elements in the population, A-Z
393.55.K85	Kunama
	History
393.7	Historiography
394	General works
	By period
394.5	Early to 1890
395	1890-1941. Italian domination
395.3	1941-1952. British administration
	Including United Nations investigations
395.5	1952-1962. Federation with Ethiopia
397	1962-1993. Annexation to Ethiopia
	Including civil war and liberation movements
397.3	1993- . Independence
	For Eritrean-Ethiopian War, 1998- , see DT388.35
398.A-Z	Regions, cities, etc., A-Z
	e.g.
	Danakil see DT390.D28
398.M3	Massaua (Massawa)
398.P8	Punt (Kingdom)
	Somalia. Somaliland and adjacent territory
	Italian and British Somaliland
	Cf. DT391+ Eritrea
	Cf. DT411+ French Territory of the Afars and Issas;
	French Somaliland; Djibouti
401	Periodicals. Societies. Serials
401.13	Congresses
401.15	Sources and documents
401.2	Gazetteers. Dictionaries, etc.
401.4	Guidebooks
401.5	General works
401.6	General special
401.7	Pictorial works
401.8	Description and travel
402	Antiquities
	For local antiquities see DT409.A+
402.2	Social life and customs. Civilization. Intellectual life
	For specific periods, see the period or reign
	Ethnography

	Eastern Africa
	Somalia. Somaliland and adjacent territory
	Ethnography -- Continued
402.3	General works
402.4.A-Z	Individual elements in the population, A-Z
402.4.B36	Bantu
402.4.R35	Rahanweyn
402.45	Somalis in foreign countries
	For Somalis in a particular country, see the country
	History
	Periodicals. Societies. Serials see DT401
402.5	Dictionaries. Chronological tables, outlines, etc.
402.6	Biography (Collective)
	For individual biography, see the specific period, reign, or place
402.8	Historiography
403	General works
403.15	Juvenile works
403.2	General special
403.25	Political history
	For specific periods, see the period or reign
	Foreign and general relations
	For general works on the diplomatic history of a period, see the period
	For works on relations with a specific country regardless of period see DT403.4.A+
403.3	General works
403.4.A-Z	Relations with individual countries, A-Z
	By period
	Early to 1889
	Including Egyptian occupation and activities of the British East Africa Company
403.5	General works
	Biography and memoirs
403.6	Collective
403.7.A-Z	Individual, A-Z
	1885-1941. British Somaliland. British Protectorate
404	General works
	Biography and memoirs
404.2	Collective
404.3.A-Z	Individual, A-Z
	1889-1941. Italian Somaliland
405	General works
	Biography and memoirs
405.2	Collective
405.3.A-Z	Individual, A-Z

Eastern Africa
  Somalia. Somaliland and adjacent territory
    History
      By period -- Continued
        1941-1960. British military administration. United
          Nations trusteeship

406	General works
	Biography and memoirs
406.2	Collective
406.3.A-Z	Individual, A-Z
	1960-
	For Somali-Ethiopian Conflict see DT387.952
407	General works
	Biography and memoirs
407.2	Collective
407.3.A-Z	Individual, A-Z
	1991-
407.4	General works
407.42	Operation Restore Hope, 1992-1993
407.43	Somalia Affair, 1992-1997
409.A-Z	Local history and description, A-Z
	e.g.
409.G58	Giuba. Oltre Giuba. Jubaland
	Jubaland see DT409.G58
	Oltre Giuba (Italian colony) see DT409.G58
	Djibouti. French Territory of the Afars and Issas. French
	Somaliland
411	Periodicals. Societies. Serials
411.13	Sources and documents
411.15	Gazetteers. Dictionaries, etc.
411.2	Guidebooks
411.22	General works
411.24	Pictorial works
411.27	Description and travel
411.4	Social life and customs. Civilization. Intellectual life
	For specific periods, see the period
	Ethnography
411.42	General works
411.45.A-Z	Individual elements in the population, A-Z
411.45.A35	Afar
	History
411.5	General works
	Foreign and general relations
	For general works on the diplomatic history of a period, see
	the period
	For works on relations with a specific country
	regardless of period see DT411.63.A+

	Eastern Africa
	Djibouti. French Territory of the Afars and Issas. French
	Somaliland
	History
	Foreign and general relations -- Continued
411.62	General works
411.63.A-Z	Relations with individual countries, A-Z
	By period
411.65	Early to 1883
	1883-1977
411.75	General works
	Biography and memoirs
411.76	Collective
411.77.A-Z	Individual, A-Z
	1977- . Independent
411.8	General works
	Biography and memoirs
411.82	Collective
411.83.A-Z	Individual, A-Z
411.9.A-Z	Local history and description, A-Z
	Danakil see DT390.D28
	East Africa. British East Africa
	Including Uganda, Kenya, and Tanzania (Collectively)
421	Periodicals. Societies. Serials
421.2	Sources and documents
421.5	Gazetteers. Dictionaries, etc.
422	Guidebooks
423	General works
423.5	Pictorial works
	Description and travel
424	Through 1799
425	1800-1950
426	1951-1980
427	1981-
428	Antiquities
428.5	Social life and customs. Civilization. Intellectual life
	For specific periods, see the period
	Ethnography
429	General works
429.5.A-Z	Individual elements in the population, A-Z
429.5.A37	Afrikaners
429.5.A38	African Americans
429.5.E27	East Indians
429.5.I7	Iranians
429.5.K35	Kalenjin
429.5.M86	Muslims
429.5.S68	South Asians

	Eastern Africa
	East Africa. British East Africa
	Ethnography
	Individual elements in the population, A-Z -- Continued
429.5.S94	Swahili-speaking peoples
	History
430	Biography (Collective)
	For individual biography, see the specific period or place
	Historiography
430.5	General works
	Biography of historians, area studies specialists, archaeologists, etc.
430.6	Collective
430.7.A-Z	Individual, A-Z
431	General works
432	General special
	Foreign and general relations
	For general works on the diplomatic history of a period, see the period
	For works on relations with a specific country regardless of period see DT432.4.A+
432.3	General works
432.4.A-Z	Relations with individual countries, A-Z
	By period
	Early to 1960 see DT431
432.5	1960-
	Uganda
433.2	Periodicals. Societies. Serials
433.213	Sources and documents
433.215	Gazetteers. Dictionaries, etc.
433.217	Place names (General)
433.22	Guidebooks
433.222	General works
433.223	General special
433.224	Pictorial works
	Historic monuments, landmarks, scenery, etc. (General)
	For local see DT433.29.A+
433.225	General works
433.226	Preservation
433.227	Description and travel
433.23	Antiquities
	For local antiquities see DT433.29.A+
433.24	Social life and customs. Civilization. Intellectual life
	For specific periods, see the period or reign
	Ethnography
433.242	General works
433.245.A-Z	Individual elements in the population, A-Z

	Eastern Africa
	East Africa. British East Africa
	Uganda
	Ethnography
	Individual elements in the population, A-Z -- Continued
433.245.A35	Acoli
433.245.B35	Bahima
433.245.B36	Batwa
433.245.B38	Bavuma
433.245.C55	Chiga
433.245.D63	Dodoth
433.245.E18	East Indians
433.245.G35	Ganda
433.245.G57	Gisu
433.245.H38	Haya
433.245.I37	Ik
433.245.K35	Karamojong
433.245.L3	Labwor
433.245.L36	Lango
433.245.L83	Lugbara
433.245.N9	Nyankole
433.245.N96	Nyoro
433.245.S24	Sapiny
433.245.S64	Soga
433.245.S92	Sudanese
433.245.T47	Teso
433.245.T66	Tooro
	History
433.252	Biography (Collective)
	For individual biography, see the specific period or reign
433.255	Historiography
433.257	General works
433.26	Political history
	For specific periods, see the period or reign
	Foreign and general relations
	For general works on the diplomatic history of a period, see the period
	For works on relations with a specific country regardless of period see DT433.263.A+
433.262	General works
433.263.A-Z	Relations with individual countries, A-Z
	By period
	Early to 1890
433.265	General works
	Biography and memoirs
433.266	Collective
433.267.A-Z	Individual, A-Z

Eastern Africa
East Africa. British East Africa
Uganda
History
By period -- Continued
1890-1962
Including the Lugard Accords, activities of the British
East Africa Company, and Buganda dominance

433.27	General works
	Biography and memoirs
433.272	Collective
433.273.A-Z	Individual, A-Z
	1962-1979. Independent
433.275	General works
	Biography and memoirs
433.279	Collective
433.28.A-Z	Individual, A-Z
433.282	1962-1971
433.283	1971-1979. Amin regime
	Including Uganda-Tanzania War, 1978-1979
	1979-
433.285	General works
	Biography and memoirs
433.286	Collective
433.287.A-Z	Individual, A-Z
433.29.A-Z	Local history and description, A-Z
	Kenya
	For works on former British East Africa as a whole see DT421+
433.5	Periodicals. Societies. Serials
433.512	Congresses
433.513	Sources and documents
433.515	Gazetteers. Dictionaries, etc.
433.517	Place names (General)
	For etymological studies, see class P
433.52	Guidebooks
433.522	General works
433.523	General special
433.524	Pictorial works
	Historic monuments, landmarks, scenery, etc. (General)
	For local see DT434.A+
433.525	General works
433.526	Preservation
433.527	Description and travel
433.53	Antiquities
	For local antiquities see DT434.A+

	Eastern Africa
	East Africa. British East Africa
	Kenya -- Continued
433.54	Social life and customs. Civilization. Intellectual life
	For specific periods, see the period or reign
	Ethnography
433.542	General works
433.545.A-Z	Individual elements in the population, A-Z
433.545.A75	Ariaal
433.545.B67	Boran
433.545.B74	British
433.545.B84	Bukusu
433.545.D54	Digo
433.545.D67	Dorobo
433.545.E27	East Indians
	Cf. DT433.545.G62 Goanese
	Cf. DT433.545.G84 Gujaratis
433.545.E45	Elmolo
433.545.E48	Embu
433.545.E53	Endorois
433.545.G55	Giryama
433.545.G62	Goanese
433.545.G84	Gujaratis
433.545.G86	Gusii
433.545.I24	Ibibios
433.545.K36	Kamba
433.545.K55	Kikuyu
433.545.K57	Kipsigis
433.545.K87	Kuria
(433.545.K88)	Kusu
	see DT433.545.B84
433.545.L63	Logooli
433.545.L85	Luo
433.545.L88	Luyia
433.545.M32	Marakwet
433.545.M33	Masai
433.545.M34	Mbere
433.545.M47	Meru
433.545.M54	Mijikenda
433.545.M87	Muslims
433.545.N34	Nandi
(433.545.N55)	Nika
	see DT433.545.M54
433.545.N83	Nubi
433.545.O74	Oromo
433.545.P36	Panjabis
433.545.P65	Pokomo

Eastern Africa
  East Africa. British East Africa
    Kenya
      Ethnography
        Individual elements in the population, A-Z -- Continued

433.545.R45	Rendille
433.545.R83	Rwandans
433.545.S26	Samburu
433.545.S75	Somalis
433.545.S77	South Asians
433.545.S83	Suba
433.545.S85	Suk
433.545.S93	Swahili-speaking peoples
433.545.T3	Tachoni
433.545.T34	Taita
433.545.T38	Taveta
433.545.T57	Tiriki
433.545.T87	Turkana
433.545.Y32	Yaaku

      History

433.552	Biography (Collective)
	For individual biography, see the specific period, reign, or place
433.555	Historiography
433.557	General works
433.558	General special
433.559	Political history
	For specific periods, see the period or reign
	Foreign and general relations
	For general works on the diplomatic history of a period, see the period
	For works on relations with a specific country regardless of period see DT433.563.A+
433.562	General works
433.563.A-Z	Relations with individual countries, A-Z
	By period
	Early to 1886
	Including Arab and Portuguese penetration; coastal domination by the Sultanate of Zanzibar
433.565	General works
	Biography and memoirs
433.566	Collective
433.567.A-Z	Individual, A-Z

<table>
<tr><td></td><td>Eastern Africa</td></tr>
<tr><td></td><td>East Africa. British East Africa</td></tr>
<tr><td></td><td>Kenya</td></tr>
<tr><td></td><td>History</td></tr>
<tr><td></td><td>By period -- Continued</td></tr>
<tr><td></td><td>1886-1920. East African Protectorate (1895-1920)</td></tr>
<tr><td></td><td>Including Anglo-German accords on Zanzibar, activities of the British East Africa Company in Kenya, and German claims to the Witu Protectorate.</td></tr>
<tr><td></td><td>Cf. DT433.27+ British East Africa Company in general, and in Uganda</td></tr>
</table>

433.57	General works
	Biography and memoirs
433.572	Collective
433.573.A-Z	Individual, A-Z
	1920-1963. Kenya Colony and Protectorate
433.575	General works
	Biography and memoirs
433.576.A2	Collective
433.576.A3-Z	Individual, A-Z
433.577	Mau Mau movement
	1963-
433.58	General works
	Biography and memoirs
433.582.A2	Collective
433.582.A3-Z	Individual, A-Z
433.583	1963-1978
433.584	1978-2002
433.586	2002-
434.A-Z	Local history and description, A-Z
	Jubaland see DT409.G58
(435)	Zanzibar
	see DT449.Z2+
	Tanzania. Tanganyika. German East Africa
	Cf. DT450+ Rwanda. Ruanda-Urundi
	Cf. DT450.5+ Burundi
436	Periodicals. Societies. Serials
	Museums, exhibitions, etc.
436.2	General works
436.32.A-Z	By place, A-Z
	Subarrange by author
437	Dictionaries. Gazetteers, etc.
437.7	Guidebooks
438	General works
438.3	Pictorial works
438.7	Historical geography
	Description and travel

	Eastern Africa
	Tanzania. Tanganyika. German East Africa
	Description and travel -- Continued
439	Early through 1918
440	1919-1980
440.5	1981-
442	Antiquities
442.5	Social life and customs. Civilization. Intellectual life
	Ethnography
443	General works
443.3.A-Z	Individual elements in the population, A-Z
443.3.A78	Asu. Pare
443.3.B35	Bantu
443.3.B37	Barabaig
443.3.B38	Baraguyu. Parakuyo
443.3.B45	Bena
443.3.B65	Bondei
	Chaga see DT443.3.W33
443.3.E38	East Indians
443.3.F56	Fipa
443.3.G64	Gogo
443.3.G88	Gusii
443.3.H37	Hatsa
443.3.H39	Haya
443.3.H67	Horombo
443.3.H88	Hutu
443.3.I8	Iraqw
443.3.I85	Italians
443.3.K33	Kaguru
443.3.K47	Kerebe
443.3.K54	Kilindi
443.3.K57	Kisongo
443.3.K87	Kuria
443.3.L84	Luguru
443.3.M34	Makonde
443.3.M36	Mamvu
443.3.M37	Masai
443.3.M39	Matengo
443.3.M47	Meru
443.3.N43	Ndendeuli
443.3.N54	Ngoni
443.3.N58	Ngulu
443.3.N92	Nyakyusa
443.3.N93	Nyamwezi
	Parakuyo see DT443.3.B38
(443.3.P37)	Pare
	see DT443.3.A78

Eastern Africa
Tanzania. Tanganyika. German East Africa
Ethnography
Individual elements in the population, A-Z -- Continued

443.3.R35	Rangi
443.3.R64	Rogoro
443.3.R88	Ruvu
443.3.S45	Shambala
443.3.S75	Sonjo
443.3.S77	South Africans
443.3.S78	South Asians
443.3.S86	Sukuma
443.3.S92	Swahili-speaking peoples
(443.3.T32)	Tabwa
	see DT650.T32
(443.3.W32)	Wabena
	see DT443.3.B45
443.3.W33	Wachaga. Chaga
443.3.W36	Wapangwa
(443.3.W39)	Wazaramo
	see DT443.3.Z37
443.3.Z35	Zanaki
443.3.Z37	Zaramo
443.3.Z53	Zigula

History

443.4	Dictionaries. Chronological tables, outlines, etc.
443.5	Biography (Collective)
	For individual biography, see the specific period, reign, or place
444	General works
445	Political history
	For specific periods, see the period or reign
	Foreign and general relations
	For general works on the diplomatic history of a period, see the period
	For works on relations with a specific country regardless of period see DT445.5.A+
445.3	General works
445.5.A-Z	Relations with individual countries, A-Z
	By period
	Early and colonial
447	General works
	Biography and memoirs
447.2.A2	Collective
447.2.A3-Z	Individual, A-Z
448	Independent, 1961-1964

Eastern Africa
  Tanzania. Tanganyika. German East Africa
    History
      By period -- Continued
        1964- , United Republic of Tanzania
          For Uganda-Tanzania War, 1978-1979 see
            DT433.283

448.2	General works
	Biography and memoirs
448.25.A2	Collective
448.25.A3-Z	Individual, A-Z
449.A-Z	Regions, cities, etc., A-Z
	e.g.
449.I7	Iringa
449.K4	Kilimanjaro
449.K45	Kilwa Kisiwani Island
	Zanzibar
449.Z2	Periodicals. Societies. Serials
449.Z22	Guidebooks
449.Z23	General works
449.Z24	Pictorial works
449.Z25	Description and travel
	History
449.Z26	General works
	By period
	Early to 1890
449.Z27	General works
	Biography and memoirs
449.Z273	Collective
449.Z274A-.Z274Z	Individual, A-Z
449.Z28	1890-1963
449.Z29	1963-

           For works about Zanzibar and Tanganyika
            treated together see DT448.2+
  Rwanda. Ruanda-Urundi
    Class here also works on Rwanda and Burundi collectively
    For works on German East Africa as a whole see
      DT436+
    For works on Burundi alone see DT450.5+

450	Periodicals. Societies. Serials
450.115	Gazetteers. Dictionaries, etc.
450.12	Place names (General)
	For etymological studies, see class P
450.13	Guidebooks
450.14	General works
450.15	General special
450.16	Pictorial works

Eastern Africa
Rwanda. Ruanda-Urundi -- Continued
Historic monuments, landmarks, scenery, etc. (General)
For local see DT450.49.A+
450.17   General works
450.18   Preservation
450.2   Description and travel
450.22   Antiquities
For local antiquities see DT450.49.A+
450.23   Social life and customs. Civilization. Intellectual life
For specific periods, see the period or reign
Ethnography
450.24   General works
450.25.A-Z   Individual elements in the population, A-Z
450.25.B38   Batwa
450.25.H86   Hutu
History
450.26   Biography (Collective)
For individual biography, see the specific period, reign, or
place
450.27   Historiography
450.28   General works
450.3   Political history
For specific periods, see the period or reign
Foreign and general relations
For general works on the diplomatic history of a period, see
the period
For works on relations with a specific country
regardless of period see DT450.33.A+
450.32   General works
450.33.A-Z   Relations with individual countries, A-Z
By period
Early to 1890. Rwanda (Kingdom)
450.34   General works
Biography and memoirs
450.35   Collective
450.36.A-Z   Individual, A-Z
1890-1916. German domination
450.37   General works
Biography and memoirs
450.38   Collective
450.39.A-Z   Individual, A-Z
1916-1945. Belgian domination. League of Nations
mandate
450.4   General works
Biography and memoirs
450.42   Collective

Eastern Africa
 Rwanda. Ruanda-Urundi
  History
   By period
    1916-1945. Belgian domination. League of Nations
     mandate
     Biography and memoirs -- Continued

450.422.A-Z	Individual, A-Z
	1945-1962. United Nations mandate. Belgian administration
450.425	General works
	Biography and memoirs
450.426	Collective
450.427.A-Z	Individual, A-Z
450.43	Civil War, 1959-1962
450.432	Gitarama coup d'etat and disolution of Rwanda-Tutsi monarchy, 1961
	1962-1994
	Including the Civil War and genocide of 1994
450.435	General works
	Biography and memoirs
450.436	Collective
450.437.A-Z	Individual, A-Z
	1994-
450.44	General works
	Biography and memoirs
450.442	Collective
450.443.A-Z	Individual, A-Z
450.49.A-Z	Local history and description, A-Z
	Burundi
	For works on German East Africa as a whole see DT436+
	For works on Rwanda and Burundi collectively and for works on Ruanda-Urundi see DT450+
450.5	Periodicals. Societies. Serials
450.515	Gazetteers. Dictionaries, etc.
450.52	Place names (General)
	For etymological studies, see class P
450.53	Guidebooks
450.54	General works
450.55	General special
450.56	Pictorial works
	Historic monuments, landmarks, scenery, etc. (General)
	For local see DT450.95.A+
450.57	General works
450.58	Preservation
450.6	Description and travel

	Eastern Africa
	Burundi -- Continued
450.62	Antiquities
	For local antiquities see DT450.95.A+
450.63	Social life and customs. Civilization. Intellectual life
	For specific periods, see the period or reign
	Ethnography
450.64	General works
450.65.A-Z	Individual elements in the population, A-Z
450.65.H87	Hutu
450.65.M87	Muslims
450.65.R86	Rundi
450.65.T87	Tutsi
	History
450.66	Biography (Collective)
	For individual biography, see the specific period, reign or place
450.67	Historiography
450.68	General works
450.7	Political history
	For specific periods, see the period or reign
	Foreign and general relations
	For general works on the diplomatic history of a period, see the period
	For works on relations with a specific country regardless of period see DT450.73.A+
450.72	General works
450.73.A-Z	Relations with individual countries, A-Z
	By period
	Early to 1890. Burundi (Kingdom)
450.74	General works
	Biography and memoirs
450.75	Collective
450.76.A-Z	Individual, A-Z
	1890-1916. German domination
450.77	General works
	Biography and memoirs
450.78	Collective
450.79.A-Z	Individual, A-Z
	1916-1945. Belgian domination. League of Nations mandate
450.8	General works
	Biography and memoirs
450.82	Collective
450.83.A-Z	Individual, A-Z
	1945-1962. United Nations mandate. Belgian administration

	Eastern Africa
	Burundi
	History
	By period
	1945-1962. United Nations mandate. Belgian administration -- Continued
450.84	General works
	Biography and memoirs
450.842	Collective
450.843.A-Z	Individual, A-Z
	1962-1993
450.85	General works
	Biography and memoirs
450.852	Collective
450.853.A-Z	Individual, A-Z
450.855	Dissolution of Burundi Tutsi monarch, 1966
	1993-
450.86	General works
	Biography and memoirs
450.862	Collective
450.863.A-Z	Individual, A-Z
450.95.A-Z	Local history and description, A-Z
	Islands (East African coast)
468	General works
468.2	Description and travel
	Ethnography
468.42	General works
468.45.A-Z	Individual elements in the population, A-Z
468.45.C45	Chinese
469.A-Z	Individual islands, A-Z
469.A6	Amirante islands
469.C7	Comoros
	Cf. DT469.M4975 Mayotte
	Madagascar
469.M21	Periodicals. Societies. Serials
469.M22	Sources and documents
469.M24	Gazetteers. Dictionaries, etc.
469.M242	Place names (General)
	For etymological studies, see class P
469.M25	Guidebooks
469.M26	General works
469.M262	General special
469.M265	Pictorial works
	Historic monuments, landmarks, scenery, etc. (General)
	For local see DT469.M37+
469.M266	General works

	Eastern Africa
	Islands (East African coast)
	Individual islands, A-Z
	Madagascar
	Historic monuments, landmarks, scenery, etc.
	(General) -- Continued
469.M267	Preservation
469.M273	Antiquities
	For local antiquities see DT469.M37+
469.M274	Social life and customs. Civilization. Intellectual life
	For specific periods, see the period or reign
	Ethnography
469.M276	General works
469.M277A-.M277Z	Individual elements in the population, A-Z
469.M277A58	Antandroy
469.M277B37	Bara
469.M277B47	Betsileo
469.M277B48	Betsimisaraka
469.M277B49	Bezanozano
469.M277G84	Gujarati
	Hovas see DT469.M277M47
469.M277M34	Mahafaly
469.M277M45	Menabe
469.M277M47	Merina
469.M277S33	Sahafatra
469.M277S35	Sakalava
469.M277T34	Taimoro
469.M277T35	Tanala
469.M277T75	Tsimahafotsy
469.M277T78	Tsimihety
469.M277V39	Vazimba
469.M277V48	Vezo
469.M277Z24	Zafimaniry
	Description and travel
	To 1810 see DT469.M31+
	1810-1900 see DT469.M32+
469.M28	1901-
	History
469.M282	Biography (Collective)
	For individual biography, see the specific period, reign or place
	Historiography
469.M283	General works
	Biography of historians, area studies specialists, archaeologists, etc.
469.M2835	Collective
469.M284A-.M284Z	Individual, A-Z

	Eastern Africa
	Islands (East African coast)
	Individual islands, A-Z
	Madagascar
	History -- Continued
	Study and teaching
469.M2848	General works
469.M2849A- .M2849Z	Local, A-Z
469.M285	General works
469.M287	General special
469.M292	Political history
	For specific periods, see the period or reign
	Foreign and general relations
	For general works on the diplomatic history of a period, see the period
	For works on relations with a specific country regardless of period see DT469.M297A+
469.M295	General works
469.M297A-.M297Z	Relations with individual countries, A-Z
	By period
	Early to 1810. Early description and travel
469.M31	General works
	Biography and memoirs
469.M312	Collective
469.M313A-.M313Z	Individual, A-Z
	1810-1885. 19th century. Hòva rule
469.M32	General works
	Biography and memoirs
469.M321	Collective
469.M322A-.M322Z	Individual, A-Z
469.M323	Radama I, 1810-1828
469.M324	Ranavalona I (Ranavalo), 1828-1861
469.M326	Radama II, 1861-1863
469.M328	Rasoherina, 1863-1868
469.M33	Ranavalona II (Ranavalo II), 1868-1883
469.M335	Ranavalona III (Ranavalo III), 1883-1897
	1885-1960. French protectorate and colony
469.M34	General works
	Biography and memoirs
469.M341	Collective
469.M342A-.M342Z	Individual, A-Z
	1960- . (Malagasy Republic)
469.M343	General works
	Biography and memoirs
469.M344	Collective
469.M345A-.M345Z	Individual, A-Z

	Eastern Africa
	Islands (East African coast)
	Individual islands, A-Z
	Madagascar -- Continued
	Local history and description
469.M37A-.M37Z	Provinces, etc., A-Z
	e.g.
469.M37A52	Ambato-Boeni
469.M37A53	Androy
469.M37N67	Nossi-Be
469.M38A-.M38Z	Cities, towns, etc., A-Z
	e.g.
	Antananarivo see DT469.M38T34
469.M38T33	Tamatave
469.M38T34	Tananarive. Antananarivo
469.M39	Mascarene Islands
	Mauritius (Ile de France)
	Including Agalega, Rodrigues, and St. Brandon
469.M4	Periodicals. Societies. Serials
469.M413	Sources and documents
469.M415	Gazetteers. Dictionaries, etc.
469.M417	Place names (General)
	For etymological studies, see class P
469.M42	Guidebooks
469.M422	General works
469.M423	General special
469.M425	Pictorial works
	Historic monuments, landmarks, scenery, etc.
	For local see DT469.M495A+
469.M426	General works
469.M427	Preservation
469.M429	Description and travel
469.M43	Antiquities
	For local antiquities see DT469.M495A+
469.M44	Social life and customs. Civilization. Intellectual life
	For specific periods, see the period
	Ethnography
469.M442	General works
469.M445A-.M445Z	Individual elements in the population, A-Z
469.M445B52	Bhojpuri
469.M445B53	Bihari
469.M445B55	Blacks
469.M445C44	Chinese
469.M445C74	Creoles
469.M445E27	East Indians
469.M445M37	Marathas
469.M445M87	Muslims

Eastern Africa
  Islands (East African coast)
    Individual islands, A-Z
      Mauritius (Ile de France)
        Ethnography
          Individual elements in the population, A-Z --
            Continued

469.M445T35	Tamil
469.M445T44	Telugu

        History

469.M45	Biography (Collective)
	For individual biography, see the specific period or place
469.M452	Historiography
	Study and teaching
469.M453	General works
469.M454A-.M454Z	By region or country, A-Z
469.M455	General works
469.M457	Political history
	For specific periods, see the period
	Foreign and general relations
	For general works on the diplomatic history of a period, see the period
	For works on relations with a specific country regardless of period see DT469.M463A+
469.M462	General works
469.M463A-.M463Z	Relations with individual countries, A-Z
	By period
	Early to 1810
	Including Dutch colonization, French control and administration of the French East India Company
	For Battle of Grand Port, 1810 see DC234.92
469.M465	General works
	Biography and memoirs
469.M466	Collective
469.M467A-.M467Z	Individual, A-Z
	1810-1968. British domination
469.M47	General works
	Biography and memoirs
469.M472	Collective
469.M473A-.M473Z	Individual, A-Z
	1968- . Independence
469.M48	General works
	Biography and memoirs
469.M482	Collective
469.M483A-.M483Z	Individual, A-Z
469.M484	1968-1992. Constitutional monarchy

	Eastern Africa
	Islands (East African coast)
	Individual islands, A-Z
	Mauritius (Ile de France)
	History
	By period
	1968- . Independence -- Continued
469.M485	1992- . Republic
	Local history and description
	Major islands and dependencies
469.M491	Agalega
	Chagos Archipelago see DS349.9.C42
	Diego Garcia see DS349.9.D53
469.M492	Rodrigues
469.M493	Saint Brandon (Cargados Carajos Shoals)
469.M495A-.M495Z	Other local, A-Z
469.M4975	Mayotte
	Nossi-Be see DT469.M37N67
	Réunion
469.R3	Periodicals. Societies. Serials
469.R32	Gazetteers. Dictionaries, etc.
469.R325	Guidebooks
469.R33	General works
469.R34	General special
469.R345	Pictorial works
	Historic monuments, landmarks, scenery, etc.
	(General)
	For local see DT469.R5A+
469.R346	General works
469.R347	Preservation
469.R35	Description and travel
469.R36	Antiquities
469.R37	Social life and customs. Civilization. Intellectual life
	For specific periods, see the period
	Ethnography
469.R38	General works
469.R39A-.R39Z	Individual elements in the population, A-Z
469.R39B74	Bretons
469.R39C48	Chinese
469.R39E28	East Indians
469.R39M87	Muslims
	History
469.R42	Biography (Collective)
	For individual biography, see the specific period, reign,
	or place
469.R425	Historiography
469.R43	General works

	Eastern Africa
	Islands (East African coast)
	Individual islands, A-Z
	Reunion
	History -- Continued
469.R432	Political history
	For specific periods, see the period
	Foreign and general relations
	For specific periods, see the period
469.R435	General works
469.R436A-.R436Z	Relations with individual countries, A-Z
	By period
	Early to 1764. Compagnie des Indes Orientales
469.R44	General works
	Biography and memoirs
469.R442	Collective
469.R443A-.R443Z	Individual, A-Z
	1764-1946
469.R45	General works
	Biography and memoirs
469.R452	Collective
469.R453A-.R453Z	Individual, A-Z
	1946-
469.R455	General works
	Biography and memoirs
469.R457	Collective
469.R458A-.R458Z	Individual, A-Z
469.R5A-.R5Z	Regions, cities, etc., A-Z
	Seychelles
469.S4	Periodicals. Societies. Serials
469.S413	Sources and documents
469.S415	Gazetteers. Dictionaries, etc.
469.S417	Place names (General)
	For etymological studies, see class P
469.S42	Guidebooks
469.S422	General works
469.S423	General special
469.S424	Pictorial works
	Historic monuments, landmarks, scenery, etc. (General)
	For local see DT469.S49A+
469.S425	General works
469.S426	Preservation
469.S427	Description and travel
469.S43	Antiquities
	For local antiquities see DT469.S49A+

Eastern Africa
Islands (East African coast)
Individual islands, A-Z
Seychelles -- Continued

469.S44	Social life and customs. Civilization. Intellectual life
	For specific periods, see the period or reign
	Ethnography
469.S442	General works
469.S443A-.S443Z	Individual elements in the population, A-Z
	History
469.S452	Biography (Collective)
	For individual biography, see the specific period, reign, or place
469.S455	Historiography
469.S457	General works
469.S46	Political history
	For specific periods, see the period or reign
	Foreign and general relations
	For general works on the diplomatic history of a period, see the period
	For works on relations with a specific country regardless of period see DT469.S463A+
469.S462	General works
469.S463A-.S463Z	Relations with individual countries, A-Z
	By period
	Early to 1814
	Including early explorations by Arabs, Portuguese and British; French colonial rule; British occupation between 1794-1814
469.S465	General works
	Biography and memoirs
469.S466	Collective
469.S467A-.S467Z	Individual, A-Z
	1814-1976. British colonial rule
	Including jurisdiction under Mauritius from 1814-1903 and British Crown Colony from 1903-1976
469.S47	General works
	Biography and memoirs
469.S472	Collective
469.S473A-.S473Z	Individual, A-Z
	1976-
469.S48	General works
	Biography and memoirs
469.S482	Collective
469.S483A-.S483Z	Individual, A-Z
469.S49A-.S49Z	Local history and description, A-Z
	West Africa. West Coast

	West Africa. West Coast -- Continued
470	Periodicals. Societies. Serials
470.15	Museums, exhibitions, etc.
470.2	Sources and documents
470.5	Guidebooks
471	General works
471.5	Pictorial works
472	Description and travel
473	Antiquities
	For local antiquities see DT477+
474	Social life and customs. Civilization. Intellectual life
	For specific periods, see the period
	Ethnography
474.5	General works
474.6.A-Z	Individual elements in the population, A-Z
474.6.B73	Brazilians
474.6.B75	British
474.6.C48	Chamba
474.6.C8	Cubans
474.6.E83	Ewe
474.6.F35	Fang
474.6.F84	Fula
474.6.G32	Gbaya
474.6.I35	Igbo
474.6.K78	Kru
474.6.M36	Mandingo
474.6.S45	Senufo
474.6.T46	Tenda
474.6.Y67	Yoruba
	History
475	General works
475.5	Biography (General)
	For individual biography, see the specific period, reign, or place
	By period
476	Early to 1884
	1884-1960. Colonial period
476.2	General works
	Biography and memoirs
476.22	Collective
476.23.A-Z	Individual, A-Z
	1960- . Independent
476.5	General works
	Biography and memoirs
476.52	Collective
476.523.A-Z	Individual, A-Z

West Africa. West Coast -- Continued
Local history and description
see DT477+

477	Upper Guinea
479	Lower Guinea
	British West Africa
491	Periodicals. Societies. Serials
493	Dictionaries. Guidebooks. Directories
494	General works
	Description and travel
496	Through 1800
497	1801-1950
498	1951-
499	Antiquities
500	Ethnography
	History
502	General works
503	Other
	Biography and memoirs
503.9	Collective
504.A-Z	Individual, A-Z
	Local
507	Ashanti Empire
	Including works on the Ashantis and the Ashanti Wars
	Cf. DT512.9.A84 Ashanti Region
	Bornu see DT515.9.B6
	Fulani Empire see DT515.9.F8
	Gambia
	Cf. DT532.25 Senegambia
509	Periodicals. Societies. Serials
509.13	Sources and documents
509.17	Place names (General)
509.2	Guidebooks
509.22	General works
509.24	Pictorial works
509.27	Description and travel
509.4	Social life and customs. Civilization. Intellectual life
	For specific periods, see the period
	Ethnography
509.42	General works
509.45.A-Z	Individual elements in the population, A-Z
509.45.M34	Mandingo
509.45.P67	Portuguese
509.45.W64	Wolof
	History
509.5	General works

West Africa. West Coast
British West Africa
Local
Gambia
History -- Continued
Foreign and general relations
For general works on the diplomatic history of a period,
see the period
For works on relations with a specific country
regardless of period see DT509.63.A+

509.62	General works
509.63.A-Z	Relations with individual countries, A-Z
	By period
509.65	Early to 1894
509.7	1894-1965. British protectorate and colony
	1965- . Independent
509.8	General works
	Biography and memoirs
509.82	Collective
509.83.A-Z	Individual, A-Z
509.9.A-Z	Local history and description, A-Z
	Ghana (Gold Coast)
	Cf. DT532.15 Ghana empire
509.97	Periodicals. Societies. Serials
510	General works
510.15	Historic monuments, landmarks, scenery, etc. (General)
	For local see DT512.9.A+
510.2	Description and travel. Guidebooks
510.3	Antiquities
510.4	Social life and customs. Civilization. Intellectual life
	Ethnography
510.42	General works
510.43.A-Z	Individual elements in the population, A-Z
510.43.A25	Abron
510.43.A34	Ada
510.43.A37	African Americans
510.43.A53	Akans
510.43.A58	Anlo
	Ashantis see DT507
510.43.B84	Buem
510.43.B85	Builsa
510.43.D33	Dagaaba
510.43.D34	Dagbani. Dagomba
510.43.E94	Ewe
510.43.F35	Fantis
510.43.F84	Fula

West Africa. West Coast
British West Africa
Local
Ghana (Gold Coast)
Ethnography
Individual elements in the population, A-Z --
Continued

510.43.G3	Gã
510.43.G65	Gonja
510.43.K37	Kasem. Kasena
510.43.K63	Koma
510.43.K65	Konkomba
510.43.K72	Krachi
510.43.K76	Krobo
510.43.K87	Kuranko
510.43.K89	Kusasi
510.43.K93	Kwahu
510.43.L42	Lebanese
510.43.L62	Lobi
510.43.M35	Mamprusi
510.43.N35	Namnam
510.43.N4	Nchumburung
510.43.N95	Nzima
510.43.S57	Sisala
510.43.S85	Swiss
510.43.T35	Tallensi. Talansi
510.43.V34	Vagala
510.43.W35	Wala
	History
510.5	General works
510.6	Biography and memoirs (Collective)
	Political and diplomatic history. Foreign and general relations. Nationalism
510.62	General works
510.63.A-Z	Relations with individual countries, A-Z
	By period
	Early to 1957
	For Ashanti Empire see DT507
511	General works
	Biography and memoirs
511.2	Collective
511.3.A-Z	Individual, A-Z
	Republic, 1957-
	1957-1979
512	General works
	Biography and memoirs
512.2	Collective

280

DT

West Africa. West Coast
British West Africa
Local
Ghana (Gold Coast)
History
By period
Republic, 1957-
1957-1979
Biography and memoirs -- Continued
512.3.A-Z   Individual, A-Z
1979-2001
512.32   General works
Biography and memoirs
512.33   Collective
512.34.A-Z   Individual, A-Z
2001-
512.42   General works
Biography and memoirs
512.43   Collective
512.44.A-Z   Individual, A-Z
512.9.A-Z   Local, A-Z
e.g.
512.9.A84   Ashanti Region
Cf. DT507 Ashanti Empire
(513)   Yorubaland. Yorubas
see DT474.6.Y67, West Africa; DT515.45.Y67, Nigeria
Nigeria
515   Periodicals. Societies. Serials
515.12   Congresses
515.13   Sources and documents
515.15   Gazetteers. Dictionaries, etc.
515.17   Place names (General)
For etymological studies, see class P
515.2   Guidebooks
515.22   General works
515.23   General special
515.24   Pictorial works
Historic monuments, landmarks, scenery, etc.
(General)
For local see DT515.9.A+
515.25   General works
515.26   Preservation
515.268   Geography
515.27   Description and travel
515.3   Antiquities
For local see DT515.9.A+

	West Africa. West Coast
	British West Africa
	Local
	Nigeria -- Continued
515.4	Social life and customs. Civilization. Intellectual life
	For specific periods, see the period
	Ethnography
515.42	General works
515.45.A-Z	Individual elements in the population, A-Z
515.45.A45	Akoko
515.45.A52	Anang
515.45.A53	Angas
515.45.A75	Armenians
515.45.A83	Atakat
515.45.A96	Awori
515.45.B5	Biase
515.45.B56	Bini
515.45.B58	Birom
515.45.B64	Bolewa
515.45.B73	Brazilians
515.45.B93	Bwatiye
515.45.D84	Dukawa
515.45.E3	Ebira
515.45.E32	Edo-speaking peoples
515.45.E34	Efik
515.45.E35	Egba
515.45.E39	Eket
515.45.E42	Ekiti
515.45.E44	Ekpeye
	Esan see DT515.45.I83
515.45.E77	Etsako
515.45.F84	Fula
515.45.G32	Gaanda
515.45.G33	Gbagyi
515.45.G34	Gbari. Gwari
(515.45.G83)	Gwari
	see DT515.45.G34
515.45.H38	Hausas
515.45.I22	Ibarapapa
515.45.I24	Ibibios
515.45.I25	Idoma
515.45.I28	Ife
515.45.I32	Igala
515.45.I33	Igbo
515.45.I34	Igbona
515.45.I347	Ijebu
515.45.I348	Ijesa

West Africa. West Coast
British West Africa
Local
Nigeria
Ethnography
Individual elements in the population, A-Z --
Continued

515.45.I35	Ijo
515.45.I36	Ika
515.45.I37	Ikwere
515.45.I43	Ilaje
515.45.I83	Ishan. Esan
515.45.I86	Isoko
515.45.I88	Itsekiri. Jekri
515.45.I93	Izere
515.45.I95	Izi
515.45.J33	Jagbe
(515.45.J44)	Jekri
	see DT515.45.I88
515.45.J83	Jukun
515.45.K33	Kadara
515.45.K332	Kadung
515.45.K334	Kagoma
515.45.K336	Kagoro
515.45.K34	Kaleri
515.45.K36	Kanuri
515.45.K64	Kofyar
515.45.K66	Koma
515.45.K68	Koro
515.45.K85	Kulung
515.45.M3	Mada
515.45.M33	Maguzawa
515.45.M35	Mambila
515.45.M39	Mbula
515.45.M62	Moba
515.45.M87	Muslims
515.45.N35	Nembe
515.45.N48	Ngwa
515.45.N55	Nkanu
515.45.N86	Nupe
515.45.O23	Obolo
515.45.O3	Ogba
515.45.O33	Ogoni
515.45.O34	Ogori
515.45.O37	Okrika
515.45.O38	Okun
515.45.O74	Oron

West Africa. West Coast
 British West Africa
  Local
   Nigeria
    Ethnography
     Individual elements in the population, A-Z --
      Continued

515.45.O88	Owan
515.45.O93	Oyo
515.45.P64	Poles
515.45.R84	Rukuba
515.45.S63	Sobo
515.45.T58	Tiv. Tivi
515.45.U24	Ubium
515.45.U35	Ujari
515.45.U54	Uneme
515.45.U74	Urhobo
515.45.Y33	Yagba
515.45.Y47	Yergum
515.45.Y67	Yoruba
515.45.Y86	Yungur

    History
515.53   Biography (Collective)
      For individual biography, see the specific period, reign,
       or place
515.55   Historiography
      Biography of historians, area studies specialists,
       archaeologists, etc.
515.552   Collective
515.553.A-Z   Individual, A-Z
      Study and teaching
515.556   General works
515.557.A-Z   By region or country, A-Z
       Subarrange by author
515.57   General works
515.58   Juvenile works
515.585   Military history
515.59   Political history
     For specific periods, see the period
    Foreign and general relations
     For general works on the diplomatic history of a period,
      see the period
     For works on relations with a specific country
      regardless of period see DT515.63.A+
515.62   General works
515.63.A-Z   Relations with individual countries, A-Z
    By period

	West Africa. West Coast
	British West Africa
	Local
	Nigeria
	History
	By period -- Continued
	Early to 1861
515.65	General works
	Biography and memoirs
515.66	Collective
515.67.A-Z	Individual, A-Z
	1861-1914. Period of colonization
515.7	General works
	Biography and memoirs
515.72	Collective
515.73.A-Z	Individual, A-Z
	1914-1960. Colony and Protectorate of Nigeria
515.75	General works
	Biography and memoirs
515.76	Collective
515.77.A-Z	Individual, A-Z
	1960- . Independence
515.8	General works
	Biography and memoirs
515.82	Collective
515.83.A-Z	Individual, A-Z
515.832	1960-1966. Balewa, Azikiwe and Ironsi administrations
	Including January 1966 coup d'état
	1966-1975. Gowon administration
	Including July 1966 coup d'état
515.834	General works
515.836	1967-1970. Civil War
	Cf. DT515.9.E3 Eastern Region. Biafra
515.838	1975-1979. Muhammad and Obasanjo administrations
	Including 1975 coup d'état
515.84	1979-1983. Shagari administration
	Including December 1983 coup d'état
515.842	1984-1993. Buhari and Babangida administrations
515.844	1993-2007. Abacha, Abubakar, and Obasanjo administrations
515.846	2007- . Yar'adua and Jonathan administrations
515.9.A-Z	Local history and description, A-Z
	e.g.
	Biafra see DT515.9.E3

West Africa. West Coast
British West Africa
Local
Nigeria
Local history and description, A-Z -- Continued
515.9.B6   Bornu
                                 Including Kanem Bornu Empire
515.9.E3   Eastern Region. Biafra
                                 For Civil War, 1967-1970 see DT515.836
515.9.F8   Fulani Empire
Sierra Leone
516   Periodicals. Societies. Serials
516.13   Sources and documents
516.15   Gazetteers. Dictionaries, etc.
516.17   Guidebooks
516.18   General works
516.19   Pictorial works
516.2   Description and travel
516.4   Social life and customs. Civilization. Intellectual life
                                 For specific periods, see the period
Ethnography
516.42   General works
516.45.A-Z   Individual elements in the population, A-Z
516.45.B57   Birwa
516.45.C73   Creoles
516.45.F85   Fula
516.45.K65   Kono
516.45.K85   Kuranko
516.45.L54   Limba
516.45.M45   Mende
516.45.S45   Sherbro
516.45.T45   Temne
516.45.W47   West Indians
516.45.Y34   Yalunka
History
516.5   General works
516.6   Political history
                                 For specific periods, see the period
Foreign and general relations
                                 For general works on the diplomatic history of a period,
                                    see the period
                                 For works on relations with a specific country
                                    regardless of period see DT516.63.A+
516.62   General works
516.63.A-Z   Relations with individual countries, A-Z
By period
516.65   Early to 1787

West Africa. West Coast
British West Africa
Local
Sierra Leone
History
By period -- Continued
1787-1961. British colony and protectorate
516.7   General works
Biography and memoirs
516.719   Collective
516.72.A-Z   Individual, A-Z
1961- . Independence
516.8   General works
1961-1991. Administrations of Milton Margai,
Albert Margai, Shaka Stevens, and Gen.
Joseph Momoh
516.815   General works
Biography and memoirs
516.819   Collective
516.82.A-Z   Individual, A-Z
1991- . Civil War
Including incursions into Sierra Leone
516.826   General works
Biography and memoirs
516.827   Collective
516.828   Individual, A-Z
516.9.A-Z   Local history and description, A-Z
e.g.
516.9.F73   Freetown
French West Africa. French Sahara. West Sahara. Sahel
521   Periodicals. Societies. Serials
523   Dictionaries. Guidebooks. Directories
524   General works
524.5   Pictorial works
Description and travel
526   Through 1800
527   1801-1950
528   1951-
529   Antiquities
Social life and customs. Civilization. Intellectual life
529.5   General works
By period, see the specific period
Ethnography
530   General works
530.5.A-Z   Individual elements in the population, A-Z
530.5.B7   Brakna
530.5.D64   Dogon

	West Africa. West Coast
	French West Africa. French Sahara. West Sahara. Sahel
	Ethnography
	Individual elements in the population, A-Z -- Continued
530.5.F34	Fang
530.5.F84	Fula
530.5.J3	Jaawambe
530.5.K64	Koniagui
530.5.L42	Lebanese
530.5.L43	Lebau
530.5.M88	Muslims
530.5.N65	Nomads
530.5.P94	Pygmies
530.5.S65	Songhai
	Tuaregs see DT346.T7
	History
532	General works
	Traditional kingdoms and empires
532.115	Adamawa (Emirate)
532.12	Denkyira (Kingdom)
532.128	Fuladu (Kingdom)
532.13	Futa-Jallon
532.14	Gajaaga
532.15	Ghana empire
	Cf. DT509.97+ Ghana
532.17	Kaabu empire
532.2	Mali empire
	Cf. DT551+ Mali Republic
532.23	Niumi (Kingdom)
532.25	Senegambia
	Cf. DT509+ Gambia
	Cf. DT549+ Senegal
532.27	Songhai Empire
	Takrur Empire see DT532.3
	Toucouleur Empire see DT532.3
532.3	Tukulor Empire. Takrur Empire
532.33	Yatenga (Kingdom)
	Foreign and general relations
	For general works on the diplomatic history of a period, see the period
	For works on relations with a specific country regardless of period see DT532.395.A+
532.39	General works
532.395.A-Z	Relations with individual countries, A-Z
	By period
532.4	Through 1884
532.5	1884-1960

West Africa. West Coast
French West Africa. French Sahara. West Sahara. Sahel
History
By period -- Continued
532.6   1960-
Biography and memoirs
533.A2   Collective
533.A3-Z   Individual, A-Z
534   Historiography
Local history and description
Benin. Dahomey
541   Periodicals. Societies. Serials
541.13   Sources and documents
541.2   Guidebooks
541.22   General works
541.24   Pictorial works
541.27   Description and travel
541.3   Antiquities
541.4   Social life and customs. Civilization. Intellectual life
For specific periods, see the period
Ethnography
541.42   General works
541.45.A-Z   Individual elements in the population, A-Z
541.45.A33   Aja
541.45.A54   Anii
541.45.B37   Bariba
541.45.D95   Dyula
541.45.F65   Fon
541.45.F85   Fula
541.45.G85   Gun
541.45.G87   Gurma
541.45.L85   Lukpa
541.45.S65   Somba
541.45.T35   Takena
541.45.T63   Tofinnu
541.45.X84   Xweda
541.45.Y65   Yoruba
History
541.5   General works
Foreign and general relations
For general works on the diplomatic history of a period,
see the period
For works on relations with a specific country
regardless of period see DT541.63.A+
541.62   General works
541.63.A-Z   Relations with individual countries, A-Z
By period

West Africa. West Coast
  French West Africa. French Sahara. West Sahara. Sahel
    Local history and description
      Benin. Dahomey
        History
          By period -- Continued
            Early to 1894

541.65	General works
	Biography and memoirs
541.66	Collective
541.67.A-Z	Individual, A-Z
	1894-1960. French territory and colony
541.75	General works
	Biography and memoirs
541.76	Collective
541.77.A-Z	Individual, A-Z
	1960- . Independent
541.8	General works
	Biography and memoirs
541.82	Collective
541.83.A-Z	Individual, A-Z
541.84	1960-1972
	Including coups d'état by Soglo and Kouandété
541.845	1972- . Kerekou Administration. 1990 multiparty restoration
	Including 1972 coup d'état, 1975 name change from Dahomey to Benin and 1977 coup attempt
541.9.A-Z	Local history and description, A-Z
	Guinea
543	Periodicals. Societies. Serials
543.13	Sources and documents
543.2	Guidebooks
543.22	General works
543.24	Pictorial works
543.27	Description and travel
543.4	Social life and customs. Civilization. Intellectual life
	For specific periods, see the period
	Ethnography
543.42	General works
543.45.A-Z	Individual elements in the population, A-Z
543.45.F84	Fula
543.45.K57	Kissi
543.45.M34	Mandingo
543.45.T65	Toma
	History
543.5	General works

	West Africa. West Coast
	French West Africa. French Sahara. West Sahara. Sahel
	Local history and description
	Guinea
	History -- Continued
543.59	Political history
	Foreign and general relations
	For general works on the diplomatic history of a period, see the period
	For works on relations with a specific country regardless of period see DT543.63.A+
543.62	General works
543.63.A-Z	Relations with individual countries, A-Z
	By period
543.65	Early to 1895
	1895-1958. French territory and colony
543.75	General works
	Biography and memoirs
543.76	Collective
543.77.A-Z	Individual, A-Z
	1958- . Independent
543.8	General works
	Biography and memoirs
543.819	Collective
543.82.A-Z	Individual, A-Z
	e.g.
543.82.T68	Touré, Ahmed Sékou
	1958-1984
543.822	General works
	Biography and memoirs
543.823	Collective
543.824.A-Z	Individual, A-Z
	1984-
543.825	General works
	Biography and memoirs
543.826	Collective
543.827.A-Z	Individual, A-Z
543.9.A-Z	Local history and description, A-Z
	Côte d'Ivoire. Ivory Coast
545	Periodicals. Societies. Serials
545.12	Congresses
545.13	Sources and documents
545.15	Gazetteers. Dictionaries, etc.
545.17	Place names (General)
	For etymological studies, see class P
545.2	Guidebooks
545.22	General works

	West Africa. West Coast
	French West Africa. French Sahara. West Sahara. Sahel
	Local history and description
	Côte d'Ivoire. Ivory Coast -- Continued
545.23	General special
545.24	Pictorial works
545.27	Description and travel
545.3	Antiquities
	For local antiquities see DT545.9.A+
545.4	Social life and customs. Civilization. Intellectual life
	For specific periods, see the period
	Ethnography
545.42	General works
545.45.A-Z	Individual elements in the population, A-Z
545.45.A27	Abron
545.45.A35	Adyukru
	Agni see DT545.45.A58
545.45.A53	Ano. Ando
545.45.A58	Anyi
545.45.A86	Avikam
545.45.B36	Baule
545.45.B45	Beng
545.45.B47	Bété
545.45.B87	Burkinabe
545.45.D34	Dan
545.45.D85	Dyula
545.45.G33	Gade
545.45.G34	Gagou
545.45.G47	Gere
545.45.G87	Guro
545.45.K77	Kru
545.45.L42	Lebanese
545.45.N93	Nyarafolo
545.45.O96	Ouobé
545.45.S44	Senufo
545.45.V47	Vere
545.45.W4	We
	History
545.52	Biography (Collective)
	For individual biography, see the specific period, reign, or place
545.55	Historiography
545.57	General works
545.58	Juvenile works
545.59	Political history
	For specific periods, see the period

West Africa. West Coast
  French West Africa. French Sahara. West Sahara. Sahel
    Local history and description
      Côte d'Ivoire. Ivory Coast
        History -- Continued
          Foreign and general relations
            For general works on the diplomatic history of a period,
              see the period
            For works on relations with a specific country
              regardless of period see DT545.63.A+

545.62	General works
545.63.A-Z	Relations with individual countries, A-Z
	By period
	Early to 1893
545.7	General works
	Biography and memoirs
545.72	Collective
545.73.A-Z	Individual, A-Z
	1893-1960
545.75	General works
	Biography and memoirs
545.76	Collective
545.77.A-Z	Individual, A-Z
	1960-1993. Houphouët-Boigny administration
545.8	General works
	Biography and memoirs
545.82	Collective
545.83.A-Z	Individual, A-Z
	1993- . Bédié, Gueï, and Gbagbo administrations
	Including 1999 coup d'état and Civil War, 2002-2007
545.84	General works
	Biography and memoirs
545.842	Collective
545.843.A-Z	Individual, A-Z
545.9.A-Z	Local history and description, A-Z
	French-speaking Equatorial Africa
	Gabon (Gaboon, Gabun)
546.1	Periodicals. Societies. Serials
546.113	Sources and documents
546.115	Gazetteers. Dictionaries, etc.
546.12	Guidebooks
546.122	General works
546.124	Pictorial works
	Description and travel
546.127	Through 1980
546.128	1981-

	West Africa. West Coast
	French West Africa. French Sahara. West Sahara. Sahel
	Local history and description
	French-speaking Equatorial Africa
	Gabon (Gaboon, Gabun) -- Continued
546.14	Social life and customs. Civilization. Intellectual life
	For specific periods, see the period
	Ethnography
546.142	General works
546.145.A-Z	Individual elements in the population, A-Z
546.145.A48	Ajumba
546.145.B35	Bantu-speaking peoples
546.145.B83	Bubi
546.145.F35	Fang
546.145.F74	French
546.145.G34	Galwa
546.145.M217	Makina
546.145.M22	Massango
546.145.M24	Mbete
546.145.M66	Mpongwe
546.145.M93	Myene
546.145.N56	Nkomi
546.145.N93	Nzabi
546.145.P86	Punu
546.145.P94	Pygmies
546.145.S55	Shira
546.145.T75	Tsogo
	History
546.15	General works
	Foreign and general relations
	For general works on the diplomatic history of a period, see the period
	For works on relations with a specific country regardless of period see DT546.163.A+
546.162	General works
546.163.A-Z	Relations with individual countries, A-Z
	By period
546.165	Early to 1886
546.175	1886-1960. French colony and territory
	1960- . Independent
546.18	General works
	Biography and memoirs
546.182	Collective
546.183.A-Z	Individual, A-Z
546.19.A-Z	Local history and description, A-Z
	e.g.
546.19.L5	Libreville

West Africa. West Coast
  French West Africa. French Sahara. West Sahara. Sahel
    Local history and description
      French-speaking Equatorial Africa -- Continued
        Congo (Brazzaville). Middle Congo

546.2	Periodicals. Societies. Serials
546.213	Sources and documents
546.215	Gazetteers. Dictionaries, etc.
546.22	Guidebooks
546.223	General works
546.224	Pictorial works
546.227	Description and travel
546.24	Social life and customs. Civilization. Intellectual life
	For specific periods, see the period
	Ethnography
546.242	General works
546.245.A-Z	Individual elements in the population, A-Z
546.245.B44	Bembe
546.245.K66	Kongo
546.245.K68	Kota
546.245.K84	Kukwa
546.245.L84	Lumbu
546.245.M35	Mbosi
(546.245.N86)	Nunu
	see DT650.N89
546.245.N93	Nzabi
546.245.T43	Teke
546.245.V54	Vili
	History
546.25	General works
	Foreign and general relations
	For general works on the diplomatic history of a
	period, see the period
	For works on relations with a specific country
	regardless of period see DT546.263.A+
546.262	General works
546.263.A-Z	Relations with individual countries, A-Z
	By period
	Early to 1910
546.265	General works
	Biography and memoirs
546.266	Collective
546.267.A-Z	Individual, A-Z
	e.g.
546.267.B72	Brazza, Pierre Savorgnan de, 1852-1905
546.275	1910-1960. French colony and territory

West Africa. West Coast
French West Africa. French Sahara. West Sahara. Sahel
Local history and description
French-speaking Equatorial Africa
Congo (Brazzaville). Middle Congo
History
By period -- Continued
1960- . Independence
Including Civil War, 1997

546.28	General works
	Biography and memoirs
546.282	Collective
546.283.A-Z	Individual, A-Z
	1997- . Sassou-Nguesso administrations
546.284	General works
	Biography and memoirs
546.285	Collective
546.286.A-Z	Individual, A-Z
546.29.A-Z	Local history and description, A-Z

Central African Republic. Central African Empire.
Ubangi-Shari

546.3	Periodicals. Societies. Serials
546.313	Sources and documents
546.315	Gazetteers
546.32	Guidebooks
546.322	General works
546.324	Pictorial works
546.327	Description and travel
546.33	Antiquities
	For local antiquities see DT546.39.A+
546.34	Social life and customs. Civilization. Intellectual life
	For specific periods, see the period
	Ethnography
546.342	General works
546.345.A-Z	Individual elements in the elements in the population, A-Z
546.345.A35	Aka
546.345.B33	Babingas
546.345.B36	Baka
546.345.B45	Benjelle
546.345.B67	Borossé
546.345.G33	Gbaya
546.345.M38	Mbum
546.345.M65	Monjombo
546.345.M67	Mpiemo
546.345.N44	Ngbaka (Lobaye)
546.345.N83	Nzakara

West Africa. West Coast
French West Africa. French Sahara. West Sahara. Sahel
Local history and description
French-speaking Equatorial Africa
Central African Republic. Central African Empire.
Ubangi-Shari
Ethnography
Individual elements in the elements in the
population, A-Z -- Continued
546.345.Z35   Zande
History
546.348   Historiography
546.35   General works
Foreign and general relations
For general works on the diplomatic history of a
period, see the period
For works on relations with a specific country
regardless of period see DT546.363.A+
546.362   General works
546.363.A-Z   Relations with individual countries, A-Z
By period
546.365   Early to 1910
1910-1960. French colony
546.37   General works
Biography and memoirs
546.372   Collective
546.373.A-Z   Individual, A-Z
1960- . Independent
546.375   General works
1960-1979
Including Central African Empire, 1976-1979
546.38   General works
Biography and memoirs
546.382   Collective
546.383.A-Z   Individual, A-Z
e.g.
546.383.B64   Bokassa I
1979-2003
546.384   General works
Biography and memoirs
546.385   Collective
546.3852.A-Z   Individual, A-Z
e.g.
546.3852.K6   Kolingba, Andre
2003-
Including 2003 coup d'état
546.3858   General works

West Africa. West Coast
  French West Africa. French Sahara. West Sahara. Sahel
    Local history and description
      French-speaking Equatorial Africa
        Central African Republic. Central African Empire.
        Ubangi-Shari
        History
          By period
            1960- . Independent
             2003- -- Continued
              Biography and memoirs

546.386	Collective
546.3863.A-Z	Individual, A-Z
546.39.A-Z	Local history and description, A-Z
	Chad (Tchad)
546.4	Periodicals. Societies. Serials
546.413	Sources and documents
546.415	Gazetteers. Dictionaries, etc.
546.42	Guidebooks
546.422	General works
546.424	Pictorial works
546.427	Description and travel
546.43	Antiquities
	For local antiquities see DT546.49.A+
546.44	Social life and customs. Civilization. Intellectual life
	For specific periods, see the period
	Ethnography
546.442	General works
546.445.A-Z	Individual elements in the population, A-Z
546.445.B34	Bagirmi
546.445.D38	Daza
546.445.G36	Gambaye
546.445.H33	Haddad
546.445.K36	Kanembu
546.445.M36	Marba
546.445.M37	Masa
546.445.M85	Mundang
546.445.N35	Nar
546.445.N43	Ngama
546.445.S25	São
546.445.S37	Sara
546.445.T4	Teda
546.445.Z33	Zaghawa
	History
546.449	Dictionaries. Chronological tables, outlines, etc.
	Historiography
546.452	General works

West Africa. West Coast
  French West Africa. French Sahara. West Sahara. Sahel
    Local history and description
      French-speaking Equatorial Africa
        Chad (Tchad)
          History
            Historiography -- Continued
              Biography of historians, area studies specialists,
                archaeologists, etc.

546.453	Collective
546.454.A-Z	Individual, A-Z
546.457	General works
546.46	Political history

For specific periods, see the period
Foreign and general relations
  For general works on the diplomatic history of a
    period, see the period
  For works on relations with a specific country
    regardless of period see DT546.463.A+

546.462	General works
546.463.A-Z	Relations with individual countries, A-Z
	By period
	Early to 1910
546.47	General works
	Biography and memoirs
546.472	Collective
546.473.A-Z	Individual, A-Z
	1910-1960
546.475	General works
	Biography and memoirs
546.476	Collective
546.477.A-Z	Individual, A-Z
	1960- . Independent

Including Civil War, 1965-

546.48	General works
	Biography and memoirs
546.482	Collective
546.483.A-Z	Individual, A-Z
	1990- . Déby administrations
546.484	General works
	Biography and memoirs
546.485	Collective
546.486.A-Z	Individual, A-Z
546.49.A-Z	Local history and description, A-Z

e.g.

546.49.L34	Lake Chad
546.49.W33	Wadai

West Africa. West Coast
French West Africa. French Sahara. West Sahara. Sahel
Local history and description -- Continued
Niger
547	Periodicals. Societies. Serials
547.13	Sources and documents
547.2	Guidebooks
547.22	General works
547.24	Pictorial works
547.27	Description and travel
547.4	Social life and customs. Civilization. Intellectual life

For specific periods, see the period
Ethnography
547.42	General works
547.45.A-Z	Individual elements in the population, A-Z
547.45.B67	Bororo
547.45.F84	Fula
547.45.H38	Hausas
547.45.K34	Kanuri
547.45.M38	Mawri
547.45.S65	Songhai
547.45.T83	Tuaregs
547.45.Z37	Zarma

History
547.48	Historiography
547.5	General works

Foreign and general relations
For general works on the diplomatic history of a period, see the period
For works on relations with a specific country regardless of period see DT547.63.A+
547.62	General works
547.63.A-Z	Relations with individual countries, A-Z

By period
547.65	Early to 1900
547.75	1900-1960. French territory and colony

1960-1993. Independent
547.8	General works

Biography and memoirs
547.82	Collective
547.83.A-Z	Individual, A-Z

1993- . Democracy
547.85	General works

Biography and memoirs
547.852	Collective
547.853.A-Z	Individual, A-Z

West Africa. West Coast
 French West Africa. French Sahara. West Sahara. Sahel
  Local history and description
   Niger -- Continued

547.9.A-Z	Local history and description, A-Z
	e.g.
547.9.N5	Niamey
	Niger River see DT360
548	West Sahara
	Senegal
549	Periodicals. Societies. Serials
549.12	Congresses
549.13	Sources and documents
549.15	Gazetteers. Dictionaries, etc.
549.17	Place names (General)
	For etymological studies, see class P
549.2	Guidebooks
549.22	General works
549.23	General special
549.24	Pictorial works
549.25	Historic monuments, landmarks, etc. (General)
	For local see DT551.9.A+
549.27	Description and travel
549.3	Antiquities
	For local antiquities see DT551.9.A+
549.4	Social life and customs. Civilization. Intellectual life
	For specific periods, see the period
	Ethnography
549.42	General works
549.45.A-Z	Individual elements in the population, A-Z
549.45.B35	Bandial
549.45.B37	Bassari
549.45.B39	Bayot
549.45.B43	Bedik
549.45.D56	Diola
549.45.F84	Fula
549.45.G85	Guineans
(549.45.H34)	Halpulaar
	see DT549.45.T68
549.45.L42	Lebou
549.45.M35	Mandingo
549.45.M37	Mandjak
549.45.M38	Mankanya
549.45.N38	Ndut
549.45.S47	Serers
549.45.S66	Soninke
	Toucouleurs see DT549.45.T68

West Africa. West Coast
 French West Africa. French Sahara. West Sahara. Sahel
 Local history and description
  Senegal
   Ethnography
    Individual elements in the population, A-Z --
    Continued

549.45.T68	Tukulor
549.45.W64	Wolof

   History
549.47 Biography (Collective)
    For individual biography, see the specific period or
    place
549.48 Historiography
549.5 General works
549.52 Juvenile works
549.55 Military history
    For individual campaigns and engagements see the
    period or reign
549.59 Political history
    For specific periods, see the period
   Foreign and general relations
    For general works on the diplomatic history of a period,
    see the period
    For works on relations with a specific country
    regardless of period see DT549.63.A+
549.62 General works
549.63.A-Z Relations with individual countries, A-Z
   By period
    Early to 1895
     Cf. DT532.25 Senegambia
549.7 General works
    Biography and memoirs
549.72 Collective
549.73.A-Z Individual, A-Z
    1895-1960
     Cf. DT551.8+ Mali (Federation)
549.75 General works
    Biography and memoirs
549.76 Collective
549.77.A-Z Individual, A-Z
    1960- . Independent
     Cf. DT551.8+ Mali (Federation)
549.8 General works
    1960-2000
549.815 General works
    Biography and memoirs

West Africa. West Coast
French West Africa. French Sahara. West Sahara. Sahel
Local history and description
Senegal
History
By period
1960- . Independent
1960-2000
Biography and memoirs -- Continued
549.82   Collective
549.83.A-Z   Individual, A-Z
2000-
549.84   General works
Biography and memoirs
549.85   Collective
549.86.A-Z   Individual, A-Z
549.9.A-Z   Local history and description, A-Z
Mali. Mali Federation. Sudanese Republic. French Sudan
Cf. DT532.2 Mali Empire
551   Periodicals. Societies. Serials
551.13   Sources and documents
551.15   Gazetteers. Dictionaries, etc.
551.2   Guidebooks
551.22   General works
551.24   Pictorial works
Historic monuments, landmarks, scenery, etc.
(General)
For local see DT551.9.A+
551.25   General works
551.26   Preservation
551.265   Geography
551.27   Description and travel
551.3   Antiquities
For local antiquities see DT551.9.A+
551.4   Social life and customs. Civilization. Intellectual life
For specific periods, see the period
Ethnography
551.42   General works
551.45.A-Z   Individual elements in the population, A-Z
551.45.B35   Bambara
551.45.B63   Bobo
551.45.B64   Bobo Fing
551.45.B68   Bozo
551.45.B84   Bwa
551.45.D45   Dendi
551.45.D64   Dogon
551.45.F85   Fula

West Africa. West Coast
French West Africa. French Sahara. West Sahara. Sahel
Local history and description
Mali. Mali Federation. Soudanese Republic. French
Sudan
Ethnography
Individual elements in the population, A-Z --
Continued

551.45.K85	Kurumba. Tellem
551.45.M36	Mandingo
551.45.M55	Minianka
551.45.M84	Muslims
551.45.S24	Samo
551.45.S65	Somono
551.45.S66	Songhai
551.45.S67	Soninke
	Tellem see DT551.45.K85
551.45.T83	Tuareg

History
551.5	General works
551.6	Political history

For specific periods, see the period
Foreign and general relations
For general works on the diplomatic history of a period,
see the period
For works on relations with a specific country
regardless of period see DT551.63.A+

551.62	General works
551.63.A-Z	Relations with individual countries, A-Z

By period
551.65	Early to 1898

1898-1959. French colony and territory
551.7	General works

Biography and memoirs
551.719	Collective
551.72.A-Z	Individual, A-Z

1959-1991
Including Mali Federation (April 1959-Aug. 1960) and
Mali Republic (1960-)
Cf. DT549.75+ Senegal
551.8	General works

Biography and memoirs
551.819	Collective
551.82.A-Z	Individual, A-Z

e.g.
551.82.K44	Keita, Modibo

1991-

West Africa. West Coast
  French West Africa. French Sahara. West Sahara. Sahel
    Local history and description
      Mali. Mali Federation. Soudanese Republic. French
        Sudan
       History
        By period
         1991- -- Continued

551.84	General works
	Biography and memoirs
551.845	Collective
551.846.A-Z	Individual, A-Z
551.9.A-Z	Local history and description, A-Z
	e.g.
551.9.T55	Timbuktu
	Mauritania
554	Periodicals. Societies. Serials
554.13	Sources and documents
554.15	Gazetteers. Dictionaries, etc.
554.17	Place names (General)
	For etymological studies, see class P
554.2	Guidebooks
554.22	General works
554.23	General special
554.24	Pictorial works
	Historic monuments, landmarks, scenery, etc. (General)
	For local see DT554.9.A+
554.25	General works
554.26	Preservation
554.27	Description and travel
554.3	Antiquities
	For local antiquities see DT554.9.A+
554.4	Social life and customs. Civilization. Intellectual life
	For specific periods, see the period
	Ethnography
554.42	General works
554.45.A-Z	Individual elements in the population, A-Z
554.45.F84	Fula
554.45.I57	Imragen
554.45.M38	Maure
554.45.M84	Muslims
554.45.S65	Soninke
	History
554.52	Biography (Collective)
	For individual biography, see the specific period, reign, or place

West Africa. West Coast
  French West Africa. French Sahara. West Sahara. Sahel
    Local history and description
      Mauritania
        History -- Continued

554.55	Historiography
554.57	General works
554.58	General special
554.583	Military history
554.59	Political history

For specific periods, see the period
Foreign and general relations
    For general works on the diplomatic history of a period,
        see the period
    For works on relations with a specific country
        regardless of period see DT554.63.A+

554.62	General works
554.63.A-Z	Relations with individual countries, A-Z

By period
  Early to 1920
    Including Arab and Berber Almoravid domination;
        early explorations by Portuguese, English and
        French; early colonization by French, and
        negotiations by Xavier Coppolani
    Cf. DT318+ Morocco
    Cf. DT532+ French West Africa
    Cf. DT532.15 Ghana empire

554.65	General works
	Biography and memoirs
554.66	Collective
554.67.A-Z	Individual, A-Z

1920-1960. French colony

554.75	General works
	Biography and memoirs
554.76	Collective
554.77.A-Z	Individual, A-Z

1960- . Independent
  Including Moroccan annexation claims
  Cf. DT346.S7 Spanish Sahara

554.8	General works
	Biography and memoirs
554.82	Collective
554.83.A-Z	Individual, A-Z
554.9.A-Z	Local history and description, A-Z

Burkina Faso. Upper Volta

555	Periodicals. Societies. Serials
555.13	Sources and documents

West Africa. West Coast
 French West Africa. French Sahara. West Sahara. Sahel
  Local history and description
   Burkina Faso. Upper Volta -- Continued

555.15	Gazetteers. Dictionaries, etc.
555.17	Place names (General)
	For etymological studies, see class P
555.2	Guidebooks
555.22	General works
555.23	General special
555.24	Pictorial works
	Historic monuments, landmarks, scenery, etc.
	(General)
	For local see DT555.9.A+
555.25	General works
555.26	Preservation
555.27	Description and travel
555.3	Antiquities
	For local antiquities see DT555.9.A+
555.4	Social life and customs. Civilization. Intellectual life
	For specific periods, see the period
	Ethnography
555.42	General works
555.45.A-Z	Individual elements in the population, A-Z
555.45.B57	Bisa
555.45.B63	Bobo
555.45.B64	Bobo Dioula
555.45.B93	Bwa
555.45.D35	Dagaaba
555.45.F85	Fula
555.45.G36	Gan
555.45.G68	Gouin
555.45.G85	Gurma
555.45.G87	Gurunsi
555.45.K37	Kasem
555.45.K62	Ko
555.45.K88	Kurumba
555.45.K9	Kusasi
555.45.L63	Lobi
555.45.L68	LoWilli
555.45.L94	Lyelae
555.45.M67	Mossi
555.45.N84	Nunuma
555.45.T82	Tuaregs
555.45.T87	Tusia
555.45.W35	Wara
	History

West Africa. West Coast
  French West Africa. French Sahara. West Sahara. Sahel
    Local history and description
      Burkina Faso. Upper Volta
        History -- Continued

555.517	Dictionaries. Chronological tables, outlines, etc.
555.52	Biography (Collective)
	For individual biography, see the specific period, reign, or place
555.55	Historiography
555.57	General works
555.59	Political history
	For specific periods, see the period or reign
	Foreign and general relations
	For general works on the diplomatic history of a period, see the period
	For works on relations with a specific country regardless of period see DT555.63.A+
555.62	General works
555.63.A-Z	Relations with individual countries, A-Z
	By period
	Early to 1897
	Including Mossi and Gourma Kingdoms; Moroccan conquest; early European explorations; invasions by Samory
	Cf. DT319 Morocco, 647-1516
555.65	General works
	Biography and memoirs
555.66	Collective
555.67.A-Z	Individual, A-Z
	1897-1960. French Protectorate and Colony
	Including administration as part of Upper Senegal-Niger (1904-1919)
	Cf. DT545+ Ivory Coast (Partition, 1932-1947)
	Cf. DT547+ Niger (Partition, 1932-1947)
	Cf. DT551+ French Sudan (Mali) (Partition, 1932-1947)
555.75	General works
	Biography and memoirs
555.76	Collective
555.77.A-Z	Individual, A-Z
	1960-1987
555.8	General works
	Biography and memoirs
555.82	Collective
555.83.A-Z	Individual, A-Z

	West Africa. West Coast
	French West Africa. French Sahara. West Sahara. Sahel
	Local history and description
	Burkina Faso. Upper Volta
	History
	By period -- Continued
	1987- . Third Republic
	Including 1987 Coup d'état
555.835	General works
	Biography and memoirs
555.836	Collective
555.837.A-Z	Individual, A-Z
555.9.A-Z	Local history and description, A-Z
	Cameroon (Cameroun, Kamerun)
	Formerly German West Africa
561	Periodicals. Societies. Serials
562	Sources and documents
563	Gazetteers. Dictionaries, etc.
563.5	Guidebooks
564	General works
	Description and travel
566	Through 1918
567	1919-1980
568	1981-
569	Antiquities
	For local antiquities see DT581.A+
569.5	Social life and customs. Civilization. Intellectual life
	For specific periods, see the period
	Ethnography
570	General works
571.A-Z	Individual elements in the population, A-Z
	Akoose see DT571.K66
571.B25	Babanki
571.B3	Babingas
571.B32	Bafia
571.B3214	Bafut
571.B322	Baka
(571.B323)	Bakwiri
	see DT571.K85
571.B33	Bali
571.B34	Bamileke
571.B35	Bamun
571.B36	Bana
571.B365	Bandjoun
571.B366	Bangwa
571.B37	Basa
571.B38	Bavëk

West Africa. West Coast
  Cameroon (Cameroun, Kamerun)
    Ethnography
      Individual elements in the population, A-Z -- Continued

571.B47	Beti
571.B67	Bororo
571.B85	Bulu
571.D33	Daba
571.D55	Dii
571.D68	Doyayo
571.D83	Duala
571.E35	Ejagham
571.E86	Eton
571.E94	Evuzok
571.F34	Fali
571.F43	Fe'Fe'
571.F64	Fon
571.F73	French
571.F84	Fula
571.G57	Giziga
571.K36	Kamwe
571.K64	Kom
571.K65	Koma
571.K66	Kossi. Akoose
571.K85	Kwiri
571.L55	Limbum
	Mafa see DT571.M39
571.M35	Maka
571.M356	Mambila
571.M36	Manda
571.M37	Mankon
571.M38	Masa
571.M39	Matakam. Mafa
571.M47	Meta
571.M84	Mumuye
571.M85	Mundang
571.N43	Ngangte
571.N45	Ngemba
571.N48	Ngwe
571.N65	Northern Mofu
571.N74	Nso
571.N78	Ntumu
571.O38	Oku
571.P44	Peere
571.P93	Pygmies
571.T54	Tikar
571.U43	Uldeme

	West Africa. West Coast
	Cameroon (Cameroun, Kamerun) -- Continued
	History
572	General works
	Foreign and general relations
	For general works on the diplomatic history of a period, see the period
	For works on relations with a specific country regardless of period see DT573.5.A+
573	Sources and documents
573.3	General works
573.5.A-Z	Relations with individual countries, A-Z
	By period
	Early to 1960
574	General works
	Biography and memoirs
574.5	Collective
575.A-Z	Individual, A-Z
	e.g.
575.D6	Dominik, Hans
	1960- . Republic
575.5	General works
	1960-1982. Ahidjo administration
576	General works
	Biography and memoirs
576.5	Collective
577.A-Z	Individual, A-Z
	1982-
578	General works
	Biography and memoirs
578.3	Collective
578.4.A-Z	Individual, A-Z
581.A-Z	Local history and description, A-Z
	Togo. Togoland
582	Periodicals. Societies. Serials
582.13	Sources and documents
582.15	Gazetteers. Dictionaries, etc.
582.2	Guidebooks
582.22	General works
582.24	Pictorial works
582.27	Description and travel
582.4	Social life and customs. Civilization. Intellectual life
	For specific periods, see the period
	Ethnography
582.42	General works
582.45.A-Z	Individual elements in the population, A-Z
582.45.A29	Adangme

West Africa. West Coast
Togo. Togoland
Ethnography
Individual elements in the population, A-Z -- Continued

582.45.A34	Aja
582.45.A54	Anii
582.45.A56	Anlo
582.45.B37	Bassari
582.45.B4	Be
582.45.C56	Chokossi
582.45.E93	Ewe
582.45.G3	Gã
582.45.G68	Gouin
582.45.K33	Kabiye
582.45.K64	Kposo
582.45.M55	Mina
582.45.M63	Moba
582.45.N38	Naudeba
582.45.S65	Somba
582.45.T45	Tem
582.45.W33	Waci
	History
582.5	General works
582.59	Political history
	For specific periods, see the period
	Foreign and general relations
	For general works on the diplomatic history of a period, see the period
	For works on relations with a specific country regardless of period see DT582.63.A+
582.62	General works
582.63.A-Z	Relations with individual countries, A-Z
	By period
582.65	Through 1884
582.7	1884-1922. German colony
	1922-1960. Partition
582.75	French Togoland (1922-1960)
	British Togoland (1922-1957) see DT511+
	1960- . Independence
582.77	General works
	1960-2005
582.8	General works
	Biography and memoirs
582.819	Collective
582.82.A-Z	Individual, A-Z
	e.g.
582.82.E94	Eyadéma, Gnassingbé

West Africa. West Coast
Togo. Togoland
History
By period
1960- . Independence
2005-

582.84	General works
	Biography and memoirs
582.85	Collective
582.852.A-Z	Individual, A-Z
	e.g.
582.852.G58	Gnassingbé, Faure
582.9.A-Z	Local history and description, A-Z
	e.g.
582.9.L65	Lomé
	Portuguese-speaking West Africa
591	Periodicals. Societies. Serials
593	Guidebooks
594	General works
	Description and travel
596	Through 1800
597	1801-1950
598	1951-
599	Antiquities
600	Ethnography
602	History
	Local history and description
	Cape Verde Islands see DT671.C2+
	Guinea-Bissau. Portuguese Guinea
613	Periodicals. Societies. Serials
613.13	Sources and documents
613.16	Guidebooks
613.17	General works
613.19	Pictorial works
613.195	Historical geography
613.2	Description and travel
613.4	Social life and customs. Civilization. Intellectual life
	For specific periods, see the period
	Ethnography
613.42	General works
613.45.A-Z	Individual elements in the population, A-Z
613.45.B35	Balanta
613.45.B54	Bijago
613.45.M36	Mandingo
613.45.P36	Papel
	History
613.5	General works

West Africa. West Coast
Portuguese-speaking West Africa
Local history and description
Guinea-Bissau. Portuguese Guinea
History -- Continued

613.6	Political history
	For specific periods, see the period
	Foreign and general relations
	For general works on the diplomatic history of a period, see the period
	For works on relations with a specific country regardless of period see DT613.63.A+
613.62	General works
613.63.A-Z	Relations with individual countries, A-Z
	By period
613.65	Early to 1879
	1879-1974. Portuguese colony and territory
613.75	General works
	Biography and memoirs
613.752	Collective
613.76.A-Z	Individual, A-Z
	e.g.
613.76.C3	Cabral, Amilcar
613.77	1879-1963
613.78	1963-1974. Revolution
	1974- . Independent
613.8	General works
	Biography and memoirs
613.82	Collective
613.83.A-Z	Individual, A-Z
613.9.A-Z	Local history and description, A-Z
	e.g.
613.9.B65	Bolama Island
	Sao Tome and Principe
615	Periodicals. Societies. Serials
615.18	General works
615.19	Pictorial works
615.2	Description and travel
615.3	Social life and customs. Civilization. Intellectual life
	Ethnography
615.42	General works
615.45.A-Z	Individual elements in the population, A-Z
	History
615.5	General works

<table>
<tbody>
<tr><td></td><td>West Africa. West Coast</td></tr>
<tr><td></td><td>Portuguese-speaking West Africa</td></tr>
<tr><td></td><td>Local history and description</td></tr>
<tr><td></td><td>Sao Tome and Principe</td></tr>
<tr><td></td><td>History -- Continued</td></tr>
<tr><td></td><td>Foreign and general relations</td></tr>
<tr><td></td><td>For general works on the diplomatic history of a period, see the period</td></tr>
<tr><td></td><td>For works on relations with a specific country regardless of period see DT615.63.A+</td></tr>
<tr><td>615.62</td><td>General works</td></tr>
<tr><td>615.63.A-Z</td><td>Relations with individual countries, A-Z</td></tr>
<tr><td></td><td>By period</td></tr>
<tr><td>615.65</td><td>Early to 1522</td></tr>
<tr><td>615.7</td><td>1522-1975. Portuguese colony</td></tr>
<tr><td>615.8</td><td>1975- . Independent</td></tr>
<tr><td>615.9.A-Z</td><td>Local history and description, A-Z</td></tr>
<tr><td></td><td>Spanish West Africa</td></tr>
<tr><td></td><td>Cf. DT330 Spanish Morocco</td></tr>
<tr><td></td><td>Cf. DT346.S7 Spanish Sahara</td></tr>
<tr><td>619</td><td>General works</td></tr>
<tr><td></td><td>Equatorial Guinea (Spanish Guinea)</td></tr>
<tr><td>620</td><td>Periodicals. Societies. Serials</td></tr>
<tr><td>620.13</td><td>Sources and documents</td></tr>
<tr><td>620.15</td><td>Gazetteers. Dictionaries, etc.</td></tr>
<tr><td>620.17</td><td>Place names (General)</td></tr>
<tr><td></td><td>For etymological studies, see class P</td></tr>
<tr><td>620.2</td><td>Guidebooks</td></tr>
<tr><td>620.22</td><td>General works</td></tr>
<tr><td>620.23</td><td>General special</td></tr>
<tr><td>620.24</td><td>Pictorial works</td></tr>
<tr><td></td><td>Historic monuments, landmarks, scenery, etc. (General)</td></tr>
<tr><td></td><td>For local see DT620.9.A+</td></tr>
<tr><td>620.25</td><td>General works</td></tr>
<tr><td>620.26</td><td>Preservation</td></tr>
<tr><td>620.27</td><td>Description and travel</td></tr>
<tr><td>620.3</td><td>Antiquities</td></tr>
<tr><td></td><td>For local antiquities see DT620.9.A+</td></tr>
<tr><td>620.4</td><td>Social life and customs. Civilization. Intellectual life</td></tr>
<tr><td></td><td>For specific periods, see the period</td></tr>
<tr><td></td><td>Ethnography</td></tr>
<tr><td>620.42</td><td>General works</td></tr>
<tr><td>620.45.A-Z</td><td>Individual elements in the population, A-Z</td></tr>
<tr><td>620.45.B45</td><td>Benga</td></tr>
<tr><td>620.45.F33</td><td>Fang</td></tr>
<tr><td>620.45.N37</td><td>Ndowe</td></tr>
<tr><td></td><td>History</td></tr>
</tbody>
</table>

	West Africa. West Coast
	Spanish West Africa
	Equatorial Guinea (Spanish Guinea)
	History -- Continued
620.46	Biography (Collective)
	For individual biography, see the specific period or place
620.47	Historiography
620.5	General works
620.6	Political history
	For specific periods, see the period
	Foreign and general relations
	For general works on the diplomatic history of a period, see the period
	For works on relations with a specific country regardless of period see DT620.63.A+
620.62	General works
620.63.A-Z	Relations with individual countries, A-Z
	By period
	Early to 1778
	Including Portuguese and Dutch claims
620.65	General works
	Biography and memoirs
620.66	Collective
620.67.A-Z	Individual, A-Z
	1778-1968
620.7	General works
	Biography and memoirs
620.72	Collective
620.73.A-Z	Individual, A-Z
	1968-
620.74	General works
	1968-1979. Regime of Macías Nguema
620.75	General works
	Biography and memoirs
620.76	Collective
620.77.A-Z	Individual, A-Z
	1979-
	Including Revolution of 1979
620.8	General works
	Biography and memoirs
620.82	Collective
620.83.A-Z	Individual, A-Z
620.9.A-Z	Local history and description, A-Z
	e.g.
620.9.A65	Annobon Island (Pagalu)
620.9.E46	Elobey Islands
	Including Corisco, Cocotiers, Mbañe and Conga

	West Africa. West Coast
	Spanish West Africa
	Equatorial Guinea (Spanish Guinea)
	Local history and description, A-Z -- Continued
620.9.F47	Fernando Po (Macías Nguema Biyogo; Bioko)
	Río Muni see DT620+
	Liberia
621	Periodicals. Societies. Serials
623	Gazetteers. Dictionaries, etc.
623.3	Place names (General)
	For etymological studies, see class P
623.5	Directories
623.7	Guidebooks
624	General works
	Description and travel
625	Through 1900
626	1901-1950
627	1951-
628	Antiquities
629	Social life and customs. Civilization. Intellectual life
	Ethnography
630	General works
630.5.A-Z	Individual, A-Z
630.5.B37	Bassa
630.5.K63	Kpelle
630.5.M35	Mano
630.5.V2	Vei
	History
630.8	Biography (Collective)
	For individual biography, see the specific period or place
631	General works
631.5	Political history
	For specific periods, see the period or reign
	Foreign and general relations
	For works on the diplomatic history of a period, see the period
632	General works
632.5.A-Z	Relations with individual countries, A-Z
	By period
	Early to 1847
	Including Grain Coast; American Colonization Society settlements
633	General works
	Biography and memoirs
633.2	Collective
633.3.A-Z	Individual, A-Z
	e.g.

	West Africa. West Coast
	Liberia
	History
	By period
	Early to 1847
	Biography and memoirs
	Individual, A-Z -- Continued
633.3.A8	Ashmun, Jehudi
	1847-1944. Republic of Liberia
634	General works
	Biography and memoirs
634.2	Collective
634.3.A-Z	Individual, A-Z
	e.g.
634.3.R6	Roberts, Joseph Jenkins
	1944-1971
635	General works
	Biography and memoirs
635.2	Collective
636.A-Z	Individual, A-Z
	e.g.
636.T8	Tubman, William V.S.
	1971-1980
636.2	General works
	Biography and memoirs
636.3	Collective
636.4.A-Z	Individual, A-Z
	e.g.
636.4.T63	Tolbert, William R.
	1980-
	Including the 1989-1996 and 1999-2003 civil wars
636.5	General works
	Biography and memoirs
636.52	Collective
636.53.A-Z	Individual, A-Z
637.A-Z	Regions, towns, etc. A-Z
	e.g.
637.G7	Grand Bassa County
637.M6	Monrovia
639	Congo (Kongo) River region
	For works by Stanley see DT351
	Congo (Democratic Republic). Zaire. Belgian Congo
641	Periodicals. Societies. Serials
643	Dictionaries. Guidebooks. Directories
644	General works
644.8	Geography
	Description and travel

West Africa. West Coast
Congo (Democratic Republic). Zaire. Belgian Congo
Description and travel -- Continued
645	Through 1880
646	1881-1950
647	1951-1980
647.5	1981-
648	Antiquities
649	Social life and customs. Civilization. Intellectual life

Ethnography
649.5	General works
650.A-Z	Individual elements in the population, A-Z
650.A38	Aka
650.A48	Alur
650.A93	Azande
	Bakongo see DT650.K66
650.B34	Balese
	Baluba see DT650.L8
650.B36	Bambute
650.B363	Bangala
650.B365	Basakata
650.B366	Bashi
	Bassonge see DT650.S55
650.B37	Basuku
650.B372	Batwa
(650.B375)	Bavili
	see DT650.V54
650.B38	Bayaka
650.B44	Bemba
650.B45	Bembe
650.B57	Bira
650.B66	Boma
650.B84	Buissi
650.B87	Bushongo
650.D44	Dengese
650.E34	Efe
650.E45	Ekonda
650.F43	Flemings
650.G46	Genya
650.G74	Greeks
650.H35	Haitians
650.H38	Havu
650.H45	Hemba
650.H54	Hima
650.H83	Hunde
650.H85	Hungana
650.H88	Hutu

West Africa. West Coast
    Congo (Democratic Republic). Zaire. Belgian Congo
        Ethnography
            Individual elements in the population, A-Z -- Continued

650.K33	Kanyok
650.K36	Kasanga
650.K39	Kela
650.K66	Kongo
(650.K68)	Kota
	see DT546.245.K68
650.K83	Kuba
650.K86	Kumu
650.L35	Lebanese
650.L38	Lele
650.L8	Luba
650.L83	Lulua
650.L86	Lunda, Northern
650.M38	Mayombe
650.M42	Mbala
650.M46	Mbole
	Mbuti see DT650.B36
650.M64	Monbuttus
650.M65	Mongo
650.M97	Muslims
650.N34	Nande
650.N45	Ngbaka
650.N48	Ngombe
650.N5	Ngongo
650.N55	Nkanu
650.N58	Nkundu
650.N85	Ntomba
650.N89	Nunu
650.N92	Nyali
650.N93	Nyanga
650.O92	Ovambo
650.P46	Pende
650.P94	Pygmies
650.R43	Rega. Warega
650.S25	Sanga
650.S53	Solongo
650.S55	Songye
650.S57	Soonde
650.S94	Sundi
650.T32	Tabwa
650.T47	Tetela
650.T65	Topoke
650.T86	Tutsi

	West Africa. West Coast
	Congo (Democratic Republic). Zaire. Belgian Congo
	Ethnography
	Individual elements in the population, A-Z -- Continued
650.V54	Vili. Bavili
650.W33	Wagenia
(650.W37)	Waregas
	see DT650.R43
650.W69	Woyo
	Yaka see DT650.B38
650.Y3	Yanzi
650.Y43	Yeke
650.Y65	Yombe
650.Z35	Zande
650.Z44	Zela
	History
	Cf. DT31+ Partition of Africa
650.17	Dictionaries. Chronological tables, outlines, etc.
	Historiography
650.2	General works
	Biography of historians, area studies specialists, archaeologists, etc.
650.3	Collective
650.4.A-Z	Individual, A-Z
	Study and teaching
650.7	General works
650.8.A-Z	By region or country, A-Z
	Subarrange by author
652	General works
653	Political history
	For specific periods, see the period
	Foreign and general relations
	For general works on the diplomatic history of a period, see the period
	For works on relations with a specific country regardless of period see DT653.5.A+
653.3	General works
653.5.A-Z	Relations with individual countries, A-Z
	By period
	Early. Congo Kingdom. Portuguese claims. Association Internationale du Congo
	Cf. DT1357+ Angola
654	General works
	Biography and memoirs
654.2	Collective
654.3.A-Z	Individual, A-Z
	Congo Free State, 1885-1908

West Africa. West Coast
  Congo (Democratic Republic). Zaire. Belgian Congo
    History
      By period
        Congo Free State, 1885-1908 -- Continued

655	General works
	Biography and memoirs
655.2.A2	Collective
655.2.A3-Z	Individual, A-Z
	Belgian Congo, 1908-1960
657	General works
	Biography and memoirs
657.2.A2	Collective
657.2.A3-Z	Individual, A-Z
	1960-
658	General works
	Biography and memoirs
658.2.A2	Collective
658.2.A3-Z	Individual, A-Z
658.22	Civil War, 1960-1965
	Including assassination of Patrice Lumumba
658.25	1965-1997. Regime of Mobuto Sese Seko
	Including Shaba Invasions of 1977 and 1978, and Kolwezi Massacre of 1978
658.26	1997- . Regime of Laurent Kabila. Administration of Joseph Kabila
663	Biography and memoirs (Collective)
665.A-Z	Local history and description, A-Z
	e.g.
665.B3	Bas-Congo (Lower Congo)
665.E4	Elisabethville. Lubumbashi
665.I55	Inkisi
665.I8	Ituri Forest. Ituri Region
665.K28	Kasai
665.K3	Katanga. Shaba
	Kinshasa see DT665.L4
665.K55	Kisangani. Stanleyville
665.K58	Kivu
665.L4	Leopoldville. Kinshasa
	Lumbumbashi see DT665.E4
665.M35	Maniema (Kasongo)
	Shaba see DT665.K3
	Stanleyville see DT665.K55
	Islands
669	General works
671.A-Z	Individual islands or groups of islands, A-Z
	Annobon Island see DT620.9.A65

	West Africa. West Coast
	Islands
	Individual islands or groups of islands, A-Z -- Continued
671.B58	Bissagos Islands (Ilhas dos Bijagós)
	Bolama see DT613.9.B65
	Canary Islands see DP302.C36+
	Cape Verde
671.C2	Periodicals. Societies. Serials
671.C212	Guidebooks
671.C215	General works
671.C22	Description and travel
671.C23	Social life and customs. Civilization. Intellectual life
	Ethnography
671.C242	General works
671.C245A-.C245Z	Individual elements in the population, A-Z
671.C2455	Cape Verdeans in foreign countries (General)
	History
671.C25	General works
	By period
671.C265	Early to 1975
	1975- . Independent
671.C28	General works
	Biography
671.C282	Collective
671.C283.A- 671.283.Z	Individual, A-Z
671.C29A-.C29Z	Local history and description, A-Z
	Elobey Islands see DT620.9.E46
	Fernando Po see DT620.9.F47
	Madeira see DP702.M11+
671.S2	Saint Helena
671.T8	Tristan da Cunha
(727-971)	Southern Africa
	see DT1001+
	Southern Africa
1001	Periodicals. Societies. Serials
	Museums, exhibitions, etc.
1005	General works
1006.A-Z	Individual. By place, A-Z
1008	Congresses
1009	Sources and documents
	Collected works (nonserial)
1011	Several Authors
1012	Individual authors
1014	Gazetteers. Dictionaries, etc.
1015	Place names (Serial)
1016	Directories

	Southern Africa -- Continued
1017	Guidebooks
1019	General works
1021	General special
1023	Pictorial works
	Historic monuments, landmarks, scenery, etc.
1025	General works
1026	Preservation
1028	Historical geography
	Description and travel
1030	Early through 1900
1032	1901-1950
1034	1951-1980
1036	1981-
1050	Antiquities
1052	Social life and customs. Civilization. Intellectual life
	For specific periods, see the period
	Ethnography
1054	General works
1055	National characteristics
1056	Ethnic and race relations
1058.A-Z	Individual elements in the population, A-Z
1058.B34	Bafokeng
1058.B53	Blacks
1058.B75	British
1058.K56	Khoikhoi
1058.K83	Kua
1058.K86	!Kung
1058.M35	Malays
1058.M87	Muslims
1058.N58	Nguni
1058.P63	Poles
1058.P65	Pondo
1058.R33	Racially mixed people
1058.S36	San
1058.T78	Tswana
1058.X55	Xhosa
1058.Z84	Zulu
	History
	Periodicals. Societies. Serials see DT1001
1062	Dictionaries. Chronological tables, outlines, etc.
1064	Biography (Collective)
	Historiography
1066	General works
	Biography of historians, area studies specialists, archaeologists, etc.
1067	Collective

	Southern Africa
	History
	Historiography
	Biography of historians, area studies specialists,
	archaeologists, etc. -- Continued
1068.A-Z	Individual, A-Z
	Study and teaching
1070	General works
1072.A-Z	By region or country, A-Z
	Subarrange by author
1079	General works
1090	Pictorial works
1092	Juvenile works
1093	Philosophy of Southern African history
1095	History of several parts of Southern Africa treated together
1096	Military history
	Political history
	For specific periods, see the period
1098	Sources and documents
1099	General works
	Foreign and general relations
	For general works on the diplomatic history of a period, see
	the period
	For works on relations with a specific country
	regardless of period see DT1105.A+
1101	Sources and documents
1103	General works
1105.A-Z	Relations with individual countries, A-Z
	By period
	Early to 1890
1107	General works
	Biography and memoirs
	Class biography under individual country except for those
	persons who are associated with more than one
	country, or who inhabited a region that does not
	correspond to a modern jurisdiction
1109	Collective
1110.A-Z	Individual, A-Z
	e.g.
1110.L58	Livingstone, David, 1812-1873
	Individual empires
1111	Karanga Empire
1113	Monomotapa
1115	Nguni States
1117	Rozwi Kingdoms
1119	Zulu Empire
	Cf. DT2400.Z85 Zululand

DT

	Southern Africa
	History
	By period
	Early to 1890 -- Continued
1123	Mfecane, ca. 1820-ca. 1840
	For Mfecane in individual countries, see the country
	1890-1975
1125	Periodicals. Societies. Serials
1126	Sources and documents
1128	Historiography
1130	General works
1132	Social life and customs. Civilization. Intellectual life
1135	Military history
1137	Political history
1139	Foreign and general relations
1142	Biography and memoirs (Collective)
1144	1890-1918
1145	1918-1945
1147	1945-1976
	1975-
1155	Periodicals. Societies. Serials
1157	Congresses
1159	Sources and documents
1161	Collected works (nonserial)
1163	Historiography
1165	General works
1166	General special
1168	Social life and customs. Civilization. Intellectual life
1170	Military history
1172	Foreign and general relations
1174	Biography and memoirs (Collective)
1177	National liberation movements
1182	1994-
1190.A-Z	Local history and description, A-Z
	e.g.
1190.K35	Kalahari Desert
1190.L56	Limpopo River and Valley
1190.Z36	Zambezi River and Valley
	Angola
1251	Periodicals. Societies. Serials
1259	Sources and documents
1264	Gazetteers. Dictionaries, etc.
1265	Place names (General)
1267	Guidebooks
1269	General works
1271	General special

	Angola -- Continued
1275	Historic monuments, landmarks, scenery, etc. (General)
	For local see DT1450+
1278	Historical geography
	Description and travel
1282	Early through 1980
1286	1981-
1300	Antiquities
	For local antiquities see DT1450+
1302	Social life and customs. Civilization. Intellectual life
	For specific periods, see the period
	Ethnography
1304	General works
1306	Ethnic and race relations
1308.A-Z	Individual elements in the population, A-Z
1308.C67	Chokwe
1308.H32	Handa
1308.H35	Hanya
1308.H48	Herero
1308.H56	Himba
1308.K66	Kongo
1308.K83	Kuanyama
1308.K88	Kuvale
1308.L68	Loanda
1308.L84	Luena
1308.L86	Lunda
1308.M36	Mashi
1308.M38	Mbundu
1308.M85	Mwila
1308.N46	Ndonga
1308.N53	Ngangela
1308.N58	Nkumbi
1308.N93	Nyaneka
1308.O83	Ovambo
1308.P68	Portuguese
1308.S35	San
1308.S68	Sosso
1308.W55	Whites
	History
	Periodicals. Societies. Serials see DT1251
1314	Biography (Collective)
	For individual biography, see the specific period
	Historiography
1316	General works
	Biography of historians, area studies specialists, archaeologists, etc.
1317	Collective

	Angola
	History
	Historiography
	Biography of historians, area studies specialists, archaeologists, etc. -- Continued
1318.A-Z	Individual, A-Z
1325	General works
1348	Political history
	For specific periods, see the period
	Foreign and general relations
	For general works on the diplomatic history of a period, see the period
	For works on relations with a specific country regardless of period see DT1355.A+
1353	General works
1355.A-Z	Relations with individual countries, A-Z
	By period
	Early to 1648
	Cf. DT654+ Congo (Kingdom)
1357	General works
	Biography and memoirs
1359	Collective
1365.A-Z	Individual, A-Z
	e.g.
1365.D53	Dias de Novais, Paulo
1365.N56	Ngola Inene, King of Ndongo
1365.N95	Nzinga, Queen of Matamba
1367	Period of conquest, 1575-1683
1369	Dutch occupation, 1641-1648
	1648-1885. Portuguese expansion
	Cf. DT654+ Congo (Kingdom)
1373	General works
	Biography and memoirs
1375	Collective
1376.A-Z	Individual, A-Z
	e.g.
1376.S56	Silva Porto, Francisco da
1378	Mbwila, Battle of, 1665
1380	Pungua-Ndongo, Siege of, 1671
1382	Separatist revolt, 1823
	1885-1961. Portuguese consolidation
1385	General works
	Biography and memoirs
1386	Collective
1388.A-Z	Individual, A-Z
	e.g.
1388.K35	Kalandula, Bailundo King

Angola
  History
    By period
      1885-1961. Portuguese consolidation
        Biography and memoirs
          Individual, A-Z -- Continued

1388.M88	Mutu ya Kevela
1390	Dembo rebellions, 1877-1919
1392	Bailundo War, 1902
1394	Mussorongo revolt, 1908
1396	Bakongo rebellion, 1913-1914

      1961-1975. Revolution

1398	Periodicals. Societies. Serials
1400	Sources and documents
1402	General works

        Military history

1405	General works
1406.A-Z	Individual events, battles, etc., A-Z
	e.g.
1406.L83	Luanda Uprising, 1961

        Foreign participation

1408	General works
1410.A-Z	By region or country, A-Z
	e.g.
1410.C83	Cuba
1413.A-Z	Special topics, A-Z
1413.P76	Propaganda
1413.R44	Registers of dead

        Biography and memoirs

1415	Collective
1417.A-Z	Individual, A-Z
	e.g.
1417.A54	Andrade, Mario Pinto de
1417.C55	Chipenda, Daniel
1417.R63	Roberto, Holden

      1975- . Independent
        For South African raids on SWAPO installations, 1978- see DT1645

1420	General works

        Biography and memoirs

1422	Collective
1424.A-Z	Individual, A-Z
	e.g.
1424.A58	Alves, Nito
1424.S38	Savimbi, Jonas
1426	Agostinho Neto, António. 1975-1979

          Class here general works on life and administration

	Angola
	History
	By period
	1975- . Independent -- Continued
1428	Civil War, 1975-2002
1430	South African invasion, 1975-1976
1432	Coup d'etat, 1977
1434	Jose Eduardo dos Santos, 1979-
	Class here general works on life and administration
1436	South African incursions, 1978-1990
	Including Lusaka Accord
	Local history and description
1450.A-Z	Provinces, districts, regions, etc., A-Z
1450.B54	Bié
1450.C33	Cabinda
1450.C85	Cunene River
1450.H83	Huambo
1450.H85	Huila
1450.K83	Kwanza (Cuanza) River
1450.M69	Moxico
1450.N36	Namibe Province. Moçâmides
1450.U55	Uige
1450.Z35	Zaire Province
	Cities, towns, etc.
1455	Luanda
1465.A-Z	Other cities, towns, etc., A-Z
	e.g.
1465.B35	Bailundo. Teixeira da Silva
1465.B46	Benguela
1465.C55	Chibia. João de Almeida
1465.H83	Huambo. Nova Lisboa
1465.K38	Kassinga. Cassinga
1465.K85	Kuito, Bié. Silva Porto
1465.L73	Lobito
1465.L83	Luachimo. Portugália
1465.L84	Luao. Teixeira de Sousa
1465.L85	Lubango. Sá da Bandeira
1465.L86	Luena. Luso
1465.M35	Malange. Malanje
1465.M42	Mbanza. Kongo. São Salvador do Congo
1465.M46	Menongue. Serpa Pinto
1465.N36	Namibe. Moçâmbides
1465.N55	Ngiva. Pereira de Eça
1465.N58	Ngunza. Novo Redondo
1465.N94	Nzeto. Ambrizete
1465.S38	Saurimo. Henrique de Carvalho
1465.U55	Uîge. Carmona

	Namibia. South-West Africa
1501	Periodicals. Societies. Serials
1509	Sources and documents
1514	Gazetteers. Dictionaries, etc.
1515	Place names (General)
1517	Guidebooks
1519	General works
1521	General special
1523	Pictorial works
1525	Historic monuments, landmarks, scenery, etc.
	For local see DT1670+
	Description and travel
1532	Through 1980
1536	1981-
1550	Antiquities
	For local antiquities see DT1670+
1552	Social life and customs. Civilization. Intellectual life
	For specific periods, see the period
	Ethnography
1554	General works
1555	Ethnic and race relations
1556	Apartheid
1557	Blacks
	Including Homelands
1558.A-Z	Individual elements in the population, A-Z
1558.A46	Afrikaners
1558.B65	Bondelswarts
1558.D35	Damara
1558.G46	Germans
1558.H45	Heikum
1558.H47	Herero
1558.H56	Himba
1558.K46	Khoikhoi
1558.K83	Kuanyama
1558.K85	!Kung
1558.K9	Kwena
1558.K95	Kxoe
1558.M33	Mbandieru
1558.M37	Mbukushu
1558.N36	Nama
1558.N46	Ndonga
1558.O83	Ovambo
1558.R45	Rehoboth Basters
1558.S36	Sambyu
1558.S38	San
1558.S83	Swedes
1558.S84	Swiss

	Namibia. South-West Africa
	Ethnography
	Individual elements in the population, A-Z -- Continued
1558.T78	Tswana
	History
	Periodicals. Societies. Serials see DT1501
1564	Biography (Collective)
	For individual biography, see the specific period
	Historiography
1566	General works
	Biography of historians, area studies specialists, archaeologists, etc.
1567	Collective
1568.A-Z	Individual, A-Z
1575	General works
1579	Political history
	For specific periods, see the period
	Foreign and general relations
	For general works on the diplomatic history of a period, see the period
	For works on relations with a specific country regardless of period see DT1585.A+
1583	General works
1585.A-Z	Relations with individual countries, A-Z
	By period
	Early to 1884
	Including Portuguese, Dutch, and British claims, and German and British settlements
1587	General works
	Biography and memoirs
1589	Collective
1595.A-Z	Individual, A-Z
	e.g.
1595.J36	Jan Jonker Afrikaner
1595.J66	Jonker Afrikaner
1597	Rehoboth Baster's settlement, 1868
1599	Walvis Bay annexation, 1878
1601	Afrikaaner Trek, 1878-1879
	1884-1915. German South-West Africa
	Including Luderitz concessions
1603	General works
	Biography and memoirs
1605	Collective
1608.A-Z	Individual, A-Z
	e.g.
1608.C57	Christian, Johannes
1608.M35	Maharero, Samuel

	Namibia. South-West Africa
	History
	By period
	1884-1915. German South-West Africa
	Biography and memoirs
	Individual, A-Z -- Continued
1608.M67	Morenga
1608.W58	Witbooi, Hendrik
1610	Afrikaaner Republic of Upingtonia, 1885-1887
1612	Witbooi Rebellion, 1893-1894
1614	Herero Uprising, 1896
1616	Bondelswarts' Uprising, 1903-1904
1618	Herero War, 1904-1907
1620	Nama War, 1904-1906
1622	Rehoboth Basters Uprising, 1915
	1915-1946. South African Mandate under authority of the League of Nations
1625	General works
	Biography and memoirs
1627	Collective
1628.A-Z	Individual, A-Z
	e.g.
1628.C57	Christian, Jacobus
1628.M78	Morris, Abraham
1630	Bondelswarts' Rebellion, 1922
1632	Rehoboth Basters' Rebellion, 1925
1634	Angola Afrikaaners' resettlement, 1925
1636	German reunification movement, 1932-1939
	1946-1990. United Nations Trusteeship. South African administration
1638	General works
	Biography and memoirs
1640	Collective
1641.A-Z	Individual, A-Z
	e.g.
1641.K36	Kapuuo, Clemens
1641.K88	Kutako, Hosea
1641.M84	Mudge, Dirk
1641.N34	Namhila, Ellen Ndeshi
1641.N85	Nujoma, Sam
1641.T75	Toivo ja Toivo, Andimba
1641.W58	Witbooi, David
1643	Cancellation of South African Mandate, 1966
1645	Armed struggle for national liberation, 1966-1990
	Including South African raids on SWAPO installations in Angola, 1978-1990
1647	Turnhalle conference, 1975-1978

	Namibia. South-West Africa
	History
	By period
	1946-1990. United Nations Trusteeship. South African administration -- Continued
1648	Transitional government, 1985-1990
1649	1990- , Independent
	Biography and memoirs
1650	Collective
1651.A-Z	Individual, A-Z
	Local history and description
1670.A-Z	Provinces, regions, etc., A-Z
	e.g.
1670.C36	Caprivi Strip
1670.D36	Damaraland
1670.E86	Etosha Pan
1670.H47	Hereroland
1670.K37	Kaokoland
1670.K38	Kavango
1670.N36	Namaland
1670.N37	Namib Desert
1670.O63	Okavango River and Swamp
1670.O83	Owambo
1670.S64	Skeleton Coast
1670.S83	Swakop River and Valley
	Cities, towns, etc.
1680	Windhoek
1685.A-Z	Other cities, towns, etc., A-Z
	e.g.
1685.B48	Bethanie
1685.K37	Karasburg
1685.L84	Luderitz. Luderitzbucht
1685.R46	Rehoboth
1685.S83	Swakopmund
1685.W35	Walvis Bay
	South Africa
1701	Periodicals. Societies. Serials
	Museums, exhibitions, etc.
1705	General works
1706.A-Z	Individual. By place, A-Z
1708	Congresses
1709	Sources and documents
1712	Collected works (nonserial)
1714	Gazetteers. Dictionaries, etc.
1715	Place names (General)
1716	Directories
1717	Guidebooks

<table>
</table>

South Africa -- Continued
1719	General works
1721	General special
1723	Pictorial works
	Historic monuments, landmarks, scenery, etc. (General)
	For local, see DT2400, DT2405, etc.
1725	General works
1726	Preservation
1727	Historical geography
1728	Geography
	Description and travel
1730	Early through 1800
1732	1801-1900
1734	1901-1950
1736	1951-1965
1738	1966-
1750	Antiquities
	For local antiquities, see DT2400, DT2405, etc.
1752	Social life and customs. Civilization. Intellectual life
	For specific periods, see the period
	Ethnography
1754	General works
1755	National characteristics
1756	Race relations
1757	Apartheid
	Blacks
	For works dealing collectively with the Bantu-speaking
	folk societies of South Africa see GN656+
1758	General works
1760	Homelands
	For individual homelands see DT2400.A+
1762	Afro-Afrikaner relations
1768.A-Z	Individual elements in the population, A-Z
1768.A57	Afrikaners
1768.A62	Americans
1768.A85	Asians
1768.B35	Bafokeng
1768.B53	Bhaca
	Blacks see DT1758+
	Boers see DT1768.A57
	Bushmen see DT1768.S36
1768.C55	Chinese
1768.C65	Colored people
1768.C68	Cornish
1768.C87	Croats
1768.C94	Czechs
1768.D88	Dutch

                        South Africa
                          Ethnography
                            Individual elements in the population, A-Z -- Continued

1768.E38	East Indians
1768.F54	Fingos
1768.F56	Flemish
1768.F73	French
	Including Huguenots
1768.G48	Germans
1768.G56	Ghoya
1768.G74	Griquas
	Hottentots see DT1768.K56
1768.I72	Irish
1768.I74	Italians
1768.J37	Japanese
1768.K53	Kgatla
1768.K56	Khoikhoi
1768.K68	Korana
1768.L45	Lemba
1768.L62	Lobedu
1768.M35	Malays
1768.M36	Mamabolo
1768.M38	Mashona
1768.M86	Muslims
1768.N37	Nama
1768.N38	Naron
1768.N42	Ndebele
1768.N45	Nguni
1768.P44	Pedi
1768.P53	Phalaborwa
1768.P65	Polish
1768.P66	Pondos
1768.P67	Portuguese
1768.R45	Rehoboth Basters
1768.R65	Rolong
1768.S36	San
1768.S43	Scandinavians
1768.S46	Scots
1768.S68	Sotho
1768.T36	Tamil
1768.T46	Tembu
(1768.T55)	Thonga
	see DT1768.T76
1768.T57	Tlhaping
1768.T76	Tsonga
1768.T89	Tswana
1768.V45	Venda

	South Africa
	Ethnography
	Individual elements in the population, A-Z -- Continued
1768.W55	Whites
1768.X57	Xhosa
1768.Z95	Zulu
1770	South Africans in foreign countries (General)
	For South Africans in a particular country, see the country
	History
	Periodicals. Societies. Serials see DT1701
1772	Dictionaries. Chronological tables, outlines, etc.
1774	Biography (Collective)
	Historiography
1776	General works
	Biography of historians, area studies specialists, archaeologists, etc.
1777	Collective
1778.A-Z	Individual, A-Z
	Study and teaching
1780	General works
1782.A-Z	By region or country, A-Z
1787	General works
1796	Military history
	For specific periods, see the period
1797	Naval history
	For specific periods, see the period
1798	Political history
	For specific periods, see the period
	Foreign and general relations
	For general works on the diplomatic history of a period, see the period
	For works on relations with a specific country regardless of period see DT1805.A+
1803	General works
1805.A-Z	Relations with individual countries, A-Z
	By period
	Early to 1652
1807	General works
	Biography and memoirs
1809	Collective
1810.A-Z	Individual, A-Z
	1652-1795. Dutch East India Company administration
1813	General works
	Biography and memoirs
1816	Collective
1817.A-Z	Individual, A-Z
	e.g.

South Africa
History
By period
1652-1795. Dutch East India Company administration
Biography and memoirs
Individual, A-Z -- Continued

1817.P53	Phalo, Xhosa chief
1817.S84	Stel, Simon van der
1817.V35	Van Riebeeck, Jan
1819	First Khoikhoi War, 1659
1821	Second Khoikhoi War, 1673-1677
1823	Huguenot settlement, 1688
1825	Xhosa Wars, 1779-1802

1795-1836. British possession

1828	General works
	Biography and memoirs
1830	Collective
1831.A-Z	Individual, A-Z
	e.g.
1831.C53	Chaka, Zulu chief
1831.D56	Dingiswayo, Zulu chief
1831.G35	Gaika, Xhosa chief
1835	Graaf-Reinet and Swellendam Rebellion, 1795
1837	Frontier Wars, 1811-1878
1839	Slaghter's Nek incident, 1815
1840	British settlers, 1820
1841	Mfecane. Difaqane, ca. 1821-1840
1843	Fiftieth Ordinance, 1828
1845	Abolition of slavery, 1834

1836-1910. British consolidation

1848	General works
	Biography and memoirs
1850	Collective
1851.A-Z	Individual, A-Z
	e.g.
1851.C48	Ceteshwayo, Zulu chief
1851.D56	Dingaan, Zulu chief
1851.D57	Dinuzulu, Zulu chief
1851.J36	Jameson, Sir Leander Starr
1851.K89	Kruger, Paul
1851.M55	Milner, Alfred
1851.P35	Panda, Zulu chief
1851.R56	Rhodes, Cecil John
1851.S37	Sarhili, Xhosa chief
1853	Great Trek, 1836-1840

For individual treks, see DT2120, DT2242, etc.
For Battle of Blood River see DT2247.B56

	South Africa
	History
	By period
	1836-1910. British consolidation -- Continued
1855	War of the Axe, 1846-1848. Seventh Xhosa War
1857	Annexation of British Kaffraria, 1847
1859	Kat River Rebellion, 1851
1861	German colonization, 1856
1863	Xhosa cattle killing. Vision of Nongquase, 1856-1857
1865	First Basuto War, 1858
1867	East Indians arrive, 1860
1869	Second Basuto War, 1865-1866
1871	Diamond rush begins, 1867
1873	Third Basuto War, 1867-1868
1874	War of Ngcayecibi, 1877-1878
	Zulu War, 1879
1875	General works
1877	Personal narratives
1879.A-Z	Individual events, battles, etc., A-Z
1879.I83	Isandhlwana, Battle of
(1879.K36)	Kambula, Battle of
	see DT1879.N55
1879.N55	Nkambule, Battle of
1879.R68	Rorke's Drift, Battle of
1879.U58	Ulundi, Battle of
1882.A-Z	Special topics, A-Z
1882.A76	Art and the war
1882.B38	Battlefields
1884	Transkei Revolt, 1880
1886	Annexation of Griqualand, 1880
1888	Rand Gold rush begins, 1886
1889	Jameson Raid, 1895
	South African War, 1899-1902
1890	Periodicals. Societies. Serials
1892	Sources and documents
1894	Causes
1896	General works
1898	Pictorial works
	Military history
1899	General works
	British Army
1900	General works
1902	Regimental histories
	Subarrange by author
	Afrikaner Army
1904	General works

	South Africa
	History
	By period
	1836-1910. British consolidation
	South African War, 1899-1902
	Military history
	Afrikaner Army -- Continued
1906	Regimental histories
	Subarrange by author
1908.A-Z	Individual events, battles, etc., A-Z
	e.g.
1908.C65	Colenso, Battle of, 1899
1908.K56	Kimberley, Siege of, 1899-1900
1908.L34	Ladysmith, Siege of, 1899-1900
1908.M34	Mafeking, Siege of, 1899-1900
1908.M35	Magersfontein, Battle of, 1899
1908.S87	Stormberg, Battle of, 1899
	Foreign participation
1911	General works
1913.A-Z	By region or country, A-Z
	Personal narratives
1915	Collective
1916.A-Z	Individual, A-Z
1918.A-Z	Special topics, A-Z
1918.B53	Blacks
1918.C64	Collaborationists
	Concentration camps see DT1918.P75
1918.I54	Influence
1918.M44	Medical care
1918.P73	Press coverage
1918.P75	Prisoners and prisons
	Including individual concentration camps
1918.P77	Protest movements
1918.P83	Public opinion
1918.R44	Religious aspects
1918.W35	War work
1918.W66	Women
1920	Peace of Vereeniging, 1902
	1902-1910
1921	General works
1922	Importation of Chinese laborers, 1904
	1910-1961. Union of South Africa
1924	General works
	Biography and memoirs
1926	Collective
1927.A-Z	Individual, A-Z
	e.g.

	South Africa
	History
	By period
	1910-1961. Union of South Africa
	Biography and memoirs
	Individual, A-Z -- Continued
1927.A34	Abdurahman, A.
1927.D83	Dube, J.L.
1927.H47	Hertzog, J.B.M.
1927.J33	Jabavu, J.T.
1927.M35	Malan, Daniel
1927.M85	Msimang, Selby
1927.P53	Plaatje, Sol
1927.S46	Seme, P. Ka. I.
1927.S68	Smuts, Jan Christiaan
	1910-1948
1928	General works
1929	Civil disobedience campaigns by Mahatma Gandhi, 1906-1914
1931	Founding of South African Native National Congress, 1912
1933	Afrikaner Rebellion, 1914
1935	Rand Revolt, 1922
1937	Founding of National Party, 1934
1937.5	Afrikaner centennial, 1936-1938
	1948-1961. Afrikaner domination
1938	General works
1939	Pass law demonstrations, 1956
1941	Sharpeville Massacre, 1960
	1961-1994. Republic of South Africa. Apartheid regime
	For South African invasion of Angola see DT1436
	For raids on SWAPO installations in Angola see DT1645
	For works on apartheid see DT1757
1945	General works
	Biography and memoirs
1948	Collective
1949.A-Z	Individual, A-Z
	e.g.
1949.B55	Biko, Steve
1949.B88	Buthelezi, Gatsha
1949.L88	Luthuli, Albert
(1949.M35)	Mandela, Nelson
	see DT1974
1949.M36	Mandela, Winnie
1949.M38	Matanzima, Kaiser
1949.M85	Mulder, Cornelius (Connie)

South Africa

History

By period

1961-1994. Republic of South Africa. Apartheid regime

Biography and memoirs

Individual, A-Z -- Continued

1949.S58	Sisulu, Walter
1949.T36	Tambo, Oliver
1951	Hendrik Verwoerd, 1961-1966
	Class here general works on life and administration
1953	National liberation and armed struggle by ANC begins, 1961-
(1955)	Rivonia Trial, 1964
	see KTL42.R58
1957	Balthazar Johannes Vorster, 1966-1978
	Class here general works on life and administration
1959	Soweto uprising, 1976
1961	Mulder scandal, 1978
1963	Pieter Willem Botha, 1978-1989
	Class here general works on life and administration
1965	Sharpeville Massacre Anniversary, 1985
1967	State of emergency, 1985-
1969	Soweto uprising anniversary, 1986
1970	F.W. de Klerk, 1989-1994
	Class here general works on life and administration
	1994- . Republic of South Africa. Government of National Unity
1971	General works
	Biography and memoirs
1971.5	Collective
1972.A-Z	Individual, A-Z
	Nelson Mandela, 1994-1999
	Class here general works on life and administration
1974	General works
1974.2	Truth and Reconciliation Commission
1975	Thabo Mbeki, 1999-
	Class here general works on life and administration
	Local history and description
	Cape Province. Cape of Good Hope
1991	Periodicals. Societies. Serials
1999	Sources and documents
2002	Collected works (nonserial)
2004	Gazetteers. Dictionaries, etc.
2005	Place names (General)
2006	Directories
2007	Guidebooks
2009	General works

	South Africa
	Local history and description
	Cape Province. Cape of Good Hope -- Continued
2012	Historic monuments, landmarks, etc. (General)
	For local see DT2400.A+
2020	Description and travel
2025	Antiquities
2027	Social life and customs. Civilization. Intellectual life
	For specific periods, see the period
2032	Ethnography. Race relations
	History
	Periodicals. Societies. Serials see DT1991
2035	Biography (Collective)
	For specific periods, see the period
2037	Historiography
2039	General works
	By period
	Early to 1795 see DT1807+
	1795-1872
2042	General works
	Biography and memoirs
2043	Collective
2044.A-Z	Individual, A-Z
	1872-1910
2046	General works
	Biography and memoirs
2048	Collective
2049.A-Z	Individual, A-Z
	1910-1994
2051	General works
	Biography and memoirs
2053	Collective
2054.A-Z	Individual, A-Z
	Eastern Cape
2058	Periodicals. Societies. Serials
2058.2	Congresses
2058.4	Sources and documents
2058.5	Gazetteers. Dictionaries, etc.
2058.6	Place names (General)
2058.7	Directories
2058.8	Guidebooks
2059	General works
2059.2	Pictorial works
2059.4	Geography
2059.5	Description and travel
2059.7	Antiquities
	For local antiquities see DT2403+

South Africa
  Local history and description
    Eastern Cape -- Continued

2059.8	Social life and customs. Civilization. Intellectual life
	Ethnography. Race relations
2060	General works
2060.2.A-Z	Individual elements in the population, A-Z
	History
	Periodicals. Societies. Serials see DT2058
2061	General works
	Biography and memoirs
2061.3	Collective
2061.4.A-Z	Individual, A-Z
	Northern Cape
2064	Periodicals. Societies. Serials
2064.2	Congresses
2064.4	Sources and documents
2064.5	Gazetteers. Dictionaries, etc.
2064.6	Place names (General)
2064.7	Directories
2064.8	Guidebooks
2065	General works
2065.2	Pictorial works
2065.4	Geography
2065.5	Description and travel
2065.7	Antiquities
	For local antiquities see DT2403+
2065.8	Social life and customs. Civilization. Intellectual life
	Ethnography. Race relations
2066	General works
2066.2.A-Z	Individual elements in the population, A-Z
	History
	Periodicals. Societies. Serials see DT2064
2067	General works
	Biography and memoirs
2067.3	Collective
2067.4.A-Z	Individual, A-Z
	Western Cape
2070	Periodicals. Societies. Serials
2070.2	Congresses
2070.4	Sources and documents
2070.5	Gazetteers. Dictionaries, etc.
2070.6	Place names (General)
2070.7	Directories
2070.8	Guidebooks
2071	General works
2071.2	Pictorial works

South Africa
  Local history and description
    Western Cape -- Continued
2071.4   Geography
2071.5   Description and travel
2071.7   Antiquities
                    For local antiquities see DT2403+
2071.8   Social life and customs. Civilization. Intellectual life
                Ethnography. Race relations
2072   General works
2072.2.A-Z   Individual elements in the population, A-Z
2072.2.C65   Colored people
                History
                  Periodicals. Societies. Serials see DT2070
2073   General works
                  Biography and memoirs
2073.3   Collective
2073.4.A-Z   Individual, A-Z
            Free State. Vrystaat. Orange Free State. Oranje Vrystaat
2075   Periodicals. Societies. Serials
2079   Sources and documents
2082   Collected works (nonserial)
2084   Gazetteers. Dictionaries, etc.
2085   Place names (General)
2086   Directories
2087   Guidebooks
2089   General works
2090   Description and travel
2097   Social life and customs. Civilization. Intellectual life
                    For specific periods, see the period
                Ethnography. Race relations
2102   General works
2103.A-Z   Individual elements in the population, A-Z
2103.G55   Ghoya
                History
                    For Great Trek see DT1853
                    For conflicts with the Sotho, the Napier Treaty and
                        Warden Line see DT2630+
                  Periodicals. Societies. Serials see DT2075
2105   Biography (Collective)
2109   General works
                  By period
                    Early to 1854. Transorangia
                        For Batlokwa Uprising, 1822 see DT2630+
2112   General works
                      Biography and memoirs
2113   Collective

South Africa
  Local history and description
    Free State. Vrystaat. Orange Free State. Oranje Vrystaat
    History
      By period
        Early to 1854. Transorangia
          Biography and memoirs -- Continued

2114.A-Z	Individual, A-Z
2116	Griqua settlements, 1803
2118	1818-1829. Mfecane. Difaqane
2120	1837-1848. Treks into Transorangia
2122	1848-1854. Orange River sovereignty

        1854-1910
          For diamond discoveries see DT1871
          For South African War, 1899-1902 see DT1890+
          Cf. DT2630+ General boundary disputes with
            Basutoland

2124	General works
	Biography and memoirs
2126	Collective
2127.A-Z	Individual, A-Z
	e.g.
2127.B83	Brand, Johannes Henricus
2127.K65	Kok, Adam III
2127.S84	Steyn, M.T.
2129	War against the Sotho, 1858
	Cf. DT2630+ Lesotho
2131	Purchase of Griqua lands, 1861
2133	War against the Sotho, 1865-1866
	Cf. DT2636 Lesotho's wars with the Orange
	Free State
2135	Treaty of Aliwal North and cession of Sotho lands,
	1869
2137	Black Flag revolt, 1875
2139	Orange River Colony, 1900-1910

        1910-1994

2142	General works
	Biography and memoirs
2144	Collective
2145.A-Z	Individual, A-Z

        1994-

2148	General works
	Biography and memoirs
2150	Collective
2151.A-Z	Individual, A-Z

    KwaZulu-Natal. Natal
      Cf. DT2400.K85 Kwazulu

South Africa
Local history and description
KwaZulu-Natal. Natal -- Continued
2181   Periodicals. Societies. Serials
2189   Sources and documents
2192   Collected works (nonserial)
2194   Gazetteers. Dictionaries, etc.
2195   Place names (General)
2196   Directories
2197   Guidebooks
2199   General works
2205   Pictorial works
            Historic monuments, landmarks, etc.
                For local, see DT2400
2205.2   General works
2205.3   Preservation
2210   Description and travel
2217   Social life and customs. Civilization. Intellectual life
                For specific periods, see the period
            Ethnography. Race relations
2222   General works
2223.A-Z   Individual elements in the population, A-Z
                    For list of elements see DT1768.A+
            History
                Periodicals. Societies. Serials see DT2181
2225   Biography (Collective)
                    For individual biography, see the specific period
2227   Historiography
2229   General works
                By period
                    Early to 1843
2232   General works
                    Biography and memoirs
2234   Collective
2235.A-Z   Individual, A-Z
                            e.g.
2235.R48   Retief, Piet
2238   Mfecane (Difaqane) beginnings, 1818-1834
2240   British settlement, 1824
2242   Treks into Natal, 1837-1846
                        Cf. DT1853 Great Trek
                    War with Dingaan, 1837-1840
                        Including death of Piet Retief
2245   General works
2247.A-Z   Special events, battles, etc., A-Z
2247.B56   Blood River, Battle of, 1838
2247.M36   Magongo, Battle of, 1840

	South Africa
	Local history and description
	KwaZulu-Natal. Natal
	History
	By period -- Continued
	1843-1910. British colony
	For works on the Zulu war, 1879 see DT1875+
	For works on the South African War, 1899-1902 see DT1890+
2250	General works
	Biography and memoirs
2252	Collective
2254.A-Z	Individual, A-Z
	e.g.
2254.K43	Keate, R.W.
2254.S54	Shepstone, Theophilus
2257	Langalibalele Rebellion, 1873
2258	Pedi War, 1879
2261	Incorporation of Zululand and Tongaland, 1897
2263	Anti-Asian riots, 1897
2265	Annexation of Vryheid, Utrecht, and Wakkerstroom, 1902
2267	Bambata Rebellion, 1907
	1910-1994
2270	General works
	Biography and memoirs
2272	Collective
2273.A-Z	Individual, A-Z
2275	Zulu-Indian riots, 1949
2278	Kwazulu-Natal Indaba, 1986-
	1994-
2280	General works
	Biography and memoirs
2282	Collective
2283.A-Z	Individual, A-Z
	Transvaal. South African Republic
2291	Periodicals. Societies. Serials
2299	Sources and documents
2302	Collected works (nonserial)
2304	Gazetteers. Dictionaries, etc.
2305	Place names (General)
2306	Directories
2307	Guidebooks
2309	General works
2310	Description and travel
2317	Social life and customs. Civilization. Intellectual life
	For specific periods, see the period

	South Africa
	Local history and description
	Transvaal. South African Republic -- Continued
	Ethnology. Race relations
2322	General works
2323.A-Z	Individual elements in the population, A-Z
2323.D88	Dutch
	History
	Periodicals. Societies. Serials see DT2291
2325	Biography (Collective)
	For individual biography, see the specific period
2329	General works
	By period
	Early to 1857
2332	General works
	Biography and memoirs
2334	Collective
2335.A-Z	Individual, A-Z
	e.g.
2335.M36	Mantatisi (Mantatee)
2335.P68	Potgieter, A.H.
2335.P84	Pretorius, Andries
2338	Batlokwa uprising under Mantatisi, 1922
2340	Ndebele in Transvaal under Mzilikazi, 1822-1837
	Cf. DT2951 Mzilikazi's invasion and occupation
	of Zimbabwe
2342	Treks into Transvaal, 1837-1852
2344	Sand River Convention, 1852
	1857-1880. South African Republic
2347	General works
	Biography and memoirs
2349	Collective
2350.A-Z	Individual, A-Z
	e.g.
2350.B88	Burgers, T.F.
2350.J68	Joubert, W.F.
2350.N53	Njabel
2350.P84	Pretorius, M.W.
2350.S45	Sekhukhune
2352	Pedi uprising under Sekhukune, 1876-1877
	War of 1880-1881. First Anglo-Afrikaner War
2354	General works
2357	Personal narratives
2359.A-Z	Individual events, battles, etc., A-Z
2359.I65	Ingogo, Battle of, 1881
2359.L35	Laing's Nek, Battle of, 1880
2359.M36	Majuba Hill, Battle of, 1881

	South Africa
	Local history and description
	Transvaal. South African Republic
	History
	By period
	War of 1880-1881. First Anglo-Afrikaner War
	Individual events, battles, etc., A-Z -- Continued
2359.P68	Potchefstroom, Siege of, 1880-1881
	1881-1910
	For Witwatersrand gold discovery see DT1888
	For Jameson raid see DT1889
2361	General works
	Biography and memoirs
2363	Collective
2364.A-Z	Individual, A-Z
2366	Stellaland and Goshen, 1882-1884
	Cf. DT2483+ Botswana
2368	Venda War, 1898
2371	1902-1910. British colony
	1910-1994
2375	General works
	Biography and memoirs
2377	Collective
2378.A-Z	Individual, A-Z
	Gauteng. Pretoria-Witwatersrand-Vereeniging
2380	Periodicals. Societies. Serials
2380.2	Congresses
2380.4	Sources and documents
2380.5	Gazetteers. Dictionaries, etc.
2380.6	Place names (General)
2380.7	Directories
2380.8	Guidebooks
2381	General works
2381.2	Pictorial works
2381.4	Geography
2381.5	Description and travel
2381.7	Antiquities
	For local antiquities see DT2403+
2381.8	Social life and customs. Civilization. Intellectual life
	Ethnography. Race relations
2382	General works
2382.2.A-Z	Individual elements in the population, A-Z
	History
	Periodicals. Societies. Serials see DT2380
2383	General works
	Biography and memoirs
2383.3	Collective

	South Africa
	Local history and description
	Gauteng. Pretoria-Witwatersrand-Vereeniging
	History
	Biography and memoirs -- Continued
2383.4.A-Z	Individual, A-Z
	Mpumalanga. Eastern Transvaal
2386	Periodicals. Societies. Serials
2386.2	Congresses
2386.4	Sources and documents
2386.5	Gazetteers. Dictionaries, etc.
2386.6	Place names (General)
2386.7	Directories
2386.8	Guidebooks
2387	General works
2387.2	Pictorial works
2387.4	Geography
2387.5	Description and travel
2387.7	Antiquities
	For local antiquities see DT2403+
2387.8	Social life and customs. Civilization. Intellectual life
	Ethnography. Race relations
2388	General works
2388.2.A-Z	Individual elements in the population, A-Z
	History
	Periodicals. Societies. Serials see DT2386
2389	General works
	Biography and memoirs
2389.3	Collective
2389.4.A-Z	Individual, A-Z
	Limpopo. Northern Province. Northern Transvaal
2391	Periodicals. Societies. Serials
2391.2	Congresses
2391.4	Sources and documents
2391.5	Gazetteers. Dictionaries, etc.
2391.6	Place names (General)
2391.7	Directories
2391.8	Guidebooks
2392	General works
2392.2	Pictorial works
2392.4	Geography
2392.5	Description and travel
2392.7	Antiquities
	For local antiquities see DT2403+
2392.8	Social life and customs. Civilization. Intellectual life
	Ethnography. Race relations
2393	General works

	South Africa
	Local history and description
	Limpopo. Northern Province. Northern Transvaal
	Ethnography. Race relations -- Continued
2393.2.A-Z	Individual elements in the population, A-Z
	History
	Periodicals. Societies. Serials see DT2391
2394	General works
	Biography and memoirs
2394.3	Collective
2394.4.A-Z	Individual, A-Z
	North-West
2396	Periodicals. Societies. Serials
2396.2	Congresses
2396.4	Sources and documents
2396.5	Gazetteers. Dictionaries, etc.
2396.6	Place names (General)
2396.7	Directories
2396.8	Guidebooks
2397	General works
2397.2	Pictorial works
2397.4	Geography
2397.5	Description and travel
2397.7	Antiquities
	For local antiquities see DT2403+
2397.8	Social life and customs. Civilization. Intellectual life
	Ethnography. Race relations
2398	General works
2398.2.A-Z	Individual elements in the population, A-Z
	History
	Periodicals. Societies. Serials see DT2396
2399	General works
	Biography and memoirs
2399.3	Collective
2399.4.A-Z	Individual, A-Z
2400.A-Z	Other regions, districts, etc., A-Z
	e.g.
2400.B66	Bophuthatswana
2400.C58	Ciskei
2400.D83	Drakensburg Mountains
2400.G39	Gazankulu
2400.G84	Great Karoo
	Homelands (General) see DT1760
2400.K35	Kaffraria
2400.K36	KaNgwana
2400.K83	KwaNdebele

	South Africa
	Local history and description
	Other regions, districts, etc., A-Z -- Continued
2400.K85	Kwazulu
	Cf. DT2181+ KwaZulu-Natal
	Cf. DT2400.Z85 Zululand
2400.L43	Lebowa
2400.L58	Little Karoo
2400.N36	Namaqualand. Little Namaqualand
2400.P66	Pondoland
2400.Q83	QwaQwa
2400.T66	Tongaland
2400.T83	Transkei
2400.V45	Venda
2400.W58	Witwatersrand
2400.Z85	Zululand
	Cf. DT2400.K85 Kwazulu
	Cities, towns, etc.
2403-2403.95	Pretoria (Table DS-DX3)
2405.A-Z	Other cities, towns, etc., A-Z
	e.g.
2405.B56	Bloemfontein
2405.C36-.C3695	Cape Town (Table DS-DX4)
2405.D88-.D8895	Durban (Table DS-DX4)
2405.E38	East London
2405.J65-.J6595	Johannesburg (Table DS-DX4)
2405.K56	Kimberley
2405.P54	Pietermaritzburg
2405.P68	Port Elizabeth
2405.S68	Soweto
	Botswana. Bechuanaland
2421	Periodicals. Societies. Serials
2428	Sources and documents
2434	Gazetteers. Dictionaries, etc.
2435	Place names (General)
2436	Guidebooks
2437	General works
2439	General special
2441	Pictorial works
2446	Historic monuments, landmarks, scenery, etc. (General)
	For local see DT2520+
2447	Geography
2448	Description and travel
2450	Antiquities
	For local antiquities see DT2520+
2452	Social life and customs. Civilization. Intellectual life
	For specific periods, see the period

Botswana. Bechuanaland -- Continued
Ethnography
2454	General works
2456	Ethnic relations. Race relations
2458.A-Z	Individual elements in the population, A-Z
2458.G27	G/wi
(2458.H36)	Hambukushu
	see DT2458.M28
2458.H47	Herero
2458.K35	Karanga
2458.K53	Kgatla
2458.K84	Kwena
2458.M28	Mbukushu. Hambukushu
2458.N45	Ngwato
2458.P44	Pedi
2458.R75	Rolong
2458.S26	San
2458.S78	Sotho
2458.T35	Tannekwe
2458.T55	Tlhaping
2458.T89	Tswana
2458.T93	Tswapong
2458.Y48	Yeye

History
   Periodicals. Societies. Serials see DT2421
2464	Biography (Collective)
	For individual biography, see the specific period

Historiography
2466	General works
	Biography of historians, area studies specialists, archaeologists, etc.
2467	Collective
2468.A-Z	Individual, A-Z
2475	General works
2478	Political history
	For specific periods, see the period

By period
   Early to 1885
      Including conflicts with Transvaal and annexation of Rolong lands
      For Stellaland and Goshen see DT2366
2483	General works
	Biography and memoirs
2485	Collective
2486.A-Z	Individual, A-Z
	e.g.
2486.S43	Sebitoane

	Botswana. Bechuanaland
	History
	By period
	Early to 1885
	Biography and memoirs
	Individual, A-Z -- Continued
2486.S44	Sechele
2488	Difaqane, 1826-1851
	Including expansion of Bakololo
	Cf. DT1123 Mfecane. Ngoni invasions
	1885-1966. Bechuanaland Protectorate. British Bechuanaland
	Including local activities of the British South Africa Company
	For Jameson Raid see DT1889
	For works on the British South Africa Company in general see DT2860
2490	General works
	Biography and memoirs
2492	Collective
2493.A-Z	Individual, A-Z
	e.g.
2493.B37	Batheon
2493.B38	Batheon II
2493.K53	Khama, Tshekedi
2493.K54	Khama III, Ngwato chief
2493.S43	Sebele I
2493.S45	Sekgoma
	1966- . Independent
2496	General works
	Biography and memoirs
2498	Collective
2499.A-Z	Individual, A-Z
2500	Seretse Khama, 1966-1980
	Class here general works on life and administration
2502	Quett Masire, 1980-
	Class here general works on life and administration
	Local history and description
2520.A-Z	Provinces, regions, etc., A-Z
	e.g.
2520.K35	Kalahari Desert
2520.M35	Makgadikgadi Pans
2520.M65	Molopo River
2520.N53	Ngami, Lake
2520.O53	Okavango River and Swamp
	Cities, towns, etc.
2523	Gaborone

	Botswana. Bechuanaland
	Local history and description
	Cities, towns, etc. -- Continued
2525.A-Z	Other cities, towns, etc., A-Z
	e.g.
2525.F83	Francistown
2525.K35	Kanye
2525.L73	Lobatse
2525.M36	Mahalapye
2525.M75	Molepolole
2525.S45	Selebi-Phikwe
2525.S47	Serowe
	Lesotho. Basutoland
2541	Periodicals. Societies. Serials
2549	Sources and documents
2554	Gazetteers. Dictionaries, etc.
2555	Place names (General)
2556	Guidebooks
2557	General works
2559	General special
2561	Pictorial works
2565	Historic monuments, landmarks, scenery, etc. (General)
	For local see DT2680.A+
2572	Description and travel
2580	Antiquities
	For local antiquities see DT2680.A+
2582	Social life and customs. Civilization. Intellectual life
	For specific periods, see the period
	Ethnography
2592	General works
2596.A-Z	Individual elements in the population, A-Z
2596.T38	Taung
	History
	Periodicals. Societies. Serials see DT2541
2604	Biography (Collective)
	For individual biography, see the specific period
	Historiography
2606	General works
	Biography of historians, area studies specialists, archaeologists, etc.
2608	Collective
2609.A-Z	Individual, A-Z
2615	General works
2618	Political history
	For specific periods, see the period

Lesotho. Basutoland
History -- Continued
Foreign and general relations
For general works on the diplomatic history of a period, see
the period
For works on relations with a specific country
regardless of period see DT2625.A+

2623	General works
2625.A-Z	Relations with individual countries, A-Z
	By period
	Early to 1868
	Including claims by Orange Free State
2630	General works
	Biography and memoirs
2632	Collective
2634.A-Z	Individual, A-Z
	e.g.
2634.M67	Moshoeshoe I
2636	Wars with Orange Free State, 1865-1868
	1868-1966. Basutoland. British Protectorate
2638	General works
	Biography and memoirs
2640	Collective
2642.A-Z	Individual, A-Z
	e.g.
2642.G75	Griffith, Chief Nathaniel
2642.M65	Mokhehke, Ntsu
2642.M66	Moorosi
2644	Cape rule, 1871-1884
2646	Moorosi Rebellion, 1879
2648	Gun War, 1880-1881
	1966- . Independent
2652	General works
	Biography and memoirs
2654	Collective
2655.A-Z	Individual, A-Z
	e.g.
2655.L45	Lekhanya, Justin
2655.M65	Molapo, Charles
2655.M67	Moshoeshoe II
	1966-1986. Leabula Jonathon
2657	General works on life and administration
2658	South African raid on Maseru, 1982
2660	1986-
	Including January, 1986 Coup d'etat
2680.A-Z	Regions, districts, etc., A-Z
	e.g.

	Lesotho. Basutoland
	Local history and description
	Regions, districts, etc., A-Z -- Continued
2680.M35	Malibamatso River
2680.M36	Maloti Mountains
	Cities, towns, etc.
2683	Maseru
2686.A-Z	Other cities, towns, etc., A-Z
	e.g.
2686.B87	Butha-Buthe
2686.Q33	Qacha's Nek
2686.Q87	Quthing
	Swaziland
2701	Periodicals. Societies. Serials
2709	Sources and documents
2714	Gazetteers. Dictionaries, etc.
2715	Place names (General)
2717	Guidebooks
2719	General works
2721	General special
2723	Pictorial works
2725	Historic monuments, landmarks, scenery, etc. (General)
	For local see DT2820+
2732	Description and travel
2740	Antiquities
	For local antiquities see DT2820+
2742	Social life and customs. Civilization. Intellectual life
	For specific periods, see the period
	Ethnography
2744	General works
2746.A-Z	Individual elements in the population, A-Z
2746.S95	Swazi
	History
	Periodicals. Societies. Serials see DT2701
2754	Biography (Collective)
	For individual biography, see the specific period
	Historiography
2756	General works
	Biography of historians, area studies specialists,
	archaeologists, etc.
2757	Collective
2758.A-Z	Individual, A-Z
2765	General works
2768	Political history
	For specific periods, see the period

	Swaziland
	History -- Continued
	Foreign and general relations
	For general works on the diplomatic history of a period, see the period
	For works on relations with a specific country regardless of period see DT2775.A+
2773	General works
2775.A-Z	Relations with individual countries, A-Z
	By period
	To 1889
2777	General works
	Biography and memoirs
2779	Collective
2780.A-Z	Individual, A-Z
	e.g.
2780.M33	Mbandzeni
2780.M78	Mswati II, King of the Swazi
2780.N58	Ngwane II
2782	Battle of Lubuya, 1854
2784	Battle of Sekhukhune's Stronghold, 1879
2786	Convention of Pretoria, 1881
	1889-1968. British rule
2788	General works
	Biography and memoirs
2790	Collective
2791.A-Z	Individual, A-Z
	e.g.
2791.B58	Bhunu
2793	Transvaal rule, 1894-1902
2795	Land partition, 1907
	1968- . Independent
2797	General works
	Biography and memoirs
2799	Collective
2800.A-Z	Individual, A-Z
	e.g.
2800.D53	Dhlamini, Mabandla
2800.D54	Dhlamini, Mfanasibili
2800.D94	Dzeliwe, Queen Regent
2800.M85	Msibi, George
2800.N86	Ntombi, Queen Regent
2802	1968-1982. Sobhuza II
	Class here general works on life and reign
2804	1982-1986. Interregnum
2806	1986- . Mswati III
	Class here general works on life and reign

	Swaziland -- Continued
	Local history and description
2820.A-Z	Regions, districts, etc., A-Z
	e.g.
2820.H56	Hhohho
2820.L43	Lebombo Plateau
2820.S55	Shisilweni
	Cities, towns, etc.
2823	Mbanane
2825.A-Z	Other cities, towns, etc., A-Z
	e.g.
2825.B86	Bunya
2825.K84	Kwaluseni
2825.M35	Manzini. Bremersdorp
2825.S58	Siteki

British Central Africa. Federation of Rhodesia and Nyasaland
  Including works on Malawi, Zambia, and Zimbabwe treated
    together
  For Zimbabwe (Southern Rhodesia) alone see DT2871+
  For Zambia (Northern Rhodesia) alone see DT3031+
  For Malawi (Nyasaland) alone see DT3161+

2831	Periodicals. Societies. Serials
2839	Sources and documents
2844	General works
2851	General special
2856	Description and travel
	History
	Periodicals. Societies. Serials see DT2831
	Biography (Collective) see DT2914
2858	General works
	By period
	Early to 1890 see DT2937+
2860	1890-1923
	Including general works on the British South Africa Company
	For activities of the Company in specific countries, see the country
2862	1923-1953. British Protectorates
2864	1953-1964. Federation of Rhodesia and Nyasaland
	Zimbabwe. Southern Rhodesia
2871	Periodicals. Societies. Serials
2879	Sources and documents
2884	Gazetteers. Dictionaries, etc.
2885	Place names (General)
2886	Guidebooks
2889	General works
2891	General special

	Zimbabwe. Southern Rhodesia -- Continued
2893	Pictorial works
	Historic monuments, landmarks, scenery, etc. (General)
	For local see DT3020+
2895	General works
2897	Preservation
2899	Geography
	Description and travel
2900	Early to 1965
2902	1965-1982
2904	1983-
2906	Antiquities
	For local antiquities see DT3020+
2908	Social life and customs. Civilization. Intellectual life
	For specific periods, see the period
	Ethnography
2910	General works
2912	Ethnic and race relations
2913.A-Z	Individual elements in the population, A-Z
2913.B38	Barwe
2913.B85	British
2913.C75	Colored people
2913.E38	East Indians
2913.E87	Europeans
2913.G68	Gova
2913.K35	Kalanga
2913.K38	Karanga
2913.K53	Kgatla
2913.M38	Mashona
2913.N44	Ndebele
2913.N49	Nguni
2913.N53	Nika
2913.P44	Pedi
2913.S55	Shona
2913.S93	Swiss
2913.T36	Tangwena
2913.T38	Tawara
2913.T45	Tembomvura
2913.T55	Tlhaping
2913.T78	Tswana
2913.Z49	Zezuru
2913.15	Zimbabweans in foreign countries (General)
	For Zimbabweans in a particular country, see the country
	History
	Periodicals. Societies. Serials see DT2871
2914	Biography (Collective)
	For individual biography, see the specific period

	Zimbabwe. Southern Rhodesia
	History -- Continued
	Historiography
2916	General works
	Biography of historians, area studies specialists, archaeologists, etc.
2917	Collective
2918.A-Z	Individual, A-Z
2925	General works
2928	Political history
	For specific periods, see the period
	Foreign and general relations
	For general works on the diplomatic history of a period, see the period
	For works on relations with a specific country regardless of period see DT2935.A+
2933	General works
2935.A-Z	Relations with individual countries, A-Z
	By period
	Early to 1890
2937	General works
	Biography and memoirs
2939	Collective
2940.A-Z	Individual, A-Z
	e.g.
2940.D66	Dombo, King of Changamire
2940.K35	Kaliphi
2940.L73	Lobengula
2940.M38	Matope
2940.M39	Mavura
2940.M95	Mzilikazi
	Monomotapa, ca. 1000-ca. 1700
2942	General works
2943	Expedition of Antonio Fernandez, 1512-1514
	Barreto Expedition, 1572 see DT3355
	Dombo's Expedition against the Portuguese, 1593 see DT3359
2945	Expedition against Kuparavidze, 1632
2947	Rozwi Empire, ca. 1700-1834
2949	Sack of Great Zimbabwe by Zwangendaba's Ngoni, 1835
	Cf. DT1123 Mfecane. Ngoni invasions
2951	Ndebele Invasions, 1838-1839
2953	Patterson Expedition, 1878
2955	Moffat Treaty, 1888
2957	Rudd Concession, 1888

	Zimbabwe. Southern Rhodesia
	History
	By period -- Continued
	1890-1923. British South Africa Company administration
	Cf. DT2860 British South Africa Company
2959	General works
	Biography and memoirs
2961	Collective
2963.A-Z	Individual, A-Z
	e.g.
2963.M64	Moffat, John
2963.S45	Selous, Frederick
2964	Pioneer Column, 1890
2966	Ndebele War, 1893
	First Chimurenga, 1896-1897. Ndebele Revolt, 1896
2968	General works
2970	Shona Revolt, 1896-1897
	1923-1953. British Crown colony
2972	General works
	Biography and memoirs
2974	Collective
2975.A-Z	Individual, A-Z
	e.g.
2975.C65	Coghlan, Charles
2975.H85	Huggins, Godfrey
2975.M64	Moffat, Howard
	1953-1965
	Cf. DT2864 Federation of Rhodesia and Nyasaland
2976	General works
	Biography and memoirs
2978	Collective
2979.A-Z	Individual, A-Z
	e.g.
2979.C55	Chikerema, James
2979.N93	Nyandoro, George
	1965-1980
2981	General works
	Biography and memoirs
2983	Collective
2984.A-Z	Individual, A-Z
	e.g.
2984.M89	Muzorewa, Abel
2984.N56	Nkomo, Joshua
2984.S58	Sithole, Ndabaningi
2984.S65	Smith, Ian
2986	Unilateral Declaration of Independence (UDI), 1965

DT

	Zimbabwe. Southern Rhodesia
	History
	By period
	1965-1980 -- Continued
	1966-1980. War of National Liberation. Second Chimurenga
2988	General works
2990	Personal narratives
2992.A-Z	Individual events, battles, etc., A-Z
2994	1979-1980. Transitional government. Lancaster House Conference
	1980- . Independent
2996	General works
	Biography and memoirs
2998	Collective
2999.A-Z	Individual, A-Z
3000	Mugabe, Robert, 1980-
	Class here general works on life and administration
	Local history and description
3020.A-Z	Regions, districts, etc., A-Z
	e.g.
3020.K38	Kariba, Lake
3020.M35	Manicaland
3020.M37	Mashonaland
3020.M38	Matabeleland
3020.M39	Matopo Hills
	Cities, towns, etc.
3022	Harare. Salisbury
3025.A-Z	Other cities, towns, etc., A-Z
	e.g.
3025.C54	Chegutu. Hartley
3025.C55	Chinhoyi. Chipinga
3025.C56	Chivhu. Enkeldoorn
3025.E85	Esigodini. Essexdale
3025.G84	Great Zimbabwe
3025.G87	Guruwe. Sipolilo
3025.G89	Gweru. Gwelo
3025.H93	Hwange. Wankie
3025.K34	Kadoma. Gatooma
3025.K84	Kwekwe. Que Que
3025.M37	Masvingo. Fort Victoria
3025.M43	Mbalabala. Balla Balla
3025.M86	Mutare. Umtali
3025.M88	Mvuma. Umvuma
3025.M94	Mwenezi. Nuanetsi
3025.N83	Nuazira. Inyazura
3025.S36	Sango. Vila Salazar

	Zimbabwe. Southern Rhodesia
	Local history and description
	Cities, towns, etc.
	Other cities, towns, etc., A-Z -- Continued
3025.S58	Shurugwe. Selukwe
3025.T85	Tsholotsho. Tjolotjo
3025.Z95	Zvishavane. Shabani
	Zambia. Northern Rhodesia
3031	Periodicals. Societies. Serials
3035	Sources and documents
3037	Gazetteers. Dictionaries, etc.
3039	Place names (General)
3041	Guidebooks
3042	General works
3044	General special
3046	Pictorial works
3048	Historic monuments, landmarks, scenery, etc.
	For local see DT3140+
3049	Geography
3050	Description and travel
3051	Antiquities
	For local antiquities see DT3140+
3052	Social life and customs. Civilization. Intellectual life
	For specific periods, see the period
	Ethnography
3054	General works
3056	Ethnic and race relations
3058.A-Z	Individual elements in the population, A-Z
3058.A63	Ambo
3058.B46	Bemba
3058.B58	Bisa
3058.C53	Chewa
3058.C56	Chokwe
3058.E38	East Indians
3058.E87	Europeans
3058.F56	Fipa
3058.G79	Gova
3058.I53	Ila
3058.K36	Kaonde
3058.K93	Kwangwa
3058.L35	Lala
3058.L36	Lamba
3058.L46	Lenje
3058.L69	Lozi
3058.L83	Luchazi
3058.L89	Luvale
3058.M35	Mambwe

Zambia. Northern Rhodesia
  Ethnography
    Individual elements in the population, A-Z -- Continued

3058.M38	Mbunda
3058.N44	Ndembu
3058.N53	Ngangela
3058.N54	Ngoni
3058.N56	Nkoya
3058.N93	Nyanja
3058.S65	Soli
3058.S68	Southern Lunda
3058.T65	Tonga
3058.T85	Tsonga
3058.U65	Unga
3058.U85	Ushi
3058.Y66	Yombe

  History
    Periodicals. Societies. Serials see DT3031

3064	Biography (Collective)

      For individual biography, see the specific period
    Historiography

3066	General works

    Biography of historians, area studies specialists, archaeologists, etc.

3068	Collective
3069.A-Z	Individual, A-Z
3071	General works
3073	Political history

      For specific periods, see the period
    Foreign and general relations
      For general works on the diplomatic history of a period, see the period
      For works on relations with a specific country regardless of period see DT3077.A+

3075	General works
3077.A-Z	Relations with individual countries, A-Z

    By period
      Early to 1890

3079	General works

        Biography and memoirs

3080	Collective
3081.A-Z	Individual, A-Z

          e.g.

3081.K35	Kanyemga, Jose do Rosario Andrade
3081.K38	Kazembe III Lukwesa
3081.K39	Kazembe IV Keleka
3081.L48	Lewanika

Zambia. Northern Rhodesia
  History
    By period
      Early to 1890
        Biography and memoirs
          Individual, A-Z -- Continued

3081.M64	Mpenzeni
3081.S43	Sebituane
3081.S56	Sipopa
3081.W48	Westbeech, George
3083	Expedition of Monteiro and Gamitto, 1831
3085	Arab and Swahili Expeditions, ca. 1840- ca. 1860
3087	Ngoni Invasions, ca. 1840-1880. Mfecane
	Cf. DT1123 Mfecane. Ngoni invasions
3089	Ndebele Invasions, ca. 1860-ca. 1880
	1890-1924. British South Africa Company administration
	For Ware Concession and British South Africa
	Company attempts to annex Katanga (Shaba)
	see DT665.K3
	For general works on British South Africa Company
	see DT2860
3091	General works
	Biography and memoirs
3093	Collective
3094.A-Z	Individual, A-Z
3097	Gwembe Tonga Uprising, 1909
3099	Lunda Uprising, 1912
3101	Luvale Uprising, 1923
	1924-1953. British Protectorate
3103	General works
	Biography and memoirs
3105	Collective
3106.A-Z	Individual, A-Z
	e.g.
3106.G78	Gore-Browne, Steward
3106.Y35	Yamba, Dauti
	1953-1964
	Cf. DT2864 Federation of Rhodesia and Nyasaland
3108	General works
	Biography and memoirs
3110	Collective
3111.A-Z	Individual, A-Z
	e.g.
3111.N58	Nkumbula, Harry
3111.W45	Welensky, Roy
	1964- . Independent

DT

	Zambia. Northern Rhodesia
	History
	By period -- Continued
	For Lumpa Church Rebellion, 1964 see BR1446.6+
	For raids of ZANU installations in Zambia see DT2988+
3113	General works
	Biography and memoirs
3115	Collective
3117.A-Z	Individual, A-Z
	e.g.
3117.K36	Kapwepwe, Simon
3119	Kenneth Kaunda, 1964-1991
	Class here general works on life and administration
3119.5	Frederick Chiluba, 1991-
	Class here general works on life and administration
	Local history and description
3140.A-Z	Provinces, regions, etc., A-Z
	e.g.
3140.B36	Bangweulu Lake and Swamp
3140.C66	Copperbelt
3140.K35	Kafue Flats
3140.M84	Muchinga Mountains
3140.V54	Victoria Falls
3140.W48	Western Province. Barotseland
	Cities, towns, etc.
3142	Lusaka
3145.A-Z	Other cities, towns, etc., A-Z
	e.g.
3145.C55	Chilialombwe
3145.C56	Chingola
3145.K33	Kabwe
3145.K58	Kitwe
3145.L58	Livingstone
3145.L83	Luanshya
3145.M85	Mufulira
3145.N46	Ndola
	Malawi. Nyasaland
3161	Periodicals. Societies. Serials
3167	Sources and documents
3169	Gazetteers. Dictionaries, etc.
3171	Place names (General)
3173	Guidebooks
3174	General works
3176	General special
3178	Pictorial works

	Malawi. Nyasaland -- Continued
3180	Historic monuments, landmarks, scenery, etc. (General)
	For local see DT3252+
3182	Description and travel
3185	Antiquities
	For local antiquities see DT3252+
3187	Social life and customs. Civilization. Intellectual life
	For specific periods, see the period
	Ethnography
3189	General works
3190	Ethnic and race relations
3192.A-Z	Individual elements in the population, A-Z
3192.C54	Chewa
3192.I85	Italians
3192.L66	Lomwe
3192.M35	Manganja
3192.N44	Ngoni
3192.N56	Nkhonde
3192.N83	Nyanja
3192.T85	Tumbuka
3192.Y36	Yao
	History
	Periodicals. Societies. Serials see DT3161
3194	Biography (Collective)
	For individual biography, see the specific period
	Historiography
3196	General works
	Biography of historians, area studies specialists,
	archaeologists, etc.
3198	Collective
3199.A-Z	Individual, A-Z
3201	General works
3204	Political history
	For specific periods, see the period
	Foreign and general relations
	For general works on the diplomatic history of a period, see
	the period
	For works on relations with a specific country
	regardless of period see DT3208.A+
3206	General works
3208.A-Z	Relations with individual countries, A-Z
	By period
	To 1891
	Including Livingstonia Central Africa Company, African
	Lakes Company and Portuguese claims
	Cf. DT2860 British South Africa Company claims on
	Mozambique and Nyasaland

Malawi. Nyasaland
  History
    By period
      To 1891 Including Livingstonia Central Africa Company,
        African Lakes Company and Portuguese claims --
        Continued

3211	General works
	Biography and memoirs
3213	Collective
3214.A-Z	Individual, A-Z
	e.g.
3214.M65	Moir, Frederick
3214.M66	Moir, John
3214.M85	Mulambwa
	1891-1953
	Including British Central Africa Protectorate and Nyasaland
	Protectorate
	For British Central Africa see DT2860
3216	General works
	Biography and memoirs
3218	Collective
3219.A-Z	Individual, A-Z
	e.g.
3219.C55	Chilembwe, John
3219.M56	Mlozi
3219.M85	Mumba, Levi
3219.S53	Sharpe, Alfred
3221	Campaign against Mlozi, 1887-1895
3223	Mpenzeni War, 1898
3225	Chilembwe Rebellion, 1915
	1953-1964
	Cf. DT2864 Federation of Rhodesia and Nyasaland
3227	General works
	Biography and memoirs
3229	Collective
3230.A-Z	Individual, A-Z
	1964- . Independent
3232	General works
	1964-1994. Banda administration
3236	General works
	Biography and memoirs
3236.3	Collective
3236.4.A-Z	Individual, A-Z
3237	Chipembere Rebellion, 1965
	1994-
3237.3	General works
	Biography and memoirs

	Malawi. Nyasaland
	History
	By period
	1964- . Independent
	1994-
	Biography and memoirs -- Continued
3237.7	Collective
3237.8.A-Z	Individual, A-Z
	Local history and description
3252.A-Z	Regions, districts, etc., A-Z
	e.g.
3252.M35	Malawi, Lake (Lake Nyasa)
3252.M85	Mulanje Mountains
3252.S55	Shire River and Valley
3252.Z65	Zomba Plateau
	Cities, towns, etc.
3254	Lilongwe
3257.A-Z	Other cities, towns, etc., A-Z
	e.g.
3257.B53	Blantyre
3257.L56	Limbe
3257.M98	Mzuzu
3257.Z66	Zomba
	Mozambique
3291	Periodicals. Societies. Serials
3293	Sources and documents
3294	Gazetteers. Dictionaries, etc.
3295	Place names (General)
3297	Guidebooks
3299	General works
3301	General special
3302	Pictorial works
3305	Historic monuments, landmarks, scenery, etc. (General)
	For local see DT3410+
	Description and travel
3308	Early through 1800
3310	1801-1980
3312	1981-
3318	Antiquities
	For local antiquities see DT3410+
3320	Social life and customs. Civilization. Intellectual life
	For specific periods, see the period
	Ethnography
3324	General works
3326	Ethnic and race relations
3328.A-Z	Individual elements in the population, A-Z
3328.B33	Ba-Ronga

	Mozambique
	Ethnography
	Individual elements in the population, A-Z -- Continued
3328.B37	Barwe
3328.C67	Chopi
3328.C69	Chwabo
3328.G73	Goans
3328.I74	Italians
3328.K85	Kunda
3328.L66	Lomwe
3328.M35	Makonde
3328.M36	Makua
3328.M38	Manyika
3328.N38	Ndau
3328.N58	Nguni
3328.N93	Nyanja
3328.P68	Portuguese
3328.R83	Rue
3328.T38	Tawara
(3328.T48)	Thonga
	see DT3328.T74
3328.T74	Tsonga
(3328.V35)	Valenge
	see DT3328.C67
3328.Y36	Yao
	History
	Periodicals. Societies. Serials see DT3291
3330	Biography (Collective)
	For individual biography, see the specific period
	Historiography
3332	General works
	Biography of historians, area studies specialists, archaeologists, etc.
3334	Collective
3335.A-Z	Individual, A-Z
3337	General works
3339	Political history
	For specific periods, see the period
	Foreign and general relations
	For general works on the diplomatic history of a period, see the period
	For works on relations with a specific country regardless of period see DT3343.A+
3341	General works
3343.A-Z	Relations with individual countries, A-Z
	By period

	Mozambique
	History
	By period -- Continued
	Early to 1505
	Including Arab and East Indian domination
3345	General works
	Biography and memoirs
3347	Collective
3348.A-Z	Individual, A-Z
	1505-1698
	Including the Captaincy of Sofala
3350	General works
	Biography and memoirs
3352	Collective
3353.A-Z	Individual, A-Z
	e.g.
3353.B38	Barreto, Francisco
3355	Barreto expedition, 1572
3357	Dutch expedition, 1604
3359	Expedition of Dombo of the Changamire, 1692-1695
	Cf. DT2942+ Monomotapa
	1698-1891
	Including border disputes with Nyasaland and claims of the
	British South Africa Company
	For general works on the British South Africa
	Company see DT2860
3361	General works
	Biography and memoirs
3363	Collective
3364.A-Z	Individual, A-Z
	e.g.
3364.B66	Bonga
3364.G68	Gouveia, Manuel Antonio de Sousa
3364.G86	Gungunhana
3364.M89	Muzila
3364.S5	Shangana
3366	Mfecan. Ngoni invasions, ca. 1820-ca. 1850
	Cf. DT1123 Mfecane. Ngoni invasions (Southern
	Africa)
3368	Zulu conquest of Lourenco Marques, 1833
3370	Attack of Sofala, 1836
3372	Attack of Inhambane, 1843
3374	Fall of Massangano, 1888
	1891-1975
	Including activities of the Companhia de Moçambique and
	the Companhia do Niassa
3376	General works

	Mozambique
	History
	By period
	1891-1975 -- Continued
	Biography and memoirs
3378	Collective
3379.A-Z	Individual, A-Z
	e.g.
3379.M66	Mondlane, Eduardo
3381	War with Shangaan, 1894-1895
3383	Campaigns in interior, 1885-1912
3385	Zambezi Rebellion, 1917
3387	National liberation struggle, 1964-1975
	1975- . Independent
	For raids against ZAPU and ZANU forces in
	Mozambique see DT2988+
3389	General works
	Biography and memoirs
3391	Collective
3392.A-Z	Individual, A-Z
3393	Samora, Machel, 1975-1986
	Class here general works on the life and administration
3394	1976-1994. Insurgency movement (RNM)
3395	Nkomati Accord, 1984
3398	Joaquim Chissano, 1986-2005
	Class here general works on life and administration
3400	Armando Guebuza, 2005-
	Class here general works on life and administration
	Local history and description
3410.A-Z	Provinces, districts, regions, etc., A-Z
	e.g.
3410.C36	Cahora Bassa. Cabora Bassa
3410.G39	Gaza
3410.I65	Inhambane
3410.M36	Manica. Vila Pery
3410.M37	Manjacaze. Muchopes
3410.M38	Maputo Province. Lourenço Marques
3410.N36	Nampula. Moçambique
3410.N53	Niassa
3410.S65	Sofala. Beira
3410.T48	Tete
3410.Z36	Zambézia
	Cities, towns, etc.
3412-3412.95	Maputo. Lourenço Marques (Table DS-DX3)
3415.A-Z	Other cities, towns, etc., A-Z
	e.g.
3415.A65	Angoche. António Enes

Mozambique
  Local history and description
    Cities, towns, etc.
      Other cities, towns, etc., A-Z -- Continued

3415.B45	Beira
3415.C36	Cantandica. Vila Gouveia
3415.C54	Chicualacuala. Malvernia
3415.C55	Chilembene. Aldeia da Madragoa
3415.C56	Chimoio. Vila Pery
3415.C58	Chokwe. Trigo de Morais
3415.C83	Cuamba. Nova Freixo
3415.G85	Guija. Vila alferes Chamusca
3415.L53	Lichinga. Vila Cabral
3415.L87	Lupichili. Olivenca
3415.M33	Macaloge. Miranda
3415.M35	Mahlazene. Santa Comba
3415.M38	Matola. Vila Salazar
3415.P45	Pemba. Porto Amelia
3415.X35	Xai-Xai. João Belo

	History of Oceania (South Seas)
1	Periodicals. Societies. Serials
	Museums, exhibitions, etc.
2	General works
2.5.A-Z	Individual. By place, A-Z
3	Congresses
4	Biography (Collective)
10	Gazetteers. Dictionaries, etc.
	Communication of information
12	General works
13	Electronic information resources
	Including computer network resources
15	Guidebooks
17	General works
18	General special
18.5	Geography
	South Sea description and travel. Voyages
19	General history of voyages and discoveries
20	Through 1800
21	1801-1897
22	1898-1950
23	1951-1980
23.5	1981-
28	Social life and customs. Social antiquities. Ethnography
	Cf. GN662 Anthropology
28.1.A-Z	Individual elements in the population, A-Z
28.1.C5	Chinese
28.1.K67	Koreans
	History
	Historiography
28.11	General works
	Biography of historians, area studies specialists, archaeologists, etc.
28.12	Collective
28.13.A-Z	Individual, A-Z
	Study and teaching
28.2	General works
28.25.A-Z	By region or country, A-Z
	Subarrange by author
28.3	General works
28.35	Military and naval history
29	Political and diplomatic history. Control of the Pacific. Colonies and possessions
	Cf. DS510.7+ Far Eastern question
	By region or country
30	United States
32	Canada

	History
	Political and diplomatic history. Control of the Pacific.
	Colonies and possessions
	By region or country -- Continued
40	Great Britain
50	France
60	Germany
65	Spain
66	Japan
67	Soviet Union
68.A-Z	Other regions or countries, A-Z
	Australia
80	Periodicals. Sources and documents. Collections. Yearbooks
82	Biography (Collective)
90	Gazetteers. Dictionaries, etc.
91	Place names (General)
	Communication of information
91.8	General works
92	Electronic information resources
	Including computer network resources
93	Monumental and picturesque
94	Preservation
95	Guidebooks. Descriptive handbooks, etc.
96	General works
96.5	Historical geography
	Description and travel
97	History of travel
	To 1788
98	Personal narratives
98.1	General works
99	1788-1836
101	1837-1850
	1851-1900
102	General works
103	Gold discovery, 1851
104	1901-1950
105	1951-1980
105.2	1981-
106	Antiquities
107	Social life and customs. Civilization. Intellectual life
	History
	Historiography
108	General works
	Biography of historians
109.A2	Collective
109.A3-Z	Individual, A-Z
109.5	Study and teaching

	Australia
	History -- Continued
110	General works
110.5	Comic and satiric works
112	Compends
112.3	Military history
112.4	Naval history
	Diplomatic history. Foreign and general relations
	For general works on the diplomatic history of a period, see the period
	For works on relations with a specific country regardless of period see DU113.5.A+
113	General works
113.5.A-Z	Relations with individual countries, A-Z
	By period
	To 1788 see DU98.1
	1788-1900
114	Sources and documents
115	General works
	Biography and memoirs
115.2.A2	Collective
115.2.A3-Z	Individual, A-Z
	1900-1945
116	General works
116.18	Foreign and general relations
	Biography and memoirs
116.2.A2	Collective
116.2.A3-Z	Individual, A-Z
	1945-
116.9	Sources and documents
117	General works
117.13	Addresses, essays, lectures
117.14	Social life and customs. Civilization. Intellectual life
117.15	Military history
117.17	Political history
117.18	Foreign and general relations
	Biography and memoirs
117.19	Collective
117.2.A-Z	Individual, A-Z
	Ethnography
	Cf. GN665+ Anthropology
120	General works
121	National characteristics
122.A-Z	Individual elements in the population, A-Z
	Afghans see DU122.P87
122.A35	Africans
122.A5	Americans

	Australia
	Ethnography
	Individual elements in the population, A-Z -- Continued
122.A63	Arabs
122.A7	Armenians
122.A73	Asians
122.A75	Assyrians
122.B34	Balts
122.B37	Basques
122.B42	Belarusians
122.B44	Belgians
122.B7	British
	Including Cornish
122.C46	Chileans
122.C5	Chinese
	Cornish see DU122.B7
122.C7	Croats
122.D8	Dutch
122.E17	East Indians
122.E2	East Timorese
	English see DU122.B7
122.E7	Eritreans
122.E8	Estonians
122.E83	Ethiopians
122.E87	Europeans
122.F5	Filipinos
122.F55	Finns
122.F73	French
122.G4	Germans
122.G7	Greeks
122.H66	Hmong
122.H8	Hungarians
122.I53	Indochinese
122.I65	Iraqis
122.I7	Irish
122.I8	Italians
122.J36	Japanese
122.K67	Koreans
122.L3	Latvians
122.L42	Lebanese
122.L5	Lithuanians
122.M3	Macedonians
122.M34	Maltese
122.M38	Mauritians
122.M87	Muslims
122.N67	Norwegians
122.P3	Pacific Islanders

DU

	Australia
	Ethnography
	Individual elements in the population, A-Z -- Continued
122.P34	Palestinian Arabs
122.P6	Poles
122.P87	Pushtuns
122.R8	Russians
122.S25	Samoans
122.S3	Scandinavians
122.S4	Scots
122.S47	Serbs
122.S54	Sikhs
122.S65	Solomon Islanders
122.S67	Sorbs
122.S73	Spaniards
122.S94	Swedes
122.S95	Swiss
122.T28	Taiwanese
122.T36	Tamils
122.T87	Turks
122.U4	Ukrainians
122.V53	Vietnamese
122.W44	Welsh
122.Y8	Yugoslavs (General)
	Aboriginal Australians
	Biography
	Including portraits
123.2	Collective
123.3.A-Z	Individual, A-Z
123.4	General works
123.5	Study and teaching
124.A-Z	Special topics, A-Z
124.A46	Agriculture
124.A53	Alcohol use
124.A57	Antiquities
124.B86	Business enterprises
124.C43	Census
124.C45	Children. Youth
124.C48	Civil rights
124.C53	Claims
124.C56	Clothing
124.C63	Communication
124.C84	Cultural assimilation
124.E36	Economic conditions
	Education see LC3501.A3
124.E46	Employment
124.E74	Ethnic identity

	Australia
	Ethnography
	Aboriginal Australians
	Special topics, A-Z -- Continued
124.E76	Ethnobotany
124.F57	First contact with Europeans
124.G68	Government relations
124.H85	Hunting
124.K55	Kinship
124.L35	Land tenure
124.M37	Material culture
124.M43	Medicine
124.M56	Missions
124.M67	Mortuary customs
	Mythology see DU124.R44
124.P47	Petroglyphs. Rock paintings
124.P64	Politics and government
124.P72	Prisoners
124.R44	Religion. Mythology
124.R57	Rites and ceremonies
	Rock paintings see DU124.P47
124.S63	Social conditions
124.S64	Social life and customs
124.S84	Suicidal behavior
124.W65	Women
	Youth see DU124.C45
	By region or state see GN667.A+
125.A-Z	By group, A-Z
	Class here works on individual named groups
125.A45	Adnyamathanha
125.A49	Alyawara
125.A56	Anmatyerre
125.A73	Aranda
125.B24	Bandjalang
125.B26	Banyjima
(125.B35)	Bindubi
	see DU125.P48
125.B38	Birragubba
125.B64	Bunuba
125.B67	Burera
(125.D35)	Dangadi
	see DU125.D5
125.D47	Dharug
125.D5	Dhungutti
125.D59	Diyari
125.D63	Djabugay
125.E17	Eastern Arrernte

Australia
Ethnography
Aboriginal Australians
By group, A-Z -- Continued

125.G33	Gadjerong
125.G37	Garawa
125.G75	Gubbi Gubbi
125.G77	Gundungurra
125.G78	Gunggari
125.G79	Gureng Gureng
125.G8	Gurindji
125.J55	Jiman
125.J57	Jinibara
125.K24	Kamberri
125.K26	Kamilaroi
125.K28	Karijini
125.K29	Karuwali
125.K3	Kaurna
125.K34	Kaytetye
125.K56	Kitja
125.K75	Kuku-Yalanji
125.K77	Kurnai
125.K85	Kwini
125.L37	Lardil
125.M28	Mandandanji
125.M29	Mandjildjara
125.M3	Mardu
125.M33	Maung
125.M52	Miriwoong
125.M54	Mirning
(125.M8)	Murngin
	see DU125.Y64
125.M83	Muruwari
125.N36	Narangga
125.N37	Narrinyeri
125.N45	Ngaanyatjarra
125.N46	Ngadjuri
125.N94	Nunggubuyu
125.N96	Nyulnyul
125.N97	Nyunga
125.P44	Pibelmen
125.P48	Pintupi. Pintubi
125.P5	Pitjantjatjara. Pitjandgara
125.R45	Rembarrnga
125.T5	Tiwi
125.T67	Torres Strait Islanders

	Australia
	Ethnography
	Aboriginal Australians
	By group, A-Z -- Continued
(125.W27)	Wailpi
	see DU125.A45
(125.W3)	Walbiri
	see DU125.W37
125.W32	Walmajarri
125.W34	Wardaman
125.W35	Waringari
125.W37	Warlpiri
125.W44	Wik-Mungkan
125.W5	Wiradjuri
125.W58	Wonnarua
125.W6	Worora
125.W66	Wotjobaluk
125.W8	Wunambal
125.W87	Wurundjeri
125.Y33	Yaburara
125.Y34	Yamatji
125.Y347	Yandruwandha
125.Y35	Yangura
125.Y37	Yankunytjatjara
125.Y39	Yanyuwa
125.Y64	Yolngu
125.Y85	Yuin
135	Other
145	Australian Capital Territory. Canberra
	New South Wales
150	Periodicals. Societies. Serials. Yearbooks
155	Gazetteers. Handbooks
155.3	Guidebooks
	General works. Description and travel
160	Through 1836
161	1837-1950
162	1951-
	History
170	General and early
	Biography and memoirs
172.A2	Collective
172.A3-Z	Individual, A-Z
	e.g.
172.M3	Macquarie, Lachlan
172.P2	Parkes, Sir Henry
172.P58	Phillip, Arthur
172.S77	Strzelecki, Sir Paul Edmund de

DU

	Australia
	New South Wales -- Continued
177	Other
	Local history and description
178	Sydney
180.A-10.Z	Other cities, regions, etc., A-Z
	e.g.
180.A8	Australian Alps
180.B56	Blue Mountains
180.B8	Broken Hill
180.F6	Forbes
180.K7	Kosciusko, Mount
180.M8	Murray River and Valley
180.N5	New Italy (Colony)
180.N56	Newcastle
180.N6	Norfolk Island
180.W3	Wagga Wagga
	Tasmania. Van Diemen's Land
182	Periodicals. Societies. Serials
	Collected works (nonserial)
183	Several authors
184	Individual authors
185	Gazetteers. Dictionaries, etc.
185.3	Guidebooks
186	General works
186.5	Pictorial works
187	Description and travel
188	Social life and customs. Civilization. Intellectual life
189	Ethnography
	History
190	Biography (Collective)
	For individual biography, see the specific period or place
191	General works
192	General special
	By period
193	Through 1803
	Biography
193.2	Collective
193.3.A-Z	Individual, A-Z
194	1803-1900
	Biography
194.2	Collective
194.3.A-Z	Individual, A-Z
195	20th century
	Biography
195.2	Collective
195.3.A-Z	Individual, A-Z

	Australia
	Tasmania. Van Diemen's Land -- Continued
198.A-Z	Regions, cities, etc., A-Z
	Victoria
200	Periodicals. Societies. Serials. Yearbooks
205	Gazetteers. Handbooks. Directories
	General works. Description and travel
210	Through 1850
212	1851-1950
213	1951-
	History
220	General and early
	Biography and memoirs
222.A2	Collective
222.A3-Z	Individual, A-Z
	e.g.
222.B8	Buckley, William
222.K4	Kelly, Edward
222.L3	Lalor, Peter
222.R8	Russel, George
222.S8	Swinburne, George
227	Other
	Local history and description
228-228.95	Melbourne (Table DS-DX3)
230.A-Z	Other cities, regions, etc., A-Z
	e.g.
230.B3	Ballarat
230.B4	Bendigo
230.G4	Geelong
	Queensland
250	Periodicals. Societies. Serials. Yearbooks
255	Gazetteers. Handbooks
260	General works. Description and travel
	History
270	General and early
	Biography and memoirs
272.A2	Collective
272.A3-Z	Individual, A-Z
	e.g.
272.K34	Kennedy, Alexander
274	Ethnography
277	Other
	Local history and description
278	Brisbane
280.A-Z	Other cities, regions, etc., A-Z
	e.g.
280.C25	Cairns

DU

	Australia
	Queensland
	Local history and description
	Other cities, regions, etc., A-Z -- Continued
280.C3	Cape York Peninsula
280.D2	Darling Downs
280.D7	Dunk Island
280.G5	Gladstone
280.M22	McPherson Range
280.M7	Moreton Bay
280.T7	Torres Strait
280.W4	Wellesley Islands
	South Australia
300	Periodicals. Societies. Serials. Yearbooks
305	Gazetteers. Handbooks
310	General works. Description and travel
	History
320	General and early
	Biography and memoirs
322.A2	Collective
322.A3-Z	Individual, A-Z
	e.g.
322.A5	Angas, George Fife
322.F5	Fisher, Sir James Hurtle
322.L6	Light, William
325	Ethnography
327	Other
	Local history and description
328	Adelaide
330.A-Z	Other cities, regions, etc., A-Z
	e.g.
330.B3	Barmera
330.E5	Encounter Bay
330.E9	Eyre Peninsula
330.G8	Gumeracha
	Western Australia
350	Periodicals. Societies. Serials. Yearbooks
	Museums, exhibitions, etc.
351	General works
351.2.A-Z	By place, A-Z
	Subarrange by author
355	Gazetteers. Handbooks
360	General works. Description and travel
	History
370	General and early
	Biography and memoirs
372.A2	Collective

	Australia
	Western Australia
	History
	Biography and memoirs -- Continued
372.A3-Z	Individual, A-Z
	e.g.
372.G3	Gaston, Albert
372.H34	Harris, Charles M.
372.K5	Kirwan, Sir John
372.S8	Stirling, Sir James
374	Ethnography
377	Other
	Local history and description
378	Perth
380.A-Z	Other cities, regions, etc., A-Z
	e.g.
380.F8	Fremantle
380.K5	Kimberley
380.N4	Nursia (Norcia)
380.R68	Rottnest Island
390	Central Australia
391	Northern Australia
	Class here works dealing collectively with the Northern territory and the northern parts of Queensland and Western Australia
	Northern Territory of Australia
392	Periodicals. Serials
394	Gazetteers. Handbooks. Guidebooks
395	General works. Description and travel
	History
396	General works
	Biography and memoirs
397.A2	Collective
397.A3-Z	Individual, A-Z
397.5	Ethnography
398.A-Z	Regions, cities, etc., A-Z
	e.g.
398.A7	Arnhem Land
398.D3	Darwin
	New Zealand
400	Periodicals. Societies. Serials. Yearbooks
405	Gazetteers. Handbooks
405.5	Guidebooks
406	Monumental and picturesque
408	General works
408.5	Preservation of historic monuments, landmarks, scenery, etc.
	Description and travel

DU

	New Zealand
	Description and travel -- Continued
409	History of travel
410	Through 1839
411	1840-1950
412	1951-1980
413	1981-
416	Antiquities
418	Social life and customs. Civilization. Intellectual life
	History
	Historiography
419	General works
	Biography of historians
419.2	Collective
419.3.A-Z	Individual, A-Z
420	General works
	Through 1840
420.12	General works
	Biography and memoirs
420.13	Collective
420.14.A-Z	Individual, A-Z
	1840-1876
420.16	General works
	Biography and memoirs
420.17	Collective
420.18.A-Z	Individual, A-Z
	1876-1918
420.22	General works
	Biography and memoirs
420.23	Collective
420.24.A-Z	Individual, A-Z
	1918-1945
420.26	General works
	Biography and memoirs
420.27	Collective
420.28.A-Z	Individual, A-Z
	1945-
420.32	General works
	Biography and memoirs
420.33	Collective
420.34.A-Z	Individual, A-Z
420.5	Military history
	Political and diplomatic history. Foreign and general relations
421	General works
421.5.A-Z	Relations with individual countries, A-Z

<table>
<tbody>
<tr><td></td><td>New Zealand</td></tr>
<tr><td></td><td>History -- Continued</td></tr>
<tr><td>422</td><td>Biography (General)</td></tr>
<tr><td></td><td>For collective or individual biography of a specific period, see the period</td></tr>
<tr><td></td><td>Ethnography</td></tr>
<tr><td>422.5</td><td>General works</td></tr>
<tr><td></td><td>Maori</td></tr>
<tr><td></td><td>Biography</td></tr>
<tr><td></td><td>Including portraits</td></tr>
<tr><td>422.8</td><td>Collective</td></tr>
<tr><td>422.82.A-Z</td><td>Individual, A-Z</td></tr>
<tr><td>423.A1</td><td>General works</td></tr>
<tr><td>423.A15</td><td>Study and teaching</td></tr>
<tr><td>423.A2-Z</td><td>Special topics, A-Z</td></tr>
<tr><td>423.A34</td><td>Aged. Older people</td></tr>
<tr><td>423.A35</td><td>Agriculture</td></tr>
<tr><td></td><td>Amusements see DU423.G3</td></tr>
<tr><td>423.A55</td><td>Antiquities</td></tr>
<tr><td></td><td>Art</td></tr>
<tr><td></td><td>see class N</td></tr>
<tr><td>423.A85</td><td>Astronomy</td></tr>
<tr><td>423.B6</td><td>Boats. Canoes</td></tr>
<tr><td></td><td>Canoes see DU423.B6</td></tr>
<tr><td>423.C44</td><td>Census</td></tr>
<tr><td>423.C5</td><td>Children. Youth</td></tr>
<tr><td>423.C56</td><td>Chronology</td></tr>
<tr><td>423.C57</td><td>Claims</td></tr>
<tr><td>423.C59</td><td>Clothing</td></tr>
<tr><td>423.C63</td><td>Cosmology</td></tr>
<tr><td>423.C8</td><td>Criminal justice system</td></tr>
<tr><td>423.C86</td><td>Cultural assimilation</td></tr>
<tr><td>423.E3</td><td>Economic conditions</td></tr>
<tr><td></td><td>Education see LC3501.M3</td></tr>
<tr><td>423.E66</td><td>Employment</td></tr>
<tr><td>423.E85</td><td>Ethnic identity</td></tr>
<tr><td>423.E87</td><td>Ethnobotany</td></tr>
<tr><td>423.E88</td><td>Ethnozoology</td></tr>
<tr><td>423.F48</td><td>First contact with Europeans</td></tr>
<tr><td>423.F5</td><td>Fishing</td></tr>
<tr><td>423.F73</td><td>French influences</td></tr>
<tr><td>423.F8</td><td>Funeral rites and ceremonies</td></tr>
<tr><td>423.G3</td><td>Games. Amusements</td></tr>
<tr><td></td><td>Government see DU423.P63</td></tr>
<tr><td>423.G6</td><td>Government relations</td></tr>
<tr><td>423.H65</td><td>Housing</td></tr>
<tr><td>423.H8</td><td>Hunting</td></tr>
</tbody>
</table>

New Zealand
   Ethnography
      Maori
         Special topics, A-Z -- Continued

423.I4	Implements
423.I53	Industries. Material culture (General)
423.I55	Information services
423.I58	Intellectual life
423.J4	Jewelry
423.K54	Kings and rulers
423.K57	Kinship
423.L35	Land tenure
	Material culture see DU423.I53
423.M38	Medicine
423.M42	Meetinghouses
	Missions see BV3665
423.M88	Museums
	Older people see DU423.A34
423.O74	Origin
423.P52	Philosophy
423.P63	Politics and government
423.P66	Population
	Religion see BL2615
423.R47	Research
423.R55	Rites and ceremonies
423.S48	Sexual behavior
423.S6	Social conditions
423.S63	Social life and customs
423.T26	Tattooing
423.T4	Textiles
423.W35	Warfare
423.W65	Women
	Youth see DU423.C5
424.A-Z	Individual tribes and cultures, A-Z
424.K38	Kāti Irakehu
424.M67	Moriori
424.N36	Nga Puhi
424.N37	Ngaa Rauru
424.N4	Ngaitahu
424.N4118	Ngāti Apa
424.N412	Ngāti Awa
424.N413	Ngāti Haua
424.N4133	Ngāti Hinga
424.N4134	Ngāti Kahungunu
424.N4137	Ngāti Kinohaku
424.N414	Ngāti Mahuta
424.N4147	Ngāti Pāhauwera

	New Zealand
	Ethnography
	Maori
	Individual tribes and cultures, A-Z -- Continued
424.N41473	Ngāti Pango
424.N4148	Ngāti Pikiao
424.N415	Ngāti Porou
424.N42	Ngāti Pukenga
424.N423	Ngāti Rangiwewehi
424.N425	Ngāti Tahu Matawhaiti
424.N43	Ngāti Tarawhai
424.N435	Ngāti Te Ata
424.N44	Ngāti Toa
424.N46	Ngāti Tuwharetoa
424.N47	Ngāti Urunumia
424.N48	Ngāti Whakaue
424.N49	Ngāti Whanaunga
424.R35	Rangitane
424.T34	Tainui
424.T4	Te Tāou
424.T83	Tuhoe
424.W3	Wai o Hua
424.W43	Whakatohea
424.5.A-Z	Other elements in the population, A-Z
424.5.A75	Asians
424.5.B75	British
424.5.C5	Chinese
424.5.C76	Croats
424.5.D35	Danes
424.5.D8	Dutch
424.5.E27	East Indians
424.5.E97	Europeans
424.5.F55	Finns
424.5.F73	French
424.5.G47	Germans
424.5.I74	Irish
424.5.I8	Italians
424.5.L37	Latvians
424.5.M87	Muslims
424.5.N67	Norwegians
424.5.P33	Pacific Islanders
424.5.P36	Panjabis (South Asian people)
424.5.P58	Poles
424.5.P6	Polynesians
424.5.S2	Samoans
424.5.S3	Scots
424.5.S33	Scots-Irish

New Zealand
  Ethnography
    Other elements in the population, A-Z -- Continued
424.5.S93   Swedes
424.5.S95   Swiss
424.5.T65   Tokelau
424.5.Y84   Yugoslavs
427   Other
              Local history and description
428   Wellington
430.A-Z   Other cities, regions, etc., A-Z
                    e.g.
430.A35   Akaroa
430.A4   Alps, Southern
                      Including Arthur's Pass, Mount Cook, etc.
430.A5   Amuri County
430.A79   Auckland (Provincial District)
430.A8   Auckland (City)
430.A83   Auckland Islands
430.B15   Banks Peninsula
430.B2   Bay of Islands
430.C3   Canterbury
430.C48   Chatham Islands
430.C5   Christchurch
430.C6   Cook Islands
430.D8   Dunedin
430.E36   Egmont, Mount
430.G7   Great Barrier Island
430.H33   Hawke's Bay
430.L9   Lyttelton
430.M35   Marlborough
430.N38   Nelson (Provincial District)
430.N4   New Plymouth
430.N5   Niue (Savage Island)
430.N6   North Island
430.O8   Otago
430.P34   Palmerston North
430.P8   Pukapuka (Island)
430.R6   Rotorua
430.S57   South Island
430.S6   Southland
430.S7   Stewart Island
430.T25   Taranaki
430.W25   Wakatipu (Lake)
430.W3   Wanganui
430.W4   Westland

(450-480)	Tasmania (Van Diemen's Land)
	see DU182+
490	Melanesia (General)
	For individual islands or groups of islands see DU520+
500	Micronesia (General)
	For individual islands or groups of islands see DU520+
510	Polynesia (General)
	For individual islands or groups of islands see DU520+
	Smaller island groups
520	Admiralty Islands
	Auckland Islands see DU430.A83
	Austral Islands see DU900
540	Banks Islands
	Bismarck Archipelago
	Cf. DU739+ Territory of New Guinea, Northeast New Guinea
550	General works
553.A-Z	Individual islands or groups of islands, A-Z
	Admiralty Islands see DU520
553.L4	Lesu
553.N35	New Britain (Neu Pommern, New Pomerania)
553.N4	New Ireland (Neu Mecklenburg, New Mecklenburg)
	Caroline Islands
560	Periodicals. Societies. Serials
563	General works. Description and travel
	History
565	General works
567	Modern
568.A-Z	Individual islands, groups of islands, cities, etc., A-Z
	Chuuk see DU568.T7
568.H3	Hall Islands
568.I3	Ifalik (Ifaluk)
568.K67	Kosrae
568.L6	Losap
568.M6	Mokil
568.N44	Ngatik
568.N6	Nomoi (Mortlock) Islands
	Pelew (Palau) Islands see DU780
568.P55	Pingelop Atoll
568.P7	Ponape (Ascension)
568.P8	Puluwat (Poloat, Polowat)
568.S37	Satawal
568.T7	Truk Islands. Chuuk
568.U5	Ulithi (Uluthi)
568.Y3	Yap (Uap)
	Cook Islands see DU430.C6
	Dangerous Islands see DU890

	Smaller island groups -- Continued
580	D'Entrecasteaux Islands
590	Ellice Islands. Tuvalu
600	Fiji Islands
	Friendly Islands see DU880
	Gambier Islands see DU680
615	Gilbert Islands. Kiribati
	Guam see DU647
	Hawaiian Islands. Hawaii
620	Periodicals. Societies. Serials
	Collected works
	Several authors
620.3	General works
620.4	Pamphlet collections
	Individual authors
620.5	General works
620.6	Pamphlet collections
621	Directories
621.5	Monumental and picturesque. Pictorial works
622	Gazetteers. Handbooks. Guidebooks
	General works. Description and travel
623	Through 1950
	For early periods to 1800 see DU626+
623.2	1951-1980
623.25	1981-
624	Antiquities
624.5	Social life and customs. Civilization. Intellectual life
	Ethnography
624.6	General works
624.65	Polynesian Hawaiians
624.7.A-Z	Other elements in the population, A-Z
624.7.A85	Asians (General)
624.7.C5	Chinese
624.7.F4	Filipinos
	Haoles see DU624.7.W45
624.7.J3	Japanese
624.7.K67	Koreans
624.7.P67	Portuguese
624.7.P83	Puerto Ricans
624.7.R87	Russians
624.7.R97	Ryukyuans
624.7.S36	Samoans
624.7.W45	Whites. Haoles
	Biography (Collective)
	For individual biography, see the specific period, reign, or place
624.9	General works

DU

Smaller island groups
Hawaiian Islands. Hawaii
Biography (Collective) -- Continued
Houses, noble families, etc.

624.95	General works
624.96.A-Z	Individual houses, families, etc., A-Z
	e.g.
624.96.K35	Kamehameha, House of

History
625	General works

Study and teaching
625.8.A-.Z8	General works
625.8.Z9	Catalogs of audiovisual materials

By period
626	Through 1778. Arrival of Captain James Cook

1778-1900
627	General works
627.1	Kamehameha I, 1784-1819
627.11	Kamehameha II, 1819-1824
627.12	Kamehameha III, 1824-1854
627.13	Kamehameha IV, 1854-1863
627.14	Kamehameha V, 1863-1872
627.15	Lunalilo, 1872-1874
627.16	Kalakaua, 1874-1891
627.17.A-Z	Biography and memoirs of contemporaries, A-Z
	e.g.
627.17.A7	Armstrong, Richard
627.17.B4	Bishop, Bernice Pauahi
627.18	Liliuokalani, 1891-1893

Overthrow of the Monarchy, 1893
627.19	Sources and documents
627.2	General works

Annexation to the United States, 1898
627.3	Sources and documents
627.4	General works

Hawaii (Territory), 1900-1959
627.5.A1-.A5	Sources and documents
627.5.A6-Z	General works

Biography and memoirs, 1891-1959
627.7.A2	Collective
627.7.A3-Z	Individual, A-Z
	e.g.
627.7.B3	Baldwin, Henry Perrine
627.7.D65	Dole, Sanford Ballard
627.7.F3	Farrington, Wallace Rider

State, 1959-
627.8	General works

Smaller island groups
Hawaiian Islands. Hawaii
History
By period
State, 1959- -- Continued
Biography and memoirs

627.82	Collective
627.83.A-Z	Individual, A-Z
628.A-Z	Islands, counties, etc., A-Z
	e.g.
628.H25	Haleakala National Park
628.H28	Hawaii (Island). Hawaii County
628.H3	Hawaii National Park
628.H33	Hawaii Volcanoes National Park
628.K3	Kauai (Kaieiewaho)
628.L3	Lanai
628.L4	Laysan
628.M3	Maui
628.M5	Midway Islands
628.M7	Molokai
628.N55	Niihau
628.O3	Oahu
629.A-Z	Cities, volcanoes, etc., A-Z
	e.g.
629.H2	Haleakala
629.H5	Hilo
629.H7	Honolulu
629.K32	Kailua (Hawaii County)
629.K5	Kilauea
629.M34	Mauna Loa
629.P3	Parker Ranch
	Hervey Islands see DU430.C6
	Northern Mariana Islands. Ladrone Islands
640	Periodicals. Societies. Serials
643	General works. Description and travel
645	History
	Individual islands, cities, etc.
647	Guam
648.A-Z	Other, A-Z
	e.g.
648.S35	Saipan
	Lagoon Islands see DU590
650	Line Islands
660	Louisiade Archipelago
	Low Archipelago see DU890
670	Loyalty Islands
680	Mangareva Islands. Gambier Islands

	Smaller island groups -- Continued
	Mariana Islands see DU640+
	Marquesas Islands
700	General works
701.A-Z	Individual islands, A-Z
	e.g.
701.F3	Fatuhiva Island
701.H5	Hivaoa Island
701.N8	Nuku-hiva Island
710	Marshall Islands
715	Nauru
	Navigators Islands see DU810+
720-720.95	New Caledonia (Table DS-DX1)
	New Guinea
739	General works
740-740.95	Papua New Guinea (Table DS-DX1)
	Including works on Papua and New Guinea (Territory)
	Papua (Indonesia). Irian Jaya. Irian Barat. Netherlands New Guinea
744	General works. Description and travel
	Ethnography
744.3	General works
744.35.A-Z	Individual elements in the population, A-Z
744.35.A8	Armati
744.35.A82	Asmat
744.35.B5	Biak
744.35.D32	Dani
744.35.E56	Eipo
744.35.F39	Fayu
	Huli see DU740+
744.35.J28	Jalé
744.35.J32	Jaqai
744.35.K33	Kaowerawédj
744.35.K34	Kapauku
744.35.K48	Ketengbau
744.35.M32	Maisin
744.35.M33	Mandobo
744.35.M34	Marind
744.35.M42	Mejprat
744.35.M55	Mimika
744.35.M66	Moni
744.35.M89	Muyuw
744.35.N32	Nalum
744.35.N56	Nimboran
744.35.P33	Papuans (General)
744.35.T38	Tause
744.35.U36	Uhunduni

DU

Smaller island groups
New Guinea
Papua (Indonesia). Irian Jaya. Irian Barat. Netherlands
New Guinea
Ethnography
Individual elements in the population, A-Z -- Continued

744.35.W37	Waropen
744.35.Y44	Yei
744.5	History
	Biography and memoirs
746.A2	Collective
746.A3-Z	Individual, A-Z
	e.g.
746.C4	Chalmers, James
746.M5	Miklukha-Maklaĭ, Nikolaĭ Nikolaevich
746.M8	Murray, Sir Hubert (Sir John Hubert P.)
747.A-Z	Local, A-Z
	e.g.
747.S8	Sukarno, Mount
760	New Hebrides. Vanuatu
	Paumotu Islands see DU890
780	Pelew (Palau) Islands
790	Phoenix Islands
800	Pitcairn Island
	Samoan Islands
810	Periodicals. Societies. Serials
812	Handbooks
813	General works. Description and travel
814	Antiquities
	History
815	General works
816	Early
	Modern. European colonization
817.A2-.A5	Sources and documents
817.A6-Z	General works
817.2	Revolution of 1899
	Biography and memoirs
818.A2	Collective
818.A3-Z	Individual, A-Z
	e.g.
818.W4	Westbrook, George Egerton L.
819.A1	American Samoa
819.A2	Samoa
	Formerly Western Samoa
819.A3-Z	Individual islands, cities, etc.
	e.g.
819.M3	Manua

	Smaller island groups
	Samoan Islands
	Individual islands, cities, etc. -- Continued
819.P3	Pagopago
	Sandwich Islands see DU620+
840	Santa Cruz Islands
850	Solomon Islands
860	Suvarrow (Suvaroff, Suwaroff) Islands
870	Tahiti and Society Islands
	Tokelau Islands see DU910
880	Tonga Islands
885	Trobriand Islands
890	Tuamotu Islands
900	Tubuai Islands
	Tuvalu see DU590
910	Union Islands
	Vanuatu see DU760
920	Wallis Archipelago
	Wellesley Islands see DU280.W4
950.A-Z	Other islands, A-Z
	e.g.
	Auckland Islands see DU430.A83
950.C5	Clipperton Island
	Easter Island see F3169
950.W28	Wake Island

DU

	History of Romanies. History of Gypsies
101	Periodicals. Societies
103	Congresses
105	Collections
115	General works
118	Popular works
120	Pamphlets, etc.
	Biography and memoirs
	Including biography of persons identified primarily with Romanies
	Cf. TR681.G9 Photographic portraits
125	Collective
127.A-Z	Individual, A-Z
	e.g.
127.P4	Petulengro, Gipsy
	History
(131)	General works
	see DX115
135	Origin
137	Ancient
141	Medieval
	Modern
	Cf. D804.5.G85 Romani victims of the Holocaust
145	General works
	By region or country see DX201+
151	Beliefs. Superstition. Religion
	Education see LC3503+
155	Magic. Fortune-telling, etc.
157	Folklore
	Music
	see Class M
(161)	Language and literature
	see PK2896+
171	Trades. Arts. Occupations
175	Wagons. Caravans
	By region or country
201	United States
205	Other American (not A-Z)
	Europe
	General works see DX145
210	Eastern Europe
	Great Britain
211	General works
213	England
215	Scotland
	Cf. DA774.4.T72 Scottish Travellers (Nomadic people)
216	Wales

	By region or country
	Europe -- Continued
217	Ireland
	Cf. DA927.4.T72 Irish Travellers (Nomadic people)
221	Austria
221.5	Bulgaria
222	Czechoslovakia. Czech Republic
222.5	Slovakia
223	Hungary
224	Romania
227	France
229	Germany
232	Greece
233	Italy
235	Netherlands
237	Belgium
241	Soviet Union
241.5	Moldova
241.8	Ukraine
242	Poland
243	Latvia
245	Scandinavian countries
247	Finland
251	Spain
255	Portugal
261	Switzerland
265	Turkey and Balkan Peninsula
268	Macedonia
269	Serbia
270	Croatia
271	Yugoslavia
	Asia
281	General works
283	India
289	Other Asian (not A-Z)
	Africa
291	General works
293	Egypt
299	Other African (not A-Z)
300	Arab countries
301	Other regions or countries (not A-Z)

DX

0.A2	Periodicals. Societies
0.A3	Sources and documents. Serials
0.A5-.Z	General works
0.2	Description and travel. Guidebooks. Gazetteers
0.3	Antiquities
0.4	Social life and customs. Civilization. Intellectual life
0.42	Ethnography
	History
0.5	General works
0.6	Biography (Collective)
	Political history. Foreign and general relations
0.62	General works
	By period
	see the specific period
0.63.A-Z	Relations with individual countries, A-Z
	By period
	Early
0.65	General works
	Biography and memoirs
0.66.A2	Collective
0.66.A3-Z	Individual, A-Z
	Colonial
0.7	General works
	Biography and memoirs
0.72.A2	Collective
0.72.A3-Z	Individual, A-Z
	20th century
0.75	General works
	Biography and memoirs
0.76.A2	Collective
0.76.A3-Z	Individual, A-Z
	Independent
0.8	General works
	Biography and memoirs
0.82.A2	Collective
0.82.A3-Z	Individual, A-Z
0.9.A-Z	Local, A-Z
	Do not use with countries that have their own "Local history and description" numbers
0.95.A-Z	Natural features such as mountains, rivers, etc., A-Z

.xA2-.xA29	Periodicals. Societies
.xA3-.xA39	Sources and documents. Serials
.xA5-.xZ	General works
.x2	Description and travel. Guidebooks. Gazetteers
.x3	Antiquities
.x4	Social life and customs. Civilization. Intellectual life
.x42	Ethnography
	History
.x5	General works
.x6	Biography (Collective)
	Political history. Foreign and general relations
.x62	General works
	By period
	see the specific period
.x63A-.x63Z	Relations with individual countries, A-Z
	By period
	Early
.x65	General works
	Biography and memoirs
.x66A2-.x66A29	Collective
.x66A3-.x66Z	Individual, A-Z
	Colonial
.x7	General works
	Biography and memoirs
.x72A2-.x72A29	Collective
.x72A3-.x72Z	Individual, A-Z
	20th century
.x75	General works
	Biography and memoirs
.x76A2-.x76A29	Collective
.x76A3-.x76Z	Individual, A-Z
	Independent
.x8	General works
	Biography and memoirs
.x82A2-.x82A29	Collective
.x82A3-.x82Z	Individual, A-Z
.x9A-.x9Z	Local, A-Z
	Do not use with countries which have their own "Local history and description" numbers
.x95A-.x95Z	Natural features such as mountains, rivers, etc., A-Z

TABLES

.A2	Periodicals. Societies. Serials
.A3	Museums, exhibitions, etc.
	Subarrange by author
.A4	Guidebooks. Gazetteers. Directories
.A5-.Z	General works. Description
.1	Pictorial works
.13	Addresses, essays, lectures. Anecdotes, etc.
.15	Antiquities
.2	Social life and customs. Civilization. Intellectual life
	History
.23	Biography
.23.A2	Collective
.23.A3-Z	Individual, A-Z
.25	Historiography. Study and teaching
.3	General works
	Sections, districts, suburbs, etc.
.4.A2	Collective
.4.A3-Z	Individual, A-Z
	Monuments, statues, etc.
.5.A2	Collective
.5.A3-Z	Individual, A-Z
	Parks, squares, cemeteries, etc.
.6.A2	Collective
.6.A3-Z	Individual, A-Z
	Streets, bridges, etc.
.7.A2	Collective
.7.A3-Z	Individual, A-Z
	Buildings
.8.A2	Collective
.8.A3-Z	Individual, A-Z
	Elements in the population
.9.A2	Collective
.9.A3-Z	Individual, A-Z
.95.A-Z	Natural features such as mountains, rivers, etc., A-Z

.x	Periodicals. Societies. Serials
.x2	Museums, exhibitions, etc.
	Subarrange by author
.x3	Guidebooks. Gazetteers. Directories
.x4	General works. Description
.x43	Pictorial works
.x45	Addresses, essays, lectures. Anecdotes, etc.
.x47	Antiquities
.x5	Social life and customs. Civilization. Intellectual life
	History
	Biography
.x53A2-.x53A29	Collective
.x53A3-.x53Z	Individual, A-Z
.x55	Historiography. Study and teaching
.x57	General works
	Sections, districts, suburbs, etc.
.x6A2-.x6A29	Collective
.x6A3-.x6Z	Individual, A-Z
	Monuments, statues, etc.
.x65A2-.x65A29	Collective
.x65A3-.x65Z	Individual, A-Z
	Parks, squares, cemeteries, etc.
.x7A2-.x7A29	Collective
.x7A3-.x7Z	Individual, A-Z
	Streets, bridges, etc.
.x75A2-.x75A29	Collective
.x75A3-.x75Z	Individual, A-Z
	Buildings
.x8A2-.x8A29	Collective
.x8A3-.x8Z	Individual, A-Z
	Elements in the population
.x9A2-.x9A29	Collective
.x9A3-.x9Z	Individual, A-Z
.x95A-.x95Z	Natural features such as mountains, rivers, etc., A-Z

.xA2-.xA29	Periodicals. Societies
.xA3-.xA39	Sources and documents. Collections
.xA5-.xZ	General works
.x2	Description and travel
.x3	Antiquities
.x4	Social life and customs. Civilization. Intellectual life
	History
.x5	General works
.x6	Biography (Collective)
	By period
.x7	Medieval and modern through 1918
.x8	1919-

.xA2-.xA29	Periodicals. Yearbooks. Societies. Directories
.xA294-.xA2959	Museums, exhibitions, etc.
	Subarrange by author
.xA3-.xA39	Sources and documents. Collections
.xA5-.xZ	General works
.x19	Historical geography
.x2	Description and travel. Dictionaries. Guidebooks. Gazetteers
.x3	Cultural property. Castles, temples, monuments, etc.
.x35	Antiquities
.x4	Social life and customs. Civilization
.x42	Elements in the population
	History
.x5	General works. Chronology
.x55	Historiography. Study and teaching
.x6	Biography and memoirs (Collective)
	For individual biography, see appropriate period or local subdivision
	By period
.x65	Early to 1600
.x7	1600-1868
.x8	1868-1945
.x85	1945-
.x9A-.x9Z	Local subdivisions of the prefecture (or the administrative subdivisions and subregions of Hokkaidō), A-Z
.x95A-.x95Z	Natural features such as mountains, rivers, etc., A-Z

TABLES

.x	General works
.x2A-.x2Z	Local, A-Z
	Biography and memoirs
.x3A1-.x3A19	Collective
.x3A2-.x3Z	Individual, A-Z

.x15	Periodicals. Yearbooks. Societies. Directories
	Museums, exhibitions, etc.
.x16	General works
.x165.A-Z	Individual. By place, A-Z
.x17	Sources and documents
.x18	General works
.x19	Historical geography
.x2	Description and travel. Dictionaries. Guidebooks. Gazetteers. Pictorial works
.x3	Cultural property. Castles, temples, monuments, etc.
.x35	Antiquities
.x4	Social life and customs. Civilization
.x42	Elements in the population
	History
.x5	General works
.x55	Historiography. Study and teaching
.x6	Biography and memoirs (Collective)
	For individual biography, see appropriate period or local subdivision
	By period
.x65	Early to 1600
.x7	1600-1868
.x8	1868-1945
.x85	1945-

TABLES

A

Abacha administration
  Nigeria: DT515.844
Abbas Hilmi, Khedive of Egypt:
  DT107.6
Abbas I the Great: DS292.6
Abbas II: DS292.8
Abbas III: DS293.8
Abbas, Khedive of Egypt
  I: DT104.7
  II: DT107.6
'Abd al-Malikis in Iran: DS269.A23
'Abd al-Qādir ibn Muḥyī al-Dīn, Amir of
  Mascara: DT294.7.A3
Abd el-Krim: DT324.92.A3
Abdullah
  I: DS154.53
  II: DS154.6
Abdur Rahman: DS365+
Abdurahman, A.: DT1927.A34
Abila (Jordan): DS154.9.A24
Abolition of slavery
  South Africa, 1834: DT1845
Abor (Indic people): DS432.A19
Aboriginal Australians: DU123.2+
Abron (African people) in Côte d'Ivoire:
  DT545.45.A27
Abron (African people) in Ghana:
  DT510.43.A25
Abu al-Kharaz, Tell: DS154.9.A28
Abu Ghaush (Israel): DS110.A22
Abū Jirāb (Egypt): DT73.A13
Abū Rawwāsh (Egypt): DT73.A137
Abu-Shushah, Tel(Israel): DS110.A25
Abu Sir Site (Jīzah) (Egypt): DT73.A14
Abū Sunbul (Egypt): DT73.A15
Abū Ẓaby: DS247.A18+
Abubakar administration
  Nigeria: DT515.844
Ābūd (Israel): DS110.A27
Abydos (Egypt): DT73.A16
Abyssinia: DT371+
Aceh (Indonesian people): DS632.A25
Achaemenidae: DS281+
Achang (Chinese people): DS731.A25

Achelnese (Indonesian people):
  DS632.A25
Achinese (Indonesian people):
  DS632.A25
Acholi (African people) in South Sudan:
  DT159.927.A35
Acholla (Extinct city)
  Tunisia: DT269.A23
Acoli (African people)
  Uganda: DT433.245.A35
Acre (Israel): DS110.A3
'Ād in Saudi Arabia: DS219.A3
Ada (African people) in Ghana:
  DT510.43.A34
Adaamawa (Emirate): DT532.115
Adab (Extinct city): DS70.5.A43
Adaima (Egypt): DT73.A17
Adanme (African people):
  DT582.45.A29
Addis Ababa (Ethiopia): DT390.A3
Adelaide (S. Aust.): DU328
Aden: DS247.A2+
Adi (Indic people): DS432.A19
Adibasis in India: DS432.A2
Adivasis in Bangladesh: DS393.83.A35
Adivasis in India: DS432.A2
Admiralty Islands: DU520
Adnyamathanha (Australian people):
  DU125.A45
Adyukru (African people) in Côte
  d'Ivoire: DT545.45.A35
Aerial operations
  Arab War, 1948-1949: DS126.96.A3
  Iraq War, 2003-: DS79.76352+
  Persian Gulf War, 1990-1991:
    DS79.744.A47
  Sino-Japanese War, 1937-1945:
    DS777.533.A35
  Vietnam War: DS558.8
Aetas in the Philippines: DS666.A3
Afar (African people) in Djibouti:
  DT411.45.A35
Afar (African people) in Ethiopia:
  DT380.4.A33
Afar (Ethiopia): DT390.D28
Afghan War, 2001-: DS371.412+

INDEX

Afghan War, 2001-
  Shok Valley, Battle, 2008:
    DS371.4123.S56
Afghan wars
  Persia: DS293
Afghanistan: DS350+
Afghanistan, Jews in: DS135.A23
Afghans in Australia: DU122.P87
Afghans in Iran: DS269.A34
Afghans in Pakistan: DS380.A35
Africa: DT1+
  Relations with U.S.: DT38+
Africa, Jews in: DS135.A25
African Americans in East Africa:
    DT429.5.A38
African Americans in Ghana:
    DT510.43.A37
African Lakes Company (Malawi):
    DT3211+
Africans in Asia: DS28.A35
Africans in Australia: DU122.A35
Africans in India: DS432.A25
Africans in Southern Asia:
    DS339.3.A34
Afridis in Pakistan: DS380.A37
Afrikaaner Republic of Upingtonia,
    1885-1887: DT1610
Afrikaaner Trek, 1878-1879: DT1601
Afrikaner centennial, 1936-1938 (South
    Africa): DT1937.5
Afrikaner domination (Union of South
    Africa): DT1938+
Afrikaner Rebellion, 1914 (Union of
    South Africa): DT1933
Afrikaners in East Africa: DT429.5.A37
Afrikaners in Namibia: DT1558.A46
Afrikaners in South Africa: DT1768.A57
Afshar (Turkish tribe) in Iran:
    DS269.A36
Agalega Island: DT469.M491
Agaria in India: DS432.A3
Agarwals in India: DS432.A34
Agha Mohammed: DS301
Agiabir Site (India): DS486.A29
Agni (African people) in Côte d'Ivoire:
    DT545.45.A58
Agostinho Neto, António: DT1426

Agriculture
  Aboriginal Australians: DU124.A46
Agriculture, Maori: DU423.A35
Ahansala (African people) in Morocco:
    DT313.3.A35
Ahirs in India: DS432.A38
Aḥmad al-Ḥa Hū, Tall: DS70.5.A46
Ahmad Seif-ed Din, Prince of Egypt:
    DT107.2.A5
Aḥmad 'Urābī (Arabi Pasha): DT107.4
Ahmed, 1909-1925: DS315+
Ahmed Shah: DS359.2
Ahom in India: DS432.A39
Ahwat Site (Israel): DS110.A38
Aims
  Iraq War, 2003-: DS79.757
Ait Atta (Berber people) in Morocco:
    DT313.3.A37
Aja (African people) in Benin:
    DT541.45.A33
Aja (African people) in Togo:
    DT582.45.A34
Ajjer in Algeria: DT283.6.A44
Ajmān: DS247.A54+
Ajumba (African people) in Gabon:
    DT546.145.A48
Ak Koyunlu: DS27.52
Ak-Kuyunli: DS289.8
Aka (African people) in Central African
    Republic: DT546.345.A35
Akans (African people) in Ghana:
    DT510.43.A53
Akaroa (New Zealand): DU430.A35
Akas in India: DS432.A44
Akāshah Site (Sudan): DT159.9.A35
Akbar: DS461.3+
Akha in Thailand: DS570.A35
Akhmīn: DT73.A28
Akhziv, Tel (Israel): DS110.T23
Akkadians: DS72.3
Akoko (African people) in Nigeria:
    DT515.45.A45
Akoose (African people) in Cameroon:
    DT571.K66
Akoris (Egypt): DT73.A29
Aksha (Sudan): DT159.9.A37
Aksum Kingdom (Ethiopia): DT390.A88

411

al Anbār: DS70.5.A5
al-'Anwāzim in Saudi Arabia: DS219.A8
Al-Aqsa Intifada, 2000-: DS119.765
al 'Asāsīf (Egypt): DT73.A82
al-Ḥuwayṭāt in Saudia Arabia:
DS219.H8
Al-Mina (Egypt): DT73.A3
Āl Murrah in Saudi Arabia: DS219.A4
Āl Zaydān in Jordan: DS153.55.A45
Alaca Höyük: DS156.A45
Alagankulam Site (India): DS486.A483
Alangan in the Philippines: DS666.A33
Alani in Central Asia: DS328.4.A43
Alas (Indonesian people): DS632.A45
Alawites in Syria: DS94.8.N67
Albania, Jews in: DS135.A28
Albert Margai administration (Sierra
Leone): DT516.815+
Alcohol use
Aboriginal Australians: DU124.A53
Aldeia de Madragoa (Mozambique):
DT3415.C55
Alexandria (Egypt)
Ancient: DT73.A4
Modern: DT154.A4
Algeria: DT271+
Algeria, Jews in: DS135.A3
Algerian Jews in Israel: DS113.8.A35
Algerian Revolution, 1954-1962:
DT295+
Algerians in Syria: DS94.8.A43
Algerians in Tunisia: DT253.2.A43
Algiers (Algeria): DT299.A5
Ali Bey: DT98.5
Allāhdino Site (Pakistan): DS392.2.A44
Alps, Southern (New Zealand):
DU430.A4
Altaic peoples in Asia: DS18
Altars
Ancient Egypt: DT68.8
Althiburos (Tunisia): DT269.A48
Alur (African people) in Congo
(Democratic Republic): DT650.A48
Alves, Nito: DT1424.A58
Alyawara (Australian people):
DU125.A49

Amaa (African people) in Sudan:
DT155.2.A53
Amanullah Khan: DS369
Amānūz in Morocco: DT313.3.A53
Ambastha Kayasthas in India:
DS432.A46
Ambato-Boeni (Madagascar):
DT469.M37A52
Ambattans in Sri Lanka: DS489.25.A43
Ambo (African people) in Zambia:
DT3058.A63
Ambrizete (Angola): DT1465.N94
Amdo in China: DS731.A53
Amenhetep IV, King of Egypt: DT87.4+
Amenhotep II, King of Egypt: DT87.3
Amenhotep III, King of Egypt: DT87.38
Amerasians in the Philippines:
DS666.A38
Amerasians in Vietnam: DS556.45.A43
American Colonization Society
settlements (Liberia): DT633+
American Samoa: DU819.A1
Americans in Australia: DU122.A5
Americans in Israel: DS113.8.A4
Americans in Japan: DS832.7.A6
Americans in Korea: DS904.6.A6
Americans in Lebanon: DS80.55.A45
Americans in South Africa: DT1768.A62
Americans in Thailand: DS570.A44
Americans in the Philippines: DS666.A4
Amhara (African people) in Ethiopia:
DT380.4.A43
Amin regime: DT433.283
Amirante Islands: DT469.A6
Amis (Taiwan people): DS799.43.A44
Ammonites: DS154.215
Amnesty
Vietnam War: DS559.8.A4
Amorites: DS72.5
Amsterdam Island (Terre australes et
antarctiques françaises):
DS349.9.A57
Amulets
Ancient Egypt: DT62.A5
Amuri County (New Zealand):
DU430.A5
Amusements, Maori: DU423.G3

An Lushan Rebellion: DS749.46
Anafa Site (Israel): DS110.A65
Anakalang (Indonesian people): DS632.A52
Anal (Indic peoples): DS432.A48
Anang (African people) in Nigeria: DT515.45.A52
Anavil Brahmans in India: DS432.A488
'Anazah (Arab tribe) in Saudi Arabia: DS219.A53
Ancient Egypt: DT57+
Andaman (and Nicobar): DS486.5.A5+
Andamanese (Indic people): DS432.A54
Ando (African people) in Côte d'Ivoire: DT545.45.A53
Andrade, Mario Pinto de: DT1417.A54
Androy (Madagascar): DT469.M37A53
Anfal Campaign, 1986-1989: DS79.718
Angami (Indic people): DS432.A546
Angas (African people) in Nigeria: DT515.45.A53
Angas, George Fife: DU322.A5
Angkola (Indonesian people): DS632.A54
Anglo-Burmese War, 1st, 1824-1826: DS475.7
Anglo-Egyptian Sudan: DT154.1+
Anglo-Egyptian War, 1882: DT107.4
Anglo-German accords on Zanzibar: DT433.57+
Anglo-Indian society: DS428
Anglo-Indians in India: DS432.A55
Anglo-Iranian Oil Dispute, 1951-1954: DS318.6
Anglo-Israelism: DS131
Angoche (Mozambique): DT3415.A65
Angola: DT1251+
Angola Afrikaaners' resettlement, 1925: DT1634
Anii (African people) in Benin: DT541.45.A54
Anii (African people) in Togo: DT582.45.A54
Animals
    Egyptology: DT62.A55

Anlo (African people) in Ghana: DT510.43.A58
Anlo (African people) in Togo: DT582.45.A56
Anmatyerre (Australian people): DU125.A56
Annam: DS556+
Annobon Island (Equatorial Guinea): DT620.9.A65
Ano (African people) in Côte d'Ivoire: DT545.45.A53
Anshan (Ancient city): DS262.A57
Antananarivo (Madagascar): DT469.M38T34
Antandroy (Malagasy people): DT469.M277A58
Anti-Asian riots, 1897 (Natal): DT2263
Anti-rightest Campaign, 1957-1958: DS778.5
Anti-war demonstrations
    Vietnam War: DS559.6+
Antinoopolis (Egypt): DT73.A7
Antioch (Extinct city): DS156.A556
Antioch in Pisidia (Extinct city): DS156.A557
Antipatris (Extinct city)
    Israel: DS110.A34
Antiquities
    Aboriginal Australians: DU124.A57
    Cape Province: DT2025
Antiquities, Maori: DU423.A55
Antisemitism: DS145
António Enes (Mozambique): DT3415.A65
Antonio Fernandez, Expedition of: DT2943
Anuak (African people) in South Sudan: DT159.927.A58
Anwal (Indic people): DS432.A56
Anyi (African people) in Côte d'Ivoire: DT545.45.A58
Ao (Indic people): DS432.A57
Apa Tanis in India: DS432.A6
Apamea on the Euphrates (Ancient city): DS156.Z48
Apartheid
    Namibia: DT1556

Apartheid
  South Africa: DT1757
Apatanin in India: DS432.A6
Aphek (Extinct city)
  Israel: DS110.A34
Aphrodisias: DS156.A63
Aphroditopolis (Egypt): DT73.A75
April Revolution, 1960 (Korea):
  DS922.43
Aqabah (West Bank): DS110.A67
Aqsá Mosque (Jerusalem):
  DS109.32.M38
Arab and Berber Almoravid domination
  (Mauritania): DT554.65+
Arab and Swahili Expeditions (Zambia):
  DT3085
Arab conquest (North Africa): DT173
Arab Cooperation Council: DS36.23
Arab countries: DS36+
Arab countries, Jews in: DS135.A68
Arab domination (Mozambique):
  DT3345+
Arab East: DS41+
Arab-Israeli conflict: DS119.7+
Arab penetration (Kenya): DT433.565+
Arab propaganda in foreign countries:
  DS63.3
Arab War
  1948-1949: DS126.9
  1967-: DS127+
  1973: DS128.1+
Arabah Valley: DS110.A683
Arabi Pasha: DT107.4
Arabia, Jews in: DS135.A7+
Arabian Peninsula: DS201+
Arabism: DS63.6
Arabs in Afghanistan: DS354.6.A7
Arabs in Africa: DT16.A72
Arabs in Algeria: DT283.4+
Arabs in Australia: DU122.A63
Arabs in foreign countries (General):
  DS36.95+
Arabs in India: DS432.A65
Arabs in Indonesia: DS632.A73,
  DS632.3.A7
Arabs in Iran: DS269.A73
Arabs in Israel: DS113.7+

Arabs in Morocco: DT313.4+
Arabs in Singapore: DS610.25.A7
Arabs in Southeast Asia: DS523.4.A73
Arabs in Sudan: DT155.2.A78
'Arad (Israel): DS110.A685
Arains in India: DS432.A67
Arains in Pakistan: DS380.A68
Arakanese in Burma: DS528.2.A73
Arameans in Egypt: DT72.A73
Arameans in Syria: DS94.8.S94
Arameans in the Middle East: DS59.A7
Aranda (Australian people): DU125.A73
Ararat: DS156.U7
Arbela Site (Israel): DS110.A689
Arbore (African people) in Ethiopia:
  DT380.4.A68
Archelaus: DS122.4
Ardashir I: DS286.2
Ardashir II: DS286.51
Ardashir III: DS287.7
Arem in Vietnam: DS556.45.A73
Argentine Jews in Israel: DS113.8.A72
Argobba (African people) in Ethiopia:
  DT380.4.A69
Ariaal (African people) in Kenya:
  DT433.545.A75
Armana, Tall (Syria): DS99.A58
Armant (Egypt): DT73.A8
Armati in Papua: DU744.35.A8
Armed struggle for national liberation,
  1966- (Namibia): DT1645
Armenia: DS161+
Armenia, Jews in: DS135.A83
Armenian Quarter (Jerusalem):
  DS109.8.A75
Armenians in Australia: DU122.A7
Armenians in Cyprus: DS54.42.A75
Armenians in Egypt: DT72.A75
Armenians in Ethiopia: DT380.4.A7
Armenians in foreign countries
  (General): DS172.2
Armenians in India: DS432.A7
Armenians in Iran: DS269.A75
Armenians in Iraq: DS70.8.A74
Armenians in Israel: DS113.8.A74
Armenians in Lebanon: DS80.55.A75
Armenians in Nigeria: DT515.45.A75

Armenians in Singapore: DS610.25.A74

Armenians in Syria: DS94.8.A83

Armenians in the Middle East: DS59.A73

Arminnā West Site (Egypt): DT73.A812

Armistice
  Arab War, 1948-1949: DS126.98

Armor
  Vietnam War: DS558.9.A75

Armored operations
  Persian Gulf War, 1990-1991: DS79.744.A75

Armstrong, Richard: DU627.17.A7

Arnhem Land (Australia): DU398.A7

Arrows
  Ancient Egypt: DT62.B6

Arsacidae: DS285

Arses: DS284.6

Arsinoe (Egypt): DT73.A8127

Arsinoites (Egypt): DT73.A813

Arsuf (Extinct city): DS110.A73

Art and the Sino-Japanese War, 1937-1945: DS777.533.A78

Art and the Vietnam War: DS559.8.A78

Art and the Zulu War: DT1882.A76

Artaxerxes I: DS284

Artaxerxes II: DS284.4

Artaxerxes III: DS284.5

Arthur's Pass (New Zealand): DU430.A4

Artillery
  Vietnam War: DS558.9.A77

Arts
  Gypsies: DX171

Arunthathiyars in India: DS432.A74

Arykanda: DS156.A64

Arzila (Morocco): DT329.A7

Ascension Island (Caroline Islands): DU568.P7

Ashanti Empire: DT507

Ashanti Region: DT512.9.A84

Ashanti Wars: DT507

Ashdod (Israel): DS110.A754

Ashikaga Shogunate: DS863.75+

Ashkelon (Israel): DS110.A76

Ashkenazim in Israel: DS113.8.A8

Ashmun, Jehudi: DT633.3.A8

Ashraf: DS293.6

Ashurnasirpal II: DS73.72

Asia, Central
  Jews in: DS135.A86

Asia, Jews in: DS135.A85

Asia Minor: DS155+

Asian Jews in Israel: DS113.8.A84

Asians in Australia: DU122.A73

Asians in Hawaii: DU624.7.A85

Asians in Japan: DS832.7.A8

Asians in New Zealand: DU424.5.A75

Asians in South Africa: DT1768.A85

Asir region: DS247.9.A83

Aṣīrah al-Shamālīyah (West Bank): DS110.A764

Asmat in Papua: DU744.35.A82

Asoka: DS451.5

Association Internationale du Congo: DT654+

Assos: DS156.A7

Assur (Ancient city): DS70.5.A7

Assurbanipal: DS73.87

Assurbelkala: DS73.58

Assyria: DS67+

Assyrians in Australia: DU122.A75

Assyrians in Iran: DS269.A88

Assyrians in Iraq: DS70.8.A89

Assyrians in the Middle East: DS59.A75

Astronomy, Maori: DU423.A85

Astyages: DS279.7

Asu (African people) in Tanzania: DT443.3.A78

Asuka period: DS855.5

Asur in India: DS432.A8

Aswan (Egypt): DT73.A88

Asyūt (Egypt): DT73.A9

Asyut Province (Egypt): DT73.A92

Atakat (African people) in Nigeria: DT515.45.A83

Atarantes in Maghrib: DT193.5.A83

Atayal (Taiwan people): DS799.43.A85

Athribis (Egypt): DT73.A93

Atlas Mountains (Morocco): DT328.A8

'Atlit (Israel): DS110.A78

Atris in Nepal: DS493.9.A87

Atrocities
  Iraq War, 2003-: DS79.767.A87
  Korean War: DS920.8+
  Persian Gulf War, 1990-1991:
    DS79.736
  Sino-Japanese War, 1937-1945:
    DS777.533.A86
  Vietnam War: DS559.2
Atuot (African people): DT155.2.A79
Auckland Islands (New Zealand):
  DU430.A83
Auckland (New Zealand)
  City: DU430.A8
  Provincial District: DU430.A79
Audumbara in India: DS432.A9
August Revolution, 1945 (Vietnam):
  DS556.815
Aurangzib: DS461.7
Austral Islands: DU900
Australia: DU80+
Australia, Jews in: DS135.A88+
Australian Alps: DU180.A8
Australian Capital Territory: DU145
Austria, Jews in: DS135.A9+
Austrian Jews in Israel: DS113.8.A88
Avedat (Israel): DS110.A8
Avikam (African people) in Côte d'Ivoire:
  DT545.45.A86
Awans in Pakistan: DS380.A94
'Awlaqī (Arab tribe) in Saudi Arabia:
  DS219.A85
Awori (African people) in Nigeria:
  DT515.45.A96
Axes
  Ancient Egypt: DT62.A9
Axum (Ethiopia): DT390.A88
Ayash (Berber people) in Morocco:
  DT313.3.A93
'Aydhāb (Egypt): DT73.A937
'Ayn al Labakhah Site (Egypt):
  DT73.A94
'Ayn Dārah, Tall (Syria): DS99.A93
'Ayn Ghazāl (Palestine): DS110.A96
'Ayn Wāqifah Site (Egypt): DT73.A95
Azande in Congo (Democratic
  Republic): DT650.A93
Azd in Saudi Arabia: DS219.A93

Azerbaijan, Jews in: DS135.A96
Azerbaijanis in Iran: DS269.A94
Azeris in Iran: DS269.A94
Azikiwe administration (Nigeria):
  DT515.832
Azim
  I: DS359.8
  II: DS364.4
Aziz Dheri Site (Pakistan):
  DS392.2.A95
Azuchi-Monoyama period: DS869.4+

B

Ba-Ronga (African people) in
  Mozambique: DT3328.B33
Bāb edh-Dhrā Site (Jordan):
  DS154.9.B32
Babangida administration
  Nigeria: DT515.842
Babanki (African people) in Cameroon:
  DT571.B25
Babar: DS461.1
Babingas (African people) in Cameroon:
  DT571.B3
Babingas (African people) in Central
  African Republic: DT546.345.B33
Babylon: DS70.5.B3
Babylonia: DS67+
Babylonia, Jews in: DS135.B2
Babylonian Exile (Jews): DS121.65
Bacchis (Egypt): DT73.B3
Badaga (Indic people): DS432.B25
Baḍaganāḍu Brāhmaṇas in India:
  DS432.B26
Badges
  Vietnam War: DS558.98+
  War and intervention, 1950-1953
    (Korea): DS920.44+
Bādīyah as-Shamāliyah (Jordan):
  DS154.9.B34
Badui (Indonesian people): DS632.B23
Bafokeng (African people) in South
  Africa: DT1768.B35
Bafokeng (African people) in Southern
  Africa: DT1058.B34

Bafut (African people) in Cameroon: DT571.B3214

Bagdis (Indic people): DS432.B27

Baggara (African people): DT155.2.B34

Bagirmi (African people) in Chad: DT546.445.B34

Bagobo (Philippine people): DS666.B27

Bagta in India: DS432.B275

Bāḥah: DS247.9.B34

Bahariya Oasis (Egypt): DT73.B33

Bahima (African people) in Uganda: DT433.245.B35

Bahnar in Vietnam: DS556.45.B3

Bahr al Ghazāl Province (Sudan): DT159.6.B34

Bahr al Ghazāl region (South Sudan): DT159.977.B37

Bahrain: DS247.B2+

Bahrain, Jews in: DS135.B26+

Bahram I: DS286.33

Bahram II: DS286.35

Bahram III: DS286.37

Bahram IV: DS286.55

Bahram V: DS286.6

Bahrām VI (Bahrām Chubin): DS287.45

Bai (Chinese people): DS731.P34

Baiga in India: DS432.B3

Bailpattars in India: DS432.B312

Bailundo (Angola): DT1465.B35

Bailundo War, 1902: DT1392

Bairwas (Indic people): DS432.B314

Bais Kshatriyas in India: DS432.B316

Bajau in Indonesia: DS632.B24

Bajau in Sabah: DS597.335.B35

Bajau in the Philippines: DS666.B3

Baka (African people) in Cameroon: DT571.B322

Baka (African people) in Central African Republic: DT546.345.B36

Baker, Sir Samuel White: DT107.2.B16

Bakhtiari in Iran: DS269.B3

Bakongo rebellion, 1913-1914: DT1396

Bakr ibn Wā'il in Saudi Arabia: DS219.B34

Bakrawallah (Indic people): DS432.B32

Bakumatsu period: DS881.2+

Bakusu (Bantu people) in Kenya: DT433.545.B84

Bakwiri (African people) in Cameroon: DT571.B323

Bal'amah Site (West Bank): DS110.B228

Balāmūn, Tall al- (Egypt): DT73.B34

Balanta (African people) in Guinea-Bissau: DT613.45.B35

Balash: DS287

Balat Site (Egypt): DT73.B35

Balathal Site (India): DS486.B345

Balāwāt: DS70.5.B35

Baldwin, Henry Perrine: DU627.7.B3

Balese (African people) in Congo (Democratic Republic): DT650.B34

Balewa administration (Nigeria): DT515.832

Balfuryah (Israel): DS110.B23

Bali (African people) in Cameroon: DT571.B33

Balī (Arab tribe) in Saudi Arabia: DS219.B345

Balija (Indic people): DS432.B324

Balinese (Indonesian people): DS632.B25

Balkan Peninsula, Jews in: DS135.B3

Balla Balla (Zimbabwe): DT3025.M43

Ballarat (Australia): DU230.B3

Baltic Sea Region, Jews in: DS135.B337

Baltic States, Jews in: DS135.B34

Balts in Australia: DU122.B34

Baluba (African people) in Congo (Democratic Republic): DT650.L8

Baluchi in Afghanistan: DS354.6.B35

Baluchi in India: DS432.B326

Baluchi in Iran: DS269.B33

Baluchi in Pakistan: DS380.B3

Baluchis in the Middle East: DS59.B34

Baluchistan: DS392.B2+

Bambara (African people) in Mali: DT551.45.B35

Bambata Rebellion, 1907 (Natal): DT2267

Bambuta (African people) in Congo (Democratic Republic): DT650.B36

Bamileke (African people) in Cameroon: DT571.B34

Bamun (African people) in Cameroon: DT571.B35

Bana (African people) in Cameroon: DT571.B36

Bāñchaṟā: DS432.B33

Banda (African people) in South Sudan: DT159.927.B36

Bandial (African people) in Senegal: DT549.45.B35

Bandjalang (Australian people): DU125.B24

Bandjoun (African people): DT571.B365

Bangala (African people) in Congo (Democratic Republic): DT650.B363

Bangash in Pakistan: DS380.B36

Bangladesh: DS393+

Bangladeshis in India: DS432.B34

Bangladeshis in Japan: DS832.7.B34

Bangwa (African people) in Cameroon: DT571.B366

Bangweulu Lake and Swamp (Zambia): DT3140.B36

Banī Ḥasan Site (Egypt): DT73.B4

Bani Hassan (Egypt): DT73.B4

Banī Naʿīm (West Bank): DS110.B25

Banī Shahr (Arab tribe) in Saudi Arabia: DS219.B35

Bani Surmah Site (Iran): DS262.B36

Baniyas in Nepal: DS493.9.B36

Banjar (Indonesian people): DS646.32.B34

Banks Islands: DU540

Banks Peninsula (New Zealand): DU430.B15

Bannú: DS392.B35

Bantian (Indonesian people): DS632.B27

Bants in India: DS432.B353

Bantu in Somalia: DT402.4.B36

Bantu-speaking peoples in Gabon: DT546.145.B35

Bantus: DT16.B2

Bantus in Tanzania: DT443.3.B35

Banū Khālid (Arab tribe) in Saudi Arabia: DS219.B36

Banū Tamim in Saudi Arabia: DS219.T34

Banyjima (Australian people): DU125.B26

Baqāh al-Gharbiȳah (West Bank): DS110.B26

Bar Kokhba Rebellion, 132-135: DS122.9

Bara (Malagasy people): DT469.M277B37

Barabaig (African people) in Tanzania: DT443.3.B37

Baraguyu in Tanzania: DT443.3.B38

Baram in Nepal: DS493.9.B37

Barānīs (Egypt): DT73.B375

Barbary States: DT181+

Barela (Indic people): DS432.B355

Bari (African people) in South Sudan: DT159.927.B37

Baria (African people) in Cameroon: DT571.B32

Bariba (African people) in Benin: DT541.45.B37

Barmera (Australia): DU330.B3

Bāroṭas (Indic people): DS432.B357

Barotseland (Zambia): DT3140.W48

Barqah (Libya): DT238.C8

Barreto expedition, 1572 (Mozambique): DT3355

Barreto, Francisco: DT3353.B38

Barri, Tell (Syria): DS99.B28

Barṭaʿa (West Bank): DS110.B27

Barwe (African people) in Mozambique: DT3328.B37

Barwe (African people) in Zimbabwe: DT2913.B38

Bas-Congo: DT665.B3

Basa (African people) in Cameroon: DT571.B37

Basadevā (Indic people): DS432.B36

Basakata (African people) in Congo (Democratic Republic): DT650.B365

Baseri tribe in Iran: DS269.B36

Bashada (African people) in Ethiopia: DT380.4.B37

Bashi (African people) in Congo (Democratic Republic): DT650.B366

Bashīt (Palestine): DS110.B28

Bāsiṭ Site (Syria): DS99.B29

Basketry
  Ancient Egypt: DT62.B27

Baskets
  Ancient Egypt: DT62.B27

Basques in Australia: DU122.B37

Basques in the Philippines: DS666.B33

Basra (Extinct city)
  Morocco: DT329.B35

Bassa (African people) in Liberia: DT630.5.B37

Bassari (African people) in Senegal: DT549.45.B37

Bassari (African people) in Togo: DT582.45.B37

Bassonge (African people) in Congo (Democratic Republic): DT650.S55

Basuko (African people) in Congo (Democratic Republic): DT650.B37

Basuto War (South Africa)
  I: DT1865
  II: DT1869
  III: DT1873

Basutoland: DT2541+, DT2638+

Bat-Shelomoh (Israel): DS110.B297

Bat Yam (Israel): DS110.B3

Batak: DS666.B34

Batak in Indonesia: DS632.B3

Batan: DS666.B36

Batek in Malaysia: DS595.2.B38

Batheon
  I: DT2493.B37
  II: DT2493.B38

Baths
  Ancient Egypt: DT62.B3

Batlokwa uprising under Mantatisi, 1922: DT2338

Batrūn (Lebanon): DS89.B39

Battle of Bizerte, 1961 (Tunisia): DT265

Battle of Omdurman, 1898
  Sudan: DT156.65

Battlefields
  Zulu War, 1879: DT1882.B38

Batwa (African people) in Congo (Democratic Republic): DT650.B372

Batwa (African people) in Rwanda: DT450.25.B38

Batwa (African people) in Uganda: DT433.245.B36

Bauddhatantis (Indic people): DS432.B367

Baule (African people) in Côte d'Ivoire: DT545.45.B36

Baum Chin in Bangladesh: DS393.83.B38

Bauris in India: DS432.B37

Bavanīlu (Indic people): DS432.B373

Bavëk (African people) in Cameroon: DT571.B38

Bavili (African people) in Congo (Democratic Republic): DT650.V54

Bavuma (African people) in Uganda: DT433.245.B38

Bawaria (Indic people): DS432.B376

Bawit (Egypt): DT73.B38

Bawo (Indonesian people): DS632.B35

Bay of Islands (New Zealand): DU430.B2

Bayaka (African people) in Congo (Democratic Republic): DT650.B38

Bayat (Turkic people) in Iran: DS269.B39

Bayot (African people): DT549.45.B39

Bayt Jirjā (Gaza Strip): DS110.B3125

Bayt Ṣafāfā (West Bank): DS110.B3127

Bayt Saḥūr (West Bank): DS110.B313

Bayt Ummar (West Bank): DS110.B315

Baytīn (West Bank): DS110.B316

Bazigar (Indic people): DS432.B38

Be (Togolese people) in Togo: DT582.45.B4

Beary (Indic people): DS432.B383

Bechuanaland: DT2421+

Bechuanaland Protectorate: DT2490+

Bédié administration (Côte d'Ivoire): DT545.84+

Bedik (African people): DT549.45.B43

Bedouins: DS36.9.B4

Bedouins in Algeria: DT283.5.B44

Bedouins in Egypt: DT72.B4
Bedouins in Iraq: DS70.8.B4
Bedouins in Israel: DS113.75
Bedouins in Jordan: DS153.55.B43
Bedouins in Lebanon: DS80.55.B43
Bedouins in Libya: DT223.2.B43
Bedouins in Saudi Arabia: DS219.B4
Bedouins in Syria: DS94.8.B4
Be'er Ṭoviyah (Israel): DS110.B3213
Be'eri Region (Israel): DS110.B3213
Beersheba (Israel): DS110.B35
Begrawia Site (Sudan): DT159.9.B34
Beira (Mozambique)
   City: DT3415.B45
   Province: DT3410.S65
Beit Jann (Israel): DS110.B364
Beja (African people) in Egypt:
   DT72.B45
Beja (African people) in Ethiopia:
   DT380.4.B45
Beja (African people) in Sudan:
   DT155.2.B44
Bekal Fort (India): DS486.B3698
Belalis Maior (Tunisia): DT269.B37
Belarus, Jews in: DS135.B38+
Belarusian Jews in Israel: DS113.8.B44
Belarusians in Australia: DU122.B42
Beldar (Indic people): DS432.B39
Belgian administration of Burundi:
   DT450.84+
Belgian administration of Rwanda:
   DT450.425+
Belgian Congo: DT641+
Belgian domination of Burundi:
   DT450.8+
Belgian domination of Rwanda:
   DT450.4+
Belgians in Australia: DU122.B44
Belgium, Jews in: DS135.B4+
Beliefs, Gypsy: DX151
Belmont Castle Site (West Bank):
   DS110.B367
Bemba (African people) in Congo
   (Democratic Republic): DT650.B44
Bemba (African people) in Zambia:
   DT3058.B46

Bembe (African people) in Congo
   (Brazzaville): DT546.245.B44
Bembe (African people) in Congo
   (Democratic Republic): DT650.B45
Bena in Tanzania: DT443.3.B45
Bendigo (Australia): DU230.B4
Bene Berak (Israel): DS110.B372
Bene Tsiyon (Israel): DS110.B3724
Beng (African people) in Côte d'Ivoire:
   DT545.45.B45
Benga (African people) in Equatorial
   Guinea: DT620.45.B45
Bengali in India: DS432.B4
Benguela (Angola): DT1465.B46
Beni Hassan (Egypt): DT73.B4
Beni Kurt: DS289.2
Beni Urriaghel (Berber people) in
   Morocco: DT313.3.W35
Beni Zurual (Berber people) in Morocco:
   DT313.3.B46
Benin: DT541+
Benjamin, Territory of (Israel and West
   Bank): DS110.B3725
Benjelle (African people) in Central
   African Republic: DT546.345.B45
Bentian Dayak (Indonesian people):
   DS646.32.B46
Benuaq (Indonesian people):
   DS632.B42
Berads (Indic people): DS432.B412
Berawan in Sarawak: DS597.367.B47
Berber Almoravid domination
   (Mauritania): DT532+
Berbers in Algeria: DT283.2+
Berbers in Maghrib: DT193.5.B45
Berbers in Morocco: DT313.2+
Bergama: DS156.P4
Berias in India: DS432.B413
Berti (African people): DT155.2.B47
Beśor Region (Israel): DS110.B3728
Besor River: DS110.B373
Bet Gan (Israel): DS110.B3925
Bet ha-Kerem (Jerusalem):
   DS109.8.B35
Bet ha-nasi (Jerusalem): DS109.8.B38
Bet She'an (Israel): DS110.B393
Bet She'arim (Israel): DS110.B3933

Bet Shemesh (Israel): DS110.B394
Bet Yeraḥ, Tel (Israel): DS110.B395
Bet Yiśra'el (Jerusalem): DS109.8.B39
Betawi (Indonesian people):
  DS632.B44
Bété (African people) in Côte d'Ivoire:
  DT545.45.B47
Betew (Indonesian people): DS632.B46
Bethanie (Namibia): DT1685.B48
Bethany (Israel): DS110.B398
Bethlehem: DS110.B4
Bethsaida (Extinct city): DS110.B476
Beti (African people) in Cameroon:
  DT571.B47
Betsileo (Malagasy people):
  DT469.M277B47
Betsimisaraka (Malagasy people):
  DT469.M277B48
Beydar, Tell (Syria): DS99.B48
Bezanozano (Malagasy people):
  DT469.M277B49
Bhaca (African people) in South Africa:
  DT1768.B53
Bhairas in India: DS432.B414
Bhamta (Indic people): DS432.B416
Bhangis in India: DS432.B417
Bhansalis (Indic people): DS432.B4177
Bhāradvājas in India: DS432.B4185
Bharia (Indic people): DS432.B419
Bharvads in India: DS432.B42
Bhāṭarā in India: DS432.B43
Bhatias in Pakistan: DS380.B5
Bhaṭṭarāīs in Nepal: DS493.9.B4
Bhil in India: DS432.B45
Bhimmā in India: DS432.B453
Bhojpuri in India: DS432.B454
Bhojpuri in Mauritius: DT469.M445B52
Bhoksa (Indic people): DS432.B455
Bhotias (Tibetan people) in India:
  DS432.B456
Bhotias (Tibetan people) in Nepal:
  DS493.9.B45
Bhovis in India: DS432.B458
Bhrgus in India: DS432.B46
Bhujela (Nepalese people):
  DS493.9.B47
Bhumij (Indic people): DS432.B47

Bhunjia in India: DS432.B475
Bhunu: DT2791.B58
Bhutan: DS491+
Biafra: DT515.9.E3
Biak in Papua: DU744.35.B5
Biase (African people) in Nigeria:
  DT515.45.B5
Biban el Moluk (Egypt): DT73.B44
Bié (Angola)
  City: DT1465.K85
  Province: DT1450.B54
Bihari in Bangladesh: DS393.83.B5
Bihari in India: DS432.B48
Bihari in Mauritius: DT469.M445B53
Bijago (African people) in Guinea-
  Bissau: DT613.45.B54
Biko, Steve: DT1949.B55
Bikol: DS666.B54
Bin 'Alī
  Administration: DT266+
Bin Barakah, al-Mahdi: DT325.92.B55
Bini (African people) in Nigeria:
  DT515.45.B56
Binjhwar in India: DS432.B49
Binyaminah (Israel): DS110.B56
Bioko (Equatorial Guinea):
  DT620.9.F47
Biological warfare
  Persian Gulf War, 1990-1991:
    DS79.744.C46
  Sino-Japanese War, 1937-1945:
    DS777.533.B55
  Vietnam War: DS559.8.C5
Bīr-koṭ-ghwaṇḍai Site (Pakistan):
  DS392.2.B57
Bir Umm Fawakhir Site (Egypt):
  DT73.B56
Biʻr Zayt (Israel): DS110.B57
Bira (African people) in Congo
  (Democratic Republic): DT650.B57
Birak, Tall (Syria): DS99.B57
Bīrānvand in Iran: DS269.B57
Birhor in India: DS432.B5
Birom (African people) in Nigeria:
  DT515.45.B58
Birragubba (Australian people):
  DU125.B38

Birwa in Sierra Leone: DT516.45.B57
Bisa (African people) in Burkina Faso:
   DT555.45.B57
Bisa (African people) in Zambia:
   DT3058.B58
Bisaya (Malaysian people):
   DS597.367.B56
Bisayas (Philippine people):
   DS666.B57
Bīshāpūr (Extinct city): DS262.B56
Bishop, Bernice Pauahi: DU627.17.B4
Biskra (Algeria): DT299.B5
Bismarck Archipelago: DU550+
Bisnrīs: DS432.B52
Bissagos Islands: DT671.B58
Bisutun Site (Iran): DS262.B57
Bithynia: DS156.B6
Bizerta (Tunisia): DT269.B6
Bizerte, Battle of 1961 (Tunisia): DT265
Blaan (Philippine people): DS666.B58
Black Flag revolt, 1875: DT2137
Black Tai: DS570.B55
Blacks
   South African War: DT1918.B53
   Vietnam War: DS559.8.B55
Blacks (from other countries) in Africa:
   DT16.B58
Blacks in China: DS731.B55
Blacks in Mauritius: DT469.M445B55
Blacks in Namibia: DT1557
Blacks in Saudi Arabia: DS219.B56
Blacks in South Africa: DT1758+
Blacks in Southern Africa: DT1058.B53
Blacks in the Middle East: DS59.B55
Blantyre (Malawi): DT3257.B53
Block statues
   Ancient Egypt: DT62.B46
Bloemfontein (South Africa):
   DT2405.B56
Blood River, Battle of, 1838 (Natal):
   DT2247.B56
Blue Mountains (Australia): DU180.B56
Blue Nile (Ethiopia): DT390.B5
Board games
   Ancient Egypt: DT62.B5
Boats
   Ancient Egypt: DT62.S55

Boats, Maori: DU423.B6
Bobo (African people) in Burkina Faso:
   DT555.45.B63
Bobo (African people) in Mali:
   DT551.45.B63
Bobo Dioula (African people) in Burkina
   Faso: DT555.45.B64
Bobo Fing (African people) in Mali:
   DT551.45.B64
Bodo (Indic people): DS432.B63
Bodrum: DS156.H3
Boers in South Africa: DT1768.A57
Bogos (African people) in Ethiopia:
   DT380.4.B6
Bokar (Indic people): DS432.B64
Bokassa I: DT546.383.B64
Bolama Island: DT613.9.B65
Bolewa (African people) in Nigeria:
   DT515.45.B64
Boma (African people) in Congo
   (Democratic Republic): DT650.B66
Bonan (Chinese people): DS731.P36
Bondei in Tanzania: DT443.3.B65
Bondelswarts in Namibia: DT1558.B65
Bondelswarts' Rebellion, 1922: DT1630
Bondelswarts' Uprising, 1903-1904:
   DT1616
Bondo (Indic people): DS432.B65
Bonga: DT3364.B66
Bongcher (Indic people): DS432.B66
Bongo (African people) in South Sudan:
   DT159.927.B66
Bontoks (Philippine people): DS666.B6
Bophuthatswana (South Africa):
   DT2400.B66
Boran (African people) in Ethiopia:
   DT380.4.B64
Boran (African people) in Kenya:
   DT433.545.B67
Bori (Indic people): DS432.B67
Borjigid in Mongolia: DS798.422.B67
Borneo: DS646.3+
Bornu (Nigeria): DT515.9.B6
Bororo (African people) in Cameroon:
   DT571.B67
Bororo (African people) in Niger:
   DT547.45.B67

Borossé (African people) in Central African Republic: DT546.345.B67
Borsippa: DS70.5.B6
Bosnia and Hercegovina, Jews in: DS135.B54+
Bote (Nepalese people): DS493.9.B68
Botha, Pieter Willem: DT1963
Botswana: DT2421+
Bougie (Algeria): DT299.B7
Boupacha, Djamila: DT295.3.B6
Bourguiba, Habib: DT264.3.B6
    Administration: DT264.35+
Bouyei (Chinese people): DS731.P84
Bows and arrows
    Ancient Egypt: DT62.B6
Boxer Rebellion: DS770+
Boy Scouts (Korean War): DS921.5.B6
Bozo (African people) in Mali: DT551.45.B68
Brahmans in Burma: DS528.2.B7
Brahmans in India: DS432.B73
Brahmans in Nepal: DS493.9.B72
Brahui in Pakistan: DS380.B7
Brakna (African people) in French West Africa: DT530.5.B7
Brand, Johannes Henricus: DT2127.B83
Brazilians in Japan: DS832.7.B73
Brazilians in Nigeria: DT515.45.B73
Brazilians in West Africa: DT474.6.B73
Brazza, Pierre Savorgnan de: DT546.267.B72
Bremersdorp (Swaziland): DT2825.M35
Bretons in Réunion: DT469.R39B74
Brisbane (Qld.): DU278
British administration (Eritrea): DT395.3
British Bechuanaland: DT2490+
British Central Africa: DT2831+
British Central Africa Protectorate (Malawi): DT3216+
British claims (Namibia): DT1587+
British colonial rule
    Seychelles: DT469.S47+
British colony
    Natal: DT2250+
    Sierra Leone: DT516.7+

British consolidation (South Africa): DT1848+
British Crown Colony
    Transvaal: DT2371
    Zimbabwe: DT2972+
British domination (Mauritius): DT469.M47+
British East Africa: DT421+
British East Africa Company
    Kenya: DT433.57+
    Somalia: DT403.5+
    Uganda: DT433.27+
British in Australia: DU122.B7
British in Israel: DS113.8.B7
British in Japan: DS832.7.B74
British in Kenya: DT433.545.B74
British in Malaysia: DS595.2.B74
British in New Zealand: DU424.5.B75
British in Pakistan: DS380.B74
British in Southern Africa: DT1058.B75
British in the Middle East: DS59.B75
British in the Philippines: DS666.B74
British in West Africa: DT474.6.B75
British in Zimbabwe: DT2913.B85
British Intervention in Afghanistan, 1839-1842: DS363
British Kaffraria, Annexation of: DT1857
British military administration
    Somalia: DT406+
British North Borneo: DS597.33+
British occupation
    Seychelles: DT469.S465+
British possession (South Africa): DT1828+
British protectorate
    Basutoland: DT2638+
    British Central Africa: DT2862
    Gambia: DT509.7
    Somalia: DT404+
    Zambia: DT3103+
British rule
    Swaziland: DT2788+
British settlements
    Namibia: DT1587+
    Natal: DT2240
British settlers, 1820
    South Africa: DT1840

British Somaliland: DT404+
British South Africa Company
  administration
  Zambia: DT3091+
  Zimbabwe: DT2959+
British Togoland: DT511+
British West Africa: DT491+
Broken Hill (Australia): DU180.B8
ʼBroṅ-pa (Tibetan people) in China:
  DS731.B76
Bru (Southeast Asian people) in
  Cambodia: DS554.46.B78
Brunei: DS650+
Bubastis Site (Egypt): DT73.B8
Bubi (African people) in Gabon:
  DT546.145.B83
Buckley, William: DU222.B8
Buddhist civilization (India): DS426
Budga Jangams (Indic people):
  DS432.B8
Budrus (West Bank): DS110.B83
Buem (African people) in Ghana:
  DT510.43.B84
Buganda dominance
  Uganda: DT433.27+
Bugis in Indonesia: DS632.B85
Bugis in Malaysia: DS595.2.B84
Bugis in Sabah: DS597.335.B84
Bugti in Pakistan: DS380.B83
Buhari administration
  Nigeria: DT515.842
Buḥayrah, al (Egypt): DT137.B8
Buhen (Sudan): DT159.9.B85
Buhid (Philippine people): DS666.B78
Builsa (African people) in Ghana:
  DT510.43.B85
Buissi (African people): DT650.B84
Bukidnon (Philippine people):
  DS666.B8
Bulakeños (Philippine people):
  DS666.B85
Bulgaria, Jews in: DS135.B8+
Bulgarians in Israel: DS113.8.B84
Bulla Regia (Tunisia): DT269.B85
Bunak (Indonesian people): DS632.B87
Bunuba (Australian people):
  DU125.B64

Bunun in Taiwan: DS799.43.B85
Bunya (Swaziland): DT2825.B86
Buqeiʻa (Israel): DS110.B97
Buraimi (Oasis): DS247.B8+
Burera (Australian people): DU125.B67
Burgers, T.F.: DT2350.B88
Burghers in Sri Lanka: DS489.25.B85
Burials
  Vietnam War: DS559.8.D38
Buriats in Mongolia: DS798.422.B87
Burji (African people) in Eastern Africa:
  DT365.45.B87
Burkina Faso: DT555+
Burkinabe (African people) in Côte
  d'Ivoire: DT545.45.B87
Burma: DS527+
Burma, Jews in: DS135.B87
Burmese in Thailand: DS570.B87
Burundi: DT450.5+
Burundi Kingdom: DT450.74+
Bushmen in South Africa: DT1768.S36
Bushongo (African people) in Congo
  (Democratic Republic): DT650.B87
Business enterprises
  Aboriginal Australians: DU124.B86
Butha-Buthe (Lesotho): DT2686.B87
Buthelezi, Gatsha: DT1949.B88
Buton (Indonesian people): DS632.B88
Buwayhids: DS288.6
Buxas (Indic people): DS432.B87
Bwa (African people) in Burkina Faso:
  DT555.45.B93
Bwa (African people) in Mali:
  DT551.45.B84
Bwatiye in Nigeria: DT515.45.B93
Byzacena (Tunisia): DT269.B98
Byzantine period (North Africa): DT172

C

Cabinda (Angola): DT1450.C33
Cabora Bassa (Mozambique):
  DT3410.C36
Cabral, Amilcar: DT613.76.C3
Cadusii in Iran: DS269.C34
Caesarea (Israel): DS110.C13

Cahora Bassa (Mozambique): DT3410.C36

Cairns (Queensland): DU280.C25

Cairo (Egypt): DT139+

Calah (Ancient city): DS70.5.C3

Caliphs, 632-1517 (Arab countries): DS38.14+

Callirrhoe Site (Jordan): DS154.9.C34

Cambodia: DS554+

Cambodian-Vietnamese Conflict: DS554.84+

Cambyses: DS282.5

Cameroon: DT561+

Cameroun: DT561+

Campaign against Mlozi, 1887-1895 (Malawi): DT3221

Campaigns in interior, 1885-1912 (Mozambique): DT3383

Canaanites: DS121.4

Canadian Jews in Israel: DS113.8.C35

Canadians in China: DS731.C35

Canary Islands, Jews in: DS135.C33

Canberra (Australia): DU145

Canes
  Ancient Egypt: DT62.W34

Canoes, Maori: DU423.B6

Canopic jars
  Ancient Egypt: DT62.C3

Cantandica (Mozambique): DT3415.C36

Canterbury (New Zealand): DU430.C3

Cape of Good Hope (South Africa): DT1991+

Cape Province (South Africa): DT1991+

Cape rule, 1871-1884 (Basutoland): DT2644

Cape Town (South Africa): DT2405.C36+

Cape Verde Islands: DT671.C2+

Cape Verde, Jews in: DS135.C35

Cape Verdeans in foreign countries (General): DT671.C2455

Cape York Peninsula (Australia): DU280.C3

Capernaum (Israel): DS110.C15

Cappadocia: DS156.C3

Caprivi Strip (Namibia): DT1670.C36

Captaincy of Sofala (Mozambique): DT3350+

Caravans
  Gypsies: DX175

Cargados Carajos Shoals: DT469.M493

Carmel, Mount (Israel): DS110.C2

Carmona (Angola): DT1465.U55

Caroline Islands: DU560+

Carthage (Tunisia): DT269.C3+

Carthaginian Empire (Tunisia): DT269.C3+

Carthaginian period (North Africa): DT168+

Casablanca (Morocco): DT329.C3

Cassinga (Angola): DT1465.K38

Caste
  India: DS422.C3
  Nepal: DS493.73

Castra Site (Israel): DS110.C27

Casualties
  Iraq War, 2003-: DS79.767.C37

Catalans in the Philippines: DS666.C36

Caucasian Jews in Israel: DS113.8.C37

Caunus: DS156.K33

Caupāla (Indic people): DS432.C38

Causes
  Iraq War, 2003-: DS79.757

Cave of the Letters (Israel): DS110.L37

Celebes: DS646.4+

Celebrations
  Korean War: DS921.9+
  Vietnam War: DS559.82+

Cemeteries
  Vietnam War: DS559.8.D38

Censorship
  Afghan War, 2001-: DS371.4135
  Iraq War, 2003-: DS79.767.P74
  Persian Gulf War, 1990-1991: DS79.739
  Vietnam War: DS559.46

Census
  Aboriginal Australians: DU124.C43

Census, Maori: DU423.C44

Central African Empire: DT546.3+

Central African Republic: DT546.3+

Central Asia: DS327+

Central Australia: DU390
Central Equatoria (South Sudan):
  DT159.977.C46
Central Sub-Saharan Africa: DT348+
Ceteshwayo, Zulu chief: DT1851.C48
Ceuta (Spain): DT329.C5
Chaamba: DT346.C5
Chad: DT546.4+
Chaga (African people) in Tanzania:
  DT443.3.W33
Chagos Archipelago (British Indian
  Ocean Territory): DS349.9.C42
Chaka, Zulu chief: DT1831.C53
Chakkiliyans in India: DS432.C43
Chakma in Bangladesh: DS393.83.C48
Chakma in Burma: DS528.2.C42
Chakma in India: DS432.C46
Chakma in Southern Asia:
  DS339.3.C45
Chaldean Catholics in the Middle East:
  DS59.A75
Chalmers, James: DU746.C4
Cham in Cambodia: DS554.46.C45
Chamārs in India: DS432.C48
Chamba (African people) in West Africa:
  DT474.6.C48
Chams in Vietnam: DS556.45.C5
Chandreseniya Bayastha Prabhus in
  India: DS432.C483
Changpa in India: DS432.C4845
Chanhu-daro (Pakistan): DS392.2.C53
Chantel (Nepalese people):
  DS493.9.C46
Chantyāla (Nepalese people):
  DS493.9.C47
Charans in India: DS432.C485
Chariots
  Ancient Egypt: DT62.C48
Charities
  Afghan War, 2001-: DS371.415
  Iraq War, 2003-: DS79.767.R43
  Korean War: DS921.3
  Sino-Japanese War, 1937-1945:
    DS777.533.R45
  Vietnam War: DS559.63
Chatham Islands (New Zealand):
  DU430.C48

Chechens in Jordan: DS153.55.C44
Chegutu (Zimbabwe): DT3025.C54
Chemical warfare
  Persian Gulf War, 1990-1991:
    DS79.744.C46
  Vietnam War: DS559.8.C5
Chen (Ch'en) dynasty: DS748.6+
Chenchu (Indic people): DS432.C488
Chepang (Nepalese people):
  DS493.9.C48
Cherchel (Algeria): DT299.C5
Cheros (Indic people): DS432.C49
Chetties in Sri Lanka: DS489.25.C45
Chewa in Malawi: DT3192.C54
Chewa in Zambia: DT3058.C53
Chewong (Malaysian people):
  DS595.2.C47
Chhetris (Nepalese people):
  DS493.9.C49
Ch'iang people in China: DS731.C48
Chibia (Angola): DT1465.C55
Chicualacuala (Mozambique):
  DT3415.C54
Chiga (African people) in Uganda:
  DT433.245.C55
Chik Baraik (Indic people):
  DS432.C495
Chikerema, James: DT2979.C55
Children
  Aboriginal Australians: DU124.C45
  Iraq War, 2003-: DS79.767.C55
  Sino-Japanese War, 1937-1945:
    DS777.533.C47
  Vietnam War: DS559.8.C53
Children, Maori: DU423.C5
Chileans in Australia: DU122.C46
Chilembene (Mozambique):
  DT3415.C55
Chilembwe, John: DT3219.C55
Chilembwe Rebellion, 1915 (Malawi):
  DT3225
Chilialombwe (Zambia): DT3145.C55
Chiluba, Frederick: DT3119.5
Chimoio (Mozambique): DT3415.C56
Chimurenga (Zimbabwe)
  I: DT2968+
  II: DT2988+

Chin Hills: DS530.8.C45
China: DS701+
China and East Asia: DS518.15
China, Jews in: DS135.C5
Chinese in Africa: DT16.C48
Chinese in Australia: DU122.C5
Chinese in Borneo: DS646.32.C5
Chinese in Brunei: DS650.43.C45
Chinese in Burma: DS528.2.C44
Chinese in Cambodia: DS554.46.C5
Chinese in East Asia: DS509.5.C5
Chinese in foreign countries (General):
  DS732
Chinese in French Indonesia:
  DS539.C5
Chinese in Hawaii: DU624.7.C5
Chinese in India: DS432.C5
Chinese in Indonesia: DS632.3.C5
Chinese in islands of the East African
  coast: DT468.45.C45
Chinese in Japan: DS832.7.C5
Chinese in Korea: DS904.6.C5
Chinese in Laos: DS555.45.C5
Chinese in Malaysia: DS595.2.C5
Chinese in Mauritius: DT469.M445C44
Chinese in New Zealand: DU424.5.C5
Chinese in Oceania: DU28.1.C5
Chinese in Réunion: DT469.R39C48
Chinese in Sarawak: DS597.367.C55
Chinese in South Africa: DT1768.C55
Chinese in Southeast Asia:
  DS523.4.C45
Chinese in Thailand: DS570.C5
Chinese in the Philippines: DS666.C5
Chinese in Vietnam: DS556.45.C55
Chinese laborers, Importation of (South
  Africa): DT1922
Ch'ing Dynasty: DS753.82+
Ching-p'o (Chinese people):
  DS731.C49
Ching (Vietnamese people):
  DS556.45.C57
Ching (Vietnamese people) in China:
  DS731.C488
Chingola (Zambia): DT3145.C56
Chinhoyi (Zimbabwe): DT3025.C55
Chino (Chinese people): DS731.C495

Chins in Burma: DS528.2.C45
Chipembere Rebellion, 1965: DT3237
Chipenda, Daniel: DT1417.C55
Chipinga (Zimbabwe): DT3025.C55
Chiru (Indic people): DS432.C52
Chissano, Joaquim: DT3398
Chitpawan Brahmans (Indic people):
  DS432.C524
Chivhu (Zimbabwe): DT3025.C56
Chodhri in India: DS432.C486
Chogha Bonut Site (Iran): DS262.C45
Chogha Mish (Iran): DS262.C46
Chokossi (African people) in Togo:
  DT582.45.C56
Chokwe in Angola: DT1308.C67
Chokwe in Zambia: DT3058.C56
Chokwe (Mozambique): DT3415.C58
Cholanaickan (Indic people):
  DS432.C54
Chopi in Mozambique: DT3328.C67
Chosŏn (Yi) dynasty: DS913+
Chosroes I: DS287.3
Chosroes II: DS287.5
Chrau in Vietnam: DS556.45.C58
Christchurch (New Zealand): DU430.C5
Christian, Jacobus: DT1628.C57
Christian, Johannes: DT1608.C57
Christian period (Egyptian antiquities):
  DT69
Christian Zionism: DS150.5
Christians
  Pakistan: DS380.C47
Christians in Algeria: DT283.6.C48
Christians in India: DS432.C55
Christians in Indonesia: DS632.C57
Christians in Iraq: DS70.8.C45
Christians in the Middle East:
  DS59.C48
Christmas Island (Kiribati):
  DS349.9.C45
Chronology, Maori: DU423.C56
Chru in Vietnam: DS556.45.C586
Chuang (Chinese people): DS731.C5
Chuar (Indic people): DS432.C57
Church of the Holy Sepulcher
  (Jerusalem): DS109.4

Churches
  Vietnam War: DS559.8.C54
Chut in Vietnam: DS556.45.C59
Chuuk: DU568.T7
Chwabo in Mozambique: DT3328.C69
Chyamlung (Nepalese people):
  DS493.9.C53
Cilicia: DS156.C5
Cillium (Tunisia): DT269.C54
Circassians in Egypt: DT72.C53
Circassians in Israel: DS113.8.C5
Circassians in Jordan: DS153.55.C57
Circassians in Syria: DS94.8.C57
Circassians in the Middle East:
  DS59.C57
Ciskei (South Africa): DT2400.C58
Citadel (Jerusalem): DS109.8.C5
City of David (Jerusalem):
  DS109.8.C54
Civil rights
  Aboriginal Australians: DU124.C48
Civil War
  Angola, 1975-2002: DT1428
  Congo (Brazzaville), 1997:
    DT546.28+
  Eritrea, 1962-: DT397
  Liberia, 1989-1996: DT636.5+
  Liberia, 1999-2003: DT636.5+
  Nigeria: DT515.836
  Rwanda, 1959-1962: DT450.43
  Sierra Leone, 1991: DT516.826+
  Sudan, 1956-1972: DT157.67
  Zaire, 1960-1965: DT658.22
Civil War, 1965-
  Chad: DT546.48+
Civil War, 1983-2005
  Sudan: DT157.672
Civil War, 2002-2007(Côte d'Ivoire):
  DT545.84+
Civilian relief
  Iraq War, 2003-: DS79.767.C58
  Persian Gulf War, 1990-1991:
    DS79.744.C58
Claims
  Aboriginal Australians: DU124.C53
Claims, Maori: DU423.C57
Cleopatra, Queen of Egypt: DT92.7

Clipperton Island: DU950.C5
Clothing
  Aboriginal Australians: DU124.C56
Clothing, Maori: DU423.C59
Clysma (Egypt): DT73.C55
Cocos Islands: DS349.9.K43
Cocotiers (Equatorial Guinea):
  DT620.9.E46
Coffins
  Ancient Egypt: DT62.C64
Coghlan, Charles: DT2975.C65
Colenso, Battle of, 1899: DT1908.C65
Collaborationists
  Sino-Japanese War, 1937-1945:
    DS777.533.C64
  South African War: DT1918.C64
Colonies and possessions
  Africa: DT31+
  Oceania: DU29
Colony and Protectorate of Nigeria:
  DT515.75+
Colored people in South Africa:
  DT1768.C65
  Western Cape: DT2072.2.C65
Colored people in Zimbabwe:
  DT2913.C75
Commerce
  Vietnam War: DS559.42
Communalism
  Bangladesh: DS393.812.C65
Communalism (India): DS422.C64
Communication
  Aboriginal Australians: DU124.C63
Communication of information
  Australia: DU91.8+
  Central Sub-Saharan Africa:
    DT349.72+
  Oceania: DU13
Communications
  Vietnam War: DS559.8.C6
Comoros: DT469.C7
Compagnie des Indes Orientales
  (Réunion): DT469.R44+
Compliance with inspections of
  UNSCOM (UN Special Commission
  on Iraw): DS79.755

Computer network resources
  Australia: DU92
  Central Sub-Saharan Africa:
    DT349.74
  Oceania: DU13
Concentration camps
  South African War: DT1918.P75
Conga (Equatorial Guinea):
  DT620.9.E46
Congo (Brazzaville): DT546.2+
Congo (Democratic Republic): DT641+
Congo (Democratic Republic), Jews in:
  DS135.C66
Congo Free State: DT655+
Congo Kingdom: DT654+
Congo River region: DT639
Conscientious objectors
  Iraq War, 2003-: DS79.767.C66
  Vietnam War: DS559.8.C63
Constantine (Algeria)
  City: DT299.C6
  Department: DT298.C7
Containment of Iraqi military operations
  Post-Persian Gulf War, 1991-:
    DS79.755
Convention of Pretoria, 1881: DT2786
Cook Islands (New Zealand):
  DU430.C6
Cook, James
  Arrival at Hawaii: DU626
Coorg in India: DS432.K56
Copperbelt (Zambia): DT3140.C66
Copts in Egypt: DT72.C7
Copts in Sudan: DT155.2.C65
Corisco (Equatorial Guinea):
  DT620.9.E46
Cornish in Australia: DU122.B7
Cornish in South Africa: DT1768.C68
Coronations
  Japan: DS824.5
Cosmology, Maori: DU423.C63
Côte d'Ivoire: DT545+
Coup d' état, 1999 (Côte d'Ivoire):
  DT545.84+
Coup d'état, 1966 (Nigeria):
  DT515.834+
Coup d'état, 1972 (Benin): DT541.845

Coup d'état, 1975 (Nigeria): DT515.838
Coup d'état, 1977 (Angola): DT1432
Coup d'état, 1985 (Sudan): DT157.673
Coup d'état, 1987 (Burkina Faso):
  DT555.835+
Coup of 1953 (Iran): DS318.6
Court life
  Japan: DS824
Creoles in Mauritius: DT469.M445C74
Creoles in Sierra Leone: DT516.45.C73
Criminal justice system, Maori:
  DU423.C8
Croatia, Jews in: DS135.C75
Croats in Australia: DU122.C7
Croats in New Zealand: DU424.5.C76
Croats in South Africa: DT1768.C87
Croesus: DS156.L9
Cromer, Evelyn Baring, 1st Earl of:
  DT107.2.C7
Crowns
  Ancient Egypt: DT62.C76
Crozet Islands: DS349.9.C75
Cua in Vietnam: DS556.45.C83
Cuamba (Mozambique): DT3415.C83
Cuanza River (Angola): DT1450.K83
Cubans in West Africa: DT474.6.C8
Cult of the pharaohs
  Ancient Egypt: DT68.3
Cultural assimilation
  Aboriginal Australians: DU124.C84
Cultural assimilation, Maori:
  DU423.C86
Cultural property
  Iraq War, 2003-: DS79.767.C85
Cultural Revolution, 1966-1976 (China):
  DS778.7
Cultus (Egyptian antiquities): DT68.2+
Cunene River (Angola): DT1450.C85
Cushites in Northeast Africa:
  DT367.45.C86
Cyaxares: DS279.5
Cyme: DS156.C87
Cypriots in foreign countries (General):
  DS54.44
Cyprus: DS54.A2+
Cyprus, Jews in: DS135.C88
Cyrenaica (Libya): DT238.C8

Cyrene (Libya): DT239.C9
Cyrus: DS282
Cyzicus: DS156.C9
Czech Jews in Israel: DS113.8.C94
Czechoslovakia, Jews in: DS135.C95+
Czechs in South Africa: DT1768.C94

D

Daba (African people): DT571.D33
Dab'ah, ad (Egypt): DT73.D25
Ḍabba in Saudi Arabia: DS219.D32
Dābūd (Temple) (Egypt): DT73.D27
Dafla (Indic people): DS432.D3
Dagaaba (African people):
  DT510.43.D33
Dagaaba (African people) in Burkina
  Faso: DT555.45.D35
Dagbani (African people) in Ghana:
  DT510.43.D34
Dagomba (African people) in Ghana:
  DT510.43.D34
Dagur (Chinese people): DS731.D33
Dahomey: DT541+
Dahshur (Egypt): DT73.D3
Daimyo: DS827.D34
Daivadnya Brahmans (Indic people):
  DS432.D32
Dakhla Oasis (Egypt): DT73.D33
Dakkalas in India: DS432.D35
Dalit Site (Israel): DS110.D3
Dalits in Nepal: DS493.9.D24
Dāliyat al-Karmil (Israel): DS110.D322
Damara in Namibia: DT1558.D35
Damaraland (Namibia): DT1670.D36
Damietta region (Egypt): DT137.D26
Dan (African people) in Côte d'Ivoire:
  DT545.45.D34
Dan (Extinct city): DS110.D33
Danagla (African people): DT155.2.D36
Danakil (Ethiopia): DT390.D28
Dandara (Egypt): DT73.D4
Danes in New Zealand: DU424.5.D35
Dangerous Islands: DU890
Dani in Papua: DU744.35.D32
Daoguang: DS757+
Darai in Nepal: DS493.9.D38

Darfur (Sudan): DT159.6.D27
Darius I: DS282.7
Darius II: DS284.3
Darius III: DS284.7
Darkhat in Mongolia: DS798.422.D37
Darling Downs (Australia): DU280.D2
Darwin (Australia): DU398.D3
Dasanetch (African people) in Ethiopia:
  DT380.4.D3
Dawāsir in Saudi Arabia: DS219.D38
Dawro (African people) in Ethiopia:
  DT380.4.D37
Dayak in Borneo: DS646.32.D9
Dayr al-Barshā (Egypt): DT73.D44
Dayr al-Zawr (Syria): DS99.D34
Dayr 'Allā, Tall: DS154.9.D34
Dayr Ayyūb (Israel): DS110.D335
Dayr Site (West Bank): DS110.D374
Daza: DT346.D38
Daza in Chad: DT546.445.D38
de Klerk, F.W., 1989-1994: DT1970
Dead, Care of
  Vietnam War: DS559.8.D38
Dead Sea: DS110.D38
Death in Japan: DS827.D4
Déby administration, Chad:
  DT546.484+
December 1983 coup d'état
  Nigeria: DT515.84
Decorations of honor
  Vietnam War: DS558.98+
  War and intervention, 1950-1953
    (Korea): DS920.44+
Defoliation
  Vietnam War: DS559.8.C5
Deganyah Alef (Israel): DS110.D4
Deioces: DS279
Deir el-Bahri Site (Egypt): DT73.D45
Deir el-Ballas Site (Egypt): DT73.D46
Deir el-Gebrawi Site (Egypt):
  DT73.D465
Deir el-Medina Site (Egypt): DT73.D47
Deis el-Shelwit Site (Egypt): DT73.D48
Delki Khadia (Indic people): DS432.D38
Dembo rebellions, 1877-1919: DT1390
Democratic People's Republic (North
  Korea): DS930+

Democratic Republic (North Vietnam): DS558.5

Demonstrations, 2010- (Tunisia): DT266+

Dendi (African people) in Mali: DT551.45.D45

Dendūr (Egypt): DT73.D49

Dengese (African people): DT650.D44

Denkyira (Kingdom): DT532.12

Denmark, Jews in: DS135.D4+

D'Entrecasteaux Islands: DU580

Deori (Indic people): DS432.D4

Dereağzı Site: DS156.D45

Derna (Libya): DT239.D4

Derr, el (Egypt): DT73.D492

Desasthas (Indic people): DS432.D43

Desertions
  Vietnam War: DS559.8.D4

Destruction and pillage
  Korean War: DS921.5.D4
  Persian Gulf War, 1990-1991: DS79.736
  Vietnam War: DS559.3

Detainees
  Iraq War, 2003-: DS79.767.D38

Devangas in India: DS432.D437

Dewar (Indic people): DS432.D44

Dharalas: DS432.D45

Dharug (Australian people): DU125.D47

Dheds in India: DS432.D47

Dhimal in India: DS432.D476

Dhimal (Nepalese people): DS493.9.D44

Dhimars in India: DS432.D48

Dhimmis: DS36.9.D47

Dhimmis in the Middle East: DS59.D47

Dhlamini, Mabandla: DT2800.D53

Dhlamini, Mfanasibili: DT2800.D54

Dhodias (Indic people): DS432.D49

Dholavira Site (India): DS486.D46

Dhors (Indic people): DS432.D494

Dhrā' el Khān Site (Jordan): DS154.9.D48

Dhubyān in Saudi Arabia: DS219.D48

Dhund in Pakistan: DS380.D48

Dhungutti (Australian people): DU125.D5

Dhurwas in India: DS432.D5

Diamond rush, 1867: DT1871

Dias de Novais, Paulo: DT1365.D53

Didaya in India: DS432.D53

Didinga (African people) in South Sudan: DT159.927.D56

Didyma (Ancient city): DS156.D5

Diego Garcia: DS349.9.D53

Diên Biên Phû: DS553.3.D5

Difaqane
  Botswana: DT2488
  Natal: DT2238
  Orange Free State: DT2118
  South Africa: DT1841

Digo (African people) in Kenya: DT433.545.D54

Dii (African people): DT571.D55

Dīmay (Egypt): DT73.D54

Dingaan, Zulu chief: DT1851.D56

Dingiswayo, Zulu chief: DT1831.D56

Dinka (African people) in South Sudan: DT159.927.D57

Dinka (Nilotic people) in Sudan: DT155.2.D56

Dinuzulu, Zulu chief: DT1851.D57

Diola (African people): DT549.45.D56

Dionysias (Egypt): DT73.D56

Diplomatic history
  Iraq War, 2003-: DS79.761
  Persian Gulf War, 1990-1991: DS79.744.D55

Displaced persons
  Afghan War, 2001-: DS371.415
  Iraq War, 2003-: DS79.767.R43
  Korean War: DS921.3
  Sino-Japanese War, 1937-1945: DS777.533.R45
  Vietnam War: DS559.63

Dissolution of Burundi-Tutsi monarchy, 1966: DT450.855

Dissolution of Rwanda-Tutsi monarchy, 1961: DT450.432

Diyala River Region (Ancient region): DS70.5.D57

Diyari (Australian people): DU125.D59

Dizi (African people) in Ethiopia:
DT380.4.D57

Djabugay (Australian people):
DU125.D63

Djamasp: DS287.2

Djibouti: DT411+

Djubi Gauhar Site (Iran): DS262.D57

Dodoth (African people) in Uganda:
DT433.245.D63

Dogon (African people) in French West
Africa: DT530.5.D64

Dogon (African people) in Mali:
DT551.45.D64

Dogras in India: DS432.D58

Dole, Sanford Ballard: DU627.7.D65

Dom (South Asian people) in India:
DS432.D587

Dombaru (Indic people): DS432.D59

Dombidasas in India: DS432.D593

Dombo, King of Changamire:
DT2940.D66

Dombo of the Changamire, Expedition
of (Mozambique): DT3359

Dome of the Rock (Jerusalem):
DS109.32.R6

Dominik, Hans: DT575.D6

Dong (Chinese people): DS731.T77

Dongria Kondh in India: DS432.D595

Dongxiang (Chinese people):
DS731.T78

Dor (Extinct city): DS110.D67

Dorla (Indic people): DS432.D6

Dorobo (African people) in Kenya:
DT433.545.D67

Dorze in Ethiopia: DT380.4.D67

Dost Mohammed: DS363

Dothan Site (West Bank): DS110.D69

Dou Donggo (Indonesian people):
DS632.D68

Doya (Bhutanese people):
DS491.76.D69

Doyayo (African people) in Cameroon:
DT571.D68

Draft resisters
Vietnam War: DS559.8.D7

Drakensburg Mountains (South Africa):
DT2400.D83

Dravidians in India: DS432.D7

Drehem (Ancient city): DS70.5.D73

Druzes in Israel: DS113.72

Druzes in Lebanon: DS80.55.D78

Druzes in Syria: DS94.8.D8

Druzes in the Middle East: DS59.D78

Du Chaillu, Paul: DT356

Duala (African people): DT571.D83

Dubai: DS247.D7+

Dube, J.L.: DT1927.D83

Dukawa (African people) in Nigeria:
DT515.45.D84

Dunedin (New Zealand): DU430.D8

Dunk Island (Australia): DU280.D7

Dur-Kurigalzu: DS70.5.D87

Dur Sharrukin (Ancient city):
DS70.5.D89

Dur-Untash (Iran): DS262.D87

Durā (Nepalese people): DS493.9.D87

Durawa in Sri Lanka: DS489.25.D87

Durban (South Africa): DT2405.D88+

Dusadhs (Indic people): DS432.D87

Dusuns in Borneo: DS646.32.D86

Dusuns in Brunei: DS650.43.D87

Dusuns in Sabah: DS597.335.D88

Dutch claims
Equatorial Guinea: DT620.65+
Namibia: DT1587+

Dutch colonization (Mauritius):
DT469.M465+

Dutch East India Company: DS642+

Dutch East India Company
administration (South Africa):
DT1813+

Dutch expedition, 1604 (Mozambique):
DT3357

Dutch in Australia: DU122.D8

Dutch in Indonesia: DS632.3.D88

Dutch in Japan: DS832.7.D8

Dutch in Malaysia: DS595.2.D88

Dutch in New Zealand: DU424.5.D8

Dutch in South Africa: DT1768.D88

Dutch in Transvaal: DT2323.D88

Dutch Jews in Israel: DS113.8.D8

Dutch occupations (Angola): DT1369

Dutch rule, 1624-1661 (Taiwan):
DS799.67

Dyak in Borneo: DS646.32.D9
Dyak in Sarawak: DS597.367.D93
Dyula (African people) in Benin:
DT541.45.D95
Dyula (African people) in Côte d'Ivoire:
DT545.45.D85
Dzeliwe, Queen Regent: DT2800.D94

E

Earlier Shu Kingdom: DS749.7+
Early European explorations (Burkino
Faso): DT555.65+
East Africa: DT421+
East African Protectorate (Kenya):
DT433.57+
East Arabia: DS247.S62+
East Asia: DS501+
East Central lake region (Central Sub-
Saharan Africa): DT361+
East Indian domination: DT3345+
East Indians arrive, 1860 (South Africa):
DT1867
East Indians in Africa: DT16.E17
East Indians in Asia: DS509.5.E3
East Indians in Australia: DU122.E17
East Indians in Central Sub-Saharan
Africa: DT352.43.E16
East Indians in China: DS731.E36
East Indians in East Africa:
DT429.5.E27
East Indians in foreign countries
(General): DS432.5
East Indians in Kenya: DT433.545.E27
East Indians in Malaysia: DS595.2.E2
East Indians in Mauritius:
DT469.M445E27
East Indians in Nepal: DS493.9.E28
East Indians in Réunion:
DT469.R39E28
East Indians in Singapore:
DS610.25.E37
East Indians in South Africa:
DT1768.E38
East Indians in Southeast Asia:
DS523.4.E28

East Indians in Southern Asia:
DS339.3.E28
East Indians in Sri Lanka: DS489.25.E3
East Indians in Tanzania: DT443.3.E38
East Indians in Thailand: DS570.E37
East Indians in the Middle East:
DS59.E27
East Indians in Uganda:
DT433.245.E18
East Indians in Zaire: DT3058.E38
East Indians in Zimbabwe: DT2913.E38
East London (South Africa):
DT2405.E38
East Malaysia: DS597.22+, DS597.22
East Pakistan: DS393+
East Timor: DS649.2+
East Timorese in Australia: DU122.E2
Eastern Africa: DT365+
Eastern Arrernte (Australian people):
DU125.E17
Eastern Cape (South Africa): DT2058+
Eastern Desert (Egypt): DT73.E27
Eastern Equatoria (South Sudan):
DT159.977.E27
Eastern Region (Nigeria): DT515.9.E3
Eastern Transvaal (South Africa):
DT2386+
Eastern Wei dynasty: DS748.7+
Eastern Zhou dynasty: DS747+
Ebal, Mount (Israel): DS110.E23
Eberhardt, Isabelle: DT294.7.E2
Ebira (African people) in Nigeria:
DT515.45.E3
Economic aspects
Iraq War, 2003-: DS79.767.E26
Persian Gulf War, 1990-1991:
DS79.738
Vietnam War: DS559.42
Economic conditions
Aboriginal Australians: DU124.E36
Economic conditions, Maori: DU423.E3
Edessa: DS156.E2
Edo period: DS870+
Edo-speaking peoples in Nigeria:
DT515.45.E32

Education
  Sino-Japanese War, 1937-1945:
    DS777.533.E38
Efe (African people) in Congo
  (Democratic Republic): DT650.E34
Efik (African people) in Nigeria:
  DT515.45.E34
Efrat (Israel): DS110.E455
Egba (African people) in Nigeria:
  DT515.45.E35
Egmont, Mount (New Zealand):
  DU430.E36
Egypt: DT43+
Egypt exploration fund: DT57+
Egypt, Jews in: DS135.E4+
Egypt, Lower: DT45
Egypt, Upper: DT45
Egyptian Jews in Israel: DS113.8.E48
Egyptology: DT57+
Eipo in Papua: DU744.35.E56
Ejagham (African people) in Cameroon:
  DT571.E35
Ekatte (Syria): DS99.E34
Eket (African people) in Nigeria:
  DT515.45.E39
Ekiti (African people) in Nigeria:
  DT515.45.E42
Ekonda (African people) in Congo
  (Democratic Republic): DT650.E45
Ekpeye (African people) in Nigeria:
  DT515.45.E44
Ekron (Extinct city): DS110.E458
Ekthariya Chhetris in Nepal:
  DS493.9.E47
el Ashmūnein (Egypt): DT73.A85
El-Kab (Egypt): DT73.E43
Elam: DS65
Elat (Israel): DS110.E46
Electronic information resources
  Australia: DU92
  Central Sub-Saharan Africa:
    DT349.74
  Oceania: DU13
Elephantine (Egypt): DT73.E45
Elisabethville (Zaire): DT665.E4
Ellice Islands: DU590
Elmolo in Kenya: DT433.545.E45

Elobey Islands (Equatorial Guinea):
  DT620.9.E46
Elot Region (Israel): DS110.E47
Embu in Kenya: DT433.545.E48
Emin Pasha: DT363
Emmaus (Israel): DS110.E5
Employment
  Aboriginal Australians: DU124.E46
Employment, Maori: DU423.E66
'En Besor Site (Israel): DS110.E58
'En Gedi (Israel): DS110.E63
'En Hatsevah Site (Israel): DS110.E643
En Hod (Israel): DS110.E645
En Shadud (Israel): DS110.E65
Encounter Bay (Australia): DU330.E5
Endorois in Kenya: DT433.545.E53
Engineering operations
  Vietnam War: DS558.85
England, Jews in: DS135.E5+
English in Australia: DU122.B7
English in the Near East: DS59.B75
English rule (India): DS463+
English-speaking countries, Jews in:
  DS135.E64
Entertainment and recreation for
  soldiers
  Sino-Japanese War, 1937-1945:
    DS777.533.E56
Environmental aspects
  Iraq War, 2003-: DS79.767.E58
  Persian Gulf War, 1990-1991:
    DS79.744.E58
Ephthalites in Central Asia:
  DS328.4.E64
Ephthalites in India: DS432.E6
Equatorial Guinea: DT620+
Erech (Ancient city): DS70.5.E65
Erg, El (Algeria): DT298.E7
Eridu (Ancient city): DS70.5.E67
Eritrea: DT391+
Eritrea, Jews in: DS135.E68
Eritrean-Ethiopian War, 1998-:
  DT388.35
Eritreans in Australia: DU122.E7
Esan (African people) in Nigeria:
  DT515.45.I83
Esarhaddon: DS73.85

Eshnunna: DS70.5.E7
Esigodini (Zimbabwe): DT3025.E85
Essaouirá (Morocco): DT329.E84
Essexdale (Zimbabwe): DT3025.E85
Estonia, Jews in: DS135.E73
Estonians in Australia: DU122.E8
Ethical aspects
　Iraq War, 2003-: DS79.767.M67
Ethiopia: DT371+
　Annexation of Eritrea: DT397
Ethiopia, Jews in: DS135.E75
Ethiopians in Australia: DU122.E83
Ethnic identity
　Aboriginal Australians: DU124.E74
　Maori: DU423.E85
Ethnic relations
　Angola: DT1306
　Botswana: DT2456
　Malawi: DT3190
　Mozambique: DT3326
　Namibia: DT1555
　Southern Africa: DT1056
　Zambia: DT3056
　Zimbabwe: DT2912
Ethnobotany
　Aboriginal Australians: DU124.E76
Ethnobotany, Maori: DU423.E87
Ethnozoology, Maori: DU423.E88
Étienne, Eugène: DT294.7.E8
Eton (African people) in Cameroon:
　DT571.E86
Etosha Pan (Namibia): DT1670.E86
Etsako (African people) in Nigeria:
　DT515.45.E77
Eurasia, Jews in: DS135.E77
Eurasians in Burma: DS528.2.E9
Eurasians in East India: DS509.5.E9
Eurasians in Indonesia: DS632.E9
Eurasians in Southeast Asia:
　DS523.4.E87
Eurasians in Southern Asia:
　DS339.3.E97
Europe, Jews in: DS135.E8+
European colonization (Samoan
　Islands): DU817+
Europeans in Africa: DT16.E95
Europeans in Algeria: DT283.6.E95

Europeans in Australia: DU122.E87
Europeans in China: DS731.E82
Europeans in India: DS432.E88
Europeans in Japan: DS832.7.E8
Europeans in New Zealand:
　DU424.5.E97
Europeans in Southeast Asia:
　DS523.4.E89
Europeans in Sri Lanka: DS489.25.E95
Europeans in Tunisia: DT253.2.E8
Europeans in Zambia: DT3058.E87
Europeans in Zimbabwe: DT2913.E87
Even-Yehudah (Israel): DS110.E76
Evenki in China: DS731.E85
Evozok (African people) in Cameroon:
　DT571.E94
Ewe (African people) in Ghana:
　DT510.43.E94
Ewe (African people) in Togo:
　DT582.45.E93
Ewe (African people) in West Africa:
　DT474.6.E83
Eyadema, Gnassingbe: DT582.82.E94
Eyre Peninsula (Australia): DU330.E9
Ezhavas in India: DS432.E95
Ezion-geber (Jordan): DS154.9.E83
Ezyon Bloc (Israel): DS110.E95

F

Fads in Japan: DS827.F34
Failaka Island: DS247.F34+
Faisal (Iraq)
　I: DS79.5
　II: DS79.53
Falashas: DS135.E75
Falashas in Israel: DS113.8.F34
Fali (African people) in Cameroon:
　DT571.F34
Fallujah, Battle of, 2004: DS79.764.F35
Fang (African people) in Equatorial
　Guinea: DT620.45.F33
Fang (African people) in French West
　Africa: DT530.5.F34
Fang (African people) in Gabon:
　DT546.145.F35

Fang (African people) in West Africa: DT474.6.F35

Fantis (African people) in Ghana: DT510.43.F35

Far East: DS501+

Far East, Jews in: DS135.E2+

Farkha, Tell el- (Egypt): DT73.F36

Farmana Site (India): DS486.F36

Farrington, Wallace Rider: DU627.7.F3

Farrokhabad, Tepe (Iran): DS262.F37

Fārūq I, King of Egypt: DT107.82

Fath Ali: DS302

Fatuhiva Island: DU701.F3

Fayṣal: DS244.6

Fayu in Papua: DU744.35.F39

Fayyūm (Egypt): DT73.F38

February Twenty Eighth Incident, 1947 (Taiwan): DS799.823

Federation of Rhodesia and Nyasaland: DT2831+

Federation of South Arabia: DS247.A2+

Federation with Ethiopia (Eritrea): DT395.5

Fe'Fe (African people) in Cameroon: DT571.F43

Fernando Po (Equatorial Guinea): DT620.9.F47

Festivals (Egyptian antiquities): DT68.4

Fezzan (Libya): DT238.F5

Fiftieth Ordinance, 1828 (South Africa): DT1843

Fiji Islands: DU600

Filipinos in Australia: DU122.F5

Filipinos in Hawaii: DU624.7.F4

Filipinos in Japan: DS832.7.F54

Finance
Persian Gulf War, 1990-1991: DS79.738
Vietnam War: DS559.42

Fingos in South Africa: DT1768.F54

Finland, Jews in: DS135.F54

Finns in Australia: DU122.F55

Finns in New Zealand: DU424.5.F55

Fipa (African people) in Tanzania: DT443.3.F56

Fipa (African people) in Zambia: DT3058.F56

First Anglo-Afrikaner War: DT2354+

First Anglo-Burmese War, 1824-1826: DS475.7

First contact with Europeans
Aboriginal Australians: DU124.F57

First contact with Europeans, Maori: DU423.F48

Fisher, Sir James Hurtle: DU322.F5

Fishing, Maori: DU423.F5

Five dynasties: DS749.6+

Five Hu and Sixteen Kingdoms: DS748.45+

Flemings in Congo (Democratic Republic): DT650.F43

Flemish in South Africa: DT1768.F56

Folklore
Gypsies: DX157

Fon (African people) in Benin: DT541.45.F65

Fon (African people) in Cameroon: DT571.F64

For (African people): DT155.2.F87

Forawa (African people): DT155.2.F87

Forbes (Australia): DU180.F6

Foreign participation
Angolan Revolution, 1961-1975: DT1408+
South African War, 1899-1902: DT1911+

Forgeries (Egyptology): DT60.5

Former Polish Eastern Territories, Jews in: DS135.F67

Fort Victoria (Zimbabwe): DT3025.M37

Fortification
Arab War, 1948-1949: DS126.96.F67

Fortune-telling
Gypsies: DX155

Founding of National Party, 1934 (Union of South Africa): DT1937

France
Iraq War, 2003-: DS79.765.F8

France and East Asia: DS518.2

France, Jews in: DS135.F8+

Francistown (Botswana): DT2525.F83

Free State (South Africa): DT2075+

Freetown (Sierra Leone): DT516.9.F73

Fremantle (Australia): DU380.F8

French colonial rule
  Seychelles: DT469.S465+
French colony
  Gabon: DT546.37+
  Mauritania: DT554.75+
French control (Mauritius):
  DT469.M465+
French East India Company (Mauritius):
  DT469.M465+
French in Australia: DU122.F73
French in Cameroon: DT571.F73
French in China: DS731.F74
French in Egypt: DT72.F7
French in French Indonesia:
  DS539.F74
French in Gabon: DT546.145.F74
French in India: DS432.F73
French in Japan: DS832.7.F74
French in Morocco: DT313.6.F73
French in New Zealand: DU424.5.F73
French in South Africa: DT1768.F73
French India: DS485.P66
French Indonesia: DS531+
French influences on Maori:
  DU423.F73
French Jews in Israel: DS113.8.F73
French protectorate
  Burkina Faso: DT555.75+
  Madagascar: DT469.M34+
  Tunisia: DT263.9+
French Sahara: DT521+
French Somaliland: DT411+
French-speaking Equatorial Africa:
  DT546.1+
French Sudan: DT551+
French territory
  Benin: DT541.75+
  Congo: DT546.275
  Guinea: DT543.75+
  Mali: DT551.7+
  Niger: DT547.75
French Territory of the Afars and Issas:
  DT411+
French Togoland: DT582.75
French West Africa: DT521+
Friendly Islands: DU880

Frontier Wars, 1811-1878 (South
  Africa): DT1837
Fuad I, King of Egypt: DT107.8
Fuḍūl in Saudi Arabia: DS219.F83
Fuel supplies
  Vietnam War: DS559.8.F83
Fujayrah: DS247.F84+
Fula (African people) in Benin:
  DT541.45.F85
Fula (African people) in French West
  Africa: DT530.5.F84
Fula (African people) in Ghana:
  DT510.43.F84
Fula (African people) in Guinea:
  DT543.45.F84
Fula (African people) in Mali:
  DT551.45.F85
Fula (African people) in Mauritania:
  DT554.45.F84
Fula (African people) in Niger:
  DT547.45.F84
Fula (African people) in Nigeria:
  DT515.45.F84
Fula (African people) in Senegal:
  DT549.45.F84
Fula (African people) in Sudan:
  DT155.2.F84
Fula (African people) in West Africa:
  DT474.6.F84
Fula in Sierra Leone: DT516.45.F85
Fuladu (Kingdom): DT532.128
Fulani Empire: DT515.9.F8
Funeral rites and ceremonies, Maori:
  DU423.F8
Funj dynasty: DT156.35
Fur (African people): DT155.2.F87
Futa-Jallon: DT532.13

G

G/wi (African people) in Botswana:
  DT2458.G27
Gã (African people) in Ghana:
  DT510.43.G3
Gã in Togo: DT582.45.G3
Gaanda (African people) in Nigeria:
  DT515.45.G32

Gabati Site (Sudan): DT159.9.G33

Gabon: DT546.1+

Gaboon: DT546.1+

Gabun: DT546.1+

Gadaba in India: DS432.G27

Gaddang (Philippine people):
DS666.G3

Gaddis (Indic people): DS432.G275

Gade (African people) in Côte d'Ivoire:
DT545.45.G33

Gadjerong (Australian people):
DU125.G33

Gagou (African people) in Côte d'Ivoire:
DT545.45.G34

Gaika, Xhosa chief: DT1831.G35

Gajaaga: DT532.14

Galela (Indonesian people):
DS632.G25

Galilee (Israel): DS110.G2

Galla (Ethiopia): DT390.G2

Gallas
Ethiopia: DT390.G2

Gallong in India: DS432.G3

Galwa (African people) in Gabon:
DT546.145.G34

Gambaye (African people) in Chad:
DT546.445.G36

Gambia: DT509+

Gambier Islands: DU680

Games
Maori: DU423.G3

Gamit (Indic people): DS432.G32

Gamo (African people) in Ethiopia:
DT380.4.G19

Gamokkalu in India: DS432.G325

Gan (Burkinabe people) in Burkina
Faso: DT555.45.G36

Gan-Yavneh (Israel): DS110.G22

Ganda (African people) in Uganda:
DT433.245.G35

Gandas (Indic people): DS432.G33

Gandhi, Mahatma
Civil disobedience campaigns
South Africa: DT1929

Gane (Indonesian people): DS632.G26

Garawa (Australian people):
DU125.G37

Garden of Gethsemane (Jerusalem):
DS109.8.G4

Garewālas (Indic people): DS432.G335

Garo in India: DS432.G34

Garos in Bangladesh: DS393.83.G37

Gaston, Albert: DU372.G3

Gatooma (Zimbabwe): DT3025.K34

Gauda Sārasvata Brāhmaṇas in India:
DS432.G37

Gaudas in India: DS432.G38

Gautamas in Nepal: DS493.9.G38

Gauteng (South Africa): DT2380+

Gawra, Tepe (Iraq): DS70.5.G38

Gayo (Indonesian people): DS632.G3

Gaza (Mozambique): DT3410.G39

Gaza Strip: DS110.G3

Gaza War, 2008-2009: DS119.767

Gazankulu (South Africa): DT2400.G39

Gbagbo administration (Côte d'Ivoire):
DT545.84+

Gbagyi (African people) in Nigeria:
DT515.45.G33

Gbari (African people) in Nigeria:
DT515.45.G34

Gbaya (African people) in Central
African Republic: DT546.345.G33

Gbaya (African people) West Africa:
DT474.6.G32

Gbaya (Central Sudanic people) in
South Sudan: DT159.927.G32

Gebelein Site (Egypt): DT73.G42

Gederah (Israel): DS110.G4

Geelong (Australia): DU230.G4

Gelo in China: DS731.G36

Gen. Joseph Momoh administration
(Sierra Leone): DT516.815+

Genghis Khan: DS22

Genya (African people) in Congo
(Democratic Republic): DT650.G46

Geography
South Africa: DT1728
Zaire: DT644.8

Georgia (Republic), Jews in:
DS135.G28

Georgian (South Caucasian) Jews in
Israel: DS113.8.G37

Georgians (South Caucasians) in Iran: DS269.G46

Georgians (South Caucasians) in Pakistan: DS380.G46

Gere (African people) in Côte d'Ivoire: DT545.45.G47

Gerf Hussein Temple (Egypt): DT73.G47

Gerizim, Mount (West Bank): DS110.G46

Germ warfare charges (Korean War): DS920.9

German colonization, 1856 (South Africa): DT1861

German colony (Togo): DT582.7

German domination of Burundi: DT450.77+

German domination of Rwanda: DT450.37+

German East Africa: DT436+

German Jews in Israel: DS113.8.G4

German reunification movement, 1932-1939 (Namibia): DT1636

German settlements
Namibia: DT1587+

German South-West Africa: DT1603+

Germans in Algeria: DT283.6.G47

Germans in Australia: DU122.G4

Germans in China: DS731.G4

Germans in Egypt: DT72.G4

Germans in Indonesia: DS632.3.G4

Germans in Japan: DS832.7.G4

Germans in Namibia: DT1558.G46

Germans in New Zealand: DU424.5.G47

Germans in Singapore: DS610.25.G47

Germans in South Africa: DT1768.G48

Germans in the Middle East: DS59.G47

Germany and East Asia: DS518.3

Germany, Jews in: DS134.2+

Gesher Site (Israel): DS110.G47

Gevat (Israel): DS110.G48

Gezer (Israel): DS110.G5

Gezer (Region) Israel: DS110.G52

Ghāmid in Saudi Arabia: DS219.G43

Ghana: DT509.97+

Ghana empire: DT532.15

Ghānchīs: DS432.G43

Gharbīyah, al (Egypt): DT137.G5

Ghasis (Indic people): DS432.G5

Ghazi I: DS79.52

Ghaznevids: DS288.7

Ghazni dynasty: DS458+

Ghor dynasty: DS458.5+

Ghoya in Orange Free State: DT2103.G55

Ghoya in South Africa: DT1768.G56

Giay in Vietnam: DS556.45.G53

Gichki in Pakistan: DS380.G52

Gilat Site (Israel): DS110.G557

Gilbert Islands: DU615

Gilgal Site (West Bank): DS110.G572

Gimiras (African people) in Ethiopia: DT380.4.G35

Gimzo (Israel): DS110.G574

Gindaros (Syria): DS99.G55

Ginegar(Israel): DS110.G577

Girsu (Extinct city): DS70.5.G57

Giryama (African people) in Kenya: DT433.545.G55

Gisu (African people) in Uganda: DT433.245.G57

Gitarama coup d'état, 1961 (Rwanda): DT450.432

Giuba (Italian Somaliland): DT409.G58

Giv'at Sha'ul (Jerusalem): DS109.8.G58

Gizeh (Egypt): DT73.G5

Giziga (African people) in Cameroon: DT571.G57

Gladstone (Australia): DU280.G5

Gnassingbé, Faure: DT582.852.G58

Goa
Portuguese colony: DS498+

Goanese in Burma: DS528.2.G63

Goanese in Kenya: DT433.545.G62

Goans (African people) in Mozambique: DT3328.G73

Goans (Indic people): DS432.G56

Godin Tepe (Iran): DS262.G6

Gogo (African people) in Tanzania: DT443.3.G64

Golan Heights (Syria): DS99.G65

Gold Coast: DT509.97+

Gold discovery, 1851 (Australia): DU103

Golden Horde: DS22.7

Golden Triangle (Southeast Asia): DS526.9

Goletta, Siege of, 1573: DT262

Golla (Indic people): DS432.G58

Gomativala Brahmans in India: DS432.G59

Gond in India: DS432.G6

Gondhalis in India: DS432.G63

Gonga (African people) in Ethiopia: DT380.4.G66

Gonja (African people) in Ghana: DT510.43.G65

Gorava (Indic people): DS432.G65

Goravālas (Indic people): DS432.G67

Gorbat (Afghanistan people): DS354.6.G67

Gordium: DS156.G6

Gordon (Sudan): DT156.6+

Gore-Browne, Steward: DT3106.G78

Gosangis in India: DS432.G68

Gouin (African people) in Burkina Faso: DT555.45.G68

Gouin (African people) in Togo: DT582.45.G68

Gourma Kingdom (Burkina Faso): DT555.65+

Gouveia, Manual Antonio de Sousa: DT3364.G68

Gova (African people) in Zambia: DT3058.G79

Gova (African people) in Zimbabwe: DT2913.G68

Government, Maori: DU423.P63

Government of National Unity (Republic of South Africa): DT1971+

Government relations
Aboriginal Australians: DU124.G68
Maori: DU423.G6

Gowon administration (Nigeria): DT515.834+

Graaf-Reinet and Swellendam Rebellion, 1795: DT1835

Grain Coast (Liberia): DT633+

Grand Bassa County (Liberia): DT637.G7

Grasia in India: DS432.G7

Grave goods
Ancient Egypt: DT62.T6

Great Andamanese in India: DS432.G74

Great Barrier Island (New Zealand): DU430.G7

Great Britain
Iraq War, 2003-: DS79.765.G7

Great Britain and East Asia: DS518.4

Great Britain, Jews in: DS135.E5+

Great Karoo (South Africa): DT2400.G84

Great Trek, 1836-1840 (South Africa): DT1853

Great Zimbabwe: DT3025.G84

Greater Khartum (Sudan): DT159.7

Greece, Jews in: DS135.G7+

Greeks in Australia: DU122.G7

Greeks in Central Sub-Saharan Africa: DT352.43.G74

Greeks in Congo (Democratic Republic): DT650.G74

Greeks in Cyprus: DS54.42.G74

Greeks in Egypt: DT72.G7

Greeks in Ethiopia: DT380.4.G72

Greeks in Sudan: DT155.2.G74

Greeks in the Middle East: DS59.G8

Greeks in Tunisia: DT253.2.G74

Griffith, Chief Nathaniel: DT2642.G75

Griqua lands, 1861, Purchase of (Orange Free State): DT2131

Griqua settlements, 1803 (Orange Free State): DT2116

Griqualand, Annexation of: DT1886

Griquas in South Africa: DT1768.G74

Gritlle Site (Turkey): DS156.G73

Guam: DU647

Guangxu: DS764+

Gubbi Gubbi (Australian people): DU125.G75

Guebuza, Armando: DT3400

Gueï administration (Côte d'Ivoire): DT545.84+

Guerrilla operations
  Korean War: DS921.5.G8
  Vietnam War: DS558.92
Guija (Mozambique): DT3415.G85
Guinea: DT543+
Guinea-Bissau: DT613+
Guineans (African people) in Senegal:
  DT549.45.G85
Gujarati (Malagasy people):
  DT469.M277G84
Gujaratis in Kenya: DT433.545.G84
Gujaratis (Indic people): DS432.G85
Gujars in India: DS432.G86
Gujars in Pakistan: DS380.G85
Gulf Cooperation Council: DS201.2
Gulf of Aqaba: DS110.45
Gumeracha (Australia): DU330.G8
Gun (African people): DT541.45.G85
Gun War, 1880-1881 (Basutoland):
  DT2648
Gundungurra (Australian people):
  DU125.G77
Gunggari (Australian people):
  DU125.G78
Gungunhana: DT3364.G86
Gurage (African people) in Ethiopia:
  DT380.4.G85
Gureng Gureng (Australian people):
  DU125.G79
Gurindji (Australian people): DU125.G8
Gurjara-Pratihāras: DS451.8
Gurkhas in Burma: DS528.2.G9
Gurkhas in India: DS432.G87
Gurkhas in Nepal: DS493.9.G8
Gurma (African people) in Benin:
  DT541.45.G87
Gurma (African people) in Burkina Faso:
  DT555.45.G85
Guro (African people) in Côte d'Ivoire:
  DT545.45.G87
Gurob (Egypt): DT73.G85
Gurungs in Nepal: DS493.9.G84
Gurunsi (African people) in Burkino
  Faso: DT555.45.G87
Guruwe (Zimbabwe): DT3025.G87
Gusii (African people) in Kenya:
  DT433.545.G86

Gusii (African people) in Tanzania:
  DT443.3.G88
Gùyùg, Khan of Mongolia: DS22.4
Gwari (African people) in Nigeria:
  DT515.45.G34, DT515.45.G83
Gwelo (Zimbabwe): DT3025.G89
Gwembe Tonga Uprising, 1909
  (Zambia): DT3097
Gweru (Zimbabwe): DT3025.G89
Gypsies: DX101+
Gypsies in Israel: DS113.8.G95

H

Habibullah: DS368
Habibullah Ghazi: DS369.2
Haddad (African people) in Chad:
  DT546.445.H33
Hadendowa (African people) in Sudan:
  DT155.2.H32
Haderah (Israel): DS110.H25
Hadiya (African people) in Ethiopia:
  DT380.4.H33
Hadramaut: DS247.H3+
Hadrami in Saudi Arabia: DS219.H34
Hafets-Hayim (Israel): DS110.H257
Haft Tepe (Iran): DS262.H34
Haifa (Israel): DS110.H28
Hāil: DS247.9.H35
Haile Selassie I, Emperor of Ethiopia:
  DT387.7+
Haitians in Congo (Democratic
  Republic): DT650.H35
Hajong in Bangladesh: DS393.83.H35
Hajong (Indic people): DS432.H28
Hakas in Burma: DS528.2.H3
Hakas in India: DS432.H3
Hakka in Singapore: DS610.25.H34
Hakkas in China: DS731.H3
Hakkas in Malaysia: DS597.335.H34
Hakkas in Taiwan: DS799.43.H35
Hakki Pikki (Indic people): DS432.H32
Halab (African people) in Sudan:
  DT155.2.H34
Hālakki Okkaligas (Indic people):
  DS432.H327
Halams (Indic people): DS432.H33

Haleakala National Park (Hawaii): DU628.H25

Haleakala (Volcano) Hawaii: DU629.H2

Halicarnassus (Ancient city): DS156.H3

Ḥalif Site (Israel): DS110.H285

Hall Islands: DU568.H3

Ḥamadyah (Israel): DS110.H286

Ḥamāmah (Palestine): DS110.H288

Hamar in Ethiopia: DT380.4.H36

Hambukol Site (Sudan): DT159.9.H36

Hambukushu (African people) in Botswana: DT2458.M28

Hammām (Arab tribe) in Tunisia: DT253.2.H35

Hammat Gader Site (Israel): DS110.H292

Hammurabi: DS73.35

Ḥamran, Mount (Israel): DS110.H295

Hamza: DS292.53

Han Dynasty: DS748+

Hana Kingdom (Syria): DS99.H296

Handa (African people) in Angola: DT1308.H32

Hani (Chinese people): DS731.H34

Hani in Vietnam: DS556.45.H35

Hanitah-Shelomi Forest (Israel): DS110.H32

Hanya (African people) in Angola: DT1308.H35

Haoles in Hawaii: DU624.7.W45

Har-Ṭov (Israel): DS110.H37

Haradum (Ancient city): DS70.5.H24

Haram Zāwiyat al 'Urbān (Egypt): DT73.H25

Harappa (Pakistan): DS392.2.H3

Harar (Ethiopia): DT390.H3

Harare (Zimbabwe): DT3022

Harari (African people) in Ethiopia: DT380.4.H38

Ḥarmal, Tall: DS70.5.H27

Haror, Tel (Israel): DS110.H346

Harris, Charles M.: DU372.H34

Hartley (Zimbabwe): DT3025.C54

Ḥaruvit (Israel): DS110.H348

Hasa Oasis: DS247.9.H37

Hasanlu (Iran): DS262.H37

Hashemite Kingdom of Jordan: DS153+

Hasi Site (Israel): DS110.T4

Hassan II, King of Morocco: DT325.92.H37

Hassaniyeh in Sudan: DT155.2.H36

Hatamoto: DS827.H37

Hatra: DS70.5.H3

Hatsa (African people) in Tanzania: DT443.3.H37

Hatshepsut, Queen of Egypt: DT87.15

Hausas (African people) in Niger: DT547.45.H38

Hausas (African people) in Nigeria: DT515.45.H38

Hausas (African people) in Sudan: DT155.2.H38

Havu (African people) in Congo (Democratic Republic): DT650.H38

Havyaka Brahmins in India: DS432.H38

Hawaii: DU620+

Hawaii County: DU628.H28

Hawaii (Island): DU628.H28

Hawaii National Park: DU628.H3

Hawaii (Territory), 1900-1959: DU627.5+

Hawaii Volcanoes National Park: DU628.H33

Hawaiian Islands: DU620+
    Annexation
        1898: DU627.3+

Hawara (Egypt): DT73.H3

Hawawish Site (Egypt): DT73.H34

Hawāzin in Saudi Arabia: DS219.H38

Hawke's Bay (New Zealand): DU430.H33

Haya (African people) in Tanzania: DT443.3.H39

Haya (African people) in Uganda: DT433.245.H38

Hayyat, Tell el- (Jordan): DS154.9.H39

Hazāras in Afghanistan: DS354.6.H3

Hazāras in Pakistan: DS380.H38

Hazna, Tall (Syria): DS99.H37

Headrests
    Ancient Egypt: DT62.H44

Health aspects
    Persian Gulf War, 1990-1991: DS79.744.M44

Health aspects
  Sino-Japanese War, 1937-1945:
    DS777.533.M42
Heard Island: DS349.9.H42
Hebron: DS110.H4
Heian period: DS855.87+
Heikum (African people) in Namibia:
  DT1558.H45
Heisei (Akihito): DS891+
Hejaz: DS247.9.H45
Heliopolis (Egypt): DT73.H42
Helwan (Egypt): DT154.H5
Hemba (African people) in Zaire:
  DT650.H45
Henrique de Carvalho (Angola):
  DT1465.S38
Heraclea Pontica: DS156.H47
Heracleopolis Magna (Egypt):
  DT73.H44
Herakleia: DS156.H48
Herat emirat: DS363.5
Herero in Angola: DT1308.H48
Herero in Botswana: DT2458.H47
Herero in Namibia: DT1558.H47
Herero Uprising, 1896: DT1614
Herero War, 1904-1907: DT1618
Hereroland (Namibia): DT1670.H47
Hermopolis Magna (Egypt): DT73.A85
Hermopolite Nome (Egypt): DT73.H45
Herod Agrippa I: DS122.7
Herod Antipas: DS122.5
Herod I the Great: DS122.3
Herod Philip: DS122.6
Hertseliyah (Israel): DS110.H47
Hervey Islands: DU430.C6
Herzog, J.B.M.: DT1927.H47
Hezhen (Chinese people): DS731.H6
Hhohho (Swaziland): DT2820.H56
Hierakonpolis (Egypt): DT73.K453
Hiligaynon (Philippine people):
  DS666.H54
Hill Kharia in India: DS432.H44
Hilo (Hawaii): DU629.H5
Hima (African people) in Congo
  (Democratic Republic): DT650.H54
Himba (African people) in Angola:
  DT1308.H56

Himba (African people) in Namibia:
  DT1558.H56
Hindu-Buddhist era
  Indonesia: DS641
Hindus in Afghanistan: DS354.6.H55
Hindus in Bangladesh: DS393.83.H54
Hisbān, Tall (Jordan): DS154.9.H57
Hisn, Kawn al- (Egypt): DT73.H57
Hissar Tepe (Iran): DS262.H57
Historical geography
  Angola: DT1278
  Libya: DT216
  South Africa: DT1727
Hittīn (Israel): DS110.H475
Hittites: DS66
Hivaoa Island: DU701.H5
Hizma Site (West Bank): DS110.H53
Hizzān in Saudi Arabia: DS219.H59
Hmar in India: DS432.H5
Hmong (Asian people): DS509.5.H66
Hmong (Asian people) in Australia:
  DU122.H66
Hmong (Asian people) in China:
  DS731.M5
Hmong (Asian people) in Laos:
  DS555.45.M5
Hmong (Asian people) in Thailand:
  DS570.M5
Hmong in Vietnam: DS556.45.H56
Ho-che (Chinese people): DS731.H6
Ho in India: DS432.H6
Hod ha-Sharon (Israel): DS110.H55
Hoga Sara (Indonesian people):
  DS632.H64
Holon (Israel): DS110.H6
Holy Sepulcher (Israel): DS109.4
Homelands
  Namibia: DT1557
  South Africa: DT1760
Honolulu (Hawaii): DU629.H7
Horemheb, King of Egypt: DT87.8
Hormizd I: DS286.31
Hormizd II: DS286.45
Hormizd III: DS286.75
Hormizd IV: DS287.4
Horombo (African people) in Tanzania:
  DT443.3.H67

Hosain: DS293.2

Hospitals
  Iraq War, 2003-: DS79.767.M43
  Korean War: DS921.25
  Sino-Japanese War, 1937-1945:
    DS777.533.M42

Hostage taking
  Lebanon
    Civil War, 1975-1990: DS87.52

Hostages
  Lebanon
    Civil War, 1975-1990: DS87.52

Hottentots (African people) in South
  Africa: DT1768.K56

Houphouët-Boigny administration (Côte
  d'Ivoire): DT545.8+

Housing, Maori: DU423.H65

Hova rule (Madagascar): DT469.M32+

Hovas in Madagascar:
  DT469.M277M47

Hoysala Karnātaka Brahmans:
  DS432.H68

Huambo (Angola)
  City: DT1465.H83
  Province: DT1450.H83

Huang Chao Rebellion: DS749.47

Huaula (Indonesian people):
  DS646.66.H82

Hudhayl in Saudi Arabia: DS219.H78

Huggins, Godfrey: DT2975.H85

Huguenot settlement, 1688: DT1823

Huguenots in South Africa:
  DT1768.F73

Hui (Chinese people): DS731.H85

Huila (Angola): DT1450.H85

Hula Valley (Israel): DS110.H77

Huli: DU740+

Humaymat Site (Jordan): DS154.9.H86

Humayun, 1530-1556 (India): DS461.2

Humayun, 1793 (Afghanistan):
  DS359.4

Hunde (African people) in Congo
  (Democratic Republic): DT650.H83

Hundred Flowers Campaign, 1956
  (China): DS778.4

Hungana (African people) in Congo
  (Democratic Republic): DT650.H85

Hungarian Jews in Israel: DS113.8.H85

Hungarians in Australia: DU122.H8

Hungary, Jews in: DS135.H9+

Huns in Central Asia: DS328.4.H85

Hunting
  Aboriginal Australians: DU124.H85

Hunting, Maori: DU423.H8

Hunza: DS392.H86

Hurfaysh (Israel): DS110.H78

Hurrians in the Middle East: DS59.H8

Hussein I (Jordan): DS154.55

Hussein, Kamil, Sultan of Egypt:
  DT107.7

Hussein, Saddam (Iraq): DS79.7

Hutu (African people) in Burundi:
  DT450.65.H87

Hutu (African people) in Congo
  (Democratic Republic): DT650.H88

Hutu (African people) in Rwanda:
  DT450.25.H86

Hutu (African people) in Tanzania:
  DT443.3.H88

Huwala in Saudi Arabia: DS219.H785

Hwange (Zimbabwe): DT3025.H93

Hyksos: DT86

I

Ibaloi (Philippine people): DS666.I12

Iban (Bornean people): DS646.32.I2

Ibaneg (Philippine people): DS666.I13

Ibans (Bornean people) in Brunei:
  DS650.43.I23

Ibans (Bornean people) in Sarawak:
  DS597.367.I23

Ibarapapa (African people) in Nigeria:
  DT515.45.I22

Ibibios (African people) in Kenya:
  DT433.545.I24

Ibibios (African people) in Nigeria:
  DT515.45.I24

Ibis Nome (Egypt): DT73.I25

Ibn Saʻūd: DS244.53

Ibrahim, Pasha of Egypt: DT104.5

Ibrim (Egypt): DT73.I27

Idangai (Indic people): DS432.I32

Idaw Martini (Berber people) in
  Morocco: DT313.3.I33
Idfū (Egypt): DT73.I3
Idoma (African people) in Nigeria:
  DT515.45.I25
Idu (Indic people): DS432.I37
Ifalik Atoll: DU568.I3
Ifaluk Atoll: DU568.I3
Ife (African people) in Nigeria:
  DT515.45.I28
Ifni (Spanish Morocco): DT330
Ifugaos in the Philippines: DS666.I15
Igala (African people) in Nigeria:
  DT515.45.I32
Igbo (African people) in Nigeria:
  DT515.45.I33
Igbo (African people) in West Africa:
  DT474.6.I35
Igbona in Nigeria: DT515.45.I34
Igorot in the Philippines: DS666.I2
Ijebu (African people) in Nigeria:
  DT515.45.I347
Ijesa in Nigeria: DT515.45.I348
Ijo (African people) in Nigeria:
  DT515.45.I35
Ik (African people) in South Sudan:
  DT159.927.I5
Ik (African people) in Uganda:
  DT433.245.I37
Ika (African people) in Nigeria:
  DT515.45.I36
Ikhnaton, King of Egypt: DT87.4+
Ikwere (African people) in Nigeria:
  DT515.45.I37
Ila (African people) in Zambia:
  DT3058.I53
Ilaje (African people) in Nigeria:
  DT515.45.I43
Ilanun (Malaysian people):
  DS597.335.I43
Ile de France: DT469.M4+
Ilhas dos Bijagós: DT671.B58
Ilkhanids: DS289
Ilokanos in the Philippines: DS666.I37
Ilongot (Philippine people): DS666.I4
Imache, Amar, 1895-1960: DT294.7.I52
Imlīḥīyah, Tall (Iraq): DS70.5.I44

Imo Incident, 1882 (Korea): DS915.52
Implements, Maori: DU423.I4
Imragen (African people) in Mauritainia:
  DT554.45.I57
Indemnity and reparation
  Sino-Japanese War, 1937-1945:
    DS777.533.I53
Independence (Eritrea): DT397.3
Independence movement, 1911
  (Mongolia): DS798.75+
Independence movement, 1919 (Korea):
  DS916.597
India: DS401+
India and East Asia: DS518.42
India, Jews in: DS135.I6+
Indian Ocean Region: DS331+
Indians
  Iraq War, 2003-: DS79.767.I53
Indo-Europeans in Asia: DS15+
Indo-Europeans in Central Asia:
  DS328.4.I53
Indo-Iranians in Asia: DS15.3
Indochinese in Australia: DU122.I53
Indochinese War: DS553+
Indonesia: DS611+
Indonesia, Jews in: DS135.I64+
Indos: DS632.I53
Industries, Maori: DU423.I53
Infanticide
  India: DS422.I5
Influence
  South African War: DT1918.I54
Information services, Maori: DU423.I55
Ingogo, Battle of, 1881: DT2359.I65
Inhambane, Attack of (Mozambique):
  DT3372
Inhambane (Mozambique): DT3410.I65
Inkisi (Zaire): DT665.I55
Inner Mongolia: DS793.M7
Insurgency
  Iraq War, 2003-: DS79.76352+
Insurgency movement (RNM)
  Mozambique: DT3394
Intellectual life
  Maori: DU423.I58
International Zone (Morocco):
  DT329.T16

Interregnum, 1982-1986 (Switzerland): DT2804

Intifada, 1987-: DS119.75, DS119.76+

Īnūlatān (Berber people) in Morocco: DT313.3.I57

Inyazura (Zimbabwe): DT3025.N83

Ionia: DS156.I6

Iqar'iyen (Berber people) in Morocco: DT313.3.I65

'Ira Site (Israel): DS110.I68

Iran: DS251+

Iran-Iraq War, 1980-1988: DS318.85

Iranians in East Africa: DT429.5.I7

Iranians in India: DS432.I75

Iranians in Israel: DS113.8.I7

Iraq: DS67+

Iraq War, 2003-: DS79.765.I72

Iraq, Jews in: DS135.I7+

Iraq-Kuwait Crisis, 1990-1991: DS79.719+

Iraq War: DS79.757+

Iraqi Jews in Israel: DS113.8.I72

Iraqi military oerations, Containment of Post-Persian Gulf War, 1991-: DS79.755

Iraqis in Australia: DU122.I65

Iraqw in Tanzania: DT443.3.I8

Ireland, Jews in: DS135.I72

Irian Barat: DU744+

Irian Jaya: DU744+

Iringa (Tanzania): DT449.I7

Irish in Australia: DU122.I7

Irish in New Zealand: DU424.5.I74

Irish in Singapore: DS610.25.I75

Irish in South Africa: DT1768.I72

Ironsi administration (Nigeria): DT515.832

Irukkuvēḷirs in India: DS432.I77

Irulas (Indic people): DS432.I78

Isandhlwana, Battle of: DT1879.I83

Isauria: DS156.I82

Ishan (African people) in Nigeria: DT515.45.I83

Isin: DS70.5.I75

Islamic antiquities: DT69.5

Islamic countries, Jews in: DS135.L4

Islamic period (Egyptian antiquities): DT69.5

Islamic Republic (Iran): DS318.72+

Islands of the East African coast: DT468+

Ismail I: DS292.3

Ismail II: DS292.5

Ismail III: DS292.55

Ismail, Khedive of Egypt: DT106

Ismail, Sultan of Morocco: DT323.5

Isnā Site (Egypt): DT73.I8

Isneg in the Philippines: DS666.I7

Isoko (African people) in Nigeria: DT515.45.I86

Israel: DS101+

Israel-Zionist propaganda in foreign countries: DS126.75

Israeli intervention, 1996 Lebanon: DS87.6

Israelis in Japan: DS832.7.I77

Italian domination (Eritrea): DT395

Italian Jews in Israel: DS113.8.I8

Italian Somaliland: DT405+

Italians in Algeria: DT283.6.I73

Italians in Australia: DU122.I8

Italians in Egypt: DT72.I8

Italians in Japan: DS832.7.I83

Italians in Libya: DT223.2.I73

Italians in Malawi: DT3192.I85

Italians in Mozambique: DT3328.I74

Italians in New Zealand: DU424.5.I8

Italians in South Africa: DT1768.I74

Italians in Tanzania: DT443.3.I85

Italians in Tunisia: DT253.2.I8

Italo-Ethiopian war, 1935-1936: DT387.8

Italy, Jews in: DS135.I8+

Itawis (Philippine people): DS666.I77

Itsekiri (African people) in Nigeria: DT515.45.I88

Ituri Forest (Zaire): DT665.I8

Ituri Region (Zaire): DT665.I8

Ivories
Ancient Egypt: DT62.I92

Ivory Coast: DT545+

Iwaak (Philippine people): DS666.I85

Iyers in India: DS432.I94

'Izbet Ṣarṭah (Israel): DS110.I93
Izere (African people) in Nigeria:
    DT515.45.I93
Izi (African people) in Nigeria:
    DT515.45.I95

J

Ja'aliyyīn (Arab people) in the Sudan:
    DT155.2.J33
Jaamwambe (African people) in French
    West Africa: DT530.5.J3
Jaba' (West Bank): DS110.J3
Jabal Mayyah Site (Sudan):
    DT159.9.J32
Jabavu, J.T.: DT1927.J33
Jacobites in the Middle East: DS59.J25
Jaffa (Israel): DS110.J3
Jagatai dynasty: DS22.5
Jagbe (African people) in Nigeria:
    DT515.45.J33
Jah Hut (Malaysian people):
    DS595.2.J27
Jahangir: DS461.5
Jains (Indic people): DS432.J223
Jaintia (Indic people): DS432.J225
Jakun (Malayan people): DS595.2.J3
Jalaris in India: DS432.J227
Jalāyirids: DS289.5
Jalé (Papuan people) in Papua:
    DU744.35.J28
Jameson Raid, 1895 (South Africa):
    DT1889
Jameson, Sir Leander Starr:
    DT1851.J36
Jan Jonker Afrikaner: DT1595.J36
Japan: DS801+
Japan and East Asia: DS518.45
Japan, Jews in: DS135.J3+
Japanese Americans
    Vietnam War: DS559.8.J35
Japanese in Africa: DT16.J34
Japanese in Asia: DS28.J3
Japanese in Australia: DU122.J36
Japanese in China: DS731.J3
Japanese in East Asia: DS509.5.J3

Japanese in foreign countries (General):
    DS832.5
Japanese in Hawaii: DU624.7.J3
Japanese in Indonesia: DS632.3.J3
Japanese in Korea: DS904.6.J3
Japanese in North Korea: DS933.3.J3
Japanese in Singapore: DS610.25.J34
Japanese in South Africa: DT1768.J37
Japanese in Southeast Asia:
    DS523.4.J36
Japanese in Taiwan: DS799.43.J3
Japanese in Thailand: DS570.J38
Japanese in the Philippines: DS666.J3
Japanese invasions, 1592-1598, of
    Korea: DS913.395+
Japanese rule, 1910-1945, of Korea:
    DS916.525+
Japanese the Middle East: DS59.J3
Jaqai in Papua: DU744.35.J32
Jarai in Southeast Asia: DS523.4.J38
Jarai in Vietnam: DS556.45.J3
Jarawa (Indic people): DS432.J229
Jarbah (Tunisia): DT268.J4
Jarmah (Libya): DT239.J35
Jatapu (Indic people): DS432.J23
Jatavs: DS432.J25
Jatigaras in India: DS432.J27
Jats in India: DS432.J3
Jaunsari (Indic people): DS432.J35
Java: DS646.17+
Javanese in Indonesia: DS632.J38
Javanese in Sri Lanka: DS489.25.J38
Jawa, Tall (Amman): DS154.9.J39
Jawlān: DS99.G65
Jaww, al: DS247.9.J38
Jayantira Panos (Indic people):
    DS432.J37
Jebel Nefusa (Libya): DT239.J4
Jekri (African people) in Nigeria:
    DT515.45.I88
Jenin (West Bank): DS110.J37
Jerba (Tunisia): DT268.J4
Jericho: DS110.J4
Jerusalem: DS109+
Jerusalem Forest (Jerusalem):
    DS109.8.J38
Jerusalem National Park: DS109.8.J4

Jewelry, Maori: DU423.J4
Jewish-Arab relations: DS119.7+
Jewish captivity, Period of (Egypt):
  DT88.5
Jewish diaspora: DS133+
Jewish identity: DS143
Jewish Quarter (Jerusalem):
  DS109.8.J45
Jewish question: DS141
Jews: DS101+
Jews in Baltic States: DS135.B34
Jews in Egypt (Ancient history):
  DS121.5
Jews in the Baltic Sea Region:
  DS135.B337
Jharkhand (India): DS485.J48+
Jhusi Site (India): DS486.J48
Jifnā (West Bank): DS110.J44
Jiman (Australian people): DU125.J55
Jin (Chin) dynasty: DS748.17+
  1115-1234: DS751.92+
  265-419: DS748.4+
Jingpo (Chinese people): DS731.C49
Jinibara (Australian people):
  DU125.J57
Jinnah, Mahomed Ali: DS385.J5
Jīyah (Gaza Strip): DS110.J58
Jīzān: DS247.9.Q58
João Belo (Mozambique): DT3415.X35
João de Almeida (Angola):
  DT1465.C55
Jochi (Mongols): DS22.1
Jogi-Nath (Indic people): DS432.J64
Johannesburg (South Africa):
  DT2405.J65+
Johfiyeh, Tell (Jordan): DS154.9.J54
John IV
  Ethiopia: DT386.7+
Jokṣer Danga Site (India): DS486.J65
Jonathan administration
  Nigeria: DT515.846
Jonathan, Leabula: DT2657+
Jonglei State (South Sudan):
  DT159.977.J66
Jonker Afrikaner: DT1595.J66
Jordan: DS153+
Jordan River: DS110.J6

Jose Eduardo dos Santos: DT1434
Joseph Kabila, Administration of:
  DT658.26
Joubert, W.F.: DT2350.J68
Journalism
  Iraq War, 2003-: DS79.767.P74
Juan (Indic people): DS432.J84
Juba (South Sudan): DT159.978.J82
Jubaland: DT409.G58
Jubanians: DS289.6
Juchen dynasty: DS751.92+
Judaea (Region): DS110.J78
Judaea, Wilderness of: DS110.J8
Judean Hills: DS110.J83
Jukun (African people) in Nigeria:
  DT515.45.J83
Jūlis (Israel): DS110.J85
Jumma in Bangladesh: DS393.83.J86
Jumūʿīyah (African people) in Sudan:
  DT155.2.J86
Jyeshṭhimalla in India: DS432.J94

K

Ka nanʿʿ in Burma: DS528.2.K22
Kaabu empire: DT532.17
Kaʿb (Arab people) in Iran: DS269.K25
Kababish (African people):
  DT155.2.K32
Kabiye (African people) in Togo:
  DT582.45.K33
Ḳabri Site (Israel): DS110.K2
Kabūd Gonbad, Kharasan (Iran):
  DS262.K32
Kabwe (Zambia): DT3145.K33
Kabyles: DT298.K2
Kabylia (Great and Little) Algeria:
  DT298.K2
Kachari in India: DS432.K15
Kachhwaha (Indic people):
  DS432.K155
Kachin in Burma: DS528.2.K3
Kadamba in India: DS432.K158
Kadar in India: DS432.K16
Kadara (African people) in Nigeria:
  DT515.45.K33
Ḳadimah Forest (Israel): DS110.K23

Kadoma (Zimbabwe): DT3025.K34

Kadung (African people) in Nigeria: DT515.45.K332

Kafa (Ethiopia): DT390.K3

Kaffa (Ethiopia): DT390.K3

Kaffraria (South Africa): DT2400.K35

Kafirs (Afghan people): DS354.6.K3

Kafue Flats (Zambia): DT3140.K35

Kagoma (African people): DT515.45.K334

Kagoro (African people) in Nigeria: DT515.45.K336

Kaguru (African people): DT443.3.K33

Kah So (Southeast Asian people) in Thailand: DS570.S65

Kahun (Egypt): DT73.K28

Kaibartas in India: DS432.K167

Kaieiewaho (Hawaii): DU628.K3

Kaikōlar in India: DS432.K17

Kaili (Indonesian people): DS632.K27

Kailua (Hawaii): DU629.K32

Kairwan (Tunisia): DT269.K3

Kaithala Vaisyas in India: DS432.K174

Kakrehta Site (India): DS486.K236

Kalahari Desert
  Botswana: DT2520.K35
  Southern Africa: DT1190.K35

Kalakaua, King of the Hawaiian Islands: DU627.16

Kalandula, Bailundo king: DT1388.K35

Kalang (Indonesian people): DS632.K28

Kalanga (African people) in Zimbabwe: DT2913.K35

Kalbelia (Indic people): DS432.K176

Kale (Extinct city): DS156.M95

Kalenjin (African people) in East Africa: DT429.5.K35

Kaleri (African people) in Nigeria: DT515.45.K34

Kalesh in Pakistan: DS380.K34

Kalinga in the Philippines: DS666.K3

Kaliphi: DT2940.K35

Kalitās in India: DS432.K177

Kallans in India: DS432.K18

Kalli Khera Mound (India): DS486.K266

Kamakura period: DS858+

Kamar in India: DS432.K187

Kamba (African people) in Kenya: DT433.545.K36

Kambata (African people) in Ethiopia: DT380.4.K34

Kamberri (Australian people): DU125.K24

Kamboh in India: DS432.K188

Kamboh in Pakistan: DS380.K37

Kambula, Battle of: DT1879.K36

Kamehameha, House of: DU624.96.K35

Kamehameha, King of the Hawaiian Islands
  I: DU627.1
  II: DU627.11
  III: DU627.12
  IV: DU627.13
  V: DU627.14

Kamerun: DT561+

Kamilaroi (Australian people): DU125.K26

Kammas in India: DS432.K19

Kamwe in Cameroon: DT571.K36

Kānaḍa Gavaḷīs (Indic people): DS432.K1905

Kanaq (Malaysian people): DS595.2.K35

Kanarese (Indic people): DS432.K1907

Kanaura (Indic people): DS432.K191

Kandh in India: DS432.K192

Kanem Bornu Empire: DT515.9.B6

Kanembu (African people) in Chad: DT546.445.K36

KaNgwana (South Africa): DT2400.K36

Kanikkaran (Indic people): DS432.K1922

Kañjārabhāṭa (Indic people): DS432.K1923

Kansari (Indic people): DS432.K1924

Kantu (Indonesian people): DS646.32.K36

Kanuri (African people) in Niger: DT547.45.K34

Kanuri (African people) in Nigeria: DT515.45.K36

Kānyakubja Brahmans: DS432.K194

Kanye (Botswana): DT2525.K35

Kanyemba, Jose do Rosario Andrade: DT3081.K35

Kanyok (African people): DT650.K33

Kaohsiung Incident, 1979 (Taiwan): DS799.834

Kaokoland (Namibia): DT1670.K37

Kaonde (African people) in Zambia: DT3058.K36

Kaothe Site (India): DS486.K325

Kaowerawédj in Papua: DU744.35.K33

Kapauku in Papua: DU744.35.K34

Kapikaya site: DS156.K27

Kapolas in India: DS432.K196

Kapsin Incident, 1884 (Korea): DS915.522

Kapuuo, Clemens: DT1641.K36

Kapwepwe, Simon: DT3117.K36

Kara Koyunlu: DS27.5

Karachi (Pakistan): DS392.2.K3

Karakorum (Extinct city)
Mongolia: DS798.9.K37

Karamojong (African people) in Uganda: DT433.245.K35

Karana (Extinct city): DS70.5.K37

Karana Kayasthas in India: DS432.K198

Karanga (African people) in Botswana: DT2458.K35

Karanga (African people) in Zimbabwe: DT2913.K38

Karanga Empire: DT1111

Karanis (Egypt): DT73.K33

Karapapaks: DS27.54

Karapapaks in Iran: DS269.K27

Kārāra in Bangladesh: DS393.83.K37

Karasburg (Namibia): DT1685.K37

Karavas in Sri Lanka: DS489.25.K3

Karbong (Indic people): DS432.K1996

Karen in Burma: DS528.2.K35

Karen in Thailand: DS570.K37

Kariba, Lake (Zimbabwe): DT3020.K38

Karijini (Australian people): DU125.K28

Kārkīs in Nepal: DS493.9.K37

Karkom Mountain (Israel): DS110.K27

Karluk (Turkic people) in China: DS731.K37

Karmah (Sudan): DT159.9.K37

Karmi'el (Israel): DS110.K313

Karnak (Egypt): DT73.K4

Karo-Batak in Indonesia: DS632.K3

Karrayu (African people) in Ethiopia: DT380.4.K36

Karuwali (Australian people): DU125.K29

Kasai (Zaire): DT665.K28

Kasanga (African people): DT650.K36

Kasem (African people) in Burkina Faso: DT555.45.K37

Kasem (African people) in Ghana: DT510.43.K37

Kasena (African people) in Ghana: DT510.43.K37

Kashgai (Turkic people) in Iran: DS269.K3

Kashmiri Pandits: DS432.K27

Kaskans in the Middle East: DS59.K3

Kasongo (Zaire): DT665.M35

Kassinga (Angola): DT1465.K38

Kat River Rebellion, 1851 (South Africa): DT1859

Katamon (Jerusalem): DS109.8.K37

Katanera Site (India): DS486.K3565

Katanga (Zaire): DT665.K3

Kathodi in India: DS432.K28

Kāti Irakehu (New Zealand people): DU424.K38

Katif Bloc (Gaza Strip): DS110.K316

Kattunaicken in India: DS432.K285

Katu in Laos: DS555.45.K37

Kauai (Hawaii): DU628.K3

Kaunda, Kenneth: DT3119

Kaundinyapura Site (India): DS486.K366

Kaunos: DS156.K33

Kaurna (Australian people): DU125.K3

Kavadh I: DS287.1

Kavadh II: DS287.6

Kavalan (Taiwan people): DS799.43.K88

Kavango (Namibia): DT1670.K38

Kaw people in Burma: DS528.2.K37

Kawa (Egypt): DT73.K45

Kawāhla in Sudan: DT155.2.K38

Kawar in India: DS432.K287
Kawm al Ahmar, al (Egypt): DT73.K453
Kaya Confederacy: DS911.775+
Kayah in Burma: DS528.2.K38
Kayamkhanis in India: DS432.K289
Kayan: DS646.32.K38
Kayasthas in India: DS432.K29
Kaytetye (Australian people): DU125.K34
Kazakhs: DS24
Kazakhs in China: DS731.K38
Kazakhs in Mongolia: DS798.422.K39
Kazakhstan, Jews in: DS135.K39+
Kazembe III Lukwesa: DT3081.K38
Kazembe IV Keleka: DT3081.K39
Keate, R.W.: DT2254.K43
Keeling Islands: DS349.9.K43
Kefar 'Azah (Israel): DS110.K34
Kefar Bar'am (Israel): DS110.K36
Kefar 'Etsyon: DS110.K375
Kefar ha-Ro'eh (Israel): DS110.K394
Kefar Ḥabad (Israel): DS110.K395
Kefar 'Otnai Site (Israel): DS110.K396
Kefar Pines (Israel): DS110.K397
Kefar Sirl̂kin (Israel): DS110.K4345
Kefar Tavor (Israel): DS110.K4346
Kefar Yeḥezḳel (Israel): DS110.K44
Kefar Yehoshu'a (Israel): DS110.K45
Kefar Yonah (Israel): DS110.K46
Keita, Modibo: DT551.82.K44
Kela (African people): DT650.K39
Kelabit in Sarawak: DS597.367.K44
Kelas (Indic people): DS432.K37
Kellia Site (Egypt): DT73.K47
Kelly, Edward: DU222.K4
Kemak (Indonesian people): DS632.K45
Kemants (African people) in Ethiopia: DT380.4.K45
Kenmu Restoration: DS863
Kennedy, Alexander: DU272.K34
Kenny in the Philippines: DS666.K4
Kenuz (African people) in Sudan: DT155.2.K46
Kenya: DT433.5+
Kenya Colony and Protectorate: DT433.575+
Kenya (Indonesian people): DS632.K46
Kenya, Jews in: DS135.K45
Kenya (Malaysian people): DS597.367.K47
Keo (Indonesian people): DS632.K47
Keramos: DS156.K46
Kerebe (African people) in Tanzania: DT443.3.K47
Kerekou administration (Benin): DT541.845
Kerguelen Islands: DS349.9.K47
Kerkouane (Tunisia): DT269.K37
Ketagalan in Taiwan: DS799.43.K48
Ketengbau in Papua: DU744.35.K48
Kgatla (African people) in South Africa: DT1768.K53
Kgatla (African people) in Zimbabwe: DT2913.K53
Kgatla in Botswana: DT2458.K53
Kha Tahoi in French Indonesia: DS539.K5
Khairwar in India: DS432.K42
Khaling in Nepal: DS493.9.K43
Khalka in Mongolia: DS798.422.K48
Khama III, Ngwato chief: DT2493.K54
Khama, Seretse, 1966-1980: DT2500
Khama, Tshekedi: DT2493.K53
Khamma in Nepal: DS493.9.K45
Khamti in India: DS432.K44
Khan, Liaquat Ali: DS385.K5
Khān Yūnus (Gaza Strip): DS110.K53
Khanate of Kiptchak: DS22.7
Khandelwals in India: DS432.K46
Khangabok Site (India): DS486.K514
Khangārota in India: DS432.K47
Khans (Iraq): DS70.5.K435
Kharga Oasis (Egypt)
  Ancient: DT73.K5
  Modern: DT154.K6
Kharia in India: DS432.K48
Khartum (Sudan): DT159.7
Khas in Nepal: DS493.9.K48
Khasi in India: DS432.K5
Khasi (Indic people) in Bangladesh: DS393.83.K45
Khatagin in Mongolia: DS798.422.K49
Khatris: DS432.K52

INDEX

Khattaks in India: DS432.K53
Khatuniyeh Site (Iraq): DS70.5.K44
Khazā'il in Iraq: DS70.8.K5
Khazraj in Saudi Arabia: DS219.K43
Khelua Site (Egypt)
  Ancient: DT73.K54
Khiamnungan (Indic people):
  DS432.K533
Khilji dynasty: DS459.2+
Khirbat Fattir (Israel): DS110.K54
Khitan Mongols: DS751.72+
Khmer Empire: DS554.62
Khmers: DS554.45
Khmers in Thailand: DS570.K48
Khmers in Vietnam: DS556.45.K5
Khmu in Laos: DS555.45.K45
Khmu' in Vietnam: DS556.45.K54
Khmu' (Southeast Asian people) in
  China: DS731.K46
Khoikhoi (African people) in Namibia:
  DT1558.K46
Khoikhoi in South Africa: DT1768.K56
Khoikhoi in Southern Africa:
  DT1058.K56
Khoikhoi War
  I: DT1819
  II: DT1821
Khokhar Rajput in Southern Asia:
  DS339.3.K56
Khomeini, Ruhollah: DS318.84.K48
Khumir (Tunisia): DT269.K4
Khuzā'ah in Saudi Arabia: DS219.K48
Khyber Pakhtunkhwa (Pakistan):
  DS392.N67
Kikuyu (African people):
  DT433.545.K55
Kilāb in Saudi Arabia: DS219.K5
Kilauea (Hawaii): DU629.K5
Kilimanjaro (Tanzania): DT449.K4
Kilindi (African people) in Tanzania:
  DT443.3.K54
Killekyatha in India: DS432.K54
Kilwa Kisiwani Island (Tanzania):
  DT449.K45
Kimberley (Australia): DU380.K5
Kimberley, Siege of, 1899-1900 (South
  Africa): DT1908.K56

Kimberley (South Africa): DT2405.K56
Kineret (Israel): DS110.K55
Kings and rulers
  Maori: DU423.K54
  Sudan: DT155.42
Kinnaura (Indic people): DS432.K545
Kinshasa (Zaire): DT665.L4
Kinship
  Aboriginal Australians: DU124.K55
Kinship, Maori: DU423.K57
Kipsigis (African people) in Kenya:
  DT433.545.K57
Kiranti in India: DS432.K55
Kiranti in Nepal: DS493.9.K57
Kirghiz in Afghanistan: DS354.6.K57
Kirghiz in China: DS731.K57
Kiribati: DU615
Kiritimati: DS349.9.C45
Kirwan, Sir John: DU372.K5
Kiryat Arba' (West Bank): DS110.K553
Kiryat Byalik (Israel): DS110.K554
Kisangani (Zaire): DT665.K55
Kish: DS70.5.K5
Kisongo (African people) in Tanzania:
  DT443.3.K57
Kissi (African people) in Guinea:
  DT543.45.K57
Kissurāh: DS70.5.K52
Kitchener (Sudan): DT156.6+
Kitja (Australian people): DU125.K56
Kitwe (Zambia): DT3145.K58
Kivu (Zaire): DT665.K58
Kızılbel Tomb: DS156.K59
Ko (African people) in Burkina Faso:
  DT555.45.K62
Koda in India: DS432.K559
Kodagu in India: DS432.K56
Kodi (Indonesian people): DS632.K6
Kofyar (African people) in Nigeria:
  DT515.45.K64
Koguryŏ Kingdom: DS911.735+
Kohalī in India: DS432.K565
Koho (Vietnamese people):
  DS556.45.K63
Koirālā in Nepal: DS493.9.K64
Kojosŏn Kingdom: DS911.62
Kok, Adam III: DT2127.K65

Kolam in India: DS432.K58
Kolami in India: DS432.K58
Kolgha in India: DS432.K583
Koli in India: DS432.K585
Kolingba, Andre: DT546.3852.K6
Koloi: DS432.K586
Koltas (Indic people): DS432.K588
Kolwezi, Massacre, 1978: DT658.25
Kom (African people): DT571.K64
Kom el-Nana Site (Egypt): DT73.T25
Kom Firin Site (Egypt): DT73.K66
Kom (Indic people): DS432.K5885
Koma (African people): DT155.2.K65
Koma (African people) in Ghana:
    DT510.43.K63
Koma (African people) in Nigeria:
    DT515.45.K66
Koma (Nigerian and Cameroonian
    people) in Cameroon: DT571.K65
Koma (Nilo-Saharan people) in South
    Sudan: DT159.927.K66
Komachi in Iran: DS269.K65
Konda Reddis in India: DS432.K5886
Kongo (African people) in Angola:
    DT1308.K66
Kongo (African people) in Congo
    (Brazzaville): DT546.245.K66
Kongo (African people) in Congo
    (Democratic Republic): DT650.K66
Kongo (Angola): DT1465.M42
Kongo River Region: DT639
Koniagui (African people) in French
    West Africa: DT530.5.K64
Konkomba (African people) in Ghana:
    DT510.43.K65
Kono in Sierra Leone: DT516.45.K65
Konsos (African people) in Ethiopia:
    DT380.4.K65
Koptos (Egypt): DT73.Q54
Koragas (Indic people): DS432.K59
Korana in South Africa: DT1768.K68
Korava in India: DS432.K6
Kordofan (Sudan): DT159.6.K67
Korea: DS901+
Korea and East Asia: DS518.47
Korean War, 1950-1953: DS918.A1+
    Armistice: DS921.7

Koreans in Australia: DU122.K67
Koreans in Central Asia: DS328.4.K6
Koreans in China: DS731.K6
Koreans in foreign countries (General):
    DS904.7
Koreans in Hawaii: DU624.7.K67
Koreans in Japan: DS832.7.K6
Koreans in Oceania: DU28.1.K67
Korku in India: DS432.K62
Koro (African people) in Nigeria:
    DT515.45.K68
Korrirāju (Indic people): DS432.K626
Korucutepe: DS156.K67
Korwa (Indic people): DS432.K63
Koryŏ period: DS912+
Kosciusko, Mount (Australia):
    DU180.K7
Kosrae Island: DU568.K67
Kossi (African people) in Cameroon:
    DT571.K66
Kota (African people) in Congo
    (Brazzaville): DT546.245.K68
Kota (Indic people): DS432.K66
Kpelle (African people) in Liberia:
    DT630.5.K63
Kposo (African people) in Togo:
    DT582.45.K64
Krachi (African people) in Ghana:
    DT510.43.K72
Kreich (African people) in South Sudan:
    DT159.927.G32
Krobo (African people) in Ghana:
    DT510.43.K76
Krongo (African people) in Sudan:
    DT155.2.K75
Kru (African people) in Côte d'Ivoire:
    DT545.45.K77
Kru (African people) in West Africa:
    DT474.6.K78
Kruger, Paul: DT1851.K89
Krui (Indonesian people): DS632.K75
Kshatriyas in India: DS432.K7
Kua in Southern Africa: DT1058.K83
Kuanyama (African people) in Angola:
    DT1308.K83
Kuanyama (African people) in Namibia:
    DT1558.K83

Kuba (Bantu people) in Congo
  (Democratic Republic): DT650.K83
Kubu (Indonesian people): DS632.K78
Kucabandiyā: DS432.K72
Kucabandiyā in Nepal: DS493.9.K83
Kudumbis in India: DS432.K73
Kui in Thailand: DS570.K84
Kuito (Angola): DT1465.K85
Kuki Chin in Burma: DS528.2.K84
Kuki Chin (South Asian people):
  DS339.3.K84
Kuki in India: DS432.K75
Kuku (African people) in South Sudan:
  DT159.927.K85
Kuku-Yalanji (Australian people):
  DU125.K75
Kukus (African people) in Egypt:
  DT72.K8
Kukwa (African people) in Congo
  (Brazzaville): DT546.245.K84
Kũḷabī in India: DS432.K754
Kulalars in India: DS432.K758
Kulawi (Indonesian people):
  DS632.K785
Kulins in India: DS432.K76
Kulu (Indic people): DS432.K77
Kulung (Nigerian people) in Nigeria:
  DT515.45.K85
Kumauni (Indic people): DS432.K778
Kumawat Kshatriyas in India:
  DS432.K779
Kumbavats in India: DS432.K78
Kumhars in India: DS432.K785
Kumu (African people) in Congo
  (Democratic Republic): DT650.K86
Kunama (African people) in Eritrea:
  DT393.55.K85
Kunbi in India: DS432.K7853
Kunchitigas in India: DS432.K7854
Kunda in Mozambique: DT3328.K85
!Kung (African people) in Namibia:
  DT1558.K85
Kung in Southern Africa: DT1058.K86
Kuntillat Jurayyah (Egypt): DT73.K75
Kuparavidze, Expedition against:
  DT2945
Kurai (Indonesian people): DS632.K8

Kuranko (African people) in Ghana:
  DT510.43.K87
Kuranko in Sierra Leone:
  DT516.45.K85
Kurdish Jews in India: DS113.8.K9
Kurdistan, Jews in: DS135.K8
Kurds in Iran: DS269.K87
Kurds in Iraq: DS70.8.K8
Kurds in Jordan: DS153.55.K86
Kurds in Lebanon: DS80.55.K87
Kurds in Pakistan: DS380.K87
Kurds in Syria: DS94.8.K8
Kurds in the Middle East: DS59.K86
Kuria (African people) in Kenya:
  DT433.545.K87
Kuria (African people) in Tanzania:
  DT443.3.K87
Kurichiya (Indic people): DS432.K786
Kurmis: DS432.K787
Kurnai (Australian people): DU125.K77
Kurumba (African people) in Burkina
  Faso: DT555.45.K88
Kurumba (African people) in Mali:
  DT551.45.K85
Kurumba in India: DS432.K8
Kusasi (African people) in Burkina Faso:
  DT555.45.K9
Kusasi (African people) in Ghana:
  DT510.43.K89
Kush (Egypt): DT73.K8
Kusu (Bantu people) in Kenya:
  DT433.545.B84
Kutako, Hosea: DT1641.K88
Kutia Kondh in India: DS432.K84
Kuvalan (Taiwan people):
  DS799.43.K88
Kuvale (African people) in Angola:
  DT1308.K88
Kuwait: DS247.K8+
Kuweit: DS247.K8+
Kwahu (African people) in Ghana:
  DT510.43.K93
Kwaluseni (Swaziland): DT2825.K84
KwaNdebele (South Africa):
  DT2400.K83
Kwangju Uprising, 1980 (Korea):
  DS922.445

Kwangwa (African people) in Zambia:
DT3058.K93

Kwanza River (Angola): DT1450.K83

KwaZulu-Natal: DT2181+

Kwazulu-Natal Indaba, 1986-:
DT2400.K85

Kwekwe (Zimbabwe): DT3025.K84

Kwena (African people) in Botswana:
DT2458.K84

Kwena (African people) in Namibia:
DT1558.K9

Kwini (Australian people): DU125.K85

Kwiri in Cameroon: DT571.K85

Kxoe (African people) in Namibia:
DT1558.K95

Kyaneai: DS156.K92

Kyme: DS156.C87

Kyrgyzstan, Jews in: DS135.K97

Kysis (Egypt): DT73.K95

L

Labwor (African people): DT433.245.L3

Laccadives: DS486.5.L3

Lachish (Israel): DS110.L3

Ladakhi: DS432.L23

Ladrone Islands: DU640+

Ladysmith, Siege of, 1899-1900:
DT1908.L34

Lagina: DS156.L34

Lagoon Islands: DU590

Lahore (Pakistan): DS392.2.L3

Lahu in China: DS731.L33

Lahu in Southeast Asia: DS523.4.L33

Lahu in Thailand: DS570.L26

Lāhūn, El (Egypt): DT73.L33

Laing's Nek, Battle of, 1880:
DT2359.L35

Lakdar, Mohamed: DT264.3.L3

Lake Chad: DT546.49.L34

Lake Nyasa (Malawi): DT3252.M35

Lakher (Indic people): DS432.L24

Lakshadweep: DS486.5.L3

Lala (African people) in Zambia:
DT3058.L35

Lalor, Peter: DU222.L3

Lalungs (Indic people): DS432.L26

Lamaholot (Indonesian people):
DS632.L33

Lamba (African people) in Zambia:
DT3058.L36

Lambadi in India: DS432.L34

Lamboya (Indonesian people):
DS632.L34

Lamet in Laos: DS555.45.L36

Lamps
Ancient Egypt: DT62.L34

Lampung: DS632.L35

Lanai (Hawaii): DU628.L3

Lancaster House Conference
(Zimbabwe): DT2994

Land partition
Swaziland: DT2795

Land tenure
Aboriginal Australians: DU124.L35

Land tenure, Maori: DU423.L35

Langalibalele Rebellion, 1873: DT2257

Lango (African people) in Uganda:
DT433.245.L36

Lao in Laos: DS555.45.L37

Lao (Southeast Asian people) in
Thailand: DS570.L28

Laos: DS555+

Laotu (Burmese people): DS528.2.L35

Lardil (Australian people): DU125.L37

Larsa (Ancient city): DS70.5.L35

Latakia (Syria): DS99.L3

Later Han dynasty: DS749.6+

Later Jin (Ch'in) dynasty: DS749.6+

Later Liang dynasty: DS749.6+

Later Shu Kingdom: DS749.7+

Later Zhou (Chou) dynasty: DS749.6+

Lati in Vietnam: DS556.45.L37

Latin American Jews in Israel:
DS113.8.L37

Latvia, Jews in: DS135.L3+

Latvian Jews in Israel: DS113.8.L38

Latvians in Australia: DU122.L3

Latvians in New Zealand: DU424.5.L37

Lauje (Indonesian people): DS632.L37

Laurent Kabila, Regime of: DT658.26

Lawa in Thailand: DS570.L3

Laysan (Hawaii): DU628.L4

League of Arab States: DS36.2

League of Nations mandate
  Burundi: DT450.8+
  Rwanda: DT450.4+
Leatherwork
  Ancient Egypt: DT62.L42
Lebanese in Australia: DU122.L42
Lebanese in Congo (Democratic
  Republic): DT650.L35
Lebanese in Côte d'Ivoire:
  DT545.45.L42
Lebanese in Egypt: DT72.L43
Lebanese in foreign countries (General):
  DS80.6
Lebanese in French West Africa:
  DT530.5.L42
Lebanese in Ghana: DT510.43.L42
Lebanese in Israel: DS113.74
Lebanon: DS80+
Lebanon, Jews in: DS135.L34
Lebanon War, 2006: DS87.65
Lebau in French West Africa:
  DT530.5.L43
Lebombo Plateau (Swaziland):
  DT2820.L43
Lebou (African people) in Senegal:
  DT549.45.L42
Lebowa (South Africa): DT2400.L43
Lekhanya, Justin: DT2655.L45
Lele (African people) in Congo
  (Democratic Republic): DT650.L38
Lemba in South Africa: DT1768.L45
Lenjie in Zambia: DT3058.L46
Leopoldville (Zaire): DT665.L4
Lepcha in Nepal: DS493.9.L44
Lepcha (South Asian people):
  DS432.L4
Leptis Magna (Libya): DT239.L4
Leptis Minor (Tunisia): DT269.L46
Lesotho: DT2541+
Lessiya, el (Egypt): DT73.L47
Lesu Island: DU553.L4
Letters, Cave of the (Israel): DS110.L37
Levant, Jews in: DS135.L4
Lewanika: DT3081.L48
Li (Hainan people) in China: DS731.L5
Li Zicheng Rebellion, 1628-1645:
  DS753.65

Liang dynasty: DS748.6+
Liao Dynasty: DS751.72+
Liberation movements
  Eritrea: DT397
Liberia: DT621+
Liberia, Incursions into Sierra Leone:
  DT516.826+
Libreville (Gabon): DT546.19.L5
Libya: DT211+
Libya, Jews in: DS135.L44+
Libyan Jews in Israel: DS113.8.L52
Licchavis in India: DS432.L5
Lichinga (Mozambique): DT3415.L53
Light, William: DU322.L6
Lij Yasu, Negus of Abyssinia: DT387.5
Liliuokalani, Queen of the Hawaiian
  Islands: DU627.18
Lilongwe (Malawi): DT3254
Limba (African people) in Sierra Leone:
  DT516.45.L54
Limbe (Malawi): DT3257.L56
Limbum (African people) in Cameroon:
  DT571.L55
Limbus in India: DS432.L55
Limbus in Nepal: DS493.9.L5
Limpopo River and Valley (Southern
  Africa): DT1190.L56
Limpopo (South Africa): DT2391+
Line Islands: DU650
Lingayats in India: DS432.L56
Lio (Indonesian people): DS632.L55
Lion Temple of Naq'a (Sudan):
  DT159.9.L55
Lisht (Egypt): DT73.L6
Lisu in Burma: DS528.2.L57
Lisu (Southeast Asian people) in China:
  DS731.L57
Lisu (Southeast Asian people) in India:
  DS432.L57
Lisu (Southeast Asian people) in
  Thailand: DS570.L56
Lithuania, Jews in: DS135.L5+
Lithuanian Jews: DS113.8.L58
Lithuanians in Australia: DU122.L5
Little Karoo (South Africa): DT2400.L58
Little Namaqualand (South Africa):
  DT2400.N36

Little Triangle (Israel): DS110.L45
Liu Song (Sung) dynasty: DS748.6+
Livingstone, David: DT1110.L58
Livingstone (Zambia): DT3145.L58
Livingstonia Central Africa Company
   (Malawi): DT3211+
Lixus (Morocco): DT329.L59
Loanda (African people) in Angola:
   DT1308.L68
Lobatse (Botswana): DT2525.L73
Lobaye (African people) in Central
   African Republic: DT546.345.N44
Lobedu in South Africa: DT1768.L62
Lobengula (Zimbabwe): DT2940.L73
Lobi (African people) in Burkina Faso:
   DT555.45.L63
Lobi (African people) in Ghana:
   DT510.43.L62
Lobito (Angola): DT1465.L73
Lod (Israel): DS110.L63
Lodha in India: DS432.L6
Lodi Dynasty: DS459.7+
Logistics
   Persian Gulf War, 1990-1991:
     DS79.744.L64
   Vietnam War: DS559.8.L64
Logooli (African people) in Kenya:
   DT433.545.L63
Lohāṇās in India: DS432.L62
Lohars in India: DS432.L63
Lois in India: DS432.L65
Lolo in Vietnam: DS556.45.L65
Lome (Togo): DT582.9.L65
Lomwe in Malawi: DT3192.L66
Lomwe in Mozambique: DT3328.L66
Lopa in China: DS731.L64
Losap (Caroline Islands): DU568.L6
Lotf-'Alī Khān: DS297
Lotuko (African people) in South Sudan:
   DT159.927.L68
Louisiade Archipelago: DU660
Lourenço Marques (Mozambique)
   City: DT3410.M38, DT3412+
Low Archipelago: DU890
Lower Congo: DT665.B3
Lower Guinea: DT479

LoWilli (African people) in Burkina Faso:
   DT555.45.L68
Loyalty Islands: DU670
Lozi in Zambia: DT3058.L69
Luachimo (Angola): DT1465.L83
Luanda (Angola): DT1455
Luanda Uprising, 1961: DT1406.L83
Luanshya (Zambia): DT3145.L83
Luao (Angola): DT1465.L84
Luba (African people) in Congo
   (Democratic Republic): DT650.L8
Lubango (Angola): DT1465.L85
Lūbiyā (Palestine): DS110.L83
Lubumbashi (Zaire): DT665.E4
Lubuya, Battle of, 1854: DT2782
Luchazi (African people) in Zambia:
   DT3058.L83
Luderitz concessions: DT1603+
Luderitz (Namibia): DT1685.L84
Luderitzbucht (Namibia): DT1685.L84
Luena (African people) in Angola:
   DT1308.L84
Luena (Angola): DT1465.L86
Lugard Accords (Uganda): DT433.27+
Lugbara (African people) in Uganda:
   DT433.245.L83
Luguru (African people) in Tanzania:
   DT443.3.L84
Lukpa (African people) in Benin:
   DT541.45.L85
Lulua (African people): DT650.L83
Lumbu (African people) in Congo
   (Brazzaville): DT546.245.L84
Lumumba, Patrica, Assassination of:
   DT658.22
Lunalilo, King of the Hawaiian Islands:
   DU627.15
Lunda (African people) in Angola:
   DT1308.L86
Lunda, Northern (African people) in
   Congo (Democratic Republic):
   DT650.L86
Lunda Uprising, 1912 (Zambia):
   DT3099
Luo (African people) in Kenya:
   DT433.545.L85
Lupichili (Mozambique): DT3415.L87

Lurs in Iran: DS269.L87

Lusaka Accord: DT1436

Lusaka (Zambia): DT3142

Lushai in Burma: DS528.2.L87

Lushai in India: DS432.L8

Lüshun, Siege of, 1904-1905753
 Port Arthur, Seige of, 1904-1095:
 DS517.3

Luso (Angola): DT1465.L86

Luthili, Albert: DT1949.L88

Luvale (African people) in Zambia:
 DT3058.L89

Luvale Uprising, 1923 (Zambia):
 DT3101

Luwians in the Middle East: DS59.L86

Luxemburg, Jews in: DS135.L8+

Luyia (African people) in Kenya:
 DT433.545.L88

Lwoo (African people) in South Sudan:
 DT159.927.L86

Lycia: DS156.L8

Lydia: DS156.L9

Lyelae (African people) in Burkina Faso:
 DT555.45.L94

Lyttelton (New Zealand): DU430.L9

M

Mã Liêng in Vietnam: DS556.45.M22

Ma'āḍīd in Saudi Arabia: DS219.M33

Ma'aleh Adumim: DS110.M218

Maanyans (Bornean people):
 DS646.32.M2

Macaloge (Mozambique): DT3415.M33

Maccabees: DS121.7+

Macedonia, Jews in: DS135.M23

Macedonians in Australia: DU122.M3

Macias Nguema Biyogo (Equatorial
 Guinea): DT620.9.F47

Macías Nguema, Regime of (Equatorial
 Guinea): DT620.75+

Macquarie, Lachlan: DU172.M3

Mactaris (Tunisia): DT269.M28

Mada (African people) in Nigeria:
 DT515.45.M3

Ma'dabā (Jordan): DS154.9.M33

Madagascar: DT469.M21+

Madigas in India: DS432.M13

Madīnat Wāṭifah, Kawn (Egypt):
 DT73.M23

Mafa (African people) in Cameroon:
 DT571.M39

Mafeking, Siege of, 1899-1900:
 DT1908.M34

Mafraq (Jordan): DS154.9.M35

Mafraq Province (Jordan):
 DS154.9.M36

Magars in Nepal: DS493.9.M3

Magdolum (Egypt): DT73.M233

Magersfontein, Battle of, 1899:
 DT1908.M35

Maghrib: DT181+

Maghs in Bangladesh: DS393.83.M3

Magic
 Gypsies: DX155

Magindanao (Philippine people):
 DS666.M23

Magnesia ad Maeander: DS156.M33

Magongo, Battle of, 1840 (Natal):
 DT2247.M36

Maguzawa (African people) in Nigeria:
 DT515.45.M33

Mah-Meri (Malaysian people):
 DS595.2.M34, DS595.2.P67

Mahadeo Koli in India: DS432.M146

Mahafaly in Madagascar:
 DT469.M277M34

Mahalapye (Botswana): DT2525.M36

Mahali in India: DS432.M15

Mahali (Indic people) in Bangladesh:
 DS393.83.M34

Maḥanayim (Israel): DS110.M26

Maḥaneh Yísra'el (Jerusalem):
 DS109.8.M34

Maharero, Samuel: DT1608.M35

Mahars in India: DS432.M154

Mahasthan Site (Bangladesh):
 DS396.9.M33

Mahatas in Nepal: DS493.9.M35

Mahdiyah (Sudan): DT156.6+

Mahesri in India: DS432.M16

Mahisyas in India: DS432.M17

Mahiyā in India: DS432.M18

Mahlazene (Mozambique): DT3415.M35

Mahmud: DS293.5

Mahmud Shah: DS359.6

Mahrattas in India: DS432.M2

Mahrine Site (Tunisia): DT269.M34

Maisin in Papua: DU744.35.M32

Maithil Brahmans in India: DS432.M23

Majangirs in Ethiopia: DT380.4.M3

Majd al-Kurūm (Israel): DS110.M27

Majdal Yābā (Israel): DS110.M274

Majha (India and Pakistan): DS485.M3493

Majlis al-Ta'āun al-'Arabī: DS36.23

Majuba Hill, Battle of, 1881: DT2359.M36

Maka (African people) in Cameroon: DT571.M35

Makasar (Indonesian people): DS632.M25

Makgadikgadi Pans (Botswana): DT2520.M35

Makhzūm in Saudi Arabia: DS219.M34

Makina (African people) in Gabon: DT546.145.M217

Makonde (African people) in Tanzania: DT443.3.M34

Makonde in Mozambique: DT3328.M35

Makua (African people) in Mozambique: DT3328.M36

Māladhārī: DS432.M235

Malagasy Republic: DT469.M343+

Malaiyaha Tamil in Sri Lanka: DS489.25.M32

Malaiyalis in India: DS432.M24

Malaku: DS646.6+

Malan, Daniel: DT1927.M35

Malange (Angola): DT1465.M35

Malanje (Angola): DT1465.M35

Malas in India: DS432.M245

Malawi: DT3161+

Malawi, Lake: DT3252.M35

Malay Archipelago: DS600+

Malay Peninsula: DS591+

Malays in Indonesia: DS632.M27

Malays in Malaysia: DS595.2.M35

Malays in Sarawak: DS597.367.M34

Malays in Singapore: DS610.25.M34

Malays in South Africa: DT1768.M35

Malays in Southeast Asia: DS523.4.M35

Malays in Southern Africa: DT1058.M35

Malays in Sri Lanka: DS489.25.M37

Malays in Thailand: DS570.M3

Malays in the Middle East: DS59.M34

Malaysia: DS591+

Malazgirt, Battle of: DS27+

Maldive Islands: DS349.9.M34+

Maldives: DS349.9.M34+

Male (African people) in Ethiopia: DT380.4.M32

Malekudiya (Indic people): DS432.M247

Maler (Indic people): DS432.M248

Malḥatah, Tel (Israel): DS110.M276

Mali: DT551+

Mali empire: DT532.2

Mali Federation: DT551+

Mali, Jews in: DS135.M234

Malī-Sainīs in India: DS432.M249

Malia Kondh (Indic people): DS432.M2493

Malibamatso River (Lesotho): DT2680.M35

Malkata Site (Egypt): DT73.M24

Mallāḥah (Palestine): DS110.M277

Mallahs in India: DS432.M2495

Maloh (Indonesian people): DS632.M275

Maloti Mountains (Lesotho): DT2680.M36

Malpaharia in India: DS432.M25

Malta, Jews in: DS135.M26

Maltese in Algeria: DT283.6.M35

Maltese in Australia: DU122.M34

Malto in India: DS432.M25

Malvernia (Mozambique): DT3415.C54

Mamabolo (African people) in South Africa: DT1768.M36

Mamanuas (Philippine people): DS666.M25

Mambai (Indonesian people): DS632.M28

Mambila (African people) in Cameroon: DT571.M356

Mambila (African people) in Nigeria: DT515.45.M35

Mambwe (African people) in Zambia: DT3058.M35

Mamelukes: DS97.4

Mamprusi (African people) in Ghana: DT510.43.M35

Mamvu (African people) in Tanzania: DT443.3.M36

Manchu invasions, 1627-1637, of Korea: DS913.615+

Manchuria: DS781+

Manchus in China: DS731.M35

Manda (African people) in Cameroon: DT571.M36

Mandaeans in Iran: DS269.M36

Mandaheccus in India: DS432.M2515

Mandailing (Indonesian people): DS632.M285

Mandandanji (Australian people): DU125.M28

Mandari (African people) in South Sudan: DT159.927.M36

Mandela, Nelson: DT1974+

Mandela, Winnie: DT1949.M36

Mandingo (African people) in Gambia: DT509.45.M34

Mandingo (African people) in Guinea: DT543.45.M34

Mandingo (African people) in Guinea-Bisseau: DT613.45.M36

Mandingo (African people) in Mali: DT551.45.M36

Mandingo (African people) in Senegal: DT549.45.M35

Mandingo (African people) in West Africa: DT474.6.M36

Mandjak (African people) in Senegal: DT549.45.M37

Mandjildjara (Australian people): DU125.M29

Mandobo (African people) in Papua: DU744.35.M33

Mang in Vietnam: DS556.45.M36

Mang (Indic people): DS432.M253

Mangalas (Indic people): DS432.M2533

Manganja in Malawi: DT3192.M35

Mangareva Islands: DU680

Manggarai (Indonesian people): DS632.M287

Mangyans in the Philippines: DS666.M3

Manica (Mozambique): DT3410.M36

Manicaland (Zimbabwe): DT3020.M35

Maniema (Zaire): DT665.M35

Manjacaze (Mozambique): DT3410.M37

Mankanya (African people) in Senegal: DT549.45.M38

Mankidia (Indic people): DS432.M254

Mankon (African people) in Cameroon: DT571.M37

Mano (African people) in Liberia: DT630.5.M35

Manobos (Philippine people): DS666.M34

Mantatee: DT2335.M36

Mantatisi: DT2335.M36

Manua: DU819.M3

Manusela (Indonesian people): DS632.M289

Manyika (African people) in Mozambique: DT3328.M38

Manyuke (Indonesian people): DS632.M29

Manzini (Swaziland): DT2825.M35

Maonan (Chinese people): DS731.M36

Maori: DU422.8+

Maporese (Indonesian people): DS632.M3

Maputo (Mozambique)
City: DT3410.M38, DT3412+

Marakwet (African people) in Kenya: DT433.545.M32

Maram (Indic people): DS432.M257

Maranao (Philippine people): DS666.M37

Marathas in India: DS432.M2, DS485.M349

Marathas in Mauritius: DT469.M445M37

Maravars in India: DS432.M26

Marba (African people) in Chad: DT546.445.M36

Marco Polo Bridge Incident, 1937 Sino-Japanese War, 1937-1945: DS777.533.M3

Mardu (Australian people): DU125.M3

Marea (Egypt): DT73.M245

Maria (Indic people): DS432.M267

Marind in Papua: DU744.35.M34

Maring (Indic people): DS432.M27

Marlborough (New Zealand): DU430.M35

Marlik Site (Iran): DS262.M37

Maroni Petrera Site (Cyprus): DS54.95.M4

Maronites in Lebanon: DS80.55.M37

Marquesas Islands: DU700+

Marrakesh (Morocco): DT329.M3

Marsá Maṭrūḥ (Egypt): DT73.M254

Marsh Arabs in Iraq: DS70.8.M37

Marshall Islands: DU710

Maru in Burma: DS528.2.M33

Marwaris in India: DS432.M28

Maryūt Lake (Egypt): DT73.M257

Masa (African people) in Cameroon: DT571.M38

Masa (African people) in Chad: DT546.445.M37

Masada (Israel): DS110.M33

Masai (African people) in Kenya: DT433.545.M33

Masai (African people) in Tanzania: DT443.3.M37

Masango (African people) in Gabon: DT546.145.M22

Mascarene Islands: DT469.M39

Maseru (Lesotho): DT2683

Mashi (African people) in Angola: DT1308.M36

Mashkan-shapir (Extinct city): DS70.5.M37

Mashona (African people) in South Africa: DT1768.M38

Mashona (African people) in Zimbabwe: DT2913.M38

Mashonaland (Zimbabwe): DT3020.M37

Masire, Quett, 1980-: DT2502

Masjid al-Aqsá (Jerusalem): DS109.32.M38

Mass media Iraq War, 2003-: DS79.767.M37

Massangano, Fall of (Mozambique): DT3374

Massaua (Eritrea): DT398.M3

Massawa (Eritrea): DT398.M3

Masvingo (Zimbabwe): DT3025.M37

Matabeleland (Zimbabwe): DT3020.M38

Matakam (African people) in Cameroon: DT571.M39

Matanzima, Kaiser: DT1949.M38

Mate (Asian people) in India: DS432.M3

Matengo (African people) in Tanzania: DT443.3.M39

Material culture Aboriginal Australians: DU124.M37

Material culture, Maori: DU423.I53

Matola (Mozambique): DT3415.M38

Matope (Zimbabwe): DT2940.M38

Matopo Hills (Zimbabwe): DT3020.M39

Mau Mau movement (Kenya): DT433.577

Maui (Hawaii): DU628.M3

Mauna Loa (Hawaii): DU629.M34

Maung (Australian people): DU125.M33

Maure (African people) in Mauritania: DT554.45.M38

Mauretania (Morocco): DT554+

Mauritania, Jews in: DS135.M3

Mauritians in Australia: DU122.M38

Mauritius: DT469.M4+

Mauritius, Jews in: DS135.M33

Mavura (Zimbabwe): DT2940.M39

Mawri (African people): DT547.45.M38

May Revolution, 1961 (Korea): DS922.44

Mayombe (African people) in Congo (Democratic Republic): DT650.M38

Mayotte: DT469.M4975

Mazkeret-Batyah (Israel): DS110.M36

Mbala in Congo (Democratic Republic): DT650.M42

Mbalabala (Zimbabwe): DT3025.M43
Mbanane (Swaziland): DT2823
Mbandieru (African people) in Namibia:
  DT1558.M33
Mbandzeni: DT2780.M33
Mbañe (Equatorial Guinea):
  DT620.9.E46
Mbanza (Angola): DT1465.M42
Mbeki, Thabo: DT1975
Mbere (African people) in Kenya:
  DT433.545.M34
Mbete (African people) in Gabon:
  DT546.145.M24
Mbole (African people) in Congo
  (Democratic Republic): DT650.M46
Mbosi (African people) in Congo
  (Brazzaville): DT546.245.M35
Mbukushu (African people) in Botswana:
  DT2458.M28
Mbukushu (African people) in Namibia:
  DT1558.M37
Mbula (African people) in Nigeria:
  DT515.45.M39
Mbum (African people) in Angola:
  DT546.345.M38
Mbunda (African people) in Zambia:
  DT3058.M38
Mbundu (African people) in Angola:
  DT1308.M38
Mbwila, Battle of, 1665: DT1378
McPherson Range (Australia):
  DU280.M22
Mea Shearim (Jerusalem): DS109.8.M4
Me'ah She'arim (Jerusalem):
  DS109.8.M4
Mech in Nepal: DS493.9.M43
Medals
  Persian Gulf War, 1990-1991:
    DS79.744.M42
  Vietnam War: DS558.98+
  War and intervention, 1950-1953
    (Korea): DS920.44+
Mēdas in India: DS432.M315
Median Empire: DS278+
Medical aspects
  Persian Gulf War, 1990-1991:
    DS79.744.M44

Medical care
  Iraq War, 2003-: DS79.767.M43
  Korean War: DS921.25
  Sino-Japanese War, 1937-1945:
    DS777.533.M42
  South African War: DT1918.M44
  Vietnam War: DS559.44
Medicine
  Aboriginal Australians: DU124.M43
Medicine, Maori: DU423.M38
Medieval Islamic civilization: DS36.85+
Medinet Habu (Egypt): DT73.M3
Medinet Madi (Egypt): DT73.M35
Mediterranean Region, Jews in:
  DS135.M43
Meetinghouses, Maori: DU423.M42
Meghavaṃsīs (Indic people):
  DS432.M32
Megiddo, Battle of: DT87.2
Megiddo (Extinct city): DS110.M4
Mehtas (Indic people): DS432.M325
Mehulash ha-ḳatan (Israel): DS110.L45
Meidum Pyramid (Egypt): DT73.M4
Meidum Site (Egypt): DT73.M4
Meiji (Mutsuhito): DS881.98+
Meinarti (Sudan): DT159.9.M44
Meitheir (Indic people): DS432.M33
Meitheis in Bangladesh: DS393.83.M44
Mejprat in Papua: DU744.35.M42
Mekan (African people) in Ethiopia:
  DT380.4.M45
Mekhadma: DT346.M5
Melanau in Sarawak: DS597.367.M44
Melanesia: DU490
Melbourne (Australia): DU228+
Melilla (Spain): DT329.M4
Memnon statue (Egypt): DT73.T32
Memons in Pakistan: DS380.M46
Memons in Sri Lanka: DS489.25.M46
Memons (Indic people): DS432.M34
Memorials
  Arab War, 1948-1949: DS126.96.M4
  Korean War: DS921.9+
  Vietnam War: DS559.82+
Memphis (Egypt): DT73.M5
Menabe in Madagascar:
  DT469.M277M45

Menaḥemiyah (Israel): DS110.M44
Menba (Chinese people): DS731.M45
Mende in Sierra Leone: DT516.45.M45
Mendes (Egypt): DT73.M54
Menelik II: DT387+
Mengüceks: DS27.53
Menongue (Angola): DT1465.M46
Mentawai (Indonesian people): DS632.M35
Meo (Indic people): DS432.M35
Mer: DS432.M37
Mergui Archipelago: DS530.8.M47
Merina in Madagascar: DT469.M277M47
Meroe (Sudan): DT159.9.M47
Meru (African people) in Kenya: DT433.545.M47
Meru in Tanzania: DT443.3.M47
Mesopotamia: DS67+
Meta (African people) in Cameroon: DT571.M47
Metals
    Ancient Egypt: DT62.M5
Mexican Americans
    Vietnam War: DS559.8.M39
Mfecane
    Mozambique: DT3366
    Natal: DT2238
    Orange Free State: DT2118
    South Africa: DT1841
    Southern Africa: DT1123
    Zambia: DT3087
Mhamais in India: DS432.M38
Miao (Asian people) in China: DS731.M5
Miao (Asian people) in Laos: DS555.45.M5
Miao (Asian people) in Thailand: DS570.M5
Micronesia: DU500
Middle Congo: DT546.2+
Middle East: DS41+
Midway Islands (Hawaii): DU628.M5
Migdal (Israel): DS110.M54
Mijikenda (African people) in Kenya: DT433.545.M54
Mikir in India: DS432.M42

Miklukha-Maklaĭ, Nikolaĭ Nikolaevich: DU746.M5
Military history
    Post-Persian Gulf War, 1991-: DS79.755
Military intelligence
    Iraq War, 2003-: DS79.767.S75
    Korean War: DS921.5.S7+
    Sino-Japanese War, 1937-1945: DS777.533.S65
    Vietnam War: DS559.8.M44
Military operations
    Persian Gulf War, 1990-1991: DS79.72, DS79.73452+
Millang in India: DS432.M424
Milner, Alfred: DT1851.M55
Milton Margai administration (Sierra Leone): DT516.815+
Mimika in Papua: DU744.35.M55
Mina (African people): DT582.45.M55
Mina in India: DS432.M43
Mina Site: DS156.M56
Minahasa (Indonesian people): DS632.M38
Minangkabau (Indonesian people): DS632.M4
Ming dynasty: DS753+
Minianka (African people): DT551.45.M55
Minoans in Egypt: DT72.M55
Minorcans in Algeria: DT283.6.M55
Minshāt abū 'Umar Site (Egypt): DT73.M72
Minyā Province (Egypt): DT73.M75
Minyong (Indic people): DS432.M434
Mir Abdallah: DS293.4
Mir Waiz: DS293.3
Miranda (Mozambique): DT3415.M33
Mirgissa (Sudan): DT159.9.M57
Miri (Indic people): DS432.M44
Miriwoong (Australian people): DU125.M52
Mirning (Australian people): DU125.M54
Mirrors
    Ancient Egypt: DT62.M58
Misgav (Israel): DS110.M557

Mishkenot sha'ananim (Jerusalem):
  DS109.8.M47
Mishmar ha-'Emek (Israel): DS110.M57
Mishmi in India: DS432.M45
Missing in action
  Korean War: DS921.5.M5
  Vietnam War: DS559.8.M5
Missions
  Aboriginal Australians: DU124.M56
Mitanni: DS66.4
Mitannians: DS66.4
Mitham Rotshild (Jerusalem):
  DS109.8.M5
Mitham Terah Sanotah (Jerusalem):
  DS109.8.M54
Mlozi: DT3219.M56
Mnong in French Indonesia:
  DS539.M58
Moba (African people) in Nigeria:
  DT515.45.M62
Moba (African people) in Togo:
  DT582.45.M63
Mobuto Sese Seko, Regime of:
  DT658.25
Moçambique: DT3410.N36
Moçâmides (Angola)
  City: DT1465.N36
  Province: DT1450.N36
Modang (Indonesian people):
  DS646.32.M64
Modi'in (Israel): DS110.M6
Moeris Lake (Egypt): DT73.M8
Moffat, Howard: DT2975.M64
Moffat, John: DT2963.M64
Moffat Treaty, 1888 (Zimbabwe):
  DT2955
Mogaveeras (Indic people): DS432.M48
Mogul Empire (India): DS461+
Mohammad Mosaddeq, Prime Minister,
  1951-1953: DS318.6
Mohammad Reza Pahlavi: DS318+
Mohammed Ali, Khedive of Egypt:
  DT104
Mohammed (Kajar dynasty): DS305
Mohammed Mirza: DS292.51
Mohammed Said, Viceroy of Egypt:
  DT105

Mohammed VI (Morocco): DT326.3
Mohenjo-daro (Pakistan): DS392.2.M6
Mohmands in India: DS432.M6
Mohmands in Pakistan: DS380.M63
Moi in French Indonesia: DS539.M6
Moinba (Chinese people): DS731.M45
Moir, Frederick: DT3214.M65
Moir, John: DT3214.M66
Moken in Burma: DS528.2.M58
Moken in Thailand: DS570.M57
Mokhehle, Ntsu: DT2642.M65
Mokil (Caroline Islands): DU568.M6
Molapo, Charles: DT2655.M65
Moldova, Jews in: DS135.M64
Molepolole (Botswana): DT2525.M75
Molokai (Hawaii): DU628.M7
Molopo River (Botswana): DT2520.M65
Moluccans, South, in Indonesia:
  DS632.M65
Moluccas: DS646.6+
Mon in Burma: DS528.2.M6
Mon in Southeast Asia: DS523.4.M65
Mon in Thailand: DS570.M6
Monastir (Tunisia): DT269.M6
Monbuttus (African people) in Congo
  (Democratic Republic): DT650.M64
Mondlane, Eduardo: DT3379.M66
Mongo (African people) in Congo
  (Democratic Republic): DT650.M65
Mongolia: DS793.M7, DS798.A1+
Mongols: DS19+
Mongols in China: DS731.M64
Monguors in China: DS731.M65
Moni in Papua: DU744.35.M66
Monjombo in Central African Republic:
  DT546.345.M65
Monomotapa
  Southern Africa: DT1113
  Zimbabwe: DT2942+
Monpa (Indic people): DS432.M63
Monpa (Indic people) in Bhutan:
  DS491.76.M66
Monrovia (Liberia): DT637.M6
Mons Claudianus Site (Egypt):
  DT73.M85
Montagnards (Vietnamese people):
  DS556.45.M6

Monteiro and Gamitto, Expedition of
(Zambia): DT3083
Monuments
Arab War, 1949-1949: DS126.96.M4
Korean War: DS921.9+
Vietnam War: DS559.82+
Moorosi: DT2642.M66
Moorosi Rebellion, 1879: DT2646
Moothans (Indic people): DS432.M64
Moplahs in India: DS432.M65
Moral and religious aspects
Arab War, 1948-1949: DS126.96.R4
Korean War: DS921.4
Persian Gulf War, 1990-1991:
DS79.744.R44
Vietnam War: DS559.64
Moral aspects
Iraq War, 2003-: DS79.767.M67
Morashah (Jerusalem): DS109.8.M57
Morenga: DT1608.M67
Moreton Bay (Australia): DU280.M7
Moria in India: DS432.M66
Moriori (New Zealand people):
DU424.M67
Moriscos in Morocco: DT313.6.M67
Moriscos in Tunisia: DT253.2.M6
Moroccan annexation claims
(Mauritania): DT554.8+
Moroccan conquest (Burkina Faso):
DT555.65+
Moroccan Jews in Israel: DS113.8.M66
Moroccan-Spanish War, 1957-1958:
DT326
Morocco: DT301+
Morocco, Jews in: DS135.M8+
Morris, Abraham: DT1628.M78
Mortlock Islands: DU568.N6
Mortuary customs
Aboriginal Australians: DU124.M67
Mortuary Temple of Amenhotep III
(Egypt): DT73.T32
Moshavah ha-Germanit: DS109.8.M58
Moshoeshoe
II: DT2655.M67
Moshoeshoe I: DT2634.M67
Moslem rule
India: DS452+

Moslem rule
Indonesia: DS641.5
Moslems: DT95+
Moso: DS731.N39
Mossi (African people) in Burkina Faso:
DT555.45.M67
Mossi Kingdom (Burkina Faso):
DT555.65+
Motion pictures about the
Arab War, 1948-1949: DS126.96.M65
Korean War: DS918.16
Vietnam War: DS557.73
Motsa (Israel): DS110.M66
Mount Cook (New Zealand): DU430.A4
Mount Herzl (Jerusalem): DS109.8.M6
Mount Scopus: DS109.8.S36
Mountains of the Moon: DT361+
Mowāmārīya (Indic people):
DS432.M67
Moxico (Angola): DT1450.M69
Mozambique: DT3291+
Mozambique, Jews in: DS135.M95
Mozan, Tall (Syria): DS99.U74
Mpenzeni: DT3081.M64
Mpenzeni War, 1898 (Malawi): DT3223
Mpiemo (African people) in Central
African Republic: DT546.345.M67
Mpongwe (African people) in Gabon:
DT546.145.M66
Mpumalanga (South Africa): DT2386+
Mru in Bangladesh: DS393.83.M78
Mrui in Burma: DS528.2.M78
Msibi, George: DT2800.M85
Msimang, Selby: DT1927.M85
Mswati, King of the Swazi
II: DT2780.M78
III: DT2806
Mubārak, Muḥammad Ḥusnī: DT107.87
Muchinga Mountains (Zambia):
DT3140.M84
Muchopes (Mozambique): DT3410.M37
Mudge, Dirk: DT1641.M84
Muduvar in India: DS432.M74
Mufulira (Zambia): DT3145.M85
Mugabe, Robert: DT3000
Muhajir in Pakistan: DS380.M83

Muhammad administration (Nigeria): DT515.838

Muhammad Nadir Shah: DS369.3

Muḥammad V, King of Morocco: DT324.92.M6

Muhammad Zahir Shah: DS369.4

Mujibur Rahman, Sheikh: DS395.7.M9

Mukden, Battle of (Russo-Japanese War): DS517.4

Mukkuvars in India: DS432.M77

Mulākānaḍu Br āhamaṇas (Indic people): DS432.M78

Mulambwa: DT3214.M85

Mulanje Mountains (Malawi): DT3252.M85

Mulao (Chinese people): DS731.M84

Mulder, Cornelius (Connie): DT1949.M85

Mulder scandal, 1978: DT1961

Multiparty restoration (Benin): DT541.845

Mumba, Levi: DT3219.M85

Mummies
Ancient Egypt: DT62.M7

Mumuye (African people) in Cameroon: DT571.M84

Munda in India: DS432.M8

Mundang (African people) in Cameroon: DT571.M85

Mundang (African people) in Chad: DT546.445.M85

Mungo Park: DT356

Munhata Site (Israel): DS110.M85

Muntafiq in Iraq: DS70.8.M86

Muong (Vietnamese people): DS556.45.M84

Muria in India: DS432.M83

Murle (African people) in South Sudan: DT159.927.M87

Murngin (Australian people): DU125.M8

Muromachi period: DS863.75+

Murray River and Valley (Australia): DU180.M8

Murray, Sir Hubert: DU746.M8

Murut in Sarawak: DS597.367.M87

Muruts in Burma: DS650.43.M87

Muruwari (Australian people): DU125.M83

Murzu in Ethiopia: DT380.4.M85

Musahar in India: DS432.M836

Muscat: DS247.M8+

Museums, Maori: DU423.M88

Musharraf, Pervez: DS389.22.M87

Muslim civilization (India): DS427

Muslims in Australia: DU122.M87

Muslims in Bangladesh: DS393.83.M87

Muslims in Burma: DS528.2.M9

Muslims in Burundi: DT450.65.M87

Muslims in Central Asia: DS328.4.M87

Muslims in Central Sub-saharan Africa: DT352.43.M87

Muslims in China: DS731.M87

Muslims in Congo (Democratic Republic): DT650.M97

Muslims in Cyprus: DS54.42.M82

Muslims in East Africa: DT429.5.M86

Muslims in Ethiopia: DT380.4.M87

Muslims in French West Africa: DT530.5.M88

Muslims in India: DS432.M84

Muslims in Kenya: DT433.545.M87

Muslims in Mali: DT551.45.M84

Muslims in Mauritania: DT554.45.M84

Muslims in Mauritius: DT469.M445M87

Muslims in Nepal: DS493.9.M87

Muslims in New Zealand: DU424.5.M87

Muslims in Nigeria: DT515.45.M87

Muslims in Réunion: DT469.R39M87

Muslims in Singapore: DS610.25.M87

Muslims in South Africa: DT1768.M86

Muslims in Southeast Asia: DS523.4.M87

Muslims in Southern Africa: DT1058.M87

Muslims in Southern Asia: DS339.3.M87

Muslims in Sri Lanka: DS489.25.M8

Muslims in Thailand: DS570.M85

Muslims in the Philippines: DS666.M8

Mussorongo revolt, 1908: DT1394

Musti (Tunisia): DT269.M87

Mutare (Zimbabwe): DT3025.M86

Muthallath (Israel): DS110.L45

Mutu ya Kevela: DT1388.M88
Muyuw in Papua: DU744.35.M89
Muzaffar-ed-Din: DS311
Muzaffarids: DS289.3
Muzila: DT3364.M89
Muzorewa, Abel: DT2984.M89
Mvuma (Zimbabwe): DT3025.M88
Mwenezi (Zimbabwe): DT3025.M94
Mwila (African people) in Angola:
   DT1308.M85
Myene (African people) in Gabon:
   DT546.145.M93
Myra (Extinct city): DS156.M95
Mythology
   Aboriginal Australians: DU124.R44
Mzilikazi (Zimbabwe): DT2940.M95
Mzuzu (Malawi): DT3257.M98

N

Nabataeans: DS154.22
Nablus (West Bank): DS110.N2
Nabonidus: DS73.93
Nabopolassar: DS73.91
Nadars in India: DS432.N25
Nadavas in India: DS432.N26
Nadir Shah: DS294
Nādōr Site (Algeria)
   City: DT299.N34
Nag' el-Scheima Site (Egypt):
   DT73.N18
Naga-ed Dêr (Egypt): DT73.N2
Naga in Burma: DS528.2.N33
Naga in India: DS432.N3
Naga (Indonesian people): DS632.N33
Nagar Brahmans in India: DS432.N28
Nage (Indonesian people): DS632.N35
Nagesia (Indic people): DS432.N313
Nahalal (Israel): DS110.N23
Nahali'el (Israel): DS110.N25
Nahariyah (Israel): DS110.N26
Naḥla'ot (Jerusalem): DS109.8.N34
Naika in India: DS432.N32
Nairs in India: DS432.N324
Najaf, Battle of, 2004: DS79.764.N35
Najd: DS247.9.N35

Nakarmīs (Nepalese people):
   DS493.9.N3
Nalum in Papua: DU744.35.N32
Nama (African people) in Namibia:
   DT1558.N36
Nama War, 1904-1906: DT1620
Namaland (Namibia): DT1670.N36
Namaqualand (South Africa):
   DT2400.N36
Namasudras in India: DS432.N35
Nambudiris in India: DS432.N354
Namhila, Ellen Ndeshi: DT1641.N34
Namib Desert (Namibia): DT1670.N37
Namibe (Angola)
   City: DT1465.N36
   Province: DT1450.N36
Namibia: DT1501+
Namibia (African people) in South
   Africa: DT1768.N37
Namnam (African people) in Ghana:
   DT510.43.N35
Nampula (Mozambique): DT3410.N36
Nande (African people) in Congo
   (Democratic Republic): DT650.N34
Nandi (African people) in Kenya:
   DT433.545.N34
Nanga Parbat (Pakistan): DS392.2.N36
Nangudi Vallalas: DS432.N36
Nantipuram (Ancient city): DS486.N314
Naqādah (Egypt): DT73.N26
Nar (African people) in Chad:
   DT546.445.N35
Nara period: DS855.68+
Narangga (Australian people):
   DU125.N36
Narmouthis (Egypt): DT73.M35
Naron (African people) in South Africa:
   DT1768.N38
Narrinyeri (Australian people):
   DU125.N37
Narseh: DS286.4
Nasiriyah, Battle of, 2003:
   DS79.764.N37
Nasr-ed-Din: DS307+
Nasser, Gamal Abdel, President United
   Arab Republic: DT107.83

Nasser, Lake (Egypt and Sudan)
  Antiquities: DT73.N27
Natal: DT2181+
Natal, Treks into: DT2242
National characteristics
  Australia: DU121
  South Africa: DT1755
National characteristics, Israeli:
  DS113.3
National liberation and armed struggle
  by ANC, 1961- (South Africa):
  DT1953
National liberation movements
  (Southern Africa): DT1177
National liberation struggle, 1964-1975
  (Mozambique): DT3387
Nationalism, Arab: DS63.5+
Naṭrūn Valley (Egypt): DT73.N28
Natsrat 'Ilit: DS110.N28
Nattukottai Chettiars in India:
  DS432.N38
Naucratis (Egypt): DT73.N3
Naudeba (African people) in Togo:
  DT582.45.N38
Nauru: DU715
Nauthars (Nepalese people):
  DS493.9.N35
Naval operations
  Arab War, 1948-1949: DS126.96.N3
Naval operatiosn
  Persian Gulf War, 1990-1991:
  DS79.744.N38
Navayats in India: DS432.N42
Navigators Islands: DU810+
Naxi: DS731.N39
Nazareth (Israel): DS110.N3
Nchumburung (African people) in
  Ghana: DT510.43.N4
Ndau (African people) in Mozambique:
  DT3328.N38
Ndebele (African people) in South
  Africa: DT1768.N42
Ndebele (African people) in Transvaal
  under Mzilikazi: DT2340
Ndebele (African people) in Zimbabwe:
  DT2913.N44

Ndebele invasions
  Zambia: DT3089
  Zimbabwe: DT2951
Ndebele Revolt, 1896 (Zimbabwe):
  DT2968+
Ndebele War (Zimbabwe), 1896-1897:
  DT2966
Ndembu (African people) in Zambia:
  DT3058.N44
Ndendeuli (African people) in Tanzania:
  DT443.3.N43
Ndhir (Berber people) in Morocco:
  DT313.3.N4
Ndola (Zambia): DT3145.N46
Ndonga (African people) in Angola:
  DT1308.N46
Ndonga (African people) in Namibia:
  DT1558.N46
Ndowe (African people) in Equatorial
  Guinea: DT620.45.N37
Ndut (African people) in Senegal:
  DT549.45.N38
Neandria: DS156.N42
Near East: DS41+
Near East, Jews in: DS135.L4
Nebuchadnessar II: DS73.92
Nefertiti, Consort of Amenhetep IV:
  DT87.45
Nefzaoua (Tunisia): DT268.N4
Negev (Israel): DS110.N4
Negritos in the Philippines: DS666.N4
Nejd: DS247.N47+
Nelson (New Zealand) Provincial
  District: DU430.N38
Nembe (African people) in Nigeria:
  DT515.45.N35
Nemrik 9 Site (Iraq): DS70.5.N35
Nemrut Daği Mound: DS156.N45
Nepal: DS493+
Nepalese in India: DS432.N46
Nepali-speaking people in India:
  DS432.N46
Nes Harim: DS110.N434
Netanyah (Israel): DS110.N46
Netherlands and East Asia: DS518.5
Netherlands, Jews in: DS135.N4+
Netherlands New Guinea: DU744+

Netsarim: DS110.N47
Netser Sireni (Israel): DS110.N475
Neu Mecklenburg Island: DU553.N4
Neu Pommern Island: DU553.N35
Neveh Etan (Israel): DS110.N48
New Britain Island: DU553.N35
New Caledonia: DU720+
New Guinea: DU739+
New Hebrides: DU760
New Ireland Island: DU553.N4
New Italy (Colony)
   Australia: DU180.N5
New Mecklenburg Island: DU553.N4
New Plymouth (New Zealand):
   DU430.N4
New Pomerania Island: DU553.N35
New South Wales: DU150+
New Zealand: DU400+
New Zealand, Jews in: DS135.N65+
New Zealanders in China: DS731.N48
Newars in Nepal: DS493.9.N4
Newcastle (Australia): DU180.N56
Nga Puhi (Maori people): DU424.N36
Ngaa Rauru (Maori people):
   DU424.N37
Ngaanyatjarra (Australian people):
   DU125.N45
Ngadjuri (Australian people):
   DU125.N46
Ngaitahu (Maori people): DU424.N4
Ngaju (Indonesian people):
   DS646.32.N45
Ngama in Chad: DT546.445.N43
Ngami, Lake (Botswana): DT2520.N53
Ngangela (African people) in Angola:
   DT1308.N53
Ngangela (African people) in Zambia:
   DT3058.N53
Ngangte (African people) in Cameroon:
   DT571.N43
Ngāti Apa (Maori people):
   DU424.N4118
Ngāti Awa (Maori people): DU424.N412
Ngāti Haua (Maori people):
   DU424.N413
Ngāti Hinga (Maori people):
   DU424.N4133

Ngāti Kahungunu (Maori people):
   DU424.N4134
Ngāti Kinohaku: DU424.N4137
Ngāti Mahuta (Maori people):
   DU424.N414
Ngāti Pāhauwera: DU424.N4147
Ngāti Pango (New Zealand people):
   DU424.N41473
Ngāti Pikiao: DU424.N4148
Ngāti Porou (Maori people):
   DU424.N415
Ngāti Pukenga (Maori people):
   DU424.N42
Ngāti Rangiwewehi (New Zealand
   people): DU424.N423
Ngāti Tahu Matawhaiti: DU424.N425
Ngāti Tarawhai (Maori people):
   DU424.N43
Ngāti Te Ata: DU424.N435
Ngāti Toa (Maori people): DU424.N44
Ngāti Tuwharetoa: DU424.N46
Ngāti Urunumia: DU424.N47
Ngāti Whakaue (Maori people):
   DU424.N48
Ngāti Whanaunga (New Zealand
   people): DU424.N49
Ngatik Atoll: DU568.N44
Ngbaka (African people) in Central
   African Republic: DT546.345.N44
Ngbaka (African people) in Congo
   (Democratic Republic): DT650.N45
Ngemba (African people) in Cameroon:
   DT571.N45
Ngiva (Angola): DT1465.N55
Ngola Inene, King of Ndongo:
   DT1365.N56
Ngombe (Bantu people) in Congo
   (Democratic Republic): DT650.N48
Ngongo (Bantu people) in Zaire:
   DT650.N5
Ngoni (African people) in Malawi:
   DT3192.N44
Ngoni (African people) in Tanzania:
   DT443.3.N54
Ngoni (African people) in Zambia:
   DT3058.N54

Ngoni invasions
  Mozambique: DT3366
  Zambia: DT3087
Ngulu (African people) in Tanzania:
  DT443.3.N58
Nguni (African people) in Mozambique:
  DT3328.N58
Nguni (African people) in South Africa:
  DT1768.N45
Nguni (African people) in Southern
  Africa: DT1058.N58
Nguni (African people) in Zimbabwe:
  DT2913.N49
Nguni States: DT1115
Ngunza (Angola): DT1465.N58
Ngwa (African people): DT515.45.N48
Ngwane II: DT2780.N58
Ngwato (African people): DT2458.N45
Ngwe in Cameroon: DT571.N48
Niamey (Egypt): DT547.9.N5
Niasese (Indonesian people):
  DS632.N52
Niassa (Mozambique): DT3410.N53
Nicaea: DS156.N5
Nicobar: DS486.5.A52
Nicobarese in India: DS432.N53
Niger: DT547+
Niger River: DT360
Nigeria: DT515+
Nigeria, Jews in: DS135.N72
Niihau (Hawaii): DU628.N55
Nika (African people) in Kenya:
  DT433.545.M54
Nika in Zimbabwe: DT2913.N53
Nile in Egypt: DT116
Nile River: DT115+
Nile River Delta (Egypt): DT73.N54
Nilotic peoples in Ethiopia:
  DT380.4.N54
Nilotic peoples in Sudan: DT155.2.N55
Nimboran (Indonesian people) in Papua:
  DU744.35.N56
Nineveh (Ancient city): DS70.5.N47
Nippur (Ancient city): DS70.5.N5
Nir 'Am (Israel): DS110.N57
Nitsanim (Israel): DS110.N58
Niue (New Zealand): DU430.N5

Niyogi Brahmans (Indic people):
  DS432.N59
Njabel: DT2350.N53
Nkambule, Battle of: DT1879.N55
Nkanu (African people) in Congo
  (Democratic Republic): DT650.N55
Nkanu (Nigerian people) in Nigeria:
  DT515.45.N55
Nkhonde (African people) in Malawi:
  DT3192.N56
Nkomati Accord, 1984 (Mozambique):
  DT3395
Nkomi (African people) in Gabon:
  DT546.145.N56
Nkomo, Joshua: DT2984.N56
Nkoya (African people) in Zambia:
  DT3058.N56
Nkumbi (African people) in Angola:
  DT1308.N58
Nkumbula, Harry: DT3111.N58
Nkundu (African people) in Congo
  (Democratic Republic): DT650.N58
Noatia (Indic people): DS432.N62
Nobility in Japan: DS827.N63
Noble families (Sudan): DT155.44+
Nocte in India: DS432.N63
Nofretete, Consort of Amenhetep IV:
  DT87.45
Nomads in Algeria: DT283.6.N6
Nomads in French West Africa:
  DT530.5.N65
Nomads in Tunisia: DT253.2.N65
Nomoi Islands: DU568.N6
Norcia (Australia): DU380.N4
Norfolk Island (Australia): DU180.N6
North Africa: DT160+
North Africans in Egypt: DT72.N67
North Africans in Israel: DS113.8.N6
North Island (N.Z.): DU430.N6
North Korea: DS930+
North Koreans in foreign countries
  (General): DS933.5
North Vietnam: DS560+
North-West province (South Africa):
  DT2396+
Northeast Africa: DT367+
Northern Australia: DU391

Northern Cape (South Africa): DT2064+
Northern dynasties: DS748.17+
Northern Dynasties (China): DS748.7+
Northern Han Kingdom: DS749.7+
Northern Mariana Islands: DU640+
Northern Morfu (African people) in
  Cameroon: DT571.N65
Northern Province (South Africa):
  DT2391+
Northern Qi (Ch'i) dynasty: DS748.7+
Northern Rhodesia: DT3031+
Northern Song dynasty: DS751+
Northern Territory of Australia: DU392+
Northern Thai: DS570.N67
Northern Transvaal (South Africa):
  DT2391+
Northern Wei dynasty: DS748.7+
Northern Zhou (Chou) dynasty:
  DS748.7+
Northern Zones (Spanish Morocco):
  DT330
Northwest Africa: DT179.2+
Northwest Frontier Province (Pakistan):
  DS392.N67
Norway, Jews in: DS135.N8+
Norwegians in Australia: DU122.N67
Norwegians in Laos: DS555.45.N67
Norwegians in New Zealand:
  DU424.5.N67
Nosairians in Syria: DS94.8.N67
Nossi-Be (Madagascar):
  DT469.M37N67
Nova Freixo (Mozambique):
  DT3415.C83
Nova Lisboa (Angola): DT1465.H83
Novo Redondo (Angola): DT1465.N58
Nso (African people) in Cameroon:
  DT571.N74
Ntomba (African people) in Congo
  (Democratic Republic): DT650.N85
Ntombi, Queen Regent: DT2800.N86
Ntumu (African people) in Cameroon:
  DT571.N78
Nu (Chinese people): DS731.N82
Nuanetsi (Zimbabwe): DT3025.M94
Nuaulu (Indonesian people):
  DS632.N83

Nuazira (Zimbabwe): DT3025.N83
Nuba (African people): DT155.2.N82
Nubi (African people) in Kenya:
  DT433.545.N83
Nubia
  Egypt: DT159.6.N83
  Sudan: DT159.6.N83
Nubians in Egypt: DT72.N83
Nuer (African people) in South Sudan:
  DT159.927.N84
Nuer in Ethiopia: DT380.4.N84
Nujoma, Sam: DT1641.N85
Nuku-hiva Island: DU701.N8
Nung in Vietnam: DS556.45.N85
Nunggubuyu (Australian people):
  DU125.N94
Nunu (African people) in Congo
  (Democratic Republic): DT650.N89
Nunuma (African people) in Burkina
  Faso: DT555.45.N84
Nupe (African people) in Nigeria:
  DT515.45.N86
Nurbāsh (Indic people): DS432.N87
Nuristani (Afghan people): DS354.6.K3
Nursia (Australia): DU380.N4
Nuzi (Ancient city): DS70.5.N9
Nyahkur in Thailand: DS570.N92
Nyakyusa (African people) in Tanzania:
  DT443.3.N92
Nyali (African people) in Congo
  (Democratic Republic): DT650.N92
Nyamwezi (African people) in Tanzania:
  DT443.3.N93
Nyandoro, George: DT2979.N93
Nyaneka (African people) in Angola:
  DT1308.N93
Nyanga (African people) in Congo
  (Democratic Republic): DT650.N93
Nyangatom (African people) in Ethiopia:
  DT380.4.N92
Nyanja (African people) in Malawi:
  DT3192.N83
Nyanja (African people) in Mozambique:
  DT3328.N93
Nyanja (African people) in Zambia:
  DT3058.N93

Nyankole (African people) in Uganda:
DT433.245.N9
Nyarafolo in Côte d'Ivoire:
DT545.45.N93
Nyasaland: DT3161+
Nyasaland Protectorate: DT3216+
Nyinba (Nepalese people):
DS493.9.N92
Nyishangba in Nepal: DS493.9.N94
Nyoro (African people) in Uganda:
DT433.245.N96
Nyulnyul (Australian people):
DU125.N96
Nyunga (Australian people):
DU125.N97
Nzabi (African people) in Congo
(Brazzaville): DT546.245.N93
Nzabi (African people) in Gabon:
DT546.145.N93
Nzakara in Central African Republic:
DT546.345.N83
Nzeto (Angola): DT1465.N94
Nzima (African people) in Ghana:
DT510.43.N95
Nzinga, Queen of Matamba:
DT1365.N95

O

O-wen-k'o in China: DS731.E85
Oahu (Hawaii): DU628.O3
Obasanjo administration
Nigeria: DT515.844
Obasanjo administration (Nigeria):
DT515.838
Obelisks
Ancient Egypt: DT62.O2
Obolo (African people) in Nigeria:
DT515.45.O23
Occupations
Gypsies: DX171
Occupied territories
Arab War, 1948-1949: DS126.96.O3
Arab War, 1967: DS127.6.O3
Oceania: DU1+
Oceania (Relations with the U.S.):
DU30

Ochollo (African people): DT380.4.O23
October Uprising 1931 (Cyprus):
DS54.85
Ogaden (Ethiopia): DT390.O33
Ogba (African people) in Nigeria:
DT515.45.O3
Ogoni (African people) in Nigeria:
DT515.45.O33
Ogori (African people) in Nigeria:
DT515.45.O34
Ogotai dynasty: DS22.3
Ohel Moshe (Jerusalem): DS109.8.O33
Oirats in Central Asia: DS328.4.O57
Oirats in Mongolia: DS798.422.O57
Okavango River and Swamp
Botswana: DT2520.O53
Namibia: DT1670.O63
Okkaligas in India: DS432.O4
Okrika (African people): DT515.45.O37
Oku in Cameroon: DT571.O38
Okun in Nigeria: DT515.45.O38
Olcha in China: DS731.O43
Older Maori: DU423.A34
Olivenca (Mozambique): DT3415.L87
Olives, Mount of (Jerusalem):
DS109.8.O4
Oltre Giuba (Italian colony): DT409.G58
Olympos (Turkey : Extinct city):
DS156.O49
Oman: DS247.O6+
Omayyads: DS97.2
Omdurman, Battle of, 1898
Sudan: DT156.65
Onge in India: DS432.O53
Operation Anaconda, 2002, (Afghan
War, 2001-): DS371.4123.O64
Operation Iron Triangle, 2006:
DS79.764.T55
Operation Restore Hope, 1992-1993
(Somalia): DT407.42
Ophel Archaeological Garden
Jerusalem: DS109.8.O62
Opium War: DS757.4+
Or Yehudah (Israel): DS110.O7
Oran (Algeria)
City: DT299.O7
Province: DT298.O8

Orang Asli in Malaysia: DS595.2.O73
Orange Free State, Claims by
  (Lesotho): DT2630+
Orange Free State (South Africa):
  DT2075+
Orange River Colony, 1900-1910
  (Orange Free State): DT2139
Orange river sovereignty (Orange Free
  State): DT2122
Oranje Vrystaat (South Africa):
  DT2075+
Oraon in Bangladesh: DS393.83.O73
Oraon in India: DS432.O7
Ordos (Mongolian people) in China:
  DS731.O73
Oriental Jews in Israel: DS113.8.S4
Orientalism
  Middle East: DS61.85
Origin, Maori: DU423.O74
Oriya (Indic people): DS432.O8
Oromo (African people) in Kenya:
  DT433.545.O74
Oromo (Ethiopia): DT390.G2
Oron in Nigeria: DT515.45.O74
Oroqen in China: DS731.O76
Orphans
  Sino-Japanese War, 1937-1945:
    DS777.533.C47
  Vietnam War: DS559.8.C53
Oshibat Site (Pakistan): DS392.2.O73
Osing (Indonesian people): DS632.O85
Osrhoene: DS156.O8
Ostraka
  Ancient Egypt: DT62.O88
Oswāls in India: DS432.O85
Otago (New Zealand): DU430.O8
Otaybah in Saudi Araba: DS219.U73
Ottoman Empire, Jews in: DS135.T8+
Ottoman period, 1517-1918 (Arab
  countries): DS38.8
Oueili, Tall al- (Iraq): DS70.5.O93
Ouermez Dere (Iraq): DS70.5.Q47
Ouled Naïl: DT346.O8
Oultanu (Berber people) in Morocco:
  DT313.3.I57
Ouobé (African people) in Côte d'Ivoire:
  DT545.45.O96

Ovambo (African people) in Angola:
  DT1308.O83
Ovambo (African people) in Congo
  (Democratic Republic): DT650.O92
Ovambo (African people) in Namibia:
  DT1558.O83
Overthrow of the Monarchy,1893
  Hawaiian Islands: DU627.19+
Owambo (Namibia): DT1670.O83
Owan (African people) in Nigeria:
  DT515.45.O88
Oxyrhynchus (Egypt): DT73.O8
Oyo (African people) in Nigeria:
  DT515.45.O93

P

Pacific, Control of the
  Oceania: DU29
Pacific Islanders in Australia: DU122.P3
Pacific Islanders in New Zealand:
  DU424.5.P33
Padagas in India: DS432.P2
Padam in India: DS432.P2115
Padma Sālēs in India: DS432.P212
Paekche Kingdom: DS911.755+
Pagalu (Equatorial Guinea):
  DT620.9.A65
Pagopago: DU819.P3
Paharia in Bangladesh: DS393.83.P33
Paharpur Site (Bangladesh):
  DS396.9.P35
Pahlavi dynasty: DS316.2+
Pai (Chinese people): DS731.P34
Pailibo (Indic people): DS432.P213
Paite (Asian people) in India:
  DS432.P214
Paiwan (Taiwan people):
  DS799.43.P34
Pakistan: DS376+
Pakpak (Indonesian people): DS632.P3
Pal Kshatriyas in India: DS432.P215
Palau Islands: DU780
Palaungs in Burma: DS528.2.P3
Palaungs in China: DS731.P35
Palawan (Philippine people):
  DS666.P34

Palestine: DS101+

Palestine problem: DS119.7+

Palestinian Arabs

  Massacre in Sabrā and Shātīlā:
    DS87.53

Palestinian Arabs in Australia:
  DU122.P34

Palestinian Arabs in Egypt: DT72.P35

Palestinian Arabs in Israel: DS113.6+

Palestinian Arabs in Jordan:
  DS153.55.P34

Palestinians in Lebanon: DS80.55.P34

Palettes

  Ancient Egypt: DT62.P34

Paliyan (Indic people): DS432.P218

Pallars in India: DS432.P22

Pallis in India: DS432.P23

Pallis in Sri Lanka: DS489.25.P35

Palmerston North (New Zealand):
  DU430.P34

Pampangan in the Philippines:
  DS666.P35

Pamphylia: DS156.P27

Panarabism: DS63.6

Panda, Zulu chief: DT1851.P35

Pāndes (Nepalese people):
  DS493.9.P35

Pang (South Asian people) in India:
  DS432.P2315

Panika in Bangladesh: DS393.83.P36

Panislamism: DS35.7

Panjabis in India: DS432.P232

Panjabis in Pakistan: DS380.P36

Panjabis in the Philippines: DS666.P36

Panjabis (South Asian people) in Kenya:
  DT433.545.P36

Panjabis (South Asian people) in New
  Zealand: DU424.5.P36

Pañjiriyarava in India: DS432.P2325

Panos (Indic people): DS432.P233

Pao-an (Chinese people): DS731.P36

Papel (African people) in Guinea-
  Bisseau: DT613.45.P36

Paphlagonia: DS156.P3

Papis in Iran: DS269.P3

Papua (Indonesia): DU744+

Papua New Guinea: DU740+

Papuans in Papua: DU744.35.P33

Paravis in India: DS432.P235

Pardhan (Indic people): DS432.P236

Pardhis (Indic people): DS432.P2365

Pare (African people) in Tanzania:
  DT443.3.A78

Pareek Brahmans: DS432.P237

Parhaiyas (Indic people): DS432.P24

Pāri (African people) in South Sudan:
  DT159.927.P37

Pariahs in India: DS432.P25

Parits in India: DS432.P255

Parji (Indic people): DS432.P26

Park ha-Sharon (Israel): DS110.P34

Park, Mungo: DT356

Parker Ranch (Hawaii): DU629.P3

Parkes, Sir Henry: DU172.P2

Parsees in India: DS432.P3

Parsees in Pakistan: DS380.P38

Parthian Empire: DS285

Partition, 1945 (Korea): DS917.43

Partition of Africa: DT31+

Pasargadae (Iran): DS262.P35

Pashai in Afghanistan: DS354.6.P37

Pasis in India: DS432.P36

Pass law demonstrations, 1956 (Union
  of South Africa): DT1939

Patidars in India: DS432.P43

Pattanavars (Indic people): DS432.P45

Patterson Expedition, 1878 (Zimbabwe):
  DT2953

Patua in India: DS432.J84

Paudi Bhuyan in India: DS432.P46

Paumoto Islands: DU890

Paundra Kshatriyas: DS432.P47

Pazeh (Taiwan people): DS799.43.P39

Peace

  Arab War, 1973: DS128.183

  Korean War, 1950-1953: DS921.75

Peace (Arab War, 1948-1949):
  DS126.983

Peace negotiations

  Persian Gulf War, 1990-1991:
    DS79.744.D55

  Vietnam War: DS559.7

Peace of Vereeniging, 1902: DT1920

Pedi (African people) in Botswana: DT2458.P44
Pedi (African people) in South Africa: DT1768.P44
Pedi (African people) in Zimbabwe: DT2913.P44
Pedi War, 1879 (Natal): DT2258
Peere in Cameroon: DT571.P44
Pelew Islands: DU780
Pella of the Decapolis (Jordan): DS154.9.P43
Pelusium (Egypt): DT73.P4
Pemba (Mozambique): DT3415.P45
Penan (Malaysian people): DS595.2.P44
Pende (African people) in Congo (Democratic Republic): DT650.P46
Pengo (Indic people): DS432.P55
Pepuza (Extinct city): DS156.P37
Per-Sopdu (Egypt): DT73.P47
Peranakan in Singapore: DS610.25.P47
Peregil Island (Morocco): DT328.P3
Pereira de Eça (Angola): DT1465.N55
Perga (Extinct city): DS156.P38
Pergamum: DS156.P4
Perikas: DS432.P56
Period of conquest (Angola): DT1367
Peroz: DS286.8
Persepolis (Iran): DS262.P4
Persian Empire: DS281+
Persian Gulf (General): DS326
Persian Gulf War: DS79.719+
Persian rule (Egypt): DT91
Personal narratives
  Arab War, 1948-1949: DS126.97
  Iraq War, 2003-: DS79.766
  Vietnam War: DS559.5
Perth (Australia): DU378
Peruvians in Japan: DS832.7.P47
Petaḥ-Tikṿah (Israel): DS110.P4
Petroglyphs
  Aboriginal Australians: DU124.P47
Petulengro, Gipsy: DX127.P4
Phalaborwa (African people) in South Africa: DT1768.P53
Phalo, Xhosa chief: DT1817.P53

Phaneromeni Site (Cyprus): DS54.95.P52
Phenicia: DS80+
Phi Tong Luang in Thailand: DS570.P48
Philae (Egypt): DT73.P5
Philippine Islands
  Commonwealth, 1935-1946: DS686+
Philippines: DS651+
Philippines, Jews in: DS135.P45
Philistines: DS90
Phillip, Arthur: DU172.P58
Philosophy, Maori: DU423.P52
Philosophy of Chinese history: DS736.5
Philosophy of Japanese history: DS834.98
Phoenix Islands: DU790
Photography
  Korean War: DS921.5.P46
Phraortes: DS279.3
Phrygia: DS156.P5
Phu Thai (Southeast Asian people) in Thailand: DS570.P49
Phuan in Thailand: DS570.P52
Pi-Ramesse (Egypt): DT73.P58
Pibelmen (Australian people): DU125.P44
Pieds noirs in Algeria: DT283.6.F7
Pietermaritzburg (South Africa): DT2405.P54
Pillage
  Persian Gulf War, 1990-1991: DS79.736
  Vietnam War: DS559.3
Pindarees in India: DS432.P6
Pingelop Atoll (Caroline Islands): DU568.P55
Pintubi (Australian people): DU125.P48
Pintupi (Australian people): DU125.P48
Pioneer Column, 1890 (Zimbabwe): DT2964
Piracy, Period of
  Algeria: DT291+
  Maghrib: DT201+
  Morocco: DT321+
  Tunisia: DT261+
Pirak (Pakistan): DS392.2.P57

INDEX

Pisidia: DS156.P58
Pitap (Indonesian people):
  DS646.32.P58
Pitcairn Island: DU800
Pitjandjara (Australian people):
  DU125.P5
Pitjantjatjara (Australian people):
  DU125.P5
Plaatje, Sol: DT1927.P53
Plant remains
  Ancient Egypt: DT62.P54
Pnar in India: DS432.P65
Pokomo (African people) in Kenya:
  DT433.545.P65
Poland, Jews in: DS134.5+
Poles in Algeria: DT283.6.P64
Poles in Australia: DU122.P6
Poles in Central Sub-Saharan Africa:
  DT352.43.P65
Poles in China: DS731.P64
Poles in India: DS432.P67
Poles in Maghrib: DT193.5.P64
Poles in New Zealand: DU424.5.P58
Poles in Nigeria: DT515.45.P64
Poles in Southern Africa: DT1058.P63
Poles in Syria: DS94.8.P64
Polish Jews in Israel: DS113.8.P64
Polish people in South Africa:
  DT1768.P65
Political antiquities
  Egyptology: DT65
Politics and government
  Aboriginal Australians: DU124.P64
Politics, Maori: DU423.P63
Poloat (Caroline Islands): DU568.P8
Polowat (Caroline Islands): DU568.P8
Polynesia: DU510
Polynesian Hawaiians: DU624.65
Polynesians in New Zealand:
  DU424.5.P6
Ponape (Caroline Islands): DU568.P7
Pondicherry (India): DS485.P66
Pondoland (South Africa): DT2400.P66
Pondos in South Africa: DT1768.P66
Pondos in Southern Africa:
  DT1058.P65
Pontus: DS156.P8

Pool of Siloam (Jerusalem):
  DS109.8.S5
Population, Maori: DU423.P66
Poravālas in India: DS432.P68
Poriyyah (Israel): DS110.P67
Port Elizabeth (South Africa):
  DT2405.P68
Port Said (Egypt): DT154.P7
Porto Amelia (Mozambique):
  DT3415.P45
Portraits
  Maori: DU422.8+
Portsmouth, Treaty of (Russo-Japanese
  War_): DS517.7
Portugal and East Asia: DS518.6
Portugal, Jews in: DS135.P7+
Portugália (Angola): DT1465.L83
Portuguese civilization (India): DS427.5
Portuguese claims
  Equatorial Africa: DT620.65+
  Malawi: DT3211+
  Namibia: DT1587+
  Zaire: DT654+
Portuguese colony and territory
  Guinea-Bissau: DT613.75+
Portuguese expansion (Angola):
  DT1373+
Portuguese Guinea: DT613+
Portuguese in Angola: DT1308.P68
Portuguese in Asia: DS28.P67
Portuguese in Gambia: DT509.45.P67
Portuguese in Hawaii: DU624.7.P67
Portuguese in India: DS498+
Portuguese in Japan: DS832.7.P67
Portuguese in Mozambique:
  DT3328.P68
Portuguese in South Africa:
  DT1768.P67
Portuguese penetration (Kenya):
  DT433.565+
Portuguese-speaking West Africa:
  DT591+
Portuguese Timor: DS649.2+
Post-Persian Gulf War, 1991-2003:
  DS79.75+
Potchefstroom, Siege of, 1880-1881:
  DT2359.P68

Potgieter, A.H.: DT2335.P68
Pottery
  Ancient Egypt: DT62.P72
Pramalai Kallans: DS432.P73
Press
  Afghan War, 2001-: DS371.4135
  Iraq War, 2003-: DS79.767.P74
  Persian Gulf War, 1990-1991:
    DS79.739
  Vietnam War: DS559.46
Press coverage
  South African War: DT1918.P73
Pretoria (South Africa): DT2403+
Pretoria-Witwatersrand-Vereeniging
  (South Africa): DT2380+
Pretorius, Andries: DT2335.P84
Pretorius, M.W.: DT2350.P84
Prisoners
  Aboriginal Australians: DU124.P72
Prisoners and prisons
  Korean War: DS921+
  Sino-Japanese War, 1937-1945:
    DS777.533.P75
  South African War: DT1918.P75
  Vietnam War: DS559.4
Prisoners of war
  Iraq War, 2003-: DS79.767.D38
Private antiquities (Egyptology): DT66
Private collections
  Egyptology: DT57.5
Propaganda
  Persian Gulf War, 1990-1991:
    DS79.739
  Revolution
    Angola, 1961-1975: DT1413.P76
  Sino-Japanese War, 1937-1945:
    DS777.533.P76
  Vietnam War: DS559.8.P65
Protection
  Korean War: DS921.3
  Sino-Japanese War, 1937-1945:
    DS777.533.R45
Protest movements
  Iraq War, 2003-: DS79.767.P76
  Persian Gulf War, 1990-1991:
    DS79.744.P74

Protest movements
  Sino-Japanese War, 1937-1945:
    DS777.533.P78
  South African War: DT1918.P77
  Vietnam War: DS559.6+
Psychological aspects
  Iraq War, 2003-: DS79.767.P79
  Korean War: DS921.5.P78
  Persian Gulf War, 1990-1991:
    DS79.744.P78
  Vietnam War: DS559.8.P7
Psychological warfare
  Korean War: DS921.5.P78
Ptolemais (Egypt): DT73.P8
Ptolemies, King of Egypt: DT92+
Pu-i (Chinese people): DS731.P84
P'u-mi (Chinese people): DS731.P844
Public antiquities
  Egyptology: DT65
Public opinion
  Arab War, 1948-1949: DS126.96.P8
  Iraq War, 2003-: DS79.767.P83
  Sino-Japanese War, 937-1945:
    DS777.533.P82+
  South African war: DT1918.P83
  Vietnam War: DS559.6+
Publicity
  Afghan War, 2001-: DS371.4135
  Persian Gulf War, 1990-1991:
    DS79.739
  Vietnam War: DS559.46
Puerto Ricans in Hawaii: DU624.7.P83
Pukapuka Island (New Zealand):
  DU430.P8
Pulang (Southeast Asian people) in
  China: DS731.P85
Pulayan in India: DS432.P76
Pulayas: DS432.P78
Puluwat (Caroline Islands): DU568.P8
Pumi (Chinese people): DS731.P844
Punan (Bornean people):
  DS646.32.P85
Pungua-Ndongo, Siege of, 1671:
  DT1380
Punjab, West: DS392.P8
Punt Kingdom (Eritrea): DT398.P8
Punu (African people): DT546.145.P86

Pupput Site (Tunisia): DT269.P85
Purum (Indic people): DS432.P8
Pushkarna Brahmans in India:
  DS432.P84
Pushtuns: DS354.58
Pushtuns in Australia: DU122.P87
Pushtuns in Pakistan: DS380.P8
Pūskān Site (Iran): DS262.P84
Puyuma (Taiwan people):
  DS799.43.P89
Pygmies: DT16.P8
Pygmies in Cameroon: DT571.P93
Pygmies in Congo (Democratic
  Republic): DT650.P94
Pygmies in French West Africa:
  DT530.5.P94
Pygmies in Gabon: DT546.145.P94
Pyramids
  Ancient Egypt: DT63+
Pyu in Burma: DS528.2.P95

Q

Qabāṭīyah (Israel): DS110.Q23
Qacha's Nek (Lesotho): DT2686.Q33
Qafṣah (Tunisia): DT269.Q24
Qajar dynasty: DS298+
Qalandar in Pakistan: DS380.Q35
Qālūniyā (Israel): DS110.Q25
Qarara Site (Egypt): DT73.Q33
Qarqur, Tall (Syria): DS99.Q228
Qashish Site (Israel): DS110.Q317
Qashqāʾī (Turkic people) in Iran:
  DS269.K3
Qaṣr-i Abū Naṣr Site (Iran): DS262.Q26
Qasr Ibrim (Egypt): DT73.I27
Qaṣr Qārūn (Egypt): DT73.D56,
  DT73.Q35
Qaṣr wa-al-Ṣayyād Site (Egypt):
  DT73.Q38
Qatar: DS247.Q3+
Qaṭīf: DS247.9.Q28
Qays: DS36.9.Q38
Qi (Ch'i) dynasty: DS748.6+
Qiang people in china: DS731.C48
Qifṭ (Egypt): DT73.Q54

Qin (Chin) dynasty
  221-207 B.C: DS747.5+
Qitmit Site (Israel): DS110.Q58
Qīzān: DS247.9.Q58
Qomemiyyut (Jerusalem):
  DS109.8.Q65
Quarries
  Egyptology: DT62.Q8
Qubaybah Site (Israel): DS110.Q75
Qubbat al-Hawā' Site (Egypt):
  DT73.Q72
Que Que (Zimbabwe): DT3025.K84
Queensland (Australia): DU250+
Quietude in Japan: DS827.Q5
Quit India Movement, 1942: DS480.82
Qumran Site (West Bank): DS110.Q8
Qūqān (Israel): DS110.Q84
Quraysh in Saudi Arabia: DS219.Q7
Qurna, el (Egypt): DT73.Q75
Qurnat Murā'i Hill (Egypt): DT73.Q76
Qusayr al-Qadīm (Egypt): DT73.Q77
Quthing (Lesotho): DT2686.Q87
QwaQwa (South Africa): DT2400.Q83

R

Ra'ananah (Israel): DS110.R22
Rabaris in India: DS432.R13
Rabha in India: DS432.R2
Rabi Das in India: DS432.R232
Race relations
  Angola: DT1306
  Botswana: DT2456
  Cape Province: DT2032
  Malawi: DT3190
  Namibia: DT1555
  South Africa: DT1756
  Southern Africa: DT1056
  Transvaal: DT2322+
  Zambia: DT3056
  Zimbabwe: DT2912
Racially mixed people in Southern
  Africa: DT1058.R33
Radama, King of Madagascar
  I: DT469.M323
  II: DT469.M326
Rade in French Indonesia: DS539.R3

Raghuvaṃsīs: DS432.R236
Rahanweyn in Somalia: DT402.4.R35
Rahaṭ (Israel): DS110.R24
Rai (Nepalese people): DS493.9.R34
Raigaras (Indic people): DS432.R238
Rajapurohitas in India: DS432.R24
Rajbangsi in India: DS432.R25
Rajbangsi (Nepalese people):
  DS493.9.R35
Rājī (Indic people): DS432.R27
Rājī (Nepalese people): DS493.9.R36
Rajput in India: DS432.R3
Rajput in Pakistan: DS380.R32
Rajuar (Indic people): DS432.R314
Rākshāina in Bangladesh:
  DS393.83.R34
Rām Allāh: DS110.R324
Rāmakṣatriya: DS432.R317
Ramat-Gan (Israel): DS110.R325
Ramat ha-Kovesh (Israel): DS110.R326
Ramat-ha-Sharon (Israel): DS110.R327
Ramat Hanadiv (Region)
  Israel: DS110.R3273
Ramat Menasheh (Israel): DS110.R328
Ramat Raḥel (Israel): DS110.R34
Ramat Yishai (Israel): DS110.R348
Ramesseum (Egypt): DT73.T33
Ramgarhia in India: DS432.R32
Ramlah (Israel): DS110.R36
Ramo (Indic people): DS432.R33
Ramon, Mount (Israel): DS110.R365
Ramot Alon (Jerusalem): DS109.8.R35
Ramses, King of Egypt
  II: DT88
  III: DT88.8
  IV: DT88.82
Ranavalona (Ranavalo), Queen of
  Madagascar
  I: DT469.M324
  II: DT469.M33
  III: DT469.M335
Rand Gold rush begins, 1886 (South
  Africa): DT1888
Rand Revolt, 1922 (Union of South
  Africa): DT1935
Rangi (African people) in Tanzania:
  DT443.3.R35

Rangitane (Maori people): DU424.R35
Raqqada (Tunisia): DT269.R35
Ras al Khaimah: DS247.R37+
Ras Taffari (Tafari Makonnen):
  DT387.6
Rashāyidah (Arab people):
  DT155.2.R37
Rasoherina, Queen of Madagascar:
  DT469.M328
Raute (Nepalese people): DS493.9.R38
Reconnaissance operations
  Vietnam War: DS559.8.R43
Reconstruction
  Korean War: DS921.8
Reddys in India: DS432.R39
Refugees
  Afghan War, 2001-: DS371.415
  Iraq War, 2003-: DS79.767.R43
  Korean War: DS921.3
  Sino-Japanese War, 1937-1945:
    DS777.533.R45
  Vietnam War: DS559.63
Rega in Congo (Democratic Republic):
  DT650.R43
Regimental histories: DS918.4+
Registers, lists, etc.
  Vietnam War: DS559
Registers of dead
  Revolution
    Angola, 1961-1975: DT1413.R44
Reḥavyah (Jerusalem): DS109.8.R45
Rehoboth Basters in Namibia:
  DT1558.R45
Rehoboth Basters in South Africa:
  DT1768.R45
Rehoboth Basters' Rebellion, 1925:
  DT1632
Rehoboth Basters' settlement, 1868:
  DT1597
Rehoboth Basters Uprising, 1915:
  DT1622
Rehoboth (Namibia): DT1685.R46
Reḥovot (Israel): DS110.R4
Rejang (Indonesian people):
  DS632.R44
Relief work
  Afghan War, 2001-: DS371.415

Relief work
  Iraq War, 2003-: DS79.767.R43
  Korean War: DS921.3
  Sino-Japanese War, 1937-1945:
    DS777.533.R45
  Vietnam War: DS559.63
Religion
  Aboriginal Australians: DU124.R44
Religion, Gypsy: DX151
Religious antiquities
  Ancient Egypt: DT68+
Religious aspects
  Iraq War, 2003-: DS79.767.R45
  Persian Gulf War, 1990-1991:
    DS79.744.R44
  South African War: DT1918.R44
Rembarrnga (Australian people):
  DU125.R45
Rembong (Indonesian people):
  DS632.R46
Rendille (African people) in Kenya:
  DT433.545.R45
Rengma (Indic people): DS432.R44
Repatriation
  Korean War: DS921.2
Repatriation of the dead
  Vietnam War: DS559.8.D38
Republic of Liberia: DT634+
Republic of South Africa: DT1945+
Republic of Vietnam: DS556+
Research, Maori: DU423.R47
Resistance movements, 1905-1945
  (Korea): DS916.59+
Retief, Piet: DT2235.R48
  Death of: DT2245+
Reunification question, 1945- (Korea):
  DS917.44+
Réunion: DT469.R3+
Revivim (Israel): DS110.R48
Revolution
  Angola, 1961-1975: DT1398+
  Equatorial Guinea, 1979: DT620.8+
  Guinea-Bissau, 1963-1974: DT613.78
Revolution, 1921 (Mongolia): DS798.8+
Reza Shah Pahlavi: DS317
Rhade in Vietnam: DS556.45.R48
Rhodes, Cecil John: DT1851.R56

Riang in India: DS432.R5
Rif (Berber people) in Morocco:
  DT313.3.R53
Rif Mountains (Morocco): DT328.R5
Rijim, Tall (Iraq): DS70.5.R54
Rimālas (Nepalese people):
  DS493.9.R55
Rinatyah (Israel): DS110.R49
Rio de Oro: DT346.S7
Rishōn le-Tsiyon (Israel): DS110.R5
Rites and ceremonies
  Aboriginal Australians: DU124.R57
Rites and ceremonies, Maori:
  DU423.R55
Rizeiqāt (Egypt): DT73.R5
Roberto, Holden: DT1417.R63
Robets, Joseph Jenkins: DT634.3.R6
Rock Chapel of Horemheb (Egypt):
  DT73.S56
Rock paintings
  Aboriginal Australians: DU124.P47
Rock Temple of el-Derr (Egypt):
  DT73.D492
Rodiya in Sri Lanka: DS489.25.R63
Rodrigues Island: DT469.M492
Roglai in Vietnam: DS556.45.R63
Rogoro (African people) in Tanzania:
  DT443.3.R64
Rohilla (Indic people): DS432.R65
Rohingya in Bangladesh:
  DS393.83.R64
Rohingya in Burma: DS528.2.R64
Rohtas Fort (Pakistan): DS392.2.R64
Rolong (African people) in Botswana:
  DT2458.R75
Rolong (African people) in South Africa:
  DT1768.R65
Roman period (North Africa): DT170
Roman rule (Egypt): DT93.A1+
Romania, Jews in: DS135.R7+
Romanian Jews in Israel: DS113.8.R65
Romanies: DX101+
Romanies in Israel: DS113.8.G95
Rorke's Drift, Battle of: DT1879.R68
Rosh ha-'Ayin (Israel): DS110.R57
Rosh Pinah (Israel): DS110.R6
Rosh Zayit Site (Israel): DS110.R65

Rotorua (New Zealand): DU430.R6
Rottnest Island (Australia): DU380.R68
Rozwi Empire, ca. 1700-1834: DT2947
Rozwi Kingdoms: DT1117
Ruanda-Urundi: DT450+
Rub 'al Khālīl: DS247.R8+
Ruc in Vietnam: DS556.45.R82
Rudd Concession, 1888 (Zimbabwe): DT2957
Rue (African people) in Mozambique: DT3328.R83
Rufa al-Hoi (African people): DT155.2.R83
Rukai (Taiwan people): DS799.43.R85
Rukuba (African people) in Nigeria: DT515.45.R84
Rulers (Sudan): DT155.42
Rundi: DT450.65.R86
Rungus (Malaysian people): DS597.335.R85
Rūpīni (Indic people): DS432.R86
Russel, George: DU222.R8
Russia (Federation), Jews in: DS134.8+
Russian Empire, Jews in: DS134.8+
Russian Jews in Israel: DS113.8.R87
Russians in Africa: DT16.R87
Russians in Australia: DU122.R8
Russians in China: DS731.R9
Russians in East Asia: DS509.5.R87
Russians in Egypt: DT72.R87
Russians in Hawaii: DU624.7.R87
Russians in Japan: DS832.7.R8
Russians in the Philippines: DS666.R85
Russians in Tunisia: DT253.2.R8
Russo-Japanese War: DS516+
Ruvu (African people): DT443.3.R88
Ruwenzori Mountains: DT361+
Ruzhen dynasty: DS751.92+
Rwanda: DT450+
Rwanda Civil War, 1994: DT450.435+
Rwanda Kingdom: DT450.34+
Rwandan Genocide, 1994: DT450.435+
Rwandans in Kenya: DT433.545.R83
Ryukyuans in Hawaii: DU624.7.R97

S

Sá da Bandeira (Angola): DT1465.L85
Sa'adim Site (Israel): DS110.S2
Sabah: DS597.33+
Sabians in Iran: DS269.M36
Sabratha (Libya): DT239.S115
Sack of the Great Zimbabwe by Zwangendaba's Ngoni, 1835: DT2949
Sacrifice, Human
  India: DS422.S2
Sadāna (Indic people): DS432.S13
Sadat, Anwar, President of Egypt: DT107.85
Sadr City, Battle of, 2008: DS79.764.B35
Ṣafāqis (Tunisia): DT269.S4
Safi I: DS292.7
Safi II (Suleiman): DS292.9
Safi (Morocco): DT329.S12
Sagalassos: DS156.S25
Sahafatra (Malagasy people): DT469.M277S33
Sahara: DT331+
Sahara (Libya): DT238.S3
Saharia (Indic people): DS432.S15
Sahel: DT521+
Sahu (Indonesian people): DS632.S32
Ṣa'īdīs (Ṣa'āyidah) in Egypt: DT72.S25
Saidu Sharif I Site (Pakistan): DS392.2.S24
Saint Brandon Island: DT469.M493
Saint Helena: DT671.S2
Saipan: DU648.S35
Saisiyat (Taiwan people): DS799.43.S24
Saka in Central Asia: DS328.4.S35
Sakalava (Malagasy people): DT469.M277S35
Ṣakhr in Jordan: DS153.55.S34
Sakkara (Egypt): DT73.S3
Sakudei (Indonesian people): DS632.S33
Śākyas in Nepal: DS493.9.S25
Salagama in Sri Lanka: DS489.25.S25
Salar (Chinese people): DS731.S24
Salghurids: DS288.9

Salisbury (Zimbabwe): DT3022
Salt, Henry: DT102.S2
Saluan (Indonesian people): DS632.S34
Samals (Philippine people): DS666.S3
Samanids: DS288.5
Samaria Region: DS110.S3
Samaritans: DS129
Samburu (African people): DT433.545.S26
Sambyu (African people) in Namibia: DT1558.S36
Samo (African people) in Mali: DT551.45.S24
Samoa: DU819.A2
Samoan Islands: DU810+
Samoans in Australia: DU122.S25
Samoans in Hawaii: DU624.7.S36
Samoans in New Zealand: DU424.5.S2
Samora, Machel: DT3393
Samory invasions (Burkina Faso): DT555.65+
Samrā' Site (Jordan): DS154.9.S27
Samurai: DS827.S3
San (African people) in Angola: DT1308.S35
San (African people) in Botswana: DT2458.S26
San (African people) in Namibia: DT1558.S38
San (African people) in South Africa: DT1768.S36
San (African people) in Southern Africa: DT1058.S36
San Chay in Vietnam: DS556.45.S24
San Diu in Vietnam: DS556.45.S25
San Marino, Jews in: DS135.S24
Sanctions
   Persian Gulf War, 1990-1991: DS79.744.S25
Sand River Convention, 1852 (Transvaal): DT2344
Sandwich Islands: DU620+
Sanga people (African people): DT650.S25
Sangar (Indic people): DS432.S16
Sangir in Indonesia: DS632.S35

Sangir in the Philippines: DS666.S34
Sango (Zimbabwe): DT3025.S36
Sankēti (Indic people): DS432.S17
Sansi in India: DS432.S18
Santa Comba (Mozambique): DT3415.M35
Santa Cruz Islands: DU840
Santal (Indic people) in Bangladesh: DS393.83.S36
Santal (South Asian people) in Nepal: DS493.9.S26
Santia (Indic people): DS432.S22
São in Chad: DT546.445.S25
São Salvador do Congo (Angola): DT1465.M42
Sao Tome and Principe: DT615+
Sao Tome and Principe, Jews in: DS135.S26
Sapiny (African people) in Uganda: DT433.245.S24
Sapua Kelas (Indic people): DS432.S25
Sara (African people) in Chad: DT546.445.S37
Sarab Site (Iran): DS262.S27
Sarābīṭ al-Khādim Site (Egypt): DT73.S35
Saraks in India: DS432.S3
Saraswats in India: DS432.S35
Sarawak: DS597.36+
Sarayūpārin Brahmans in India: DS432.S357
Sarbadarids: DS289.4
Sardanapalus: DS73.87
Sardis (Ancient city): DS156.S3
Sargon II: DS73.8
Sarhili, Xhosa chief: DT1851.S37
Sarmi (Indonesian people): DS632.S37
Sasak (Indonesian people): DS632.S38
Sassanian Empire: DS286+
Sassanids: DS186+
Satawal (Caroline Islands): DU568.S37
Satnāmīs (Indic people): DS432.S359
Saʿūd: DS244.56
Saudi Arabia: DS201+
Saurashtra in India: DS432.S36
Saurashtrians in India: DS432.S36
Saurimo (Angola): DT1465.S38

Savage Island (New Zealand): DU430.N5

Savara (Indic people): DS432.S37

Savimbi, Jonas: DT1424.S38

Sawu (Indonesian people): DS632.S39

Sayyālah (Egypt): DT73.S38

Sayyid dynasty: DS459.6

Scandinavia, Jews in: DS135.S32

Scandinavians in Australia: DU122.S3

Scandinavians in South Africa: DT1768.S43

Scarabs
  Ancient Egypt: DT62.S3

Science and technology
  Persian Gulf War, 1990-1991: DS79.744.S34
  Vietnam War: DS559.8.S3

Scopus, Mount: DS109.8.S36

Scots in Africa: DT16.S35

Scots in Australia: DU122.S4

Scots in New Zealand: DU424.5.S3

Scots in South Africa: DT1768.S46

Scots-Irish in New Zealand: DU424.5.S33

Sealand (Arabian Peninsula): DS247.S4+

Search and rescue operations
  Korean War: DS921.5.S4
  Vietnam War: DS559.8.S4

Sebele I: DT2493.S43

Sebitoane: DT2486.S43

Sebituane: DT3081.S43

Sechele: DT2486.S44

Secret service
  Iraq War, 2003-: DS79.767.S75
  Korean War: DS921.5.S7+
  Sino-Vietnam War, 1937-1945: DS777.533.S65

Secularism
  India: DS422.S43

Sedang in Vietnam: DS556.45.S44

Sekgoma: DT2493.S45

Sekhukhune: DT2350.S45

Sekhukhune's Stronghold, Battle of, 1879: DT2784

Sekia el Hamra: DT346.S7

Seksawa (Berber people) in Morocco: DT313.3.S44

Selebi-Phikwe (Botswana): DT2525.S45

Seletar (Malaysian people): DS595.2.S37

Seleucia Babylonia: DS70.5.S45

Seleucia on the Euphrates (Ancient city): DS156.Z48

Seleucia on the Tigris: DS70.5.S45

Seleucids: DS284.9

Seljuks: DS27+
  Persia: DS288.8

Selous, Frederick: DT2963.S45

Selukwe (Zimbabwe): DT3025.S58

Selung in Burma: DS528.2.M58, DS528.2.S34

Semang (Malayan people): DS595.2.S4

Semang (Malaysian people) in Thailand: DS570.S42

Seme, P. Ka I.: DT1927.S46

Semelai (Malaysian people): DS595.2.S43

Semiramis: DS73.74

Semites in Asia: DS16

Senegal: DT549+

Senegal, Jews in: DS135.S34

Senegambia: DT532.25

Sengoku period: DS868+

Sennacherib: DS73.83

Sennar (Sudan): DT159.6.S46

Senoi (Indonesian people): DS632.S45

Senoi (Malaysian people): DS595.2.S3

Senoi (Malaysian people) in Thailand: DS570.S44

Sentinelese (Indic people): DS432.S42

Senufo (African people) in Côte d'Ivoire: DT545.45.S44

Senufo (African people) in West Africa: DT474.6.S45

Separatist revolt, 1823 (Angola): DT1382

Sephardim: DS133+

Sephardim in Israel: DS113.8.S4

Sepphoris (Extinct city)
  Israel: DS110.S43

Seppuku: DS827.S46

Serbia, Jews in: DS135.S35+
Serbs in Australia: DU122.S47
Serers (African people) in Senegal: DT549.45.S47
Serowe (Botswana): DT2525.S47
Serpa Pinto (Angola): DT1465.M46
Serra East Site (Sudan): DT159.9.S47
Seventh Xhosa War: DT1855
Sexual behavior, Maori: DU423.S48
Seychelles: DT469.S4+
Sgaw Karen (Southeast Asian people): DS570.S46
Sha'ar ha-Golan Site (Israel): DS110.S5
Shaba Invasions, 1977-1978: DT658.25
Shaba (Zaire): DT665.K3
Shabani (Zimbabwe): DT3025.Z95
Shabwa: DS247.7.S52
Shagari administration (Nigeria): DT515.84
Shāh'dizh (Iran): DS262.S48
Shāhjahān: DS461.6
Shahr-i Sokhta (Iran): DS262.S515
Shahsevan in Iran: DS269.S53
Shahwani in Pakistan: DS380.S45
Shaikia (Arab people): DT155.2.S45
Shaka Stevens administration (Sierra Leone): DT516.815+
Shalmaneser
  I: DS73.45
  II: DS73.73
  III: DS73.75
  IV: DS73.78
Shambala (African people) in Tanzania: DT443.3.S45
Shammar in Saudi Arabia: DS219.S38
Shan State: DS530.8.S45
Shandar (Bangladeshi people): DS393.83.S43
Shang (Yin) dynasty: DS744+
Shangaan, War with (Mozambique): DT3381
Shangana: DT3364.S5
Shanhūr (Egypt): DT73.S5
Shans in Burma: DS528.2.S5
Shans in Thailand: DS570.S52
Shapur I: DS286.3

Shapur II: DS286.5
Shapur III: DS286.53
Shāpūr (Iran): DS262.S52
Sharārāt in Saudi Arabia: DS219.S43
Shāriqah, ash: DS247.S5+
Sharīqiyah Governorate (Egypt): DT73.S53
Sharon, Plain of (Israel): DS110.S53
Sharonah (Israel): DS110.S534
Sharpe, Alfred: DT3219.S53
Sharpeville Massacre, 1960 (South Africa): DT1941
Sharpeville Massacre Anniversary, 1985: DT1965
Sharqīyah (Saudi Arabia): DS247.9.S52
Shārūnah Site (Egypt): DT73.S54
Shaybān in Saudi Arabia: DS219.S45
Shaykh Ḥasan Site (Syria): DS99.S39
Shayzar Site (Syria): DS99.S395
She (Chinese people): DS731.S54
Shechem (Extinct city)
  West Bank: DS110.S543
Shefar'am (Israel): DS110.S546
Sheikh Jarrah (Jerusalem): DS109.8.S44
Shekhunat ha-nHabashim (Jerusalem): DS109.8.S45
Shenyang, Siege of (Russo-Japanese War): DS517.4
Shephelah: DS110.S555
Shepstone, Theophilus: DT2254.S54
Sherbro (African people) in Sierra Leone: DT516.45.S45
Sherdukpen in India: DS432.S45
Shere Ali: DS364+
Sherpas in Nepal: DS493.9.S5
Shī'ah in Lebanon: DS80.55.S54
Shiites in Iraq: DS70.8.S55
Shiites in Saudi Arabia: DS219.S47
Shikmonah (Extinct city)
  Israel: DS110.S557
Shilluk (African people) in South Sudan: DT159.927.S55
Shilluks (African people): DT155.2.S46
Shiloh (Extinct city): DS110.S558
Shiltā (Israel): DS110.S57

Ships
  Ancient Egypt: DT62.S55
Shira (African people): DT546.145.S55
Shire River and Valley (Malawi):
  DT3252.S55
Shisilweni (Swaziland): DT2820.S55
Shivalli Brahmans in India:
  DS432.S455
Shivta (Extinct city): DS110.S58
Shoes
  Ancient Egypt: DT62.S57
Shok Valley, Battle, 2008:
  DS371.4123.S56
Shomerah (Israel): DS110.S585
Shompen in India: DS432.S46
Shona (African people) in Zimbabwe:
  DT2913.S55
Shona Revolt, 1896-1897 (Zimbabwe):
  DT2970
Shōwa (Hirohito): DS888.15+
Shubat-Enlil (Syria): DS99.S44
Shudras in India: DS432.S47
Shuḥūḥ in Saudi Arabia: DS219.S58
Shuja Shah: DS359.7
Shurugwe (Zimbabwe): DT3025.S58
Shuwayrah, Tall (Syria): DS99.S5
Shuyūkh (West Bank): DS110.S59
Si La in Vietnam: DS556.45.S5
Sibo (Chinese people): DS731.S57
Sidamas in Ethiopia: DT380.4.S5
Siddhi (Indic people): DS432.S49
Siddi (Indic people): DS432.S49
Siddiquis (South Asian people):
  DS339.3.S53
Sierra Leone: DT516+
Sikhs: DS432.S5
Sikhs in Australia: DU122.S54
Sikhs in Malaysia: DS595.2.S55
Sikhs in Singapore: DS610.25.S54
Sikligars in India: DS432.S6
Silla Kingdom: DS911.715+
Silsila, Gebel el-. (Egypt): DT73.S56
Silva Porto (Angola): DT1465.K85
Silva Porto, Francisco da: DT1376.S56
Simelungun (Indonesian people):
  DS632.S5
Simithu (Tunisia): DT269.S57

Sin, Tall: DS99.S55
Sinai Peninsula (Egypt): DT137.S55
Sind: DS392.S5+
Sindhi in India: DS432.S64
Sindhi in Pakistan: DS380.S53
Sindhollus in India: DS432.S66
Singapore: DS608+
Sinhalese in Sri Lanka: DS489.25.S5
Sino-French War, 1884-1885: DS549
Sino-Japanese Conflict, 1931-1933:
  DS777.5+
Sino-Japanese War, 1894-1895:
  DS764.4+
Sino-Japanese War, 1937-1945:
  DS777.52+
Sino-Vietnamese Conflict, 1979:
  DS559.915+
Sinope: DS156.S6
Sipolilo (Zimbabwe): DT3025.G87
Sipopa: DT3081.S56
Sippar (Ancient city): DS70.5.S55
Sīrāf (Iran): DS262.S57
Siraiki in Pakistan: DS380.S55
Siraya in Taiwan: DS799.43.S57
Sisalo (African people) in Ghana:
  DT510.43.S57
Sisulu, Walter: DT1949.S58
Sisupalgarh (Extinct city): DS486.S576
Siteki (Swaziland): DT2825.S58
Sithole, Ndabaningi: DT2984.S58
Siwa Oasis (Egypt): DT154.S5
Six dynasties: DS748.17+
Siyalk, Tepe (Iran): DS262.S59
Skeleton Coast (Nambibia):
  DT1670.S64
Slaghter's Nek incident, 1815 (South
  Africa): DT1839
Slave kings of Delhi: DS459+
Slavs in the Islamic World:
  DS35.625.S55
Slovakia, Jews in: DS135.S55+
Slovenia, Jews in: DS135.S57+,
  DS135.S57
Smerdis: DS282.6
Smith, Ian: DT2984.S65
Smuts, Jan Christiaan: DT1927.S68

So (Southeast Asian people) in
Thailand: DS570.S65
Sobhuza II: DT2802
Sobo (African people) in Nigeria:
DT515.45.S63
Social aspects
Iraq War, 2003-: DS79.767.S63
Korean War: DS921.5.S63
Sino-Japanese War, 1937-1945:
DS777.533.S62
Vietnam War: DS559.8.S6
Social conditions
Aboriginal Australians: DU124.S63
Social conditions, Maori: DU423.S6
Social life and customs
Aboriginal Australians: DU124.S64
Social life and customs, Maori:
DU423.S63
Socialist Republic of Vietnam:
DS559.912+
Society Islands: DU870
Sofala, Attack of (Mozambique):
DT3370
Sofala (Mozambique): DT3410.S65
Soga (African people) in Uganda:
DT433.245.S64
Sogdians (Chinese people):
DS731.S63
Solgas (Indic people): DS432.S69
Soli (African people) in Zambia:
DT3058.S65
Solomon Islanders in Australia:
DU122.S65
Solomon Islands: DU850
Solongo (African people) in Congo
(Democratic Republic): DT650.S53
Somali-Ethiopian Conflict, 1977-:
DT387.952
Somalia: DT401+
Somalia Affair, 1992-1997: DT407.43
Somaliland: DT401+
Somalis in Ethiopia: DT380.4.S65
Somalis in foreign countries (General):
DT402.45
Somalis in Kenya: DT433.545.S75
Somanis in India: DS432.S7
Somavasī Kshatriyas: DS432.S73

Somba (African people) in Benin:
DT541.45.S65
Somba (African people) in Togo:
DT582.45.S65
Somono (African people) in Mali:
DT551.45.S65
Song (Sung) dynasty: DS751+
Songhai (African people) in French
West Africa: DT530.5.S65
Songhai (African people) in Mali:
DT551.45.S66
Songhai (African people) in Niger:
DT547.45.S65
Songhai Empire: DT532.27
Songye (African people) in Congo
(Democratic Republic): DT650.S55
Soninke (African people) in Mali:
DT551.45.S67
Soninke (African people) in Senegal:
DT549.45.S66
Soninke in Mauritania: DT554.45.S65
Sonjo (African people) in Tanzania:
DT443.3.S75
Sonowal Kachari (Indic people):
DS432.S735
Soods: DS432.S74
Soonde in Congo (Democratic
Republic): DT650.S57
Sorbs in Australia: DU122.S67
Sosso (African people) in Angola:
DT1308.S68
Sotho (African people) in Botswana):
DT2458.S78
Sotho (African people) in South Africa:
DT1768.S68
Sotho, War against the (Orange Free
State)
1858: DT2129
1865-1866: DT2133
Soudanese Republic: DT551+
Souhtern Tang Kingdom: DS749.7+
South Africa: DT1701+
South Africa, Jews in: DS135.S6+
South African administration
Namibia: DT1638+
South African in foreign countries
(General): DT1770

South African incursions, 1978-:
DT1436

South African invasions, 1975-1976
(Angola): DT1430

South African Jews in Israel:
DS113.8.S65

South African Mandate: DT1625+

South African Mandate, 1966,
Cancellation of: DT1643

South African Native National Congress,
1912, Founding of: DT1931

South African Republic: DT2291+

South African War, 1899-1902:
DT1890+

South Africans in Tanzania:
DT443.3.S77

South Asians in East Africa:
DT429.5.S68

South Asians in Kenya: DT433.545.S77

South Asians in Tanzania:
DT443.3.S78

South Island (N.Z.): DU430.S57

South Moluccas: DS646.69.S69

South Seas: DU1+

South Vietnam: DS556+

South-West Africa: DT1501+

Southeast Asia: DS520+

Southern Africa: DT1001+

Southern Anhui Incident, 1941:
DS777.534

Southern Asia: DS331+

Southern dynasties: DS748.17+

Southern Han Kingdom: DS749.7+

Southern Lunda (African people) in
Zambia: DT3058.S68

Southern Ming dynasty: DS753.75

Southern Ping (Jing Nan) Kingdom:
DS749.7+

Southern Rhodesia: DT2871+

Southern Song dynasty: DS751+

Southern Sudan question: DT157.67,
DT157.672

Southern Territories (Algeria):
DT298.S6

Southern Zones (Spanish Morocco):
DT330

Southland (New Zealand): DU430.S6

Southwestern Asia: DS41+

Soviet Jews in Israel: DS113.8.R87

Soviet occupation of Afghanistan:
DS371.2

Soviet Union and East Asia: DS518.7

Soviet Union, Jews in: DS134.8+

Soweto (South Africa): DT2405.S68

Soweto uprising, 1976: DT1959

Soweto uprising anniversary, 1986:
DT1969

Spain, Jews in: DS135.S7+

Spaniards in Algeria: DT283.6.S62

Spaniards in Australia: DU122.S73

Spaniards in Israel: DS113.8.S72

Spaniards in Taiwan: DS799.43.S73

Spanish Guinea: DT620+

Spanish Morocco: DT330

Spanish Sahara: DT346.S7

Spanish West Africa: DT619+

Sparterie: DT62.S67

Sphinxes
Ancient Egypt: DT62.S7

Spies
Iraq War, 2003-: DS79.767.S75
Korean War: DS921.5.S7+
Sino-Japanese War, 1937-1945:
DS777.533.S65

Spoons
Ancient Egypt: DT62.S73

Śreshṭhas in Nepal: DS493.9.S74

Sri Lanka: DS488+

Sri Lankans in India: DS432.S76

Sri Lankans in Malaysia: DS595.2.S64

Srimali Brahmans in India: DS432.S77

Srngavāla Brahmans (Indic people):
DS432.S78

St. John's Christians in Iran:
DS269.M36

Stanleyville (Zaire): DT665.K55

State of emergency, 1985-
South Africa: DT1967

Stel, Simon van der: DT1817.S84

Steles
Ancient Egypt: DT62.S8

Stellaland and Goshen, 1882-1884:
DT2366

Stewart Island (New Zealand): DU430.S7

Steyn, M.T.: DT2127.S84

Stieng in Vietnam: DS556.45.S75

Stirling, Sir James: DU372.S8

Stodpa (Indic people): DS432.S83

Stormberg, Battle of, 1899: DT1908.S87

Straits of Tirin: DS110.45

Straits Settlements: DS591+

Strzelecki, Sir Paul Edmund de: DU172.S77

Sub-Saharan Africa, Central: DT348+

Suba (African people) in Kenya: DT433.545.S83

Ṣūbā (Palestine): DS110.S83

Subanuns in the Philippines: DS666.S8

Subarnabaniks: DS432.S86

Sudan: DT154.1+

Sudan, Jews in: DS135.S85

Sudanese in Cairo, Egypt: DT146.6.S83

Sudanese in Uganda: DT433.245.S92

Sudanese Republic: DT551+

Sudugadusiddha (Indic people): DS432.S87

Suez Canal: DT154.S9

Sūhāj Province (Egypt): DT73.S85

Sui Dynasty: DS749.2+

Sui in China: DS731.S88

Suicidal behavior
  Aboriginal Australians: DU124.S84

Suk (African people) in Kenya: DT433.545.S85

Sukarno, Mount: DU747.S8

Sūkās, Tall: DS99.S75

Sukuma (African people): DT443.3.S86

Sulawesi: DS646.4+

Sulaym in Saudi Arabia: DS219.S84

Sulod (Philippine people): DS666.S85

Sulung (Indic people): DS432.S88

Sum in Afghanistan: DS354.6.S9

Sumaq Site
  Israel: DS110.S85

Sumarā (Indic people): DS432.S9

Sumatra: DS646.1+

Sumbanese (Indonesian people): DS632.S89

Sumerians: DS72

Ṣummeil (Palestine): DS110.S86

Sun Yat-sen: DS777.A2+

Sundanese (Indonesian people): DS632.S9

Sundi (African people) in Congo (Democratic Republic): DT650.S94

Sunnites in the Middle East: DS59.S86

Sunuwar (Indic people): DS432.S94

Sunuwar (South Asian people) in Nepal: DS493.9.S94

Superstition, Gypsy: DX151

Supplies
  Arab War, 1948-1949: DS126.96.S94
  Vietnam War: DS559.8.S9

Suri in Ethiopia: DT380.4.S87

Surt Site (Libya): DT239.S87

Susa (Ancient city): DS262.S9

Sushen (Manchurian people): DS731.S95

Susita (Extinct city): DS110.S87

Sutaeans: DS72.52

Suvaroff Islands: DU860

Suvarrow Islands: DU860

Suvedīs (Nepalese people): DS493.9.S965

Suwaroff Islands: DU860

Suyala Th+ap+as (Nepalase people): DS493.9.S97

Swabians in Africa: DT16.S94

Swahili-speaking peoples in East Africa: DT429.5.S94

Swahili-speaking peoples in Eastern Africa: DT365.45.S93

Swahili-speaking peoples in Kenya: DT433.545.S93

Swahili-speaking peoples in Tanzania: DT443.3.S92

Swakop River and Valley (Namibia): DT1670.S83

Swakopmund (Namibia): DT1685.S83

Swazi (African people): DT2746.S95

Swaziland: DT2701+

Sweden, Jews in: DS135.S87+

Swedes in Australia: DU122.S94

Swedes in Cyprus: DS54.42.S94
Swedes in Ethiopia: DT380.4.S94
Swedes in Namibia: DT1558.S83
Swedes in New Zealand: DU424.5.S93
Sweyhat, Tell (Syria): DS99.S86
Swinburne, George: DU222.S8
Swiss in Australia: DU122.S95
Swiss in Ghana: DT510.43.S85
Swiss in Namibia: DT1558.S84
Swiss in New Zealand: DU424.5.S95
Swiss in Zimbabwe: DT2913.S93
Switzerland, Jews in: DS135.S9+
Sydney (Australia): DU178
Syria: DS92+
Syria, Jews in: DS135.S95
Syriac Christians in India: DS432.S965
Syriac Christians in Syria: DS94.8.S94
Syriac Christians in the Middle East:
  DS59.S94
Syrian Christians in the Near East:
  DS59.J25
Syrians in Egypt: DT72.S9

T

Taaisha in Sudan: DT155.2.T36
Taanach (Extinct city)
  West Bank: DS110.T13
Ta'anakh Region: DS110.T15
Tabo Site (Sudan): DT159.9.T33
Tabor, Mount (Israel): DS110.T2
Tabwa (African people) in Congo
  (Democratic Republic): DT650.T32
Tachoni (African people) in Kenya:
  DT433.545.T3
Tadmur (Syria): DS99.P17
T'aebong Kingdom, 901-918: DS911.86
Tagalos in the Philippines: DS666.T2
Tagals in the Philippines: DS666.T2
Tagbanuas in the Philippines:
  DS666.T3
Taghlib (Arab tribe) in Saudi Arabia:
  DS219.T32
Tagin (Indic people): DS432.T17
Tāhā Husayn: DT107.2.T3
Tahirids: DS288.4
Tahiti Islands: DU870

Tahmasp I: DS292.4
Tahmasp II: DS293.7
Taḥrīr Province (Egypt): DT137.T3
Tai Phakes (Indic people): DS432.T27
Tai Ping Tian Guo: DS758.7+
Tai (Southeast Asian people):
  DS523.4.T35
Tai (Southeast Asian people) in China:
  DS731.T27
Tai (Southeast Asian people) in East
  Asia: DS509.5.T3
Tai (Southeast Asian people) in India:
  DS432.T26
Tai (Southeast Asian people) in Laos:
  DS555.45.T35
Tai (Southeast Asian people) in
  Vietnam: DS556.45.T35
Tai Turung in India: DS432.T28
Tai Yong (Southeast Asian people) in
  Thailand: DS570.T34
Taika reform: DS855.6
Taïlakh (Kazakh people) in Mongolia:
  DS798.422.T34
Taimoro (Malagasy people):
  DT469.M277T34
Tainu (Maori people): DU424.T34
Taiping Rebellion: DS758.7+
Taishō (Yoshihito): DS885.8+
Taita (African people) in Kenya:
  DT433.545.T34
Taiwan: DS798.92+
Taiwanese in Australia: DU122.T28
Taj Majal: DS486.A3
Tajikistan, Jews in: DS135.T34
Tajiks in Afghanistan: DS354.6.T35
Tajiks in China: DS731.T29
Tajiks in Israel: DS113.8.T3
Takena (African people) in Benin:
  DT541.45.T35
Takhak in India: DS432.T53
Takht-i-Sulayman (Iran): DS262.T35
Takla Makan Desert (China):
  DS793.T337
Takrur Empire: DT532.3
Talal I: DS154.54
Talang Mama (Indonesian people):
  DS632.T35

Talansi (African people) in Ghana: DT510.43.T35

Taliban regime (Afghanistan), 1996-2001: DS371.3+

Talieng in Laos: DS555.45.T36

Talismans
Ancient Egypt: DT62.T24

Tallense (African people) in Ghana: DT510.43.T35

Taman (Bornean people): DS646.32.T35

Tamang (Nepalese people): DS493.9.T35

Tamatave (Madagascar): DT469.M38T33

Tambo, Oliver: DT1949.T36

Tamil in French Indonesia: DS539.T36

Tamil in India: DS432.T3

Tamil in Malaysia: DS595.2.T36

Tamil in Mauritius: DT469.M445T35

Tamil in Singapore: DS610.25.T34

Tamil in South Africa: DT1768.T36

Tamil in Sri Lanka: DS489.25.T3

Tamils in Australia: DU122.T36

Tamim in Saudi Arabia: DS219.T34

Tammburi(Indic people): DS432.T29

Tanala in Madagascar: DT469.M277T35

Tananarive (Madagascar): DT469.M38T34

Tanawalis in Pakistan: DS380.T3

Tang (T'ang) dynasty: DS749.3+

Tanganyika: DT436+

Tangier Zone (Morocco): DT329.T16

Tangkhul in India: DS432.T32

Tangsa in India: DS432.T33

Tangut: DS751.82+

Tangwena (African people) in Zimbabwe: DT2913.T36

Tanimbar (Indonesian people): DS632.T36

Tanis (Egypt): DT73.T2

Tank warfare
Korean War: DS921.5.T35

Tanka (Chinese people): DS731.T3

Tannekwe (African people) in Botswana: DT2458.T35

Tanninim Site (Israel): DS110.T22

Tanoli in Pakistan: DS380.T35

Ṭanṭūrah (Palestine): DS110.T225

Tanzania: DT436+

Taokas (Taiwan people): DS799.43.T42

Taphis (Egypt): DT73.T23

Ṭāq-e Bostān Site (Iran): DS262.T4

Taranaki (New Zealand): DU430.T25

Tarbīkhā (Israel): DS110.S585

Tarkhan Site (Egypt): DT73.T244

Tarkhanewala-Dera Mound (India): DS486.T37

Tarshīḥā (Israel): DS110.T227

Tasaday (Philippine people): DS666.T32

Tasmania: DU182+

Tatars: DS25

Tatars in China: DS731.T34

Tats in Iran: DS269.T38

Tattooing, Maori: DU423.T26

Taungtha in Burma: DS528.2.T38

Tause in Papua: DU744.35.T38

Tausug in the Philippines: DS666.T33

Taut Batu (Philippine people): DS666.P34

Taveta in Kenya: DT433.545.T38

Tawara in Mozambique: DT3328.T38

Tawara in Zimbabwe: DT2913.T38

Tawfīq, Khedive of Egypt: DT107.3+

Tawilan Site (Jordan): DS154.9.T38

Taxila (Pakistan): DS392.2.T3

Tay' in Saudi Arabia: DS219.T38

Tay Nung: DS556.45.T39

Tboli: DS666.T36

Tchad: DT546.4+

Te Tāou (New Zealand people): DU424.T4

Tebtunis Site (Egypt): DT73.T247

Technology
Persian Gulf War, 1990-1991: DS79.744.S34

Teda: DT346.T4

Teda (African people) in Chad: DT546.445.T4

Teichiussa (Extinct city): DS156.T45

Teixeira da Silva (Angola): DT1465.B35

Teixeira de Sousa (Angola):
  DT1465.L84
Teke (Bantu people) in Congo
  (Brazzaville): DT546.245.T43
Tel Akhziv (Israel): DS110.T23
Tel Aviv (Israel): DS110.T3+
Tel-Yosef (Israel): DS110.T397
Tell Duweir (Israel): DS110.L3
Tell ed Duweir (Israel): DS110.L3
Tell el-Amarna (Egypt): DT73.T25
Tell el-Farkha (Egypt): DT73.F36
Tell el Hasī (Israel): DS110.T4
Tell en-Nasbeh: DS110.T5
Tellem (African people) in Mali:
  DT551.45.K85
Telugu in Burma: DS528.2.T43
Telugu in India: DS432.T4
Telugu in Mauritius: DT469.M445T44
Tem in Togo: DT582.45.T45
Tembomvura (African people) in
  Zimbabwe: DT2913.T45
Temne (African people) in Sierra Leone:
  DT516.45.T45
Temple (Jerusalem): DS109.3
Temple Mount (Jerusalem): DS109.28+
Temple of Ammon (Egypt): DT73.K4
Temple of Luxor (Egypt): DT73.T3+
Temples
  Ancient Egypt: DT68.8
Temuan (Malayan people):
  DS595.2.T45
Ten Kingdoms: DS749.7+
Ten lost tribes of Israel: DS131
Tenda (African people) in West Africa:
  DT474.6.T46
Tenggerese (Indonesian people):
  DS632.T38
Territorial questions
  Arab War, 1948-1949: DS126.96.T4
Teso (African people) in Uganda:
  DT433.245.T47
Tete (Mozambique): DT3410.T48
Tetela (African people) in Congo
  (Democratic Republic): DT650.T47
Tétouan (Morocco): DT329.T4
Tetum (Indonesian people): DS632.T4
Textiles, Maori: DU423.T4

Thado in Burma: DS528.2.T45
Thado in India: DS432.T46
Thai Deng in Laos: DS555.45.T48
Thai Deng in Vietnam: DS556.45.T53
Thailand: DS561+
Thailand, Jews in: DS135.T54
Thais in China: DS731.T53
Thais in Malaysia: DS595.2.T53
Thakali (Nepalese people):
  DS493.9.T45
Thakuri in India: DS432.T48
Thamud in Saudi Arabia: DS219.T45
Thamugadi City (Algeria): DT299.T5
Thao (Taiwan people): DS799.43.T45
Thapli Site (India): DS486.T484
Thaqif in Saudi Arabia: DS219.T47
Tharu in India: DS432.T49
Tharus in Nepal: DS493.9.T47
Thebes (Egypt): DT73.T3+
Theodore II (Ethiopia): DT386.3
Thonga in Mozambique: DT3328.T74
Thonga in South Africa: DT1768.T76
Thos in Vietnam: DS556.45.T58
Thoti in India: DS432.T495
Thracians in Sudan: DT155.2.T45
Three Kingdoms: DS748.2+
Thugga (Tunisia): DT269.T48
Thugs (India): DS422.T5
Thutmose III, King of Egypt: DT87.2
Thysdrus (Tunisia): DT269.T52
Tiananmen Square Incident, 1989:
  DS779.32
Tibbu: DT346.T4
Tiberias (Israel): DS110.T6
Tiberias Lake (Israel): DS110.T62
Tibesti Mountains (Libya): DT238.T5
Tibet: DS785+
Tibetans in China: DS731.T56
Tibetans in India: DS432.T5
Tibetans in Nepal: DS493.9.T53
Tibeto-Burman peoples: DS25.5
Tidjani, Aurélie (Picard): DT294.7.T5
Tigalas (Indic people): DS432.T52
Tiglath-Pileser
  I: DS73.53
  III: DS73.76
Tigre (Ethiopia): DT390.T5

Tigrinya (African people) in Ethiopia: DT380.4.T54

Tīh Plateau (Egypt): DT137.T54

Tikar (African people) in Cameroon: DT571.T54

Tiles
  Egyptian antiquities: DT62.T45

Tille Mound: DS156.T54

Tilmen (Extinct city): DS156.T55

Timbuktu: DT551.9.T55

Timgad (Algeria): DT299.T5

Timma Site (Israel): DS110.T63

Timor: DS646.5+

Timor (Indonesian people): DS632.T5

Timor-Leste: DS649.2+

Timor Timur: DS649.2+

Timur, 1336-1405 (Mongols): DS23

Timur, 1773-1793 (Afghanistan): DS359.3

Timurides (Mongols): DS23.1

Timurids
  Persia: DS289.7

Tinguianes in the Philippines: DS666.T5

Tipura in Bangladesh: DS393.83.T57

Tipurs in India: DS432.T54

Tirah: DS392.T5

Tirat Karmel (Israel): DS110.T66

Tirich Mīr Mountain: DS392.T54

Tiriki (African people) in Kenya: DT433.545.T57

Tiruray (Philippine people): DS666.T6

Tiv (African people) in Nigeria: DT515.45.T58

Tivi (African people) in Nigeria: DT515.45.T58

Ṭiwāl al-Sharqī Site (Jordan): DS154.9.T57

Tiwi (Australian people): DU125.T5

Tiyars in India: DS432.T56

Tjolotjo (Zimbabwe): DT3025.T85

Tlemcen (Algeria): DT299.T55

Tlhaping in Botswana: DT2458.T55

Tlhaping in South Africa: DT1768.T57

Tlhaping in Zimbabwe: DT2913.T55

Toba-Batak (Indonesian people): DS632.T62

Tobelo in Indonesia: DS632.T63

Toda in India: DS432.T6

Tofinnu (African people) in Benin: DT541.45.T63

Togo: DT582+

Togoland: DT582+

Toilet articles
  Ancient Egypt: DT62.T5

Toivo ja Toivo, Andimba: DT1641.T75

Tokelau: DU424.5.T65

Tokelau Islands: DU910

Tokhari in China: DS731.T6

Tokuguwa period: DS870+

Tolaki in Indonesia: DS632.T65

Tolbert, William R.: DT636.4.T63

Tolemaide (Libya): DT239.T6

Toma (African people) in Guinea: DT543.45.T65

Tombs
  Ancient Egypt: DT62.T6

Tonga in Zambia: DT3058.T65

Tonga Islands: DU880

Tongaland, Incorporation of (Natal): DT2261

Tongaland (South Africa): DT2400.T66

Tonghak Incident, 1894 (Korea): DS915.53

Tongzhi: DS763.5+

Toṅ'sā" in Burma: DS528.2.T65

Tools
  Ancient Egypt: DT62.T65

Tooro (African people) in Uganda: DT433.245.T66

Topoke in Congo (Democratic Republic): DT650.T65

Toradjas in Indonesia: DS632.T7

Torghuts in Mongolia: DS798.422.T67

Torres Strait (Australia): DU280.T7

Torres Strait Islanders (Australian people): DU125.T67

Toto in India: DS432.T66

Touggourt (Algeria): DT299.T7

Toure, Ahmed Sekou: DT543.82.T68

Trades
  Gypsies: DX171

Transitional government
  Namibia: DT1648

Transitional government
  Zimbabwe: DT2994
Transjordan: DS153+
Transkei Revolt, 1880: DT1884
Transkei (South Africa): DT2400.T83
Transorangia: DT2112+
Transorangia, Treks into: DT2120
Transportation
  Sino-Japanese War, 1937-1945:
    DS777.533.T73
  Vietnam War: DS559.8.T7
Transvaal: DT2291+
Transvaal rule, 1894-1902: DT2793
Transvaal, Treks into: DT2342
Treaties (Vietnam War): DS559.7
Treaty of Aliwal North and cession of
  Sotho lands, 1869 (Orange Free
  State): DT2135
Tree Shelter Site (Egypt): DT73.T74
Trigo de Morais (Mozambique):
  DT3415.C58
Trilokpur Mound (India): DS486.T75
Tripoli (Libya)
  City: DT239.T7
Tripolitania: DT238.T8
Tristan da Cunha Islands: DT671.T8
Trobriand Islands: DU885
Trucial Oman: DS247.T8+
Trucial States: DS247.T8+
Truk Islands: DU568.T7
Truku (Taiwan people): DS799.43.T66
Truth and Reconciliation Commission
  (Republic of South Africa): DT1974.2
Trysa (Extinct city): DS156.T79
Tsana Lake (Ethiopia): DT390.T8
Tsefat (Israel): DS110.T77
Tsholotsho (Zimbabwe): DT3025.T85
Tsimahafotsy in Madagascar:
  DT469.M277T75
Tsimihety in Madagascar:
  DT469.M277T78
Tsogo (African people) in Gabon:
  DT546.145.T75
Tsonga in Mozambique: DT3328.T74
Tsonga in South Africa: DT1768.T76
Tsonga in Zambia: DT3058.T85
Tsou (Taiwan people): DS799.43.T74

Tsovah (Israel): DS110.T82
Tswana (African people) in Botswana:
  DT2458.T89
Tswana (African people) in Namibia:
  DT1558.T78
Tswana (African people) in South Africa:
  DT1768.T89
Tswana (African people) in Southern
  Africa: DT1058.T78
Tswana (African people) in Zimbabwe:
  DT2913.T78
Tswapong (African people) in Botswana:
  DT2458.T93
Tuamotu Islands: DU890
Tuang (African people): DT2596.T38
Tuareg in Mali: DT551.45.T83
Tuaregs in Algeria: DT283.6.T83
Tuaregs in Burkina Faso:
  DT555.45.T82
Tuaregs in Libya: DT223.2.T83
Tuaregs in Niger: DT547.45.T83
Tuaregs in Sahara: DT346.T7
Tubman, William V.S.: DT636.T8
Tubuai Islands: DU900
Tuggurt (Algeria): DT299.T7
Tughlak dynasty: DS459.4+
Tuhoe (Maori people): DU424.T83
Tujia (Chinese people): DS731.T74
Tukulor (African people) in Senegal:
  DT549.45.T68
Tukulor Empire: DT532.3
Tulu in India: DS432.T8
Tulung (Tibeto-Burman people) in
  China: DS731.T76
Tumbuka (African people) in Malawi:
  DT3192.T85
Tundjung (Indonesian people):
  DS632.T95
Tung (Chinese people): DS731.T77
Tung-hsiang (Chinese people):
  DS731.T78
Tungusic peoples in China: DS731.T8
Tunis (Tunisia): DT269.T8
Tunisia: DT241+
Tunisia, Jews in: DS135.T7+
Tunisian Jews in Israel: DS113.8.T83

Tunnels
  Vietnam War: DS559.8.T85
Tuqan, Tell (Syria): DS99.T86
Ṭūr (Egypt): DT73.T87
Turco-Italian War, 1911-1912: DT234
Turkana (African people) in Kenya:
  DT433.545.T87
Turkey, Jews in: DS135.T8+
Turkic peoples: DS26+
Turkish Jews in Israel: DS113.8.T85
Turkish provinces, regions, etc.:
  DS51.A+
Turkish rule (Egypt): DT97+
Turkmen in Afghanistan: DS354.6.T87
Turkmenistan, Jews in: DS135.T85
Turkomans in Iran: DS269.T8
Turkomans in Iraq: DS70.8.T85
Turkomans in Israel: DS113.8.T86
Turks in Australia: DU122.T87
Turks in Cyprus: DS54.42.T87
Turks in Iran: DS269.T82
Turks in Iraq: DS70.8.T86
Turks in Libya: DT223.2.T85
Turks in the Middle East: DS59.T8
Turnhalle conference, 1975: DT1647
Tusia (African people) in Burkina Faso:
  DT555.45.T87
Tutenkhamun, King of Egypt: DT87.5
Tutsi (African people) in Burundi:
  DT450.65.T87
Tutsi in Congo (Democratic Republic):
  DT650.T86
Tuttul (Extinct city)
  Syria: DS99.T88
Tuvalu: DU590
Tuvinians in Mongolia: DS798.422.T85
Twat: DT346.T8

U

U.S. Marine headquarters, Bombing of
  (Lebanon): DS87.53
Uap (Caroline Islands): DU568.Y3
Ubangi-Shari: DT546.3+
Ubium (African people) in Nigeria:
  DT515.45.U24
Ucai in India: DS432.U25

Udayagiri Site (India): DS486.U295
Uduk (African people): DT155.2.U38
Uduk (African people) in South Sudan:
  DT159.927.U38
Ufzul: DS364.2
Uganda: DT433.2+
Uganda, Jews in: DS135.U32
Uganda-Tanzania War, 1978-1979:
  DT433.283
Uhunduni in Papua: DU744.35.U36
Uîge (Angola)
  City: DT1465.U55
  Province: DT1450.U55
Uighur: DS27.56
Uighur (Turkic people) in China:
  DS731.U4
Ujari (African people) in Nigeria:
  DT515.45.U35
Ukheidar: DS70.5.U4
Ukraine, Jews in: DS135.U4+
Ukrainian Jews in Israel: DS113.8.U4
Ukrainians in Australia: DU122.U4
Ukrainians in East Asia: DS509.5.U35
Ulad Stut in Morocco: DT313.5.U4
Uldeme in Cameroon: DT571.U43
Ulithi (Caroline Islands): DU568.U5
Ulladans in India: DS432.U4
Ultānu (Berber people) in Morocco:
  DT313.3.I57
Ulundi, Battle of: DT1879.U58
Uluthi (Caroline Islands): DU568.U5
'Umayri, Tall al- (Jordan): DS154.9.U4
Umm al-Jimāl Site (Jordan):
  DS154.9.U45
Umm al Marā, Tall (Syria): DS99.U46
Umm al-Nār Island: DS247.U45+
Umm Hammad, Tall (Jordan):
  DS154.9.U47
Umma (Ancient city): DS70.5.U44
Umtali (Zimbabwe): DT3025.M86
Umvuma (Zimbabwe): DT3025.M88
UN Special Commission on Iraq:
  DS79.755
'Unayzah: DS247.U5+
Underground movements
  Sino-Japanese War, 1937-1945:
    DS777.533.U53

Uneme (African people) in Nigeria: DT515.45.U54

Unga (African people) in Zambia: DT3058.U65

Unilateral Declaration of Independence (UDI), 1965 (Zimbabwe): DT2986

Union Islands: DU910

Union of South Africa: DT1924+

United Arab Emirates: DS247.T8+

United Nations investigations (Eritrea): DT395.3

United Nations mandate
  Burundi: DT450.84+
  Rwanda: DT450.425+

United Nations trusteeship
  Namibia: DT1638+
  Somalia: DT406+

United Republic of Tanzania: DT448.2+

United States
  Annexation of Hawaii: DU627.3+
  Iraq War, 2003-: DS79.765.U5+

United States and East Asia: DS518.8

United States and the Islamic world: DS35.74.U6

Unity (South Sudan): DT159.977.U65

UNSCOM inspections, Compliance with: DS79.755

Untouchables
  India: DS422.C3

Upper Guinea: DT477

Upper Nile (South Sudan): DT159.977.U67

Upper Ta'oih (Southeast Asian people) in Vietnam: DS556.45.U66

Upper Volta: DT555+

Upper Zohar (Israel): DS110.U65

Uppina Kolaga Okkaligas (Indic people): DS432.U65

'Uqayl in Saudi Arabia: DS219.U72

Ur (Ancient city): DS70.5.U7

Urak Lawoi' in Thailand: DS570.U73

Ural-Altaic peoples in Asia: DS17

Urartu (Kingdom): DS156.U7

Ureu (Tunisia): DT269.U73

Urfa: DS156.E2

Urhobo (African people) in Nigeria: DT515.45.U74

Urkesh (Syria): DS99.U74

Ushabti
  Ancient Egypt: DT62.U84

Ushi (African people) in Zambia: DT3058.U85

'Utaybah in Saudi Arabia: DS219.U73

Uthina (Tunisia): DT269.U78

Utica (Tunisia): DT269.U8

Utrecht, Annexation of (Natal): DT2265

'Uza Site (Israel): DS110.U99

Uzbekistan, Jews in: DS135.U92

Uzbeks in Afghanistan: DS354.6.U82

Uzbeks in China: DS731.U8

Uzbeks in Israel: DS113.8.U92

V

Vāḍabalija in India: DS432.V29

Vagala in Ghana: DT510.43.V34

Vāgheras: DS432.V33

Vaidu in India: DS432.V34

Vaiphei (Indic people): DS432.V35

Vaiṣṇava Okkaligas (Indic people): DS432.V36

Vaisyas in India: DS432.V37

Valangai (Indic people): DS432.V376

Valayars (Indic people): DS432.V38

Valenge (African people) in Mozambique: DT3328.C67

Valley of the Kings (Egypt): DT73.B44

Valley of the Queens (Egypt): DT73.V34

Van Diemen's Land: DU182+

Van Kieu (Southeast Asian people) in Vietnam: DS556.45.V34

Van Riebeeck, Jan: DT1817.V35

Van (Turkey): DS51.V3

Vanavarayar in India: DS432.V39

Vandals (North Africa): DT171

Vanuatu: DU760

Vazimba in Madagascar: DT469.M277V39

Veddahs in Sri Lanka: DS489.25.V4

Vei (African people) in Liberia: DT630.5.V2

Vellalas in India: DS432.V4

Venda in South Africa: DT1768.V45

Venda (South Africa): DT2400.V45

Venda War, 1898: DT2368

Vere (African people) in Côte d'Ivoire: DT545.45.V47

Vessels
Ancient Egypt: DT62.V47

Veterans
Persian Gulf War, 1990-1991: DS79.744.V47
Vietnam War: DS559.72+

Vettuvar in India: DS432.V48

Vezo (Malagasy people): DT469.M277V48

Victoria (Australia): DU200+

Victoria Falls (Zambia): DT3140.V54

Vietnam: DS556+

Vietnam (Democratic Republic): DS560+

Vietnam War: DS557+

Vietnamese in Australia: DU122.V53

Vietnamese in China: DS731.V53

Vietnamese in Laos: DS555.45.V54

Vietnamese in Thailand: DS570.V5

Vila Alferes Chamusca (Mozambique): DT3415.G85

Vila Cabral (Mozambique): DT3415.L53

Vila Gouveia (Mozambique): DT3415.C36

Vila Pery (Mozambique)
City: DT3415.C56
Province: DT3410.M36

Vila Salazar
Mozambique: DT3415.M38
Zimbabwe: DT3025.S36

Vili (African people) in Congo (Brazzaville): DT546.245.V54

Vili (African people) in Congo (Democratic Republic): DT650.V54

Vision of Nongguase, 1856-1857: DT1863

Volubilis (Morocco): DT329.V6

Vorster, Balthazar Johannes, 1966-1978: DT1957

Vounous Site (Syria): DS54.95.V68

Vryheid, Annexation of (Natal): DT2265

Vrystaat (South Africa): DT2075+

W

Wa (Burmese people) in China: DS731.W32

Wa in Burma: DS528.2.W32

Wabena (African people) in Tanzania: DT443.3.W32

Wachaga (African people) in Tanzania: DT443.3.W33

Waci (African people) in Togo: DT582.45.W33

Wadai (Chad): DT546.49.W33

Wagenia (African people) in Congo (Democratic Republic): DT650.W33

Wagga Wagga (Australia): DU180.W3

Waghri in India: DS432.W27

Wagons
Gypsies: DX175

Wahhabi movement: DS242

Wai o Hua (Maori people): DU424.W3

Wailpi (Australian people): DU125.A45

Waizeru Zauditu: DT387.6

Wakatipu Lake (New Zealand): DU430.W25

Wake Island: DU950.W28

Wakhi in Afghanistan: DS354.6.W34

Wakkerstroom, Annexation of (Natal): DT2265

Wala in Ghana: DT510.43.W35

Walking sticks
Ancient Egypt: DT62.W34

Wallis Archipelago: DU920

Walmajarri (Australian people): DU125.W32

Walung in Nepal: DS493.9.W35

Walvis Bay annexation, 1878: DT1599

Walvis Bay (Namibia): DT1685.W35

Wambule Rai in Nepal: DS493.9.W36

Wana (Indonesian people): DS632.W34

Wang-ku (Turkic people) in China: DS731.W35

Wanganui (New Zealand): DU430.W3

Wankie (Zimbabwe): DT3025.H93

Wapangwa (African people) in Tanzania: DT443.3.W36

War for Union with Greece, 1955-1959 (Cyprus): DS54.86

War Kabud Site (Iran): DS262.W37
War of Attrition, Middle East, 1969-
   1970: DS127.95
War of National Liberation (Zimbabwe):
   DT2988+
War of Ngcayecibi, 1877-1878: DT1874
War of the Axe, 1846-1848: DT1855
War with Dingaan, 1837-1840:
   DT2245+
War with Italy, 1895-1896: DT387.3
War with Orange Free State, 1865-1868
   (Lesotho): DT2636
War work
   Sino-Japanese War, 1937-1945:
      DS777.533.W37
   South African War: DT1918.W35
Wara (African people) in Burkina Faso:
   DT555.45.W35
Wardaman (Australian people):
   DU125.W34
Warega in Congo (Democratic
   Republic): DT650.R43
Warfare, Maori: DU423.W35
Waringari (Australian people):
   DU125.W35
Warli in India: DS432.W3
Warlpiri (Australian people):
   DU125.W37
Waropen in Papua: DU744.35.W37
Warrap (South Sudan):
   DT159.977.W37
Waryaghar (Berber people) in Morocco:
   DT313.3.W35
Wazaramo (African people) in Tanzania:
   DT443.3.W39
Waziristan: DS392.W3
We (African people) in Côte d'Ivoire:
   DT545.45.W4
Weapons
   Persian Gulf War, 1990-1991:
      DS79.744.S34
Wei dynasty: DS748.17+
Welensky, Roy: DT3111.W45
Wellesley Islands (Australia):
   DU280.W4
Wellington (New Zealand): DU428
Welsh in Australia: DU122.W44

West Africa: DT470+
West Bank: DS110.W47
West Central Africa: DT356
West Coast (Africa): DT470+
West Indians in Sierra Leone:
   DT516.45.W47
West Sahara: DT521+, DT548
West Sudan: DT356
Westbeech, George: DT3081.W48
Westbrook, George Egerton L.:
   DU818.W4
Western Australia: DU350+
Western Bahr el Ghazal (South Sudan):
   DT159.977.W47
Western Cape (South Africa): DT2070+
Western Desert (Egypt): DT137.W4
Western Equatoria (South Sudan):
   DT159.977.W48
Western Province (Zambia):
   DT3140.W48
Western Sahara: DT346.S7
Western Samoa: DU819.A2
Western Wall (Jerusalem):
   DS109.32.W47
Western Wei dynasty: DS748.7+
Western Zhou dynasty: DS747+
Westland (New Zealand): DU430.W4
Wewewa (Indonesian people):
   DS632.W48
Whakatohea (Maori people):
   DU424.W43
White Lotus Rebellion: DS756.3+
Whites in Africa: DT16.W45
Whites in Angola: DT1308.W55
Whites in Asia: DS28.W46
Whites in Hawaii: DU624.7.W45
Whites in South Africa: DT1768.W55
Wik-Mungkan (Australian people):
   DU125.W44
Windhoek (Namibia): DT1680
Wiradjuri (Australian people):
   DU125.W5
Witbooi, David: DT1641.W58
Witbooi, Hendrik: DT1608.W58
Witbooi Rebellion, 1893-1894: DT1612
Witu Protectorate
   German claims: DT433.57+

Witwatersrand (South Africa): DT2400.W58

Wolof (African people) in Gambia: DT509.45.W64

Wolof (African people) in Senegal: DT549.45.W64

Women
 Aboriginal Australians: DU124.W65
 Iraq War, 2003-: DS79.767.W66
 Korean War: DS921.5.W64
 Persian Gulf War, 1990-1991: DS79.744.W65
 Sino-Japanese War, 1937-1945: DS777.533.W65
 South African War: DT1918.W66
 Vietnam War: DS559.8.W6

Women, Maori: DU423.W65

Wonnarua (Australian people): DU125.W58

Worora (Australian people): DU125.W6

Wotjobaluk (Australian people): DU125.W66

Woyo (African people) in Congo (Democratic Republic): DT650.W69

Wu Kingdom: DS749.7+

Wunambal (Australian people): DU125.W8

Wurundjeri (Australian people): DU125.W87

Wuyue Kingdom: DS749.7+

X

Xai-Xai (Mozambique): DT3415.X35

Xavier Coppolani negotiations (Mauritania): DT554.65+

Xerxes I: DS283

Xerxes II: DS284.2

Xhosa (African people) in South Africa: DT1768.X57

Xhosa (African people) in Southern Africa: DT1058.X55

Xhosa cattle killing: DT1863

Xhosa in Sri Lanka: DS489.25.X56

Xhosa Wars, 1779-1802: DT1825

Xi Xia (Hsi Hsia) dynasty: DS751.82+

Xia (Hsia) dynasty: DS743

Xianfeng: DS758+

Xin (Hsin) dynasty: DS748.162+

Xinh Mun in Vietnam: DS556.45.X56

Xuantong: DS773+

Xweda (African people) in Benin: DT541.45.X84

Y

Yaaku (African people) in Kenya: DT433.545.Y32

Yaburara (Australian people): DU125.Y33

Yāfiʻ in Saudi Arabia: DS219.Y34

Yagba (African people) in Nigeria: DT515.45.Y33

Yagur (Israel): DS110.Y26

Yahya, Tapah-ye (Iran): DS262.Y3

Yaka in Congo (Democratic Republic): DT650.B38

Yakans in the Philippines: DS666.Y33

Yakha in Nepal: DS493.9.Y35

Yakub: DS364.6

Yalu, Battle of (russo-Japanese War): DS517.15

Yalunka (African people) in Sierra Leone: DT516.45.Y34

Yamāmah: DS247.Y35+

Yamatji (Australian people): DU125.Y34

Yamba, Dauti: DT3106.Y35

Yami (Taiwan people): DS799.43.Y35

Yamphu (Nepalese people): DS493.9.Y36

Yāmūn (West Bank): DS110.Y27

Yanadi in India: DS432.Y3

Yandruwandha (Australian people): DU125.Y347

Yangura (Australian people): DU125.Y35

Yankunytjatjara (Australian people): DU125.Y37

Yanoaḥ (Israel): DS110.Y29

Yanyuwa (Australian people): DU125.Y39

Yanzi (Bantu people) in Congo (Democratic Republic): DT650.Y3

Yao in Malawi: DT3192.Y36
Yao in Mozambique: DT3328.Y36
Yao (Southeast Asian people): DS523.4.Y36
Yao (Southeast Asian people) in China: DS731.Y3
Yao (Southeast Asian people) in Thailand: DS570.Y35
Yao (Southeast Asian people) in Vietnam: DS556.45.Y36
Yap (Caroline Islands): DU568.Y3
Yar'adua administration Nigeria: DT515.846
Yatenga (Kingdom): DT532.33
Yaudheya (Indic people): DS432.Y35
Yavne'el (Israel): DS110.Y387
Yazdegerd I: DS286.57
Yazdegerd II: DS286.7
Yazdegerd III: DS287.8
Yei in Papua: DU744.35.Y44
Yeke (African people) in Congo (Democratic Republic): DT650.Y43
Yemen: DS247.Y4+
Yemen, Jews in: DS135.Y4
Yemenis in Indonesia: DS632.3.Y45
Yemenis in Jordan: DS153.55.Y46
Yemenites in Egypt: DT72.Y44
Yemenites in Israel: DS113.8.Y4
Yemin Moshe (Jerusalem): DS109.8.Y45
Yerava in India: DS432.Y44
Yergum (African people) in Nigeria: DT515.45.Y47
Yerukala in India: DS432.Y47
Yesud ha-Ma'alah (West Bank): DS110.Y42
Yeye (African people) in Botswana: DT2458.Y48
Yezidis in Iraq: DS70.8.Y49
Yi (Chinese people): DS731.Y5
Yirka (Israel): DS110.Y53
Yokne'am (Israel): DS110.Y64
Yolngu (Australian people): DU125.Y64
Yom ha-zikaron (Memorial Day): DS126.82
Yombe (African people) in Congo (Democratic Republic): DT650.Y65

Yombe (African people) in Zambia: DT3058.Y66
Yoruba (African people) in Nigeria: DT515.45.Y67
Yoruba (African people) in West Africa: DT474.6.Y67
Yoruba in Benin: DT541.45.Y65
Youth
   Aboriginal Australians: DU124.C45
Youth, Maori: DU423.C5
Yuan dynasty: DS752+
Yugoslavia, Jews in: DS135.Y8+
Yugoslavian Jews in Israel: DS113.8.Y83
Yugoslavs in Australia: DU122.Y8
Yugoslavs in New Zealand: DU424.5.Y84
Yugur (Chinese people): DS731.Y83
Yuin (Australian people): DU125.Y85
Yungur (African people) in Nigeria: DT515.45.Y86
Yuruks: DS27.55
Yusufzais in Pakistan: DS380.Y85

Z

Zafimaniry in Madagascar: DT469.M277Z24
Zaghawa (African people) in Chad: DT546.445.Z33
Zaghawa (African people) in Sudan: DT155.2.Z34
Zahrān in Saudi Arabia: DS219.Z34
Zahrat adh-Dhra' 1 (Jordan): DS154.9.Z35
Zaire: DT641+
Zaire Province (Angola): DT1450.Z35
Zaman Shah: DS359.5
Zamār (Nīnawá): DS70.5.Z35
Zambezi Rebellion, 1917 (Mozambique): DT3385
Zambezi River and Valley (Southern Africa): DT1190.Z36
Zambézia (Mozambique): DT3410.Z36
Zambia: DT3031+
Zambia, Jews in: DS135.Z35

Zanaki ((African people) in Tanzania: DT443.3.Z35
Zande (African people): DT352.43.Z35
Zande (African people) in South Sudan: DT159.927.Z36
Zande in Central African Republic: DT546.345.Z35
Zanzibar: DT449.Z2+
Zar Dheri Site (Pakistan): DS392.2.Z37
Zaramo ((African people) in Tanzania: DT443.3.Z37
Zarma (African people) in Niger: DT547.45.Z37
Zarqā' (Jordan): DS154.9.Z37
Zauditu, Waizeru, Empress of Ethiopia: DT387.6
Zāwiyat al-Amwāt Site (Egypt): DT73.Z35
Zay (African people) in Ethiopia: DT380.4.Z39
Zayd ibn Layth in Saudi Arabia: DS219.Z39
Zayt Mountain: DT73.Z39
Zebulon Valley (Israel): DS110.Z38
Zela (African people): DT650.Z44
Zeliangrong (Indic people): DS432.Z44
Zeme (Indic people): DS432.Z46
Zeugma (Ancient city): DS156.Z48
Zezuru (African people) in Zimbabwe: DT2913.Z49
Zhou (Chou) dynasty: DS747+
Zhuang (Chinese people): DS731.C5
Zigula ((African people) in Tanzania: DT443.3.Z53
Zikhron Ya'akov (Israel): DS110.Z5
Zikim Site (Israel): DS110.Z53
Zimbabwe: DT2871+
Zimbabwe, Jews in: DS135.Z56
Zimbabweans in foreign countries (General): DT2913.15
Zionism: DS149+
Zir'īn (Israel): DS110.Z64
Ziwiyē: DS262.Z58
Ziyarids: DS288.56
Zomba (Malawi): DT3257.Z66
Zomba Plateau (Malawi): DT3252.Z65
Zoroastrian civilization, Early: DS267

Zoroastrians in Iran: DS269.Z65
Zou (Indic people): DS432.Z68
Zubaydāt (West Bank): DS110.Z75
Zulu (African people) in South Africa: DT1768.Z95
Zulu (African people) in Southern Africa: DT1058.Z84
Zulu conquest of Lourenco Marques, 1833: DT3368
Zulu Empire: DT1119
Zulu-Indian riots, 1949 (Natal): DT2275
Zulu War, 1879: DT1875+
Zululand, Incorporation of (Natal): DT2261
Zululand (South Africa): DT2400.Z85
Zuwaya in Libya: DT223.2.Z87
Zvishavane (Zimbabwe): DT3025.Z95

GPO U.S. GOVERNMENT PRINTING OFFICE: 2012–372–396/40019